W9-ALU-973

# Credits

**President**
Roland Elgey

**Publisher**
Joseph B. Wikert

**Publishing Director**
Jim Minatel

**Editorial Services Director**
Elizabeth Keaffaber

**Managing Editor**
Sandy Doell

**Director of Marketing**
Lynn E. Zingraf

**Senior Series Editor**
Chris Nelson

**Acquisitions Editor**
Stephanie Gould

**Product Directors**
Mark Cierzniak
Benjamin Milstead

**Production Editor**
Elizabeth A. Bruns

**Editors**
Danielle Bird
Thomas Cirtin
Mark Enochs
Lisa M. Gebken
Patrick Kanouse
Susan Ross Moore
Kelly Oliver
Caroline D. Roop
Maureen A. Schneeberger
Kathy Simpson

**Assistant Product
Marketing Manager**
Kim Margolius

**Technical Editors**
MagnaStar, Inc.
Joseph Carpenter
Jeffrey Erickson
John Ostlund
Joseph L. Weber

**Technical Specialist**
Nadeem Muhammad

**Operations Coordinator**
Patricia J. Brooks

**Editorial Assistant**
Andrea Duvall

**Book Designer**
Ruth Harvey

**Cover Designer**
Dan Armstrong

**Production Team**
Stephen Adams
Brian Buschkill
Jason Carr
Kim Cofer
Chad Dressler
Jenny Earhart
Trey Frank
Sonja Hart
Damon Jordan
Daryl Kessler
Clint Lahnen
Stephanie Layton
Michelle Lee
Linda Quigley
Laura Robbins
Kelly Warner
Todd Wente
Paul Wilson

**Indexers**
Tim Griffin
Joy Dean Lee

*First, to my parents, who still have no idea what I'm talking about. Second, to John Mickevich and Charles Sumner for holding down the fort so I could take the time to write this book. Last and forever, to sweet Jeanne Marie, who's the cream in my coffee.*

*—AN*

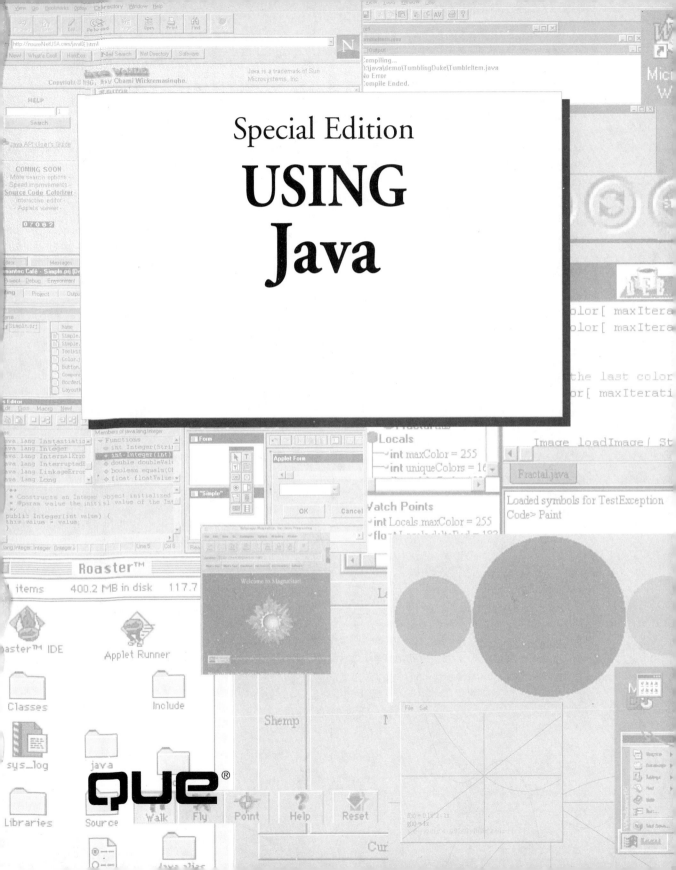

# Special Edition
# USING Java

*Written by Alexander Newman*

*with*

| | |
|---|---|
| *Jerry Ablan* | *Suresh K. Jois* |
| *Michael Afergan* | *Ira Krakow* |
| *Amber Benson* | *Kevin M. Krom* |
| *Eric Blossom* | *Mary Pietrowicz* |
| *Lee Brintle* | *Mark Waks* |
| *Joe Carpenter* | *Gregory A. Walsh* |
| *Luke Cassady-Dorion* | *Joseph L. Weber* |
| *Jay Cross* | *Scott Williams* |
| *Simeon Greene* | *Mark Wutka* |

que®

# Special Edition Using Java

**Copyright© 1996 by Que® Corporation**

Library of Congress Catalog No.: 95-71750

ISBN: 0-7897-0604-0

98 97 96     6 5 4 3 2 1

Interpretation of the printing code: the rightmost double-digit number is the year of the book's printing; the rightmost single-digit number, the number of the book's printing. For example, a printing code of 96-1 shows that the first printing of the book occurred in 1996.

Screen reproductions in this book were created using Collage Plus from Inner Media, Inc., Hollis, NH.

Composed in *Stone Serif* and *MCPdigital* by Que Corporation

# About the Authors

**Alexander Newman** has been executive director of the Sun User Group, the parent organization of Java-SIG—the national Java Users Group since 1993. His frequent commentary on the Sun/SPARC community appears regularly in *SunExpert* and *Sun Observer*. Despite the hi-tech environment he is submersed in, Alex prefers to think of himself as a "technologist," rather than a "technician"; studying what technology does, rather than how it does it. He has contributed to several technical conferences and symposia, including SunWorld and the various Sun User Group conferences, and is founding chair of the annual "Computers and the Law" symposium. He grew up in New York City and currently lives in Boston, MA. (Introduction, chapters 1, 30, appendix D)

**Jerry Ablan** (**munster@mcs.net**) is best described as a computer nut. Involved in computers since 1982, he has worked on and owned a variety of microcomputers including several that are no longer manufactured. Jerry is the president of netGeeks (**http://www.netgeeks.com**), an Internet consulting firm in Chicago, Illinois. He is also the coauthor of the *Web Site Administrator's Survival Guide* from Sams.net Publishing. (Chapters 4, 18)

**Michael Afergan** (**mikea@ai.mit.edu**) began working with Java as early as the spring of 1995 through his research work at the MIT AI Labs. Since then, he has carefully studied its growth, developing practical applets for companies as an independent consultant. Michael is also a founding member of TeamJava, a network of Java professionals and also wrote a chapter for *Java Unleashed* on multiuser environments. Although 18, Michael has been programming for 10 years and even taught a class on computer science at MIT. Captain of his high school wrestling team, he has been accepted for early admission to Harvard University. (Chapters 10, 11, appendix C)

**Amber Benson** is a software contractor and free-lance writer, specializing in object-oriented technology, graphical user interfaces, C++, and Java. She has a master's degree in computer science from the University of Colorado. She has worked in both the scientific and business computing communities, and ran her own software development company for 10 years. Most recently, she was a member of the software engineering development team for the OI Object Interface toolkit. She is coauthor of the *OI User's Guide* and the *XKB X Key-*

board *Extension Library Specification.* She telecommutes from her Montana mountain home, where she also raises world-class dressage horses. (Chapter 17)

**Eric Blossom** is a consulting software engineer for Blossom Associates West (**http://www.BlossomAssociates.Com**). He grew up in New York, attended college in Indiana and now lives in Berkeley, California. He has a bachelor's degree from Earlham College and a master's degree in mathematics from the University of California at Berkeley. He can be reached at **Eric@BlossomAssociates.Com**. (Chapters 26, 27)

**Lee Brintle** is the president and founder of Leepfrog Technologies, Inc. (**http://www.leepfrog.com**), located in Iowa City, Iowa. He has written a variety of World Wide Web browsers and servers, including a cable television web browser. His company specializes in custom database programming for the Web and providing direct access to the Internet. Lee has developed a trusted third-party user authentication security system for use on the Web, and also has tinkered with parallel processing and distributed databases. He was introduced to the distributed security and database arena by a too-healthy dose of the original MUDs. Lee received a bachelor's degree in computer science from the University of Iowa, and can be reached at **lbrintle@leepfrog.com**. (Chapter 30)

**Joe Carpenter** is a senior in computer science at Marquette University in Milwaukee, Wisconsin. His Web creations have won a number of awards, including the coveted "Cyber Star" award from *Virtual City* Magazine, as well as the Point Communications "Top 5% of the Web" award. He is currently a programmer for MagnaStar, Inc., the world's first Java-only consulting firm. He can be reached at **lungfish@magnastar.com**. His home page can be seen at **http://studsys.mscs.mu.edu/~carpent1**. (Appendix D)

**Luke Cassady-Dorion** (**luke@iliad.com**) is currently studying computer science at Drexel University (**http://www.drexel.edu**) in Philadelphia, PA. He is head of Java development at Odyssey Systems Corporation (**http://www.iliad.com**) and founder of the Philadelphia Java Users' Group (**http://www.iliad.com/PhillyJUG**). (Chapter 5, appendix D)

**Jay Cross** has been working in the field of software development for about 20 years. His main focus has been financial and business applications involving databases, and large heterogeneous distributed systems. He devotes his spare time and Web-surfing both to home and family, and to such hobbies as old time baseball, ancient astronomy, improvisational comic theatre, and model rockets. (Chapters 7, 8, 9, 13, 16)

**Simeon Greene** works for CIGNA International, an insurance company in Philadelphia PA, where he is a systems analyst, as well as the technical member of a small staff responsible for establishing the company's Web site. Simeon is also a computer engineering student at Drexel University. He handles various projects involving Java and other programming languages. His current residence is in Philadelphia, PA, but he was born in Trinidad. You can contact him at **smgree@ix.netcom.com**, or check out his home page at **http://www.well.com/~smgree**. (Chapter 2)

**Suresh K. Jois** is an interactive media technologist with expertise in Java, VRML, Software Agents, graphics, and video. He has worked for Sun Microsystems, SiliconGraphics, and the Internet Shopping Network. At Sun, he witnessed the birth of Java (then called Oak), and later at ISN, developed the very first Java-based commerce application. He is also deep into the creative and social aspects of interactive media, with interests in computer art, animation, music, and applications of Networked Virtual Reality to rehabilitation and health-care. (Chapters 6, 14)

**Ira Krakow** is an independent software developer who specializes in developing customized client-server databases and in integrating database and Internet technologies. He is the author of two books and many articles on computer related topics. He has over 23 years of experience in all aspects of computer technology. On the Internet, Ira publishes a daily personal finance newsletter (persfin-digest) where anyone can have his or her personal finance questions answered by professionals. His wife (Sandy), and two children (Sam and Laura), live in Stoneham, Massachusetts. You can reach him at **ikrakow@shore.net** and his Web page is **http://www.tiac.net/users/ikrakow**. (Chapter 28)

**Kevin M. Krom** is a software engineer at Carnegie Group, Inc., in Pittsburgh, PA. Since graduating from Purdue University in 1992, he has worked on both GUI-driven, knowledge-based systems and embedded microprocessor control systems, using object-oriented analysis and design techniques on a variety of platforms. He can be reached at **krom@cgi.com** or **http://www.city-net.com/~krom/**. (Chapters 19, 23, appendix D)

**Mary Pietrowicz** is a software engineer with the National Center for Supercomputing Applications, Software Development Group (NCSA-SDG) in

Champaign, IL. She develops software tools in Java and other languages for the Federal Consortium Team. Prior to joining NCSA, Mary provided computer-aided software engineering (CASE) consulting and support for Motorola's Paging Division, developed software for network adapter cards for Ungermann-Bass, and developed two-way radio software and radio service software for Motorola's Land Mobile Product Sector. Mary lives in Champaign with her husband and daughter. (Chapter 15, appendix E)

**Mark Waks** is a general languages mavin, who has worked in every major programming language (and most of the minor ones) over the past 15 years. He currently specializes in cutting-edge Web tools, and has been actively involved in the debates over the development of VRML since the start of serious discussion about the language. (Chapter 29)

**Gregory A. Walsh** is a founding member of TeamJava, and president of ARTEC Communications. Greg has consulted organizations on their use of technology to support organizational communication, learning, responsiveness, and agility since 1982. He is experienced in developing distance education and performance support systems, introducing new technologies, and facilitating high performance workgroups. He promises potential clients that the members of TeamJava will deliver "astonishingly wonderful" results to their projects. You can find him at **http://www.artec.com**. (Appendix D)

**Joseph L. Weber** is the vice president of Research and Development at MagnaStar Inc., the first Java-only development company. He is on the judging panel at the Java Application Review System (JARS), a founder for Team Java, and is the current moderator for Java-SIG, the national Java Special Interest Group. Joe is also a frequent contributor to *Java World* Magazine and holds an electrical and computer engineering degree from Marquette University. You can reach him at **jweber@magnastar.com** or **http://www.magnastar.com**. (Chapters 16, 24, 25)

**Scott Williams** is cofounder of The Willcam Group where he is the senior technology specialist. He writes and teaches on technical and business aspects of UNIX, C/C++, the Internet, and Java. He is also editor of *The Open Systems Letter*. He lives and works in Toronto, Canada. (Chapters 3, 12, appendix B)

**Mark Wutka** has spent the last seven years tinkering around with distributed object-oriented systems for a major airline. He is rumored to have developed some useful applications. (Chapters 20, 22, 23, 31)

# Acknowledgments

The publisher and authors would like to thank the members of TeamJava, a global network representing some of the premiere Java Consultants in the world, for springing into action at the last possible minute before this book went to bed. Their quick action allowed us to include the most "up-to-date" information on the just released MacintoshJDK, as well as Natural Intelligence's "Roaster" in this book.

Thanks to all, but in particular, to James A. Squires, initial founder of TeamJava and a programming consultant since 1978.

I'd like to thank the folks at Sun Expert for publishing my first article on Java many, many moons ago. This in turn led to my revising that article, and selling it to the guys at BoardWatch, or promising it to them, anyway. They never actually got it because when Cheryl Willoughby from Que contacted BoardWatch looking for a few good Java authors, the fellows at BoardWatch were good enough to point her in my direction. *Special Edition Using Java* took over my life for a while, and the article for BoardWatch fell by the wayside (sorry guys, I'll get it to you soon).

A book of this size could not possibly have been the work of one person (especially not me). There was a team of authors, editors, and production people who each had to do his or her job in order for everything to come together into the package you're currently holding. While I'm not aware of everyone at Que who contributed to this massive project, I'd like to single out some people there (and at other places) for their contributions to this effort.

I worked with a number of terrific people at Que, inluding Stephanie Gould, Jim Minatel, and Elizabeth Bruns. However, there are a lot of people at Que whose names I never learned who had a great deal of impact on making this book what it is.

Besides the people at Que, there are some folks I'd like to single out for their assistance and support. I'd like to thank Mark Waks, not only for his contribution to the book, but for several long discussions on what the book should and could cover; Mark Schuldenfrei at the X Consortium for pointing me towards material on Broadway; and Peter Salus for sitting down with me and giving me some small idea of what to expect from the business of writing a book.

—AN

## We'd Like To Hear from You!

As part of our continuing effort to produce books of the highest possible quality, Que would like to hear your comments. To stay competitive, we *really* want you, as a computer book reader and user, to let us know what you like or dislike most about this book or other Que products.

You can mail comments, ideas, or suggestions for improving future editions to the address below, or send us a fax at (317) 581-4663. Our staff and authors are available for questions and comments through our Internet site, at **http://www.mcp.com/que**, and Macmillan Computer Publishing also has a forum on CompuServe (type **GO QUEBOOKS** at any prompt).

In addition to exploring our forum, please feel free to contact me personally to discuss your opinions of this book: I'm **mcierzniak@que.mcp.com** on the Internet, and **76245,476** on CompuServe.

Thanks in advance—your comments will help us to continue publishing the best books available on new computer technologies in today's market.

Mark Cierzniak
Product Director
Que Corporation
201 W. 103rd Street
Indianapolis, Indiana 46290
USA

# Contents at a Glance

Appendixes

# Contents

## 7 The Parts of the Language                           **121**

## 8 Tokens in Depth                                       **133**

## 9 Types in Depth                                        **151**

## 10 Classes in Depth — 163

## 13  Statements in Depth                                   245

## 14 Extending Java with Standard Language    257

# III Writing an Applet    267

## 15 The Basics of Applet Construction    269

## 16 Writing an Applet Explored — 293

## 17 Debugging Your Java Code — 309

## 21  AWT                                                          405

## 25  More About Java Applications: Threads      547

## 26  Protocol Handlers      567

## 27 **Content Handlers**

## 28 **Communications and Networking**

# VI The Future of Java 613

## 29 Java and VRML 615

## B The Java System API    **701**

## C Java Language Grammar         **787**

## D  Installation of the Java Developers Kit   809

## E  Glossary   819

## F  The Java-SIG Library of Applets   827

# Introduction

*by Alexander Newman*

## Is This Book for You?

If you're interested in Java, the new programming platform from Sun Microsystems that has taken the World Wide Web by storm, this book is for you. Whether you have only heard of Java and are curious to learn more, or already have a great deal of experience with Java, *Special Edition Using Java* has something to offer you.

The team of writers that put this book together brought a broad range of experience to it. The team included people who had a great deal of Java expertise and people who knew very little Java but had a great deal of programming experience. This wide variety of perspectives enabled us to cover all the issues that occur when a person wants to learn Java. Whether you are a beginner or an expert, someone who was involved in the production of this book represented your perspective. In fact, you could look at *Special Edition Using Java* as being several books in one.

If you're new to Java and object-oriented programming, this book covers basic concepts and builds on them with each chapter. Don't worry if you don't understand any given topic the first time through; *Special Edition Using Java* takes a very hands-on approach to learning. If you don't want to get involved in the nuts and bolts of Java programming right away, the CD-ROM that's included with this book enables you to be a Web wizard without having to develop your own applets.

Intermediate readers are the most difficult audience to write for. Everybody doesn't know something; the problem is that "something" is different for each reader. This book is organized in such a way that it allows you to brush up on a weak area or to quickly locate the answer to a single tough question. This book covers the difficult middle ground, firms up your grasp on the basics, and prepares you to tackle some of advanced topics.

For experienced Java users, this book examines some of the underlying concepts of the Java machine and discusses tough topics such as Java security. The book covers building your own applets with Java and with other languages. The book also provides in-depth coverage of the Java tools, and examines the advantages and disadvantages of Java-compatible technology.

# History of Java

What is Java, and where did it come from? Surprisingly, this hot new technology has been around for years. In 1990, a team of Sun researchers developed some concepts for a new direction in high-tech, consumer-driven technology. Even in 1990, it was obvious that computers were everywhere and were the driving force behind many of the products in the home: the VCR, the microwave oven, the security system, even the stereo system. Unfortunately, almost everyone regarded computers—especially the ones made by Sun Microsystems—as being too weird, too geeky, and too hard to use. Sun, which felt that it had lost a major opportunity by not getting in on the ground floor of the PC explosion, launched a strange new project which would become Java: technology for everyday people.

Patrick Naughton, a programmer at Sun and a friend of Scott McNealy, the president of Sun, was going to quit his job. Sun was going nowhere, and NeXT Computer, Inc., with its cutting-edge NeXTstep operating system, was leading the next wave of the computer revolution. To McNealy's credit, when Naughton said that he was leaving, McNealy asked for a complete report on everything that Naughton felt Sun was doing wrong—and for suggestions on how to fix those problems. Naughton produced the report, and McNealy passed it along to Sun's entire management chain.

The results were astounding. Hundreds of Sun higher-ups agreed with Naughton. One of the people in whom Naughton's report struck a resonant chord was James Gosling. Gosling, whom Sun co-founder Bill Joy calls "the world's greatest programmer," carried a lot of clout with Sun's management. Gosling said that "somewhere along the way [Sun has] lost touch with what it means to produce a quality product."

Backed by luminaries such as John Gage, Sun's science-office director, a group of Sun employees batted ideas around until the small hours of the morning, when they came up with the governing principles for a new project:

- Keep the team small enough to fit around a table at a restaurant.
- The consumer market is where we want to be. And consumers won't come to us; we have to go to them.
- Let the computing environment become what it's going to become, with one parameter: keep it small.
- The hardware should be simple to use and intuitive—in short, computers for real people.

If the principles seemed to be vague, they were equally exciting. With the backing of John Gage, Naughton pitched the idea to Wayne Rosing, the president of Sun Laboratories—a subsidiary of Sun Microsystems. The request seemed ludicrous. Naughton wanted to keep the project secret from everyone except the top executives of Sun—so secret, in fact, that the team was going to relocate away from Sun's corporate headquarters (and away from the corporate mentality that could erode and undermine creative concepts). The team's hardware and software wouldn't have to be compatible with Sun's existing architecture, and on top of everything else, Naughton wanted a budget of $1 million for the first year.

He got it.

Wayne Rosing brought the proposal to Scott McNealy, and after the meeting, Rosing expected to deliver everything that Naughton had asked for. In the next 24 hours, two more of Sun's top executives put their support behind the project, and the team, code-named Green, was born. The team consisted of Naughton, programmer Jim Gosling, and engineer Mike Sheridan, whom Sun had hired after it bought out his startup company.

The sky was the limit. The Green Team could do whatever it wanted. The question, of course, was what the team wanted to do. After some discussion, said Naughton, the team decided that "the third wave of computing would be driven by consumer electronics." Hardware and software would no longer be specialized purchases; consumers would be able to buy software at local record stores.

Gosling brought up the doorknob paradigm during a company retreat in Squaw Valley, California, near Lake Tahoe. Gosling commented that computer chips were showing up everywhere, even in the doorknobs of the rooms at the ski lodge. The Green Team saw a contradiction: even though computer technology was used in all common consumer electronics products (such as stereo systems, television sets, and VCRs), each product required its own interface. In other words, to control three devices, consumers had to have three remote controls and to understand programming for three devices. Then, as now, most people didn't have the understanding. It didn't take much to see that with a little hardware engineering, common devices could not only be made to work together, but also improved.

The Green Team, expanded to include Ed Frank, one of Sun's hardware engineers, finally had its mission: to create a simple device that controlled a variety of day-to-day electronics products. The team moved out of Sun's offices in April 1991 and set up camp in offices above a bank in Menlo Park, hoping that some of Edison's creative genius still lingered in the town. The team did everything as differently from Sun as it could, distancing itself from Sun's corporate mentality physically, culturally, and electronically.

Why was the distance necessary? Mike Sheridan said, "We thought if we stayed over there [at Sun], we would end up with just another workstation." The team ended up building its own machine out of cannibalized parts of Nintendo Gameboys and Sharp television sets, but the language was the real challenge.

After months of banging his head against a wall, Gosling had an epiphany at a rock concert in Mountain View. Instead of seeing the wires, speakers, and automated light show that everyone else was watching, Gosling saw the "packets flowing down the wires and making everything happen." He realized that existing programming languages weren't going to do it. C++ was close, but because that language had come from the computer side of things, its emphasis was on speed, not reliability. In consumer electronics, reliability is more important than speed, and C++ programs had a tendency to break at unpredictable times. In addition, the interfaces were inconsistent. To survive in the consumer marketplace, the software interfaces needed to fit together as regularly as a light bulb fits into a light socket. Gosling needed a new programming language.

As it turned out, Gosling nearly had the answer in his back pocket. He had been tinkering with a replacement language for C++ at home (not surprising when you realize that he wrote his first computer language when he was 14). In the meantime, Naughton had been developing the device's interface: a series of graphic animations. The two men brought the halves of the language together, and by August 1991, a new language called Oak (named for a tree outside Gosling's window) was born.

A year later, the Green Team was demonstrating its baby for Scott McNealy. A hand-held device with no keyboard, no buttons (not even a power switch), and a tiny screen, the prototype didn't look like a computer at all. The interface was invisible. You touched the screen to turn it on and controlled the action on the screen with a fingertip—no keyboard, no tablet and pen, no mouse. A cartoon house appeared on-screen, along with a cartoon tour guide, Duke. Duke was shaped like one of the rank insignias on the old "Star Trek" TV series and the red nose of W.C. Fields. Controlling the house, and Duke, was easy: you moved your finger along the screen from the front hall to the living room. In the living room, an icon that represented a TV schedule rested on the coffee table. You flipped through the guide, selected a movie, and dragged the movie's icon to the virtual VCR. The VCR was programmed, and it told you so with a satisfying "ka-ching" tone.

Nothing like this had been seen before, and McNealy was ecstatic; this was what he needed to crush Apple, IBM, Microsoft, and Hewlett-Packard.

In September 1992, Sun set up the Green Team as FirstPerson, Inc., a Sun subsidiary. Wayne Rosing moved over from Sun Labs to run the new company. Sheridan, who felt that he should have been the one picked to run the company, quit. It wasn't an smooth changing of the guard, but life went on...and went wrong.

Somehow, even this perfect technology wasn't taking off. The chips were too expensive to manufacture, and Sun lost a lucrative contract with Time-Warner to its crosstown rival, Silicon Graphics, Inc. Time-Warner was interested only in a promise of set-top boxes, priced at less than $300 each, for its interactive television project. SGI made the promise but delivered the boxes more than a year late—at a cost of nearly $3,000 each. The project failed all around. (To show how circular the world is, Jim Clark, SGI's founder, later gave up on interactive TV to embrace the World Wide Web—and to found Netscape, Inc., the company that would develop the popular Netscape Navigator browser that would incorporate and drive Java.)

FirstPerson managed to dodge the bullet of promising to deliver something it couldn't, but ultimately, the Green Team project was a failure, and the company was dissolved in 1994. It took Bill Joy to rescue Oak from oblivion.

Joy, one of the co-founders of Sun, is unique in the annals of computing; he's a hacker who writes glorious code but is respected by businesspeople. In 1992, Joy pulled up stakes and headed from California to Aspen, Colorado, where he established a small Sun research lab.

Joy, who saw an opportunity for Oak in the dramatic emergence of the World Wide Web, put Gosling and Naughton back to work on Oak while he went to work convincing Sun the project was worth saving. Joy's idea was to follow Netscape's Internet Play model and release Java for free over the Internet. Internet Play is the "profitless" approach to market share: by giving your product away for noncommercial use, you can make it the standard. Some opponents equate this method with price dumping. Price dumping is a practice used by companies who take a longer view of developing market share. You release a product at a lower cost than it costs you to produce it—sometimes you give it away. By keeping your price drastically below your competitors' prices, you can gain control of the market. Price dumping is illegal in the United States. So far, there are no laws against giving your product away.

Oak hit some legal snags, including the fact that its name was too close to that of another product. In January 1995, Oak was renamed Java—which, incidentally, doesn't stand for Just Another Vague Acronym; it doesn't stand for anything.

Today, Joy's vision of free and accessible technology is a reality, although not one that Sun may be entirely happy with yet. Sun still needs to make sure that Java becomes the standard; then, even more important, it needs to figure out how to make money from the product. Selling commercial licenses seems to be the way to go. Rather than go head-to-head with Sun over Java, on December 7, 1995, Microsoft signed a letter of intent with Sun for a Java-technology source license. Additionally, Microsoft agreed in principle to give Sun two things: Microsoft's reference implementation of the Java virtual machine, and the applet application programming interface (AAPI) for Windows.

This deal was important. By integrating Java into its Explorer browser, Microsoft provided Java with a huge base of previously untapped Windows users. In addition, it was a major endorsement from the world's largest software firm that Sun's Internet technology is top-notch and goes a long way toward establishing Java as the *de facto* open standard for programming on the Internet.

With Java, Sun established the first programming language that wasn't tied to any particular operating system or microprocessor. Applications written in Java will run anywhere, eliminating one of the biggest headaches for computer users: incompatibility between operating systems and versions of operating systems. Where Java goes from here is up to Sun, Microsoft… and you.

# Java and the Web

Until the personal-computing revolution of the 1970s and 1980s, working on a computer meant working on a large, shared mainframe. Users never actually touched the computer, which lived in some basement or air-conditioned room; they worked on terminals. Users shared both the terminals and the computer's processing power with other users on the system. Communicating with other users was easy; a user simply moved a piece of data from one place on the computer to another.

Personal computers changed intercomputer communication. A personal computer put all the computing power that a user could want right on his own desktop, eliminating the need to share a terminal or cycles with anyone else. Unfortunately, if a user wanted to send a message to someone else, he couldn't. Someone had to figure out how to allow all the individual computers to talk to each other without being dependent on one another. The company that developed the solution that became the standard was Xerox Corporation; the solution was Ethernet.

Ethernet was limited, however, in that it primarily connected computers at a single site. The Internet ultimately linked multiple sites and became the operating system for which the World Wide Web became a command-line interpreter. Just as a windowing system allows easy access to an operating system, the Web facilitates use of esoteric, arcane UNIX commands such as Telnet, FTP, and Gopher. And, of course, the Web brought us Java.

To understand why Java has taken off so quickly, all that you really need to know is this: before Java, the World Wide Web was limited to still images; after Java, the Web was capable of supporting animation, graphics, games, and a wide range of special effects. Java effectively allows you run a program on someone else's computer across the Internet—exciting stuff, particularly when you realize what's pushing Web technology. The Web seems to have infiltrated areas where even ubiquitous e-mail can't. No company ever put its e-mail address in its television commercials, but many non-technology-oriented companies, ranging from movie studios to real estate agencies, have discovered the Web.

If you're not familiar with the World Wide Web, it can be a little difficult to understand. Like most of the topics that this book deals with, the Web is buzzword-friendly. The Web could be described as an interactive, global, platform-neutral, hypermedia information retrieval system—but no one would know what that description means. Because some of the terms in that description apply to Java as well as the Web, the following sections touch on them.

## The Web Is an Interactive...

Thanks to Java, the Web is more interactive now than it's ever been, but even before Java came along, the Web was considered to be interactive. All that *interactive* means in this context is that you can do more with a Web page than just look at it.

Almost all Web pages contain *links*, which enable you to move around the page, the site, or even the Web at the click of a button. Besides links, Web pages can have forms; people who access pages with forms can fill in information requested by that pages owner. Sometimes forms aren't open-ended. A person who designs a form can limit the responses by installing a set of buttons—each button representing one possible response. Buttons are great if you want to quantify the responses.

What a user can do with the information he or she supplies is up to the designer of the Web page. Sometimes, you fill out a form in order to request more information, as with a search engine. The information you provide can also be appended to a file on the server that hosts the Web page. The form that you fill out can even be mailed to someone who you couldn't reach using the options presented on that page. So you can order goods, sign up for mailing lists, or get more information.

Although Web pages tend to look like brochures, they certainly don't have to behave like them. This is even more true now that Java has come along.

## The Web Is an Interactive, Global...

The World Wide Web is literally that: worldwide. The Web uses the structure of the Internet to distribute and receive information. Everywhere that the Net goes, the Web can go. Web servers operate on almost every continent and in hundreds of languages.

## The Web Is an Interactive, Global, Platform-Neutral...

"Platform-neutral" is a cryptic way of saying "it doesn't matter what hardware you run your server on or what hardware I run my browser on." Like the Internet, the World Wide Web isn't limited to a single architecture or operating system. You access the Web by using a specialized piece of software called a *browser*, and you can use whatever kind of browser is best for you. Only a few Java-compatible browsers are available; the book talks about them in a later chapter. If you're using a Macintosh, you need to make sure that your browser is compatible with your hardware, not with anyone else's. It doesn't matter whether the machine that you're connecting to (called a *server*) is another Macintosh, an IBM PC, a Sun workstation, or some other brand of computer.

Bear in mind, however, the Web is an outgrowth of the Internet and that most advances in Internet technology happen first on UNIX systems. The reason is simple: the Internet was developed on UNIX machines, and UNIX still is the dominant platform on the Internet. Don't feel that you need to run out and buy a UNIX workstation, though. Like most things, computer technology is demand-driven. Sooner or later (and sooner, if demand exists), the technology that you want will make the move to personal computers.

## The Web Is an Interactive, Global, Platform-Neutral, Hypermedia...

If you ask someone who uses the Web what makes it better than other information services, the most common answer is, "It's cooler." Hypertext is what makes the Web cool. The advantage of hypertext over plain printed material (such as this book, for example) is that in a hypertext document, if you come across a something which looks interesting, you usually can click it to get details. Hyperlinks can be used intradocument (such as footnotes) or interdocument—that is, from one page to another, and many times even from one World Wide Web site to another. The advantage of hyperlinks over footnotes is that hyperlinks allow you to access documents which are related to each other instantly.

Hypertext is a non-linear method of organizing text. Individual elements (words, pictures, addresses, etc.) point to one another. Hyperlinks are elements (words, pictures, etc.) within a hypertext document that point towards other elements.

Until recently, even though the Web encompassed more than simple text, it was commonly called a hypertext system. When the Web was created, it really was just text, and the hyperlinking technology was borrowed from single-user machines. With the introduction of Java, and with the development of VRML, the Virtual Reality Modeling Language (see chapter 28), and other nontext technologies, the Web has truly moved from hypertext to hypermedia, as documents begin to do more and more. The difference, of course, between hypertext and hypermedia, is that in hypertext, words connect largely to words or still images, while in hypermedia elements that connect to one another can be words, pictures, sounds, even applications.

### The Web Is an Interactive, Global, Platform-Neutral, Hypermedia Information Retrieval System

Almost everything on the Web is information. Whether the information in question is a copy of the president's recent State of the Union address or pictures of bikini-clad beauties, the Web allows you to retrieve information entered by other people, and vice versa.

# How This Book Is Organized

*Special Edition Using Java* is organized in seven major sections.

Part I, "Getting and Installing Java," introduces the underlying concepts of the Java programming language, as well as practical information such as where to get Java and how to install it on your computer.

Part II, "The Java Language," covers the basics of programming in this C/C++-like language, including classes, multithreading, types, expressions, and statements. This part of the book also discusses Java security.

Part III, "Writing an Applet," explores the construction of applets (Java's mini-programs) from concept to finished program. This part describes several applets in detail and shows you how to write your own.

Part IV, "Using Applets in Web Pages," teaches you how to apply what you learned in parts I through III to the World Wide Web. Installing applets isn't difficult, but you need to be aware of what requirements exist and what system resources Java can consume.

Part V, "Advanced Java," focuses on Java applications. Although much of the thrust of Java today is toward applet-building, Java is a robust language, fully capable of supporting large and intricate programs. Like applications developed in other languages, Java applications (unlike applets) don't require a browser.

Part VI, "The Future of Java," discusses where you can expect to go with Java in the near and not-so-near future. This part of the book pays particular attention to the interaction of Java and VRML (Virtual Reality Modeling Language).

Part VII is made up of reference material: the appendixes and the glossary. There are six appendixes, ranging in topics of the Java API to the Java-SIG Library of Applets.

# Conventions Used in This Book

Before reading *Special Edition Using Java* you should be aware of several conventions that the book uses.

Program code is printed in a `monospace font`. Anything that you see in that font, you should type. *Variables* in program code appear in `monospace italics`. The specific word that a variable represents varies, according to the situation; you need to enter the appropriate data.

*Italics* also are used for definitions. Terms are defined the first time that they appear in the book; some terms also appear in the glossary (appendix E).

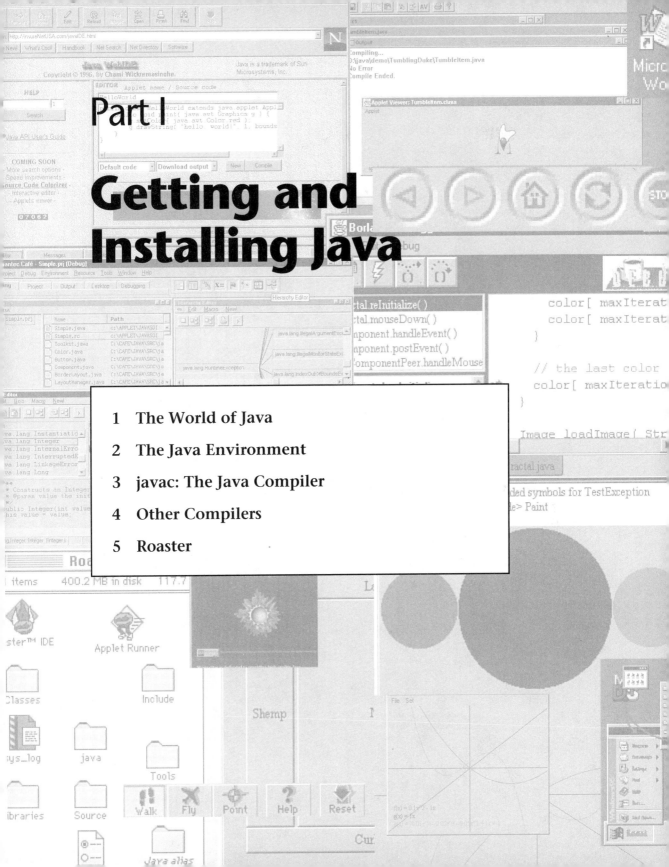

# Part I

# Getting and Installing Java

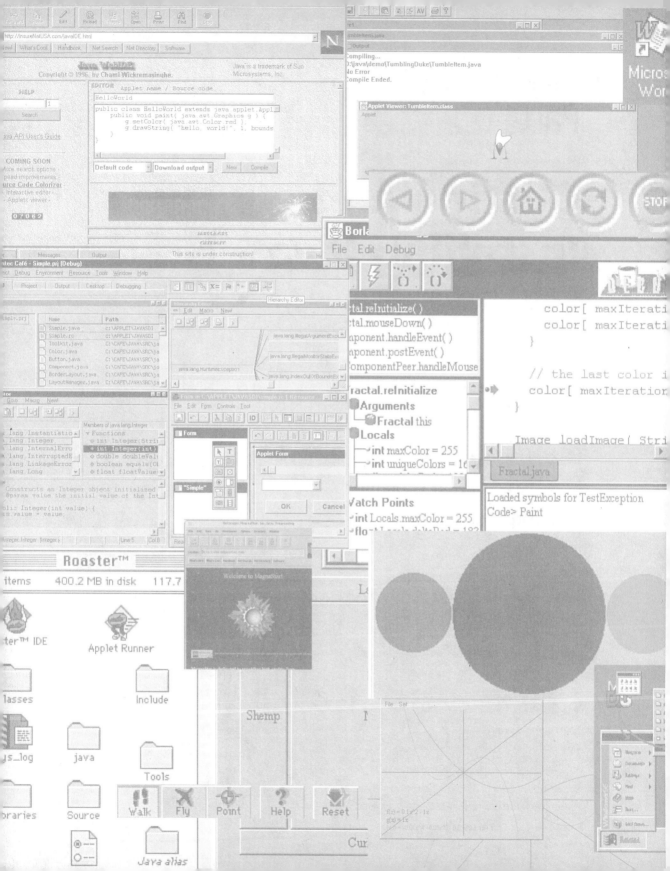

# CHAPTER 1

# The World of Java

*by Alexander Newman*

In this chapter, we'll talk a little bit about what Java is, in general terms. Java is in many ways similar to program languages that have gone before it, but there are a few key differences. Fortunately, the fact that there's a standard vocabulary used to describe computer languages makes our job a little easier.

Throughout the upcoming chapter, we'll see that Java's features are really all interrelated. You can't talk about Java security without discussing the fact that Java is interpreted by the browser. You can't discuss the fact that Java is interpreted as well as compiled without touching on architecture independence—and architecture independence is the cornerstone of Java's portability.

In this chapter you'll learn:

- Why Java is so popular
- How Java interracts with HTML
- Java's defining qualities
- Some of the differences between Java and C++

## Why Is Java so Hot?

You can make up whatever coffee metaphors you like, but there's no getting around the fact that Java is the most exciting thing to hit the Internet since the World Wide Web. That's because it fills a need—several needs, in fact. With Java, programmers are able to deliver what everyone who uses the Web has been clamoring for—true interactivity.

First of all, Java is a programming language. Languages are used to compose a set of instructions which a computer follows. These groups of instructions are called programs, applications, executables, or, in the case of Java, applets.

Java can also be used to build stand-alone programs, called applications, just like any other programming language. It's the applets that are the most innovative thing about Java.

Java applets, as discussed in the introduction, add life to the World Wide Web. By "life" I mean that with Java you can add animation, local data searches, and a wide variety of other functions and features that just weren't possible without the Java environment. It's not surprising that companies from Netscape to America Online have jumped on-board the Java bandwagon to design the next generation of browsers.

This brings us to browsers. In order to look at the Web, you need a *browser*. A browser is an application that runs over the Internet and interprets HTML code. There are graphical and non-graphical browsers, but we're interested in the graphical ones only (the ones that can display pictures on your screen). There are a lot of browsers available. Currently only two support Java: Netscape 2.0 and HotJava.

Netscape 2.0 can be downloaded from

**http://www.netscape.com/**

Currently HotJava is available for Windows 95, Windows NT, and Sun's Solaris 2.x platforms. Other systems, including Mac OS 7.5, are in the works and should be available soon. HotJava can be downloaded from

**http://www.javasoft.com/**

Browsers aren't the only way to view applets. Sun has a utility called Appletviewer. Unfortunately, Appletviewer, which is currently available for Sun's Solaris operating system, Windows, and the Macintosh, doesn't interpret HTML code. It only shows applets.

For example, the Webpage called Example1.html contains the following code:

```
<title>Jumping Box</title>
<hr>
<H2>The Amazing Jumping Box!</H2>
<P>
<applet code=MouseTrack.class width=300 height=300>
</applet>
<P>
<H3>Stunning and amazing -- a game of skill for children of all
ages!</H3>
<hr>
<a href="MouseTrack.java">The source.</a>
```

Figure 1.1 shows that file, Example1.html using Sun's Applet Viewer.

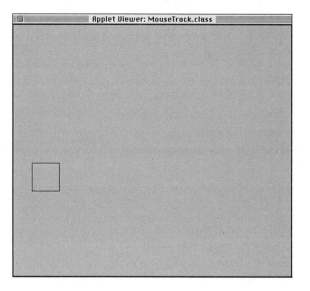

**Fig. 1.1**
Example1.html viewed with Applet Viewer.

Looking at this Web page through the applet viewer, we lose all of the text. On the other hand, if we look at it through a Java-powered browser (in this case, Netscape Navigator 2.0 for the Macintosh), we not only can see the applet, but the text ("Stunning and amazing—a game of skill for children of all ages!") as well.

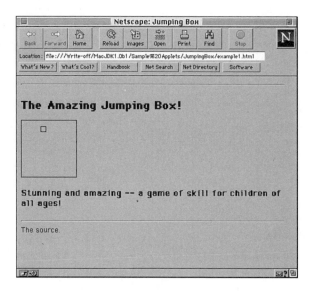

**Fig. 1.2**
Example1.html viewed with Netscape Navigator.

Java is a complete programming environment and comes with its own set of tools, including a compiler (javac) and a debugger (jdb). We'll talk about both the compiler and the debugger in depth later on. For now, it's important to get a basic grasp of how the Java compiler acts upon what you write to develop bytecode.

Byte code format is halfway between the code you write (source code) and the code the computer reads (which is a machine language specific to the architecture of each type of computer). In other words, the Java compiler takes your relatively short Java source code and breaks it down (lengthens it, really) into a longer set of instructions that are ready to be run on a computer—once the specifics of that computer are known.

Bytecode consists of a lot of the material produced by a normal compiler, but stops just before conforming the code to the particulars of a specific architecture or operating system. The bytecode is passed along to the run-time environment. The *run-time environment* interprets and checks the integrity and security of bytecode, then dynamically applies specifics based on the parameters found in the HTML code, system configurations, and environmental variables.

# What Is Java?

Now that we've established the difference between a browser (HotJava, Netscape) and a programming language (Java), it's time to get down to what Java is.

The folks who designed Java hoped to solve some of problems they saw in modern programming. As we said, Java's core principles developed out of a desire to build software for consumer electronics. Like those devices, the language needed to be compact, reliable, portable, distributed, realtime, and embedded.

Like most modern products, Java can be defined neatly in a set of buzzwords. Sun Microsystems' official definition of Java is:

Java: A simple, object-oriented, distributed, interpreted, robust, secure, architecture neutral, portable, high-performance, multithreaded, and dynamic language.

## Java Is Simple...

Even though the Java developers decided that C++ was unsuitable for their purposes, they designed Java as closely to C++ as possible. This was done in order to make the system more familiar, more comprehensible, and to shorten the time necessary to learn the new language. One of Java's greatest appeals is that, if you're a programmer, you already know how to use it. Ninety percent of the programmers working these days use C, and almost all object-oriented programming is done in C++.

Another goal of the designers was to eliminate support for multiple class inheritance, operator overloading, and extensive automatic coercion of data types—several of the poorly understood, confusing, and rarely used features of C++. Also omitted from Java were header files, pre-processor, pointer arithmetic, structures, unions, or multi-dimensional arrays. They were selective and retained features that would ease development, implementation, and maintenance of software, while omitting things that would slow a developer down. For example, even though operator overloading was eliminated (which lets programmers exist when operators have more than one semantic interpretation), they kept method overloading.

Here's the now-famous "Hello World" program, rendered as a Java applet:

```
import java.awt.*;

public class applet extends java.applet.Applet {
        public void paint(Graphics g)
        {
                g.drawString("Hello world!", 25, 25);
        }
}
```

Figure 1.3, below shows the "Hello World" applet and HTML code for the page "example1.html" in Sun's applet viewer. Not very exciting, but we've got to start small.

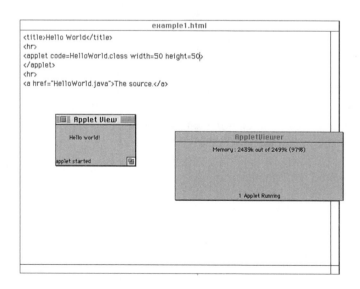

**Fig. 1.3**
HelloWorld applet, as seen with Applet Viewer.

Another problem faced by C and C++ programmers is storage management, which is the allocation and freeing of memory. Ordinarily, a C programmer needs to keep a careful eye on how much memory the program is using. When a chunk of memory is no longer being utilized, the programmer needs to make sure the program frees it up so it can be reused. This is even harder than it sounds, especially in large programs, and is the main cause for memory leaks and bugs.

When programming in Java, you don't need to worry about those problems.

The Java system has an embedded auto garbage collection. The garbage collector simplifies Java programming, but at the expense of making the system more complicated. Because it has automatic garbage collection, Java not only makes programming easier, it also dramatically cuts down on the number of bugs and eliminates the hassle of memory management.

## Java Is Small

One of the features of Java which Sun neglected to mention in its definition was Java's size—or lack of it. As a side effect of being simple, Java is very small. Remember that one of the original goals of Java was to facilitate the construction of software that ran stand-alone in small machines. The original *7 module that Java was developed for had only 3Mb of main memory. Java can happily run on personal computers with at least 4Mb of RAM or even VCRs, telephones, or doorknobs.

The size of the basic interpreter and class support is about 40K of RAM; adding the basic standard libraries and thread support (essentially a self-contained microkernel) adds an additional 175K. The combined total of approximately 215K is significantly smaller than comparable programming languages and environments.

## Java Is Simple (Small), Object-Oriented...

Java is an object-oriented language. That means that it's part of a family of languages that focuses on defining data as objects and the methods that may be applied to those objects. As we've said, Java and C++ share many of the same underlying principles; they just differ in style and structure. Simply put, object-oriented (OO, for short) languages describe interactions among data objects. To make an analogy with medicine, an "object-oriented" doctor would be interested in holistic medicine—examining the body (or object) as a whole first, and the vaccines, diets, and medicine (the tools) used to make your health improve after that. A "non-object-oriented" doctor would think primarily of his tools.

Many OO languages support multiple inheritance, which can sometimes lead to confusion or unnecessary complications. Java doesn't; as part of its "less-is-more" philosophy, Java supports only single inheritance. That means that each class can inherit from only one other class at any given time. This avoids the problem of a class inheriting classes whose behaviors are contradictory or mutually exclusive.

Having said that, we should point out that, while Java does not support multiple inheritance per se, it does support abstract classes, which can implement multiple inheritances. Abstract classes allow programmers to define methods for interfaces and worry about how the methods will be implemented later. This bypasses a lot of the problems inherent in actual multiple inheritance while still retaining most of the advantages.

Each class, whether abstract or not, defines the behavior of an object through a set of methods. All the code used for Java is divided into classes. Behaviors can be inherited from one class to the next, and at the head of the class hierarchy is the class called "Object." This is illustrated in figure 1.1, which shows a class called "meat" that inherits from class "Food," which, as all classes ultimately do, inherits from the class called OBJECT.

Objects can also implement any number of interfaces (or abstract classes, remember?). The Java interfaces are a lot like the Interface Definition Language interfaces. That similarity means that it's easy to build a compiler from IDL to Java.

That compiler could be used in the CORBA (Common Object Request Broker Architecture) system of objects to build distributed object systems. Is this good? Yes. Both IDL interfaces and the CORBA system are used in a wide variety of computer systems, and this facilitates Java's platform independence, which we'll talk more about later.

As part of the effort to keep Java simple, not everything in this object-oriented language is an object. Booleans, numbers, and other simple types are not objects, but Java does have wrapper objects for all simple types. Wrapper objects allow all simple types to be implemented as though they were classes.

Object-oriented design is also the mechanism which allows modules to "plug and play." The object-oriented facilities of Java are essentially those of C++, with extensions from Objective C for more dynamic method resolution.

## Java Is Distributed...

An essential characteristic of client/server applications like Java is the ability to share both information and the data processing workload. The term "distributed" describes the relationship between system objects, whether these objects are on remote or local systems. One of the great things about Java applets and applications is that they can open and access objects across the Web via URLs as easily as they can access a local file system.

Another bonus for Java programmers is the extensive library of routines built into the language. This allows Java applications and applets to cope easily with TCP/IP protocols like HTTP and FTP. Currently, some of the other protocols which are in common on the Web—protocols like gopher, mailto, or news—haven't been implemented in Java, but they will be in future releases.

The beauty of the distributed system is that multiple designers, at multiple remote locations, can collaborate on a single project. For example, by using Java, a distributed OO steam engine builder application that supports collaboration from other engine builders (at either remote or local sites) could be built. Using the OO steam engine builder, collaborators can work together to develop a better (faster, economical, etc.) machine.

## Java Is Interpreted (and Compiled)...

Strictly speaking, that's true, although in reality Java is both interpreted and compiled. In fact, only about 20 percent of the Java code is interpreted by the browser—but this is a crucial 20 percent. Both Java's security and its ability to run on multiple platforms stem from the fact that the final steps of compilation are handled locally.

A programmer first compiles Java source into byte code, using the Java compiler. This byte code is binary and architecture-neutral (we'll also use the term "platform-independent"—they mean the same thing). This byte code isn't complete until it's interpreted by a Java run-time environment, usually a browser. Since each Java run-time environment is for a specific platform, the final product is going to work on that specific platform.

This is good news for developers. It means that Java code is Java code is Java code, no matter what platform you're developing for or on. That means you could write and compile a Java applet on your UNIX system and install the applet on your Web page. Three different people on three different machines—each with its own environment—can take a peek at your new applet. Provided each of those three people was running a Java-capable browser, it wouldn't matter whether they were on an IBM, an H-P, or a Macintosh. Using Java means that only one source of Java code needs to be maintained for the byte code to run on a variety of platforms. One pass through a compiler for multiple platforms is good news for programmers.

Be aware that, because Java byte code is interpreted, Web pages with applets frequently take much longer to load than those without. That's due, in part, to the fact that the byte code that will become the applets you see contains more compile-time data than is typically used in non-interpreted situations. The byte code is downloaded to your system, much as the HTML code or images that make up a Web page are. Then a series of run-time procedures check its security or robustness.

Why is this combination of compilation and interpretation a positive feature? First, it facilitates security and stability. The Java environment contains an element called the linker, which checks data coming into your machine to make sure that it contains neither deliberately harmful files (security) nor files that could disrupt the functioning of your computer (robustness).

---

**Caution**

Despite the assurances of Sun and the Java team, you're not completely safe when using Java. There are still too many variables. An example of this can be seen at the Missile Commando site (**http://www.sdsu.edu/~boyns/java/mc/**).

See chapter 7 for more information on Java security.

---

Second, and more importantly, this combination of compilation and interpretation alleviates concerns about version mismatches.

The fact that the final portion of compilation is being done by a platform-specific device, which is maintained by the end-user, relieves the developer of the responsibility of maintaining multiple sources for multiple platforms. Interpretation also allows data to be incorporated at run-time, which is the foundation of Java's dynamic behavior.

## Java Is Robust...

"Robust" is simply computerspeak for how reliable a language is. The more robust a language is, the less likely that programs written in this language will crash and the more likely it is that they will be bug-free. Strongly typed languages (like Java or C++) allow extensive compile-time checking, meaning any bugs can be found early. "Strongly typed" means that most of the data type checking isn't performed at run-time, rather it's performed during compilation.

Simply put, Java can't cause programs to crash. That's obviously a feature because crashes are a bad thing. At a minimum, they're inconvenient. At most, they can cost you many hours of work, or worse. A Java program can't cause a crash because it doesn't have permission to access all of your computer's memory. Programs written in other languages can traditionally access, and therefore change, any part of your system's memory, but Java has a built-in limitation. Java programs can access only a restricted area of memory, so they can't change a value that is not meant to change.

Unlike C++, which has a lot of loopholes in compile-time checking (particularly method/procedure declarations), Java requires declarations and doesn't support C-style implicit declarations. Implicit declarations are bad; C++ supports them mostly to be compatible with the older C language. They state that if a method is implicitly declared, then type information isn't available, which defeats the type-checking process. In short, with implicit declarations a C++ programmer can (deliberately or through oversight) do an end-run around the safety built into strong type-checking. A Java programmer can't do that.

As a final safety check, Java has the linker. The linker is part of the run-time environment. It understands the type system and during run-time repeats many of the type-checks done by the compiler to guard against version mismatch problems.

Robustness is in many ways Java's most important feature. Despite the release of the "gold" version of Java, it is still very much an experimental language and is still in the development stages. Java's stability—its robustness—encourages people to use it as a development platform. It allows programmers to focus on programming, rather than chasing bugs or memory leaks. And the more people work with Java, the closer it grows to becoming the standard that Sun hopes it can be.

## Java Is Secure...

Java's security is still something that remains to be proven. The concept of allowing another site to upload executables sight unseen to your machine is something that just doesn't sit right with many computer and Internet professionals. The simple truth is, viruses are out there, and no one wants to infect their machine by downloading a binary from the Net.

Some of the other features, such as robustness and the fact that Java is both interpreted and compiled, are aids to security. For example, the fact that Java programs can't access memory means they can be safely executed. Mostly, Java is secure because it was designed to be.

As we've said. Java programs are first compiled into byte-code instructions, proto-programs, which are verified. Byte-code instructions, unlike other instruction sets, are not platform specific and contain extra type information.

This type information can be used to verify the program's legality and to check for potential security violations.

Java uses a new and unique approach to calling functions. Traditionally, PC programs call functions by a numeric address. Since this address is just a numeric sequence and that sequence can be constructed any way the programmer likes, any number can be used to tell the program to execute a function. This provides a level of anonymity that makes it impossible to tell which functions actually will be used when the program is run.

Java, on the other hand, uses names. Methods and variables can be accessed only by name, which means that determining which methods and functions are actually used is easy. This *verification* process is used to ensure the byte code has not been contaminated or altered and that it conforms to Java language constraints.

Even if a "bad" applet somehow managed to slip through the verification process, the amount of damage it could do is extremely limited. That's because Java applets are executed in a restricted environment. Within this environment, the Java applet is not permitted to execute certain dangerous functions unless the end user allows it to.

## Java Is Architecture Neutral...

The team that designed Java was well aware that if Java was to support applications on networks, it would have to support a variety of systems with a variety of CPU and operating system architectures. A Java application can execute anywhere on the network, or on the Internet, because the compiler generates an architecture-neutral object file format—the compiled code is executable on many processors, provided that processor is running a Java-savvy browser.

Once a Java program is written, it stays written. It doesn't need to be recompiled for each different platform. The Java language is the same on every computer. There's no "Java for Windows" or "Java for Macintosh." This isn't a new concept for the Web; HTML scripting works the same way. However, HTML code is good for only one thing, generating Web pages. Java, on the other hand, is a full-fledged programming language. A platform-independent language is not only useful for networks but also for single system software distribution. Currently, application writers developing software for the present computer market have to produce multiple versions of their application: one for each platform they want their software to run on. Current trends in the personal computer market, like Apple moving off the 68000 processor, make developing software that runs on all platforms almost impossible. With Java, the same version of the application runs on all platforms.

This is possible because, as we discussed earlier, the Java compiler generates bytecode instructions and not binaries. The bytecode instructions are easy to interpret on any machine, although they are not oriented towards a particular platform, and easily translated into native machine code at runtime.

## Java Is Portable...

Java's architecture neutrality makes the concept of porting from one platform to another a little redundant. But even beyond platform independence, Java's use of standards for data types eliminates the "implementation dependent" aspects of the specification that are found in C and C++.

For example, in Java the sizes of the primitive datatypes are specified, as is the behavior of arithmetic on them. Two examples that Sun uses are that *int* always means a signed two's complement, 32-bit integer, and *float* always means a 32-bit IEEE 754 floating point number. Computer technology has advanced to the point where making a decision like this is possible. Almost all interesting CPUs share these characteristics. Further, the Java libraries define portable interfaces for the three most common platforms: UNIX, Windows, and the Macintosh.

But even beyond that, the Java system itself was built to be portable. Javac, the Java compiler, is written in Java, and the run-time environment is written in ANSI C with a portability boundary, which is essentially POSIX Interpreted. The Java interpreter can execute Java bytecodes directly on any machine to which the interpreter has been ported. Using Java speeds the development process, and that speed allows developers to explore directions they might not have had time for using a system that didn't support linking. Linking, since it's a lighter-weight and a more incremental process, only enhances the speed of the development process.

The linker also facilitates the debugging process. Since more compile-time information is carried over (therefore and available) at run-time as a part of the bytecode stream, the linker is able to check types. Dynamic type-checking further enhances debugging.

Ease of portability will go a long way towards establishing Java as a commonly used development platform. Remember that most of the software business is just that, a business. Businesses are interested in making money, and one of the best ways to make money is to capture marketshare. Before Java, if you wanted to develop a software product that run on the Macintosh and under Windows and on UNIX, there was a lot of redundancy on your development team—in fact, there were usually multiple development teams, one for each platform. This drastically increases overhead. With Java, you're essentially developing for several platforms simultaneously. The necessity of porting is nearly eliminated.

## Java Is High Performance...

Java's not high performance in the sense of "faster than a comparable C++ routine." In fact, it's almost the same speed. In benchmark tests run by Sun Microsystems on one of their SPARCStation 10 machines, the performance of byte codes converted to machine code is almost indistinguishable from native C or C++. Of course, that doesn't take into account the time of run-time compilation.

Interpreted byte code performance is fine for most usual tasks, but there are certainly situations which call for higher performance. In those instances, the interpreted byte codes may not be the way to go, especially when you consider that the byte code format was designed with generating machine codes in mind. The process of generating machine code from byte code is pretty simple and produces reasonably good code.

## Java Is Multithreaded...

The human brain is multithreaded. It can easily handle thousands of tasks simultaneously. You can be talking on the telephone while listening to the radio while pouring yourself a glass of orange juice while pinning the telephone to your ear with your shoulder while thinking about your plans for the weekend while noticing that the dishes need to be done while...

Computers aren't that good and probably won't ever be. However, a powerful computer application can deal with many simultaneous actions. Multithreading is how they accomplish this. Unfortunately, C and C++ lend themselves towards a single-threaded program, which hampers your ability to develop multithreaded programs. Java couldn't be restricted to a single-threaded construction.

What multithreading means, to Java users, is that they don't have to wait for the application to finish one task before beginning another. For example, if you were playing a dungeon adventure game, one thread could be handling the mathematics of the combat you were in, while another was taking care of the graphics. Multithreading eliminates a lot of lag time when compared to single-threading. On a personal computer, it means you see a lot less of the hourglass or wristwatch icon which we all know is the computer's way of saying "Don't rush me."

Java's sophisticated set of synchronization primitives are integrated into the language, making them more robust and much easier to use. That's not original to Java. A lot of the style of integration is based on Xerox's Cedar/Mesa system. But if it's not broken, don't fix it. Java's primitives are based on C. Anthony Hoare's 20 year-old monitor and condition variable paradigm.

What this built-in multithreading means to programmers is that constructing multithreaded programs is a lot easier in Java. The synchronization features eliminated much of the difficulties of dealing with a multithreaded environment's unpredictable nature. Things don't always happen in the same order.

Remember that the benefits of multithreading (better interactive responsiveness, real-time behavior) depend a lot on the underlying platform. Java applications are MP-Hot—they run better on a multi-processor machine—and stand-alone Java run-time environments have good real-time behavior. This will slow down if you're running a Java application on top of Windows, the Macintosh, Windows NT, or UNIX operating systems. Homogeneity is the best way to get performance out of any operating environment, and Java is no exception.

## Finally, Java Is Dynamic

Java is a more dynamic language than C or C++. Unlike either of those languages, Java was designed to adapt to an evolving environment.

One of the major problems in development that uses C++ is that you can unwittingly or unwillingly become dependent on someone else. This is due to *class libraries*, a collection of plug and play components. Since C++ code has to be implemented in class libraries, if you license and use a second party's class library in your software, and that company subsequently alters or upgrades that library, you're more than likely going to have to respond. This response could be almost anything up to and including recompiling and redistributing your own software.

Now bearing that in mind, imagine the problems that can result if your customer is in an environment where he gets your (old) software and the second party's updated libraries independently. What happens if the library producer distributes an upgrade to their libraries? To your customers, it looks like all of the software you've built them (using those libraries, but the customer may not know that) breaks. It's possible—but extremely difficult—to write programs in C++ and still avoid this problem, but the resulting programs are hardly worth it. Essentially it means not using any of the language's OO features directly.

Java, on the other hand, makes the interconnections between modules later. This is both a more effective and easier to follow use of the object-oriented paradigm, and also neatly avoids the library problem. Because Java delays the binding of modules, libraries can be upgraded and changed at will. Methods and instance variables can be added or deleted without any negative impact on the library clients.

> **Caution**
>
> Having said that, you should be aware that it is possible to substitute different vesions of a class at run-time with disasterous consequences.  If you remove a method from one class, without recompiling the entire program, eliminating all *.class files, the applet/application will throw a very very vague exception.

Like Objective C, Java understands *interfaces*. Similar to classes, interfaces are simply any specification of a set of methods that an object responds to. Unlike classes, interfaces support multiple-inheritance, plus they can be used more flexibly than the usual class inheritance structure, which is quite rigid.

In a C or C++ program, if you have a pointer to an unknown type object, there is no way to find out. The compiler makes the assumption that you're not doing anything incorrectly. With Java, on the other hand, casts are checked at both compile-time and run-time, so determining the type of an object based on the run-time type information is easy. Because of this run-time checking, Java casts are more trustworthy than those in C++.

Further, it's possible to look up the definition of a class given a string containing its name. This is possible because class definitions are contained in the class named Class, and Class has a run-time representation. This allows you to compute a data type name and easily have that name dynamically-linked into a running system.

Lisp, TCL and Smalltalk are often used for prototyping because they are extremely dynamic. Dynamic languages are good for prototyping because of their flexibility. You can put off a lot of decisions. Like Java, the above languages are known for their robustness, and programmers don't have to worry about memory getting corrupted. This quality is one of Java's many good points.

One reason that dynamic languages are good for prototyping is that they don't require you to pin down decisions early on. Although it's dynamic, Java requires programmers to make choices explicitly, but there are safeguards built into the Java environment to keep a poor choice from crashing your program. For example, if you write a method invocation and get it wrong, you are alerted to the error when you try to compile the source. Method invocation error is covered the same way.

# Differences between Java and C++

Throughout this chapter we've discussed some of the features of the Java language in terms of their differences or similarities to the C++ programming language. There are a few issues that didn't fit well into Sun's feature list, but are worth pointing out anyway.

Certainly the biggest difference between Java and C/C++ is that Java has true arrays instead of linked lists of pointers. Java's pointer model eliminates the possibility of overwriting memory and corrupting data, and allows subscript checking to be performed. C++, on the other hand, has pointer arithmetic instead of true arrays. In addition, it is not possible to turn an arbitrary integer into a pointer by casting.

There's also the issue of speed. With all the talking we've done about how efficient Java is, you'd expect it to be significantly faster than C++, right? Not so. C++ is almost 20 times as fast as Java. This is still "fast enough," and developers are working on code generators to enable Java programs to run nearly as quickly as those written in C++. ❖

## CHAPTER 2
# The Java Environment

*by Simeon Greene*

Now that you have the Java Development Kit installed and decompressed, you can get to work, and you'll need to know a bit about your work environment.

The JDK environment is command-line driven and, unlike some programming languages, does not look attractive just sitting there. In other words, the Java environment is not graphical, as are other popular languages like Visual C++ or Visual Basic, which use a GUI (Graphical User Interface) environment.

Command-line driven also means that you call JDK's tools, including the compiler, from the command prompt (DOS prompt for Windows NT and 95), and you create the text of the Java file (`filename.java`) using an ASCII text editor such as the MS-DOS Editor or WinEdit.

This chapter discusses the Java environment. The main topics to be covered are

- Customizing the Java environment
    - How to use the Java environment tools from any directory (adding \java\bin to the path).
    - How to reduce retyping commands (using the DOSKey program).
    - How to organize files and directories.
- Testing your installation
    - How to test your installation on a Java applet.
    - How to test your installation on a Java application.
- The Java environment tools
    - What are the functions of the appletviewer tool?
    - What are the functions of the functions of the Java Compiler (javac)?

- • What are the functions of the Java Interpreter (java)?
- • What are the functions of the Java Disassembler (javap)?
- • What are the functions of the javah tool?
- • What are the functions of the Java Documentation Generator (javadoc)?
- • What are the functions of the Java Debugger (jdb)?
- ■ Environment variables
  - • What is the WWW_HOME environment variable?
  - • What is the HOTJAVA_HOME environment variable?
  - • What is the HOTJAVA_READ_PATH environment variable?
  - • What is the HOTJAVA_WRITE_PATH environment variable?
  - • What is the CLASSPATH environment variable?

| **Note** |
| --- |
| This chapter covers only the features of 1.0 and 2.0 versions of the JDK, provided by Sun Microsystems (the versions downloaded from **http://www.sun.com/**). Other tools and Java compilers are available from third party vendors but are not discussed in this chapter. |

# Customizing the Java Environment

In a moment you'll put your installation to the test. Before you do this, however, you may find it helpful to customize your Java environment. Although this step may seem unnecessary—since at a glance there doesn't seem to be much of an environment to customize—you might have to thank these seemingly insignificant tips for saving your fingers from repetitive typing or preventing your hair from being pulled out when none of the Java tools seem to work!

| **Tip** |
| --- |
| It is good practice to make the tools of the environment accessible from all directories on your system. For Microsoft Windows NT and Windows 95 users, this is achieved by placing the directory containing the tools in the path statement of the autoexec.bat file. |

## Adding \Java\bin to the Path

The Java compiler as well as the other tools are located in the directory [MyDrive]:\[MySubdir]\java\bin, where [drive] is the letter of the drive where the JDK resides, and [MySubDir] is the name of the subdirectory, if any, in which Java was installed (decompressed). To make these files accessible from any other drive, or directory, edit your autoexec.bat file, and add [MyDrive]:\[MySubdir]\java\bin to the path statement (if your directory structure is different, you will need to make the necessary adjustments). Figure 2.1 shows the path statement in my autoexec.bat file that has the location of my \java\bin directory added to it.

---

**Note**

For Windows 95 users, the autoexec.bat file can be edited by using SysEdit (System Editor). SysEdit can be executed by clicking on the Start Button, selecting Run, and then typing **sysedit** in the text box provided.

---

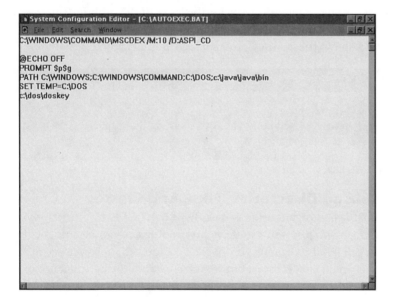

**Fig. 2.1**
The \java\bin directory added to the path statement in the autoexec.bat file.

## Using DOSKey To Reduce Retyping Commands

The DOS program, DOSKey, is a TSR (Terminate and Stay Resident) program that has as one of its many functions the ability to store text that the user has typed in a memory lookup table of some sort, and allow the user to scroll through this table to find commands or executable text (program names) that have already been entered. This can become very useful in the Java environment because many commands may have to be called numerous times.

The case of having to recompile is one example. With DOSKey installed, you need to type this command only once. If your code produces errors (and believe me it will!) on the first compile, you will need to recompile and then edit the file again. This becomes a tedious typing routine, especially if you need to do it six or seven times, or if you're not an avid typist. DOSKey can limit this routine to as little as two keys.

The Up Arrow allows you to scroll up the memory table and find text that has already been used. Instead of retyping **javac filename.java** (to recompile your code), you could simply use the Up Arrow key to scroll through the memory table until you found `javac filename.java` and then hit enter. The Down Arrow key is used to scroll down the table, and the Escape Key is used to clear the entry.

DOSKey has some other interesting features, but these are not discussed in this chapter or in this book. For more information on DOSKey, type **doskey/?** at the command prompt. To have DOSKey installed on your system, just add [DosDrive]:\[DosSubdir]\DOSKey to the end of your autoexec.bat file, where [DosDrive] is the letter of the drive in which DOS is installed, and [DosSubdir] is the name of your DOS subdirectory. Figure 2.1 shows the DOSKey program loaded in my autoexec.bat file.

### Tip

To clear the command history table, use Alt+F7. To view this table, use F7. DOSKey will lose stored commands when you exit from DOS. Use Alt+Tab to switch tasks rather than quitting DOS.

## Organizing Directories, Files, and Classes

File structure and organization can easily be overlooked by an anxious programmer who just wants to delve into coding and not be bothered by aesthetics or good programming "hygiene." You will, however, see in the upcoming chapters that organization is in fact vital to the performance of your Java applications and applets. Some good principles to follow are to:

- Create a project subdirectory (c:\JavaProjects) to store all your other subdirectories, and files related to Java.

- Separate files in various subdirectories according to type. For example, create a Java subdirectory (c:\JavaProjects\Java) to store files of type filename.java, and a Classes subdirectory (c:\JavaProjects\Classes) to store files of type filename.class.

- Keep a consistent, and meaningful naming scheme for all filenames, and directories.

# Testing Your Installation

Now, after all this preparation, see if your installation works. Test both Java applets and Java applications since each are handled differently by your system and the Java environment.

▶ Java applets are covered in chapter 15, "The Basics of Applet Construction," p. 269, and Java applications are covered in chapter 23, "Java Applications," p. 501.

| Note |
| --- |
| A Java application is just what the name implies—a stand-alone Java program that is executed on your system by using the Java Interpreter. A Java applet is usually a remote Java program executed by a Web Browser (Netscape 2.0 for example). The Browser locates the applet by referencing its HTML tag (<applet code="myApplet" width = somewidth height = someheight> </applet>) embedded in a Web Page. |

## Testing with a Java Applet

There is no better way to test our installation on an applet than to actually write one. The following applet is a fairly simple one, and there is no need to skip to chapter 15, "The Basics of Applet Construction," so that you can understand applets better and then return to this test. This applet is also available on the CD.

Follow the these steps to test an applet in the Java environment.

### Creating a Test Applet

Using an editor (I use MS-DOS Editor), create a new file called FancyHello.java by typing in the following:

```
/*
 First java applet. This applet will be used to test my installation.
*/

import java.awt.*;

public class FancyHello extends java.applet.Applet {

        Font        f;
        int         xpos,ypos;
        String      HelloString;
        FontMetrics fm;

        public void paint (Graphics g) {
                HelloString = "Hello World!";
                f = new Font("Helvetica", Font.BOLD +
```

```
Font.ITALIC,24);
                 fm = getFontMetrics(f);
                 g.setFont(f);

                 g.setColor(Color.blue);
                 xpos = (this.size().width -
fm.stringWidth(HelloString)) / 2;
                 ypos = (this.size().height -
fm.stringWidth(HelloString)) /2;

                 g.drawString(HelloString, xpos, ypos);
        }
    }
```

(Don't worry about the syntax for now; it will be explained in later chapters.)

Save this file as FancyHello.java in your Java subdirectory.

### Compiling a Test Applet

From the command prompt, and within the same subdirectory in which you saved your java file, type

### javac FancyHello.java

Since Java is case-sensitive, take care to type everything exactly as it appears here. In a few seconds your command prompt will reappear. If you receive an error after the compiler is finished, check your code for typographic errors.

---

### Troubleshooting

*Whenever I try to compile within a specific subdirectory, I get the error* Bad command or filename.

Your \java\bin directory is probably not in your path statement. You can check your path statement for this directory by typing path at the command prompt. If this subdirectory does not appear in the path statement, you can add it by editing the autoexec.bat file. You must restart your system in order for this statement to be executed and the \java\bin directory to be added to your path.

---

Providing that the compiler returned no errors, the file FancyHello.class should have been automatically created in the same subdirectory. This is the compiled version of the Java code you just entered, and contains the byte codes that are necessary to execute your Java program.

### Testing Appletviewer—Viewing the Applet

Now that you're done with compiling, your Java program is ready to execute.

But didn't we say before that applets were remote Java programs executed by a World Wide Web Browser? How could we test our applet without putting it out on the Internet?

Fortunately, the JDK comes with a tool called "appletviewer," which allows you to view test your Java applets stand-alone.

---

**Note**

If you have a Java compatible browser such as Netscape Navigator 2.0, you can also test your applets stand-alone by clicking File, then selecting Open file, and finally selecting the HTML document with the embedded applet tag in it, or by typing directly into the "Go to" edit box:

**file:///[drive]:\[subdir]\HTMLfile.html**

Figure 2.2 shows the FancyHello Applet displayed in Netscape 2.0.

---

**Caution**

If you're using the alpha version of the HotJava browser, then you will be unable to view applets created with other versions of the JDK. In order to view the applet, you must acquire a Browser capable of viewing version applets, or use the appletviewer.

---

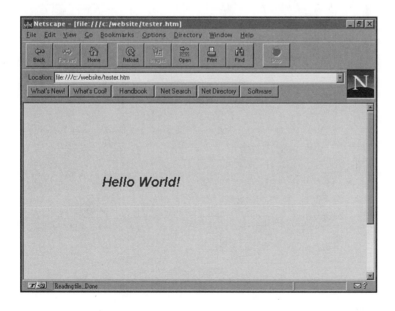

**Fig. 2.2**
An applet displayed using Netscape 2.0.

This is a great time-saver to say the least, since you will often need to customize your applets before you actually put them out on the Internet. Appletviewer executes applets via the same method a Web Browser does, and so it requires an HTML file with the applet tag specifying the compiled Java program (javafile.class) that is to be run.

If you have created HTML documents before, then you probably have an HTML editor, and you can use this editor to create a new HTML document and embed the applet tag within it. Since this is only a test applet, you can use any text editor to create the following HTML document:

```
<HTML>
<HEAD>
<TITLE>Testing My Installation</TITLE>
<BODY>
<APPLET CODE="FancyHello.class" WIDTH=400 HEIGHT=400>
</APPLET>
</BODY>
</HTML>
```

Save this file as test.html in the same subdirectory as FancyHello.class. Now type

**appletviewer test.html**

at the command prompt. You should then get a copyright notice screen (see fig. 2.3), to which you should respond by clicking the "Accept" button. If the HTML document above was entered correctly, your applet should now appear on your screen as shown in figure 2.4 .

**Fig. 2.3**

Appletviewer's copyright screen.

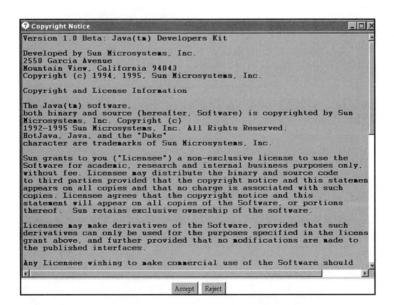

**Fig. 2.4**
The FancyHello
Applet displayed
using appletviewer.

If what you see is what you get, then you know for sure that your JDK can
successfully run applets. If errors have occurred even after you double-check
your code for typos, or nothing happens when you call the specified commands, then it is possible that you have not installed the JDK correctly (see
appendix D, "Installation of the Java Development Kit," and follow the steps
there), or the JDK you downloaded is corrupted and therefore needs to be
downloaded again.

Now that you know your Java applet works, let's test a Java application to see
if our JDK works with Java applications as well.

## Testing with a Java Application

We'll make the coding of our test Java application a lot simpler than our previous example of the applet. If this example compiles and runs successfully,
then your JDK should work for more complex code.

### Creating a Test Application

Using your text editor, create a new file to be called TestApp.java and enter
the following program:

```
class TestApp {
        public static void main(String args[]) {
                System.out.println("My Java installation
works...");
        }
}
```

Save this file as TestApp.java in your Java files subdirectory.

### Compiling the Test Application

At the command prompt type

**javac TestApp.java**

If you typed everything correctly, the compiler should automatically create the file `TestApp.class` in the same subdirectory as `TestApp.java`.

### Using the Java interpreter To Run Your Application

The Java Interpreter is used to run a Java program stand-alone. When called, the Interpreter looks for the `void main(String args[])` method specified in the application, and begins execution of the application from there.

At the command prompt type

**java TestApp**

Your installation works fine with applications and applets (if the previous test was also successful).

---

**Troubleshooting**

*Problem: I already checked for typos: everything checks out fine and the code even compiles, but when I try to run the application by typing **java TestApp.class** I get the following error:* `Can't find class TestApp/class`.

When running a Java Application you need to specify the class name only, and not the class extension. The file should execute correctly if you type **java TestApp** instead.

---

# The Java Environment Tools

The JDK comes with a collection of tools that is used with Java programs to perform various functions. This section discusses these tools and lists their various functions. The Java environment tools consist of the following:

- ■ appletviewer (for viewing Java applets stand-alone)
- ■ javac (the Java compiler)
- ■ java (the Java interpreter)
- ■ javap (the Java disassembler)
- ■ javah (for creating C header files, and stub files)

- javadoc (for creating HTML documents on the applet)
- jdb (the Java debugger)

These tools should all be located in the \java\bin directory. To use any of these tools, type its syntax (options described in this section should be typed without the square brackets [ ]) at the command prompt.

## The Appletviewer Tool

The appletviewer tool allows you to view your applet as a stand-alone Java program. It requires an HTML file with the applet tag embedded in it as shown in previous examples. This tool is the only one of the JDK collection that has a Graphical User Interface.

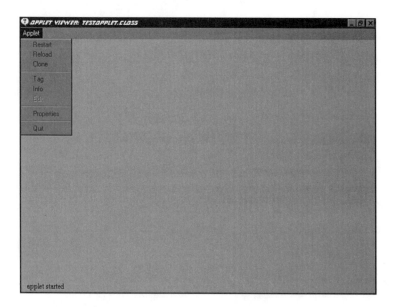

**Fig. 2.5**
Applet Viewer's
GUI Interface.

### The Appletviewer's Applet Menu
- Restart—Restarts the applet using the current settings.
- Reload—Reloads the applet. Changes in the class file will be applied upon reload.
- Clone—Clones (duplicates) the current applet, using the same settings to create another appletviewer instance.

Getting and Installing Java

- Tag—Shows the HTML applet tag that was used to run the current applet, as well as any parameters that were passed to the applet from the HTML tag (see fig. 2.6.).

- Info—Shows special information about the applet that was set within the applet's program (see fig. 2.7.).

- Properties—Shows the appletviewer security properties. These settings allow you to configure Appletviewer for a network environment that includes a Firewall Proxy, or an HTTP proxy, using the relative proxy server, and proxy port boxes. The Network access box allows you to select the type of network access that appletviewer is allowed. The choices are No network access, Applet Host (default), and Unrestricted. The Class access box allows you to chose what kind of access— Restricted or Unrestricted—you would like Appletviewer to have on other classes (see fig. 2.8.).

- Quit—Closes the appletviewer window and terminates the applet.

**Fig. 2.6**
The Window associated with Appletviewer's Tag menu item.

▶ See chapter 17, "Debugging Your Java Code," p. 309, for more on debugging your Java applets.

Appletviewer has the following syntax:

```
appletviewer [-debug] html_file
```

where -debug is the option of running appletviewer from within the Java debugger.

**Fig. 2.7**
The Window associated with Appletviewer's Info menu item.

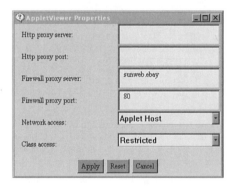

**Fig. 2.8**
The Window associated with Appletviewer's Properties menu item.

## javac (The Java Compiler)

The Java compiler is what actually converts your file—filename.java—into Java bytecode. This bytecode is then stored in a class file—filename.class. Both applets, as well as applications, are compiled using javac. javac has the following syntax:

```
javac [options] filename.java
```

The options for javac are listed in table 2.1:

| Table 2.1 javac Options | |
|---|---|
| **Options** | **Description** |
| -nowrite | This option tells the compiler to compile the code, but to not create the class file. This is useful for testing your syntax without creating files, or overwriting previously created classes. |
| -nowarn | This option turns off the compiler's warning messages. (Warning messages are displayed when the compiler wants to inform you of errors that might occur at run-time, but they do not affect compilation.) |
| -verbose | This option tells the compiler to display information on the source, while it is compiling. This information includes all classes being loaded, the time it takes to load these classes in milliseconds, as well as the total time it takes to compile the source code in milliseconds. |
| -d *dir* | This option tells the compiler to use the directory *dir* as the first directory of a package. |
| -classpath dirs | This option tells the compiler to look in the directories, listed in dirs for classes included in the source file. Multiple directories are separated by colons.  For example: javac -classpath \java\demos : \MyDir\MyClasses Myfile.java |
| -debug | This option runs the compiler in debug mode and steps through the source code adding compiler comments. |
| -o | This option tells the compiler to make the program's methods inline. Making the methods inline actually speeds up execution since the entire method body will be inserted wherever it is called by the program, instead of having multiple calls refer to a single method. |
| -g | This option is used to prepare the bytecodes for debugging. |

▶ See chapter 3, "javac: The Java Compiler," p. 49, for more information on the Java compiler.

## java (The Java Interpreter)

The Java interpreter is what you use to run your compiled Java application. The syntax for the Interpreter is

```
java [options] classname
```

where classname includes only the name of the class and not the extension (.class). The Java Interpreter options are listed in table 2.2:

**Table 2.2  Java Interpreter Options**

| Options | Description |
| --- | --- |
| -help | This option tells the interpreter to display all of the options. |
| -version | This option tells the Interpreter to display the version of the JDK that was used to compile the source code. |
| -v | (also -verbose) This option tells the Interpreter to display all the classes as they are loaded. (Performs the same functions as in the javac tool.) |
| -cs | (also -checksource)  This option makes the interpreter check if the source code is newer (not yet compiled) than its class file. If this is the case, then the new version of source is compiled. |
| -noasyncgc | This option turns off asynchronous garbage collection. |
| -verbosegc | This option tells the Interpreter to print out a message each time garbage collection occurs. |
| -verify | This option tells the Interpreter to verify all classes that are loaded. |
| -noverify | This option turns off class verification. |
| -verifyremote | This option tells the Interpreter to verify classes that were imported or inherited. |
| -mx *val* | This option sets the maximum Java heap size to the value specified by *val*. The minimum heap size is 1kb (-mx *1k*) and the default is 16mb (-mx *16m*). (Use the letters "m" and "k" to specify megabytes or kilobytes for the value of *val*.) |
| -ms *val* | This option sets the initial Java heap size to the value specified by *val* . The minimum heap size is 1kb (-mx *1k*) and the default is 1mb (-mx *1m*). (Use the letters "m" and "k" to specify mega-bytes or kilobytes for the value of *val*.) |
| -ss *val* | This option is used to set the value of the stack size for a C process to the value specified in *val*. The stack size must be greater than 1kb (-ss 1k). |
| -oss *val* | This option is used to set the stack size of a Java process to the specified value in *val*. (-ss and -oss will be covered in later chapters.) |
| -debug | This option is used with remote Java files that are to be debugged later with the jdb tool. The Interpreter will generate a password for you that will be used in the jdb's -password option (see table 2.3). |
| -prof | This option tells the Interpreter to output profiling information to file \java.prof. |

## javap (The Java Disassembler)

The Java Disassembler is used to disassemble already compiled Java bytecode. After disassembling the code, information about the member variables and methods are printed. The syntax for the Java Disassembler is:

```
javap [options] classnames
```

Multiple classes can be disassembled. Use a single space to separate each class. The options available for the Disassembler are shown in table 2.3 .

| Table 2.3 | javap Options |
| --- | --- |
| **Option** | **Description** |
| -version | This option tells the compiler to display the version of the JDK that javap is being executed from. |
| -p | This option tells the disassembler to print out private as well as public member variables and methods. (By default, javap prints out only public member variables and methods.) |
| -c | This option tells the disassembler to disassemble the source file and display the bytecodes produced by the compiler. |
| -h | This option tells the disassembler to output information on the particular class in C header file to be used by a C program that wants to use the methods in that class. |
| -classpath dirs | This option tells the disassembler to look for class files included in the source file in the specified directories - *dirs*. For multiple directories, a colon is used to separate each directory. |
| -verify | This option runs the verifier on the source, and checks the classes being loaded. |
| -v | (verbose) This option causes the disassembler to display information on the source code in detail as it disassembles. |

## javah (C Header, and Stub File Creation)

The javah tool creates C header and stub files needed to extend your Java code with the C language. (Chapter 14 talks about extending Java in more detail). The syntax of the javah tool is

```
javah [options] classname
```

where classname is the name of the Java class file without the .class extension. Javah options are listed in table 2.4.

| Table 2.4 javah Options | |
|---|---|
| **Option** | **Description** |
| -stubs | This option tells the javah tool to create stub files instead of the default-header files. |
| -d *dir* | This option tells the javah tool what directory to create the header or stub files in. |
| -v | This option tells the javah tool to print out the status as it creates the header or stub file. |
| -o *filename* | This option tells the javah tool to put the sub and header files into the file specified by *filename*. This file could be a regular text file or even a header (*filename.h*) or stub (*filename.c*) file. |
| -version | This option causes the javah tool to print out the build version. |

## The javadoc Tool (Documentation Generator)

The javadoc tool creates an HTML file based on the tags that are embedded in the /** */ type of comments within a Java source file. These HTML files are used to store information about the classes and/or methods and, since they are in an HTML format, hyperlinks to other Web Pages that might be related to your Java program. Javadoc was actually used by the creators of the JDK to create the Java API Documentation (refer to **http://www.sun.com/** for more information). You can view the API online and you can also see the source code used to generate it in your \java\src\java directory. Table 2.5 shows the tags that are recognizable by javadoc. (These tags are inserted between the special comment indicators (/** */) and are ignored by the compiler.)

| Table 2.5 javadoc Tags | |
|---|---|
| **Tag** | **Description** |
| @see *class* | This tag puts a *"See also"* link in the HTML file to the class specified by *class*. |
| @see *class#method* | This tag puts a *"See also"* link in the HTML file to the method specified by *method*. |
| @param *param descr* | This tag is used to describe method arguments. |
| @version *ver* | This tag specifies the version of the program. |
| @author *name* | This tag includes the author's name in the HTML file. |
| @return *descr* | This tag is used to describe a method's return value. |
| @exception *class* | This tag is used to create a link to the Exceptions thrown by the class specified by *class*. |

### jdb (The Java Debugger)

▶ See chapter 17, "Debuggung Your Java Code," p. 309, for more on the Java debugger.

The Java debugger is the debugging tool for the Java environment. The debugger is completely command-line driven. You can use the debugger to debug files located on your local system or files that are located on a remote system. For remote Java files, the jdb must be used with the -host and -password options described in table 2.6. The jdb also consists of a list of commands that will not be covered in this chapter.

| Table 2.6  jdb Options | |
| --- | --- |
| **Options** | **Description** |
| -host hostname | This option tells the jdb where the remote Java program resides. Where hostname is the name of the remote computer (example—`well.com`, `sun.com`, etc.). |
| -password *password* | This option passes to the jdb the password, for the remote Java file, issued by the Java Interpreter using the -debug option. |

# The Environment Variables

The environment variables are settings used to determine the HotJava and Java Interpreter environments for your system.

> **Note**
>
> The environment variables are used by HotJava, and not Netscape. If you do not use the HotJava Browser, you may want to skip this section, or you may just want to skim through it to gain some knowledge on HotJava.

The environment variables are as follows:

- WWW_HOME
- HOTJAVA_HOME
- HOTJAVA_READ_PATH
- HOTJAVA_WRITE_PATH
- CLASSPATH

## The WWW_HOME Environment Variable

This environment variable sets the HotJava default URL for the home page.

## The HOTJAVA_HOME Environment Variable

This environment variable sets the directory where HotJava will search for the necessary files that are needed to run the Browser.

## The HOTJAVA_READ_PATH Environment Variable

This environment variable tells HotJava the directory where file read access is allowed to applets. This can be used as a security precaution for applets that might read unauthorized information.

## The HOTJAVA_WRITE_PATH Environment Variable

This environment variable tells HotJava which directories are allowed to be written to by applets. Similar to HOTJAVA_READ_PATH, this variable can be used as a security measure to control the ability of applets writing files on your system.

## The CLASSPATH Environment Variable

This environment variable determines where all classes are imported from. Use semicolons to separate classes. ❖

# CHAPTER 3

# javac: The Java Compiler

*by Scott Williams*

Some programming languages, such as C and Fortran, are compiled languages: the source code is compiled into machine code that is unique to the target hardware platform and operating system. Other languages, such as APL and lisp, are interpreted languages: the source code is executed by running it through an interpreter. Both approaches have their strengths and weaknesses. Compiled programs tend to be faster and more efficient, but the compiled program can be run on only one hardware platform and operating system. Interpreted programs tend to be less efficient but potentially can be run, without change, on any platform for which an interpreter exists.

Java is both compiled and interpreted. The Java compiler, called *javac*, compiles (translates) the Java source code into an intermediate-level code called *byte codes*. These byte codes are not directly executable on any hardware platform that is currently in existence; rather, the codes are interpreted by the Java interpreter, which can operate either by itself or as part of a Web browser such as Netscape.

The fact that Java is both compiled and interpreted can give you, the Java programmer, the best of both worlds. A program that you write in Java will be efficient (because it is compiled) and capable of running on a multitude of platforms (because it is interpreted).

In this chapter, you learn the following:

- **How to get started with the Java compiler**

  The Java compiler is easier to use than it seems. You'll find that out when you compile and run your first Java program.

- **How the Java directories are organized**

  The Java Development Kit is split across a number of directories. This chapter covers those directories that are significant to the compiler.

■ **How to use the various compiler options**

The Java compiler supports a number of options that vary its operation. You'll learn about those in this chapter.

■ **How to troubleshoot common compiler problems**

You'll learn to recognize and solve some of the problems that you may encounter with the Java compiler, especially when you use it for the first time.

# Finding javac on Your System

▶ See "Installation of the Java Development Kit," p. 809

The installation process creates a hierarchy of directories, beginning with a directory called java. When we installed Java on our system, we put the java directory below a root-level directory called Languages, but you can put yours wherever you think is best, including directly below the root. After installation, then, we have the following directories on our machine:

| Directory | What You'll Find There |
| --- | --- |
| \java\bin | Programs that make up the Java Development Kit (the JDK): the compiler, the interpreter, the debugger, and so on |
| \java\lib | Standard Java classes supplied with the JDK |
| \java\include | Header files for use in combining Java and C/C++ programs |
| \java\demo | Demonstration programs that familiarize you with the JDK |

The javac compiler resides in the \java\bin directory.

---
**Note**

Remember that UNIX uses a forward slash (/) where DOS uses a back slash (\). On a UNIX machine, then, the path to the javac compiler would be something like /java/bin/javac, while on a DOS machine, it would be something like \java\bin\javac. The main java directory could be somewhere other than directly below the root.

---

# Understanding the Two Forms of the Compiler

Most modern compilers are *optimizing* compilers. After an optimizing compiler has performed the translation step (translating source code into object code) it goes through an additional step in which the object code is optimized either to use memory more efficiently, or to use less CPU time, or both. The Java compiler comes in two forms. The javac compiler is an optimizing compiler and is the one you will usually use. The javac_g compiler is a nonoptimizing version and is intended primarily for debugging purposes, generating bytecodes for interpretation by jdb or some other compatible debugger.

Both compilers, javac and javac_g, have the same syntax, so everything that this chapter covers applies equally to both compilers. The chapter uses javac in all its examples, but you could use javac_g in exactly the same ways.

# Using the javac Compiler

You invoke the javac compiler from the command line. The general syntax is as follows:

```
javac [ options ] filename
```

The options govern the behavior of the compiler. The file name is the name of the file that contains the Java source code that you want to compile. The javac compiler requires that source code be contained in files whose names end with the .java extension. Because the options are not required (they really are options; they're optional!), the following example is a valid invocation of the compiler:

```
javac HelloWorldApp.java
```

If all goes well—meaning, in this example, that HelloWorldApp.java contains valid Java source code for a class called HelloWorldApp—the javac compiler compiles the source code into Java byte codes and stores the output in a file called HelloWorldApp.class.

Suppose that you want to create a file called HelloWorldApp.java, containing the code as shown in listing 3.1.

**Listing 3.1  HelloWorldApp.java**

```
class HelloWorldApp
  {
  public static void main (String args[])
    {
    System.out.println ("Hello, world!");
    }
  }
Listing 3.1  A simple "Hello World" Java application.
```

◀ See "The Java Environment Tools," p. 38

Don't worry too much about what all the code means; we'll be covering the syntax for the language in detail in part two of this book (chapters 6 through 14).

Figure 3.1 shows what happens when you use javac to compile this program and then use java, the Java interpreter, to run it.

**Fig. 3.1**

The javac compiler reads in the .java file and generates the .class file from it, ready for interpretation by java, the Java interpreter.

---

### File Extensions

C and C++, like many other languages, have certain conventions and defaults for the names of your files. File names that end with .c might be C source code files; those that end with .cpp might be C++ source code files; and those that end with .obj might be object code files. For most C and C++ development systems, these defaults are easy to override. The rules in Java programming, however, are not so easy to break:

- Java source-code files have names that end in .java.

- Java compiler output is stored in files with names that end in .class.

---

# More on Understanding Java Directories

As you learned earlier in this chapter, the byte codes that are generated by the javac compiler are stored in a file with the extension .class. These .class files are roughly equivalent to the .`obj` object files or .`exe` executable files that are generated by other compilers. The difference, of course, is the fact that the .`class` files contain not machine language but byte codes that are ready for interpretation by the Java interpreter.

By default, the .`class` files are created in the same directory as the .`java` source file, but this default is easy to change. If you want to store your .class files elsewhere, you can use the -d option of the javac command to have the compiler create the .`class` files elsewhere. Consider the following example:

```
javac -d MyClasses HelloWorldApp.java
```

In this case, the .`class` file generated by javac is stored in the MyClasses directory.

> **Note**
>
> Some operating systems, such as UNIX, use permissions on directories (and on files, for that matter) to determine what kinds of access you have. When the javac compiler generates its output, it must create the .`class` file. Make sure that you have permission to create files (in UNIX, write permission) in the directory in which the Javac compiler is to generate the .`class` file.

# Finding Your Classes: the *CLASSPATH* Variable and *-classpath*

Take a moment to consider how regular executable programs are invoked from the command line. When a user of MS-DOS or UNIX types the name of a program on the command line and presses Enter, the command interpreter looks for an executable program of the specified name and, if it finds that program, loads the program into memory and begins execution. The *PATH* variable determines where the command interpreter looks for the executable program.

A very similar situation exists in Java. The only problem is that Java programs are not executable in the traditional sense; they are loaded and executed directly by the Java interpreter, by a browser such as Netscape, or by a utility such as AppletViewer (part of the Java Development Kit). Because these files aren't executable by the operating system, the *PATH* variable isn't going to help you.

## The *CLASSPATH* Variable

Where the operating system uses the *PATH* variable to find executables, Java uses the *CLASSPATH* variable to find classes. The *CLASSPATH* variable is a list of directories, delimited either by semicolons (Windows 95 or Windows NT) or colons (UNIX). Java searches these directories, in order, for the appropriate .class file.

The *CLASSPATH* variable isn't of interest only to the run-time system. As you see in later chapters, Java classes often depend on one another for much of their functionality. If you are creating your own classes to be used by other classes, you must tell the compiler where to find those classes, just as you would tell the interpreter. When the javac compiler needs to load one of your classes, it searches, in order, through the directories listed in the *CLASSPATH* variable.

> **Note**
>
> The directory that holds the system classes (\java\lib, for example) always is ap-
> pended to your *CLASSPATH* variable. In other words, you should have to specify
> directories in *CLASSPATH* only for additional classes that you create.

If you are using a PC running Windows, for example, you might add the following line to your autoexec.bat file to add the \project\classes directory to
the *CLASSPATH* variable:

```
SET CLASSPATH=.;C:\project\classes
```

> **Tip**
>
> Remember that changes to the autoexec.bat file don't take effect until you reboot
> your computer. Be sure to reboot after adding the above line to your autoexec.bat.

## The *-classpath* Option in javac

Permanent settings for the *CLASSPATH* variable normally are set in an
autoexec.bat file or (on UNIX systems) in a shell startup file such as .profile.
For a temporary change of *CLASSPATH*, you can use the -classpath option in
the javac compiler. The directory list specified in the -classpath option temporarily overrides the contents of the *CLASSPATH* variable. Note that in the following example we've explicitly included the location of the system classes:

```
javac -classpath .;C:\java\lib\classes.zip;C:\develop\classes
➥Payroll.java
```

In this example, java compiles the file Payroll.java and, if necessary, searches
the current directory, followed by the system library (C:\java\lib\classes.zip)
followed by C:\develop\classes, for any additional classes. The equivalent
command on a UNIX system would be:

```
javac -classpath .:/java/lib/classes.zip:/develop/classes
➥Payroll.java
```

---

**Note**

In order to conserve disk space (and to save time when downloading), the system classes are now supplied in one archive file called `classes.zip`. The Java run-time system and the javac compiler are both able to search for classes in directories, or in `.zip` archives.

---

**Note**

The syntax for the *CLASSPATH* variable or for the `-classpath` argument is similar to the syntax for the *PATH* variable in DOS or UNIX. For PC users on Microsoft platforms, the path is a list of directories separated by semicolons (;). For UNIX users, the path is a list of directories separated by colons (:).

---

# Using Other Compiler Options

Two options in the compiler affect the kinds of messages that the compiler generates:

`-nowarn`   Like most compilers, javac generates warning messages when it is compiling code that is syntactically correct but that may point to an error of some sort on the part of the programmer. The `-nowarn` option suppresses the display of these messages.

`-verbose`   In normal operation, unless errors or warnings must be reported, the javac compiler does its job quietly. The `-verbose` option causes the compiler to print messages about source files that it is compiling and class files that it is loading. You may find using this option to be quite enlightening, particularly in the early days, as you gain experience with Java.

The `-verbose` option is available also in the java interpreter. The option causes the interpreter to display a short message each time it loads a new class file.

The final two compiler options affect the kind of output generated by javac:

-g     This option gives you access to additional information if you use debugging tools such as jdb to debug your Java programs. By default, only line numbers are available to you at debugging time. If you have compiled the program with the -g option, however, javac generates debugging tables that provide information on local variables as well.

-0     This option causes the compiler to optimize the output for greater speed, at the possible expense of greater memory consumption, by inlining static, final, and private methods.

---

**Note**

*Inlining* is a technique that is familiar to C++ programmers. When a method or function is compiled inline, its code is generated at the location where the method is invoked, which means that the code will be executed at runtime without the additional overhead of a function call.

The best place to consider inlining is when short methods are invoked many times from one location in the source code (like a method invoked from within a loop that is repeated many times). In such a situation, the overhead associated with the method invocation will be high when compared to the total processing for the method.

---

**Caution**

Because code for inlined methods is duplicated at each place the method is invoked, the resulting code can be larger and can require more memory in which to run.

---

# Troubleshooting

Here are some of the common problems that you might encounter with the javac compiler, especially when you are using it for the first time.

## You Cannot Invoke the javac Compiler

If you attempt to invoke the javac compiler and get the error message `file not found` (in UNIX) or `Bad command or file name` (in Windows), you probably did not set your *PATH* variable correctly. The operating system uses this variable to determine where to look for programs such as javac. Your *PATH* is

set in the autoexec.bat file (on PC platforms) or in a startup script such as
.profile (on UNIX systems). The *PATH* variable must contain the name of your
Java bin directory—for example, \java\bin or \tools\java\bin.

> **Tip**
>
> On a DOS system, remember to reboot your system to have the changes to the
> `autoexec.bat` take effect. If you are on a UNIX system, be sure to log out and log
> back in again to have the changes to your .profile take effect.

## javac Can't Find Your Classes or the System Classes

If you get any of the following error messages, the compiler is unable to
locate either your classes or the system classes:

```
Unable to initialize threads

Cannot find class

Class (or superclass) not found
```

This problem has several possible causes. If you are getting error messages like
the ones in the preceding list, try the following procedures:

- Make sure that your system classes are in the directory in which they
  were installed. This directory will be \java\lib if you installed Java directly below the root, or in a path such as \Languages\java\lib if you
  installed Java below a subdirectory (in this case, Languages).

- Check to see whether the directory list in your *CLASSPATH* variable includes the system directory mentioned in the preceding paragraph, as
  well as any directories for classes that you may have added. Use the set
  command to determine whether your *CLASSPATH* is set correctly. (In
  either DOS or UNIX, the *set* command is issued by typing *set* on the
  command line, and pressing *Enter*.)

- If you are trying to use only system classes (none of your own), try not
  setting the *CLASSPATH* variable at all; use the default setting. This method
  isn't reliable, however, if you moved any of your directories after installation. If you have moved the system classes, try moving them back to
  the directory into which they were installed (e.g. \java\lib). If you
  haven't made such a change, using the default *CLASSPATH* setting may
  clean up any errors that you made in setting *CLASSPATH*.

- If you are using the -classpath option of the javac command, make
  sure that you included the system directories in your list. Because the

*Getting and Installing Java*

-classpath option overrides the CLASSPATH variable, the system directories will no longer be searched by default, so you must list them
explicitly.

Recall the earlier example of a possible DOS command:

```
javac -classpath .;C:\java\lib\classes.zip;C:\develop\classes
Payroll.java
```

And the equivalent UNIX command:

```
javac -classpath .:/java/lib/classes.zip:/develop/classes
Payroll.java
```

■ If you are having trouble finding classes in your own directory, make
sure that the first directory in the CLASSPATH variable or the argument of
the -classpath option is the dot (.), representing the current directory.
Adding the dot in this way causes your current directory to be searched
first, before any other directories are searched.

■ The system classes are now provided in a file called classes.zip. This
file can be left intact—in its zipped state—in the lib directory. If you
decide to unzip this file—a move that is not recommended—then
be sure that your CLASSPATH includes the directory that contains the
unzipped classes.

## Caution

Many DOS-based unzip programs do not correctly handle long file names. Such
utilities will truncate the names of the classes contained in classes.zip. Either leave the
classes.zip as-is—in its zipped state—or be sure to unzip it with a utility that understands long file names.

## .zip File Formats

A .zip file is an archive; it can potentially contain many other files or directories. The
.zip file format was initially popularized on the PC, but is now supported on a wide
variety of operating platforms. To "unzip" a .zip file means to extract the component files from the archive. The Java system classes come in a .zip file—an archive—
called classes.zip. There is no need to unzip this archive.

■ Make sure that you spelled everything correctly—and remember that
Java is case-sensitive. If you called your class HelloWorldApp, for example, its name is not helloworldapp.

## javac Rports a Sntax Eror

Like all compilers everywhere in the world, javac is very adept at reporting syntax errors, such as misspellings, missing punctuation, and incorrect use of keywords. In all of these cases, the compiler lists the error and attempts to direct you to the appropriate line of code. Keep in mind, however, that errors on one line of code sometimes won't be discovered until a line or two later. If the line to which javac is directing you seems to be perfectly OK, check the few lines before it; a more subtle error may be lurking in those lines.

## You Ecounter a Bg

Like all software, javac (and the rest of the JDK) contains a few *bugs*— problems that weren't caught before the software was released. Sun maintains a list of the known bugs at **http://java.sun.com/JDK-1.0/ knownbugs.html**. Checking this site periodically is worthwhile; you can see whether the trouble that you are having has already been reported by someone else. ❖

# CHAPTER 4
# Other Compilers

*by Jerry Ablan*

The Java language and compiler were developed primarily on UNIX-based systems. UNIX systems are not known for their well-developed user interface. Usually, UNIX machines run X-Windows, but you still must use a command-line interface to enter commands. Only the newer UNIX operating environments have the niceties of Microsoft Windows or the Macintosh. Creating command-line interface programs for UNIX is easy, fast, and completely natural to UNIX developers.

Because of these and possibly other factors, the Java Developer's Kit (JDK) currently does not include an integrated development environment, or *IDE*. Sometime in the future, the JDK may include an IDE, but this niche most likely will be filled by third-party products. As you'll see in this chapter, some interesting entries have surfaced in this arena.

In addition to third-party IDEs, third-party compilers will arrive. As with any language, there are developers who feel that there is a market for another compiler. Just look at how many C and C++ compilers are currently available.

In this chapter, you'll learn about:

- Integrated Development Environments

  This chapter discusses some of the more interesting IDEs that have surfaced, both public-domain and commercial.

- Third-Party Compilers

  This chapter discusses a few Java compilation options and a new public-domain compiler.

# Integrated Development Environments

An integrated development environment, or IDE, is a unique programming setting in which you have all the necessary tools at your fingertips. Generally, a source-code editor is the centerpiece of the program. Arranged around it are a compiler, a debugger, and other development tools. Better IDEs allow for a certain amount of extensibility. This enables a developer to customize his or her work environment for maximum productivity.

One of the first IDEs for IBM PCs and compatibles was Turbo Pascal from Borland International. This program was an editor and compiler bundled into one neat little package. The program was fast, and it produced tight, fast executables. Borland later enhanced the concept to produce Turbo C and then Turbo C++. Microsoft responded with what it called the Programmer's Workbench. This product was not as slick as the Turbo packages but was very extensible. Some people argue that Turbo C started the compiler wars between Borland International and Microsoft.

In any case, myriad compilers are available today, and a different IDE comes with each one. Each IDE is the producer's vision of the way programmers should work, and that vision is the best (according to the software maker). Unfortunately, all programmers have different methods to their madness and tend toward no commonality. Therefore, many IDEs are available today and have been for quite some time.

The compilers for Pascal, C, and later C++, had no IDE available initially—only the simple command-line tools. Java is no exception. Currently there is no IDE available from Sun Microsystems for Java development. This will most likely change in the future.

Before the official version 1.0 of Java was released, several IDEs were available for Java. By the end of 1996, a complete IDE probably will be available from each major compiler maker, including Borland, Microsoft, and Symantec. In fact, in the first half of 1996, the following products became available:

■ Borland Debugger for Java

Borland produced the first graphical debugger for Java. It works as a stand-alone debugger option for the JDK, and is integrated into their Borland C++ 5.0, which includes Java support.

■ Symantec Café

A complete visual integrated development and debugging environment for Java.

- Borland C++ 5.0

    Borland's famous IDE enhanced to include Java support.

Today, several of note—public-domain and commercial—deserve a closer look. Those environments are JavaMaker, Diva for Java, Java WebIDE, Kalimantan, Roaster, Symantec Café, and Borland C++.

> **Note**
>
> Visual C++ version 4 from Microsoft is extensible enough to be used as an IDE for Java. This is not really a stand-alone Java IDE and does not warrant mention in this chapter, but it can be configured to be useful. This information is available at the following URL:
>
> **http://www.ivas-as.attistel.co.uk/java/vc-java.htm**

So without further ado, let's look at some IDEs.

## JavaMaker
**http://net.info.samsung.co.kr/~hcchoi/javamaker.html**

JavaMaker, written by Heechang Choi in 1995, is a simple public-domain IDE for the Windows 95 and Windows NT platforms. JavaMaker provides a simple editor, compiler, and applet viewer launcher. Figure 4.1 shows the JavaMaker main window.

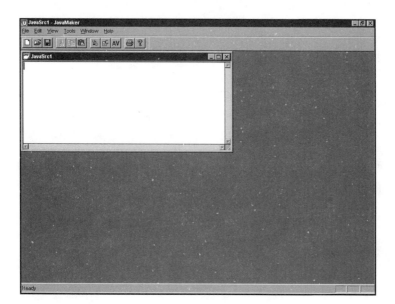

**Fig. 4.1**
The JavaMaker main window is a standard Windows application with support for multiple source code windows to be opened at once.

At startup, JavaMaker provides a blank document window for creating a new class. You can close that window and open an existing class. When a class is loaded or a new class is saved, JavaMaker places the name of the class at the top of the main window and the document window. Figure 4.2 shows a loaded class.

**Fig. 4.2**

The JavaMaker system is shown with the TumbleItem class loaded.

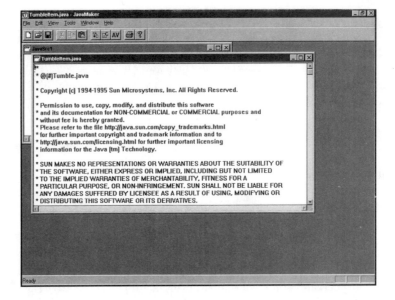

After you have loaded a class, or typed a new one into the entry window, your next step is compilation. JavaMaker provides a Tools menu that contains several options, the first of which is Compile. This option starts the Java compiler, javac, and places the output of the compiler in a new window called Output, as shown in figure 4.3.

If errors occur, the output window displays them, along with the numbers of the lines on which they occurred. One nice feature of JavaMaker is the fact that when you double-click the error message, the cursor moves to the offending line in your source-code window. If your class was compiled properly, you can run the AppletViewer tool to view your applet. Figure 4.4 shows the AppletViewer command in the Tools menu.

**Fig. 4.3**
The compilation
output is shown in
a separate window.

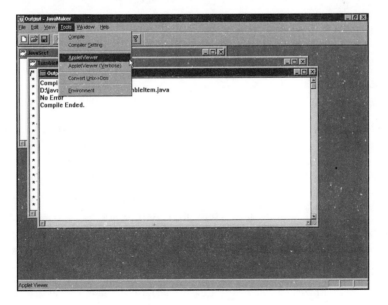

**Fig. 4.4**
The AppletViewer
is launched from
the Tools menu.

AppletViewer runs in its own window and runs the class that was currently
active in JavaMaker. Figure 4.5 shows AppletViewer running the TumbleItem
class that comes with the JDK.

**Fig. 4.5**
The AppletViewer runs the Java applet that you are currently working on in JavaMaker.

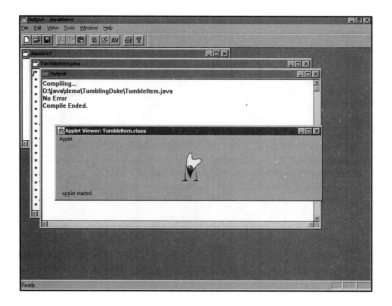

JavaMaker is a simple IDE that offers only a bundled editor, compiler, and launcher tool. JavaMaker is a good improvement over the command-line tools and should speed your development effort.

## Diva for Java
### http://www.inch.com/~friskel

Diva for Java, formerly known as Javaside, is an IDE from Quintessential Objects, Inc. The IDE is available for the Windows 95 and Window NT platforms, and requires the JDK. Diva more closely models the Visual C++ version 4.0 development environment than JavaMaker does. Diva even associates itself with .java files, so that when such a file is opened from the Windows Explorer or via a shortcut, the Diva application starts automatically. At the time of this writing, Diva for Java was only available in an alpha state. The alpha and beta versions are available free from the URL above. However, the 1.0 release of Diva for Java will be a commercial product.

Diva for Java utilizes a project system. This system manages the source code files that are part of your applet or application. Projects can include multiple source code files. When you create a new project with Diva, you insert new files into the project. Usually with Java, each file is a separate class; therefore a complex project will have many source-code files. The management of these files can get out of hand quickly. Having the IDE manage the project is a very nice feature.

Figure 4.6 shows the Diva startup-tips screen.

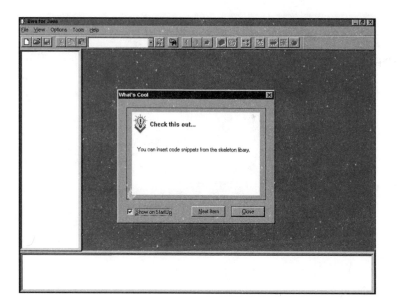

Along the left side of the screen is the project view, which details the files
that make up the current project. You can create new projects that include
Java source code, HTML, and special Diva Design documents (.jad files).
These design documents are created with the Diva Designer. There is more
information about the Diva Designer coming right up.

At the bottom of the screen is the compiler output window, which displays
all output from the compiler. You can double-click errors to move directly to
the correct place in the source code. The current file appears in a new window above the output window, allowing you to edit and manipulate the file.

When you insert a new file into the project, the software asks you what type
of file you want to add: Java, HTML, or Diva Design document.

If you select Diva Design Document, the Diva Designer window opens (see
fig. 4.7).

The Diva Designer allows you to create Diva Design documents. The interface
is similar to other window prototyping tools. Objects are available on a pal-
ette. These objects can then be selected and placed on your window. Once
placed, the objects can be given names. These names are used when Diva for
Java generates source code for your applet. After you've laid out the objects
you want on your program's window, you can have Diva generate a class file
around your design.

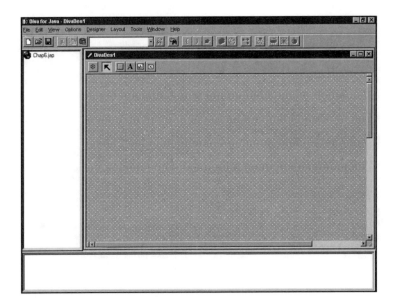

Before Diva can generate your source code, you must select the type of application template that Diva will use. The selections include a basic application with a frame or an applet. Figure 4.8 shows the selection window. This list can also be extended. Instructions for customization are included in the Diva distribution.

**Fig. 4.8**
The application
selection window

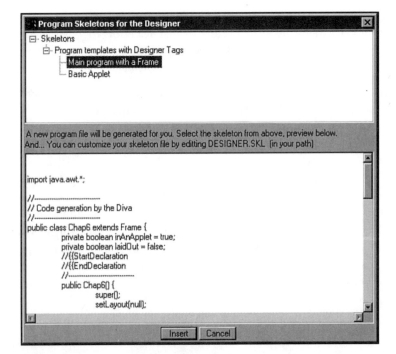

The coolest thing about Diva is the source-code-window navigation panel, which is displayed next to the source code at all times. This window represents the code in a treelike graphic. At the base, or root, of the tree is the Java source file itself. At the next level up are the imported libraries; the top level shows the class or classes defined in the file. All variables, methods, and extensions appear below the class. Simply click a variable or method, and you are instantly taken there in the source code window. This feature is very nice. Figure 4.9 shows a source code window with the class navigation panel.

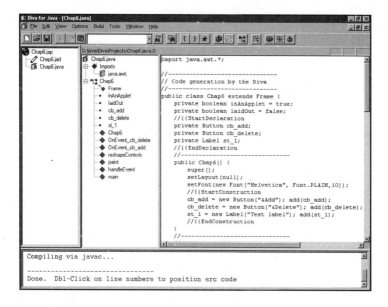

**Fig. 4.9**
The class navigation panel allows you to move about your class by method.

Even though this is the pre-release version of Diva, it is still a useful program. The release 1.0 version of Diva should be a good entry into the IDE arena.

## Java WebIDE
### http://insureNetUSA.com/javaIDE.html

Java WebIDE, written by Chami Wickremasinghe, is not just a public Web-based compiler; it is a nearly complete IDE written entirely with HTML and Java/JavaScript. You access it only via the World Wide Web. There is nothing to download and it is completely free. All the compilation is done at the Web site, not locally. Figure 4.10 shows the Java WebIDE in action.

Included in this unique IDE are an editor, compiler, and the entire JDK documentation online. You can enter your code in the editor and then click the Compile button. The output then is available for downloading via the compilation screen (see fig. 4.11).

All in all, using the Java WebIDE is a unique experience. If you are looking for an integrated debugger, Java WebIDE is not your IDE. If your development needs are small, the Java WebIDE may be just the ticket.

**Fig. 4.10**
The Java WebIDE is an IDE implemented completely with HTML.

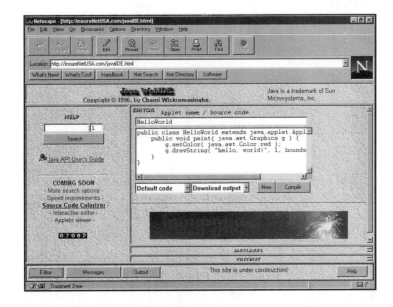

**Fig. 4.11**
Java WebIDE shows this screen when compilation is successful.

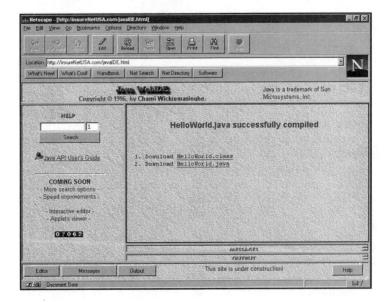

## Kalimantan
http://acsl.cs.uiuc.edu/~phelps/kalimantan/

Kalimantan (formerly known as Espresso) is a set of public-domain tools for creating and debugging Java applets and applications. Although Kalimantan is not a full-blown IDE, it deserves mention in this chapter because it includes some non-command-line utilities. These utilities are an Inspector and a Debugger. The Inspector is a tool that allows the programmer to fully explore the contents of an object. The Debugger allows the programmer to set breakpoints in a Java application or applet and then to use the Inspector to inspect the source code and variables (see fig. 4.12). All of the Kalimantan tools are written in Java, so they are portable to any operating system that supports Java.

These tools are very much like the Smalltalk programming environment; the only portion that's missing is the class browser. To overcome this limitation, the Kalimantan tool set is bundled with another tool set called dejava (Development Environment for Java), which includes a class and method browser, among other features. These tools run in any platform that supports Java. However, they have only been tested in Windows 95 and Sun Solaris.

## Roaster
http://www.natural.com/pages/products/roaster/index.html

Roaster, from Natural Intelligence, Inc., is the first commercial Java IDE available for the Macintosh. The features of Roaster include an editor, a compiler, a debugger, and a class disassembler.

According to the release notes, Roaster works only with PowerPC Macintoshes, not with 680X0-microprocessor-based Macs. In addition, the product still supports only the first release of JDK, even though the 1.0 release of JDK is out. The compiler is not yet working properly, so the manufacturer recommends using the compiler that comes with the JDK. Java's Abstract Windows Toolkit is not fully supported, and no source-level debugging is available, a fact that makes the debugger somewhat useless.

## Symantec Café
http://www.symantec.com/lit/dev/javaindex.html

Symantec Café is a commercial Java IDE built on Symantec's C/C++ IDE product. First available with the version 7.2, the upgrade is downloadable from Symantec's FTP site as an upgrade. The upgrade allows for the development of Java applets. Symantec Café is now available as a complete, stand-alone, Java development environment. Figure 4.13 shows the Café system.

**Fig. 4.12**
The Debugger window shows the source code of the currently running applet.

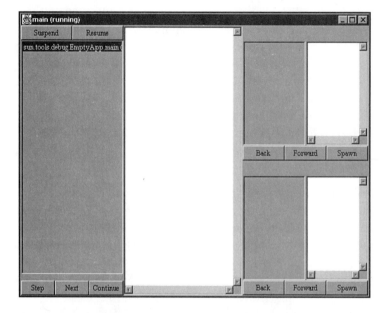

**Fig. 4.13**
The Symantec Café product has multiple windows from which to view the current project.

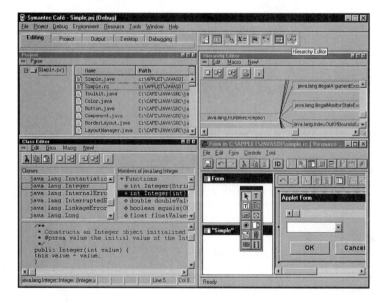

Café provides a graphical Java class hierarchy diagram that is created on the fly by the IDE. This diagram helps the developer understand the layout of the Java class library and where the classes created by the developer belong. Café also provides a class editor, which allows the developer to work on the classes in his or her project. Editing by a class view is much easier to deal with than individual source code files are.

Café also includes two wizard-like features called AppExpress and ProjectExpress. These features generate a complete, fully functional Java applet skeleton that can be enhanced and revised through the Café system.

## Borland C++ Version 5.0
**http://www.borland.com/Product/Lang/cpp5/index.html**

It would be sad if the granddaddy of all IDEs didn't throw its hat into the ring. Borland International recently announced that version 5.0 of its C++ development environment will include complete Java support. This support includes integration with the JDK, a programmer's editor, and a graphical source-level debugger. The debugger itself is written in Java and is the first of its kind. This product became available in March of 1996. Figure 4.14 shows the Borland Debugger.

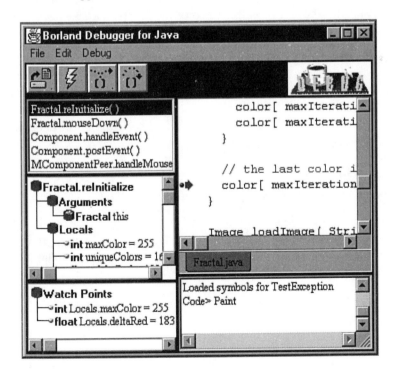

**Fig. 4.14**
The Borland Debugger for Java is written entirely in Java.

At the time when this chapter was written, not much information about the Borland C++/Java product was available. The new IDE is likely to be built on the version 4.5 product, which includes features such as a class editor/ browser, an extendible programmer's editor, and AppExpert.

AppExpert, the shining star of the Borland development tool, is very similar to Symantec's AppExpress and Microsoft's AppWizard. AppExpert allows a developer to build an application from the ground up; it then creates all the support tools and scripts needed to compile and run the target application.

Borland has promised Java support in AppExpert. Symantec already has support, and Microsoft probably will, too, at some time.

# Other Java Compilers

Because Java source code is compiled in a byte code that is interpreted instead of executed, just about anyone who has the desire and the know-how can create a Java compiler. As the language evolves and matures, more and more compilers will arise. The speed of these compilers will be the defining factor of their success.

At the time when this chapter was written, two third-party Java compilers were available. The first compiler is part of the Roaster package from Natural Intelligence, which is discussed earlier in this chapter. The second compiler is EspressoGrinder, which is discussed in the next section.

Public compilers also are available. A public compiler is a Web-based interface to Java's javac program. The purpose of public compilation is to provide compilation access to people who have platforms for which the JDK is not available. The third-party and public compilers are discussed in more detail in the following sections.

## EspressoGrinder
**http://www.icsi.berkeley.edu/~phlipp/espresso/**

EspressoGrinder is the first replacement compiler for Java. The compiler's most notable features are its size and speed. EspressoGrinder is approximately half the size of the Java compiler javac and twice as fast (in compilation speed).

> **Note**
>
> *Compilation speed* is the time that it takes the program to compile the Java program, not the speed at which the program executes.

EspressoGrinder is available for UNIX and Windows 95 systems. This product requires that the JDK version 1.0 be installed.

The compiler is part of a larger ongoing project by the EspressoGrinder team to make better tools and languages available to more computer professionals. One part of this project involves providing a native-code generator for Java. The native-code, in conjunction with an interpreter, would allow for increased performance and speed unseen today. For more information about their project, check out:

**http://www.icsi.berkeley.edu/~phlipp/espresso/Project/**

## Black Star Public Java Compiler
**http://mars.blackstar.com/compiler.html**

The JDK does not support some UNIX and microcomputer platforms. Also, some people may not be able to install and run the JDK. This can be because of lack of resources or sufficient permission on the target computer. What is someone to do who cannot run the Java compiler but wants to develop Java applications? Enter the public compiler.

Because the Java compiler produces a byte code that is interpreted instead of executed, the compiler does not require execution on the target machine. The compiler can run anywhere, really. All that is needed is the compiled `.class` file for it to run. This feature opened the door for the Black Star public compiler.

The compiler accepts as input an upload from a client; it then passes this upload to the Java compiler (javac) for compilation. Figure 4.15 shows the compiler main page.

One of the newer browser features is the capability to upload files to a Web server. The Black Star site takes advantage of this feature. The Web site allows you to upload your Java source code directly to the server. If your browser is not capable of uploading a file, you are also able to hand-enter your source code. This method is called the text-entry method of compilation. The text-entry method is available on another Web page at the Black Star site. Again, complete instructions are given.

**Fig. 4.15**
The Black Star public compiler Web site has complete instructions for its use.

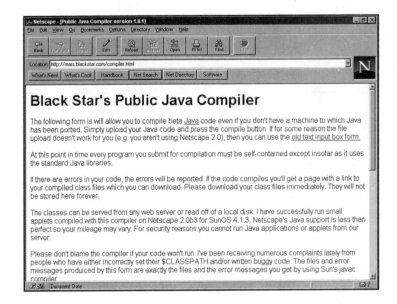

After compilation, if no errors occur, the public compiler produces a page that has links to your compiled class files. These files need to be downloaded to your system via this page. No other access is available. Figure 4.16 shows the Compiler output page.

**Fig. 4.16**
The output of the compiler as well as links to your compiled class are displayed on a new Web page.

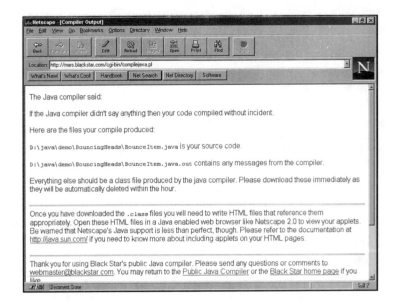

## The Java Public Compiler

**http://www.innovation.ch/java/java_compile.htm**

This site is another public interface to Java's compiler, javac. This interface is a little bit nicer than the Black Star Web site. The site allows for up to five source files and other options. Figure 4.17 shows the input system.

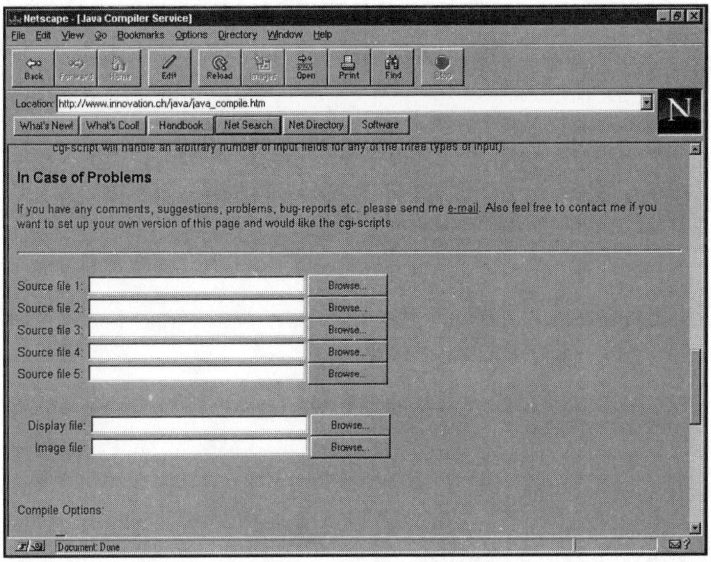

**Fig. 4.17**
The Java Compiler Service site has a much nicer interface than the Black Star site.

Getting and Installing Java

After you enter the names of your source code files, you can select the options that you want the Java compiler to use. This feature allows you to compile in verbose mode or in debug mode. Figure 4.18 shows the available compilation options.

When the compiler finishes compiling your source code, your browser displays the Compilation Results page (see fig. 4.19). Simply click the class file that you want to download, and the file is transferred to your machine. Compilation could not be easier.

**Fig. 4.18**

The Compiler Service's Java allows you to select any of the compilation options available in the javac program.

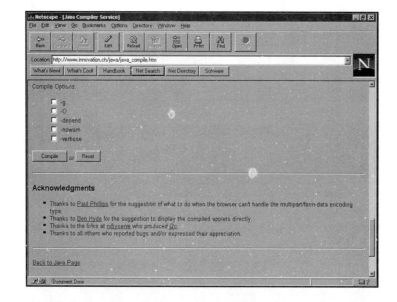

**Fig. 4.19**

The compilation results.

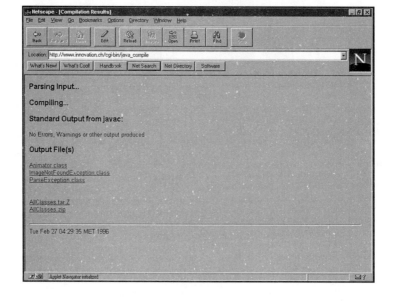

# CHAPTER 5

# Roaster

*by Luke Cassady-Dorion*

There are multiple Java development environments which you could choose to work in. This chapter teaches how to use Natural Intelligence's Roaster. Once you finish this chapter you will fully understand all the features which Roaster brings to the Macintosh. And once you become an accomplished Java programmer, this chapter should serve as a reference to you as you work with Roaster.

This chapter will teach you how to:

- Enter code for an applet or application into the code editor
- Learn to recognize the special methods which Roaster uses to aid you in finding errors in your source
- Take advantage of the vast number of utilities which Roaster's toolbar provides
- Compile and run both applets and applications within the environment
- Take advantage of the debugger to find the errors in your source

## Introducing Roaster

Natural Intelligence filled a void in the Mac Programming community when they released their Java Development Environment in January of 1996. Previous to this, Mac programmers wishing to get a jump on learning Java were unable to without jumping to other platforms. Roaster allows Mac programmers to create Java applets for use on World Wide Web pages, and also allows for the creation of minimal use applications. (Development of applications with Roaster is covered later in the chapter.)

## What Roaster Can Do for You

Roaster is Natural Intelligence's Integrated Development Environment (IDE) for the Macintosh. The program is a powerful tool for developing Java Applets (and partial applications) on the Macintosh. These Applets can be used in your Web creations to bring new energy to static environments.

Buzzwords aside, Roaster enables you to create some very cool stuff. Java, unlike HTML, does have a steep learning curve, especially for new programmers. Roaster will do nothing for you if you cannot program in Java.

## Installing Roaster

The current version of Roaster is version Developer Release 1.1.

> **Note**
>
> As is the case in the computer industry, information is current only for about 10 minutes. This text is based on Developer Release 1.1 of Roaster and press releases current at this time of writing. A new version of Roaster is expected quite soon, and Roaster Pro should be out in May 1996.

This version, however, is not the one which was mastered on the CD. The CD ships with version DR1.0, and the update is available from Natural Intelligence's Web site at **http://www.natural.com/pages/products/ roaster/updatenoterdr1.html**, or by contacting them at 617-876-4876. To install the CD, drag its contents to your hard drive, and then move the Roaster VM extension from the For Extensions folder to the extensions folder on your hard drive. You will notice a variety of free software which Natural Intelligence has bundled on the CD. None of this is required to run the program, but is quite useful; this chapter, in fact, was written using BBEdit. Restart your computer, and Roaster is ready to go. If you are having troubles with running Roaster, make sure that you copied all of the files shown in figure 5.1.

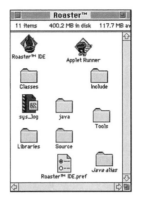

**Fig. 5.1**
Once installed on
your computer,
Roaster will
present itself with
the window shown
here.

# The Roaster Interface

After the programming experts develop an application, the information systems experts take over and shape the product's interface into what users feel comfortable interfacing with. Natural Intelligence, in developing the product, was well aware of the fact that an interface can make or break a product. All commands are easy to locate and are not masked with confusing names.

> **Tip**
>
> Before you begin developing your first applet, sit down and familiarize yourself with the environment. You will be happy with the control you have over the application.

## Introducing the Integrated Development Environment

Unlike the Java Developers Kit for the Mac, Roaster is a complete Integrated Development Environment (IDE); this involves a combination of a powerful text editor, interpreter, and compiler all in one. Roaster also bundles a debugger with their environment.

The IDE that Natural Intelligence has created for Roaster integrates a version of their powerful QuickCode Pro editor with a suite of Java development tools. This includes the Sun javac compiler and also their own compiler. The combination of these two compilers provides for increased user flexibility. The Java developer can opt to choose from Sun's compiler which is not as fast as the Natural Intelligence's own compiler, but tends to generate fewer compile time errors than that of the Natural Intelligence compiler. Or the Natural Intelligence compiler, while faster, is still deep in development. To switch between the two compilers, choose from the Edit menu, Preferences, and then click on the Compiler icon. If you are confused, look at the screen shot in figure 5.2; this is what you should see on your screen.

> **Note**
>
> Roaster still classifies their compiler as "icky" and recommends that for the time being you use Sun's compiler.

**Fig. 5.2**
Natural Intelligence combines two compilers with their development environment. The NI compiler promises to go above and beyond Sun's compiler in both speed and class support in the near future.

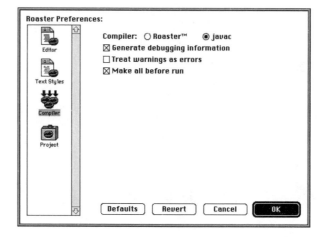

To manage an increasingly large amount of project files, Roaster incorporates a hierarchical project manager system. This system displays all project files in a window, which supports a drag-and-drop interface. This enables you to add files to the project simply by dragging them to the project window. You will find this especially helpful as your projects grow in size and begin containing many project files.

The Roaster interface puts their development tools right at your fingertips. Their versatile code editor supports multiple clipboards; you will find this extremely helpful when managing code snippets. All Roaster menu commands have associated keyboard shortcuts, thus cutting down on the annoying keyboard to mouse exchange which often bothers programmers.

## Roaster's Special QuickCode Pro

With Roaster, Natural Intelligence includes a special version of QuickCode Pro, their popular code editor.

The editor supports syntax coloring, and brace flashing to instantly notify a user if a brace has been accidently omitted. Take a look at figure 5.3, this window shows an applet that you will be developing later in the chapter. Note how the editor deals with the code, pretty cool huh? The colors and text style used for special words are configurable by choosing Edit, Preferences, Text Styles. At this time it's not possible to add words to the database of special words; it is unclear if this will be possible in future releases. It is possible from this section to turn off syntax coloring, and also to set the display font.

```
                        helloAuthor.java

import java.awt.*;

public class helloAuthor extends java.applet.Applet {

    String greeting = "Hello Luke";
    Font myFont = new Font("Helvetica", Font.PLAIN, 24);

    public void paint(Graphics g) {
        g.setFont(myFont);
        g.setColor(Color.magenta);
        g.drawString(this.greeting, 10, 50);
    }

}

Line: 14  ▲ 299
```

**Fig. 5.3**
Note how the code editor deals with your code. Special words are colored, and new sections are automatically indented.

**Tip**

There is no real reason to turn off syntax coloring; if the preset colors bother you, feel free to adjust them. Once you become accustomed to the colors, you will catch code errors much faster.

## Using Quick Code Pro's Toolbar

One of the code editor's most useful capabilities is its customizable toolbar. The toolbar includes a method browser, two powerful find utilities, book marking utilities, and a quick commenting tool. The toolbar also allows for complete control over both named and unnamed clipboards, code balancing, both redefined and user-defined macros, text shifting, and incorporates support for multi-platform file formats. Control over the toolbar was designed with human-computer interface guidelines constantly in mind.

The method browser is a pop-up menu which when held down displays a running total of all methods in the current window. The methods are displayed using the convention **class_name.method_name**; again, as your projects begin to grow in size, this tool will prove invaluable. Figure 5.4 shows how the method browser displays the available methods, to instantly go to a specific method, simply choose it from the pop-up menu.

**Fig. 5.4**

The method browser provides a hierarchical list of all methods which you have developed so far in the current file.

```
                        BounceItem.java
Ni  [icons]
      public    BounceImage.play
      if (pare  BounceImage.BounceImage
         pare   BounceImage.move
      }         ◇ BounceImage.paint
      }         BounceImage.step
                BounceItem.BounceItem
      public    BounceItem.makeImages    arent) {
      this.par  BounceItem.run
      width =   BounceItem.init
      height =  BounceItem.start
      }         BounceItem.stop
                BounceItem.paint
      public void move(float x1, float y1) {
      x = x1;
      y = y1;
      }

      public void paint(Graphics g) {
      int i = index;

      if (parent.bounceimages[i] == null) {
         i = 0;
      }
      g.drawImage(parent.bounceimages[i], (int)x, (int)y, null);
      }

      public void step(long deltaT) {
      boolean    collision_x = false;
      boolean    collision_y = false;

      float jitter = (float)Math.random() * .01f - .005f;

      x += Vx * deltaT + (Ax / 2.0) * deltaT * deltaT;
      y += Vy * deltaT + (Ay / 2.0) * deltaT * deltaT;
      if (x <= 0.0f) {
Line: 79  ∆ 2443:2448
```

---

**Note**

If you are wondering what methods are, don't worry, we'll explain all of this later in the book.

---

The two included find utilities are a Quick Find tool for locating repeated occurrences of a string, and a Zip Find tool for more advanced searching capabilities. To use the Quick Find tool, simply highlight a string in the development window, and then click the Quick Find icon. This will search from the current selection to the bottom of the file. To search from the current selection up to the top of the file, option-click the Quick Find icon.

 The Zip Find utility allows for some more advanced searching techniques. To use this tool choose Configure Zip Find... from the menu accessible under its icon in the toolbar, and enter a search string when prompted. In addition to entering a search string, the Zip Find tool allows for a variety of search options to be configured from this menu. Clicking the OK button causes the Zip Find menu to update itself, containing a listing by line number of all occurrences of your string. Figure 5.5 shows how the code editor brings you instantly to the location of a string occurrence.

The search criteria feature is also added to the pull-down menu to accommodate repeating this task. To go to an occurrence of the string, simply select it from the pull-down menu. To perform search and replace commands, choose Search, Find; this menu allows more complex searching capabilities.

```
Bounceitem.java

public void play(int n) {
if (parent.sounds[n] != null) {
    parent.sounds[n].play();
}
}

public BounceImage(BounceItem parent) {
this.parent = parent;
width = 65;
height = 72;
}

public void move(float x1, float y1) {
x = x1;
y = y1;
}

public void paint(Graphics g) {
int i = index;

if (parent.bounceimages[i] == null) {
    i = 0;
}

g.drawImage(parent.bounceimages[i], (int)x, (int)y, null);

public void step(long deltaT) {
boolean    collision_x = false;
boolean    collision_y = false;

float jitter = (float)Math.random() * .01f - .005f;

x += Vx * deltaT + (Ax / 2.0) * deltaT * deltaT;
y += Vy * deltaT + (Ay / 2.0) * deltaT * deltaT;
if (x <= 0.0f) {

Line: 79  △ 2443:2446
```

```
Configure Zip Find...
Graphics

Line 79 : public void paint(Graphics g) {
Line 246 : public void paint(Graphics g) {
```

**Fig. 5.5**
Note how selecting a found word from the menu instantly highlights its location in the text.

To accommodate quick movement to commonly referenced parts of your code, you can add jump points with the Bookmark tool. Just select the location in your code which needs to be book marked, and click in the bookmark icon.

> **Note**
>
> Try this out; the paper clip, which appears over the icon, indicates that a bookmark has been added. Option-clicking the bookmark icon will void its link.

To reference that location in the future, simply click the icon. The number of your project's bookmarks is limited only by your system's memory. See the end of this section for more information on customizing the toolbar.

Java supports multiple styles of commenting: one for individual lines, one for blocks of text, and another which is used to develop documentation. You can control these first two types of commenting via the toolbar. If you want to comment out a single line of text, place the cursor at the start of the text and click the comment icon. Option-clicking the icon while you have a block of text highlighted will comment out that whole block.

Two toolbar utilities, which you will no doubt use over and over, are the named and unnamed clipboards. These utilities allow for intelligent managing of multiple code snippets. Figure 5.6 shows the clipboard utility as it manages multiple code snippets.

**Fig. 5.6**
This figure shows the addition of new text to a clipboard. Note all of the other tools available to the clipboard utility.

Named clipboards are used more when dealing with commonly used code. To load something to a named clipboard, select the text, and from the named-clipboard pull-down menu, choose Cut or Copy, New; the editor will then prompt you for a name for this code. This code can now be referenced by name from the named-clipboard pull-down menu. These snippets are in range for the entire project, thus you can copy and paste between project windows with increased ease.

## Tip

If you attempt to add a new entry to a named clipboard, and it does not seem to load, make sure that the window has been saved to disk. Currently it is not possible to add to the named clipboards on a new, unsaved window.

The unnamed clipboards are used more for code which will be accessed only a few times. To load code into these clipboards, select the code and use the standard clipboard management tools—just like you did with the named clipboards—under the unnamed clipboard pull-down menu. When an unnamed clipboard is storing data, its icon changes to a clipboard with a piece of paper attached. These clipboards also have a range of the entire project. In addition to the standard suite of clipboard commands, there is added support for some advanced commands which you will find helpful. Take a second to familiarize yourself with these menu commands; again, you will find them very helpful.

## Note

Of course, you can use the traditional clipboard commands from the Edit menu. These are useful for inter-application text manipulation.

Locating a missing parenthesis, brace, or bracket can be a source of programming headache, especially as the wee hours of the morning approach when your eyes blur everything together. The code balancing utility will test for matching parenthesis, braces, and brackets. As methods become increasingly developed, this utility becomes very helpful. To take advantage of the utility, place the cursor at an open section marker, and, when clicked, the utility highlights the text as far as the corresponding close section marker.

As the number of Roaster projects worked on increases, the amount of code which is repeated also increases. This can range from standard comment headers to developed event loops. To accommodate this, the toolbar can take advantage of macros.

> **Tip**
>
> Macros are definitely a very cool utility. I take advantage of them by building macros around all of my commonly used methods. I then never have to retype them! I also program basic method frameworks to macros, and then only have to modify them to create new methods. Remember they stay in range for any project which you develop, so unless you delete them, they are around forever.

To define a macro select the text in your code which will be reproduced, and choose Macro, New Macro, and then enter the text of the macro into the window which appears. You are presented with a dialog box asking for a macro name and identifier. The name is displayed in the macro menu, and the identifier is used to reference the macro in other macros, giving you the ability to create nested macros. To use a macro in your code, either choose the macro by name from the macro menu, or assign a keyboard shortcut to it. You can assign a keyboard macro by selecting Configure Hot Keys from the NI menu in the toolbar. Figure 5.7 shows how to accomplish this.

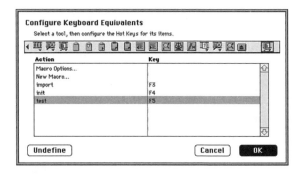

**Fig. 5.7**
Adding keyboard shortcuts to commonly used functions can help to increase productivity. I use them to automatically place in overused parts of code.

Select this menu item, click the macro name from the menu which appears, and then press the hot key combination you want to associate with the macro. In addition to user-definable macros, there is also a set of built-in macros which include: Date, Time, User name, and Window name. You can modify the macros' names by choosing Macro, Macro Options.

When code demands the addition of a new loop at the center of the method, a programmer who uses proper formatting techniques will indent their code one tab stop farther. Moving code a tab stop to the right or left can be shortcut by selecting the code, and clicking either the Shift Left or Shift Right icons.

Java's cross-platform, object-oriented nature leads to situations where code you wrote on one platform might be compiled on a different platform. This can cause problems because Macs, UNIX systems, and Windows-based systems all treat text files in a slightly different manner. To accommodate this, Roaster has added the File Format utility to the toolbar. This utility brings up a menu which enables you to select your code's format.

To recognize each icon's command, place the mouse over the icon and a small help box appears to give the utility's name. This is true for all toolbar utilities. You also can display the utility's name in the toolbar if you would prefer. Note how the first method is being performed in figure 5.8.

**Fig. 5.8**
Holding your mouse over any one icon for a second or so will display its function.

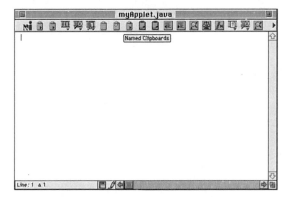

To configure the toolbar, choose Configure Toolbar from the pull-down menu which is displayed from the NI icon on the top-left side of the toolbar. The configuration window displays a scrolling list of all toolbar utilities, and a picture of the current toolbar. To add a new icon to the toolbar, simply drag the utility name to the toolbar. The utility is displayed as either text, icon, or both (depending on user selection) in the toolbar. The individual entries can be dragged into any order which the programmer finds useful.

To remove an icon from the toolbar, simply drag its entry to the trashcan icon which is displayed conveniently in the toolbar configuration window. Figure 5.9 shows all of this in action.6

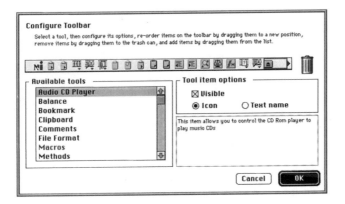

**Fig. 5.9**
Configuring the toolbar is as easy as dragging and dropping the desired utility onto the toolbar—if programming were only this easy.

The toolbar allows for multiple instances of a single utility; this is helpful, especially when defining a series of clipboards to organize your code. A scrolling system is established to accommodate more entries than will fit in the toolbar.

**Tip**

For a description of each toolbar utility, click its entry in the configuration window.

The Audio CD Utility enables you to control your audio CDs while engaging in long, Java-enhanced coding sessions. It is always part of my toolbar, but then I hooked up my stereo to the audio-out jacks on my computer.

## The IDE Windows

The Roaster IDE uses a Project Manager Window to organize the files which your project utilizes. To start a new project choose Project, New Project. The current release of Roaster requires that all projects use the **project_name._** (+) naming convention. Also, if you are developing an applet with your project, Roaster requires that the class which extends `java.applet.Applet` have the same name with which it is saved.

The Project Manager supports full drag-and-drop capabilities. To add a file to your project, simply drag it from the finder to the project manager window. The project manager allows the grouping of your code under separate headings. Next to the code's name in the Project Manager Window is a pop-up menu which displays, using a hierarchical menu system, the name of all classes and their associated methods. This is shown in figure 5.10.

**Fig. 5.10**
Choosing a method in one of your project files is as easy as selecting its name from the pop-up menu.

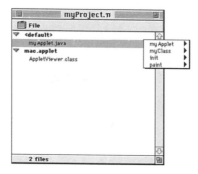

# Your First Roaster Project

It is important to step through a sample project to show how one would build an Applet or Application with Roaster.

## Developing an Applet

To launch Roaster, double-click its icon in the finder. This brings you into the Roaster IDE. The IDE includes all tools necessary for developing the project itself.

> **Tip**
>
> To actually view the applet, it is necessary to use the Applet Runner.

Choose Project, New Project when prompted, create a new folder for your project, and then enter a name for your project. For your sample project, use the name **hello._**. Creating a new project brings up the Project Manager window (for more information about the Project Manager, see the previous section). A new project contains no files; as you build your project you will add to this window. All applets in Roaster require the addition of the **AppletViewer.class** to add this project to your project window choose Add Files... from the project window. Navigate to the AppletViewer.class file which is nested deeply in the various Roaster subfolders. To find the file, open the Roaster folder, and then open the Classes folder; dig into the Mac folder, and finally you will find the file nested inside the Applet folder. Highlight the file, click Add File, and then click Done.

**Tip**

This whole process can be simplified by taking advantage of the drag-and-drop features of the Project Manager; simply drag the file onto the Project Manager window.

Create a new file by choosing File, New. Into this new window, enter the following code:

```
import java.awt.Color;
import java.awt.Graphics;
import java.awt.Font;
public class helloAuthor extends java.applet.Applet {
    String greeting = "Hello Luke";
    Font myFont = new Font("Helvetica", Font.PLAIN, 24);
     public void paint(Graphics g) {
        g.setFont(myFont);
          g.setColor(Color.magenta);
          g.drawString(this.greeting, 10, 50);
      }
}
```

**Tip**

As you enter the text notice how the text changes color. As you become familiar with the Roaster environment, you will begin to know which words change color, and which stay black. This is extremely helpful in finding typos as you generate code.

Now that you have the above text entered, choose File, Save. When prompted, name the file **helloAuthor.java** and save it in the same folder as your project. Note that at this time Roaster requires you to name your source file with the same name as your class, and requires the source files to be in the same folder as the project. Choose Project, Add Window. This adds the file to your Project Manager. Of course you could drag the source file into the Project Manager yourself. As the number of files which your project manager contains begins to grow, you will want to group and order them in the Project Manager.

Now that you have a complete project choose Project, Compile. If you have no errors, Roaster adds a file to your project folder with the .class naming convention. This file is your byte-code, and can be distributed for viewing on many Web pages. Unless you are terribly satisfied with my chapter, and wish to say "Hello" to me all over the Internet, I am sure that you will not want to place this applet on your Web pages.

To view your applet, one more thing is still necessary: the HTML code which defines the layout of your page. Create a new file by choosing File, New, and entering the following text into it:

```
<html>
    <head><title>Hello Author</title></head>

    <body>
        <applet code="helloAuthor.java" width=300 height=60>
        </applet>
    </body>
</html>
```

The preceding HTML is obviously quite minimalistic. This is because the Applet Runner will only interpret the <applet> tags and is not a complete Web browser. There obviously is no need to place any other miscellaneous HTML around the page. The file needs to be saved in the same folder as your project, and must be named **example1.html.** This file name requirement was hard-coded by Sun, and Natural Intelligence plans to allow for any .html name in the future. Now you are ready to check out the applet. Figure 5.11 shows what the final output for the applet is.

**Fig. 5.11**
Once you get the applet up and running, you should see output similar to what is pictured here.

Choose Run from the project menu, or drag the html file on top of the Applet Runner to launch that application. Assuming that everything has been entered correctly, there should be a magenta-colored greeting directed toward me in a gray-colored box.

## Developing an Application

As previously stated, the DR1.1 release of Roaster will not compile stand-alone application into native code.

> **Note**
>
> Watch for Roaster Pro in May; this will enable you to compile your application into code native to many platforms. Think of how easy it will be to develop cross-platform products in the future!

It is, however, quite possible to view Java applications with the Applet Runner. Now close your current project, and create a new project (remember how to do this?). This time don't add the AppletViewer.class to your project. This file is only for applet projects. Create a new window, and enter the following text:

```
class heyLuke {
    public static void main (String args[]) {
        System.out.println("Another exciting creation");
    }
}
```

Save the file as heyLuke.java and add it to your project window. Before you can run the application, you need to tell Roaster that your file is an application, and that it should be the startup file.

> **Note**
>
> In the case of applets, the startup file is the AppletViewer.class; Roaster automatically specifies this when you add the file.

To indicate that **heyLuke.java** is your startup file, highlight it in the project window, and choose Set Startup File from the project window. Notice the arrow which now appears next to the file name? More kudos to Natural Intelligence's adherence to human-computer interface guidelines. Now that the file has been ear marked as your startup file, you are ready to run the application. Choose Run from the project window, and what do you know? More fun from the Java department. The output for this application is shown in figure 5.12. Try playing around with the application a little. Can you make it output the text in color? If not don't worry, by the time that you finish this book, you will be able to do anything that you want with Java.

**Fig. 5.12**
This is the output
for our complex
application. Hey
what will these
brilliant program-
mers think of
next?

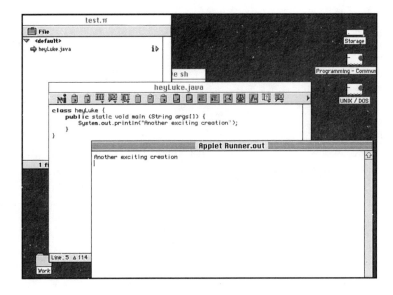

## Applets versus Applications

The decision on whether to develop an applet over an application depends on the scope of your project. Often a project can seem to exist in both the applet, application categories, and sometimes two versions of a product will be developed. Applications due to the fact that they do not require a Web browser interface allow for greater flexibility. The security issues which an applet possesses do not exist with applet development. As you become increasingly familiar with the language, it will become much easier to decide which route your projects need to take.

# Roaster's Capabilities

While Roaster is an advanced Java development environment, it does still have some room for growth. Note that at the time of this writing, neither Roaster Pro nor DR2.0 of the current environment have been released. These programs promise to bring many enhancements to the Roaster environment.

## Roaster's Java Support

Currently Roaster supports only one release specification of the JDK. At the time of this writing, Sun has released the JDK in its final 1.0 state. Natural Intelligence has been doing a great job keeping up with advancements in this ever-changing market, and it plans to support a more advanced version of the JDK.

While Roaster supports only one release of the JDK, it does not fully implement its current state. Some of these reasons are due to restrictions placed on Roaster by the Mac OS, and other reasons stem from Natural Intelligence's rush to get this product into the hands of developers. These restrictions are far from limiting; one can develop a complex project with Roaster.

> **Note**
>
> While Roaster does not support some aspects of the current specification, it will still generate proper byte-code; thus browsers on other platforms will be able to fully use the applet.

The restrictions the Mac OS places on Roaster are possible to override, but doing so is not a desirable thing for Mac programmers to do. Doing this means overriding many toolbox calls, and this can make the program highly incompatible with future releases of the system software (including 7.5.3). If you have never programmed for the Mac before, the toolbox might be something new to you. The toolbox contains a series of functions which deal with the Mac's graphical interface, memory management schemes, and other Mac-specific functions. Java supplies its own methods to deal with these situations, including the Abstract Window Toolkit (AWT), thus a Java programmer does not need to bother with toolbox calls. All translation to the Mac interface is taken care of by the geniuses who write the Applet Runner software.

Currently the Mac OS requires applications to have a standard look and feel. Roaster's Applet Runner has done a great job of making Java projects conform to that look and feel. For example, the AWT lets users create text areas of varying background colors; on a Mac, text areas are always white, thus any calls to change a text area's background color are ignored. Also it is obviously a rare occasion that, on a Mac, pop-up menus will appear in a font other than preset system font. Roaster's applet viewer will conform to this by not interpreting any calls to menu font change. Java also allows for a Windows feel by supporting window iconization. This will not occur with Roaster's applet viewer. Any programmer wishing to develop for the Mac, even in Java, should familiarize himself with the Mac toolbox. Apple's Inside the Macintosh series is a great resource for toolbar programming.

In addition to a slightly "Mac-ified" version of Java support, Roaster has not fully implemented the JDK in its current state. This poses a little problem, however, and it must be remembered that the release of Roaster as of this writing is a developer's release, and that it is not expected to be in its final polished form. The most obvious omissions to the Roaster environment are the lack of net and audio support. Again, look for .net support in DR2.0. The Applet Runner which comes with the Mac JDK from Sun does have net support, and thus it is possible to view applets which take advantage of this class with their Sun Applet Runner. Also at this point, jpegs are unsupported by Roaster, all images that a developer may want to display must be in GIF format. Finally, the File Dialog is also currently unsupported.

### Applet Support versus Application Support

Currently much of the hype surrounding Java development is related to applet development. However, Java's application building qualities are perhaps even more powerful. It is possible to develop applications which, for example, dynamically update themselves over their network. Thus a company never needs to worry that a staff member might not be using the latest version of a software product. It is estimated that companies spend millions of dollars just in physically making sure that all products are kept up-to-date. As a Java programmer, your applications—if they support this capability—will have a much higher selling value.

Roaster currently supports a minimal version of application development. Roaster Pro, which may be out at the time that this is published, will allow for complete stand-alone application development. This includes pure bytecode development, and also native code development for multiple platforms.

To write an application with Roaster, develop your source code in the traditional manner, and then in the project window highlight the file which contains your main() method, and choose Set Startup File from the project menu. Then when you run the application, the Applet Viewer will be able to properly interpret your code. Note when doing this, make sure that you do not include the **AppletViewer.class** or the Applet Viewer will get confused. The **AppletViewer.class** is used solely for applet development.

# Debugging Your Code

Of all the hours that you will spend working on code, most of your time will be spent on debugging. This might range from finding a missing semicolon (my favorite), to dealing with incorrect variable handling. Finding errors in Java-based projects is, for the most part, much easier than in projects developed in languages such as C++. This is due in part to Java's automatic garbage collection, and decreased dependence on pointers. There are plenty of situations where you will not be able to troubleshoot your code merely by examining it and will need to turn to a debugging utility.

In the development of Roaster, Natural Intelligence opted not to include Sun's dbx debugging library and decided to develop its own graphical debugging environment. At present the debugger is not in any way a complete product and is probably the most underdeveloped component of the IDE. This, however, does not stop you from using the debugger to solve problems with a project, and Natural Intelligence promises to deliver a full force debugging tool in the coming months.

To work with the debugger, a .class file must be developed first. This means that unless you are able to work out all syntax errors and get the code to compile correctly, you will not be able to use the debugging tool.

> **Note**
>
> Natural Intelligence's compiler is not too intelligent when it comes to describing errors in your source, thus fixing these errors can be more time-consuming than is really necessary.

To run the debugger, open the project on which you will be working. If you have not already compiled the code, now is a prime time to this; as stated earlier, the .class file is required for the debugger to run. Once the project is open, choose Project, Enable Debugging.

> **Tip**
>
> Note the check which appears next to the debugger menu option; this indicates that the debugger will take over operation once the project is run.

You will notice that your code has been shifted to the right about 1cm, and there is now a thin gray line running down the page. You can click to the left of the line to set a debugging breakpoint. Figure 5.13 shows a class file being debugged.

> **Note**
>
> A breakpoint is a point in your class file where the debugger will automatically pause execution.

**Fig. 5.13**

The debugger at work. Natural Intelligence debugger will let you step through your class file, tracing the path of a variable.

To set the breakpoints for the .class file, just open up this file and insert them in the fashion described previously. If you are totally unsure where to set your breakpoints, there are a suite of tools which will help you locate the problem. These tools are displayed on the toolbar which is displayed when the debugger is fired up. Well, let's fire up the debugger and look at a program!

---

**Note**

In this release of the debugger, breakpoints placed in the source code will be ignored. This is partially due to the fact that the debugger does not support source level debugging. This is currently one of the biggest weaknesses with the debugger; Natural Intelligence plans to release a debugger with source level debugging capabilities in the future.

---

Choose Project, Enable Debugger, Run (see figure 5.14). The debugger now displays your .class file with a small green arrow next to the first instruction in the code. The debugger only executes a line of code when you give it permission. This is quite helpful as you are able to step through the program and trace exactly what happens line by line. If errors are deeply nested within the program, this can be a rather tedious process—you might want to have a hot pot of coffee sitting at your side! The debug toolbar displays a series of icons which allow you to control the execution of the program. One other window that you might want to bring up at this point is Windows, Current Object Inspector. This window displays the values of the instance variables of the current object.

```
Project
 New Project...           ⇧⌘N
 Open Project...          ⇧⌘O
 Set Current Project

 Add Files...             ⇧⌘A
 Add Window               ⇧⌘W
 Remove Files
 Reset File Paths

 Set Startup File         ⇧⌘F

 Update Method List       ⇧⌘U
 Clear Method List

 Compile                   ⌘K
 Compile HTML Documentation
 Make                      ⌘M

✓Enable Debugger          ⇧⌘D
 Run                       ⌘R
```

**Fig. 5.14**

The Project window with debugging enabled. Note that once debugging is enabled, it stays enabled until you turn it off.

> **Note**
>
> At this point in time, it is not possible to view local variables within a method.

From this point there are a variety of options which you can choose to take over program control.

Clicking Run executes your code up to the point where either a break point occurs, the program terminates, or the program crashes. If you already have a good idea of where your program is causing errors, you might want to place a breakpoint before that line, and then execute the code until you encounter the line.

You probably don't know where your code is beginning to generate errors and will want to start with another one of the tools.

The Step Over button executes your code one line at a time. This is very useful (and sometimes tedious, if you have to step through hundreds of lines of code) for tracking the exact values of instance variables.

If in your trace through the file you encounter a call to a subroutine, the Step In button moves the trace into the subroutine.

To move out of the subroutine, and continue the trace at the source of the call, click the Step Out button.

> **Note**
>
> Note that clicking this does not exactly cause the program to jump back to the source of the call. The subroutine's execution is finished, and thus any computations performed on variables are still in scope.

The Step Over Continuous button is basically the combination of the Run and Step Over buttons. Basically it runs through your program line-by-line, but never steals control away from the user.

While the Run button only stops program execution when it hits a breakpoint (or in the other cases stated above), it is possible to stop this operation with the Stop button on the debug toolbar. If in the course of this operation your code involves a call to a subroutine, the debugger will not show what is happening in that call. The subroutine will, of course, still be executed, but this will all happen behind the scenes.

If your debugging needs involve the examination of all subroutines, the Step Into Continuous button will bring you through all subroutines one line at a time. Again the Stop button pauses the execution at that current line of code.

If during the course of your debugging, a sudden flash of brilliance tells you the source of your error (or if you just figure it out), clicking the Kill button (aren't geeks violent?), returns you to the text editor. Remember that once the debugger is enabled, it must be manually disabled for normal execution.

## Where Roaster Is Going

Well as is obvious, Roaster is quite an advanced program. It does have a way to go, but the developer release program makes your investment well worth it. Unfortunately Natural Intelligence is not too forthcoming about details of exactly when new enhancements will be released; they do say the DR2.0 will incorporate a class browser, and will have complete Applescript support. It also will let programmers use the java.net classes, and finally the term "programmers" will extend to 68K programmers with this release.

Natural Intelligence is also to be commended on its technical support; a post to its mailing list at **java-mac@natural.com** is usually answered by a competent staff member within 10 hours. When I was first starting to use Roaster, I was constantly posting questions to the group, only to have my problems solved right away! ❖

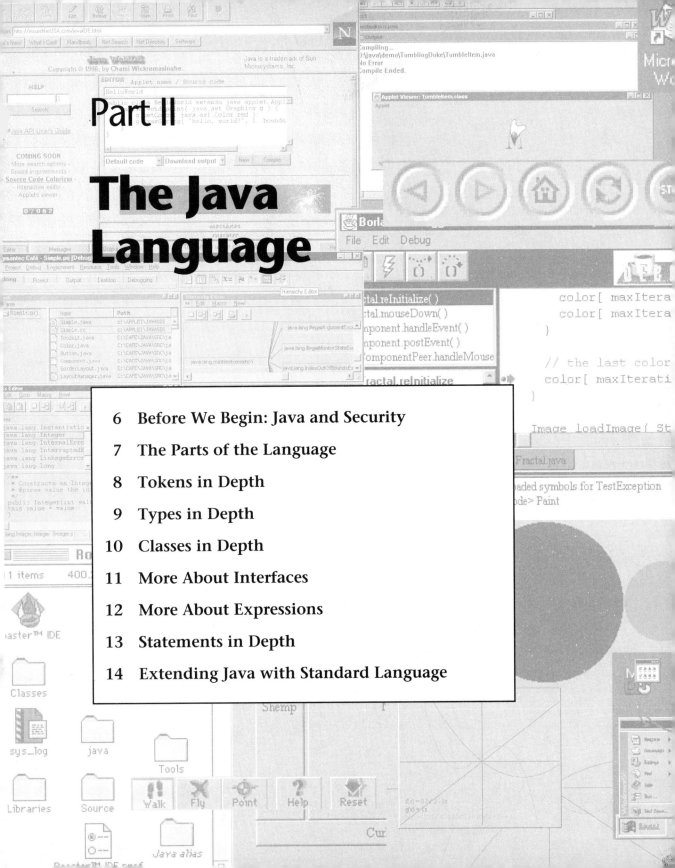

# Part II

# The Java Language

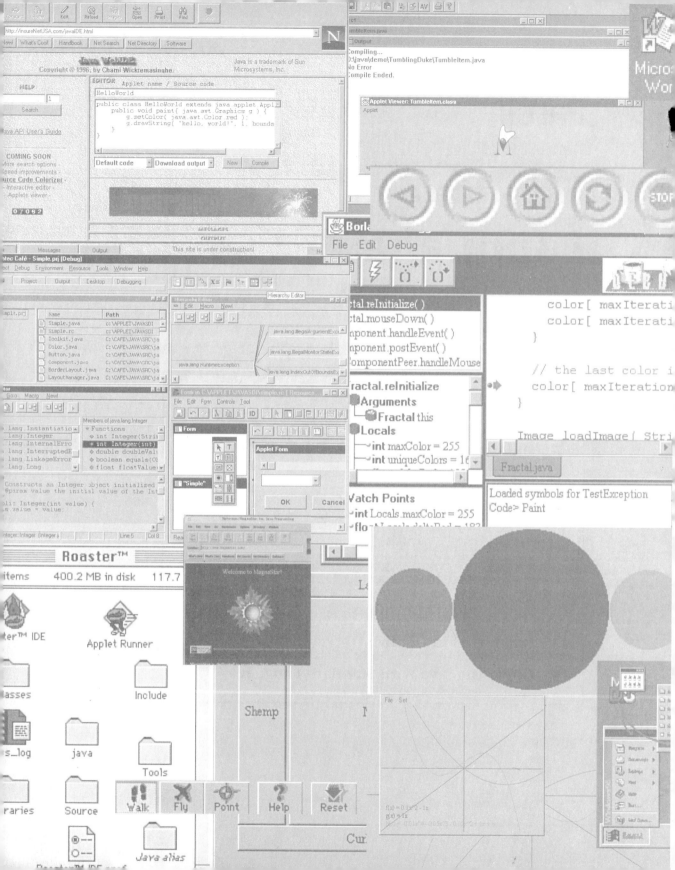

## CHAPTER 6

# Before We Begin: Java and Security

*by Suresh K. Jois*

## Introduction

In this chapter we discuss security in networked computing environments, specifically in the context of the Java programming language.

We will begin by a generic discussion of security of networked computing environments, such as the Internet. We will then arrive at a precise definition of the security problem, and propose a strategy to develop security mechanisms. We will then examine the Java security architecture, and conclude with a brief discussion of open and evolving issues related to Java security.

When you finish reading this chapter, you will have a good understanding of security issues related to networked computing in general, and of the Java security architecture in particular.

### The Internet, Java, and Security

The Internet, especially with the Web and Java, is rapidly evolving from a limited set of computer networks, into a mass-market, consumer-oriented, mainstream medium for delivering diverse forms of information. Earlier generation mass media, such as TV, have four important attributes which make them zero-security-risk systems:

- **They are unidirectional systems**: Information travels just one way, from the producer device (say a TV station) to the consumer device (your TV set). No private or confidential information goes out of the consumer device.

- **They are one-to-many systems**: There is usually just one producer device (TV station) transmitting to several consumer devices. So there are fewer staging grounds for malicious security attacks.

- **Transmitter identity is fixed, and is not concealed**: A TV station usually transmits on a fixed frequency. So in a given geographical area, it is easy to identify the origin of a broadcast.

- **Information transmitted is just passive content**: Once information reached the consumer device, it simply played in a fixed sequence, and went away—a TV program never persists on your equipment unless you specifically record it on a VCR. Also, a TV program itself does not have any ability to directly control your TV or VCR. So security of the consumer device was never an issue. A TV station cannot broadcast anything that can lock up your TV controls or upset its color balance.

The Internet (and consequently the Web and Java) has exactly the opposite characteristics, on each of the above attributes:

- **It is a bidirectional system**: Information travels both ways between your computer and the Internet.

- **It is a many-to-many system**: Anyone can in principle transmit arbitrary pieces of information from any computer to any other computer. So there are orders of magnitude more potential staging grounds for security breaches.

- **Transmitter identity is programmable, and can be concealed**: The identity of a computer on the Internet is software programmable, and can be concealed through several techniques, all collectively called *spoofing*.

- **Information transmitted can be active programs**: Anyone can send out both data and programs to any computer connected to the Net. This is precisely what Java applets are—encapsulations of data and programs which travel across the network and execute on your computer. And precisely what the applet program does on your computer is entirely up to the programmer.

The above four characteristics are the major source of the power, flexibility, and dynamism of the Internet (and the Web and Java). However, they are also the source of most potential security issues related to Java. In the following sections we will examine the above attributes of the Net in general, and Java in particular, and delineate their security implications. We will then present the specific security risk-minimizing mechanisms built into the core of the Java architecture.

## Brief Outline of This Chapter

This chapter is organized into six sections. Following this introduction, we will explore the issue of security of networked computing in general, and define the security problem associated with executable content. We will propose a six-step approach to construct a viable and flexible security mechanism.

We will outline the security approach taken by the Java language architecture, in the context of the six-step approach. We will also telescope in at greater detail on Java architectural components that implement security mechanisms.

As with any new technology, there are several open questions related to Java security, which are still being debated on the Net and other forums. We will briefly examine some of them.

Finally, there is a list of references and resources for further information on Java security.

# Executable Content and Security

In this section we will analyze the concept of security in the general context of interactivity on the Web implemented via executable content.

We will first examine the duality of Security versus Interactivity on the Web, and examine the evolution of the Web as a medium in the context of this duality. We will see that the security problem is most acute at the highest level of interactivity provided by executable content such as a Java applet.

Next, we will arrive at a definition of the security problem, in the context of executable content. The chapter will conclude with a delineation of security breach/attack scenarios.

## Interactivity versus Security

As mentioned briefly in the introduction above, a unique attribute of the Internet (and the Web) that makes it a powerful interactive mass medium is the ability to transmit information consisting of data and executable programs, using a language like Java. This is called transportable code, or Executable Content. In this subsection, we will explore the relationship between security and interactivity achieved with executable programmatic extensions to either the server or the browser or both. It turns out there is almost an inverse relationship—more executable extensions means less security (and hence more risk) on both the server and the client ends.

The Web in its original form, and the underlying HTTP protocol, allowed only data to be sent from a server to the browser. This arrangement was not qualitatively different from the TV model, where the receiving device is a passive renderer of data sent by the transmitting device. This made real interactivity over the Web pretty difficult. Web users were limited to simply browsing static content served up by the server. But at this level, the Web was also the most secure, both on the server side and the client (browser) side. The only potential security risk on the server side was that a browser could request directory and content listings of the server's file-system. But that could be prevented by server side access-control. On the browser side, a potential security risk was that the server could send a huge document, which could overload the client Operating System. But this was preventable by process resource caps enforced by most operating systems.

HTML forms and server-side CGI scripts allowed for a limited degree of interactivity. But this interactivity was very expensive and cumbersome, because data had to be constantly shuttled back and forth between the server and the browser. Also, the server had the burden of keeping track of the state of interaction for each of the multitude of browsers connected to it. From the security standpoint, CGI scripts opened up a breach on the server side, in that improperly written CGI scripts could be tricked into doing dangerous things like executing file-system delete commands on the server.

The concept of helper-apps and browser plug-ins was the next step forward in making the Web more interactive. In this model, a content provider shipped a custom program to users who installed it alongside their Web browsers. Subsequently, when appropriate data arrived at the browser, the helper app would kick in and render (or "play") the data. The helper app could also interact with the server independent of the Web browser. This allowed for true two-way interactivity. But this entailed that a user blindly trust the helper-app/plug-in to be safe and benign. The security implication was the potential for trojan-horse style attacks.

Helper apps could be looked upon as a two-part implementation of the executable content model, where the executable portion is shipped upfront, and the data portion is shipped on demand. The next logical step was true executable content, using a language like Java. With Java, anything going across the wire is a full-fledged program. This makes the Web truly interactive, since the browser becomes infinitely adaptive and extensible. A lot of the computational load can be more equitably shared between the server and the browser. And the content served can be richer and more complex. But this also opens up the full spectrum of security risks associated with any kind of program—from bugginess to intentional malicious behavior.

So, while more executable content means richer interactivity, it also means higher security risks. This means that any implementation of executable content, such as Java or Java-enabled Web browsers, should also be designed from the ground up with multistage security features. Users of a Java-enabled Web browser should not have to worry that a Java applet might be deleting files or sending private information out of their computers.

## The Security Problem Defined

In this subsection, we will define precisely what constitutes the security problem entailed by and associated with executable content, and outline a solution strategy for this problem. This will form a frame of reference within which Java security features will be explained in subsequent sections of this chapter.

Any computer program has essentially unrestricted access to the computer's resources, within the confines of access controls defined by the operating system. A program developed by a local user of the computer is implicitly trusted as not being a security risk. Any consequences of the program's behavior—intentional or due to bugs—are accepted and borne by the user.

A program arriving from outside the computer via the network has to be greeted by the user with a similar degree of trust, and allowed a similiar degree of access to the computer's resources, to serve any useful purpose. But the program was written by someone else, under no contractual or transactional obligation to the user. If this someone was a hacker, the executable content coming in could be a malicious program with the same degree of freedom as a local program.

Does the user have to completely restrict the outside program from accessing any resource whatsoever on the computer? Of course not. This would cripple the ability of executable content to do anything useful at all. A more complete and viable security solution strategy would be a six-step approach:

**Step 1**: Pre-visualize all potential malicious behavior and attack scenarios.

**Step 2**: Reduce all such malicious behavior to a minimal orthogonal basis set.

**Step 3**: Construct a programming environment/computer language which implicitly disallows the basis set of malicious behaviors, and hence by implication, all potential malicious behavior.

**Step 4**: Logically or, if possible, axiomatically prove that the language/environment is indeed secure against the intended attack scenarios.

**Step 5**: Implement and allow executable content using only this proven secure language.

**Step 6**: Design the language such that any new attack scenarios arising in the future can be dealt with by a corresponding set of countermeasures, which can be retrofitted into the basic security mechanisms.

Working backwards from the above solution strategy, the security problem associated with executable content can be stated as consisting of the following six subproblems:

- What are the potential target resources and corresponding attack scenarios
- What is the basic minimal set of behavioral components that can account for the above scenarios
- How to design a computer language/programming environment, that implicitly forbids the basic set of malicious behavior
- How to prove that such a language/environment is indeed secure as claimed
- How to make sure that incoming executable content has indeed been implemented in, and has originated from, the trusted language
- How to make the language future-proof, i.e., extensible to co-opt security strategies to counter new threats arising in the future

As we will see, Java has been designed from the ground up to address most (but probably not all) of the security problem as defined above. Before we move on to Java security architecture itself, we will identify the attack targets and scenarios in the next subsection.

## Potential Attack Scenarios and Targets of Executable Content

In this subsection, we will list the various possible attack scenarios and resources on a user's computer likely to be targeted by a potentially malicious, external, executable, content module.

Attack scenarios could belong to one of the following categories (this is not an exhaustive list):

- Damage or modify integrity of data and/or execution state of programs.
- Collect and smuggle confidential data out.

- Lock up resources, making them unavailable for legitimate users and programs.
- Steal resources for use by an external unauthorized party.
- Cause non-fatal but low-intensity unwelcome effects, especially on output devices.
- Usurp identity and impersonate the user or user's computer, to attack other targets on the network.

The following table lists the resources that could potentially be targeted, and the type of attack they could be subject to. A good security strategy will assign security/risk weights to each resource, and design an appropriate access policy for external executable content.

| | Damage Integrity | Smuggle Information | Lock Up/ Deny Usage | Steal Resource | Non-fatal Distraction | Impersonate |
|---|---|---|---|---|---|---|
| File system | X | X | X | X | X | |
| Confidential data | X | X | X | | X | X |
| Network | X | X | X | X | | X |
| CPU | | X | X | X | | |
| Memory | X | X | X | X | | |
| Output Devices | | X | X | X | X | |
| Input Devices | | X | X | | X | |
| OS, program state | X | | X | X | X | |

# Java Approach to Security

In this section, we will move forward from the generic discussion of security issues related to executable content, and take a broad look at the fundamental implicit security mechanisms built into Java by its designers, in reference to the six-step approach outlined in the previous section.

### Step 1: Visualize all attack scenarios

Instead of coming up with every conceivable attack scenario, the Java security architecture posits potential targets of a basic set of attack categories, very similiar to the attack scenario matrix above.

Specifically, the Java security model covers the following potential targets:

- Memory
- Client file system
- OS/program state
- Network

against the following attack types listed in the table:

- Damage integrity of software resources on client machine
- Lock up/deny usage of resource on client machine
- Smuggle information out of client machine
- Impersonate client machine

### Step 2: Construct a basic set of malicious behavior

Instead of arriving at a basic set of malicious behavior, Java posits a basic set of security hotspots, and implements a mechanism to secure each of these hotspots:

- Java language mechanism and compiler
- Java compiled class file
- Java byte code verifier and interpreter
- Java runtime system, including class loader, memory, and thread manager
- Java external environment, such as Java Web browsers and their interface mechanisms
- Java applets and degrees of freedom allowed for applets (which constitute executable content)

### Step 3: Design security architecture against above behavior set

Construct a programming environment/computer language which implicitly disallows the basic set of malicious behaviors, and hence by implication, all potential malicious behavior.

You guessed it—this language is Java !

### Step 4: Prove security of architecture

Logically or, if possible, axiomatically prove that the language/environment is indeed secure against the intended attack scenarios.

Security mechanisms built into Java have not (yet) been axiomatically or even logically proven to be secure. Instead, Java encapsulates all of its security mechanism into distinct and well-defined layers. Each of these security loci can be observed to be secure by inspection, in relation to the language design framework and target execution environment of Java language programs and applets.

**Step 5: Restrict executable content to proven secure architecture**

The Java class file checker and bytecode verifier achieve this objective.

**Step 6: Make security architecture extensible**

Design the language such that any new attack scenarious arising in the future can be dealt with by a corresponding set of countermeasures, which can be retrofitted into the basic security mechanisms.

The encapsulation of security mechanisms into distinct and well-defined loci, combined with the provision of a Java Security Manager class, provides a generic mechanism for incremental enhancement of security.

# Architecture and Implementation of Java Security Mechanisms

In this section, we will examine specific details of security mechanisms built into Java.

## Security Built into the Java Language Itself

The first tier of security in Java is the language design itself—the syntactical and semantic constructs allowed by the language. The following is an examination of Java language design constructs with a bearing on security.

### Strict Object-Orientedness

Java is fully object-oriented, with every single, primitive data structure (and hence derived data structures) being a first class, full-fledged object. This ensures that all the theoretical security advantages of OOP permeate the entire syntax and semantics of programs written in Java:

- Encapsulation and hiding of data behind private declarations
- Controlled access to data structures via public methods only
- Incremental and hierarchical complexity of program structure
- No operator overloading

### Final Classes and Methods

Classes and methods can be declared as FINAL, which disallows further subclassing and method overriding. This prevents malicious modification of trusted and verified code.

### Strong Typing and Safe Typecasting

Typecasting is security checked both statically and dynamically, which ensures that a declared compile-time type of an object is strictly compatible with eventual run-time type, even if the object transitions through type-casts and coercions. This prevents malicious type camouflaging.

### No Pointers

This is possibly the strongest guarantor of security built right into the Java language. Banishment of pointers ensures that no portion of a Java program is ever anonymous. Every single data structure and code fragment has a handle which makes it fully traceable.

### Language Syntax for Thread-Safe Data Structures

Java is multithreaded. Java language enforces thread-safe access to data structures and objects. Chapter 25 examines Java threads in detail, with examples and application code.

### Unique Object Handles

Every single Java object has a unique hash-code associated with it. This means that the state of a Java program can be fully inventoried at any time.

## Security in Compiled Java Code

At compile time, all the security mechanisms implied by the Java language syntax and semantics are checked, including conformance to private and public declarations, type-safeness, and initialization of all variables to a guaranteed known value.

### Class Version and Class File Format Verification

Each compiled class file is verified to conform to the currently published official class file format. The class file is checked for both structure, and consistency of information within each component of the class file format. Cross-references between classes (via method calls or variable assignments) are verified for conformance to public and private declarations.

Each Java class is also assigned a major and minor version number. Version mismatch between classes within the same program is checked.

### Byte Code Verification

Java source classes are compiled into byte codes. The byte code verifier subjects the compiled code to a variety of consistency and security checks. The verification steps applied to byte code include:

- Check for stack underflows and overflows
- Validity of register accesses
- Correctness of byte-code parameters
- Dataflow analysis of byte code generated by methods, to ensure integrity of stack and objects passed into and returned by a method

### Name Space Encapsulation Using Packages

Java classes are defined within packages. Package names qualify Java class names. Packages ensure that code coming from the network is distinguished from local code. An incoming class library cannot maliciously shadow and impersonate local trusted class libraries, even if both have the same names. This also ensures unverified, accidental interaction between local and incoming classes.

### Very Late Linking and Binding

Late linking and binding ensure that the exact layout of run-time resources, such as stack and heap is delayed as much as possible. This constitutes a roadblock to security attacks utilizing specific assumptions about the allocation of these resources.

## Security in the Java Run-Time System

The default mechanism of run-time loading of Java classes is to fetch the referred class from a file on the local host machine. Any other way of loading a class, including from across the network, requires an associated ClassLoader. A ClassLoader is a subtype of the standard Java ClassLoader class which has methods that implement all the consistency and security mechanisms and apply them to every class that is newly loaded.

For security reasons, the ClassLoader cannot make any assumptions about the byte code. The byte code could have been created from a Java program compiled with the Java compiler, or it could have been created by a C++ compiler modified to generate Java byte code. This means the ClassLoader kicks in only after the incoming byte code has been verified.

ClassLoader has the responsibility of creating a namespace for downloaded code, and resolving the names of classes referenced by the downloaded code. The ClassLoader enforces package-delimited namespaces.

### Automatic Garbage Collection and Implicit Memory Management

In C and C++, the programmer has the explicit responsibility to allocate and deallocate memory, and keep track of all the pointers to allocated memory. This often is a maintenance nightmare, and a major source of bugs resulting from memory leaks, dangling pointers, null pointers, mismatched allocation and deallocation operations.

Java eliminates pointers, and with it the programmer's obligation to explicitly manage memory. Memory allocation and deallocation are automatic, strictly structured, and fully type-safe. Java uses garbage collection to free unused memory instead of explicit programmer mediated deallocation. This eliminates memory-related bugs as well as potential security holes. Manual allocation and deallocation allows unauthorized replication, cloning and impersonation of trusted objects, as well as attacks on data consistency.

### SecurityManager Class

SecurityManager is a generic and extensible locus for implementing security policies, and providing security wrappers around other parts of Java, including class libraries and external environments (such as Java-enabled browsers and native methods). The SecurityManager class itself is not intended to be used directly (each of the checks defaults to throwing a security exception). It is a shell class, intended to be fleshed out via subclassing, to implement a specific set of security policies.

Among other features, it has methods to

- Determine whether a security check is in progress.
- Check to prevent the installation of additional ClassLoaders.
- Check if dynamic libraries can be linked (used for native code).
- Check if a class file can be read from.
- Check if a file can be written to.
- Check if a network connection can be created.
- Check if a certain network port can be listened to for connections.
- Check if a network connection can be accepted.
- Check if a certain package can be accessed.
- Check if a new class can be added to a package.
- Verify security of a native OS system call.

## Security of Executable Code Implemented as Java Applets

The major source of security threats from and to Java programs is Java code coming in from across the network, and executing on the client machine. This class of transportable Java programs is called Java applets. Java applets have a very distinct set of capabilities and restrictions within the language framework, especially from the security standpoint.

### File System and Network Access Restrictions on Applets Arriving from the Network

Applets loaded over the network have the following restrictions imposed on them:

- Cannot read or write files on the local file system
- Cannot create, rename, or copy files and directories on the local file system
- Cannot make arbitrary network connections, except to the host machine they originally came from. This would be the host domain name specified in the URL of the HTML page which contained the APPLET tag for the applet, or the hostname specified in the CODEBASE parameter of the APPLET tag. Numeric IP address of the host will not work.

The above strict set of restrictions on access to a local file system apply to applets running under Netscape Navigator 2.0 versions. The JDK 1.0 Appletviewer slightly relaxes the above, by letting the user define a specific explicit list of files that can be accessed by applets.

### External Code Access Restrictions on Applets

Applets cannot:

- Call external programs, via such system calls as fork or exec.
- Manipulate any Java threadgroups except their own thread group rooted in the main applet thread.

### System Information Accessible from Applets

Applets can read some system properties by invoking System.getProperty (String key). Applets under Netscape 2.0 have unrestricted access to these properties. Sun JDK 1.0 appletviewer allows individual control over access to each property. The following table lists the type of information returned for various values of key.

| key | Information returned |
|---|---|
| java.version | Java version number |
| java.vendor | Java vendor-specific string |
| java.vendor.url | Java vendor URL |
| java.class.version | Java class version number |
| os.name | Operating system name |
| os.arch | Operating system architecture |
| file.separator | File separator (e.g., "/") |
| path.separator | Path separator (e.g., ":") |
| line.separator | Line separator |

### System Information Not Accessible from Applets

The following information is not accessible to applets under Netscape 2.0.
JDK 1.0 appletviewer allows user controllable access to one or more of these
resources.

| key | Information returned |
|---|---|
| java.home | Java installation directory |
| java.class.path | Java classpath |
| user.name | User account name |
| user.home | User home directory |
| user.dir | User's current working directory |

### Applets Loaded from the Local Client File System

There are two different ways that applets are loaded by a Java system.
An applet can arrive over the network, or can be loaded from the local file
system. The way an applet is loaded determines its degree of freedom.

If an applet arrives over the network, it is loaded by the `ClassLoader`, and is
subject to security checks imposed by the `ClassLoader` and `SecurityManager`
classes. If an applet resides on the client's local file system in a directory listed
in the user's `CLASSPATH` environment variable, then it is loaded by the file
system loader.

From a security standpoint, locally loaded applets can:

■ Read and write the local file system
■ Load libraries on the client

- Exec external processes on the local machine
- Exit the Java virtual machine
- Skip being checked by the byte code verifier

# Open Issues on Java Security

Having examined the issue of security of executable content both in general and specifically in the framework of Java, we will now examine some aspects of security not fully addressed by the current version of the Java architecture. We will also see if, for some types of threats, 100 percent security can be achieved at all.

The following components of the Java architecture, are the loci of security mechanisms:

- Language syntax, semantics
- Compiler and compiled class file format and version checker
- Byte code verifier and interpreter
- Java run-time system, including `ClassLoader`, `SecurityManager`, memory, and thread management
- Java external environment, such as Java Web browsers and their interface mechanisms
- Java applets and degrees of freedom allowed for applets (which constitute executable content)

However, security provided by each of these layers can be diluted, or defeated in some ways, with varying degrees of difficulty:

- Data layout in the source code can be haphazard and exposed despite hiding and control mechanisms provided by Java syntax.

    This can lead to security breaches, if for instance, access and assignment to objects are not threadsafe, or, data structures that ought to be declared private are instead exposed as public resources.

- The run-time system is currently implemented in a platform-dependent non-Java language such as C. The only way to ensure it is not compromised is by licensing it from Sun, or comparing it with a reference implementation.

This can lead to a security compromise, if instead of using Sun's own run-time system or a provably verified clone, someone uses a home-brew or no-name version of the runtime which has diluted versions of the class loader or byte code verifier.

■ The interface between Java and external non-Java environments such as Web browsers may be compromised.

Security issues which cannot easily be addressed within Java (or any other mechanism of executable content for that matter) include:

■ Stealing of CPU resources on client side. I could send an applet to your computer that uses your CPU to perform some computation, and return the results back to me.

■ Applets can contain nasty or annoying content (images, audio, or text). If this happens often, users will have to block applets on a per-site basis. User-definable content filtering should be integrated into the standard Java class library.

■ An applet can allocate an arbitrary amount of memory.

■ An applet can start up an arbitrary number of threads.

■ Security compromises arising out of inherent weaknesses in Internet protocols, especially those that were implemented before the Java and executable content burst on the scene.

One generic way to deal with security problems is for Java applet classes to be sent encrypted and digitally signed. The `ClassLoader`, `SecurityManager`, and even the byte code verifier can include decryption and signature verification methods built-in.

These and other open issues related to Java security are topics of ongoing debates and exploration of specific and involved security breach scenarios, especially on online forums. The next and final section of this chapter has pointers to references and sources of further information on this topic.

# References and Resources on Java and Network Security

**UseNet Newsgroups**

alt.2600

comp.risks

comp.lang.java

comp.infosystems.www.

**Web Sites**

Drew Dean and Dan S. Wallach, *Security Flaws in the HotJava Web Browser*, November 3, 1995.

> **ftp://ftp.cs.princeton.edu/reports/1995/501.ps.Z**

James Gosling and Henry McGilton, *The Java Language Environment: A White Paper*, Sun Microsystems, May 1995.

> **ftp://java.sun.com/docs/JavaBook.ps.tar.Z**

Sun Microsystems, *HotJava!: The Security Story*.

> **http://java.sun.com/1.0alpha3/doc/security/security.html**

Sun Microsystems, *The Java Language Specifications: Version 1.0 Beta*.

> **http://java.sun.com/JDK-beta/psfiles/javaspec.ps**

Frank Yellin, *Low Level Security in Java*, Sun Microsystems.

> **http://java.sun.com**

Sun Microsystems, *FAQ - Applet Security*.

> **http://java.sun.com**

Joseph A. Bank, *Java Security*, Massachusetts Institute of Technology,

> **http://www-swiss.ai.mit.edu/~jbank/javapaper/javapaper.html**

# CHAPTER 7

# The Parts of the Language

*by Jay Cross*

Now that you have installed Java and learned about its security features, the next step is to learn the Java language. If you are an experienced C or C++ programmer, most parts of this language will seem very familiar. C programmers will need to adjust to the object paradigm, but Java uses it about as simply as has ever been expressed. Otherwise, it will still be fairly simple; Java has few extraneous features.

In this chapter, an overview of the parts of the language is presented. In subsequent chapters, more detailed views of these parts is presented. These parts are given in seven categories: Tokens, Types, Expressions, Statements, Classes, Interfaces, and Packages. From these parts, ideas can be expressed in Java as applications or applets.

In this chapter, you will learn:

- The English language terms used to describe the Java language.
- The groupings of parts of the Java language.
- What Packages are in Java.
- What Classes and Interfaces are in Java.
- What Statements are in Java.
- What Expressions are in Java.
- What Types are in Java.
- What Tokens are in Java.
- How these parts relate to each other in the Java language.

Looking from the largest to the smallest, Java applets and applications import prepackaged utilities from Packages such as Graphics, or widgets. (Java's equivilent to libraries or class libraries). Packages are made up of classes and interfaces (the self-contained units which may be imported). The java awt package has class definitions for Graphics, Color, Font, and many more. A class is defined by a declaration and a block of statements, as seen in the ubiquitous HelloWorld examples. Most statements contain expressions. Expressions describe what is done with types of data (such as "Radius * Radius * Pi") ; and tokens are the characters and groups of characters which the compiler recognizes for building up expressions and statements.

**Fig. 7.1**

(a) Java applications and applets are classes, which may use other classes and interfaces imported from packages. (b) Java classes are defined using a block of statements. (c) Java statements and expressions are built using tokens. (d) Java statements can contain expressions of compatible types.

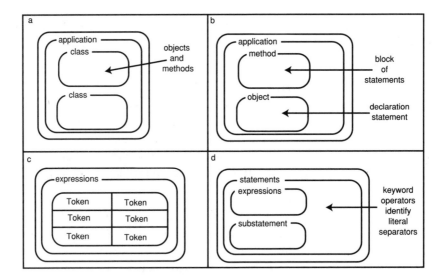

These parts are described from the most basic to the highest level.

# Tokens

For a compiler to convert a human readable file to machine instructions, it must first determine what tokens or symbols are expressed in the code. This is true for any computer language. By analogy, the same idea can be applied to human language and philosophy.

◀ javac is described on p. 49.

When Java code is fed to the Java Compiler (javac), it parses the code into individual tokens. In Java, as with most computer languages, there are five types of tokens: identifiers, keywords, literals, operands, and separators. Java code may also contain comments and white space (spaces, tabs, and line feeds), which are a great aid to human readability, but do not affect the interpretation of the application or applet. See table 7.1.

### Table 7.1    The Types of Tokens in the Java Language

| Type | Description | Examples |
|---|---|---|
| Keyword | Words that are an essential part of the language definition. | public, class, static, void, String, else, if, synchronized, this, while |
| Identifier | Names for classes, objects, variables, constants, labels, methods, etc. Composed of unicode alpha-numerics, with the first character being a non-numeric. | HelloWorld, main, args, System, out, println, j, n32e20 |
| Literal | Used for entering explicit values for variables or constants. These may be numeric, Boolean, character, or strings. | "Hello World", 6, 257L, 7Ex, 6.0225e+23d, true |
| Separator | Symbols used to indicate where groups of code are divided and arranged. | ( ) { } [ ] ; , . |
| Operator | Characters and combinations of characters that identify an operation to be done on one or more variables or constants. | +, -, *, /, <<, >>, |
| White Space | Non-meaningful characters that may be placed between any of the above in any order of quantity. Used to add clarity to the appearance of the source code. | [space], [tab], [end-of-line], [formfeed] |
| Comment | Further aid and abet the conveying of meaning of the source code to human readers. | // Comment until the next end-of-line /* Embedded comment */ |

Java code uses the 16-bit Unicode character set (not 8-bit ASCII). This allows the use of alphabets other than the Latin/English one. The compiler expects Unicode. All literals are in Unicode. When javac is done, the result is in the form of machine-independent Java bytecode.

▶ More details about the individual token types, plus comments and white space, are available on p. 133.

## Types

Type for a computer language refers to how a primitive object (i.e. a variable) is represented in the computers storage facilities. It also usually has ramifications pertaining to what operations can be one with it, and to it. For example, many computer languages forbid direct arithmetic operations on a character string, unless there is an implied instruction to first attempt to convert the string to a number.

Java has eight primitive types, including six numeric types, plus one Boolean and one character type. Java also allows arrays of any of these types, which are described briefly in table 7.2 below.

| Table 7.2   Primitive Data Types in the Java Language | |
| --- | --- |
| **Type** | **Description** |
| byte | 8 bit two's-compliment integer with values between $-2^7$ and $2^7$-1 (-128 and 127) |
| short | 16 bit two's-compliment integer with values between $-2^{15}$ and $2^{15}$-1 (-32,768 and 32,767) |
| int | 32 bit two's-compliment integer with values between $-2^{31}$ and $2^{31}$-1 (-2,147,483,648 and 2, 147,483,647) |
| long | 64 bit two's-compliment integer with values between $-2^{63}$ and $2^{63}$-1 (+/- 9.2 x $10^{18}$, roughly the number of stars in 10 million large galaxies, or the number of bits in 3 million uncompressed HDTV feature length movies) |
| float | 32 bit single precision floating point numbers using the IEEE 754-1985 standard (+/- about $10^{39}$) |
| double | 64 bit double precision floating point numbers using the IEEE 754-1985 standard. (+/- about $10^{317}$) |
| char | 16 bit Unicode characters. For alpha-numerics, these are the same as ASCII with the high byte set to 0. |
| boolean | These have values of either true or false. |

None of the numeric types are unsigned. This is one way in which Java is different from C or C++. This helps to simplify the usage of the language, and eliminates a subtle variety of errors that has plagued C programmers for decades. Of the six numeric types, there are four integer types: byte (8-bit signed), short (16-bit signed), int (32-bit signed), and long (64-bit signed), and two floating point types: float (32-bit) and double (64-bit). Note that literal floating point expressions (such as 3.14159) are interpreted by default to be of type double.

Boolean variables are type Boolean, and have values of true or false. These types cannot have integer operations done to them, or have values other than true or false. C or C++ programmers may have seen Booleans as a typedef in their local programming environment. Java has no typedef statement.

As stated earlier in the overview of tokens, characters in Java store 16-bit Unicode values, not the 8-bit ASCII that C and C++ programmers are familiar with. For the most part this should not result in much of an adjustment; it means that strings take up twice as much space, and that internationalization is easier.

▶ Types are examined in more detail on p. 151.

# Expressions

Expressions in Java are very similar to expressions in C or C++. They express a value either directly, or by being a means of computing the value; or they can be control-flow expressions, which express the sequence of program execution. These expressions can include constants, variables, keywords, operators and other expressions. Some valid Java expressions are:

```
7
3.141592654
2^32 -1
3*i
(14-i) * (3+j)
(i>64) && (i<73)
j++
k<<7
(k>128) ? true : false
```

Java does not support the creation of compound statements using the comma operator, except within the initialization and continuation clauses of loop statements.

Thus:

```
k=25, j=36;
```

is not by itself a valid statement, but it may be included in the initialization (or continuation) clause of a loop:

```
for (k=25, j=36; j+k < 65; j++, k++) {
// statements in the loop...
}
```

▶ The lists of keywords and operators are presented on p. 133.

# Statements

Statements in Java are similar to statements in C or C++, and, to a lesser degree, like many other computer languages such as Pascal, Ada, Basic, Fortran, and Cobol. Statements are executed in sequence (except as described by control-flow statements, or exception statements). They are executed for their effect, and do not of themselves have any value.

Java has several different types of statements as described below in table 7.3:

<table>
<tr><td colspan="2">**Table 7.3  Types of Statements in the Java Language**</td></tr>
<tr><td>**Statement**</td><td>**Description**</td></tr>
<tr><td>**Empty Statement**</td><td>These do nothing, and may be useful during program development as a place holder. This is the same as in C and C++.</td></tr>
<tr><td>**Labeled Statement**</td><td>Any statement may begin with a label. Such labels must not be keywords, already declared local variables, or previously used labels in this module. Except for their use with Jump statements, labels are identical to their C and C++ counterparts. Labels in Java may be used as the arguments of Jump statements which are desribed later in this list.</td></tr>
<tr><td>**Expression Statement**</td><td>Most statements are expression statements. The Java language specification lists seven types of Expression statements: **Assignment, Pre-Increment, Pre-Decrement, Post-Increment, Post-Decrement, Method Call**, and **Allocation Expression**.</td></tr>
<tr><td>**Selection Statement**</td><td>These choose one of several control flows. As in C and C++, there are three types of selection statements in Java: **if, if-else**, and **switch-case-default**.</td></tr>
<tr><td>**Iteration Statement**</td><td>These specify how and when looping will take place. There are three types of iteration statements, which, except for jumps and labels are identical to their C and C++ counterparts: **while, do**, and **for**.</td></tr>
<tr><td>**Jump Statement**</td><td>Jump Statements pass control to the beginning or end of the current block, or to a labeled statement. Note that there is **no goto** statement in Java. The optional label argument on the break and continue statements are not part of C or C++. Such labels must be in the same block, and continue labels must be on an iteration statement. These</td></tr>
</table>

▶ The details and nature of these statements are presented on p. 245.

| Statement | Description |
|---|---|
| | statements have implications for synchronization statements in the block, as well. The four types of Jump statement are **break**, **continue**, **return**, and **throw**. Throw statements are an important part of the exception mechanism. |
| **Synchronization Statement** | These are used used for handling issues with multi-threading. The **synchronized** and **threadsafe** keywords are used to mark variables which may or may not require locks against simultaneous use. |
| **Guarding Statement** | Guarding statements are used for safe handling of code that may cause exceptions (such as divide by zero). These statements use the **try**, **catch**, and **finally** keywords. |
| **Unreachable Statement** | These generate an error at compile time. |

# Classes

In the context of computer languages, classes are a piece of the object paradigm. If you are familiar with the world of object-oriented programming, you will find Java refreshingly simple. If you are not, you will need to learn the object paradigm if you are going to use Java. Java is purely object-oriented. You cannot write a procedural program in Java.

It is beyond the scope of this book to teach object-oriented programming. However, here are a few notes that should be enough to get you started.

Take a look at the Hello World example; the whole program is the definition of a trivial object:

```
public class HelloWorld {
   public static void main(String Args[]) {
          System.out.println("Hello World");
   }
}
```

The hello world example does so little that it shows very little about how a class is defined. It does show that a class that does something can be created with five lines of code (two of which are closing curly braces). When compiled with javac, it creates a file called HelloWorld.class which has the class expressed as machine independent byte-codes that Java can execute on any machine on which it resides. Later class examples will show instance variables, static members, inheritance, and methods including creators and destructors. Classes are to objects as types are to variables. A variable is an instance of a type. (For example, a place in memory that the compiler is told contains a byte, has the value 0000 0110 in it. This instance of a byte has the value 6.) An object is a instance of a class. The hello world example creates a definition of a class, which, when run, creates an object that writes the text "Hello World" to the screen.

Classes are different from types in many ways. They can be composed of a mixed assortment of types and other classes. They can inherit properties from parent classes. They can have operations (called Methods in the object paradigm) as part of their definition. Perhaps most importantly, it is the definition of these classes that is the job of the programmer.

C programmers often consider classes to be like structure definitions, in which the structure may contain procedures that pertain to the data in the structure. People experienced with relational databases can consider a class to be like a table, with the tables columns being like the classes instance variables and the tables triggers being like the classes methods. In neither case is the correlation perfect, but it is a good place to start.

▶ Classes are discussed in much more detail on p. 163, and in Appendix C, p. 787.

Traditionally, teachers of the object paradigm like to describe a class as a template, from which objects are created. Also, from such a template, a more specific class may be defined. For instance, we might imagine a class which is describes a room. This class might have features for dimensions, and for methods for placement of windows, doors, sockets, lights, etc. This class might work well for describing offices and bedrooms, but you may want to extend the class definition for describing a kitchen or bathroom with methods for placement of other fixtures. See figure 7.2.

Classes are discussed in much more detail in a chapter 10 and in appendix C.

**Fig. 7.2**
In this figure we see a room of a hypothetical class "Room" on the left. It has the simple features of a room. On the right we see a room from a child class of "Room." In this case the child class is "BathRoom." It has the extra features of a bathtub, and a sink.

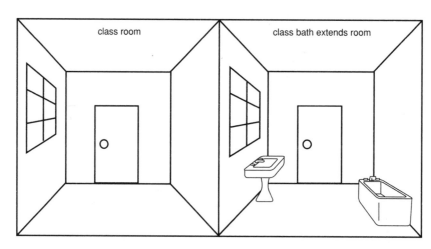

# Interfaces

There is no multiple inheritance in Java. Object-oriented programming relies on the creation of subclasses from broad parent classes. For example, you could imagine that Class TwoDoorSedan could be a subclass of Class Car. It inherits properties from Class Car, and has some properties of its own that Car does not have. In C++ and some other object-oriented languages, an allowance was made for inheriting properties from two distinct parent Classes. For example Class AmphibiousCar might inherit from Class Car, and from Class MotorBoat. This is called multiple inheritance. Readers familiar with C++ are well aware that multiple inheritance makes object-oriented programming more complex.

Java's creators knew about the value of multiple inheritance, but found a simpler way to fill the same needs, while reducing ambiguity and general doubt about usage. It is known as an *interface*. An interface is a collection of methods declarations and constants that one or more Classes of Objects will use. Interfaces cannot contain variables or code to specifically implement any method.

With a bit of a change in how you define it, Interfaces allow making the Class AmphibiousCar inherit from both Class MotorBoat and Class Car, because (you may imagine) there may need to be both motorboat-like and car-like variables in the class (e.g., TireSize (from Car) and GunwaleLength (from MotorBoat)). Real programming examples that can't be done just as easily with the interface construct are proving very rare.

Commonly seen examples of interfaces tend to be lists of methods for printing or acquiring data, for specifying how forms will look on the screen, and for defining how classes might deal with some contained feature such as images or bodies of text.

Getting back to the AmphibiousCar: in Java, an inexperienced programmer might let the Class AmphibiousCar inherit from either Car or MotorBoat, and the other features (MotorBoat-like or Car-like) would need to be built into the subclass and maintained there to imitate the features of non-inherited class. This would result in maintenance trouble. Clever programmers, anticipating this rare object duality could create the parent classes using interfaces to specify the common methods for each. Then, the AmphibiousCar class would have a list of methods that need to be implemented, and javac would point out when some feature had not been fleshed out.

**Listing 7.1    An Example to Demonstrate Using Interfaces for Multiple Inheritance**

```
Interface WheeledVehicle {
     String GetTireSize();
     int GetNumberOfTires();
}
Interface FloatingVehicle {
     int GetGunwaleLength();
     int GetTransomStrength();
}
Class Car Implements WheeledVehicle {
     protected String TireSize;
     protected int NumberOfTires;
     // note many necessary methods not included, see chaps 11 & 12.
     public String GetTireSize() {
            return TireSize;
     }
     public int GetNumberOfTires() {
            return NumberOfTires;
     }
}
Class AmphibiousCar extends Car Implements FloatingVehicle {
     protected int GunwaleLength;
     protected int TransomStrength;
     // note many necessary methods not included, see chaps 11 & 12.
     public int GetGunwaleLength() {
            return GunwaleLength;
     }
     public int GetTransomStrength() {
            return TransomStrength;
     }
}
```

In the above example, the keyword "implements" is used to identify a list (in these cases a one-element list) of interfaces used by the class.

Interfaces are a simple but important part of the Java language, and are discussed less fancifully and in much more detail in chapter 11.

# Packages

Packages in Java are groups of Classes. These are like libraries in many computer languages. A package of Java classes typically will contain related classes. From the above fanciful examples we can imagine a package called Transportation, which would have numerous Classes defined in it, such as Car, Boat, Airplane, Train, Rocket, AmphibiousCar, SeaPlane, etc. Applications that deal with items of this sort might benefit from importing our imaginary Transportation Package. This is done by a line that must come before the definition of any class in the file, as follows:

```
// FILE: TravelAgencyApp.java
import Transportation.*;
// ... the import statement having been demonstrated,
//   the rest of the Application is omitted.
// End of File
```

While a package may contain many classes (related or not), each file that goes into creating a package may contain at most one public Class definition. The package statement at the beginning of the file tells Java that this class is part of a package, as follows:

```
// FILE: Car.java
package Transportation;
// ... definition of the Car Class
// End of File
// FILE: Boat.java
package Transportation;
// ... definition of the Boat Class
// End of File
```

Note that you do not need to import a package to use classes in a package, but doing so affords a shorthand way to refer to classes defined in the package. Specifically, in the above example, if the Package was not imported, to create an object of Class Car, you would need to write:

```
new Transportation.Car()
```

Whereas if the Transportation package was imported you could write:

```
new Car()
```

Packages are more than just a shortcut. They are a way of keeping things organized.

Java comes with a built-in set of packages:

**Table 7.4    Standard Java Packages**

| Package | Description |
| --- | --- |
| java.applet | Contains classes needed to create Java applets that will run under Netscape 2.0 (or greater), HotJava, or other Java-compatible browsers. |
| java.awt | Contains classes helpful in writing platform-independent Graphic User Interface (GUI) applications. This comes with several subpackages, including java.awt.peer, and java.awt.image. |
| java.io | Contains classes for doing I/O (input & output). This is where the data stream classes are kept. |
| java.lang | Contains the essential Java classes. It is implicitly imported, so you don't need to. |

(continues)

The Java Language

| Table 7.4 | Continued |
|-----------|-----------|
| **Package** | **Description** |
| java.net | Contains the classes used for making network connections. These are used in tandem with java.io for reading and writing data from the network. |
| java.util | Contains the leftovers, such as encoding, decoding, vectors, stacks, etc. |

Additional packages are available commercially. ❖

# CHAPTER 8
# Tokens in Depth

*by Jay Cross*

*Tokens* are to computer language as words and punctuation are to human language. William of Ockham (a noted 14th Century Scholar famous for his support of simplicity) in his *Summa Logicae* went to great lengths to describe his theory of terms. While it is beyond the scope of this book to explain Ockham fully, the sense of it is that (for example) the word "chair" is not *a chair*, but rather a symbol—a reader or listener conjures up the thought of a chair when he reads or hears the word.

Using the same analogy, *tokens* are terms in source languages for computers. If a programmer declares a token "counter" to represent a short integer (a 16-bit number described later in this chapter), then the compiler recognizes the token "counter" every time it is used in that context as referring to a specific 16 bits of memory somewhere. Any operations performed on "counter" are done with the value contained in those 16 bits; not with the token (the characters c, o, u, n, t, e, r), but with what that token represents to the compiler.

To accurately describe a task to a compiler, a description language needs to have a strict and unambiguous grammar structure. Java's grammar is fairly simple and elegant. You can begin understanding Java by learning about the tokens from which the more complex forms of expression are composed. These include *keywords*, *identifiers*, *literals*, *separators*, and *operators*. A Java program may also contain *white space* and *comments* that have no meaning to the compiler but are permitted for the sake of making the code's meaning clear to human readers—especially its author(s).

In this chapter you will learn:

- What the reserved words are in the Java language.
- How to create user-defined names and labels.

- The many ways to express values for constants.
- What the limits are in the ranges of the types of numbers that may be expressed.
- What separators are.
- What the various operators do.
- Why even though the compiler ignores them, comments and white space are important.

# Keywords

There are certain sequences of characters that have special meaning in Java; these sequences are called *keywords*. Some of them are like verbs, some like adjectives, and some like pronouns. Some of them are tokens that are saved for later versions of the language, and one (goto) is a vile oath from ancient procedural tongues that may never be uttered in polite Java.

The following is a list of the 56 keywords you can use in Java. When you know the meanings of all these terms, you will be well on your way to being a Java programmer.

**Table 9.1   The 56 Keywords Used in Java**

| | | | |
|---|---|---|---|
| abstract | boolean | break | byte |
| case | cast | catch | char |
| class | const | continue | default |
| do | double | else | extends |
| final | finally | float | for |
| future | generic | goto | if |
| implements | import | inner | instanceof |
| int | interface | long | native |
| new | null | operator | outer |
| package | private | protected | public |
| rest | return | short | static |
| super | switch | synchronized | this |
| throw | throws | transient | try |
| var | void | volatile | while |

The keywords byvalue, cast, const, future, generic, goto, inner, operator, outer, rest, and var are reserved, but have no meaning in Java 1.0. Programmers experienced with other languages such as C, C++, Pascal, or SQL may know what these terms might eventually be used for. For the time being, you won't use these terms, and Java is much simpler and easier to maintain without them.

The tokens true and false are not on this list; technically, they are literal values for Boolean variables or constants (Boolean and other literals are described in the section on literals later in this chapter). As such, programmers should refrain from using them as identifiers (user-defined names or labels).

Because these terms have specific meaning in Java, you can't use them as identifiers for something else, such as variables, constants, class names, and so on. However, they can be used as part of a longer token, for example:

```
public int abstract_int;
```

Also, because Java is case-sensitive, if a programmer is bent on using one of these words as an identifier of some sort, you can use an initial uppercase letter. While this is possible, it is a very bad idea in terms of human readability, and it results in wasted man-hours when the code must be improved later to this:

```
public short Long;
```

It can be done, but for the sake of clarity and mankind's future condition, please don't do it.

There are numerous Classes defined in the standard packages. While their names are not keywords, the overuse of these names may make your meaning unclear to future people working on your application or applet.

# Identifiers

*Identifiers* are terms chosen by the programmer that become tokens representing variables, constants, classes, objects, labels (which are like nouns), and methods (which are like verbs). As noted in the previous section, identifiers cannot be identical to Java keywords.

Identifiers in Java are a sequence of Unicode letters and digits of unlimited length. (Actually, the length may be limited by the maximum file size on the applet or application developer's system. Practically, this would limit an identifier to being less than two billion characters.) The first character of an identifier must be a letter. All subsequent characters must be letters or numerals.

They do not need to be Latin letters or digits; they could be from any alphabet that Unicode supports, such as Arabic-Indic, Devanagari, Bengali, Tamil, Thai, or many others. For various historical and practical considerations, the underscore (_) and the dollar sign ($) are considered letters and may be used as any character in an identifier, including the first one.

Two tokens are the same identifier only if they are of equal length and if each character in the first token is exactly the same as its counterpart in the second token. This is case-sensitive and language-sensitive. This means that Latin letters are different from matching Greek letters, and letters with accents are different from letters without.

Most application developers are forever walking the line of compromise between choosing identifiers that are short enough to be quickly and easily typed without error and those that are long enough to be descriptive and easily read. Either way, in a large application it is useful to choose a naming convention that reduces the likelihood of accidental reuse of a particular identifier.

**Table 9.2  Examples of Legal and Illegal Identifiers**

| Legal Identifiers | Not Legal Identifiers |
| --- | --- |
| HelloWorld | 9HelloWorld |
| counter | count&add |
| HotJava$ | Hot Java |
| ioc_Queue3 | 65536 |
| ErnestLawrenceThayersFamousPoemOfJune1888 | non-plussed |

In the above illegal examples, the first is forbidden because it begins with a numeral. The second has an illegal character (&) in it. The third also has an inappropriate character—the blank space. The fourth is a literal number ($2^{16}$) and cannot be used as an identifier. The last one contains yet another bad character—the hyphen or minus sign. Java would try to treat this last case as an expression containing two identifiers and an operation to be performed on them.

# Literals

*Literals* are tokens representing values to be stored in bytes, shorts, ints, longs, floats, doubles, Booleans, and chars. In addition, literals are used to represent values to be stored in string types. The following statements contain literals:

```
int j=0;

long GrainOfSandOnTheBeachNum=1L;

short Mask1=0x007f;

static String FirstName = "Ernest";

static Char TibetanNine = '\u1049'

boolean UniverseWillExpandForever = true;
```

Clearly, there are several types of literals. In fact, the Java Language Specification gives five major types of literals, some of which have subtypes. The five major types are:

- Boolean literals
- Character literals
- Floating point literals
- Integer literals
- String literals

The following five sections of this chapter give more information about the different types of literals.

## Boolean Literals

There are two *Boolean literals*: `true` and `false`. There is no null value, and there is no numeric equivalent.

## Character Literals

*Character literals* are enclosed in single quotes. This is true whether the character value is Latin alphanumeric, an escape sequence, or any other Unicode character. Single characters are any printable character except hyphen (-) or backslash (\). Some examples of these literals are `'a'`, `'A'`, `'9'`, `'+'`, `'_'`, and `'~'`.

The escape sequence character literals are of the form `'\b'`. That is within single quotes, a backslash followed by one of the following:

- another character (b, t, n, f, r, ", ', or \)
- a series of octal digits
- a u followed by a series of hex digits expressing a non-line-terminating Unicode character

The meaning of the items from the first bulleted item above is probably familiar to C and C++ programmers, and anyone else should quickly recognize it as needing a special way to represent the following:

| Escape Literal | Meaning |
|---|---|
| '\b' | \u0008   backspace |
| '\t' | \u0009   horizontal tab |
| '\n' | \u000a   linefeed |
| '\f' | \u000c   form feed |
| '\r' | \u000d   carriage return |
| '\"' | \u0022   double quote |
| '\'' | \u0027   single quote |
| '\\' | \u005c   backslash |

Character literals mentioned in the second bulleted item above are called *octal escape literals*. They can be used to represent any Unicode value from '\u0000' to '\u00ff' (the traditional ASCII range). In octal (base 8), these values are from \000 to \377. Note that octal numerals are from 0 to 7 inclusive. Some examples of these octal literals are:

| Octal Literal | Meaning |
|---|---|
| '\007' | \u0007   bell |
| '\101' | \u0041   'A' |
| '\141' | \u0061   'a' |
| '\071' | \u0039   '9' |
| '\042' | \u0022   double quote |

Character literals of the type in the last bulleted item above are interpreted very early by javac. As a result, using the escape Unicode literals to express a line termination character such as carriage return or line feed results in an end-of-line appearing before the terminal single quote mark. The result is a compile-time error. Examples of this type of character literal appear as the first six characters of each listing under the "Meaning" heading above.

Don't use the \u format to express an end-of-line character. Use the \n or \r characters instead.

## Floating-Point Literals

*Floating-point literals* have several parts. They appear in the following order:

| Part | Is it Required? | Examples |
| --- | --- | --- |
| Whole Number Part | Not if fractional part is present. | 0, 1, 2, ..., 9, 12345 |
| Decimal Point | Not if exponent is present. Must be there if there is a fractional part. | . |
| Fractional Part | Can't be present if there is no decimal point. Must be there if there is no whole number part. | 0, 1, 14159, 718281828, 41421, 9944 |
| Exponent | Only if there is no decimal point. | e23, E-19, E6, e+307, e-1 |
| Type Suffix | No. In the absence of a type suffix, the number is assumed to be double precision. | f, F, d, D |

Note that the whole number part does not have to be a single numeral; case is not important for the *e* or *E* that is the first character of the exponent, or for the *f*, *F*, *d*, or *D* that indicates the type. As a result, a given number can be represented in several different ways as a literal. 1003.45 could be represented in the following ways (among many others):

1003.45, 1.00345e3, 100.345E+1
100345e-2, .00100345e6, 0.00100345e+6

Of these, the first two are the ways numbers should be represented, but the others get the point across to javac just as well. Because there is no type suffix on any of them, they are all interpreted as double-precision numbers.

Single-precision floating-point literals produce compile-time errors if their values are non-zero and have an absolute value outside the range from 1.40239846e-45f to 3.40282347e+38f. Likewise, the range for the non-zero absolute values of double-precision literals is 4.94065645841246544e-324 to 1.7976931348623157e+308.

## Integer Literals

*Integer literals* may be expressed as decimal (base 10), octal (base 8), or hexadecimal (base 16) numbers, with an optional uppercase L ('L') or lowercase L ('l') at the end. If the L is at the end, the number is interpreted as a long (64-bit) integer.

Decimal-integer literal tokens are identified by Java as beginning with a non-zero digit. Octal-integer literal tokens are recognized by the leading zero; they may not contain the numerals 8 or 9. Hexadecimal-integer literal tokens are known by their distinctive 'zero-X' at the beginning of the token. Hex numbers are composed of the numerals 0 through 9—the numerals representing the values from 10 through 15 are the Latin letters A through F. Case is not important for the letters used representing hexadecimal-integer literals (a, A, b, B, c, C, d, D, e, E, f, F, x, X, l, L).

The largest and smallest values for integer literals are given in these three formats:

| | |
|---|---|
| Largest 32-bit integer literal | 2147483647 |
| | 017777777777 |
| | 0x7fffffff |
| Most negative 32-bit integer literal | -2147483648 |
| | 020000000000 |
| | 0x80000000 |
| Largest 64-bit integer literal | 9223372036854775807L |
| | 0777777777777777777777L |
| | 0x7fffffffffffffffL |
| Most negative 64-bit integer literal | -9223372036854775808L |
| | 01777777777777777777777L |
| | 0xffffffffffffffffL |

Attempts to represent integers outside this range result in compile-time errors.

## String Literals

*String literals* have zero or more characters enclosed in double quotes. These characters may include the escape sequences listed in the "Character Literals" section. Both double quotes must appear on the same line of the source code, so strings may not directly contain a new line character. To achieve the new line effect, you must use an escape sequence such as \n or \r.

The double-quote (") and backslash (\)characters must also be represented using escape sequences (\" and \\).

If you need to use a longer string than can be conveniently placed on one source code line, a string may be created from concatenating two or more smaller strings with the string concatenation operator (+).

Some examples of string literals follow:

```
"Java"
"Hello World!\n"
"The Devanagari numeral for 9 is \u096f "
"Do you mean the European Swallow or the African Swallow?"
"****ERROR 9912 Date/Time 1/1/1900 00:01"
        + " predates last backup: all files deleted!"
"If this were an actual emergency"
```

# Separators

*Separators* are single-character tokens, which (as their name implies) are found between other tokens. There are nine separators, which are loosely described below:

| | |
|---|---|
| ( | Used both to open a parameter list for a method and to establish a precedence for operations in an expression. |
| ) | Used both to close a parameter list for a method and to establish a precedence for operations in an expression. |
| { | Used to begin a block of statements, or an initialization list. |
| } | Used to close a block of statements, or an initialization list. |
| [ | Precedes an expression used as an array index. |
| ] | Follows an expression used as an array index. |
| ; | Used both to end an expression statement and to separate the parts of a 'for' statement. |
| , | Used as a list delimiter in many contexts. |
| . | Used both as a decimal point and to separate such things as package name from class name from method or variable name. |

# Operators

Operators express which operation is to be performed on a given value or values. Here they are described in several related categories.

There are 37 character sequences that are tokens used as *operators*. (C and C++ users will find most of them very familiar.) There are the five arithmetic operators (+, –, *, /, %), six assignment operators (=, +=, *=, –=, /=, %=), a decrement operator (– –), an increment operator (++), four bitwise arithmetic operators (&, |, ^, ~), three bitwise shifting operators (<<, >>, >>>), six bitwise assignment operators (&=, |=, ^=, <<=, >>=, >>>=), six comparison operators (==, !=, <. >, <=, >=), three logical comparison operators (&&, ||, !), and two that act as an if-then-else when used together (?, :).

## Arithmetic Operators

The *arithmetic operators* take two values, integer or floating point, and return a third value whose type can be determined as follows: two integer types (byte, short, int, or long) produce an int or a long (long if and only if one of the operands was a long, or the result can only be expressed as a long). Two floating point types produce a floating point type (if either is a double, it produces a double). An integer and a floating point produce a floating point result. Note that the plus-sign operator also acts as the string concatenation operator.

+ addition operator

– subtraction operator

* multiplication operator

/ division operator

% modulus operator (gives the remainder of a division)

The following code fragment shows these operators in an integer context. The use of the operators is syntactically the same for floating point numbers.

**Listing 9.1   Examples Using Arithmetic Operators**

```
byte j = 60;                // set the byte j's value to 60
short k = 24;
int l = 30;
long m = 12L;
long result = 0L;

result = j + k;             // result gets 84: (60 plus 24)
result = result / m;        // result gets 7: (84 divided by 12)
result = j - (2*k + result); // result gets 5: (60 minus (48 plus 7))
result = k % result;        // result gets 4: (remainder 24 div by 5)
```

## Arithmetic Assignment Operators

With the exception of the (direct) assignment operator (=), the *arithmetic assignment operators* are a little bit of a shortcut. Like the arithmetic operators above, they can be used with both integers and floating point values. With each of these operators, the result is placed in the left operand.

| | |
|---|---|
| = | assignment operator |
| += | add and assign operator |
| −= | subtract and assign operator |
| *= | multiply and assign operator |
| /= | divide and assign operator |
| %= | modulus and assign operator |

The following code fragment shows these operators in an integer context. The use of the operators is syntactically the same for floating point numbers.

**Listing 9.2    Examples Using Arithmetic Assignment Operators**

```
byte j = 60;                   // set the byte j's value to 60
short k = 24;
int l = 30;
long m = 12L;
long result = 0L;

result += j;                   // result gets 60: (0 plus 60)
result += k;                   // result gets 84: (60 plus 24)
result /= m;                   // result gets 7: (84 divided by 12)
result -= l;                   // result gets -23: (7 minus 30))
result = -result;              // result gets 23: (-(-23))
result %= m;                   // result gets 11: (remainder 23 div by 12)
```

## Increment/Decrement Operators

The *increment* and *decrement operators* are used with one integer or floating point operand (they are unary operators). The increment operator (++) adds one to the operand. If the operator appears before the operand, the increment occurs before the value is taken for the expression. If it appears after the operand, the addition occurs after the value is taken. Similarly, the decrement operator (– –) subtracts one from the operand, and the timing of this is in relation to evaluation of the expression that it occurs in.

| | |
|---|---|
| ++ | increment operator |
| – – | decrement operator |

The following code fragment shows these operators in an integer context. The use of the operators is syntactically the same for floating point numbers.

**II**

**The Java Language**

**Listing 9.3   Examples Using Increment and Decrement Operators**

```
long counter = 1000000;     // start at a million.
double fpcounter = 0;       // start with a clean slate.
double fpsum = 0;           // no additions so far.

// compute the sum of all the numbers from one to a million.
while (counter-- > 0) {     // using a million on the first iteration.
    fpsum += ++fpcounter;   // fpcounter incremented before use.
}
```

In the above example, counter is decremented as the test to get out of the loop. In the first iteration, it has a value of a million; in the last iteration, it starts with a value of one. Within the loop, fpcounter is incremented before adding it to the fpsum variable, so the very first iteration has a value of 1—even though it is initialized to 0. In the last iteration, it has a value of a million. The value of fpsum is a little less (due to round-off error) than 500,000,500,000.0, which would have been more easily, but less instructively, computed using n(n+1)/2.

## Bitwise Arithmetic Operators

*Bitwise arithmetic* is not complicated. If you are unfamiliar with it, there may be some new ideas here that will be difficult to learn from a short section in a book. If this is important but difficult for you, try reading a general computer science book for a section on this subject. For starters, let's just say that bitwise arithmetic is used for setting and testing single bits and combinations of individual bits within a variable. Generally, it is not good programming style to do this without a very good reason. Most of these reasons involve communicating with hardware devices or storing information as densely as possible. In the following examples, you will be using variables of type byte because they are the simplest to see. It is assumed that you understand the meaning of hexadecimal numbers. Bitwise arithmetic is defined for the four integer and char types, but not for the floating point, or Boolean types.

|   |   |
|---|---|
| **&** | bitwise arithmetic And operator |
| \| | bitwise arithmetic Or operator |
| ^ | bitwise arithmetic Xor operator |
| ~ | bitwise arithmetic Compliment operator |

First, a bit of elementary computer science: Ignoring sign for a moment, a byte is composed of 8 bits. Each bit has a value of 1 or 0. You assign values to each of the bits as 128, 64, 32, 16, 8, 4, 2, 1, ($2^7$, $2^6$, $2^5$, $2^4$, $2^3$, $2^2$, $2^1$, $2^0$)—if the low seven bits are set, the byte has the value of 1+2+4+8+16+32+64 = 127. In hexadecimal, we call this 0x7f [7 is 0111 (4+2+1), and f is 1111 (8+4+2+1)].

The four bitwise arithmetic operators are called And, Or, Xor, and Compliment. If you And (&) one byte with another and put the result in a third byte, the resulting byte has bits = 1 only when both of the operands had bits in that position = 1. Thus, if 0x7f (0111_1111) is Anded with 0x34 (0011_0100), the result is 0x34 because all the one bits in 0x34 were set to one in the other number. Similarly:

```
0x4f & 0x22 = 0x02     (0100_1111) & (0010_0010) = (0000_0010)
0x3c & 0xa5 = 0x24     (0011_1100) & (1010_0101) = (0010_0100)
```

As you can see, the Anding process always results in the same or fewer bits set to one.

If you Or (|) one byte with another and put the result in a third byte, the resulting byte has bits = 1 when either of the operands had a bit in that position = 1. So, as shown previously:

```
0x4f ¦ 0x22 = 0x6f     (0100_1111) ¦ (0010_0010) = (0110_1111)
0x3c ¦ 0xa5 = 0xbd     (0011_1100) ¦ (1010_0101) = (1011_1101)
```

The process of Oring always results in the same or more bits set to one.

If you Xor (^) (exclusive or) one byte with another and put the result in a third byte, the resulting byte has bits = 1 when the corresponding bit is set in exactly one of the two operand bytes. Thus:

```
0x4f ^ 0x22 = 0x6d     (0100_1111) ^ (0010_0010) = (0110_1101)
0x3c ^ 0xa5 = 0x99     (0011_1100) ^ (1010_0101) = (1001_1001)
```

Complementing (~) is a unary bitwise operation. When a byte is complemented, all the bits are inverted. Thus, ~(0x7f) = 0x80.

## Bitwise Shifting Operators

*Bitwise shifting operations* rotate the bits in an integer. The bits of the first operand are rotated by the number of positions given in the second operand. In the case of the shift left, it is always a zero that is shifted in at the right; it is the equivalent of multiplying by 2 to the second operand power. The normal shift right operator propagates the sign bit. This is like dividing by a power of 2. The shift right with zero fill propagates a zero from the left.

    <<      bitwise shift left operator

    >>      bitwise shift right operator

    >>>     bitwise shift right with zero fill operator

The following examples may be instructive:

```
0x4f << 1 = 0x9e    (0100_1111) << 1 = (1001_1110)
0x3c << 2 = 0xf0    (0011_1100) << 2 = (1111_0000)
0x4f >> 1 = 0x27    (0100_1111) >> 1 = (0010_0111)
0xf0 >> 2 = 0xfc    (1111_0000) >> 2 = (1111_1100)

0x4f >>> 1 = 0x27   (0100_1111) >>> 1 = (0010_0111)
0xf0 >>> 2 = 0x3c   (1111_0000) >>> 2 = (0011_1100)
```

## Bitwise Assignment Operators

By now it should be fairly obvious what the *bitwise assignment operators* do. They take a value, do the appropriate bitwise operation with the second operand, and place the result as the contents of the first operand.

&=      bitwise assignment And operator

|=      bitwise assignment Or operator

^=      bitwise assignment Xor operator

<<=     bitwise assignment shift left operator

>>=     bitwise assignment shift right operator

>>>=    bitwise assignment shift right with zero fill operator

## Comparison Operators

*Comparison operators* compare two integers or floating point numbers and return a Boolean value (true or false) depending on the relationship between the operands.

==      equality operator

!=      inequality operator

<       less than operator

>       greater than operator

<=      less than or equal operator

>=      greater than or equal operator

> **Note**
>
> Variables of type char have their values treated as unsigned 16-bit integers (values 0 to 65535) for use by comparison operators. See the chapter on Types for more detail.

These operators are often used in "if" or "while" statements that require a Boolean value to determine whether to execute a block of code. The following code fragment shows the use of one of these operators:

---

**Listing 9.4    An Example Using a Comparison Operator**

```
int big = 100;
int small = 2;

if (big >= small) {
    System.out.println("All is right with the world");
}
```

---

**Caution**

Note that the equality operator is two successive equal signs. A single equal sign is
the assignment operator and has a very different meaning.

---

## Logical Comparison Operators

The *logical comparison operators* take Boolean operands and produce Boolean
results. The logical Not operator is unary.

    **&&**        logical And operator

    **||**         logical Or operator

    **!**          logical Not operator

The logical And operator returns true only if both operands are true. The logical Or operator returns false only if both operands are false. The logical Not
operator returns true only if the operand is false.

Oddly, in most computer languages, including Java, there is no logical Xor
operator.

## If-Then-Else Operators

This operator is part of the C language. Enough people use it that it was not
expunged in the stripping down of C and C++ to make clean, new Java. It is a
shorthand for the If () {} else {} construct. Perhaps these code fragments
will make usage of these operators clear:

---

**Listing 9.5    An Example Using the If-Then-Else Operator**

```
int j = 5;
int k = 10;
long max = 0;

max = k>j ? k : j;    // for easily understood Java code,
                      // use this construct sparingly.
```

---

In this example, max is assigned the value k if the Boolean expression preceding the question mark (?) is true. It is assigned the value of j if that expression is false. The result in this case is that it always gets the greater of the two.

# White Space

Technically, *white space* is not a token. White space can be inserted into a Java application's source code without affecting the meaning of the code to the compiler. White space is composed of space characters, horizontal tab characters, new line characters, carriage returns, and form feeds. These characters can be anywhere except within a token.

White space is optional, but because proper use of it has a big impact on readability and consequently maintainability of the source code for an application or applet, its use is highly recommended. Let's take a look at the ever popular HelloWorld App written with minimal use of white space:

```
public class HelloWorld{public static void main(String
args[]){System.out.println("Hello World");}}
```

Clearly, it is a little harder to ferret out what this application does, or even that you have started at the beginning and ended at the end. Choose a scheme for applying meaningful white space, and follow it. Then you stand a better chance of knowing which close curly brace (}) matches which open curly brace ({).

# Comments

Java supports three styles of *comments*. Comments are not tokens and neither are any of their contents. These comments are referred to here as Traditional comments (from the C language tradition), javadoc comments (a minor modification of the above), and C++ style comments for the additional style introduced in C++.

## Traditional Comments

The first is the traditional C-style comment that begins with a slash-star (/*) and ends with a star-slash (*/). These can begin and end anywhere except within a string literal, character literal, or another comment.

Comments of this sort can span many lines or be contained in a single line (outside of a token). Comments cannot be nested. Thus, if you try to nest them, the opening of the inner one is not detected by the compiler, and the closing of the inner one ends the comment, and subsequent text is interpreted as tokens. This usually results in a compile-time error. Two examples of comments of this sort are seen in the following code fragment:

---

**Listing 9.6    An Example with Two Traditional Comments**

```
/* The following is a code fragment
 * that is here only for the purpose
 * of demonstrating a style of comment.
 */

double pi = 3.141592654  /* close enough for now */ ;
```

---

## javadoc Comments

The second style of comment in Java is a special case of the first. It has the properties mentioned previously, but the contents of the comment may be used in automatically generated documentation by the javadoc tool. Avoid inadvertent use of this style if you plan to use javadoc.

## C++ Style Comments

The third style of comment begins with a slash-slash (//), and ends when the current source code line ends. These comments are especially useful for describing the intended meaning of the current line of code. The following instructive code fragment demonstrates the use of this style of comment:

---

**Listing 9.7    An Example Using Traditional and C++ Style Comments**

```
for (int j = 0, boolean Bad = false;    // initialize outer loop
j < MAX_ROW;                            // repeat for all rows
j++) {
    for (int k = 0;                     // initialize inner loop
    k < MAX_COL;                        // repeat for all
columns
    k++) {
        if (NumeralArray[j][k] > '9') {  // > highest numeric?
            Bad = true;                  // mark bad
        } /* close if > '9' */
        if (NumeralArray[j][k] < '0') {  // < lowest numeric?
            Bad = true;                  // mark bad
        } /* close if < '0' */
    } /* close inner loop */
} /* close outer loop */
```

---

II

The Java Language

# CHAPTER 9
# Types in Depth

*by Jay Cross*

Baseball players can be sorted into types: sluggers, contact hitters, defensive replacements, fireballers, control pitchers—the list is long. In the case of ball players, they have enough in common with each other that it may not make much of a difference to the final outcome of a game if the type of player were to be confused. The 1927 Yankees (arguably the best ball club in history) would probably still have won quite a few games if they had occasionally switched the role of a pitcher for a heavy-hitting outfielder (Babe Ruth). Similarly, in *Casey at the Bat*, by Ernest Lawrence Thayer, we read that Flynn was type "lulu" and Blake was type "cake," but both of them hit safely, while much to everyone's surprise, Casey, (type "mighty batsman") struck out swinging. All of these ballplayers (types) belong to the object "Mudville Nine," which is an instance of the class "ball club." Types are important concerning humans and their endeavors, but are far less definable than data types in a computer.

Even on the smallest level, information can be stored in a computer in a variety of formats. The way that bits in a 32-bit integer are interperated is very different from the way that bits of a like-sized, floating-point number are used. Both of these interpretations are very different from bits in a string with a unicode-decimal representation of a number. It goes without saying that all of these formats are very different from a 32-bit memory address, which points to where one of these numbers is stored. Because the computer's processor follows a specific sequence of bit manipulations to do a calculation, treating a 32-bit number as the wrong type will produce a good result once in 4,294,967,296 instances. Java makes it difficult to make this kind of error by accident.

In the this chapter you will learn the following:

- How Booleans are treated in Java
- How char variables are stored
- The four types of integers in Java
- The parts of a floating point number
- The limits on casting variables and expressions from one primative type to another
- The limits of the values of each type
- How to declare arrays

There are four groups of types in Java: *Primative types*, *Array types*, *Class types*, and *Interface types*. This chapter will cover Primative types and Arrays of Primative types. Classes and interfaces will be covered in great detail in chapters 10, "Classes in Depth," and 11, "More About Interfaces." There is one section in this chapter that covers each of the broad primative types (the four types of integers are treated collectively, as are the two floating-point types), plus one for arrays, and a summary.

# Boolean Variables in Depth

Visualize Booleans in Java as representing one bit. Therefore, a Boolean has exactly two possible values: true or false. There is no other value. In some computer languages, a Boolean may have a multitude (if booleans in C are defined based on the unsigned byte, they have 255 values that mean `true`) of possible values, of which one means `false` and the rest usually mean `true`, but in Java there are only two values. This makes Java beautiful, elegant, and harder to abuse.

## Default Value
The default value of a Boolean variable is `false`.

## Operations on Booleans
Operators in Java have particular meanings for use with boolean expressions. Many of the same operator symbols are used as with other types of expressions. In most cases, the meanings are a natural extension from the operations performed on integer types. The operations shown in table 9.1 can be performed on Booleans.

| Table 9.1 | Operations on Boolean Expressions | |
|---|---|---|
| **Operation** | **Name** | **Description** |
| = | Assignment | As in `tf = true;` |
| == | Equality | This produces a true if the two Boolean operands have the same value (true or false). It produces false, otherwise. This is equivalent to not exclusive or (NXOR). |
| != | Inequality | This produces a true if the two Boolean operands have different values (one true, the other false). It produces false, otherwise. This is equivalent to exclusive or (XOR). |
| ! | Logical NOT | If the operand is false, the output is true, and vice versa. |
| & | AND | Produces a true if and only if both operands are true. |
| ¦ | OR | Produces a false if and only if both operands are false. |
| ^ | XOR | Produces true only if exactly one (exclusive OR) operand is true. |
| && | Logical AND | Same result for Booleans as described for &. |
| ¦¦ | Logical OR | Same result for Booleans as described for ¦. |
| ?: | if-then-else | Requires a Boolean expression before the question mark. |

## Booleans in Control Flow Statements

Booleans (and Boolean expressions) are the only type that may be used in the true clause of the control flow statements as seen in the following code fragment:

```
boolean TestVal = false;
int IntVal = 1;
...
if (TestVal) {} else {}
if (IntVal != 1) {} else {}
...
while (TestVal) {}
while (IntVal == 0) {}
...
do {} while (TestVal)
do {} while (IntVal == 0)
for (int j=0; TestVal; j++) {}
for (int j=0; IntVal < 5; j++) {}
```

In the above code fragment, the comparisons of the integer IntVal to an integer constant value are a very simple Boolean expression. Naturally, much more complicated expressions could be used in the same place.

C and C++ programmers beware: Assignments of other types cannot be used as a Boolean expression. Because the function (or method) getc returns an int, not a Boolean, you can no longer use your old friend:

```
if (c=getc()) {}  //  !! Valid in C, but not in Java !!
```

You must use an explicit comparison to zero to get the same result. Object references must be explicitly compared to null.

## Casting and Converting Booleans

▶ Briefly, casting and converting are the ways that Java allows the use of a variable of one type in an expression of another type. Casting and converting are covered in much more detail on p. 245.

There is no direct way to cast or convert a Boolean to any other type. If you are intent on getting an integer to have a 0 or 1 value based on the current value of a Boolean, use an if-else statement, or imitate the following code:

```
int j;
boolean tf;
...
j = tf?1:0;          // integer j gets 1 if tf is true, and 0
otherwise.
```

Conversion the other way can be done with zero to be equal to false, and anything else equal to true, as follows:

```
int j;
boolean tf;
...
tf = (j!=0);     // Boolean tf is true if j is not 0, false other-
wise.
```

---

**Note**

Boolean types are a new feature in Java, not found in C and C++. To some, this stricter adherence to typing may seem oppressive. On the other hand, this may eliminate the pervasive ambiguity that has resulted in countless lost man-hours from the world's intellectual workforce in the form of chasing many hard-to-detect programming errors.

---

# Character Variables in Depth

Characters in Java are 16-bit Unicode characters. The Unicode standard allows for the use of many different languages' alphabets. The Latin alphabet, numerals, and punctuation have the same values as the ASCII character set, with a byte full of zeros as the high order bits.

Characters can be operands in any integer operation and can be treated as 16-bit unsigned integers. The result of the binary operations (operations with two operands) will be either an `int` or a `long` according to the same rules that the integers follow (except that if both operands are `char`, the result is a `char`). Recovering the result as a `char` requires an explicit cast back to `char`. The unary operations, such as the assignment operations, logical negation, and the increment and decrement operations, do not need explicit casting. Because they are unsigned, the unary sign operators (+ and –)—not to be confused with the binary operations of addition and subtraction (which use the same symbols)—have no meaning with `char` type operands, and result in casting to `int`.

The default value for a `char` variable is \u0000.

## Operations on Characters

The operations listed in table 9.2 can be performed with `char` type variables as at least one of the operands.

**Table 9.2    Operations on *char* Expressions**

| Operation | Description |
| --- | --- |
| =, +=, -=, *=, /= | Assignment operators |
| ==, != | Equality and inequality operators |
| <, <=, >, >= | Inequality operators |
| +, - | Unary sign operators |
| +, -, *, / | Addition, subtraction, multiplication, and division operators |
| +=, -=, *=, /= | Addition, subtraction, multiplication, division, and assign operators |
| ++, -- | Increment and decrement operators |
| <<, >>, >>> | Bitwise shift operators |
| <<=, >>=, >>>= | Bitwise shift and assign operators |
| ~ | Bitwise logical negation operator |
| &, ¦, ^ | Bitwise AND, OR, and exclusive or (XOR) operators |
| &=, ¦=, ^= | Bitwise AND, OR, exclusive or (XOR), and assign operators |

◀ See "Character Literals" on p. 137 in chapter 8 (Tokens in Depth) for more about the char type and Unicode.

### Casting and Converting Characters

Characters can be cast in the same way 16-bit (short) integers are cast; that is, you can cast it to be anything. If you cast into a smaller type, you will lose some data. Note that if you are using the Han character set (Chinese, Japanese, or Korean), you can lose data by casting a char into a short (16-bit integer), because the top bit will be lost.

# Floating-Point Variables in Depth

Floating-point numbers are represented by the types float and double. Both of these follow the specifications defined in *IEEE Standard for Binary Floating-Point Arithmetic*, ANSI/IEEE Std. 754-1985 (IEEE, New York). For those unfamiliar with floating-point numbers, they are different from integers, which (except for a negative numbers) are a straight base-2 representation of the integers you probably are familiar with from grade school. Floating-point numbers have a group of bits that are used for holding a sign and mantissa, and another group of bits for representing an exponent (base 2 with an offset). There are a few special configurations of the bits with special meanings such as negative infinity, zero, positive infinity, and not a number (which is the result of zero divided by zero among other things).

The fact that these floating-point numbers follow this specification, no matter what machine the application or applet is running on, is one of the details that makes Java so portable. Many older implementations of other languages execute the floating-point operations as defined for the floating-point registers in their arithmetic logic unit, resulting in some minor variations from machine to machine in the least significant bits. This can be the cause of some consternation when the calculations involve money in some way. The downside for Java is that if the processor running the application doesn't support ANSI/IEEE 754-1985 in hardware, some extra bit shuffling has to occur with each floating-point calculation done, causing somewhat slower performance. On the upside, except possibly for Cray, almost no machines that don't follow 754 have been made in the last five years.

### Limits of Floating-Point Values

Aside from the values mentioned in the preceding section of negative infinity, zero, positive infinity, and not a number, float type numbers can have absolute values from 1.40239846e–45f to 3.40282347e+38f. Likewise, the range for the non-zero absolute values of double-precision numbers is 4.94065645841246544e–324d to 1.7976931348623157e+308d. The default value for a floating-point variable is 0.0f for a float, and 0.0d for a double.

## Operations on *floats* and *doubles*

Many of the operations that can be done on integers have an analogous operation that can be done on floating-point numbers. The main exceptions are the bitwise operations. It is easy to imagine how meaningless it would be to shift bits from the mantissa into the exponent. The operators which may be used in expressions of type float or double are given in table 9.3 below.

**Table 9.3   Operations on *float* and *double* Expressions**

| Operation | Description |
| --- | --- |
| =, +=, -=, *=, /= | Assignment operators |
| ==, != | Equality and inequality operators |
| <, <=, >, >= | Inequality operators |
| +, - | Unary sign operators |
| +, -, *, / | Addition, subtraction, multiplication, and division operators |
| +=, -=, *=, /= | Addition, subtraction, multiplication, and division, and assign operators |
| ++, -- | Increment and decrement operators |

The equality and inequality operators produce a Boolean result, no matter what type the operands are.

When a binary operation has two floats as operands, the result is a float. When a binary operation has at least one double as an operand, the result is a double. When a binary operation has a float or double as one operand, and an integer as the other, the result is the same type as the float or double.

## Casting and Converting *floats* and *doubles*

The float and double types can be cast to any other type except Boolean. Casting it into a smaller type can result in a loss of data. Casting to an integer results in a loss of the fractional part, rounding towards zero (i.e. truncating the fractional part).

Java floating-point numbers are rounded using the IEEE 754 "round to nearest" mode of rounding. When converting a float or double to some kind of integer, numbers are truncated towards zero.

No exceptions are produced by Java when performing floating-point arithmetic. Overflow (a condition that occurs when an operation produces a result larger than the largest number that may be expressed by the given type), or division of anything but zero by zero and similar operations result in the infinity and negative infinity type values, which are meaningful using the comparison operators. Underflows (resulting when an operation produces a non-zero number smaller than the smallest that may be expressed by the given type) result in special values called positive zero or negative zero. Division of zero by zero type calculation generates the not-a-number value, which produces a false in any comparison.

# Integer Variables in Depth

There are four types of integers in Java. They are byte, short, int, and long. These are all signed two's compliment numbers, with 8, 16, 32, and 64 bits, respectively.

## Two's Compliment Notation

The term *two's compliment* will be familiar to most computer scientists. It is a way of representing negative integers with bits. In fact, very nearly all computers use this method for storing integers. Commercial computing has developed to the point where most programmers won't need to know about the details of this notation, but out of respect for the past, your own inner satisfaction, or some hardware device-related need, read on.

As in the section of chapter 8, "Tokens in Depth," that deals with the bitwise arithmetic and shifting operators, we will use 8 bit (type byte) numbers as our example, but be aware that these ideas extend quite naturally to the longer integer types. We can see how the number 5 would be represented in a byte. It is $2^2+2^0$ (4+1), so the lowest and second-to-lowest bits are ones and the rest are zeros:

    5 = 0000_0101 = 0x05

But how do we represent -5? It would be conceptually simple to just use the top bit as a sign bit, and leave it at that, which means that -5 would be 0x85. It is not done this way primarily because there is a way (two's compliment arithmetic) that offers much simpler algorithms for binary arithmetic and type conversions. In two's compliment arithmetic, subtracting one from zero produces the same result as if there had been some higher order byte with a number in it. See table 9.4 below.

### Table 9.4  Representing Some Negative Numbers

```
256 - 1 = 255   // 1_0000_0000-1 = 0_1111_1111   (0x0100-1 = 0x00ff)
  0 - 1 = -1    //   0000_0000-1 =   1111_1111   (0x00-1 = 0xff)
 -1 - 1 = -2    //   1111_1111-1 =   1111_1110   (0xff-1 = 0xfe)
 -1 - 2 = -3    //   1111_1111-2 =   1111_1101   (0xff-2 = 0xfd)
 -1 - 3 = -4    //   1111_1111-3 =   1111_1100   (0xff-3 = 0xfc)
 -1 - 4 = -5    //   1111_1111-4 =   1111_1011   (0xff-4 = 0xfb)
```

Naturally, the same argument holds for operations with the whole range of integers.

To calculate what (-1) multiplied by a number will look like in two's compliment notation, simply subtract one from the number, and then flip every bit.

> **Note**
>
> Don't confuse this with the logical compliment called one's compliment. With the logical compliment, you don't subtract anything, you just flip every bit. This is done in Java with the logical NOT (!) and compliment (or bitwise logical negation) (~) operators.

One feature of two's compliment notation is that the sign bit is repeated from the highest bit down to, but not including, the most signifigant bit of the number. This is what the term *sign extend* refers to. This is also why two (as opposed to one) shift right (>>, >>>) operators are needed. The >>> operator simply shifts the bits, and inserts zero bits at the high end. The >> operator replicates the top bit as it shifts.

## Limits on Integer Values

Integers can have values in the following ranges.

| Integer Type | Minimum Value | Default Value | Maximum Value |
|---|---|---|---|
| byte | -128 | (byte) 0 | 127 |
| short | -32,768 | (short) 0 | 32,767 |
| int | -2,147,483,648 | 0 | 2,147,483,647 |
| long | -9,223,372,036,854,775,808 | 0L | 9,223,372,036,854,775,807 |

Note that the maximum number for a long is enough to provide a unique ID for one transaction per second for every person on the planet for the next fifty years. It is also the number of grains in about a cubic mile of sand. Yet, if a project is undertaken to count the black flies in Maine, or to catalog surveillance frames from every street corner in the world, surely the cry will arise for 128-bit integers.

## Operations on Integers

The operations listed in table 9.5 can be performed with four integer type variables as at least one of the operands.

**Table 9.5 Operations on Integer Expressions**

| Operation | Description |
| --- | --- |
| =, +=, -=, *=, /= | Assignment operators |
| ==, != | Equality and inequality operators |
| <, <=, >, >= | Inequality operators |
| +, - | Unary sign operators |
| +, -, *, / | Addition, subtraction, multiplication, and division operators |
| +=, -=, *=, /= | Addition, subtraction, multiplication, division, and assign operators |
| ++, -- | Increment and decrement operators |
| <<, >>, >>> | Bitwise shift operators |
| <<=, >>=, >>>= | Bitwise shift and assign operators |
| ~ | Bitwise logical negation operator |
| &, ¦, ^ | Bitwise AND, OR, and exclusive or (XOR) operators |
| &=, ¦=, ^= | Bitwise AND, OR, and exclusive or (XOR) and assign operators |

The equality and inequality operators produce a Boolean result, no matter what type the operands are. The rest of this section refers to the other operations.

Binary operations with integer operands produce either an int or a long (never a byte or short, unless explicitly cast as such). The result will be a long only if one of the operands was a long or if the result won't fit into an int without overflowing.

## Casting and Converting Integers

The four integer types can be cast to any other type except Boolean. Casting into a smaller type can result in a loss of data. Casting to a floating-point number (float or double) will probably result in the loss of some precision, unless the integer is a whole power of two (for example, 1, 2, 4, 8…).

## Overflows and Exceptions

If some operation creates a number exceeding above mentioned range, no overflow or exception is indicated. The low bits that fit are the result. (For a result cast as a byte, 127+1=–128, 127+9 =–120, and 127+127=–2.) An ArithmeticException will be thrown if the right-hand operand in an integer divide or modulo operation is zero.

# Arrays in Depth

There are three types of reference variables: classes, interfaces, and arrays. Classes and interfaces are complicated enough that they each get their own chapter; but arrays are comparatively simple and are covered here with the primative types.

An *array* is an indexed collection of objects of one particular type. These can be arrays of Booleans, chars, bytes, shorts, ints, longs, floats, doubles, arrays, or objects. There are three separate steps in the creation of an array: declaring it, allocating the memory for it, and populating it. It is possible to do two or more of these steps in the same statement. Several examples of creating arrays of long types are shown in the following code fragment:

```
long Primes[] = new long[1000000];     // declare an array and
                                       // assign some memory to hold it.
long[] EvenPrimes = new long[1];       // Either way, it's an array.
EvenPrimes[0] = 2;                          // populate the array.

// now declare an array with an implied new and partially populate.
long Fibonacci[1000] = {1, 1, 2, 3, 5, 8, 13, 21, 34, 55, 89, 144};

long Perfects = {6, 28};               // creates two element
array.

long BlackFlyNum[];                         // declare an array.
                                            // Default value is
null.

BlackFlyNum = new long[2147483647];    // Array indexes must be
type int.

// declare a two dimensional array and populate it.
long TowerOfHanoi[3][10] = {{10,9,8,7,6,5,4,3,2,1},{},{}};

long[][][] ThreeDTicTacToe;                 // Uninitialized 3D
array.
```

There are a number of points worth noting here.

- The array Primes is type long. The variable EvenPrimes is an array of longs.
- Indexing of arrays starts with 0 (as in C and C++).
- You can partially populate an array on initialization.
- Array indexes must either be type int (32-bit integer) or be able to be cast as an int. As a result, the largest possible array size is 2,147,483,647. Most Java installations would fail with arrays anywhere near that size, but that is the maximum defined by the language.

■ When populating an array, the rightmost index sequences within the innermost curly braces.

## Differences with Arrays Between C or C++ and Java

In Java, arrays must be created dynamically, using the new command. An array in Java is a variable, not a pointer. In Java, you cannot reference an array element that hasn't been created; therefore, memory is protected from either walking off the end or uninitialized pointer corruptions, which are common in C. ❖

# CHAPTER 10

# Classes in Depth

*by Michael Afergan*

To write a Java program, whether an applet or application, it is necessary to understand the underlying structure of all Java programs: classes. Java is based on an object-oriented outlook on code, viewing programs as an aggregation of several objects—constructs specifically designed to accomplish a given task. Nevertheless, it is classes that create and define the properties of these objects. By allowing developers to adopt the object-oriented model and presenting developers with a powerful library of tools developed from classes, Java becomes an interesting and powerful language.

In this chapter, you explore in detail how to create and use classes. More specifically, you cover:

- The theory behind classes and object-oriented programming
- The syntax of creating a class
- The idea and implementation of inheritance
- Fields, Methods, and access to them
- Integrating a class within another

## What Are Classes?

From a very simple viewpoint, *classes* define the state and behavior of an object. An assembly of data and tools to handle the data, classes are clearly defined tools that may be integrated, combined, and extended to create powerful yet lucid programs.

In terms of code, every class has two portions: the properties that define the class and the ability to manage these properties, with the latter giving the class its utility. The properties, called *fields*, are essentially variables that may be accessed by the entire class and possibly by other classes as well. The tools to handle the fields, called *methods*, are similar to functions in such languages as C. However, they are slightly different from functions inasmuch as they are provided with complete access to the fields, or *state*, of the class.

In a practical sense, a class is a group of related information and methods, placed together for utility. For example, if you were creating a game, you might want to have one class to handle the board. This class would contain all the information about the board (player positions, and so on) as well as the appropriate methods required to manage the board, such as moving a piece, and checking the validity of a move. By creating the game board in this manner, we not only encapsulate the necessary game board functionality in the class, but also enable ourselves to use such a class in an applet or application, making use of its methods and fields.

# Why Use Classes?

When dealing with classes, it is important to remember that classes do not enable us as programmers to do anything more than what we would be able to do without them. Then why use them? The answer to this is similar to the reason why large companies are divided into departments and sub-departments. Organizing hundreds of people with thousands of tasks, the department architecture provides for a simple distribution of tasks and responsibilities. Furthermore, because the billing department knows how to bill customers, the sales department does not need to worry about the details of this process. Finally, this process of distributing tasks may be extended to the departments, thereby creating sub-departments—all of which contribute to creating an efficient company.

However, the power of object-oriented programming extends beyond the simple ability to encapsulate functionality in objects. A great deal of the appeal of OOP is its ability to provide for inheritance—the ability to create new classes based on old classes. Using the example of the game board, in an object-oriented architecture, we are able to create new "board" classes that inherit the properties of the old board, such as the layout and moving mechanisms. The beauty of this is that in this new class, we are now able to build upon these structures. For example, the new game may require that certain locations remain hidden until they are explored. Therefore, the new board class may have the added capability of keeping track of those locations that have been explored by the player.

**Object-Oriented Programming Jargon**

Because these new classes inherit the properties of another class, they are referred to as *child classes* or *subclasses*. Consequently, the class from which they are derived is called a *parent* or *superclass*.

An *instance* of an object is a specific copy of that object. While classes can define objects, it is still necessary to create a copy of the class before using it. In the declaration `String name`, name is an instance of the String class.

Furthermore, due to the length of its name, object-oriented programming is often abbreviated as OOP (as will be the case in this chapter).

Another benefit of enclosing data and methods in classes is the OOP characteristic of *encapsulation*, the ability to effectively isolate and insulate information from the rest of your program. By creating isolated modules, once you have developed a complete class to perform a certain task, you may effectively forget the intricacies of that task and simply utilize the methods provided by the class. This means that while you may later have to significantly change the inner workings of a given class, as long as the methods used to gain access to the class do not change, you do not need to modify the rest of your program. Furthermore, by placing the data within the class and creating the appropriate methods to manipulate it, you may seal the data off from the rest of the program, thereby preventing accidental corruption of the data.

Furthermore, the allure of the OOP approach of creating self-sustaining modules is enhanced by the fact that children of a given class are still considered to be of the same "type" as the parent. This feature, called *polymorphism*, enables you to perform the same operation on diffrent types of classes, as long as they share a common trait. While the behavior of each class might be diffrent, you know that the class will be able to perform the same operation as its parent because it is of the same family tree. For example, if you were to create a `Vehicle` class, you may later choose to create `Truck` and `Bike` classes, each of which extended the `Vehicle` class. Although bikes and trucks are very different, they are both still vehicles! Therefore, everything that you are permitted to do with an instance of the `Vehicle` class you may also do with an instance of the `Truck` or `Bike` classes. As an example, if you had a method that accepted an instance of the `GameBoard` class as one of its parameters, and you derived a class named `NewGameBoard` that extended the `GameBoard` class, you would still be able to pass instances of `NewGameBoard` to the same method.

---

**What's so New About Object-Oriented Programming?**

The answer is: plenty and not much. Contrary to the belief of many, OOP is not the antithesis of the top-down approach to programming. Conversely, OOP actually emphasizes a modular view of programming by forcing you to break down your task into manageable components, each with a specific function. However, unlike procedural functions, which are simply pieced together to form a program, objects are living "creatures" that have the ability to manage themselves, running concurrently with other operations and even existing after the rest of the program has terminated. It is this ability to exist and work with objects as a separate entity that makes OOP a nice match for Java, a network-based language.

---

**Caution**

Note that in the previous example, while every bike and truck is also a vehicle, a vehicle is not necessarily a bike or a truck. Thus, while the Bike and Truck classes can be treated just like the Vehicle class in Java, you may not perform an operation reserved for the Bike class on an instance of the Vehicle class.

---

Finally, inasmuch as Java is designed to be a web-based programming language, it is a good match for the OOP property of dynamic binding, the ability to link code "on the fly" during execution as needed. Consequently, if you look carefully at the bottom of the Netscape screen when you are loading an applet or the prompt from which the appletviewer was spawned, you will see that the browser does not load "the applet" as an entity, but rather a .class file which is often dependent on several other classes residing on the server. Nevertheless, when writing your code, you do not need to worry about how this binding will occur or where the other classes will be loaded from.

# Classes in Java

As stated earlier, classes are the essential building block in any Java applet or application. Each class that you create will build upon some of the classes already created by Sun to enable it to function, and will finally be fleshed out and brought to life with the code that you add. In accordance with the object-oriented paradigm, you may later choose to build upon older programs or to enhance your program by creating new classes that will perform certain tasks for you.

**Bigger and Better Java**

You will note that Java itself is built from classes made available to the general public in the JDK. While there are some limitations, a large number of the classes that make up the Java architecture may themselves be extended. Consequently, you may tailor the classes in the Java API library, especially those in the AWT, to meet your particular needs—thereby creating your own "version" of Java!

---

Before you start creating large programs, you must first learn how to create simple classes. In terms of syntax, there are two parts to a class in Java: the declaration and the body. Listing 10.1 is a simple class (that fulfills some of the requirements of the simple game board discussed earlier). Examine this listing to get an idea of what constitutes a class. You can refer to this listing again later as your understanding of classes grows.

**Listing 10.1  File Name—Source Code for Sample Class**

```
public class GameBoard
{
/* This is the begining a simple game board class that provides the     basic */
/* structures necessary for a game board.  It may easily be */
/* extended to create a richer game board. */

    private static final int WIDTH      =    10;  /* These are    constants */
/* that you want to */     private static final int HEIGHT     =    10;  /* keep
   ➥as standards */
    private static final int EMPTY      =     0;

    private int board[][];
       // This array will keep track of the board

    public String myname;                // what game is being played

    public GameBoard (String gamename) {
        board = new int[WIDTH][HEIGHT];
        myname = new String(gamename);
        }

    public final void cleanBoard() {
        for (int i = 0; i < WIDTH; i++)
            for (int j = 0; j < HEIGHT; j++)
                board[i][j] = EMPTY;
    }

    public synchronized void setSquare(int x, int y, int value) {
        board[x][y] = value;
        }
    public synchronized boolean isEmpty(int x, int y) {
        if (board[x][y] == EMPTY)
```

(continues)

II

The JAVA Language

```
                return(true);
           return(false);
                  }
    }
```

## Declaring a Class

In general, Java class declarations have the form:

```
    modifiers   class NewClass    extends NameofSuperClass      implements
    NameofInterface
```

where everything in italics is optional. As you can see, there are four properties of the class that may be defined in the declaration:

- Modifiers
- Class Name
- SuperClasses
- Interfaces

> **Note**
>
> Declaration in Practice: `public class GameBoard`
>
> You will note that the class declaration need not be very complex, and most often is very simple. In this example, only one modifier, `public`, was used; no other classes or interfaces were required.

### Modifiers

The modifiers in a class declaration determine how the class can be handled in later development. While they are usually not extremely important in developing the class itself, they become very important when you decide to create other classes, interfaces, and exceptions that involve that class.

When creating a class, you may choose to accept the default status or you may employ one of the three modifiers: `public`, `final`, or `abstract`.

**"Friendly" Classes.** Example: `class PictureFrame`

If you choose not to place a modifier in front of the class declaration, the class is created with the default properties. Therefore, you should be aware of what these properties are.

By default all classes are assigned the "friendly" level of access. This means that while the class may be extended and employed by other classes, only those objects within the same package may make use of this class.

**Public Classes.** Example: `public class PictureFrame`

By placing the modifier `public` in front of the class declaration, the class is defined to be public. Public classes are, as their name implies, accessible by all objects. This means that they can be used or extended by any object, regardless of its package.

Also note that public classes must be defined in a file called `ClassName.java`.

**Final Classes.** Example: `final class PictureFrame`

Final classes may not have any subclasses, and are created by placing the modifier `final` in front of the class declaration.

At first the reason for doing so may not be evident. Why would you want to prevent other classes from extending your class? Isn't that one of the appeals of the object-oriented approach?

While this is true it is important to remember that the object-oriented approach effectively enables you to create many versions of a class (by creating children that inherit its properties but nevertheless change it somewhat). Consequently, if you are creating a class to serve as a standard (for example, a class that will handle network communications), you would not want to allow for the possibility of classes that would handle this function in a different manner. Thus, by making the class final you prevent this possibility and ensure consistency.

**Abstract Classes.** Example: `abstract class PictureFrame`

An abstract class, denoted by the modifier `abstract`, is a class in which at least one method is not complete. This state of not being finished is referred to as abstract.

How can a finished class not be complete? In the case of a grammar-checking class that is to be implemented in many languages, there are several methods that would have to be changed for each language-dependent version class. To create a cleaner program, instead of creating an `EnglishChecker`, a `FrenchChecker`, and a `SpanishChecker` class from scratch, you could simply create a `GrammarCheker` class in which the language-specific methods were declared as `abstract` and left empty. When ready, you could then create the language-specific classes which would extend the abstract `GrammarCheker` class and would fill in the blanks by redefining these methods with actual code. While you would still end up with separate classes for each language, the heart of your code would be in the GrammarChecker class, leaving only the language-dependent portions for the specific classes. (You will deal more with abstract methods and the topic of overriding methods later in this chapter in the sections "Abstract" and "Overriding," respectively.)

> **Note**
>
> Because they are not complete, you may not create instances of abstract classes.

### Class Name

There is not much to discuss with regards to the class name inasmuch as the options are virtually endless and the ramifications virtually nonexistent. Like all other Java identifiers, the only requirements on a class name are that it begin with a letter, the character '–' or '$,' contain only Unicode characters above hex 00C0 (basic letters and digits, as well as some other special characters), and not be the same as any Java keyword (such as void or int). Also, it is general practice to capitalize the first letter in the name of any class.

> **Tip**
>
> Although only required for public classes, it is generally a good practice to name the file in which class NewClass is defined as NewClass.java. This is because doing so enables you to compile AnyClass that uses NewClass even if NewClass has not been compiled yet.
>
> If you attempt to use a currently uncompiled class in AnyClass, the compiler will first compile these classes before it compiles AnyClass. Thus, if AnyClass is dependent on NewClass, NewClass must be compiled before compilation of AnyClass concludes.
>
> If, however, you had placed the code for NewClass in a file named AnotherName.java, the compiler would be unable to find and thus unable to compile NewClass. Therefore, it would also be unable to compile AnyClass.
>
> Finally, and even more importantly, by placing NewClass in NewClass.java you will be able to find the source code for NewClass more easily.

### Super Classes

By specifying the names of other classes after the extends keyword, you are able to build upon other classes in typical OOP fashion as explained earlier in this chapter in "Why Use Classes?".

By extending a superclass, you are making your class a new copy of that class, but are allowing for growth. If you were simply to leave the rest of the class blank (and not do anything different with the modifiers), the new class would behave identically to the original class. Your new class will have all the fields and methods declared and/or inherited in the original class.

> **Note**
>
> public class MyClass extends Applet {
>
> Does the above example look familiar? If you look at the source of any applet, you will see that its declaration resembles the above example. In fact, you probably have been extending the `java.applet.Applet` class without even knowing what you were doing.
>
> Remember the methods that you have been able to use in your applets such as `showStatus()`, `init()`, and `keyDown()`? Did they appear out of thin air? No, they are drawn from the `java.applet.Applet` class or one of the classes that it extends, such as `java.awt.Component`.
>
> By extending the `java.applet.Applet` class, your applet class is able to access and/or implement these methods, thereby providing your applet with a great deal of power.

Furthermore, note that every class in Java is considered to be a an `object`. Therefore, every class is derived from the `java.lang.Object` class in some form. As a result, if you do not declare your class as extending any other class, it is by default considered to extend the `java.lang.Object` class.

> **Note**
>
> Multiple-inheritance does *not* exist in Java. Thus, unlike C++, Java classes may have only one superclass.

### Interfaces

As discussed in chapter 11, interfaces, much like abstract classes, provide for the creation of pseudo-classes of entirely abstract methods. By implementing an interface, any non-abstract class must override all methods declared in the interface.

By implementing an interface, you guarantee that the class will possess certain properties. Consequently, choosing to implement an interface may provide you with a great deal of flexibility in later development.

▶ See "More About Interfaces," p. 207

The JAVA Language

> **Caution**
>
> If you choose to implement an interface, be sure to override every method declared in the interface! If you don't, you must make your method abstract.

# Methods

Like C functions and C++ methods, Java methods are the essence of the class and are responsible for managing all tasks that will be performed by the class. While the actual implementation of the method is contained within the method's body, like classes, a great deal of important information is defined in the method declaration.

## Declaration

In general, method declarations have the form:

```
access_specifier   modifier  return_value    nameofmethod    (parameters)
➡throws ExceptionList
```

where everything in italics is optional.

### Access Specifiers

Like classes, it is often wise to restrict access to the methods of a given class. However, the considerations involved are even more important for methods. While all methods in a given class are accessible by all other methods in the class, there may be certain necessary tasks that you may not want other objects to be able to perform.

In the example of the game board class, you may later decide to develop a multiplayer game. In such a program, moving a piece would not be as simple an operation as changing the value of a given square, but would require other tasks, such as informing other clients of the move. As a result, we would not want to allow other objects to access the setSquare() method, for changing the board without notifying the other players would ruin the game. Therefore, it would be necessary for each move to pass through a publicly accessible wrapper method, such as movePiece(), which would in turn call such private methods as setSquare() and notifyClients(). As a result, the game board would have complete control over the movement of the pieces, and the master class would not need to worry about these processes. Finally, if the networking protocols specified in the notifyClient() method had to change for any reason, there would be no need to change the program itself, only the `notifyClients()` method, since the master class never knew that `notifyClients()` even existed.

Finally note that each class may have only one access modifier. It makes little sense for a method to be both public and private!

**public.** Example: `public void toggleStatus()`

`public` is the most relaxed access status that may be applied to a method. In addition to being accessible to all methods in the class, a public method is accessible to all classes regardless of their lineage or their package. One should make an effort to limit the number of public methods in a class.

**protected.** Example: `protected void toggleStatus()`

`protected` methods are identical to `public` methods except for the fact that they cannot be accessed by objects outside of the current package.

---

### Troubleshooting

*If you are having a compile-time error caused by an attempt to access a method not visible to the current scope, you may have some trouble diagnosing the source of your problems. This is because the error message will not tell you that you are attempting to access a protected method. Instead it will resemble the following:*

```
No method matching paramString() found in class java.awt.TextArea.
```

(Note that `java.awt.TextArea.paramString()` is a protected method in java.awt.TextArea.)

This is because the restricted methods are effectively hidden from the nonprivileged classes. Therefore, when compiling a class that does not meet the security restrictions, such methods are hidden from the compiler.

Also note that you will encounter a similar error message when trying to access a private or friendly method outside of its range of access as well as when you attempt to access a field from an unprivileged class.

---

**private.** Example: `private void toggleStatus()`

`private` is the highest degree of protection that may be applied to a method. A `private` method is only accessible by those methods in the same class.

If a method deals with the inner workings of a class, and you do not want to make it accessible to subclasses of the current class, you should make it private.

**friendly.** Example: `void toggleStatus()`

Like classes, if you fail to specify an access modifier, the method will be considered friendly. Friendly methods are accessible both within the class and the package. However, friendly methods are not accessible to subclasses of the current class.

**private protected.** Example: `private protected void toggleStatus()`

Those methods declared to be `private protected` are accessible to both the class and any subclasses, but not the rest of the package nor any classes outside of the current package. This means that while subclasses of the given class may invoke private protected methods of a given class, instances of the given class in its subclasses cannot.

For example:

```
class NetworkSender {
    private protected void sendInfo(String mes) {
            out.println(mes);
            }
    }

class NewNetworkSender extends NetworkSender {
    void informOthers(String mes) {
        NetworkSender me;
        me = new NetworkSender();

        super.sendInfo(mes); // this is legal
        me.sendInfo(mes);    // this is not
        }
    }
```

The first statement invokes `sendInfo()` as a method belonging to the superclass of `NewNetworkSender`. This is legal because private protected methods are accessible to subclasses. However, the second statement is illegal because it attempts to invoke `sendInfo()` on an instance of the NetworkSender class. Even though `NewNetworkSender` is a subclass of `NetworkSender`, it is referencing `sendInfo()` not as a method belonging to its superclass, but rather as a method belonging to an instance of `NetworkSender`.

> **Note**
>
> While the above statement accurately describes how private protected methods should work, as of the 1.0 release they do not behave in this manner.
>
> While the proper access is provided, subclasses were unable to successfully override private protected methods. While the subclass code would compile properly and

execute, the original method, not the new method, would be executed even when the newer method was called.

This bug should be fixed as of the 1.01 release.

## Modifiers

Like class modifiers, method modifiers allow you to set properties for the method such as where it will be visible and how subclasses of the current class will interact with it.

**static.** Example: `static void toggleStatus()`

Static, or class, variables and methods are closely related. You learn about both—and their relationship to the `static` keyword—here.

It is important to differentiate between the properties of a specific instance of a class and the class itself. In the following code, you create two instances of the `Elevator` class and perform some operations with them.

**Listing 10.2   Hotel.java—Hotel Example with Instance Methods**

```java
class Elevator {
      boolean running = true;
      void shutDown() {
            running = false;
         }
}

class FrontDesk {
    private final int EVENING = 8;
    Elevator NorthElevator, SouthElevator;

    FrontDesk() {                          // the class constructor
        NorthElevator = new Elevator();
        SouthElevator = new Elevator();
        }

    void maintenance(int time) {
            if (time == EVENING)
                NorthElevator.shutDown();
            }

    void displayStatus() {
        // code is very inefficient, but serves a purpose
            System.out.print("North Elevator is ");
            if (!(NorthElevator.running ))
            System.out.print("not ");
            System.out.println("running.");
```

(continues)

The JAVA Language

```
 Listing 10.2   Continued
            System.out.print("South Elevator is ");
        if (!(SouthElevator.running ))
                System.out.print(" not ");
        System.out.println("running.");
            }
        }
    }
public class Hotel {

    public static void main(String args[]) {
        FrontDesk lobby;
        lobby = new FrontDesk();

        System.out.println("It's 7:00.  Time to check the
        ➥elevators.");
        lobby.maintenance(7);
        lobby.displayStatus();

        System.out.println();
        System.out.println("It's 8:00.  Time to check the
        ➥elevators.");
        lobby.maintenance(8);
        lobby.displayStatus();

    }

}
```

Both NorthElevator and SouthElevator are instances of the Elevator class.
This means that each is created with its own running variable, and its own
copy of the shutDown() method. While these are initially identical for both
elevators, as you can see from the previous example, the status of running
in NorthElevator and SouthElevator will not remain equal once the
maintenance() method is called.

Consequently, if compiled and run, the previous code will produce the
following output:

```
C:\dev>\jdk\java\bin\java Hotel

It's 7:00.  Time to check the elevators.

North Elevator is running.

South Elevator is running.

It's 8:00.  Time to check the elevators.

North Elevator is not running.

South Elevator is running.
```

> **Note**
>
> In the previous example, you will notice a rather funny looking method named
> FrontDesk(). What is it? As you will see in "Constructors" later in this chapter, this
> is the constructor method for the FrontDesk class. Called whenever an instance of
> FrontDesk is created, it provides you with the ability to initialize fields and perform
> other such preparatory operations.

Variables and methods such as running and shutDown() are called *instance variables* and *instance methods*. This is because every time the Elevator class is instantiated, a new copy of each is created. In the previous example, while the value of the running variable certainly can change because there are two copies of it, changing one does not change the other. Therefore, we are able to track the status of the NorthElevator and SouthElevator separately.

However, what if we wanted to define and modify a property for *all* elevators? Examine the following example and note the additions:

**Listing 10.3    Hotel2.java—Hotel Example with Static Methods**

```java
class Elevator {
      boolean running = true;
      static boolean powered = true;
      void shutDown() {
              running = false;
          }
      static void togglePower() {
        powered = !powered;
                }
}

class FrontDesk {
private final int EVENING = 8;
private final int CLOSING = 10;
private final int OPENING = 6;
Elevator NorthElevator, SouthElevator;

    FrontDesk() {
       NorthElevator = new Elevator();
       SouthElevator = new Elevator();
       }

    void maintenance(int time) {
         if (time == EVENING)
         NorthElevator.shutDown();
```

(continues)

---

**Listing 10.3  Continued**

```
                    else if ( (time == CLOSING) || (time == OPENING) )
                        Elevator.togglePower();
                    }

            void displayStatus() {
            // code is very inefficient, but serves a purpose
                System.out.print("North Elevator is ");
                if (!(NorthElevator.running ))
               System.out.print("not ");
                System.out.println("running.");

                System.out.print("South Elevator is ");
            if (!(SouthElevator.running ))
                    System.out.print(" not ");
            System.out.println("running.");

            System.out.print("The elevators are ");
             if (!(Elevator.powered  ))
               System.out.print("not ");
            System.out.println("powered.");
                }
        }

    public class Hotel2 {
        public static void main(String args[]) {
            FrontDesk lobby;
            lobby = new FrontDesk();

            System.out.println("It's 7:00.  Time to check the
            ➥elevators.");
            lobby.maintenance(7);
            lobby.displayStatus();

            System.out.println();
            System.out.println("It's 8:00.  Time to check the
            ➥elevators.");
            lobby.maintenance(8);
            lobby.displayStatus();

            System.out.println();
            System.out.println("It's 10:00.  Time to check the
            ➥elevators.");
            lobby.maintenance(10);
            lobby.displayStatus();
            }
    }
```

---

In this case, the variable powered is now a static variable and the method
togglePower() is a static method. This means that each is now a property of
all Elevator classes, not the specific instances. Consequently, invoking either

the NorthElevator.togglePower(), SouthElevator.togglePower(), or Elevator.togglePower() method would change the status of the powered variable in *both* classes.

Consequently, the code would produce the following output:

```
C:\dev>\jdk\java\bin\java Hotel2
It's 7:00.  Time to check the elevators.
North Elevator is running.
South Elevator is running.
The elevators are powered.

It's 8:00.  Time to check the elevators.
North Elevator is not running.
South Elevator is running.
The elevators are powered.

It's 10:00.  Time to check the elevators.
North Elevator is not running.
South Elevator is running.
The elevators are not powered.
```

Placing the static modifier in front of a method declaration makes the method a static method. While nonstatic methods may also operate with static variables, static methods may only deal with static variables and static methods. Consequently, if you are creating a method that deals only with static variables, it is a good practice to make the method a static method. Also, if you are creating a method that will run in a loop for the lifetime of the class—such as a thread to read from a socket—and you want to share that information with all instances of the class, you could do so by making the method static. As a result, although you may create many instances of the class, you will only create one copy of the method—thereby saving yourself a good deal of memory.

**abstract.** Example: abstract void toggleStatus();

Abstract methods are simply methods that are declared, but are not implemented in the current class. It is therefore the responsibility of the class's subclasses to override and implement these methods.

You declare an abstract method by placing the keyword abstract in front of the method name and replacing the method body with a simple semicolon. Therefore a complete abstract method would have the following form:

```
abstract boolean checkStatus();
```

It is the responsibility of subclasses of the abstract class to override all abstract methods and provide their implementation. This is done by creating a new method in the subclass with the same name and parameter list as the abstract method. (See "Overriding" later in this chapter for more information on this process.) If a subclass does not override all abstract methods, it too must be declared to be abstract.

Also note that neither static methods nor class constructors may be declared to be abstract. Furthermore, you should not make abstract methods final, inasmuch as doing so prevents you from overriding the method.

**final.** Example: `final void toggleStatus()`

By placing the keyword final in front of the method declaration, you prevent any subclasses of the current class from overriding the given method. This ability enhances the degree of insulation of your classes, for you ensure that the functionality defined in this method will never be altered in any way.

In the game board example, you will notice that the `cleanboard()` method is declared as final. Because this method is vital and should not change, it is declared as final to ensure that all subclasses of the game board class possess the proper `cleanboard()` method.

**native.** Example: `native void toggleStatus();`

▶ See "Native Methods," p. 258

Native methods are methods that you wish to use, but do not want to write in Java. Native methods are most commonly written in C++, and can provide several benefits such as faster execution time. Like abstract methods, they are declared simply by placing the modifier native in front of the method declaration and by substituting a semicolon for the method body.

However, it is also important to remember that the declaration will inform the compiler as to the properties of the method. Therefore, it is imperative that you specify the same return type and parameter list as can be found in the native code.

**synchronized.** Example: `synchronized void toggleStatus()`

▶ See "What Are Threads?" p. 547

By placing the keyword synchronized in front of a method declaration, you can prevent data corruption that may result when two methods attempt to access the same piece of data at the same time. While this may not be a concern for simple programs, once you begin to use threads in your programs, this may become a serious problem.

In the original game board example, consider what would happen if you had two threads running in the main program, one which used the `setSquare()` method to enable the player to move some blocks, and another which used the `isEmpty()` method to continually determine if there was a direct path to the finish. What would happen if the second thread called the `isEmpty()` method to check a certain space just as the other thread was using the `setSquare()` method to move that same block? Would it find the square empty, occupied, neither?

To avoid this problem, you make the two methods synchronized. In a given object, no two synchronized methods may run at the same time. Once one is called, it obtains a "lock" on the object. Thus, if another synchronized method is called, the second will wait until the first is completed and has relinquished its lock on the object. In this manner, you prevent such access problems created by having two concurrently running threads each requiring access to the same data. By placing the `synchronized` modifier in front of both methods, neither may run at the same time as the other.

### Returning Information

While returning information is one of the most important things that a method can do, there is little to discuss by way of details about returning information. Java methods may return any data type ranging from simple ones such as integers and characters to more complex objects. (This means that you can return things such as strings as well.)

Keep in mind that unless you use the keyword `void` as your return type, you must return a variable of the type specified in your declaration.

As an example, the following method is declared to return a variable of type `boolean`. This is accomplished by employing the `return()` (either `true` or `false`) statements in the third and fourth lines.

```
public synchronized boolean isEmpty(int x, int y) {
     if (board[x][y] == EMPTY)
          return(true);
     return(false);
          }
```

### Method Name

The rules regarding method names are quite simple and are the same as any other Java identifier: Begin with a Unicode letter (or an underscore or dollar sign) and continue with only Unicode characters.

There are, however, two twists in Java's naming structure that are worth examination. In the next two sections we will describe and discuss both.

**Overloading.** Assume that you were expanding your GameBoard class to accept input from a wide variety of sources—the keyboard, the mouse, a text file, and so on—each of which was supplying information to the move() method. Each would present the move() method with a different type of data—a character, integers, or a string, respectively. Therefore, it seems as if you would be forced to create three new methods, parseCharInfo(), parseIntInfo(), and parseStringInfo(), each of which would then call the move() method—a real headache!

However, Java provides you with a rather convenient means of sidestepping this naming problem. While you cannot avoid the fact that you will still need to write appropriate handling methods for each data type, you could instead use the one method name, parseInfo(), which had three definitions:

```
public class GameBoard
{
...
private void parseInfo(String move) {
    // parse string
    move(...);
    }
private void parseInfo(int key) {
    // parse keyboard move
    move(...);
    }
private void parseInfo(int x, int y) {
    // parse mouse click
    move(...);
    }

public int updateBoard(Event evt) {
// checks 3 sources of data, but is able to use the same
// method name for all 3
    if ( infoInFile() )
        parseInfo( readInfo() );        // readInfo() would return a String
    else if ( validKeyboardMove(evt) )
        parseInfo( evt.key );
    else if ( validMouseMove(evt) )
        parseIfno(evt.x, ext.y);
    }

}
```

While the details of updateBoard() and move are not important, the fact that you have three definitions of the parseInfo() method is extremely significant. This process, called *overloading*, extends the OOP theory of isolation by permitting you to simply call the parseInfo() method without worrying about passing the correct data type—as long as you have created a corresponding `parseInfo()` method.

Overloading a method, the process of creating several methods with the same name but different parameter signatures, provides you with a great deal of flexibility. At run time the program will determine which version of the `parseInfo()` method is most appropriate for your use and call it appropriately.

When you later deal with constructors, you will see how this feature enables you to create the same class in several different manners.

---

**Parameter Signature versus Parameter List**

When discussing overloading and overriding it is important to distinguish between a method's parameter signature and its parameter list. A method's parameter signature defines the order and type of the parameters that will be passed to a method (such as `int`, `String`, or `boolean`). A method's parameter list is more specific for it also names these variables (for example, `int size`, `String name`, `boolean running`). While declaring a method with the same name but a different parameter signature will overload a method, declaring a new method with the same parameter signature but a different parameter list will not.

Declaring two methods with the same name and the same parameter signature in the same class is illegal. Look at the example shown in the following table:

---

| Illegal | Legal |
|---|---|
| public void testme(int size) | {<br>....<br>}<br>public void testme(int size, String name) {<br>...<br>} |
| private void testme(int height) | {<br>...<br>}<br>public void testme(String name, int size) {<br>...<br>} |

**Overriding.** While creating two methods with the same name and parameter signature within the same class is illegal, one of the purposes of extending a class is to create a new class with added functionality. Although this may be handled by creating new methods and variables, you may want to change some of the methods in your old class as well. Reusing your Elevator class from before:

```
class Elevator {
    ...
    private boolean running = true;
    ...
    void shutDown() {
        running = false;
        }

    }
```

you are still able to extend the Elevator class, maintain most of its properties, but change some as well. Consequently, if you wanted to create a SaferElevator class which made sure that the elevator car was empty before stopping, you could do so with the following code:

```
class SaferElevator extends Elevator {
    ...
    void shutDown() {
        if ( isEmpty() )
            running = false;
        else
            printErrorMessage();
        }
    }
```

Note that overriding is accomplished only if the new method has the same name and parameter signature as the method in the parent class. If the parameter signature is not the same, the new method will *overload* the parent method, not *override* it.

Also note that methods may not be overridden to become more protected.

### Parameter List

Simply put, the parameter list in the list of information that will be passed to the method. It is in the form:

```
DataType VariableName, DataType VariableName, ...
```

and may consist of as many parameters as you want.

Do note, however, that if you have no parameters, Java requires that you simply leave the parentheses empty. (This is unlike other languages which permit you to omit a parameter list, or C which requires the keyword `void`.) Therefore, a method that took no parameters would have a declaration resembling:

```
public static final void cleanBoard()
```

### Throwing Exceptions

Exceptions provide you with an excellent way of handling the various run-time problems that you may encounter in the execution of your Java program. A good program will be flexible enough to recover from user mistakes and other problems. In fact, most statements in the API that can encounter problems throw exceptions, thereby requiring that you surround it with appropriate error-handling routines.

```
...
try {
    queue.deQueue();
    queue.displayStatus();
}
catch (Exception e) {
    queue.reset();
}
```

The above code, attempts to perform some operations on a queue. If, however, there is a problem, the problem is dealt with properly since the possibly problematic statements are enclosed in a `try-catch` block. If any of the statements within this block "throws" an exception, it is properly "caught" by the `catch` statement and handled. (We will deal with the try-catch construct and exceptions in detail in chapter 15.) However, in order to appropriately deal with thrown exceptions, you must first learn how they are thrown.

The process of creating a method that throws an exception is two tiered. First, you must list those types of exceptions that may be thrown. This is accomplished by placing these exceptions in the exception list of our method declaration.

---

**Note**

Instead of listing all the types of exceptions that may be thrown, you may also list a more general type of exception (such as java.lang.Exception). This would enable you to throw any exception that was derived from java.lang.Exception.

However, it is considered bad practice to list a very general exception if you are able to choose a more specific one instead. By listing a more detailed exception you provide readers of your code and the compiler with more information—enhancing the readablity and efficiency of your code.

---

The second step is the act of throwing the exception. This is performed by using the `throw` statement followed by an appropriate exception somehow derived from java.lang.Throwable. (The exception may be either one of the ones native to Java or one that you have created yourself.) Consequently, we could rewrite the `shutDown()` method from the `SafeElevator` class in the following manner:

```
void shutDown() throws NotEmptyException{
            if ( isEmpty() )
                 running = false;
            else
                 throw new NotEmptyException();
            }
    }
```

where `NotEmptyException` was a throwable Exception that you had created yourself.

---

**Note**

Notice the use of the new operator in the throw statement. As you will see later, the new operator creates a new object of the type specified. Therefore, the above throw statement will create a new `NotEmptyException` object which it will then throw to the calling statement.

If, however, you first catch an exception before throwing it, there is no need to use the new operator in your `throw` statement, as seen below. (The reason for this is that in order for the exception to have been thrown, it must have already been created somewhere.)

```
void closeConnection(Socket connection) throws
➥java.lang.Exception{
    try {
        connection.close();
        }
    catch (Exception e) {
        // any handling code would go here
        throw e;
        }
}
```

---

## Constructors

Constructors are very special methods with unique properties and a unique purpose. Constructors are utilized to set certain properties and perform certain tasks when instances of the class are created.

```
public GameBoard (String gamename) {
    board = new int[WIDTH][HEIGHT];
    myname = new String(gamename);
    }
```

Constructors are identified by having the same name as the class itself. Thus, in the `GameBoard` class, the name of the constructor is `GameBoard()`. Secondly, constructors do not specify a return argument because they will be used to return the instance of the class itself. (For more information on this, see the section on the `new` operator.)

In general, constructors are used to initialize the class's fields and perform various tasks related to creation, such as connecting to a server or performing some initial calculations.

Also note that overloading the constructor enables you to create an object in several different manners. For example, by creating several constructors, each with a different set of parameters, you could enable yourself to create an instance of the `GameBoard` class specifying the name of the game, the values of the board, both, or neither. You will note that this practice is prevalent in the Java libraries themselves. As a result, you can create most data types (such as `java.lang.String` and `java.net.Socket`) while specifing varying degrees and types of information.

---

### Tip

Most programmers choose to make their constructors public. This is because if the level of access for the constructor is less than the level of access for the class itself, another class may be able to declare an instance of your class but will not be able to actually create an instance of that class.

However, this loophole may actually be used to your advantage. By making your constructor private, you may enable other classes to use static methods of your class without enabling them to create an instance of it.

---

Finally note that constructors cannot be declared to be `native`, `abstract`, `static`, `synchronized`, or `final`.

# Referring to Parts of Classes

Now that we have begun to develop classes, let us examine how they may be used in other classes. As discussed earlier in "Why Use Classes," Java classes may contain instances of other classes, which are treated as variables. However, you may also deal with the fields and methods of these class type reference variables. To do so, Java utilizes the standard dot notation used in most OOP languages. Examine the following example:

```
public class Checkers
{
    private GameBoard board;

    public Checkers() {
        board = new game board("Checkers");
        board.cleanBoard();
        }
    ...

    public void movePiece(int player, int direction) {
        java.awt.Point    destination;
        ...
        if (board.isEmpty(destination.x, destination.y) )
            // code to move piece
        }

    private void showBoard(Graphics g) {
        g.drawString(board.myname,100,100);
        drawBoard(g);
        }
}
```

You can see that if board is an instance in the GameBoard class, the variable myname is referenced by board.myname.

---

**Caution**

Notice that the variable myname is referred to as board.myname *not* as GameBoard.myname. If you try to do so, you will get an error resembling:

```
Checkers.java:5: Can't make a static reference to non-static variable
myname in class GameBoard.
```

This is because GameBoard is a *type* of class while board is an *instance* of the class. As discussed earlier, when you deal with board, we deal with a specific copy of the GameBoard class. Because myname is not a static variable, it is not a property of the GameBoard class, but rather a property of the instances of that class. Therefore, it cannot be changed or referenced by using GameBoard as the variable name.

Note, however, that you are able to change *static* variables in this manner.

### "This" Special Variable

You have seen how to refer to other classes. However, what if you want the class to refer to itself? While the reasons to do so may not seem so obvious at first, being able to refer to itself is a capability very important for classes. Consequently, in Java code, the variable this is used whenever it is necessary to explicitly refer to the class itself.

In general, there are two situations which warrant use of the this variable. The first is the case where there are two variables in your class with the same name—one belonging to the class and one belonging to a specific method. As you will see later in "Scope," using the this.variablename syntax enables you to refer to the variable belonging to the class.

Another situation which lends itself nicely to using the this variable is when a class needs to pass itself as an argument to a method. Often when you create applets that employ other classes, it is desirable to provide those classes with access to such methods as showStatus(). For example, if you are creating a Presentation applet class and wanted to utilize a simple TextScroll class to display some text across the status bar at the bottom of the screen, you would need to provide the TextScroll class with some means of utilizing the showStatus() method belonging to the applet. The best way to do this is to create the TextScroll class with a constructor method that accepted an instance of the Presentation applet class as one of its arguments. As seen in the following example, the TextScroll class would then be able to display the information across the bottom of the Presentation class' screen.

```
public class Presentation extends Applet {
    TextScroll scroller;

    public void init() {
        ...
        scroller = new TextScroll(this, length_of_text);
        scroller.start();
    }
    ...
}

class TextScroll extends Thread {
    Presentation screen;
    String newMessage;
    boolean running;
    int size;

    TextScroll(Presentation appl, int size) {
        screen = appl;
    }
```

```
public void run() {
    while (running) {
    displayText();
    }
}

void displayText() {
    // perform some operations to update what should
    // be displayed (newMessage)

    screen.showStatus(newMessage);
    }
}
```

▶ See "What Are
Threads?"
p. 547

While the concepts of threads and their uses will be discussed in later chapters, note the use of the special this variable in the init() method of the Presentation class as well as the result. This technique is extremely useful and powerful.

### "Super" Special Variable

Along the same lines as this, the special variable super provides access to a class's superclass. This is useful when overriding a method, for when doing so you may want to use code from the old method as well. For example, if we were creating a new class NewGameBoard that extended the game board class and was overriding the setSquare() method, we might employ the super variable to use the former code without recopying all of it.

```
class NewGameBoard extends game board {

    private static int FIXEDWALL  = 99;
    // permanent wall, cannot be moved

public static synchronized void setSquare(int x, int y, int value)      {
            if (board[x][y] != FIXEDWALL)
                super.setSquare(x,y,val);
            }
        }
```

In the preceding example, you use the super variable to refer to the original version of the setSquare() method, found in the GameBoard class. By doing so, you save yourself the headaches of recopying the entire method.

You should also examine how you do the same thing if you were dealing with the constructor method of the NewGameBoard() class. While it is not much different, its syntax may seem confusing at first.

```
public NewGameBoard(String gamename) {
    // new code would go here
    super(gamename);
    }
```

Note that on a simplistic level, super can be considered equivalent to GameBoard. Consequently, since GameBoard() is the name of the original constructor method, it may be referred to as super().

# Variables

Obviously, variables are an integral part of programs and thus classes as well. In chapter 8, you examined the various types of variables, but you must also consider how they are employed in your programs and the different roles they may assume. Therefore, when creating variables, whether they are as simple as integers or as complex as derived classes, you must consider how they will be used, what processes will require access to the variables, and what degree of protection you want to provide to these variables.

◀ See "Literals," p. 137

The ability to access a given variable is dependent on two things: the access modifiers used when creating the variable and the location of the variable declaration within the class.

---

### Class Fields versus Method Variables

In a class there are two types of variables: those belonging to the class itself and those belonging to specific methods.

Those variables declared outside of any methods but within a given class (usually immediately after the class declaration and before any methods) are considered to be fields of the class. These variables are referred to as *fields* of the class and accessible to all methods of the class.

In addition, one may declare variables within a method. These variables are local to the method and may only be accessed within that method.

Because method variables exist only for the lifetime of the method, they therefore cannot be accessed by other classes. Consequently, you cannot apply any access modifiers to method variables.

---

While it is possible to make every field accessible to every class, this is not a prudent practice. First of all, you would be defeating a great deal of the purpose of creating your program from classes. Why do you choose appropriate class names instead of class1, class2, class3, and so on? Simply to create a clean program that is easy to code, follow, and debug. For the same reason, by creating various levels of protection, you capsulize your code into self-sufficient and more logical chunks.

II

**The JAVA Language**

Furthermore, inasmuch as OOP is heavily dependent on the modification of code that you have written beforehand, access restrictions prevent you from later doing something that you shouldn't. (Keep in mind that preventing access to a field does not prevent use of it.) For example, in creating a `Circle` class, there will most likely be several fields that will keep track of the properties of the class, such as `radius`, `area`, `border_color`, and so on, many of which may be dependent on each other. Although it may seem logical to make the `radius` field public (accessible by all other classes) consider what would happen if a few weeks later you decided to write the following:

```
class Circle {
  int radius, area;
...
}

class GraphicalInterface {
Circle ball;
...
void animateBall() {
for (int update_radius = 0; update_radius <= 10; update_radius++){
      ball.radius = update_radius
        paintBall(ball.area, ball.border_color)
            ...
          }
      }
   }
```

This code would not produce the desired result. Although the

```
ball.radius = update_radius
```

statement would change the radius, it would not affect the `area` field. As a result, you would be supplying the `paintBall()` method with incorrect information.

In the next few sections you will examine the various ways of regulating access and solving the above problem.

## Modifiers

Like the modifiers for classes and methods, access modifiers determine how accessible certain variables will be to other classes. However, it is important to realize that access modifiers apply only to the global fields of the class—those variables declared before any methods. It makes little sense to speak of access modifiers for variables within methods because they exist only while the method is executing and then "collected" to free up memory for other variables.

---

**Why Not Make All Variables Fields?**

Inasmuch as all fields of a class are accessible to all methods in a given class, why shouldn't you make all variables fields—global to all methods in the class?

The first reason is that by doing so, you would be wasting a great deal of memory. While local variables (those variables declared within the methods themselves) exist only while the method is executing, fields must exist for the lifetime of the class. Consequently, instead of allocating memory for dozens of fields, by making many of your variables local you are able to use the same piece of memory over and over again.

The second reason is that making all your variables global would create sloppy programs that were hard to follow. If you are going to be using a counter only in one method, why not declare it in that method? Furthermore, if all of your variables are global, someone reviewing your code (or you a few weeks later) would have no idea where the variables were obtaining their values from since there would be no logical path of values being passed from method to method.

---

### friendly
Example: `int size;`

By default, fields are assigned the "friendly" level of access. This means that while accessible to other classes within the same package, they are not accessible to subclasses of the current class nor classes outside of the current package.

### public
Example: `public int size;`

Identical to the public access modifier for methods, the public modifier makes fields visible to all classes, regardless of their package, as well as all subclasses. Again, one should make an effort to limit public fields.

### protected
Example: `protected int size;`

Protected fields may be accessed by all subclasses of the current class, but are not visible to classes outside of the current package.

### private
Example: `private int size;`

The highest degree of protection, `private` fields are accessible to all methods within the current class. They are, however, not accessible to any other classes nor are they accessible to the subclasses of the current class.

### private protected

Example: `private protected int size;`

Private protected fields, like `private protected` methods, are accessible within the class itself as well as within subclasses of the current class.

> **Two Birds of a Feather**
>
> Like the private protected modifier for classes, the private protected modifier for fields does not work as of the 1.0 JDK for a similar reason. Although you are able to redeclare private protected fields in subclasses and assign them new values, if you create an instance of the new class, the field will be created with the value from the superclass, not the new value.
>
> Again, this problem should be resolved as of the 1.01 release.

### static

◀ See "Static Methods," p. 175

Example: `static int size;`

As with methods, placing the modifier `static` in front of the field declaration makes the field a static, commonly referred to as a class, field. Static fields are fields of the class whose value is the same in all instances of the class. Consequently, changing a static field in one class will affect that field in all instances of the given class. Static fields may be modified in both static and nonstatic methods.

For more information on static fields and static methods see the explanation of "Static" in the "Methods" section.

### final

Example: `final int SIZE = 5;`

Although Java does not have pre-processor `#define-type` statements nor constants, there is a very simple way of creating constants, fields whose values cannot change while the program is running. By placing the modifier `final` in front of a field declaration, you tell the compiler that the value of the field may not change during execution. Furthermore, because it cannot change elsewhere, it is necessary to set the value of all final fields when they are declared as seen in the example above.

If the value cannot change, why not use the value itself within the program? The answer to this is twofold. First, while the value of constants cannot change within your code, you may later change the initial value of a constant

without having to change the value of each use of the constant. Furthermore, by using constants, your code becomes a lot cleaner and easy to follow. For example, in the GameBoard class, using 0 as a check for an empty space would not always make sense to a reader of your code. However, using the final field EMPTY and assigning it the value 0 makes the code a lot easier to follow.

> **Note**
>
> By convention, all letters of constants are capitalized. Furthermore, to save memory, constants are usually made static as well.

> **Note**
>
> Although not ignored in the 1.0 release, there are two additional modifiers for fields.
>
> When dealing with many threads, there are several problems that can result when multiple threads attempt to access the same data at the same time. While a majority of these problems can be solved by making certain methods synchronized, in future release of Java, you will be able to declare certain fields as threadsafe. Such fields would be handled extra carefully by the Java runtime environment. In particular, the validity of each volatile field will be checked before and after each use.
>
> The other heralded keyword, transient, is related closely with Sun's plans to enable the creation of persistent Java applets. In such an environment, transient fields would not be part of the persistent object.

## Using Methods to Provide Guarded Access

While it may be advantageous to restrict access to certain fields in your class, it is nevertheless often necessary to provide some form of access to these fields. A very intelligent and useful way of doing this is to allow access to restricted fields through less restricted methods, such as in the following example:

```
class Circle {
    private static int PI = 3.1415;
    private int radius, area;
    private Color border_color;

    public void setRadius(int update_radius) {
        radius = update_radius;
        area = PI * radius * radius;
        }
```

```
          public Color getColor() {
               return(border_color);
               }
          public int getRadius() {
               return(radius);
               }
          public int getArea() {
               return(area);
               }
     }
     class GraphicalInterface {
          Circle ball;
          ...
          void animateBall() {
               for (int update_radius = 0; update_radius <= 10;
               ➥update_radius++){
                    ball.setRadius(update_radius);
                    paintBall(ball.getArea(), ball.getColor() );
                    }
               ...
          }
     }
```

By limiting access to the radius field to the setRadius() method, you ensure that any change of the radius will be followed by an appropriate change of the area variable. Because you have made the two fields private, you must also provide yourself with the means of accessing them through the various "get"-type methods. These methods are commonly referred to as *accessor methods* because they provide access to otherwise inaccessible fields. While at first this may seem a bit cumbersome, its benefits by far outweigh its negatives. As a result, it is a very widely used approach and is extremely prevalent in the Java API libraries on which Java is heavily dependent.

## Scope

While it is important to consider the level of access that other objects will have to your fields, it is also important to consider how visible the fields and method variables will be *within* your class. Where the variable is accessible, a property called its scope is a very important topic. In general, every variable is accessible only within the block (delimited by the curly braces { and } ) in which it is declared. However, there are some slight exceptions to this rule. Examine the following code:

```
     class  CashRegister {
          public int total;
          int sales_value[];
          Outputlog log;
```

```
void printReceipt(int total_sale) {
    Tape.println("Total Sale = $"+ total_sale);
    Tape.println("Thank you for shopping with us.");
    }

void sellItem(int value) {
    log.sale(value);
    total += value;
    }

int totalSales() {
    int num_of_sales, total = 0;
    num_of_sales = log.countSales();

    for (int i = 1; i <= num_of_sales; i++)
        total += sales_value[i];
    return(total);
    }
}
```

Now examine some of the variables and their scope:

| Variable Name | Declared As | Scope |
|---------------|-------------|-------|
| total | Field global to `CashRegister` class | Entire class* |
| total | Local to `totalSales()` method | Within `totalSales()` |
| log | Field global to `CashRegister` class | Entire class |
| value | Parameter to `sellItem()` | Within `sellItem()` |
| i | Local to `totalSales()` within for loop | Within the `for` loop |

There are several things to note from the table. We will start with the simplest variable, `log`. `log` is a field of the CashRegister class and is therefore visible throughout the entire class. Every method in the class (as well as other classes in the same package) may access `log`. Similarly simple is `value`. Although it is declared as a parameter, it is nevertheless local to the method `sellItem()` in which it was declared. While all statements in `sellItem()` may access `value`, it may not be accessed by any other methods. Slightly more confusing is the variable `i`, which is declared not at the beginning of a method but within a `for` statement. Like `log` and `value` which exist only within the block in which they were defined, `i` exists only within the `for` statement in which it was defined.

Finally, you arrive at the problem of having two `total` variables with overlapping scope. While the `total` field is accessible to all methods, a problem seems to arise in the `totalSales()` method. In such cases, using the multiply-defined identifier refers to the most local definition of the variable. Therefore, while having no impact on the rest of the class, within the `totalSales()`the identifier `total` refers to the local variable `total`, not the global one.

While using an identifier as a field and method variable name does not cause many problems and is considered an acceptable practice, it is preferable to chose a different (and more descriptive) identifier such as `total_sales` to avoid this problem.

> **Note**
>
> While you are able to use the same identifier as a field and a variable within a method, this does not apply to all code blocks within your code. For example, declaring `num_of_sales` as your counter within the `for` block would produce an error.

> **Tip**
>
> If you do create a method variable with the same name as a field and need to refer to the field rather than the method variable, you may do so with the `this` variable, as explained earlier in this chapter in " 'This' Special Variable."

# Creating and Destroying Objects

Memory management is a topic very important to all computer languages. Whenever you create a new instance of a class, the Java runtime system will set aside a portion of memory in which to store the information pertaining to the class. However, when the object "falls out of scope," or is no longer needed by the program, this portion of memory is freed to be used again by other objects.

While Java hides most of these operations from the programmer, it does provide you with some chances to optimize your code by performing certain additional tasks. While requiring you to explicitly allocate memory for each new object with the new operator, it also allows you to specialize your new object (by using its constructor methods), and to ensure that it leaves no loose ends when it is destroyed.

---

**Memory Management—C versus Java**

Unlike C and C++, which provide the programmer with a great deal of control over memory management, Java performs many of these tasks for you. Most notably, in its aptly called "garbage collection," Java automatically frees objects when there are no references to the given object, thereby making C++ free() method unnecessary.

Furthermore, when creating a new object, you do not need to specify the amount of memory requested, but rather the name of the object requested. This also means that when the new statement returns a reference to the allocated portion of memory, it will already have been assigned the proper data type and thus will not require a cast as in C.

---

## Creating Objects with the new Operator

When creating an instance of a class, it is necessary to set aside a piece of memory to store various information. However, when you declare the instance at the beginning of a class, you are merely telling the compiler that a variable with a certain name will be used in the class. Consequently, it is necessary to actually create the variable using the new operator. Examine the following code used earlier:

```
public class Checkers
{
     private GameBoard board;
     public Checkers() {
          board = new GameBoard("Checkers");
          board.cleanBoard();
          }
     ...
```

You will see that although we declared the variable board to be of type GameBoard in the third line, we must also create it in the fifth line using the new operator. The syntax of a statement involving the new operator is:

```
instanceofClass = new ClassName(optional_parameters);
```

Quite simply, the line tells the compiler to allocate memory for an instance of the class, and assigns the name of the instance to the section of memory. In doing so, the compiler also calls the class' constructor method if one has been defined. If a specific constructor method has been defined, it passes the appropriate parameters to it as seen in the game board example above.

II

The JAVA Language

If, however, the constructor does not take any parameters or if no constructor method has been defined, no parameters are necessary. For example, when you create a new instance of a `java.lang.String`, you employ the same procedure, but need only write:

```
title = new String();
```

## Pointers: Fact or Fiction?

Java claims not to possess pointers, and as a result prevents the programmer from making some of the mistakes associated with pointer handling. Nevertheless, while it chooses not to adopt a pointer-based mindset, Java is forced to deal with the same issues of allocating memory and creating references to these locations in memory.

Thus, while assigned a different name, references are Java's version of pointers. Although you cannot perform some of the intrusive operations with pointers as you can with C, you will notice the striking parallels between pointer assignment and object creation. Like declaring a pointer, you must first declare a reference, which is not a complete variable inasmuch as it does not refer to a portion of memory yet. Then you must allocate adequate memory and assign the reference to it. Furthermore, since you may later decide to set a reference equal to another type of the same variable, Java's system of references is extremely analogous to C's system of pointers—and inherently should be inasmuch as they accomplish the same task.

While Java's implementation effectively hides the behavior of pointers from the programmer and shields him from their pitfalls, it is nevertheless a good idea to consider what is occurring behind the scenes when you create and refer to a variable.

## Using the *finalize()* Method

Belonging to the `java.lang.Object` class, and thus present in all classes is the `finalize()` method. Empty by default, this method is called by the Java runtime system during the process of garbage collection, and thus may be used to clean up any ongoing processes before the object is destroyed. For example, in a class that deals with sockets, it is good practice to close all sockets before destroying the object defined by the class. Therefore, one could place the code to close the sockets in the `finalize()` method. Once the instance of the class was no longer being used in the program and was destroyed, this method would be invoked to close the sockets as required.

For example,

```
public class NetworkSender
{
```

```
      private Socket me;
      private OutputStream out;

      public NetworkSender(String host, int port) {
         try {
             me = new Socket(host,port);
             out = me.getOutputStream();
         }
         catch (Exception e) {
            System.out.println(e.getMessage());
            }
      }

      public void sendInfo(char signal) {
              try {
                  out.write(signal);
              out.flush();
          }
              catch (Exception e) {
                  System.out.println(e.getMessage());
                       }
           }

   public void disconnect() {
    System.out.println("Disconnecting...");
          try {
              me.close();
          }

      catch (Exception e)
         System.out.println("Error on Disconnect" + e.getMessage());

      System.out.println("done.");
   }
/* In this case finalize() is the identical to disconnect() /*
/* and only attempts to ensure closure of the socket in the /*
/* case that disconnect() is not called. */

  protected void finalize() {
     System.out.println("Disconnecting...");
     try {
         me.close();
     }
     catch (Exception e)
        System.out.println("Error on Disconnect" + e.getMessage());

     System.out.println("done.");
   }

}
```

Note that `finalize()` is declared to be protected in java.lang.Object and thus must remain protected or become less restricted.

---

**Caution**

While the `finalize()` method is a legitimate tool, it should not be relied upon too heavily inasmuch as garbage collection is not a completely predictable process. This is because garbage collection runs in the background as a low priority thread and is generally performed when you have no memory left.

Consequently, it is a good practice to attempt to perform such "clean-up" tasks elsewhere in your code, resorting to `finalize()` only as a last resort and when failure to execute such statements will not cause significant problems.

---

# Synchronized Blocks

While synchronized methods can handle the problem of multiple threads attempting to access the same information, a similar problem can arise when multiple threads attempt to access the same information through an explicit reference. To solve problems created by this scenario, you may employ the synchronized keyword again, this time to create a *synchronized block*.

```
class Game {
    ScoreKeeper recorder;
    ...
    synchronized (recorder) {
        System.out.println("Player One Score: " +
        ➥recorder.score[1]);
        System.out.println("Player Two Score: " +
        ➥recorder.score[2]);
    }
}
```

Like synchronized methods, synchronized blocks lock up the specified object while executing. In addition, like synchronized methods, synchronized blocks will not start if another synchronized process is running.

---

**Note**

While synchronized methods lock the current class, synchronized blocks lock the specified class during execution. In the above example, the instance named `recorder`, not the Game class would be locked.

# Summary

Classes are the building blocks of all Java programs. Consisting of fields and methods which may employ these fields in accomplishing a given task, classes enable you to encapsulate an object's behavior and state in a self-sustaining unit. Employing the object-oriented programming view of code, Java's classes can be used by other classes both as a foundation for new classes and as a class type variable.

When creating the class itself, as well as the class's fields and methods, there are several modifiers that you may use to specify how they will interact with other classes. These modifiers will determine how the class, method, or field will interact with other classes.

**Table 10.1   Table of Modifiers for Classes, Methods, and Fields**

| Modifier | Effect on Classes | Effect on Methods | Effect on Fields |
|----------|-------------------|-------------------|------------------|
| default (friendly) | Visible to subclasses and class within the same package | Can be called by methods belonging to classes within the same package | Accessible only to classes within the same package |
| public | Visible to subclasses and classes regardless of their package | Can be called by methods in subclasses and all classes regardless of their package | Accessible only to subclasses and all classes regardless of their package |
| private | Classes cannot be private | Can only be called by methods within the current class | Accessible only to methods within the current class |
| private protected | Not applicable to classes | Can only be called by methods within the current class and subclasses | Accessible only to methods within the current class and subclasses |

(continues)

**Table 10.1    Continued**

| Modifier | Effect on Classes | Effect on Methods | Effect on Fields |
|---|---|---|---|
| static | Not applicable to classes | Method is shared by all instances of the current class | Field is shared by all instances of the current class. |
| abstract | Some methods are not defined. These methods must be implemented in subclasses | Contains no body and must be overridden in subclasses | *Not applicable to fields.* |
| final | The class may not be used as a superclass | The method may not be overridden in any subclasses | *Variable's value cannot be changed.* |
| native | Not applicable to classes | This method's implementation will be defined by code written in another language | *Not applicable to fields.* |
| synchronized | Not applicable to classes | This method will seize control of the class while running. If another method has already seized control, it will wait until the first has completed. | *Not applicable to fields.* |

In addition to modifiers, class declarations have the form

```
modifiers    class NewClass    extends NameofSuperClass
➡implements NameofInterface
```

and may utilize the final two options to add preexisting functionality to the class.

Methods are the OOP equivalent of functions and provide the class with its functionality. Method declarations have the form

```
access_specifier  modifier   return_value   nameofmethod   (parameters)
➡throws ExceptionList
```

The access specifiers and modifiers are listed previously. The return type is the data type (or void) that will be returned from the method after execution. Parameters are the information that will be passed to a method when it is called. Finally, the exception list specifies those exceptions that may be thrown by the method. The actual throwing of exceptions is performed with the throw statement.

Constructors are special methods that share the name of the class and that do not specify a return type. They are called when an instance of the class is created.

Two important facets of the naming methods are the ability to overload and override methods. Method overloading is the process of creating several methods with the same name but different parameters to enable you to perform the same task with different types of data. Method overriding is the act of creating a new method with the same name and parameter list as a method in the class's superclass. Consequently, the method in the subclass, not the superclass, will be used when the method is called.

Fields are variables declared outside of the scope of individual methods but within a class. These variables are said to define the "state" of the instance, and may be accessed by all methods in the class as well as other classes depending on the access modifier used when declaring the field.

In addition to fields, you may also declare variables within your methods. These variables however exist only while the method is executing and thus cannot be accessed outside of the particular method.

To the runtime system, objects are portions of memory set aside to keep track of the various properties of the object, such as its fields and methods. Therefore, it is necessary to not only declare instances of classes, but also to create them (by reserving sufficient memory) with the new command. The syntax for such a command is instanceofClass = new ClassName(optional_arguments);

Note that class constructors are called when the object is created. Therefore, this is when you are able to pass information to these constructors by way of any paramaters specified in the constructor. ❖

The JAVA Language

II

# CHAPTER 11

# More About Interfaces

*by Michael Afergan*

While classes define objects, interfaces help to define classes. Somewhat resembling classes in syntax, interfaces are used when you want to define a certain functionality to be used in several classes, but are not sure exactly how this functionality will be defined by these classes. By placing such methods in an interface you are able to outline common behavior and leave the specific implementation to the classes themselves.

Interfaces are Java's substitute for C++'s feature of multiple inheritance, the practice of allowing a class to have several superclasses. While it is often desirable to have a class inherit several sets of properties, for several reasons, the creators of Java decided not to allow multiple inheritance. Java classes, however, can implement several interfaces, thereby enabling you to create classes that build upon other objects without the problems created by multiple inheritance.

Although not very complex, interfaces are rather useful. In this chapter we will discuss:

- **The syntax of creating an interface**

    Before we can use an interface, we must first develop it. As we will see, the syntax and process for doing so resembles that of classes quite closely and is very uncomplicated.

- **Implementing interfaces in classes**

    Because interfaces define only abstract methods, the next step is to create some classes that will actually implement these methods. This is done by creating a class that "implements" the given interface.

■ **Using interfaces as types**

All classes that implement a given interface will share a set of methods. Therefore, we may perform certain operations such as classes without worrying how the methods were implemented or what else is included in the class.

# What Are Interfaces?

Interfaces are the underprivileged first cousins of classes. While classes have the ability to define an object, interfaces define a set of methods and constants to be implemented by another object. From a practical viewpoint, interfaces help to define the behavior of an object by declaring a set of characteristics for the object. For example, knowing that a person is an athlete does not define his or her entire personality, but does ensure that he or she will have certain traits and abilities. Thus, by later implementing an interface, you ensure that a class will possess these abilities.

Interfaces define only abstract methods and final fields, but cannot specify any implementation for these methods. As a result, like abstract classes, it is the responsibility of any classes that implement an interface to specify the implementation of these methods.

In general, interfaces enable you as a programmer to define a certain set of functionality without having any idea as to how this functionality will be later defined. As an example, the java.lang.Runnable interface provides you with a tremendous amount of power and flexibility. That is partly because although it defines one method, run(), it places no limitations on the way in which you may define run() in other classes. Therefore, you may place virtually anything within the run() method of your class and still have it treated as a class implementing the Runnable interface. When developing a class that implements an interface, you are able to develop the class-specific implementation of these methods. Consequently, when using such classes, you are able to depend on the fact that these methods will be implemented, without having to worry about *how* these methods are implemented.

Another excellent example is the java.applet.AppletContext interface. The interfaces defines a set of methods that return information regarding the environment in which an applet is running, such as the appletviewer or a Web browser. While the java.applet.Applet class depends on the methods declared in the AppletContext interface, it nevertheless does not need to worry about *how* these methods obtain their information but can be assured that they *will* somehow. Therefore, we can use the same applet class and the same methods (such as `java.applet.Applet.showStatus()`) in a variety of environments without worrying about how these methods are implemented.

# Creating an Interface

The syntax for creating an interface is extremely similar to that for creating a class. However there are a few exceptions. Most significant is the fact that none of the methods in your class may have a body, nor may you declare any variables that will not serve as constants. Nevertheless, there are some important things that you may include in an interface definition.

Here is an example of an interface, a class that implements the interface, and a class that uses the derived class. Look it over to get an idea as to how interfaces are used and where we are going in this chapter. As we go on, we will thoroughly examine each portion.

---

**Listing 11.1    An Application of an Interface**

```
interface Product {
    static final String MAKER = "My Corp";
    static final String PHONE = "555-123-4567";

    public int getPrice(int id);

}
class Shoe implements Product {
    public int getPrice(int id) {
        if (id == 1)
            return(5);
        else
            return(10);
    }
    public String getMaker() {
        return(MAKER);
    }
}
class Store {
    static Shoe hightop;

    public static void init() {
        hightop = new Shoe();
    }

    public static void main(String argv[]) {
        init();
        getInfo(hightop);
        orderInfo(hightop);
    }
```

(continues)

```
Listing 11.1   Continued

    public static void getInfo(Shoe item) {
        System.out.println("This Product is made by "+
        ➥item.MAKER);
        System.out.println("It costs $" + item.getPrice(1) + '\n');
    }

    public static void orderInfo(Product item) {
        System.out.println("To order from " +item.MAKER + " call
        ➥" + item.PHONE + ".");
        System.out.println("Each item costs $" +
        ➥item.getPrice(1));
    }
}
```

## The Declaration

Interface declarations have the syntax:

> *public* interface NameofInterface *extends InterfaceList*

where everything in italics is optional.

### Public Interfaces

By default, interfaces may be implemented by all classes in the same package. By making your interface public, you allow classes and objects outside of the given package to implement it as well.

```
Tip

Like public classes, public interfaces must be defined in a file named
<NameofInterface>.java.
```

### Interface Name

The rules for an interface name are identical to those for classes. The only requirements on the name are that it begin with a letter, an underscore character, or a dollar sign, contain only Unicode characters (basic letters and digits, as well as some other special characters), and not be the same as any Java keyword (i.e., extends or int). Again, like classes, it is common practice to capitalize the first letter of any interface name.

> **Tip**
>
> Additionally, while only required for public interfaces, it is a good practice to place all interfaces in a file named `<NameofInterface>.java`. This will enable both you and the Java compiler to find the source code for your class.
>
> Thus, while the Product interface is not public, we should still declare it in a file named `Product.java`.

### Extending Other Interfaces

In accordance with the OOP theory of inheritance, Java interfaces may also extend other interfaces as a means of further developing previously coded interfaces. The new subinterface will inherit all the methods and static constants of the superinterfaces in the same manner as how subclasses inherit the properties of superclasses.

While interfaces are allowed to extend other interfaces because they cannot define any methods, interfaces may not define the methods declared in the interfaces that they extend. Instead, it will be the responsibility of any class that implements the derived interface to define both the methods declared in the derived interface *and* any methods defined in the extended interfaces.

As an example, the following lines are the declarations of two separate interfaces, each of which extends a previously defined interface:

```
interface MonitoredRunnable extends java.lang.Runnable
interface NetworkedDataOuput extends java.io.DataOuput
```

The first declaration could be used to create a more detailed Runnable interface, perhaps including some of the features that can be found in `java.lang.Thread`.

The second declaration could belong to an interface defining an additional set of methods pertaining to network communications. Both these methods and the methods declared in the `java.io.DataOutput` interface would be found in any classes implementing the new `NetworkedDataOutput` interface.

> **Note**
>
> Interfaces cannot extend classes.

II

The Java Language

Remember that if you implement an extended interface, you must override *both* the methods in the new interface and the methods in the old interface as seen in listing 11.2.

---

**Listing 11.2    Implementing a Derived Interface**

```
interface MonitoredRunnable extends java.lang.Runnable {
    public boolean isRunning();
}

class Fireworks implements MonitoredRunnable {
    private boolean running;        // keeps track of state

    void run() {
            shootFireWorks();
            }

    boolean isRunning() {           // provides access to other
                                    ➥objects without
            return(running);        // allowing them to change the
                                    ➥value of running

            }

}
```

---

Note that since `Fireworks` implements `MonitoredRunnable` it must override `isRunning()`, declared in `MonitoredRunnable`, and `run()`, declared in `Runnable`.

---

**Note**

Notice that while classes implement interfaces as a means of inheriting their properties, interfaces extend other interfaces. This is because the extends keyword allows for further development of code while the implements keyword simply causes a given class to acquire the properties of an `interface`.

---

If extending more than one interface, separate each by a comma.

## The Interface Body

While it cannot specify any specific implementation, the body of an interface does specify its properties. While a majority of the benefits of interfaces come from their ability to declare methods, interfaces may also possess final variables.

For example, by declaring the `MAKER` variable in the `Product` interface, you declare a constant that will be employed by all classes implementing the `Product` interface.

Another nice example of final fields in interfaces can be found in the
`java.awt.image.ImageConsumer` interface. The interface defines a set of
final integers that will serve as standards for interpreting information.
Because the `RANDOMPIXELORDER` variable equals 1, classes that implement
the ImageConsumer interface will be able to understand that the value of 1
means that the pixels will be sent in a random order.

### Methods

The main purpose of interfaces is to declare abstract methods that will be
defined in other classes. As a result, if you are dealing with a class that implements an interface, you can be assured that these methods will be defined in
the class. While this process is not overly complicated, there are some important things that should be noticed.

The syntax for declaring a method in an interface is extremely similar to declaring a method in a class. The only significant difference is that in contrast
to methods declared in classes, methods declared in interfaces cannot possess
bodies.

As stated above, an interface method consists of only a declaration. For example, the following two methods are complete if they are defined in an
interface:

```
public int getPrice(int id);
public void showState();
```

However in a class, they would require method bodies:

```
public int getPrice(int id) {
   if (id == 1)
           return(5);
   else
           return(10);
   }

public void showState() {
   System.out.println("Massachusetts");
   }
```

While the method declaration does not determine how a method will behave, it nevertheless defines its behavior by defining what information it
needs and what (if any) information will be returned. Since the method
implementations will be dependent on the methods declarations specified in
the interface, it is important that you consider the necessary properties of the
method—its return value, parameters, and exception list—and how they will
impact the rest of your code.

Method declarations in interfaces have the following syntax:

```
public return_value  nameofmethod  (parameters)  throws
➥ExceptionList;
```

where everything in italics is optional. Also note that unlike normal method declarations in classes, declarations in interfaces are immediately followed by a semicolon.

**Tip**

Note that method declarations in interfaces resemble method declarations in Java classes and function declarations in C++ classes.

**Note**

While it is possible to use the keyword public when declaring methods, all methods in interfaces are naturally public regardless of the presence or absence of the public modifier.

Also note that you may not use any of the other standard method modifiers, (including native, static, synchronized, final, private, protected, or private protected) when declaring a method in an interface.

**Variables**

Although interfaces are generally employed to provide abstract implementation of methods, they may also possess variables. Nevertheless, because you cannot place any code within the bodies of the methods, all variables declared in an interface must be fields global to the class. Furthermore, regardless of the modifiers used when declaring the field, all fields declared in an interface are always public, final, and static.

**Tip**

While all fields will be created as public, final, and static, you do not need to explicitly state this in the field declaration. All fields will be created as public, static and final regardless of the presence of these modifiers.

Nevertheless, it is good practice to explicity define all fields in interfaces as public, final, and static to remind yourself (and other programmers) of this fact.

As seen in the previous `Product` interface, interface fields, like final static fields in classes, are used to define constants that can be accessed by all classes that implement the interface.

Lastly, since all fields are final, they must be initialized when they are declared the interface itself.

# Implementing Interfaces

Now that we have seen how to create interfaces, let us examine how they are used in developing classes. Here is an example of a class that implements our `Product` interface:

**Listing 11.3   Implementing an Interface**

```
class Shoe implements Product {
    public int getPrice(int id) {
        if (id == 1)
                return(5);
        else
                return(10);
        }
    public String getMaker() {
        return(MAKER);
        }
    }
```

Of course, the code in the class can deal with functions other than those relating to the interface. Nevertheless, in order to fulfill the requirements of implementing the `Product` interface, the class must override the `getPrice(int)` method inasmuch as it is originally declared in the interface. Because it is the only method declared in the interface, it therefore is the only method that must be found in the `Shoe` class.

## Overriding Methods

As we have seen, declaring a method in an interface is often a good practice. However, the method cannot be used until it is overriden in a class implementing the given method.

A method declaration in an interface determines much of the method's behavior by defining such things as the method name, return type, and parameter signature. However, when overriding such a method, there are also several aspects that may be changed. In fact, the only part of the method that cannot change is its name.

**Tip**

Remember that if you implement an interface, you are required to override all methods declared in the interface. Failure to do so will make your class abstract.

### Modifiers

As discussed earlier, methods declared in interfaces are by default assigned the public level of access. Because you cannot override a method to be more private than it already is, all methods declared in interfaces and overridden in classes *must* be assigned the public access modifier.

Of the remaining modifiers that may be applied to methods, only `native` and `abstract` may be applied to methods originally declared in interfaces.

### Parameter List

Interface methods define a set a of parameters that must be passed to the method. Consequently, declaring a new method with the same name but a different set of parameters than the method declared in your interface will overload the method, not override it.

While there is nothing wrong with overloading methods declared in interfaces, remember that it is also important to implement the method declared in the interface. Therefore, unless you declare your class to be abstract, you must override each method, employing the same parameter signature as in your interface. This means that while the names of the variables may change, their order and types may not.

**Tip**

If the method `String createName(int length, boolean capitalized)` is declared in an interface, here are some valid and invalid examples of how to override it.

| Valid | Invalid |
|---|---|
| `String createName(int a, boolean b)` | `String createName(boolean capitalized, int length)` |
| `String createName(int width, boolean formatted)` | `String createName(int length)` |

### Exceptions.

◀ See "Throwing Exceptions," p. 185

> **Tip**
>
> In Java, the term "exception" has two definitions. In a general sense, an exception is an unwanted occurrence. Every programmer, through instruction or experience, learns that it is a good idea to place error-handling code in every program to prevent such things as improper input and division by 0. Such unwanted and undefined functions must be handled.
>
> Java has special constructs for handling such problems. Java Exceptions are objects created when an exception is encountered. These objects are then returned from the method to the calling object and must be dealt with. This process of returning exceptions is called "throwing" exceptions and is performed with a `throw` statement. Dealing with exceptions is called "catching," and is accomplished by placing statements that may throw exceptions in a `try-catch` block.

In order to throw an exception, the exception type (or one of its superclasses) must be listed in the exception list for the method. However, when dealing with interface methods, exceptions are an exception. Here are the rules for overriding methods that throw exceptions:

1. The new exception list may only contain exceptions listed in the original exception list, or subclasses of the originally listed exceptions.

2. The new exception list does not need to contain any exceptions, regardless of the number listed in the original exception list. (This is because the original list is inherently assigned to the new method.)

3. The new method may throw any exception listed in the original exception list or derived from an exception in the original list regardless of its own exception list.

In general, the exception list of the method declared in the interface, *not* the redeclared method determines which expectations can and cannot be thrown.

While it is good practice to list those exceptions that the new method may throw in the class declaration of the method, you do not need to include an exception list in the redeclaration of methods first declared in interfaces.

For an example, examine the interface and method declarations in listing 11.4.

**Listing 11.4    Alternate Exception Lists**

```
interface Example {
     public int getPrice(int id) throws java.lang.RuntimeException;
     }

class User implements Example {
     public int getPrice(int id) throws java.awt.AWTException
     ➥{   // Illegal - Reason 1
                              // java.awt.AWTException is not a
                              ➥subclass of java.lang.RuntimeException
     /// method body
     }
      public int getPrice(int id) {
             if (id == 6)
                     throw new java.lang.IndexOutOfBoundsException();
                     ➥// Legal - Reason 2
                                 //IndexOutOfBoundsException is
                                 ➥derived from RuntimeException
             else
                     ...
             }
     public int getPrice(int id) throws
     ➥java.lang.IndexOutOfBoundsException {  // Legal - Reason 1
                             // IndexOutOfBoundsException is derived
                             ➥from RuntimeException
             if (id == 6)
throw new java.lang.ArrayIndexOutOfBoundsException();   // Legal -
Reason 3
                     //       ArrayIndexOutOfBoundsException
                             ➥is derived from
                             ➥IndexOutOfBoundsException
             ...
             }
```

## Body

When creating a class that implements an interface, one of your chief concerns will be the creation of bodies for the methods originally declared in the interface. Unless you decide to make the method native, it is necessary to create the body for every method originally declared in your interface if you do not wish to make your new class abstract. Nevertheless, the actual implementation and code of the body of your new method are entirely up to you. This is one of the nice things about using interfaces. While the interface ensures that in a non-abstract class, its methods will be defined and will return an appropriate data type, the interface places no further restrictions or limitations on the method bodies.

> **Note**
>
> While a non-abstract class that implements an interface is assured to possess every method declared in the interface, it does not assure you that these methods will be implemented properly. In fact, creating a method body consisting simply of opening and closing curly braces (`{ }`) will satisfy the requirements of a method whose return type is `void`.
>
> While doing this will trick the compiler into believing that you have satisfied the requirements of implementing an interface, doing so can create many problems. As we will later see, we can perform nice operations with classes that implement interfaces because we know that every method in the interface is implemented in the class. However, if the method exists in name only, we will not obtain the desired result.
>
> Consequently, do not cheat yourself by overriding interface methods with inadequate method bodies. If for some reason you are unable to create an effective method, rethink your use of the interface.

# Using Interfaces from Other Classes

We have examined how to create interfaces and how to build classes based on interfaces. However, interfaces are not useful unless we are able to develop classes that will either employ the derived classes or the interface itself.

As we will see, there are several ways in which classes that implement interfaces can be employed in other classes. Nevertheless, all uses hinge on one certain ability: being assured of the fact that the methods and fields declared in the interface will be defined in the given class.

## Using an Interface's Fields

Although the fields of an interface must be both static and final, they nevertheless can be extremely useful in your code. As discussed earlier, they must serve as constants, but even in this limited role, as seen in listing 11.5 and listing 11.6, they serve to clarify your code and provide with with valuable information.

As seen in the following example, any field of an interface may be referenced using the standard dot notation as `InterfaceName.field`. This will provide you with access to descriptive constants (as seen in listing 11.5), as well as information (such as `MAKER` in the `Product` interface).

---

**Listing 11.5    Using the Constant Fields of an Interface**

```
class MyImageHandler {
/* The java.awt.image.ImageConsumer interface defines certain
   ➥constants to serve as indicators.
STATICIMAGEDONE, which  is set to equal 3, informs the consumer that
➥the image is complete.*/
    ImageConsumer picture;

    void checkStatus(boolean done) {
        if (done)

    picture.imageComplete(ImageConsumer.STATICIMAGEDONE);
        }
}
```

---

Because STATICIMAGEDONE is a public field of the ImageConsumer interface it may be referenced as ImageConsumer.STATICIMAGEDONE.

## Using Interfaces as Types

Another nice feature of interfaces is the fact that any instance of a class that implements a given interface must possess the abstract methods declared in the interface. (If the class did not override and implement these methods, it would be abstract and thus you could not create an instance of it.) Consequently, it is possible to refer to types of objects that implement a given interface inasmuch as they will all possess a common set of methods. Although the classes may differ significantly in their task and implementation, classes that implement a given interface may be dealt with in a similar manner without any worry as to how the methods are implemented.

### As a Parameter Type

In the following example, we create a simple application that employs the Shoe class developed earlier. Because the Shoe class implements the Product interface, we may deal with the instances of the Shoe class either as standard Shoe objects or as objects based on the Product interface. Although both approaches produce the same results, treating the instance of Shoe as an object based on the Product interface provides us with a more flexible and useful way of using the resources provided by the Product interface.

---

**Listing 11.6  Using an Interface as a Parameter Type**

```
class Store {
    static Shoe hightop;

    public static void init() {
        hightop = new Shoe();
```

```
        }

    public static void main(String argv[]) {
        init();
          getInfo(hightop);
          orderInfo(hightop);
      }

    public static void getInfo(Shoe item) {
        System.out.println("This Product is made by "+ item.MAKER);
        System.out.println("It costs $" + item.getPrice(1) + '\n');
        }

    public static void orderInfo(Product item) {
        System.out.println("To order from " +item.MAKER + " call " +
        ➥item.PHONE + ".");
        System.out.println("Each item costs $" + item.getPrice(1));
        }
    }
```

## Output:

```
C:\dev>\jdk\java\bin\java Store
This Product is made by My Corp
It costs 5

To order from My Corp call 555-123-4567.
Each item costs 5
```

In the above example, the getInfo() methods treats hightop as a simple class with certain methods and fields. However, the interesting example is orderInfo(), which extracts almost the same information without knowing anything about a Shoe. Since a Shoe meets the requirements of a Product, we are able to implicitly cast a Shoe to become a Product. As a result, since we know that the Product interface declares certain features, we can be sure that these features, such as the getPrice() method, are present in the parameter item.

---

**Note**

You will notice that in treating hightop as a Product, we are implicitly casting it as a new data type without specifically stating so in our code. While the compiler has no trouble doing this, we could substitute that line of code in the Store class for the following:

```
    orderInfo( (Product)hightop);
```

The above statement would accomplish the same goal and is often more clear inasmuch as it shows that orderInfo() accepts a Product, not a Shoe as its argument.

---

In this simplistic example, it is not necessary to use the Product type as our argument. However, its utility becomes apparent when we have multiple classes, each of which implements the same interface. For example, consider a more elaborate Store class with several items, all of which implemented the Product interface—such as in listing 11.7. While it would be necessary to create a different getInfo() method for each item class, we could retain the same orderInfo() method inasmuch as each class was guaranteed to have a MAKER and PHONE field as well as a getPrice(int) method.

**Listing 11.7  Using an Interface as a Type to Deal with Several Classes**

```java
interface Product {
    String MAKER = "My Corp";
    static final String PHONE = "555-123-4567";
    public int getPrice(int id);
    public void showName();
}
class Book implements Product {
    public int getPrice(int id) {
        if (id == 1)
            return(20);
        else
            return(30);
    }
    public void showName() {
        System.out.println("I'm a book!");
    }
}
class Shoe implements Product {
    public int getPrice(int id) {
        if (id == 1)
            return(5);
        else
            return(10);
    }
    public void showName() {
        System.out.println("I'm a shoe!");
    }

}
class store {
    static Shoe hightop;
    static Book using_java;

    public static void init() {
        hightop = new Shoe();
        using_java = new Book();
}

    public static void main(String argv[]) {
        init();
```

```
        orderInfo(hightop);
        orderInfo(using_java);
    }

    public static void orderInfo(Product item) {
        item.showName();
        System.out.println("To order from " +item.MAKER + " call " +
        item.PHONE + ".");
        System.out.println("Each item costs " + item.getPrice(1));
        }

    }
```

```
Output:
C:\ev>\jdk\java\bin\java Store
I'm a shoe!
To order from My Corp call 555-123-4567.
Each item costs 5
I'm a book!
To order from My Corp call 555-123-4567.
Each item costs 20
```

### As a Reference

While an interface contains no implementation code, it is nevertheless possible to create a reference to an interface. Much like pointers in C, simply attempting to invoke a method on a instance of an interface will create a NullPointer exception during execution. What then is the purpose of creating such a reference?

As stated earlier, it is possible to create a NullPointer exception when dealing with references to objects. The idea behind the following example is valid. However, we cannot attempt to use the reference until after we have assigned it to an object.

```
public interface Helper  {
   public int performOp(int id);
}
public class User {
    static Helper inst;
    public static void main(String args[]) {
        inst.getPrice(6);
    }
}
```

The above code will compile.  However, examine the output:

```
java.lang.NullPointerException
        at User.main(user.java:3)
```

To remedy this problem, we must (as done in listing 11.8) insert at least one more line, assigning the reference to an object that implements the Helper interface.

The usefulness of an instance-type reference variable comes in the fact that you may assign it to an instance of a class that implements the interface. As seen in listing 11.8, by doing so, we are able to access those methods and fields declared in the interface inasmuch as we are guaranteed that they will be present in the class.

### Listing 11.8    Using an Interface as a Variable Type

```
class InventoryTracker {
    static Product commodity;

    public InventoryTracker(Product item) {
        commodity = item;
        }

    public static void orderInfo() {
        System.out.println("To order from " + commodity.MAKER +
        ➥" call "
        ➥+ item.PHONE + ".");
        System.out.println("Each item costs $" +
commodity.getPrice(1));
        }
    }
```

In the above example, the InventoryTracker constructor can be called using any class that implements the Product interface as the parameter. Regardless of the specific class, knowing that it implements the Product interface enables us to create a reference to the object. Since we know that the object must contain a getPrice(int) method and a MAKER and PHONE field, we are therefore able to create an orderInfo() method without even knowing what type of object was passed to the constructor method. ❖

# CHAPTER 12

# More About Expressions

*by Scott Williams*

Expressions—combinations of operators and operands—are one of the key building blocks of the Java language, as they are of many programming languages. Expressions allow you to do arithmetic calculations, concatenate strings, compare values, perform logical operations, and manipulate objects. Without expressions, a programming language is dead—useless and lifeless.

You've already seen expressions, mostly fairly simple ones, in other chapters in this book. Chapter 9 in particular showed you that operators—one of the two key elements in an expression—form one of the main classifications of Java tokens, along with such things as keywords, comments, and so on. In this chapter, you take a closer look at how you can use operators to build expressions—in other words, how to put operators to work for you.

In this chapter, you take a look at the following:

- What expressions are
- Java operators and how to use them
- The rules for building expressions: operator associativity, precedence, and the order of evaluation
- Type conversions and casts
- How Java expressions compare to C and C++ expressions

## What Is an Expression?

There are all kinds of technical definitions of what an expression is, but at its simplest, an *expression* is what results when operands and operators are joined together according to the syntax rules of the language. As such, expressions are usually used to perform operations—manipulations—on variables or values. In table 12.1, you see legal Java expressions.

| Table 12.1 Legal Java Expressions | |
|---|---|
| **Name of Expression** | **Example** |
| Additive expression | x+5 |
| Assignment expression | x=5 |
| Array indexing | sizes[11] |
| Method invocation | Triangle.RotateLeft(50) |

In fact, because you don't always need operators, the following are also legal Java expressions, just as they would be legal in C or C++:

arithmetic constant       5

variable       x

◄ See "Opera-
tors," p. 141

As seen in Chapter 9, operators are one of the key categories of tokens in the Java language. Java operators can take one, two, or three operands. Operators that take a single operand are called *unary* or *monadic* operators. Some unary operators come before the operand (these are called *prefix* operators), while others come after the operand (these are called *postfix* operators). These expressions both use unary operators:

−n

k++

Operators that take two operands are called *binary* or *dyadic* operators. These expressions both make use of binary operators:

x=5

a+b

Java also includes one operator—the *conditional* operator—that takes three operands. It is called a *ternary* or *triadic* operator. You'll learn about it a little later in this chapter.

A complete table of all the Java operators is provided at the end of this chapter.

# Arithmetic Expressions

Virtually every programming language provides a mechanism for arithmetic calculations. In Java, such calculations would be performed in arithmetic expressions. Because you are already no doubt familiar with such arithmetic expressions from other languages, let's start with them.

## The Binary Arithmetic Operators

Most of the arithmetic operators in Java are binary operators—they take two operands. The binary arithmetic operators in Java are split into two groups:

- Multiplicative operators. Some examples are multiplication (*), division (/), and remainder after division (%).

- Additive operators. Some examples are addition (+) and subtraction (–).

The multiplication, division, addition, and subtraction operators need little explanation. Each produces a value which is equivalent to the result of the corresponding mathematical operation performed on the same quantities. If you've read chapter 9, you remember that there are some type conversion rules that are important here. You'll handle that issue in more detail in "Type Conversions" later in this chapter. For now, assume that operations on integers produce an integer result, while operations on floating-point values produce floating-point results.

▶ See "Type Conversions," p. 231

## The Remainder Operator (%)

The *remainder operator* deserves some special attention. (C and C++ programmers are familiar with the use of this operator with integer operands.) In general, the expression

```
x%y
```

yields the remainder after y has been divided into x. Consider the following examples:

| Operation | Remainder |
|-----------|-----------|
| 10 % 3 | 1 |
| 15 % 4 | 3 |
| 49 % 7 | 0 |

Java extends the remainder operator a little, by defining its operation with floating-point operands as well. The value it produces is still the "remainder after division," as in the following examples:

| Operation | Remainder |
|-----------|-----------|
| 12%2.5 | 2.0 |
| 15.5%4 | 3.5 |

The technical formula for determining the value of x%y where at least one of x or y is of floating-point type is as follows:

```
x - ( (int)(x/y) * y)
```

The (int) operator is an example of the cast operator. Its syntax is the same as in C and C++. You read about it in more detail later in this chapter.

---

**Note**

In C, the % operator is commonly referred to as *modulus* and can only be applied to integral operands. The term "modulus" comes from the word "modulo," common in algebra and number theory; two integers are said to be "congruent modulo *n*" if their difference is a multiple of *n*.

---

### Unary Arithmetic Operators

There are two unary arithmetic operators in Java:

- Unary arithmetic negation, such as –

- Opposite of the above, such as +

The unary negation simply produces the arithmetic negation of its numeric operand. Thus, an expression like -x simply produces the arithmetic negative of whatever the value is of x. The unary + operator was first introduced in ANSI C, and was introduced primarily for "symmetry" with the unary negation. It simply produces the value of its operand; in other words, it essentially does nothing!

# How Expressions Are Evaluated

At the beginning of this chapter, you learned that expressions are just combinations of operators and operands. And while that definition may be true, it's not always very helpful. Sometimes you need to create and use pretty complex expressions—maybe to perform some kind of complicated calculation or other long involved manipulation. You need deeper understanding of how Java expressions are created and evaluated. In this section, you look at three major tools that will help you in your work with Java expressions: operator associativity, operator precedence, and order of evaluation.

### Operator Associativity

The easiest of the expression rules is associativity. All the arithmetic operators are said to *associate* left-to-right. This means that if the same operator appears more than once in an expression—as in a+b+c, for example—then the leftmost occurrence will be evaluated first, followed by the one to its right, and so on. Consider the following assignment statement:

```
x = a+b+c;
```

In this example, the value of the expression on the right of the = is calculated and assigned to the variable x on the left. In calculating the value on the right, the fact that the + operator associates left-to-right means that the value of a+b is calculated first, and the result is then added to c. The result of that second calculation is what will be assigned to x.

---

**Note**

Notice that in the previous example, a+b+c, the same operator appears twice. It's when the same operator appears more than once—as it does in this case—that you apply the associativity rule.

---

You would use the associativity rule in evaluating the right-hand sides of each of the following assignment statements:

```
volume = length * width * height ;
OrderTotal = SubTotal + Freight + Taxes ;
PerOrderPerUnit = Purchase / Orders / Units ;
```

## Precedence of Java Operators

When you have an expression that involves different operators, the associativity rule doesn't help much. The associativity rule helps figure out how combinations of the same operator would be evaluated. Now you need to know how expressions using combinations of different operators are evaluated.

Like most programming languages, and like basic arithmetic, Java operators conform to strict rules of precedence. The multiplicative operators (*, /, and %) have higher precedence than the additive operators (+ and –). In other words, in a compound expression that incorporates both multiplicative and additive operators, the multiplicative operators are evaluated first. Consider the following assignment statement, which is intended to convert a Fahrenheit temperature to Celsius:

```
Celsius = Fahrenheit - 32 * 5 / 9;
```

Because the * and / operators have higher precedence, the sub-expression 32*5/9 is evaluated first (yielding the result 17) and that value is subtracted from the Fahrenheit variable. Clearly, this isn't going to give you a correct conversion from Fahrenheit to Celsius.

Whenever you need to change the order of evaluation of operators in an expression, you can use brackets. Any expression within brackets is evaluated first. To perform the correct conversion above, you would write:

```
Celsius = ( Fahrenheit - 32 ) * 5 / 9;
```

> **Note**
>
> Interestingly, there are some languages that do not use rules of precedence. Some languages, like APL for example, use a straight left-to-right or right-to-left order of evaluation, regardless of the operators involved.

These precedence rules would help you with the following examples:

```
NewAmount = (Savings + Cash) * ExchangeRate ;
TotalConsumption = (Distance1 + Distance2) * ConsumptionRate ;
```

The precedence of the unary arithmetic operators—in fact all unary operators—is very high; it's above all the other arithmetic operators. This means that in the following example, you multiply the value -5 times the value of Xantham:

```
Ryman = -5 * Xantham;
```

## Order of Evaluation

Many people, when they first learn a language, confuse the issue of operator precedence with order of evaluation. The two are actually quite different. The precedence rules help you determine which operators come first in an expression, and help you determine what the operands are of an operator. For example, in the following line of code, the operands of the * operator are a and (b+c):

```
d = a * (b+c) ;
```

The order of evaluation rules, on the other hand, help you to determine not when *operators* are evaluated, but when *operands* are evaluated. In some programming languages, like C and C++, the order of evaluation is not well-defined. But in Java, the order of evaluation of operands is always well-defined. Here are three rules that should help you remember how an expression will be evaluated:

- For any binary operator, the left-hand operand is evaluated before the right-hand operand.

- Operands are always evaluated fully before the operator is evaluated; for example, before the operation is actually performed.

- If a number of arguments are supplied in a method call, separated by commas, the arguments are evaluated strictly left-to-right.

---

**Note**

In C and C++, there are a number of "loopholes" in the precedence rules: situations in which the order of evaluation of operands is not guaranteed. The three rules you just learned about make things much clearer in Java. There is nothing about the evaluation of Java expressions that is implementation-specific: if an expression is evaluated one way on one Java system, it is evaluated identically in all Java systems.

---

# Type Conversions

As you know, Java is a typed language. In fact, Java can be called strongly typed, because it performs extensive type-checking (to help detect programmer errors) and imposes strict restrictions on when values can be converted from one type to another. There are really two different kinds of conversions. *Explicit conversions* occur when you deliberately change the data type of a value; *ad hoc conversions* can happen without your intervention, even without your knowledge.

## Ad Hoc Type Conversions

Java performs a number of ad hoc type conversions when evaluating expressions, but the rules are simpler and more controlled than in the case of C or even C++.

For unary operators, the situation is very simple: operands of type `byte` or `short` are converted to `int`, and all other operands are left as-is.

For binary operators, the situation is only slightly more complex. For operations involving only integral operands, if either of the operands is `long`, then the other is also converted to `long`; otherwise, both operands are converted to `int`. The result of the expression is an `int`, unless the value produced is so large that a `long` is required. For operations involving at least one floating point operand, if either of the operands is `double`, then the other is also converted to `double` and the result of the expression is also a double; otherwise, both operands are converted to `float`, and the result of the expression is also a float. Consider the expressions in listing 12.1.

---

**Listing 12.1  Some Mixed Expressions Showing Type Conversions**

```
short Width;
long Length, Area;
double TotalCost, CostPerFoot;

// In the multiplication below, Width will be converted to a
// long, and the result of the calculation will be a long.
Area = Length * Width;

// In the division below, Area will be converted to a double,
// and the result of the calculation will be a double
CostPerFoot = TotalCost / Area ;
```

---

## Conversions and the Cast Operator

The cast operator consists of a type name within round brackets. It is a unary operator with high precedence and comes before its operand. The cast operator produces the value of its operand, converted to the type named within the brackets. You saw an example of the cast operator in the previous section called "Remainder Operator." It was:

```
x - ( (int)(x/y) * y)
```

When x is divided by y in this example, the type of the result is either floating point or integer, depending on the types of x and y. Either way, the value of x/y is explicitly converted to type `int` by the cast operator.

◄ See "Declaring a Class," p. 168

Note that not all conversions are legal. Values of any arithmetic type can be cast to any other arithmetic type. Boolean values cannot be cast to any other type. Casting objects is a little more tricky, but the general rule is that an object of one class can be cast to a superclass but not to a subclass.

Because casting involves an unconditional type conversion (if the conversion is legal), it is also sometimes known as *type coercion*.

# Addition of Strings

In Java, strings are native data types, and the concatenation of strings is supported using the + operator. The behavior of the + operator with strings is just

The Java Language

what you'd expect. In the following expression, the strings referenced by variables String1 and String2 will be concatenated:

```
String1 + String2
```

If a non-string value is added to a string, it is converted to a string before concatenation. This means, for example, that a numeric value can be added to a string. The numeric value is converted to an appropriate sequence of digit characters which are concatenated to the original string. All the following are legal string concatenations:

```
"George " + "Burns"
"Burns" + " and " + "Allen"
"Fahrenheit" + 451
"Answer is: " + true
```

# Comparison Operators

Java incorporates a full slate of operators for comparing two or more quantities. There are really two different categories of these operators:

- Relational operators. Designed to determine ordering: whether some quantity is greater than another, whether some letter is less than another, and so on.

- Equality operators. Don't help determine ordering; they just tell you whether two values are the same or not.

## The Relational Operators

Java supports the *relational operators* in the following list. Each takes numeric operands (integral or floating point) and produces a Boolean result.

| Operator | Boolean Result |
| --- | --- |
| < | Less than |
| <= | Less than or equal to |
| > | Greater than |
| >= | Greater than or equal to |

The precedence of the relational operators is below that of the arithmetic operators, but above that of the assignment operators. Thus, the following two assignment statements produce identical results:

```
result1 = a+b < c*d ;
result2 = (a+b) < (c*d) ;
```

The associativity is left-to-right, but this feature isn't really very useful. It may not be immediately obvious why, but consider the following expression:

```
a < b < c
```

The first expression, a<b, is evaluated first, and produces a value of `true` or `false`. This value then would have to be compared to c. Since a Boolean cannot be used in a relational expression, the compiler will generate a syntax error.

> **Note**
>
> In C and C++, the relational operators produce an integer value of 0 or 1, which can be used in any expression expecting an integer. Expressions like the following are legal in C or C++, and will generate compiler errors in Java:
>
> ```
> RateArray [ day1 < day2 ]
> NewValue = OldValue + ( NewRate > OldRate ) * Interest;
> ```

## The Equality Operators

The following *equality operators* are very similar to the relational operators, with slightly lower precedence:

| Operator | Boolean Result |
|----------|----------------|
| ==       | Is equal to    |
| !=       | Is not equal to |

The equality operators can take operands of virtually any type. In the case of the primitive data types, the values of the operands are compared. However, if the operands are some other type of object, the operands must refer to exactly the same objects. Consider the following example:

```
String1 == String2
```

In this example, String1 and String2 must refer to the same string—not to two different strings that happen to contain the same sequence of characters, but to exactly the same string.

The associativity of these operators is again left-to-right. You've seen that the associativity of the relational operators is really not useful to you as a programmer. The associativity of the equality operators is only slightly more useful. Take a look at the following example:

```
StartTemp == EndTemp == LastRace
```

Here the variables `StartTemp` and `EndTemp` are compared first, and the Boolean result of that comparison is compared to `LastRace`, which must be Boolean. If `LastRace` is of some non-Boolean type, the compiler will generate an error.

---

**Caution**

Writing code that depends on this kind of subtlety is considered to be extremely poor form. Even if you understand it completely when you write it, chances are you'll be as mystified as everyone else when you try to read it a few weeks or months later. Try to use constructs in your code that are easily read. If there is some reason that you must use an expression like the one just given, be sure to use comments to explain how the expression operates and, if possible, why you've chosen to implement your algorithm that way.

---

# Logical Expressions

In computing, it is not uncommon to need to combine values using the logical operations of And, Or, and Exclusive Or. You are probably familiar with these operations from previous experience. When you are programming in Java, you have the ability to perform such logical operations in two different ways:

- *Short-turn operators*. Only operate on Boolean values.
- *Bitwise operators*. Operate on each bit in a pair of integral operands.

## The Bitwise Operators

The *bitwise operators* in Java allow you to perform a logical operation on a pair of Boolean operands, or on each bit in a pair of integral operands. Such an operation is relatively rare, but might be necessary when you're having to manipulate the individual bits in a control word from a database record, or when manipulating hardware registers or performing other low-level programming. These operations also potentially enable you to pack data more densely when memory is at a premium, though the extra processing overhead and programming difficulty would rarely make this worthwhile.

Begin by making sure that you're comfortable with the idea of an integral value being made up of individual bits. (If this is old hat to you, feel free to skip a few paragraphs to the discussion of the operators).

For now, consider only integral values of type byte—for example, occupying one byte (eight bits) of memory. Each of the eight bits can have the value of 0 or 1. The value of the whole quantity is determined by using *base 2 arithmetic*, meaning that the rightmost bit means a value of 0 or 1; the next bit means a value of 0 or 2; the next means a value of 0 or 4, and so on. Table 12.2 shows a number of examples.

| Table 12.2 Some Base 10 Values and Their Base 2 Equivalents | | | | | | | | |
|---|---|---|---|---|---|---|---|---|
| Base 10 Value | 128 | 64 | 32 | 16 | 8 | 4 | 2 | 1 |
| 17 | 0 | 0 | 0 | 0 | 1 | 0 | 0 | 0 | 1 |
| 63 | 0 | 0 | 0 | 1 | 1 | 1 | 1 | 1 | 1 |
| 131 | 0 | 1 | 0 | 0 | 0 | 0 | 0 | 1 | 1 |
| 75 | 0 | 0 | 1 | 0 | 0 | 1 | 0 | 1 | 1 |

The numeric quantities in table 12.2 are all positive integers, and I've done that on purpose. Negative numbers are a little more difficult to represent. In fact, for any integral quantity in Java, the leftmost bit is reserved for the sign-bit. If the sign-bit is 1, then the value is negative. The rest of the bits in a negative number are also determined a little differently than the way I've described, but don't worry about that now. Floating-point numbers also have their own special binary representation, but that's beyond the scope of this book.

The three binary bitwise operators perform the logical operations of And, Or, and Exclusive Or (sometimes called Xor) on each bit in turn. The three operators are:

- Bitwise AND: &
- Bitwise OR: |
- Bitwise Exclusive OR:

The operands of the bitwise operators can also be Boolean, in addition to being of any integral type. In the case of operands of integral type, the operation is performed on each bit in the operands in turn. In case you're a bit rusty on the rules for logical operations, table 12.3 summarizes them for you.

**Table 12.3   Summary of Logical Operations**

| bit1 | bit2 | bit1 & bit2 | bit1 \| bit2 | bit1  bit2 |
|------|------|-------------|--------------|------------|
| true | true | true | true | false |
| true | false | false | true | true |
| false | true | false | true | true |
| false | false | false | false | false |

Table 12.4 shows the results of each of these operations performed on two sample values.

**Table 12.4   Bitwise Operation Examples**

| Expression | Binary Representation |
|------------|-----------------------|
| 11309 | 0010 1100 0010 1101 |
| 798 | 0000 0011 0001 1110 |
| 11309 & 798 | 0000 0000 0000 1100 |
| 11309 \| 798 | 0010 1111 0011 1111 |
| 11309 ^ 798 | 0010 1111 0011 0011 |

The precedence of the bitwise logical operators is below that of the equality operators.

◄ See "Bitwise Arithmetic Operators," p. 144

## The "Short-Turn" Logical Operators

There are two additional binary logical operators:

- Logical And: &&
- Logical Or: ||

These operators behave very much as the bitwise operators do, with two main exceptions. First, the logical operators may only take Boolean operands. Second, the operands are evaluated left-to-right; if the value of the expression is determined after evaluating the left-hand operand, the right-hand operand will not be evaluated. In the following example, if x is indeed less than y, then m and n are be compared:

```
(x<y) || (m>n)
```

If the left-hand side of the previous expression produces the Boolean value true, then the result of the whole expression is true, regardless of the result of the comparison m>n. Note that in the following expression using the bitwise operator, m and n are compared regardless of the values of x and y:

```
(x<y) ¦ (m>n)
```

The precedence of the two logical operators is below that of the bitwise operators just discussed.

### The Unary Logical Operators

There are two *unary logical operators*:

- Logical negation of Boolean operand: !
- Bitwise negation of integral or Boolean operand: ˜

> **Note**
>
> For integral operands, this operator is the "bit flipper"—each bit in its operand is toggled. What was 0 becomes 1, what was 1 becomes 0.

Both these operators have high precedence, equivalent to that of the other unary operators.

Take a look at the following example, which shows a combination of the logical negation and the short-turn logical &.

```
if (!dbase.EOF & dbase.RecordIsValid() )
```

Because the logical negation has high precedence, it is evaluated first. If EOF refers to End of File, you might check in the first operation to see if you hit end of file on this database. If you haven't, then the second operand is evaluated, which in this case is a method invocation that might determine the validity of the record. The key to understanding is that if the first operand is false—in other words you *have* hit end of file—then you don't check for a valid record.

## The Shift Operators

There are three *shift operators* in Java:

- Left shift: <<
- Signed right shift: >>
- Unsigned right shift: >>>

These are binary operators, taking integral operands. The left-hand operand is the value to be shifted, while the right-hand operand is the number of bits to shift by. The left shift and the unsigned right shift populate the vacated spaces with zeroes. The signed right shift populates the vacated spaces with the sign bit. The following examples are for 8-bit quantities of type byte, but the same principles would apply to larger quantities:

| x   | x<<2     | x>>2     | x>>>2              |
|-----|----------|----------|--------------------|
| 31  | 00011111 | 01111100 | 0000011100000111   |
| –17 | 11101111 | 10111100 | 1111101100111011   |

The precedence of the shift operators is above that of the relational operators, but below the additive arithmetic operators.

C and C++ programmers should note that while the right shift of signed values in those languages is platform-specific behavior that will vary from system to system, all shifts in Java are well-defined.

◀ See "Bitwise Shifting Operators," p. 145

### Hardware Architecture

The C and C++ languages attempt to be general enough to match the underlying hardware as closely as possible—regardless of what that hardware architecture might be. Programmers using those languages endure considerable complexity in the language as a result. The Java designers took a different approach. Java assumes an underlying hardware architecture that uses a 2's-complement representation for negative numbers, and that uses the IEEE 754 standard for floating-point arithmetic. The result is that Java programmers only have to learn the behavior of one platform. There is virtually nothing in the Java language that is "platform-specific."

# The Conditional Operator

The conditional operator is the one ternary or triadic operator in Java, and operates as it does in C and C++. It takes the following form:

```
expression1 ? expression2 : expression3
```

In this syntax, expression1 must produce a Boolean value. If this value is true, then expression2 is evaluated, and its result is the value of the conditional. If expression1 is false, then expression3 is evaluated, and its result is the value of the conditional.

Consider the following examples. The first is using the conditional operator to determine the maximum of two values; the second is determining the minimum of two values; the third is determining the absolute value of a quantity:

```
BestReturn = Stocks > Bonds ? Stocks : Bonds ;
LowSales = JuneSales < JulySales ? JuneSales : JulySales ;
Distance = Site1-Site2 > 0 ? Site1-Site2 : Site2 - Site1 ;
```

In reviewing these examples, think about the precedence rules, and convince yourself that none of the three examples requires any brackets in order to be evaluated correctly.

# The Increment and Decrement Operators

The increment and decrement operators are unary operators that add and subtract, respectively, the value 1 (or 1.0) from the operand:

- Increment: ++
- Decrement: −−

The operand must be a variable, and may be of any numeric type. The operator may come before the operand (called the prefix case) or after the operand (called the postfix case). In the prefix case, the value of the expression is the value of the operand before incrementing. In the postfix case, the value of the expression is the value of the operand after incrementing. Table 12.5 illustrates the two cases.

**Table 12.5  Comparing the Prefix and Postfix Increment Operators**

| Prefix Case | Postfix Case |
| --- | --- |
| Length = 12.5; | Length = 12.5; |
| NewLength = ++Length; | OldLength = Length++; |
| Following these two statements, | Following these two statements, |
| Length has value 13.5 | Length has value 13.5 |
| NewLength has value 13.5 | OldLength has value 12.5 |

◀ See "Increment/Decrement Operators," p. 143

The increment and decrement operators have high precedence equivalent to that of the other unary operators.

# The Assignment Operators

Java has two different kinds of assignment operators: the simple assignment, and the compound assignment. All the assignment operators have low precedence.

## The Simple Assignment

The simple assignment is the operator you are probably already familiar with:

    =  assignment

This binary operator takes the value of its right-hand operand and stores it in the left-hand operand. The left-hand operand must be a variable. The value of the right-hand operand is converted, if necessary, to the data type of the left-hand operand.

> **Note**
>
> In C, almost any data type can be converted to almost any other across an assignment statement. In Java, conversions between numeric data types are only performed if they do not result in loss of precision or magnitude. Any attempted conversion that would result in such a loss produces a compiler error.

Like most other operators, the assignment operator also produces a result, that being the value of the left-hand operand after the assignment, which means that a statement like the following is legal, if extremely bad form:

    a = (b=7) + 3;

This assigns the value 7 to b, and the value 10 to a.

The assignment operators associate right-to-left, so that the two assignments below are both legal and produce identical results:

    a=b=c;
    a=(b=c);

In each case, the value of c is assigned to b, after which the value of b is assigned to a. Multiple assignments of this form are generally considered to be poor form.

## Compound Assignment Operators

The compound assignment operators have the following form:

```
*= %=    +=      -=      <<=     >>=
/= &=    ^=      |=      >>>=
```

The compound assignment operator behaves as follows, for a binary operator op:

```
expression1 op= expression2
```

is equivalent to

```
expression1 = expression1 op expression2
```

except that expression1 is only evaluated once. All the following are legal assignment statements in Java:

```
Location += DownShift ;
NewValue -= Taxes ;
Loan *= InterestRate ;
Cost /= Units ;
BitMask <<= 3 ;
```

> **Note**
>
> The simple assignment operator takes operands of virtually any type; the value on the right is converted to the type of the variable on the left, with a compiler error if the conversion cannot be performed. The compound assignments, on the other hand, because they depend on the underlying binary operations, can only be used with operands of primitive type.

# The Instanceof Operator

The binary instanceof operator takes two operands: an object on the left and a class name on the right. If the object on the left is indeed an instance of the class on the right (or any of its subclasses), then this operator returns a Boolean value of true. Otherwise, it returns false. The use of instanceof in the following example prevents an exception being thrown at runtime in the initialization of my_car:

```
if ( your_car instanceof MotorVehicle )
    MotorVehicle my_car =(MotorVehicle) your_car;
```

# The "High Precedence" Operators

Here are the last three Java operators:

- Field selection: .
- Array subscripting: []
- Method invocation: ()

These three operators have very high precedence—the highest in the Java language.

# Of Special Interest to C Programmers

Because Java is an evolutionary outgrowth of C and C++, it's understandable that the expression syntax for the three languages is so similar. If you already know C, it's important that you keep in mind that the three languages are only similar—not identical.

The most important difference, without question, is that order of evaluation is guaranteed in Java, and is generally undefined or implementation-specific in C:

◄ See "Order of Evaluation," p. 230

- In simple expressions like a+b
- In bizarre expressions like a[i]=(i=7);
- In method invocations like a.b(c,d,e);

In Java, the remainder, increment, and decrement operators are defined for all numeric data types; in C only for integers.

Relational and equality operators in Java produce a Boolean result; in C they produce results of type int. Furthermore, the logical operators in Java are restricted to Boolean operands.

Java supports native operations on strings—including string concatenation and string assignment. C does not support strings.

In C, using the right-shift operator on a signed quantity results in implementation-specific behavior. Java, by using two different right-shift operators—one which pads with zeroes and the other that does sign-extension—avoids this confusion.

# Summary—The Operator Table

You've now learned about all the Java operators—the building blocks of Java expressions. Here is the final precedence table (see table 12.6) with the highest precedence operators at the top. Operators on the same line are of equal precedence. All these operators associate left-to-right, except the unary operators, assignments, and the conditional. For any single operator, operand evaluation is strictly left-to-right, and all operands are evaluated before operations are performed.

**Table 12.6   The Complete Java Operator Table**

| Description | Operators |
|---|---|
| High Precedence | . [] () |
| Unary | + – ~ ! ++ ––      instanceof |
| Multiplicative | * / % |
| Additive | + – |
| Relational | < <= >= > > |
| Equality | == != |
| Bitwise And | & |
| Bitwise Xor | ^ |
| Bitwise Or | \| |
| Short-turn And | && |
| Short-turn Or | \|\| |
| Conditional | ?: |
| Assignment | =  *op=* |

# CHAPTER 13
# Statements in Depth

*by Jay Cross*

Statements in Java are like sentences in human languages. In a way, the demand that things expressed in a computer language be very precise and error free makes it more difficult to use a computer language than a human one. On the other hand, in a computer language, there is generally only one tense (the imperative), as opposed to the thirty-eight or so that make up the Romance languages. There are only a hundred or so predefined keywords and other tokens. Even throwing in all the commercially available classes and their public methods still leave Java much smaller than the hundred thousand to half a million words that English has incorporated. Java's keywords, operators, classes, and methods are very seldom as heavily overloaded as words in human language. It is always possible to determine which definition of a term is intended in Java statements.

Expressing something is more than just stringing terms together. In human languages or computer languages you must make statements, and statements have specific forms. The forms of Java statements are described in the following sections.

In this chapter about Java statements you will learn:

- What statements in Java are
- What blocks of statements are, and where they can be used
- What empty statements are
- How and why to label a statement
- How to construct declaration statements
- What an expression statement is
- Control flow using selection, iteration, and jump statements

- What synchronization and Guarding statements are
- What happens if the compiler finds an unreachable statement

# Blocks and Statements

Methods and Static initializers in Java are defined by blocks of statements. A block of statements is a series of statements enclosed within curly braces ({}). When a statement's form calls for a statement or substatement as a part, a block may be inserted in the substatement's place.

A block of statements has its own local scope for the statements within it. This means that local variables may be declared within this block, which are unavailable outside the block, and whose very existence is extinguished when the block has completed execution. (In most systems, they are stored on a stack.)

There is nothing in the definition of Java that prevents the programmer from breaking code into blocks even though they are not specifically called for, but it is seldom done. The following code fragment demonstrates this legal but seldom done technique:

```
String Batter;
Short Inning, Out, Strikes;
Batsman Casey;                          // Object of class Batsman.
...
If ((Inning == 9) && (Out==2) && (Batter.equals("Casey"))) {
    Casey.manner("ease");
    Casey.bearing("pride");
    {
                                        // Begins new block for no
                                        // ➥reason.
        int OnlyExistsInThisBlock = 1;
        Casey.face("smile");
        Casey.hat("lightly doff");
    }
                                        // Ends superfluous
                                        // ➥blocking.

}
```

Notice that this fragment contains two complete blocks. One is the substatement of the If statement, and the other is the unneeded block, which contains the unused integer OnlyExistsInThisBlock. Experienced programmers know that if there are two blocks, A and B, A cannot contain part of B unless A contains all of B. Syntactically this is because the curly braces ({}) are always interpereted in a nested fashion.

# Empty Statements

It is legal to create an empty statement in Java. This is a statement that holds a place in the code but does nothing. Some programmers find this handy for holding labels or for some other trick that may make program maintenance a bit easier. To the compiler, it looks like an extra semicolon. The following code fragment shows four empty statements together.

```
while (strike++ < 2) {
    Casey.RubHands("dirt");
    Casey.WipeHands("shirt");
    ;;;;                        // four empty statement here for emphasis.
    Casey.WatchPitch();
}
```

# Labeled Statements

Any statement in Java can have a label. The actual label has the same properties as any other identifier; it cannot have the same name as a keyword or already declared local identifier. If it has the same name as a variable, method, or type name that is available to this block, then within that block, the new label takes precedence and that outside variable, method, or type is hidden. It has the scope of the current block. The label is followed by a colon.

Labels are only used by the break and continue Jump statements described below. The details of this use are given in the section entitled "Jump Statements."

An example of labeled statements appears in the following code fragment:

```
writhing:
    Pitcher.GrindsBall("Hip");
    Casey.eye("Defiance Gleams");
    Casey.lip("Curling Sneer");
pitch:    while (strike++ < 2) {
            if (strike < 2) continue pitch;
            break writhing;
    }
```

The statement, writhing, is simple labeling of an expression statement, in this case, a method call from a rather complicated object called Pitcher. The statement pitch is labeling an iteration statement (while). This label is used as a parameter for the continue statement.

# Declarations

In short, a declaration statement defines a variable, whether class, interface, array, object, or primitive type. The form of such a statement depends on which of the five types is being declared.

## Class Declaration

◀ Classes and their declarations are described more fully in chapter 11.

A class declaration is composed of the following six parts which are put together in this order.

| | | |
|---|---|---|
| **Class modifiers** | **Optional** | These are the keywords abstract, final, or public. One class cannot have both final and abstract as modifiers. |
| **Class** | **Required** | the keyword class. |
| **Identifier** | **Required** | This has the same properties as any other identifier. See Chapter 9. |
| **Super** | **Optional** | the keyword extends followed by a type name. The type must be an accessible class, that is not final. |
| **Interfaces** | **Optional** | the keyword implements followed by a comma-separated list of interfaces. |
| **Class Body** | **Required** | See Chapter 11. |

## Interface Declaration

◀ Interfaces and their declarations are described more fully in chapter 12.

An interface declaration is composed of the following five parts, which are put together in this order.

| | | |
|---|---|---|
| **Interface modifiers** | **Optional** | These are the keywords abstract or public. All interfaces are abstract, but the modifier may be used for clarity. |
| **Interface** | **Required** | the keyword interface. |
| **Identifier** | **Required** | This has the same properties as any other identifier. See Chapter 9. |
| **Extends Interfaces** | **Optional** | the keyword extends followed by a comma-separated list of interface identifiers. |
| **Interface Body** | **Required** | See Chapter 12. |

## Array Declaration

Array declarations are composed of the following parts.

| | | |
|---|---|---|
| **Array modifiers** | **Optional** | These are the keywords, `public`, `protected`, `private`, or `synchronized`. |
| **TypeName** | **Required** | The name of the type or class being arrayed. |
| **brackets** | **Required** | [ ]. |
| **Initialization** | **Optional** | For more details about initialization see the end of Chapter 10. |
| **Semicolon** | **Required** | ; |

◀ Arrays and their declarations are described more fully in chapter 12.

## Object Declaration

When an object is declared, a reference is created for it. That reference only points to an object if an object is initialized or assigned to that reference. An object declaration has the following parts:

| | | |
|---|---|---|
| **Object modifiers** | **Optional** | These are the keywords, `public`, `protected`, `private`, or `synchronized`. |
| **TypeName** | **Required** | The name of the class that this object is an instance of. |
| **Initialization** | **Optional** | For more details about initialization see Chapter 11. |
| **Semicolon** | **Required** | ; |

◀ Objects and their declarations are described more fully in chapter 11.

## Primitive Type Declaration

When a variable of a primitive type is declared, storage space for that variable is created. If there is no value assigned to it by an explicit initialization clause, it takes on the default value which is zero for the numeric and char types, and false for Booleans. A declaration for a primitive type is composed of the following parts:

| | | |
|---|---|---|
| **Array modifiers** | **Optional** | These are the keywords, `public`, `protected`, `private`, or `synchronized`. |
| **TypeName** | **Required** | The name of the type: `boolean`, `char`, `byte`, `short`, `int`, `long`, `float`, or `double`. |
| **Initialization** | **Optional** | For more details about initialization see chapter 10. |
| **Semicolon** | **Required** | ; |

◀ Primitive types and their declarations are described more fully in chapter 10.

**II**

**The Java Language**

# Expression Statements

The Java Language Specification lists seven kinds of Expression statements. They are Assignment, Pre-increment, Pre-decrement, Post-Increment, Post-decrement, Method call, and Allocation Expression.

All of the Expression statements are terminated with a semicolon.

All side effects of an expression statement will have taken effect before the next statement is executed.

A Java Assignment statement may have an expression on the right side of the assignment operator (=). This expression can be any of the seven types of expression statements. Only the right side of such an assignment may be cast.

Note that even though Java is fairly strongly typed, it is legal for the return value of a nonvoid method to be called without assignment (implicitly casting it as void).

The following code fragment gives a sample of each of the seven types of expression statements:

```
Inning = 9;                 // Assignment: put the value 9 in
                            //    Inning.
++strike;                   // PreIncrement: adds 1 to strike before
                            //        the statement is evaluated.
--strike;                   // Predecrement: subtracts 1 from strike
                            //        before the statement is
                            //    evaluated.
pitch++;                    // PostIncrement: adds 1 to pitch after
                            //        the statement is evaluated.
pitch--;                    // Postdecrement: subtracts 1 from pitch
                            //        after the statement is
                            //    evaluated.
Umpire.Said("Strike One"); // Method Call: Invokes the method 'Said'
                            //        for the object Umpire, with
                            //        "Strike One" as a parameter.
byte Score[][];
Score = new byte[2][12];   // Allocation Expression: allocates
                            //    space
                            //        for the array 'Score'.
```

◀ More details about the use of the allocation statement for creating space for instances of arrays and objects can be found in chapters 10 and 11.

An expression statement may be considerably more complex than those in the preceding fragment, and parentheses may be used to affect the order in which the various subexpressions are evaluated.

# Selection Statements

Java supports three types of selection statements: if, if-else, and switch. These are very similar to the statements of the same type found in C and C++.

## *if* statements

An if statement tests a Boolean variable or expression to determine whether to execute a statement or block of statements. If the Boolean is true, the block is executed; if not, program control passes to the next statement after the block. An example of an if statement is shown in the following code fragment:

```
if (umpire.says.equals("Strike two")){    // equals method returns boolean
    Croud.cry("Fraud");                    // method call
    Strike++;                              // last statement in if block.
}
Casey.face("Christian charity");           // 1st statement after if block.
```

In this example if the object umpire's method **"says"** returns a string "Strike two," then the block will be executed, and control is passed to the next statement. If the string returned says something else (such as "Strike one," "Strike too," "STRIKE TWO," or "Play Ball") then the next statement executed will be the call to the face method for the object Casey.

## *if-else* statements

An if-else statement is very similar to the if statement, except that it has an else clause. An else clause passes control to a statement or block if the Boolean evaluated in the if portion of the statement was false. An example of an if-else statement appears in the following code fragment:

```
if (strike != 2)
    Casey.lip("Curling Sneer");            // single substatement
                                           ➥(could have been a block)
else {
    Casey.teeth("Clenched in hate");       // block of
                                           ➥substatements
                                           (could have been single)
    Casey.bat.pound("Plate");
}
```

In this example, the if clause has one statement. The else clause controls a block of two statements. Experienced programmers will recognize that the one substatement of the if clause could have been an if statement, which would lead to some ambiguity as to which if the else was attached to. In the absence of curly braces, Java resolves this ambiguity by connecting the else with the next most recent "elseless" if statement in the block. If there are none, a compile-time error is generated.

## *Switch* Statements

A switch statement permits passing control to one of many statements within its block of substatements, depending on the value of the expression in the statement. Control is passed to the first statement following a case label with the same value as the expression. If there are none, control passes to the first statement after the "default" label. If there is no default label, control passes to the first statement after the switch block. The switch expression and case label constants must all evaluate to either byte, short, char, or int. No two case labels in the same switch block can have the same value.

Labels do not affect the control flow. Control continues on through one of these labels as if it weren't there. As a consequence, multiple labels can precede the same line of code. As a general practice, programmers put a break statement at the end of each labeled section of code to prevent executing more than one set of statements.

An example of the switch statement is included in the following code fragment:

```
switch (strike) {
case 0:
case 1:
    Casey.lip("Curling Sneer");
    break;
case 2:
    Casey.teeth("Clenched in hate");
    Casey.bat.pound("Plate");
    break;
default:
    System.out.println("Strike out of range");
}
```

In this example, we assume that strike is a compatible integer type (e.g., int). Control passes to the correct line, depending on the value of strike. If strike doesn't have one of the values it should have, a programmer-defined error message is printed.

switch statements are much like the statements of the same name in C and C++.

# Iteration Statements

Programmers use iteration statements to control sequences of statements that are repeated according to run-time conditions.

Java supports three types of iteration statements: while, do, and for. These are very similar to the statements of the same type found in C and C++, with the exception that continue and break statements in Java have optional parameters which can change their behavior (compared with C and C++, where these statements have no parameters) within the substatement blocks. You will read more about the use of parameters in break and continue statements later in this chapter.

## *while* Statements

The `while` statement tests a Boolean variable or expression, and if it is true, executes the substatement or block repeatedly until it is false. When the variable or expression is false, control is passed to the next statement after the `while` statement's substatement or block. An example of a `while` statement appears in the following code fragment.

```
while (Casey.RoundingTheBasepads==true) {
    Crowd.cry("Hooray for Casey");
}
```

In this example, it is clear that the expression might not be true initially, and if not, the block in the substatement will never be executed. If it is true, this block of code is executed repeatedly until it is not true, or until a `jump` statement (not appearing in this code fragment) is executed, and passes control to a statement outside the loop.

## *do* Statements

The do statement is much like the `while` statement. In fact, it has a `while` clause at the end. Like the `while` statement above, the expression in the `while` statement must be a Boolean. The primary reason that a programmer chooses to use a do statement instead of a `while` statement is if the block of code needs to be executed at least once, no matter what.

```
do {
    Crowd.cry("Kill the Umpire!");
} while (umpire.says.equals("Strike two"));
```

In this example, the method `Crowd.cry` is invoked at least once no matter what. But as long as the `umpire.says` method returns the string `"Strike two"`, the `Crowd.cry` method is called over and over again.

## *for* Statements

`for` statements are the most complicated of the three iteration statements. Yet `for` statements are complicated by some useful features, which make them the most used of the three. The `for` statement is composed of:

| | |
|---|---|
| **for (** | The text string `"for"` followed by optional whitespace, followed by an open paren "(" |
| **initialization clause** | Contains a comma-separated series of declaration and assignment statements terminated by a semicolon. The declarations have a scope of the `for` statement and its substatements only. The assignments are made once, before the first iteration of the substatement or block. |

| | |
|---|---|
| **test clause** | Contains a Boolean variable or expression which is evaluated once per loop. If it is false, control passes to the next statement after the `for` statement and its substatement or block. This clause is terminated by a semicolon. |
| **increment clause** | Contains a comma-separated series of expressions which are evaluated once per iteration of the loop. These are usually used to increment an index that is being tested in the test clause. There is no semicolon at the end of this clause. |
| **)** | This is the close paren character ")" |
| **substatement or block** | This is the block of code which is to be repeated. |

An example of a `for` loop appears in the following code fragment:

```
for (int ball=0, int strike=0; (ball<4) && (strike<3);
➥System.out.println("Here's the
pitch"), Pitcher.pitch()) {
    if (Ump.CallPitch.equals("Strike")) {
        strike++;
        System.out.println("Strike " + strike);
    }
    else if (Ump.CallPitch.equals("Ball")) {
        ball++;
        System.out.println("Ball " + ball);
    }
    else
        break;
}
```

In this example, the initialization clause declares and initializes two variables, `ball` and `strike`. The test clause returns `false` if either ball four or strike three is called, and the iteration clause calls `println`, and the pitch method for the object `Pitcher`.

The loop itself prints the ball or strike number, and goes back to the top of the loop. If `Ump.CallPitch` does not return a ball or strike, the loop is exited prematurely. It is beyond the scope of this fragment to account for foul balls and do-overs.

## *Jump* Statements

Java has four kinds of `Jump` statements : `break`, `continue`, `return`, and `throw`.

## *break* Statements

The substatement blocks of loops and switch statements can be broken out of by use of the break statement. An unlabeled break statement passes control to the next line after the current (innermost) iteration (while, do, or for loop) or switch statement. With a label, control may be passed to a statement with that label in the current method. If there is a finally clause of a currently open try statement within the loop, that clause will be executed before control is passed.

You will find a description of the try, catch, and finally statements below, with a more detailed explanation of their use in chapters that explore writing applets.

Those who mock good programming practices will be pleased to note that the labeled break statement can be made to act as the expunged-from-Java goto statement.

The code fragments in this chapter contain several examples of unlabeled break statements.

## *continue* statements

A continue statement may only appear within the substatement block of an iteration statement (while, do, or for). The effect of the unlabeled continue statement is to skip the remainder of the statements in the innermost iteration statement's block, and go on to the next pass through the loop. The label parameter permits the programmer to choose which level of nested iteration statements to continue with.

If there is a finally clause for a currently open try statement within the indicated level of nesting, that clause will be executed before control is passed.

## *return* statements

A return statement passes control to the caller of the method, constructor, or static initializer containing the return statement. If the return statement is in a method that is not declared void, it may have a parameter of the same type as the method.

If there is a finally clause for a currently open try statement, that clause will be executed before control is passed.

## *throw* statements

A throw statement signals a run-time exception. It takes an argument which is an object. This object is normally of a subclass of Exception.

When the throw statement is encountered, execution is suspended. Levels of enclosing statements (statements with substatements or blocks) are closed until a catch clause is found with a formal argument which is a superclass of the type in the throw statement.

The finally clause of any try statements are executed along the way as they are encountered.

More details about throw statements are available in Chapter 18.

# Synchronization Statements

Java has a keyword synchronized which some sources list as a type of statement, and others list as a modifier in declarations. It is part of Java being multithreaded, and is covered in more detail in chapters 23, 24, and 25.

# Guarding Statements

Java has three kinds of statements called Guarding Statements. These are try, catch, and finally. These statements are used to set up exception handling around a method which could possibly generate an exception. To some limited degree they are like the switch-case-default statements mentioned previously. In this analogy, the try statement is like the switch statement. Instead of an integer parameter, the try statement takes a block of code. If an exception occurs which is not handled by some inner try-catch-finally type handler, then execution of the block is suspended, and control is passed to the catch statement with the right object type as an argument.

The catch statements have the exception handler objects as arguments.

The finally statements permit wrapping up essential things (such as closing files) before execution is halted.

# Unreachable Statements

It is possible to write a method that has lines of code which can never be reached. Lines between an unconditional return statement, and the next label, or end of the block are the clearest example. It can be written, but it can't be compiled. A compile-time error is generated. ❖

# CHAPTER 14

# Extending Java with Standard Language

*by Suresh K. Jois*

This chapter explores the topic of interfacing Java language programs with programs (or functions) written in other languages.

In this chapter, you will learn

- The pros and cons of outfitting non-Java language code with Java modules
- How to interface a simple C language program to a Java program
- How to interface C++ with Java
- Alternative ways to get non-Java programs to work with Java programs
- Sources of further information on this topic

## Adapting Software to the Internet Era

The Internet and its core enabling technologies, such as the Web, Java, and VRML, have rapidly emerged from the backwaters of university and corporate research labs and have been transformed into mainstream, consumer-oriented mass media. These new media are rapidly complementing or even replacing traditional consumer electronic devices and creating completely new application markets.

This wave of change and emergence of new media markets has created entirely new applications as well as repositioning opportunities for old applications (software, hardware, and services).

One good example of such repositioning of application software is the Internet-enabling of personal finance software, which used to be strictly confined to the users' desktops. But with additional modules added on to provide network connectivity, the old accounting and check balancing programs are being transformed almost entirely into a personalized virtual bank branch office.

The emergence of executable content and transportable code technologies, such as Java, will cause even more transformations in traditional software applications. But in the face of extremely rapid evolution of Internet technology standards, what is the best strategy for vendors of existing stand-alone, shrink-wrapped software to leverage their existing code-base and customer-base and rapidly co-opt emerging technologies, such as Java? One possible answer to this question—getting legacy code written in non-Java languages, such as C and C++, to work with Java—is the topic of this chapter.

### Native Methods: Co-Opting Non-Java Programs into the Java Method Invocation System

The approach described in this chapter is a standard feature of Java called *native methods*. The term *native* refers to such languages as C and C++. To interface with Java, functions written in these languages are compiled into dynamically loadable objects (dynamic shared libraries on UNIX platforms and DLLs on Microsoft Windows 95/NT platforms) and encapsulated inside a Java method call. At runtime, Java invokes these functions much like it would call any Java method. Thus, Java methods implemented in a language other than Java are called native methods.

# Mixing Java with Other Languages: What You Gain and What You Lose

The unique features of Java that make it very suitable for networked applications, including executable content using applets, are its properties of full OOP model, robustness, compactness, security, dynamic, and so on. Java has been designed from the ground up to avoid several deficiencies found in older languages, such as C and C++. Mixing non-Java programs with Java code could undermine some of these unique attributes of Java.

On the other hand, Java is so new that there is not yet a whole lot of production quality, commercial grade software base out on the market. Also, software engineers well versed in large-scale Java development are still a minority, and there is a huge installed base of C and C++ software. This makes a compelling case for taking the native method interface route to quickly migrate non-Java.

The following is a list of pros and cons of constructing a system containing Java and native methods.

Pros:

- You can quickly leverage and co-opt existing code base.

- You can create an easy migration path (via the method interface) for later downstream full rewrite of code in Java.

- You can exploit particular application-specific efficiencies and strengths of non-Java languages.

- In some situations, this native method interfacing might be the only option, especially when source code is not available for alternative migration paths.

Cons:

- Native methods do not go through the Java runtime security mechanisms described in Chapter 6, "Before We Begin: Java and Security," such as the Classloader and bytecode verifier. Thus, they could subvert Java security.

- Native methods are platform dependent, so they cannot be used in applets to deliver executable content.

- The current Java native method interface is matched to the C function call sequence only, so programs written in such languages as C++ have to be encapsulated in C wrappers before being finally linked to Java.

- They present additional software engineering overheads during the compilation, testing, and delivery phases.

# Interfacing Java with C Language Programs

This section details the exact process you need to follow to convert a simple C program to work with a Java program via the native method interface.

The example used in this section has the very simple behavior of printing out the contents of the current directory it is running in. The example program has two Java classes: the first implements the `main()` method for the overall program, and the second, called `ListDirJava`, has one method—a native method implemented in C that displays the contents of the current directory.

Perform the following seven basic steps to interface a C program with a Java program via the native method interface:

1. Write the Java code.
2. Compile the Java code using javac.
3. Create the `.h` file using javah.

4. Create a stubs file using javah.

5. Write the C function as a .c file.

6. Create a dynamically loadable object module from the .h file, the stubs file, and the .c file that you created in steps 3, 4, and 5.

7. Run the program.

## Step 1: Write the Java Code

Listing 14.1 implements a class named ListDirJava that declares and calls the native C function. Enter this code into a class file called ListDirJava.java.

---

**Listing 14.1   Declare and Call Native Method**

```
class ListDirJava {
    public native void ListDirC();

    static {
        System.loadLibrary("liblistdir");
    }
}
```

---

The native keyword signals the ClassLoader that the implementation for the ListDirJava class's ListDirC() method is written in another programming language. This definition provides only the method signature for ListDirC() and does not provide any implementation for it. The implementation is done in a separate C language source file.

The C code that implements ListDirC() must be compiled into a dynamically loadable object and loaded into the Java class that requires it. Loading the object into the Java class connects the implementation of the native method to its definition.

The following code fragment from the ListDirJava() class in listing 14.1 loads the appropriate library, named liblistdir.

```
static {
    System.loadLibrary("liblistdir");
}
```

Next, in a separate source file named Main.java, create a Java Main class that instantiates ListDirJava and calls the ListDirC() native method (see listing 14.2).

---

**Listing 14.2   Main Program Class for *ListDirJava***

```
class Main {
    public static void main(String args[]) {
```

```
            new ListDirJava().ListDirC();
    }
}
```

It is clear from the previous code fragment that you call a native method the same way you would call a true Java method. Any arguments to pass into the method can be passed into the parentheses after the method name. The ListDirC() method doesn't take any arguments.

## Step 2: Compile the Java Code

Use javac to compile the Java code that you wrote in step 1.

## Step 3: Create the .h File

In this step, use the javah utility to generate a C header file (an .h file) from the ListDirJava.java class. The header file contains a structure that encapsulates the ListDirJava class on the C side and a C function definition for the implementation of the native method ListDirC() defined in the Java class. On UNIX platforms, you use the following command in your shell to run javah on the ListDirJava class:

```
% javah ListDirJava
```

By default, javah places the new .h file in the same directory as the class file. Javah generates the header file with the same name as the class name appended with a .h extension. Therefore, the command shown previously generates a file named ListDirJava.h. Its contents will look like listing 14.3:

**Listing 14.3   Header File Generated by java.h**

```
/* DO NOT EDIT THIS FILE--it is machine generated */
#include <native.h>
/* Header for class ListDirJava */

#ifndef _Included_ListDirJava
#define _Included_ListDirJava

typedef struct ClassListDirJava {
    char PAD;    /* ANSI C requires structures to have a least one member */
} ClassListDirJava;
HandleTo(ListDirJava);

extern void ListDirJava_ListDirC(struct HListDirJava *);
#endif
```

You can see that the header file contains a definition for a structure named ClassListDirJava. The members of this structure mirror the members of the corresponding Java class. The fields in the structure correspond to instance variables in the class. But because ListDirJava does not have any instance variables, there is just a dummy field in the structure. The members of the structure enable the C function to reference Java class instance variables.

In addition to the C structure that mirrors the Java class, the header file also contains a C function prototype:

```
extern void ListDirJava_ListDirC(struct HListDirJava *);
```

This is the prototype for the C function that you implement in step 5. You must use this exact same function prototype when you write the actual C function. If `ListDirJava` contained any other native methods, their function prototypes appear here as well. The name of the C function is derived from the Java package name, the class name, and the name of the Java native method. Thus, the native method, `ListDirC()`, within the `ListDirJava` class becomes `ListDirJava_ListDirC()`. In this example, there is no package name because `ListDirJava` is in the default package.

The C function has one parameter even though the native method defined in the Java class has none. You can think of the parameter as being similar to the `this` variable in C++. However, in this example, it is ignored.

## Step 4: Create a *stubs* File

Now, use javah with the stubs option on the Java class to create a `stubs` file. On UNIX systems you use the command

```
% javah -stubs ListDirJava
```

The `stubs` file contains C code that actually maps the Java class to its parallel C structure. By default, javah will place the resulting stub file in the same directory as the class file. Like the `.h` file that javah generated in step 3, the name of the `stubs` file is the same as the class name with `.c` appended to the end. In this case, the `stubs` file is called `ListDirJava.c`. It will look like the code listing below.

> **Listing 14.4   *stubs* File Generated by java.h**

```
/* DO NOT EDIT THIS FILE--it is machine generated */
#include <StubPreamble.h>

/* Stubs for class ListDirJava */
/* SYMBOL: "ListDirJava/ListDirC()V", Java_ListDirJava_ListDirC_stub
*/
stack_item *Java_ListDirJava_ListDirC_stub(stack_item *_P_,struct
execenv *_EE_) {
        extern void ListDirJava_ListDirC(void *);
        (void) ListDirJava_ListDirC(_P_[0].p);
        return _P_;
}
```

For the purposes of this discussion, all you need to know about the stubs file is that you will later compile it into the dynamically loadable library that you create in step 6.

## Step 5: Write the C Function

Now write the actual C code for the native method in a C source file. The function that you write must have the same name as in the function prototype generated with javah into the ListDirJava.h file in step 3. The function prototype generated looks like this:

```
extern void ListDirJava_ListDirC(struct HListDirJava *);
```

The C code for this function looks like the following. You could, of course, embellish it in any way except returning any value back to the calling function. Create the C code in a file called ListDirC.c (see listing 14.5).

**Listing 14.5   C Code Implementing the Native Method**

```
#include <StubPreamble.h>
#include "ListDirJava.h"
#include <stdio.h>
void ListDirJava_ListDirC(struct HListDirJava *this) {
system("ls -l\n");return;
}
```

As you can see, the C function uses the C system() function call to list the contents of the current directory.

Listing 14.5 works as is for UNIX users. Users of Microsoft Windows NT/95 and Macintosh platforms should use the directory list command specific to their operating system. The C file includes three C header files:

- StubPreamble.h provides hooks for the C code to interact with the Java runtime system. When writing native methods, you must always include this file in your C source files.

- The ListDirJava.h file that you generated in step 3 contains the C structure that mirrors the Java class for which you are writing the native method and the function prototype for the native method you are writing in this step.

- Any other standard C header files, such as stdio.h, that you might need specifically for your C code are included.

## Step 6: Create a Dynamically Loadable Library

In this step, use appropriate commands specific to your operating system to turn the C code you wrote in step 5 into a dynamically linked library or object file. The command should include both the C file containing the native method implementation as well as the stubs file generated in step 4.

```
% cc -G ListDirJava.c ListDirC.c -o liblistdir.so
```

If necessary, use the -I flag to indicate to the compiler where to find the various header files. The C compiler will create a file liblistdir.so in the current directory. On the DOS shell under Windows 95/NT, assuming you are using Microsoft Visual C++ 2.x to generate DLLs, the command looks like the following:

```
C:\> cl ListDirJava.c ListDirC.c -Feliblistdir.dll -MD -LD javai.lib
```

> **Note**
>
> javai.lib must be the last argument to the C compiler. If necessary, add the directory path containing the Java source files to the environment variable, INCLUDE, and the directory path containing the Java libraries to the environment variable, LIB.

## Step 7: Run the Program

And finally, use java—the Java interpreter—to run the program. You should see some output showing the contents of your current directory in a format appropriate to your operating system. If you see an exception like the following, then you don't have a library path set up:

```
java.lang.NullPointerException
    at java.lang.Runtime.loadLibrary(Runtime.java)
    at java.lang.System.loadLibrary(System.java)
    at ListDirJava.(ListDirJava.java:5)
    at java.lang.UnsatisfiedLinkError ListDirCat Main.main(Main.java:3)
```

The library path is a list of directories that the Java runtime system searches when loading dynamically linked libraries. Set your library path now, and make sure that name of the directory where the liblistdir library lives is a part of the library path list.

If you see the following exception, then you have a library path set in your environment, but the name of the directory where the liblistdir library resides is not a part of the path list:

```
java.lang.UnsatisfiedLinkError no liblistdir in LD_LIBRARY_PATH
    at java.lang.Throwable.(Throwable.java)
    at java.lang.Error.(Error.java)
```

```
    at java.lang.LinkageError.(LinkageError.java)
    at java.lang.UnsatisfiedLinkError.(UnsatisfiedLinkError.java)
    at java.lang.Runtime.loadLibrary(Runtime.java)at
    java.lang.System.loadLibrary(System.java)
    at ListDirJava.(ListDirJava.java:5)
    at java.lang.UnsatisfiedLinkError ListDirC
    at Main.main(Main.java:3)
```

Modify your library path, and make sure that the name of the `liblistdir` library is a part of it.

# Interfacing Java with C++ Programs

There is a degree of resemblance between Java and C++ in that both are object oriented and a lot of the operator syntax looks similar. This might lead people to believe that it is relatively straightforward to migrate C++ code to Java. But this is not entirely true.

From an interfacing point of view, the following characteristics differentiate Java from C++:

- The Java native method runtime interface calls the actual dynamic object via a C function calling sequence, not C++.

- In C++, the name of a function in the object file is not the same as the name used by the programmer in the C++ source code. Thus, a C++ method might actually have a completely different name in the object file. This is called *name mangling* and is an inherent feature of all C++ compilers.

The consequence of the previous two factors is that if you want to call a C++ method from Java, you cannot use the same name you assigned the method in C++. Currently, the only way to interface C++ to Java is to create a C wrapper around the C++ methods and call the C wrapper functions from Java via the native method interface.

The additional downside of doing this includes the following:

- C++ exceptions cannot be easily handled when the Java program is executing.

- You need to properly handle parameter passing all the way between Java and the actual C++ code.

- There might be a performance penalty due to this indirection.

Also, from a complete source-level migration point of view, you need to be aware of these additional important differences between C++ and Java:

II

**The Java Language**

- C++ templates have no corresponding construct in Java.
- C++ has pointers; Java does not.
- C++ has multiple inheritance; Java does not.
- Strings and array syntax and semantics are different between C++ and Java.
- C++ has operator overloading; Java does not.

# Alternative Ways To Interface Java with Non-Java Language Programs

Native methods are not the only way to interface C or C++ programs with Java. In fact, this might not even be possible if the functionality of the non-Java program cannot be neatly segmented and encapsulated into some sort of an API with C bindings and turned into a dynamic shared object.

In such cases, the following alternative approaches may be taken to get the Java program to work with the non-Java language program:

- Structure the two programs as a client/server or producer/consumer system, communicating over a socket.
- Structure the two programs such that they exchange data by reading and writing files.
- An emerging option is to use the capability of some C and C++ compilers to directly generate Java byte code and class files.

# Resources for Further Reading

Interfacing Java with non-Java language programs is an evolving topic. The most topical and current sources of information on this are the following:

- The Sun Web site at URL **http://www.javasoft.com**.
- UseNet newsgroups **comp.lang.java** and **comp.lang.c++**. These newsgroups can be accessed using the UseNet newsreader programs from your Internet Access provider.
- Internet search engines, especially Dejanews at URL **http://www.dejanews.com**.

# Part III

# Writing an Applet

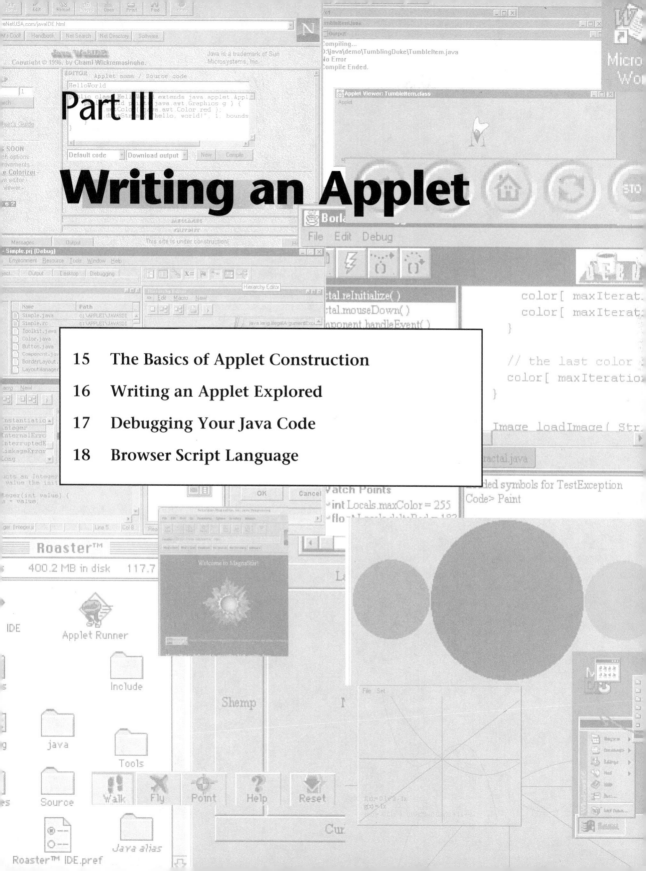

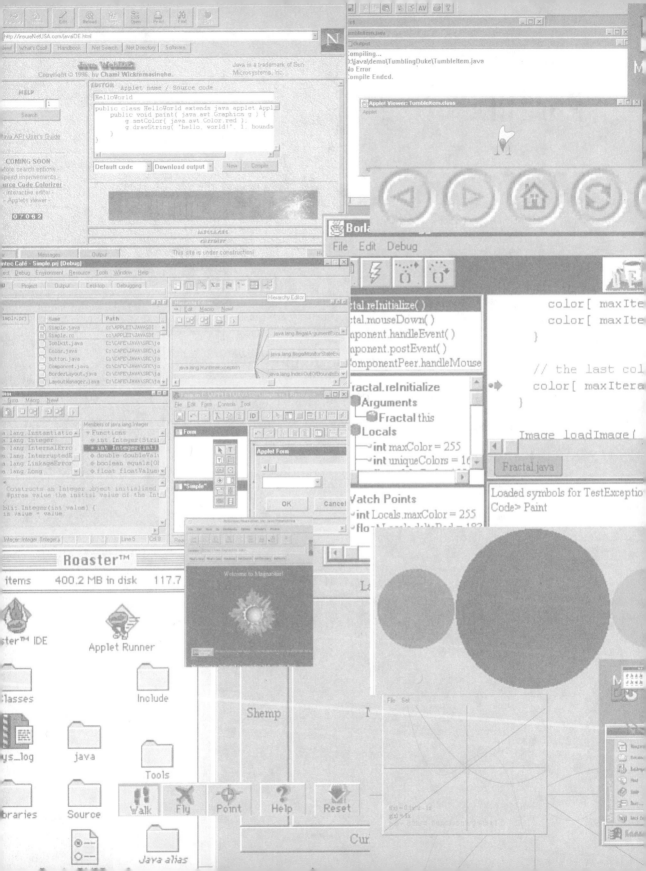

# CHAPTER 15

# The Basics of Applet Construction

*by Mary Pietrowicz*

Until recently, the Web had static documents made up of text and graphics—period. If you wanted to do something more interesting, you had to rely on an external application launched from the browser. Often, users didn't have these applications available.

Now, you are no longer limited to mere text and graphics. Today's browsers can run programs written in Java called applets. Using Java applets, browsers can run animations, play audio, and interact with the user. Anyone with a Java-capable browser can run an applet, no matter what kind of computer is used. And, your users don't have to install anything. They just load the page that contains your applet.

In this chapter, you will learn

- The parts of a simple applet
- The difference between instance variables and class variables
- The way to control access to variables and methods in applets
- The capabilities the applet class gives to applets
- The lifecycle of an applet
- The limitations of applets

## Preparing To Write Applets

Consider writing an applet when you

1. Need something other than static text and graphics. For example, an applet that calculates monthly mortgage payments would be useful on a page that posts current interest rates.

2. Need "flash" factor. Attention-grabbing animations, sounds, and executable programs are useful for announcements and advertisements.

**3.** Want to make an application readily available on the web to all kinds of people using all kinds of machines.

◀ See "The Java Environment," p. 29

First, you'll need to create a development environment for your applets. At a minimum, you'll need places to put the applet code, sound files, images, and associated HTML pages.

In our discussion and examples, we will use the following directories:

| | |
|---|---|
| /html | For .html files |
| /html/audio | For .au files |
| /html/classes | For .java and .classes files |
| /html/images | For .gif or .jpeg image files |

Before you try to write applets, make sure that Java is installed correctly.

Also make sure that you have either the Java appletviewer or a Java-capable browser available.

---

**Tip**

It's handy to have both the appletviewer and a Java-capable browser around when you are debugging an applet. Often it's faster to try out new code with the appletviewer, and any resulting error messages are easy to see.

---

## A First Look at a Simple Applet

Let's look at a simple applet called "ImgSound." ImgSound displays a picture of a cat and plays a "meow" sound until the reader leaves the page. Figure 15.1 shows what ImgSound looks like when it's running.

ImgSound's files fit into the development environment as shown in table 15.1 below.

**Table 15.1 Location of ImgSound Files in the Development Environment**

| Directory | ImgSound Files |
|---|---|
| /html | ImgSound.html |
| /html/audio | meow.au |
| /html/classes | ImgSound.class<br>ImgSound.java |
| /html/image | cat.gif |

**Fig. 15.1**
The ImgSound
applet displays
a picture of a
cat and plays a
"meow" sound
while it is running.

## Including an Applet in HTML

To include an applet in an HTML document, insert an <APPLET> </APPLET>
tag pair at the point where the applet should go. Listing 15.1 below shows
how ImgSound.html includes the ImgSound applet.

The <APPLET> element specifies five things:

1. The name of the applet
2. The directory containing the applet code, relative to the HTML
   document
3. The width in pixels of the applet
4. The height in pixels of the applet
5. The parameters passed to the applet

**Tip**

To display a different image and play another sound, just change the value= assignments in the PARAM statements below.

**Listing 15.1** *ImgSound.html* Includes the *ImgSound* Applet

```
<HTML>
<HEAD>
<TITLE> Meowing Cat Applet </TITLE>
</HEAD>
<BODY>
<P>
The Cat's Meow...
<P>
<HR>
<APPLET code="ImgSound.class" codebase="./classes" width=500
height=400>
<PARAM name=picture-url value=../image/cat.gif>
<PARAM name=sound-url value=../audio/meow.au >
</APPLET>
<HR>
</BODY>
</HTML>
```

You can do much more with the <APPLET> tag. If you want to learn more about the <APPLET> tag, skip ahead to chapter 19, "Adding an Applet to an HTML Document."

## Examining the ImgSound Applet

Examine the ImgSound applet in listing 15.2 below. ImgSound loads an image called cat.gif (a picture of a cat) and a sound called meow.au. After initialization is complete, the applet displays the cat picture and meows. The applet will continue to meow until the user leaves the page or selects the browser and presses any keyboard key. The meowing will resume when the user reenters the page.

**Listing 15.2** *ImgSound.java* Displays an Image and Plays a Sound

```
// ImgSound
//
// Description:
//    ImgSound is an applet that displays an image and plays a sound
//    when the applet starts.

import java.awt.*;
import java.applet.*;
import java.net.*;

public class ImgSound extends java.applet.Applet
{
  // URLs
  private String img_url = null;
```

```
private String sound_url = null;

// Panels and canvases that the applet uses.
Canvas c_north = null;

// Images that the applet uses.
Image img_1 = null;

// Sounds that the applet uses.
AudioClip sound_clip = null;

// The background color
Color bkgnd;

public void init()
{
  // Set up the display.
  setLayout(new BorderLayout());
  bkgnd = new Color(255, 255, 255);  // White
  setBackground(bkgnd);
  c_north = new Canvas();
  add("North", c_north);

  // Read in the parameters from the HTML document.
  img_url = getParameter("picture-url");
  sound_url = getParameter("sound-url");

  // Load image and sound clip.
  MediaTracker tracker = new MediaTracker(this);
  img_1 = getImage(getCodeBase(), img_url);
  tracker.addImage(img_1, 0);
  try
  { tracker.waitForID(0); }
  catch (InterruptedException e)
  { System.out.println("Image Load Failure"); }

  sound_clip = getAudioClip(getCodeBase(), sound_url);

}

public void start()
{
    // Play the sound over and over.
    sound_clip.loop();
}

public void stop()
{
   // Quiet.
   sound_clip.stop();
}

public void paint(Graphics g)
{
   if (img_1 != null)
   {
```

(continues)

III

Writing an Applet

**Listing 15.2 Continued**

```
        g.drawImage(img_1, 0, 0, getBackground(), c_north);
    }
}

public boolean keyDown(Event evt, int key)
{
    // Quiet.
    sound_clip.stop();
    return true;
}
}
```

ImgSound has four main components:

**1.** Import statements

**2.** A class definition

**3.** Variables

**4.** Methods

The import statements let your applet use Java classes and methods. They are similar to "#include" directives in C.

**Tip**

All applets must import java.applet.Applet in the file that contains the applet class definition. Including java.applet.* will include `java.applet.Applet`. Applets with user interfaces (most applets!) will include `java.awt.*`, too.

This applet's class definition is:

```
    public class ImgSound extends java.applet.Applet
```

A different applet "X" would have a similar applet class definition:

```
    public class X extends java.applet.Applet
```

Note that all applet class definitions extend `java.applet.Applet`.

**Note**

Because ImgSound "extends java.applet.Applet," ImgSound inherits all of java.applet.Applet's methods and variables.

Look for the variable definitions `img_url`, `sound_url`, `c_north`, `img_1`, `sound_clip`, and `bkgnd`. Find the methods `init()`, `start()`, `stop()`, `paint(Graphics g)`, and `keyDown(Event evt, int key)`. Each variable and method is inside the ImgSound class. All applet variables and methods belong to and are declared inside of a class.

Let's take a closer look at ImgSound's methods.

The `init()` method makes the applet ready to run. It reads parameters, sets up the display, and reads in the image and sound clip. These activities happen only once. They do not need to be repeated if the applet stops temporarily.

In this case, `start()` is very simple. It just plays a sound over and over. `start()` is the point of entry if ImgSound temporarily starts and resumes.

The `stop()` method stops the sound from playing. `stop()` is the point of exit if ImgSound stops temporarily.

The `paint(Graphics g)` draws the image on the display.

The `keyDown(Event evt, int key)` method stops the meow sound when the user selects the applet and presses a keyboard key.

> **Note**
>
> Applets that make noise like this one can be annoying. It's a good idea to provide a way to stop the noise. The method `keyDown(Event evt, int key)` in ImgSound stops the noise when a key is pressed. Just select the applet by clicking it, then press any keyboard key.

# Variables and Methods

As we saw in the previous example, Java variables are always declared within the boundaries of a class. If their declarations appear inside a method, then they are visible only in the method. We will focus on variables declared outside of methods. They belong to the class. We will learn the difference between class and instance variables. We will also learn how to control access to variables and methods.

> **Note**
>
> The information in this section applies to both applets and applications.

## Instance Variables versus Class Variables

Java allocates new space in memory for instance variables whenever new objects are instantiated from classes. In contrast, Java allocates space for class variables only once per class.

For example, the class Secret Numbers below stores 3 numbers of a secret code or combination.

```
class Secret_Numbers
{
   int first = 0;
   int second = 0;
   int third = 0;
}
```

An applet code segment could create new secret numbers for anyone who needed a combination. For example,

```
Secret_Numbers Steves_numbers = new Secret_Numbers();
Steves_numbers.first = 1;
Steves_numbers.second = 2;
Steves_numbers.third = 3;

Secret_Numbers Marys_numbers = new Secret_Numbers();
Marys_numbers.first = 4;
Marys_numbers.second = 5;
Marys_numbers.third = 6;
```

The two sets of numbers are distinct. With the two "new" commands, Java has created two objects with space for two copies of the integers first, second, and third. If we print Steves_numbers and Marys_numbers, they have different values. An applet code segment that prints the numbers looks like this:

```
System.out.println("Steves_numbers.first = "+Steves_numbers.first);
System.out.println("Steves_numbers.second =
➥"+Steves_numbers.second);
System.out.println("Steves_numbers.third = "+Steves_numbers.third);
System.out.println("Marys_numbers.first = "+Marys_numbers.first);
System.out.println("Marys_numbers.second = "+Marys_numbers.second);
System.out.println("Marys_numbers.third = "+Marys_numbers.third);
```

The printed output looks like this:

```
Steves_numbers.first = 1
Steves_numbers.second = 2
Steves_numbers.third = 3
Marys_numbers.first = 4
Marys_numbers.second = 5
Marys_numbers.third = 6
```

In short, Java creates an object with space for instance variables every time a class is instantiated with the "new" command.

In contrast, Java allocates space for class variables only once. Each instance of the class shares the class variables. An instance that changes a class variable value changes the value for all instances!

The keyword "static" in a variable declaration indicates a class variable. Let's modify the Secret_Numbers class so that each of its variables is a class variable.

```
class Secret_Numbers
{
  static int first = 0;
    static int second = 0;
    static int third = 0;
}
```

As before, we assign the secret numbers.

```
Secret_Numbers Steves_numbers = new Secret_Numbers();
Steves_numbers.first = 1;
Steves_numbers.second = 2;
Steves_numbers.third = 3;

Secret_Numbers Marys_numbers = new Secret_Numbers();
Marys_numbers.first = 4;
Marys_numbers.second = 5;
Marys_numbers.third = 6;
```

The printed output is different!

```
Steves_numbers.first = 4
Steves_numbers.second = 5
Steves_numbers.third = 6
Marys_numbers.first = 4
Marys_numbers.second = 5
Marys_numbers.third = 6
```

Steves_numbers and Marys_numbers are the same because the two instances share the same copies of the variables first, second, and third.

## Controlling Access to Variables and Methods

Access control determines how applets can read and modify variables and call methods. The examples below show how to enable or prevent access among the classes and subclasses in your applets. Java makes decisions about access based on whether

- The variable is in the same class as the reference
- The variable is in the same package as the reference
- The variable is a superclass of the reference
- The variable is a subclass of the reference

Java provides the following keywords for controlling access:

- private
- public
- protected
- private protected

*Private* means that references are illegal outside the scope of the immediate class. *Public* means that references are legal anywhere. The *protected* modifier, in general, limits references to the scope of the class, its subclasses, and the class's package. A subclass, however, can't access a superclass's protected variables. The *private protected* modifier limits references to the scope of the class and its subclasses.

If no keywords are used, then references are legal within the package. Sometimes this is called *friendly* access.

Now let's look at some examples. We've modified the Secret_Numbers class to contain another number, a method to print all the numbers, and a method to print the first number. What else has changed? The methods and variables have access modifiers.

**Listing 15.3** *Secret_Numbers.java* **Shows How To Apply Access Modifiers to Variables and Methods**

```
package A;

public class Secret_Numbers
{
    private int first = 0;
    private protected int second = 0;
    protected int third = 0;
    public int fourth = 0;

    void print_secret_numbers()
    {
        System.out.println("first = "+first);
        System.out.println("second = "+second);
        System.out.println("third = "+third);
        System.out.println("fourth = "+fourth);
    }

    private protected void print_first()
    {
        System.out.println("first = "+first);
    }
}
```

What happens if a class Get_Secrets from the same package tries to access Secret_Number's variables and methods?

Get_Secrets *can* access third, fourth, and print_secret_numbers(). Accessing "third" and "print_secret_numbers()" is legal because Get_Secrets and Secret_Numbers belong to the same package. The variable "fourth" is accessible from any class because it is public.

Get_Secrets *cannot* access first, second, and print_first(). The variable first is private, so no other class can access it directly. second and print_first()are out of reach because Get_Secrets is not a subclass of Secret_Numbers.

---

**Listing 15.4  *Get_Secrets* Tries To Access *Secret_Numbers*'s Variables and Methods**

```
package A;

import A.Secret_Numbers;

public class Get_Secrets
{
   void get_all(Secret_Numbers nums)
   {
     int a = nums.first;              // Illegal - can't access a
                                      ➥private variable directly.
     int b = nums.second;            // Illegal - Get_Secrets is not
                                      ➥a subclass of Secret_Numbers.
     int c = nums.third;             // OK
     int d = nums.fourth;            // OK
     nums.print_secret_numbers();    // OK
     nums.print_first();             // Illegal - Get_Secrets is not
                                      ➥a subclass of Secret_Numbers.

   }
}
```

---

What happens if a class from another package, Safecracker, tries to access Secret_Number's variables and methods?

Since Safecracker is not a subclass of Secret_Numbers, it can't access print_first() and second. Since Safecracker doesn't belong to the same package, it can't access print_secret_numbers() and third. Accessing first, a private variable, is illegal. Accessing fourth, a public variable, is always legal.

This listing is Safecracker.java on the CD-ROM.

**Listing 15.5  Class *Safecracker* Tries To Access *Secret_Numbers*'s Variables and Methods**

```
package B;

import A.Secret_Numbers;

class Safecracker
{
  void crack_safe(Secret_Numbers nums)
  {
    nums.print_secret_numbers();    // Illegal - Safecracker not
                                    //➥in the same package as
                                    //➥Secret_Numbers
    nums.print_first();             // Illegal - Safecracker not a
                                    //➥subclass of Secret_Numbers.
    int a = nums.first;             // Illegal - Can't access a
                                    //➥private variable directly.
    int b = nums.second;            // Illegal - Safecracker not a
                                    //➥subclass of Secret_Numbers.
    int c = nums.third;             // Illegal - Safecracker not in
                                    //➥same package and not a subclass.
    int d = nums.fourth;            // OK
  }
}
```

Finally, what happens if a class from another package, `Another_Num`, tries to access `Secret_Number`'s variables and methods? Note that `Another_Num` is a subclass of `Secret_Number`.

`Another_Num` can't access `print_secret_numbers()` because `Another_Num` and `Secret_Numbers` belong to different packages. It can't access `nums.first` because first is declared private, but it can access the public variable `nums.fourth`. `Another_Num` can't access `nums.second` and `nums.third` because a subclass can't access a superclass's protected variables. `Another_Num` can, however, access its own inherited copy of `third` and run its own inherited `print_first()` method.

**Note**

It's legal for a subclass to access its own inherited copies of protected variables and methods. It's not legal, however, for a subclass to access a superclass's copy of the same protected variables and methods.

---

**Listing 15.6   Class *Another_Num* Tries To Access *Secret_Numbers*'s Variables and Methods**

```
package B;

import A.Secret_Numbers;

class Another_Num extends Secret_Numbers
{
  int fifth = 0;

  public void get_other_numbers(Secret_Numbers nums)
  {
    nums.print_secret_numbers();    // Illegal - Another_Num not in
                                    // ➥the same package.
    int a = nums.first;             // Illegal - can't access a
                                    // ➥private variable directly.
    int b = nums.second;            // Illegal - can't access a
                                    // ➥superclass's private
                                    // ➥protected variables.
    int c = nums.third;             // Illegal - can't access a
                                    // ➥superclass's protected
                                    // ➥variables.
    int d = nums.fourth;            // OK

    this.print_secret_numbers();    // Illegal - not in same
                                    // ➥package.
    int e = this.third;             // OK - accessing the subclass's
                                    // ➥protected variable.
    this.print_first();             // OK - accessing the subclass's
                                    // ➥protected method.
  }
}
```

---

# The Applet Class

As we saw in listing 15.2, applets are defined with the statement of the form

```
access_modifier class classname extends java.applet.Applet
```

This means that the applet `classname` inherits methods and variables from the Applet class.

> **Note**
>
> A closer look reveals that the applet class itself inherits from a long chain of classes. In short, a class that extends `java.applet.Applet` can use variables and methods (including constructors) from `java.lang.Object`, `java.awt.Component`, `java.awt.Container`, and `java.awt.Panel`.
>
> Take a minute to investigate which variables and methods are available to applets.

## How To Use the Applet Class Methods

The methods in the applet class provide ways for applets to

1. Handle parameters
2. Get images
3. Get and play sound clips
4. Interact with the browser or appletviewer
5. Manage lifecycle events cleanly, e.g., loading, starting, stopping, restarting, and quitting

We have already used some of these methods in the previous examples.

### Handling Parameters

The example in listing 15.1 shows how to pass parameters to an applet from an HTML document. Listing 15.2 shows how the applet code retrieves the parameters. The getParameter() method reads a parameter in an applet.

```
// Read in the parameters from the HTML document.
    img_url = getParameter("picture-url");
    sound_url = getParameter("sound-url");
```

> **Note**
>
> Note that parameters are passed in as type String.

The getParameterInfo() method returns a string listing all the parameters the applet understands. For each parameter, the string specifies the name, type, and description.

### Getting Images

The getImage(URL, String) method loads image files for the applet to use. For example, in listing 15.2, the line

```
    img_1 = getImage(getCodeBase(), img_url);
```

loads the image img_url.

### Getting and Playing Sound Clips

We have already seen the methods for getting audio clips. In listing 15.2, the line

```
    sound_clip = getAudioClip(getCodeBase(), sound_url);
```

loads the applet's sound.

The `play(URL, String)` method plays a sound clip. If the sound has already been loaded, though, you can play it with the technique used in listing 15.2:

```
// Play the sound over and over.
    sound_clip.loop();
```

### Interacting with the Applet's Environment

The `getAppletContext()` method returns an object you can use to get information about and control the environment. Specifically, it returns type AppletContext (an interface). AppletContext methods allow you to

- Find out what applets are running on the same page as your applet
- Get the context of another applet and run its methods
- Send messages to other applets
- Get images and audio clips

The `getAppletInfo()` method lets you provide information about an applet. Override this method by putting something like this in your applet:

```
public String getAppletInfo()
{ return "Applet Name, version 1.0, date, author, copyright date";
}
```

We used `getCodeBase` in listing 15.2. The line

```
img_1 = getImage(getCodeBase(), img_url);
```

uses `getCodeBase()` to get the URL of the directory containing ImgSound. The `getImage` method constructs the image URL from `getCodeBase()` and `img_url`.

The `getDocumentBase()` method is similar to `getCodeBase()`, except that `getDocumentBase()` returns the URL to the directory containing the applet's HTML document.

There are many more methods in the applet class for interacting with the applet's environment:

- The `isActive()` method determines whether an applet is active. Use this method to check the state of another applet by calling `AppletContext()`, calling `getApplets()` on the context, and calling `isActive` on a particular applet.
- Use `SetStub()` to set up a new AppletStub interface. Implementors of new applet viewers will use this.
- Use `ShowStatus(String)` to post messages into the browser's status area.
- The `resize(Dimension)` method resizes an entire applet.

### Managing an Applet's Lifecycle

Java provides a mechanism for applets to take control at key moments when certain events occur. The init(), start(), stop(), and destroy() methods are called when the applet loads, begins executing, stops executing, and unloads, respectively. If an applet needs to do something at one of these key stages, just override the method by including your own implementation of it in the applet.

Let's take a closer look at these methods in the next section.

# The Structure of an Applet

The applet class and its superclasses provide methods that the system calls when key events occur. When we want to do something in response to an event, we just override the corresponding method. Suppose that an applet needed to print the word "Beep!" when the user pressed the mouse button. Since the system calls mouseDown(event, int, int) when the user presses a mouse button, we would override the mouseDown method in component by putting a method in our applet with the same format.

```
public boolean mouseDown(Event evt, int x, int y)
{ System.out.println("Beep!"); }
```

The system calls methods for "lifecycle" events, too. When an applet loads, the system calls the init() method. When initialization is complete, the system calls the start()routine to begin execution. The system also calls start()to resume execution. The stop()method is called to halt execution, and the destroy()method is called to do any remaining cleanup before the applet is unloaded.

---

**Note**

Entering the applet's page causes the system to call start(), and exiting the applet's page causes the system to call stop().

---

**Tip**

You can use your own stop() method to stop things like sounds, display updates, and calculations. Users won't be able to appreciate display updates to your applet if they are no longer viewing the applet. Users will be very annoyed if an applet continues to make noise after they have left the page, too!

Applets selectively override these methods. Most applets will have an `init()` method to do a one-time initialization. This is the place to initialize variables, load images, etc.

> **Tip**
>
> Think of an applet as a dark room in your house. When you buy the house, you connect the electricity (`init`). When you go into the room, you turn on the light (`start`). When you leave the room, you turn the light off (`stop`). When you sell the house, you disconnect the electricity (`destroy`).

Listing 15.7 below shows how an applet moves from state to state. This applet is ImgSound from the previous example—with a few modifications. The applet ImgSound2 overrides `init()`, `start()`, `stop()`, and `destroy()`. Whenever the system calls one of these methods, it plays an appropriate sound (a different one for each method). It also appends `initializing`, `starting up`, `stopping`, or `destroying` to a text area at the bottom of the screen. When the applet loads, you will see "Initializing. Starting up." in the text window and will hear sound clips for the `init()` and `start()` methods. Figure 15.2 shows the ImgSound2 applet running.

**Fig. 15.2**
The ImgSound2 Applet displays state change information and plays sounds to mark changes in state.

III

**Writing an Applet**

If you leave the page and return later, you will see that the text window has changed. Before, the text window just displayed Initializing. Starting Up.

Now it says, Initializing. Starting Up. Stopping. Starting Up. When you left the applet's page, the stop() method ran, appended "Stopping." to the text area on the screen, and played the audio clip for the stop() method. When you returned, the start() method ran again, appended "Starting Up." to the text area, and played the audio clip for the start() method. Figure 15.3 shows how the text area changes when you leave the applet's page and return later.

**Fig. 15.3**
The ImgSound2 Applet text shows that you have left the page and returned; "Stopping. Starting Up." has been appended.

---

**Listing 15.7** *ImgSound2.java* **Tracks the Applet Lifecycle**

```
// ImgSound2
//
// Description:
//    ImgSound2 is an applet that displays an image and plays a sound
//    ➥when
//    the applet starts.  It also displays the state trail of the
//    ➥applet.
//    When the applet changes states, it plays a sound clip
//    ➥indicating
//    the state just entered.

import java.awt.*;
import java.applet.*;
import java.net.*;

public class ImgSound2 extends java.applet.Applet
{
  // URLs
  private String img_url = null;
```

```java
private String start_url = null;
private String stop_url = null;
private String init_url = null;
private String destroy_url = null;

// Display objects that the applet uses.
Canvas c_north = null;
TextField tf_south = null;
StringBuffer str = null;

// Images that the applet uses.
Image img_1 = null;

// Sounds that the applet uses.
AudioClip init_clip = null;
AudioClip start_clip = null;
AudioClip stop_clip = null;
AudioClip destroy_clip = null;

// The background color
Color bkgnd;

// Minimum delay time between sounds
Long time_delay;


// Workspace
String scratch;

public void init()
{
  // Read parameters passed in from HTML document.
  img_url = getParameter("picture-url");
  init_url = getParameter("init-url");
  start_url = getParameter("start-url");
  stop_url = getParameter("stop-url");
  destroy_url = getParameter("destroy-url");
  scratch = getParameter("delay");
  time_delay = new Long(scratch);

  // Set up the screen.
  setLayout(new BorderLayout());
  bkgnd = new Color(255, 255, 255);   // White
  setBackground(bkgnd);
  c_north = new Canvas();
  tf_south = new TextField();
  add("North", c_north);
  add("South", tf_south);

  // Read in images.
  MediaTracker tracker = new MediaTracker(this);
  img_1 = getImage(getCodeBase(), img_url);
  tracker.addImage(img_1, 0);
  try
  { tracker.waitForID(0); }
```

(continues)

**Listing 15.7 Continued**

```
      catch (InterruptedException e)
      { System.out.println("Image Load Failure"); }

      // Read in sound clips.
      init_clip = getAudioClip(getCodeBase(), init_url);
      start_clip = getAudioClip(getCodeBase(), start_url);
      stop_clip = getAudioClip(getCodeBase(), stop_url);
      destroy_clip = getAudioClip(getCodeBase(), destroy_url);

      // Display the state, and play audio indicator.
      str = new StringBuffer("Initializing. ");
      tf_south.setText(str.toString());
      init_clip.play();
      this.delay(time_delay.longValue());
   }

   public void start()
   {
      // Display the state.
      str  = str.append("Starting up. ");
      tf_south.setText(str.toString());

      // Play "start" audio indicator.
      start_clip.play();
      this.delay(time_delay.longValue());
   }

   public void stop()
   {
      // Display the state.
      str = str.append("Stopping. ");
      tf_south.setText(str.toString());

      // Play "stop" audio indicator.
      stop_clip.play();
      this.delay(time_delay.longValue());
   }

   public void destroy()
   {
      // Display the state.
      str = str.append("Destroying. ");
      tf_south.setText(str.toString());

      // Play "destroy" audio indicator.
      destroy_clip.play();
      this.delay(time_delay.longValue());
   }

   public void paint(Graphics g)
   {
      if (img_1 != null)
      {
```

```
            g.drawImage(img_1, 0, 0, getBackground(), c_north);
      }
  }

  private void delay(long wait_time)
  {
      for (int i=0; i<wait_time; i++)
      { i=i+1; }
  }
}
```

# An Applet Template

Let's take what we've learned, generalize, and create a template for building applets.

First, a Java applet must include the appropriate import statements. The most common import statements are provided in the Template below. Just uncomment what you need. If only a few objects from a package are needed, include the objects explicitly instead. For example, the statement

```
    import java.applet.Applet;
```

includes the Applet class and nothing else from the applet package.

Next, be sure to include a class definition that "extends java.applet.Applet." This is the main class for the applet.

Then, list instance variables, class variables, and methods. The variables and methods can appear in any order, but grouping the variables in one section and the methods in another makes the code easy to read.

Finally, decide which methods the applet needs to override. Consider at least init(), start(), stop(), destroy(), and paint(). These are frequently replaced.

**Listing 15.8** *ImgSound2.java* **Tracks the Applet Lifecycle**

```
// Name of Class (the file name and class name should be the same)
//
// Description:
//    Insert an appropriate description.
//

// Import Statements:
// Uncomment what you need to include, or insert a statement to import
// a specific item, e.g., "import java.applet.Applet;".
```

*(continues)*

**Listing 15.8 Continued**

```
// import java.applet.*;
// import java.awt.*;
// import java.awt.image.*;
// import java.awt.peer.*;
// import java.io.*;
// import java.lang.*;
// import java.net.*;
// import java.util.*

// Top-level class declaration for the applet.
public class Template extends java.applet.Applet
{
  //  Insert instance variable declarations here.


  //  Insert methods here.


  //  Methods you might need to override.
  //  public void init()
  //  {
  //  }

  //  public void start()
  //  {
  //  }

  //  public void stop()
  //  {
  //  }

  //  public void destroy()
  //  {
  //  }

  //  public void paint(Graphics g)
  //  {
  //  }
}
```

# Applet Limitations

Before you roll up your sleeves and rush into writing applets, let's take a minute to understand what an applet can't do. In general, applets loaded from the network are not allowed access to the local machine. Most limitations are there—on purpose—for security reasons.

■ Applets can't access files from the client machine.

■ Applets can't create files on the client machine.

- Applets can't make network connects except back to the host machine where the applet came from.
- Applets can't start any programs on a client machine.
- Applets can't load libraries.
- Applets can't define native method calls.
- Applets can't halt execution of the interpreter (can't call `System.exit()`).

These limitations are necessary! The security restrictions prevent applets from doing harmful things across the net like

1. Reading and downloading private files from machines
2. Writing viruses or destroying data on machines
3. Running potentially destructive programs on random machines on the network
4. Talking directly to the client machine and making selective modifications

This means you can't

1. Post a useful file from a friendly network machine to the host machine, without the client machine having to run httpd
2. Prompt the client machine to run helper routines for the applet
3. Use files on the client
4. Make a call to System.exit() for debugging or other purposes

If applet restrictions prevent you from doing work you need to do, consider writing a Java application instead. Applications can make network connections, access files, run programs, go native, load libraries, and make calls to `System.exit()`. On the other hand, applications don't have browsers built into them and don't have the ability to display HTML, jump to links, etc. Applications also are not as visible over the network as applets are. Weigh your requirements carefully when deciding between writing an applet and writing an application. ❖

III

**Writing an Applet**

# CHAPTER 16

# Writing an Applet Explored

*by Jay Cross*

No matter how well you know the fairly simple rules of the game "Chess," you cannot be very good at it without playing the game. Likewise, there is something reassuring about creating your own simple application to be certain that you really do have a grasp of a computer language.

Though Java is a fine object-oriented language in its own right, it has come to prominence because of its usefulness in creating applets that can be run by any browser that supports Java. In this chapter we explore the creation of applets, and examine the obvious and subtle uses of Java's language and packaged features used by these applets.

## Hello World

In chapter 15 you learned the basics of applet construction. In this chapter you will look at three real applets, starting with a complete Hello World applet. Create a file called `HelloMudvilleApplet.java` with your favorite text editor, and copy listing 16.1 into it.

**Listing 16.1** *HelloMudvilleApplet.java* **Source Code**

```
import java.awt.Graphics;
import java.awt.Color;
import java.awt.Font;
public class HelloMudvilleApplet extends java.applet.Applet {
    Font f = new Font("Ariel", Font.BOLD, 24);
    Public void paint(Graphics g) {
        g.setColor(Color.blue);          // Set the color
        g.setFont(f);                    // Set the font
        g.drawString("Hello Mudville!", 10, 60);
    } /* end of paint method */
} /* end of HelloMudvilleApplet */
```

The first thing that you need to do in any java file, including this one, is to import any class files you wish to use from other packages. You can use these classes to reduce the amount of programming you need to do. In HelloMudville you need to import three classes from the java.awt package: Graphics, Color, and Font. Color and Font will be used to change the attributes of the text for "Hello Mudville." Graphics will be used to actually paint the text "Hello Mudville" onto the screen. After you have taken care of the administrative duties of importing other classes, the next thing to do is declare the class definition for HelloMudvilleApplet.

```
public class HelloMudvilleApplet extends java.applet.Applet {
```

HelloMudville is created as a public class. All applets must be declared to be public, or the browser won't be able to actually add the applet to the page. Next, note that all applets must extend java.applet.Applet.

The next step in an applet is to declare the class variables. For HelloMudville there is one variable called f. You can use f to change the font type used to display "Hello Mudville" much the same as you would change the font in a word processor.

Once all the variables have been declared you can start declaring the methods. The only method in HelloMudvilleApplet is paint. It overrides the paint method from Applet, and is called any time your HelloMudville applet needs to be drawn on the screen.

**Listing 16.2   The *paint* Method for HelloMuddvilleApplet**

```
public void paint(Graphics g) {
    g.setColor(Color.blue);        // Set the color
    g.setFont(f);              // Set the font
    g.drawString("Hello Mudville!", 10, 60);
  } /* end of paint method */
```

The first thing the paint method does is set the Color to blue, and change the font. In this case the font is set to f, the font variable we specified earlier. Finally, the paint method draws the string "Hello Mudville" to the screen.

**Note**

Notice, that when the color and font are set, you are actually setting the attributes of g, a Graphics object. Once you have used the setColor method on a Graphics object, anything you draw in that screen afterwards will be in that color. After the setFont method all text drawn to that graphic would be in the new font. However, if

> for some reason you had two Graphics objects, the only one affected by this change would be g; if you went to draw to the other object it would be in the old color and font.

With all the code in place, compile the HelloMudville applet with javac. To do this type:

```
javac HelloMudvilleApplet.java
```

**Tip**

In order to compile a Java application you must have the JDK installed.

To view the applet, you need to create an HTML file. For this applet, create a file called HelloMudville.html and copy the text from listing 16.3 into it.

**Listing 16.3    HTML File for Use with HelloMudville Applet**

```
<HTML>
<HEAD>
<TITLE>The Hello Mudville Applet:</TITLE>
</HEAD>
<BR>
<APPLET CODE="HelloMudvilleApplet.class" WIDTH=300 HEIGHT=60>
Does your browser support Java?
</APPLET>
</BODY>
</HTML>
```

Now, you can run the applet using the appletviewer or Netscape. To load the applet in Netscape you will need to open the file HelloMudville.html as shown in figure 16.1. Don't open the HelloMudvilleApplet.class or HelloMudville.java files, that won't work.

To view the HelloMudville applet with appletviewer as seen in figure 16.2 type:

```
appletviewer HelloMudville.html
```

**III**

**Writing an Applet**

**Fig. 16.1**
HelloMudville
as seen from
the Netscape
Navigator

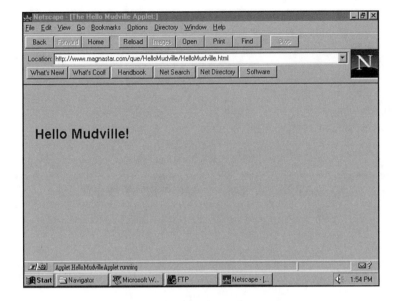

**Fig. 16.2**
HelloMudville
as seen from
applet viewer.

# Developing an Applet Concept

Java can be used to do nearly anything that can be done with a computer. On the other hand, you may not want to go to the trouble of creating an applet that does something much more easily done some other way. For example, HTML (HyperText Markup Language) already provides an excellent and easy facility for displaying static text. HTML easily accommodates displaying static images, loading text files, running applications such as ftp, or collecting user information through static forms.

Java is especially good for handling moving, or highly interactive components of Web pages. Java applets can also be very simple, as seen above. If you are new to object-oriented programming you should probably start small. As a beginner you would probably benefit from studying the source code of as many applets as you have time for, looking for techniques to handle common situations.

# A Blinking Word Applet

The following applet shown in listing 16.4 was written by Arthur van Hoff as a simple example of a Java applet. This one is a bit more complex than the "HelloMudville" applet above. It shows a few more techniques that make up useful applets.

**Listing 16.4    Blink.java—Source Code for Blink Applet**

```java
import java.awt.*;
import java.util.StringTokenizer;

public class Blink extends java.applet.Applet implements Runnable {
  Thread blinker;        // declare an uninitialized Thread
  String lbl;            // declare an uninitialized String variable
  Font font;             // declare an uninitialized Font object
  int speed;             // declare a 32 bit integer speed = 0

public void init() {
    // The font is not a runtime parameter.
    font = new java.awt.Font("TimesRoman", Font.PLAIN, 24);

    // get the blink speed from HTML or set to default.
    String att = getParameter("speed");
    speed = (att == null) ? 400 : (1000 /Integer.valueOf(att).intValue());

    // get the text to display from HTML or set to "Blink"
    att = getParameter("lbl");
    lbl = (att == null) ? "Blink" : att;
  }

public void start() {
    blinker = new Thread(this);
    blinker.start();
  }

public void paint(Graphics g) {
    // declare and initialize some variables.
    int x = 0, y = font.getSize(), space;
    int red = (int)(Math.random() * 50);
    int green = (int)(Math.random() * 50);
    int blue = (int)(Math.random() * 256);
    Dimension d = size();

    // set Font and Color, and get letter sizes.
    g.setColor(Color.black);
    g.setFont(font);
    FontMetrics fm = g.getFontMetrics();
    space = fm.stringWidth(" ");

    // go through a loop to place the words, and
    //  set their color.
```

(continues)

**Listing 16.4  Continued**

```
        for (StringTokenizer t = new StringTokenizer(lbl)
      ➡t.hasMoreTokens() ; ) {
          String word = t.nextToken();
           // will the word fit on this line? If not, new line.
          int w = fm.stringWidth(word) + space;
          if (x + w > d.width) {
            x = 0;
            y += font.getSize();
          }
          if (Math.random() < 0.5) {
            g.setColor(new java.awt.Color((red + y * 30) % 256, (green
            ➡+ x / 3) % 256, blue));
          } else {
            g.setColor(Color.lightGray); // invisible
          }
          g.drawString(word, x, y);
          x += w;
        }
    }

  public void stop() {
      blinker.stop();
    }

  public void run() {
      while (true) {
        try {Thread.currentThread().sleep(speed);}
        catch (InterruptedException e){}
        repaint();
      }
    }
  }
}
```

As with HelloMudville, the first thing that you need to do in the Blink
applet is import the classes which you intend to borrow. With Blink, a number of the elements in the java.awt package are used, so rather than importing each of them individually, the entire package is installed, by importing
java.awt.*

The variables declared for Blink, are very similar to those for HelloMudville,
however, we have added one significant one: Thread blinker. Since Blink
will be doing more than displaying information once, we need to create a
Thread in which to process our work.

The first method that Blink has is the init method. init is overridden from
Applet, and is called the first time the applet is started.

Usually, `init` is used to set up information specific about the applet. `Blink`'s init method is no exception. `Blink` uses the `init` method to set the `font` variable, which in `HelloMudville` was set right with the variable instantiation. Next `Blink` retrieves information from its HTML file. This is done with the `getParameter` method. As you will see in listing 16.5, the speed of the applet can be configured in the Web page. Using `getParameter` and the HTML file to set variables makes it possible to configure an Applet without having to actually change the code, and recompile the applet each time.

In case the parameter is not actually placed in the HTML file, it is necessary to make sure that `getParameter` actually returned a value, and if not, set it to a default value. This is what is accomplished in the line.

```
speed = (att == null) ? 400 : (1000 / Integer.valueOf(att). intValue());
```

If you're familiar with C or C++, this line will make perfect sense to you. If not, this is what happens: speed is set to the value produced by the `?` operator. The `?` operator evaluates `att==null` (if no parameter is present `getParameter` will return `null`), and if it is true it will return the first parameter, so speed will be set to 400. If `att==null` is false, the `?` operator will return the second parameter so speed will be set to 1000 divided by the value from the HTML file.

The second method in `Blink` is the `start` method. Once again, `start` is overridden from the Applet class. `start` is called each time your program is rerun. This happens each time a user leaves a Web page and comes back to it, as well as a number of other times. In `Blink` the only thing that is done in the `start` method is to create and start a `Thread`.

The third method in `Blink` is `paint`. `paint` is overridden from Applet (are you seeing a pattern here?). The `paint` method in `Blink` is much more complicated from the one in `HelloMudville`. First, `Blink` has half a dozen variables. These are used for various reasons throughout the `paint` method. The variables x, y, and space are used to position the text; red, green, and blue are used to set the color of the text, and d stores the size of the applet, so your text won't run outside the boundary.

The most significant thing to happen occurs in the `for` loop. Here, the entire string is tokenized. In other words, each of the words in the string is broken out into it's own token.

A check is then made to make sure that the word won't go outside of the window. After all, you want to be able to see the entire word. The color is then set and the text is drawn to the screen.

III

Writing an Applet

The fourth method in Blink is stop. stop is called anytime someone switches off of the web page. All stop actually does is stop the Thread for Blink. However, this is an important step, it is very irresponsible to have your applet continue to run when the user can't see it, and may not even return. Unless you have a really good reason not to, all applets should stop their Threads in the stop method.

The fifth and final method in Blink is run. run is an important method because it is where the actual processing for our Thread takes place. It is also the first one we have encountered which is not overridden from the Applet class. run, however, is required for any class which implements Runnable. The run method of Blink is a very simple one. The run method simply goes to sleep for a time, and then calls repaint, which in turn will cause the paint method to be called.

That is the end of the Applet source code. To try it, create the Blink.class file by compiling Blink.java using javac.

**javac Blink.java**

You must also create the HTML file. Copy the following into a file called Blink.html. This can then be viewed with either Netscape or appletviewer as seen in figure 16.3. Notice the string "Oh, somewhere . . ." This is the line that will be displayed by Blink. Right below that you should see the <param> tag for speed which was discussed when you looked at the init method.

---

**Listing16.4   HTML File for Use with Blink**

```
**listing 16.4: Blink.html**
<title>Blinking Text</title>
<hr>
<applet code="Blink.class" width=300 height=100>
<param name=lbl value="Oh, somewhere in this favored land the sun is
shining bright; The band is playing somewhere, and somewhere hearts
are light.">
<param name=speed value="4">
</applet>
<hr>
<a href="Blink.java">The source.</a>
```

---

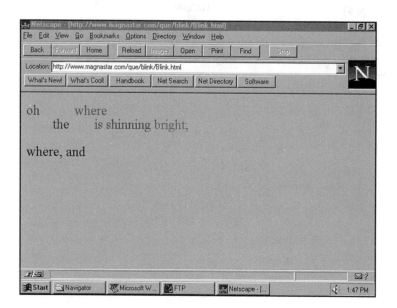

**Fig. 16.3**
Blink as seen
when run from
Netscape.

# A Complex Applet

The applet liveButton shown in listing 16.5 is a bit more complicated. The liveButton applet pays attention to such things as, when the mouse moves into the field of view of the applet, the mouse button being clicked on the applet, or the mouse being dragged across the applet (with the button down). It is also an example of how data can be changed at anytime, and needs to be synchronized.

### Listing 16.5   liveButton.java

```
/* ----------------------------------------------------------------
 * liveButton , Copyright (c) 1995 MagnaStar Inc, All Rights Reserved.
 * Permission to use, copy, modify, and distribute this software and its
 * documentation for NON-COMMERCIAL purposes and without fee is hereby
 * granted, provided that this copyright notice and appropiate documention
 * appears in all software that contains this code, or is derived from it.
 *
 * MagnaStar Inc. MAKES NO REPRESENTATIONS OR WARRANTIES ABOUT THE
 * SUITABILITY OF THE SOFTWARE, EITHER EXPRESS OR IMPLIED, INCLUDING BUT NOT
 * LIMITED TO THE IMPLIED WARRANTIES OF MERCHANTABILITY, FITNESS FOR A
```

(continues)

```
* PARTICULAR PURPOSE, OR NON-INFRINGEMENT. MagnaStar Inc. SHALL NOT
  ➥BE LIABLE
* FOR ANY DAMAGES SUFFERED BY LICENSEE AS A RESULT OF USING, MODIFY
  ➥ING OR
* DISTRIBUTING THIS SOFTWARE OR ITS DERIVATIVES.
*
* You may reach MagnaStar Inc. at info@magnastar.com
* P.O. Box 70, Waupun, WI 53963
*
* For more information see:
* http://www.magnastar.com                                    */

import java.awt.*;
import java.applet.*;
import java.net.URL;

public class liveButton extends java.applet.Applet implements
➥Runnable {
//Normal is the image which is displayed normally
Image Normal;
//Live is the image which moves, once the mouse first enters the
➥applet
Image Live;
//theSound is a sound that is played the first time the mouse enters
➥the applet
AudioClip theSound;
//status is true when the mouse is in the button area
boolean status;
//Tracker is used to monitor the loading of the images
MediaTracker Tracker;
//This thread is where we process the animation
Thread thisThread;
//locationX,locationY, goDown and goRight track the live image
int locationX=0,locationY=0;
boolean goDown=true, goRight=true;


public void init(){
 String param;
 status=false;
 Tracker = new MediaTracker(this);

 //Get the normal gif, by default we will take Normal.gif
 param=getParameter ("normal");
 if (param==null)
  Normal=getImage(getDocumentBase(),"Normal.gif");
 else
  Normal=getImage (getDocumentBase(),param);
 Tracker.addImage(Normal,0);

 //Get the live gif, but default we will take Live.gif
 param=getParameter ("live");
 if (param==null)
```

```
    Live=getImage(getDocumentBase(),"Live.gif");
  else
    Live=getImage (getDocumentBase(),param);
  Tracker.addImage(Live,1);

  //Get the sound byte, by default it is welcome.au
  param=getParameter("sound");
  if (param==null)
   theSound=getAudioClip(getDocumentBase(),"welcome.au");
  else
    theSound=getAudioClip(getDocumentBase(),param);
}

public void start(){
 thisThread = new Thread(this);
 thisThread.start();
}

public synchronized void paint(Graphics g){
 g.drawImage(Normal,0,0,size().width,size().height,null);
 if(status)
  g.drawImage(Live,locationX,locationY,null);
}

public void update(Graphics g){
 paint(g);
}

public void stop(){
 thisThread.stop();
}

public synchronized boolean mouseEnter(Event e,int x, int y){
 if (!status){
  status=true;
  theSound.play();
  }
 repaint();
 return false;
}


public synchronized boolean mouseDown(Event e,int x, int y){
 locationX=x;
 locationY=y;
 return true;
}


public synchronized boolean mouseDrag(Event e,int x, int y){
 if(x>locationX)
  goRight=true;
 else
  goRight=false;
 if(y>locationY)
  goDown=true;
```

(continues)

Writing an Applet

III

**Listing 16.5  Continued**

```
  else
   goDown=false;
  locationX=x;
  locationY=y;
  return true;
 }


 public void run(){
  //start all the images downloading
  while (!Tracker.checkAll(true)){
   repaint();
   try{
    thisThread.sleep(100);
    } catch(Exception e){}
   }
  repaint();
  //once the images have been loaded go through the following loop to
    ➥animate
  //the Live image if the mouse is over the button
  while (true){
   if (status){
    if (goDown){
     if((locationY+=3)>(size().height-Live.getHeight(null)))
      goDown=false;
     }
    else{
     if ((locationY-=3)<0)
      goDown=true;
     }
    if (goRight){
     if((locationX+=3)>(size().width-Live.getWidth(null)))
      goRight=false;
     }
    else{
     if((locationX-=3)<0)
      goRight=true;
     }
    repaint();
    }
   try{
    thisThread.sleep(50);
    }catch(Exception e){}
   }
 }

}//end class liveButton
```

As with the rest our applets, the first thing that liveButton does is import
several classes. Notice that, like Blink, liveButton imports whole packages
of classes. This eliminates the need to specify each and every class from a

particular class which you want to add. However, it does slightly increase the load on the virtual machine because it must keep track of all of them, even the ones which are not in use. Because of this, since only one class is used from the java.net package, liveButton only imports java.net.URL rather than the entire package.

liveButton declares a number of variables for the class. The advantage of declaring variables in the class scope, is that they can be used by any of the methods directly. However, it is also a good idea not to abuse this technique.

The init method for liveButton is very similar to the one you looked at from Blink. Several variables are fixed based on parameter values in the HTML file. However, in the case of liveButton these values are the names of graphic and sound files. These names cannot be used directly though, they must be converted into an URL. Take a look at a snippet from the init method shown in listing 16.6.

### Listing 16.6   Code Snippet from *init* Method of liveButton

```
param=getParameter ("normal");
 if (param==null)
  Normal=getImage(getDocumentBase(),"Normal.gif");
 else
  Normal=getImage (getDocumentBase(),param);
 Tracker.addImage(Normal,0);
```

In the Blink example, since all that you were getting from the <param> tag was the string which you would display, there was not much that you did with it in the init. In this case, you want to actually get the image which is specified by the parameter. To do this the getImage method from Applet is called.

So what is the getDocumentBase() doing in there? Well, the odds are you don't want to have to type the complete URL for the image in the HTML file. Why not use the relative URL of the HTML page? getDocumentBase() allows you to do just that. By using getDocumentBase() in conjunction with the file name, you can type:

```
<param name=normal value="MyGif.gif">
```

Rather than having to type:

```
<param name=normal value="http://www.mycorp.com/theDoc/dir/TheMyGif.gif">
```

The paint method for liveButton is actually much simpler than that for Blink, since much less is done here. The background image (Normal) is drawn, and then the Live image is drawn on top of it.

The next method after paint is update. update works much the same as paint. However, there are two important differences. First, paint is called each time the applet appears for the first time, or is partially revealed (such as when you page up and down on a Web page, and part of the applet disappears). update is called every other time the applet needs to be painted (for "update" changes). By default update clears the applet and then calls paint. The problem with this is that it causes a really nasty flicker. To overcome this, liveButton overrides the update method from applet, and without erasing the panel, calls paint.

If you look down a few more methods from update, you will see several methods called mouseEnter, mouseDown, and mouseDrag. Each of these methods is called when an appropriate action occurs. In the case of mouseDown this is called each time the mouse button is pressed within the applet, mouseDrag is called each time the mouse is moved with the mouse button down. mouseEnter is called each time the mouse arrow enters the Applet. The mouse button does not need to be pressed in order for mouseEnter to be called. However, for a reason which I'm sure made sense to Sun, each time the mouse button is pressed, before mouseDown is called, the mouseExit and mouseEnter methods are called too. While this is occasionally useful, more often it means you cannot do as much with the mouseEnter method as you might like to.

Each of the mouse methods causes something to happen to the live image. Before the mouse first enters the applet, the live image is not even drawn (go back and look at the paint method). When the mouse button is pressed, the live image moves to where the user has clicked, and as the mouse is dragged, the image follows. So what is the key word synchronized doing in the declaration for each of these methods? Since all these methods are changing information, it is important to make sure that they don't change it while paint is trying to use it. In the case of liveButton, changing information in the middle of the paint would not really cause much of a problem; however, in bigger applications it can cause chaos.

The last method for liveButton is run. As with all Runnable classes, run is the method where all the work must take place. The liveButton run method is no different. The first thing that is done in the run method is a block that looks like this:

```
//start all the images downloading
 while (!Tracker.checkAll(true)){
  repaint();
  try{
   thisThread.sleep(100);
   } catch(Exception e){}
  }
```

This block has been added to illustrate the use of the `ImageTracker`. In Java, when the `getImage` method is called (as you did back in the `init` method) the `Image` is not actually downloaded immediately. The system actually waits until the graphic is needed before it starts to download it. In addition, even after it is drawn, there is no guarantee that it is all there. To handle this situation, the `MediaTracker` class was added to the java.awt package. You actually created a `MediaTracker` object called `Tracker` back in the `init` method, but we didn't talk about it there. In the `run` method you will use the `Tracker` object to find out when all of the images have completed loading. Until they all have loaded, you keep repainting, which has the effect of redrawing the image onto the screen as it loads.

Once, all the images have been loaded, the `run` method enters a loop where it moves the `Live` image around. This is mostly a logical event, so it is left to you to muddle through it except for one thing. If you look into the loop, you will see two references to `Live.getHeight(null)` and `Live.getWidth(null)`. `Live` is an `Image`, and to obtain its height and width you need to use these methods from the `Image` class. However, if you had not waited for all the images to be completely loaded, there is a chance that the height and width would not be available. In this case the method would return a -1. Because this can happen (image information being requested, when it's not yet available) there is an interface called `ImageObserver` which can be used to monitor the state of the image as it downloads. It is important to realize what the `null` parameter is doing in ImageObeserver. You are telling the method that you don't want to be informed when the height and width information is available, and it should be sent to no one (null). You can do this because we already know the graphics are available, and so should their information. However, this will not always be the case in your own applets.

To compile the `liveButton` applet, once again you must use javac.

```
javac liveButton.java
```

The HTML file for `liveButton` is shown in listing 16.7. Aside from the different parameter names, the HTML file for `liveButton` is almost exactly the same as the one you created for `Blink`.

### Listing 16.7 HTML File for Use with liveButton Applet

```
<applet code="liveButton.class" width=424 height=99>
<param name=normal value="banner.gif">
<param name=live value="sunbrst.gif">
<param name=sound value="welcome.au">
<param name=link value="http://www.magnastar.com">
</applet>
```

III

**Writing an Applet**

**Fig. 16.4**

`liveButton` as seen
when run from
Netscape on a
UNIX machine.

# CHAPTER 17

# Debugging Your Java Code

*by Amber Benson*

In this chapter, you learn

- Why you would want to use a debugger
- How to start the `jdb` `debugger`
- How to set breakpoints and control execution
- How to list code at breakpoints and examine variables
- How to manipulate threads and the function stack
- How to catch and handle exceptions
- A simple example gets you started debugging

`jdb` is a command-line debugger for Java applications and applets. By using a debugger, you can avoid inserting print statements throughout your code, which you have to remove later, to learn the values of variables during execution. Instead you set breakpoints, `jdb` stops at the breakpoints, and you can print out variable values via commands to `jdb`. If you discover you have not pinpointed the location of a bug, you can then set new breakpoints, or move through the code at various granularities: you can continue to the next breakpoint, or execute the next line of code, or step into any function which may be called in the next line of code. You can always list the code surrounding the point at which the code is stopped. You can also examine the call stack at any time the code is stopped or suspended.

Using `jdb` you can move through the threads in your code with ease. You can focus `jdb`'s attention on any given thread, and you can suspend and resume execution of any or all threads independently. This gives you a fine control over your program which may allow you to solve bugs which would otherwise be extremely difficult to find.

You can also instruct jdb to catch exceptions, whether they are caught in your program or not. Once caught, you can then examine variables and the stack, just as if you had set a breakpoint at that point in the code.

You can use jdb to debug either a stand-alone application or an applet, using the appletviewer in debug mode. You can use jdb to inspect and debug your programs running under either a local or a remote Java interpreter.

# An Example—StockTicker Program

The example used in this chapter is a StockTicker program—a stand-alone application, not an applet. It continuously reads stock market price data and displays it in its own window. For brevity's sake we have removed any code that sized the window—it appears as merely a window frame and you must resize it with your mouse. At regular intervals, the StockTicker moves the display left one character, thus giving the appearance of a stock ticker. In a real live stock ticker application the data would be from an incoming data source, probably on the Net, but in this example it comes from static data and just simulates incoming data. We did this so you can run the example locally, without having a network connection or access to a stock quotation service. The StockTicker has three threads—the main thread, a StockReader, and a ShiftPainter.

```
import java.awt.*;
import java.net.URL;
public class TheStockTicker {
        public static void main( String[] argv ) {
                Frame          mainWin;      // Top level window
                StockTicker    ticker;       // Ticker object
                mainWin = new Frame( "Stock Ticker" );
                mainWin.setLayout( new BorderLayout() );
                ticker = new StockTicker();
                ticker.show();
                mainWin.add( "Center", ticker );
                mainWin.show();
                mainWin.layout();
                ticker.begin();
        }
}
 class StockTicker extends java.awt.Canvas {
        static       int    MAXLENGTH = 1000;
        ➥// max length ticker string
        static       int    HZMARGIN = 20;
        ➥// horizontal margin space
        static       int    VTMARGIN = 5;
        ➥// vertical margin space
        String              tickerStr = null;
        ➥// text left to print
```

```
int                    paintX, paintY;
➥// x origin and Y origin (baseline) for painting
ShiftPainter           shifter = null;
➥// thread controlling painting of ticker
boolean                paused = false;
➥// true => ticker is not scrolling
Thread                 reader = null;
➥// thread controlling reading of stock data
public void begin() {
        // Get the stock data feed going
        if (reader == null) {
                reader = new StockReader( this );
                reader.start();
        }
        // Get the shifter going
        if (shifter == null) {
                shifter = new ShiftPainter( this );
                shifter.start();
        }
        return;
}
public void stop() {
        shifter.stop();
        reader.stop();
        return;
}
public void paint(Graphics g) {
        if (tickerStr != null) {
                if ((paintX == 0) && (paintY == 0)) {
                        paintY = g.getFontMetrics()
                        ➥.getMaxAscent() + VTMARGIN;
                        paintX = HZMARGIN;
                }
                g.drawString( tickerStr, paintX, paintY
);
        }
        return;
}
public synchronized boolean shiftData() {
        boolean        shifted;
        ➥// true => data was actually shifted
        shifted = false;
        // Determine if we need to shift (text is longer
        ➥than display area)
        if (tickerStr != null && getGraphics()
        ➥.getFontMetrics().stringWidth( tickerStr ) +
                2 * HZMARGIN > size().width) {
                if ( tickerStr.length() >= 1) {
                ➥// Do the shift
                        tickerStr = tickerStr.substring( 1 );
                        shifted = true ;
```

```
                                }
                        }
                        return( shifted );
                }
                public synchronized void append( String data ) {
                        if (tickerStr == null)
                        ➥// Fill up the ticker string
                                tickerStr = data;
                        else
                                tickerStr = tickerStr + data;
                        if (tickerStr.length() > MAXLENGTH)
                        ➥// Truncate if string growing too big
                                tickerStr = tickerStr.substring(
                                ➥tickerStr.length() - MAXLENGTH );
                        repaint();
                        if (shifter != null && shifter.isWaiting())
                                shifter.resume();
                        return;
                }
        }
        class StockReader extends Thread {
                StockTicker            tickerData;
                ➥// objectholding the ticker data
                static final String[] dummyData = { "PARQ: 8.5", "PARQ:
                ➥10.2", "PARQ: 7.3" };
                static int             i = 0;
                StockReader( StockTicker t)          { tickerData = t; }
                public void run() {String newData; // new data read from
                                                   ➥stock info service
                URL stockURL;// connection to stock data server
                Object dataPipe; // content from stock data server
                do {newData = readTicker();// Fill up the ticker string
                if (newData != null)tickerData.append( "" + newData );
                try {// Wait for the next time to poll sleep(10000);
                }catch (InterruptedException e) {
                }} while (newData != null);
                }String readTicker() {StringpollData;
                        // data from poll of stock info
                        pollData = dummyData[i];
                        i = ++i % 3;
                        return( pollData );
                }}class ShiftPainter extends Thread {
                StockTicker tickerWin;
                // Window to paint in boolean stalled;
                // true => we are stalled, waiting for more text
                ShiftPainter( StockTicker st ){ tickerWin = st; stalled =
                ➥false; }
                public void run() {do {try {sleep(100);
                                }
                                catch (InterruptedException e) {
                                }
                                tickerWin.repaint();
                                // Shift string one position to the left
                                if (tickerWin.shiftData() == false) {
                                        stalled = true;
                                        suspend();
```

```
                }
            } while ( true ) ;
        }
        public boolean isWaiting() {
                return( stalled );
        }
    }
```

# Preparing for Debugging

If you are going to look at local (stack) variables in your debug session, you must first compile your classes with the -g option:

```
    javac -g <className>.java
```

The resulting compilation of your application is unoptimized byte code, which jdb needs to access the symbol tables for local variables.

---

**Note**

Do not confuse javac_g with javac  -g. javac_g is an unoptimized version of javac, and as such is suitable for use if you think you are having compiler problems or are doing a port, so that you might need to debug the compiler itself. javac_g does not produce unoptimized byte code of your application, which is what you need to debug your application.

---

# Starting *jdb*

Since jdb is command-line oriented, you start jdb from the prompt in an xterm or an MS-DOS prompt window. Typically you start a jdb session in the directory that contains the classes you intend to debug, although that is not necessary (see the -classpath option, which follows). You can start a jdb debugging session in one of two ways. You can have jdb start the Java interpreter with the class to be debugged, or you can start jdb and ask it to attach to a running Java interpreter. jdb accepts the same options as the Java interpreter; it also has a few of its own, as shown in the following sections.

## Starting *jdb* to Debug a Complete Application

To start jdb and the Java interpreter in one command (jdb starts the Java interpreter), use:

```
    jdb <className>
```

Once you start jdb, it responds in the xterm or MS-DOS window from which you started jdb with three lines similar to the following:

```
Initializing jdb...

0x139f408:class(TheStockTicker)

>
```

Since none of your code has yet executed, you see nothing more than these three lines in the xterm. Used this way, jdb starts the Java interpreter with any specified command line arguments, loads the specified class, and stops before executing the class's first executable instruction.

If your classes are in a different directory or directories, start jdb with the command line argument classpath, specifying all the directories jdb should look in for classes:

```
jdb -classpath <classPath> <className>
```

You must specify the complete path to classes.zip in the classpath argument, in addition to the path to your classes. For example, on a Windows system:

```
jdb -classpath C:/mystuff/myclasses;C:/java/java1_0/lib/classes.zip
➥MyApp
```

And on a UNIX system:

```
jdb -classpath /usr/mystuff/myclasses:/usr/java/java1_0/lib/
➥classes.zip MyApp
```

You can also start the program with the Java interpreter, then start jdb as a separate process and attach it to the running program. To do this, you must start the execution of your program with the -debug option. Doing this will cause Java to print a password before beginning execution of the program. The password can then be used as a command line argument to jdb; jdb will attach to the process with that password. If you wish to run the Java program on one machine and jdb on a different one, use the -host option when starting jdb:

```
java -debug <className>

jdb [-host <hostname>] -password <password>
```

If you have a program which takes input from the standard input, you must use this second method to debug it. Once jdb is started, any input typed is treated as input to jdb. Using the second method, you can have one input stream for your program, and one for jdb.

### Starting *jdb* to Debug an Applet

To debug an applet using jdb, start the appletviewer with the
-debug command line argument. This starts jdb, which then starts the
appletviewer but stops before any executable appletviewer line is executed.
Once you type run, execution in appletviewer begins, and each applet in the
HTML file is started in a separate window:

```
appletviewer -debug <htmlFileName>
```

Once you start the appletviewer in debug mode, jdb responds with three
lines similar to the following:

```
Initializing jdb...
0x139f408:class(sun.applet.AppletViewer)

>
```

Since none of your code has yet executed, you see nothing except these three
lines in the xterm.

# The *jdb* Prompt

If you start jdb with no command line arguments, whether or not you have
loaded a class, the jdb prompt is the following:

```
>
```

However, once you type run, the prompt is the name of the thread which has
jdb's attention. By default, this is the main thread, and the jdb prompt is:

```
main[1]
```

If you point jdb at another thread using the thread command, the prompt
changes to that of the new thread. Using the StockTicker example, the command thread 5 causes the prompt to change to the following:

```
Screen Updater[1]
```

The number in brackets indicates the stack level context. If you give the up
or down command, the number in brackets changes to show the stack level.
Continuing with the StockTicker example, after the command thread 5, a
command of up 2 causes the prompt to change to:

```
Screen Updater[3]
```

Each time you enter a command, jdb executes the command and then
redisplays the prompt, regardless of the state of the program being debugged.

Each of the commands listed in the remainder of this chapter is a command
to be typed at the jdb prompt.

III

Writing an Applet

# Specifying the Source Path and Loading Classes

The command use with no argument causes jdb to list the path it is using to find the source code. use followed by a file path changes the source file path to the one specified. This is the path jdb follows to find the source code (*.java) when listing code in response to the list command:

```
use [source file path]
```

If you started jdb with no arguments, or if you wish to load a new class that has not yet been loaded as a result of program execution, use load <className>:

```
load <className>
```

# Listing Parts of the Program and Program Organization

You can use most of these commands regardless of the state of the program. They return correct responses whether the program is running, stopped at a breakpoint, or any or all threads are suspended. The only exception to this is the list command, which does not list source code unless the program is suspended or stopped at a breakpoint.

### *classes*

The classes command causes jdb to list all the currently known classes. This includes all the Java classes, as well as the classes in your program.

### *methods*

You must specify a class name with the methods command; jdb lists all the methods for the specified class:

```
methods <class id>
```

Using the StockTicker example, the command methods ShiftPainter causes jdb to list the following:

```
void <init>(StockTicker)
void run()
boolean isWaiting()
```

### *list* **[line number]**

In order to list lines of source code, the program must be stopped at a breakpoint or you must have already specified a thread of interest and have suspended that thread. If you use the list command at any other time, jdb responds with the following:

```
No thread specified.
or
Current thread isn't suspended.
```

A command of list with no argument causes jdb to list the source code surrounding the breakpoint or the point at which the thread was suspended. list with a line number argument causes jdb to list the source code surrounding the specified line.

If the thread is suspended rather than stopped at a breakpoint, in order for the context to be correct so that the list command can find the correct code to list, you must specifically set the thread context via the thread command, and then you may need to move up the stack using the up command to set the stack context to your program's code.

If the source for the classes being debugged is not in the default classpath (or the classpath specified by the -classpath command line argument), jdb cannot list the source. See the use command above for specifying a file path to the source.

### memory

The memory command causes jdb to report the memory usage of the program at that point in time. Both the free memory and the total memory are reported.

# Threads

You can examine all the threadgroups and threads currently in existence in your program. You can also change jdb's focus from one thread to another, and suspend and resume execution of any or all threads. You may, for example, need to suspend one thread while you step through another to a certain point, then resume the first thread, examining variable values along the way.

### threadgroups

The threadgoups command lists all the threadgroups in the program. They are listed prefaced by an incremental index number, followed by the class name (java.lang.ThreadGroup), followed by the threadgroup handle, followed by the threadgroup name. Only threadgroups of threads which have been started are shown.

**III**

**Writing an Applet**

Using the StockTicker example, the `threadgroups` command produces the following output:

```
1. (java.lang.ThreadGroup)0x13930b8 system
2. (java.lang.ThreadGroup)0x13939c0 main
3. (java.lang.ThreadGroup)0x13a0b50 TheStockTicker.main
```

### *threads* [threadgroup]

Typing `threads` causes `jdb` to list all the threads in the default threadgroup, which is normally the first non-system group. `threads <threadgroup>` causes `jdb` to list all the threads in the specified threadgroup. Use the threadgroup name (the last element in a `threadgroups` command output line) to specify the threadgroup in the `threads` command. Threads are listed prefaced by an incremental index number. The last item on the thread line is the condition of the thread. Only the threads that have been started are shown.

Using the StockTicker example, the command `threads TheStockTicker.main` issued while the stock ticker program is running produces the following output:

```
Group TheStockTicker.main:
1. (java.lang.Thread)0x13a09f8      AWT-Win32          running
2. (java.lang.Thread)0x13a0a50      AWT-Callback-Win32 running
3. (StockReader)0x13a0cb0           Thread-2           cond. waiting
4. (ShiftPainter)0x13a0d10          Thread-3           running
5. (sun.awt.ScreenUpdater)0x13a0da8 Screen Updater     cond. waiting
```

### *suspend* [thread id(s)]

The suspend command with no arguments suspends all non-system threads. `suspend` followed by one or more thread ids suspends those threads only. The `thread id` argument is the index number of the thread in the current threadgroup; the indexes begin at 1 in each threadgroup and are the first item displayed in response to the `threads` command. Thus, if you are interested in a thread belonging to a threadgroup other than the default (normally the first non-system group), you must first specify the threadgroup via the `threadgroup` command.

If you wish to list the code where the thread is suspended, you may need to use the `thread` command and the `up` command to set the thread context and the stack frame context to the appropriate section of code. See the `list` command.

## *resume* [thread id(s)]

The resume command with no arguments resumes all suspended threads. resume followed by one or more thread ids resumes those threads only. The thread id argument is the index number of the thread in the current threadgroup; the indexes begin at 1 in each threadgroup and are the first item displayed in response to the threads command. Thus, if you are interested in a thread belonging to a threadgroup other than the default (normally the first non-system group), you must first specify the threadgroup via the threadgroup command.

## *threadgroup* <name>

If you are interested in a thread in a threadgroup other than the default, you must specify that threadgroup via the threadgroup command. The name argument should be the threadgroup name that is the last item displayed on a line in response to the threadgroups command.

## *thread* <thread id>

You can specify a thread of interest to jdb via the thread command. The thread id is the index number of the thread in the current threadgroup; the index numbers begin at 1 in each threadgroup and are the first item displayed in response to the threads command. Thus, if you are interested in a thread belonging to a threadgroup other than the default (normally the first non-system group), you must first specify the threadgroup via the threadgroup command. Once you have specified a thread of interest, you can examine its stack.

# Breakpoints

If you want your program to stop so you can examine variables or step through it one line at a time, you must set a breakpoint, which is essentially a stop sign telling the debugger to stop the program when execution reaches that point in the code. You can either instruct jdb to stop at a certain line number or in a method for a class.

## *stop in* <class id>.<method>

This command causes jdb to set a breakpoint at the first executable statement in the method specified.

### stop at <class id>:<line>

This command causes jdb to set a breakpoint at the specified line number.

---

**Note**

Note that if you have more than one class in your .java file, you must specify the class containing the code when you specify the line number, even if the class name is different than the file name. For example, if the StockTicker example were stored in a file named The StockTicker.java, and if you wanted to stop at line 117, which is the

```
    tickerWin.repaint();
```

line near the bottom, you must type

```
    stop at ShiftPainter:117
```

---

### clear <class id>:<line> and clear <class id>.<method>

These clear commands clear the specified breakpoint.

### clear and stop

The clear or stop command with no arguments causes jdb to list the currently set breakpoints.

# Controlling Execution

You may want to set breakpoints before executing any lines of code, so jdb does not start execution of your application or applet until you type run. Then, once the program is stopped at a breakpoint, you may want to continue on to the next breakpoint, or execute the next line of code in the current function, or step into any other functions that are called in the current line of code. These commands allow you to control the granularity of program execution.

### run <class> [args]

jdb does not execute any class until instructed to run. If you started jdb with a classname as a command line argument, you can issue the run command with no arguments to start execution of that class. When starting a stand-alone application, execution starts at the main method for the class. For applets, execution starts at the init method. If you load the class(es) via a load command, or have not loaded any classes, you must specify the class name as an argument to the run command. The optional args should be the command line arguments for the class being run.

Once the program is stopped at a breakpoint, you can control execution from that point via the step, next, or cont command.

### step

When execution is stopped, issuing the step command causes jdb to execute the current line. If the current line contains a call to a method, jdb steps into the method, stopping at the first executable line in the called method.

### next

When execution is stopped, issuing the next command causes jdb to execute the current line. If the current line contains a call to a method, jdb executes that method, completes the execution of the current line, and stops at the line following this one in the current method.

### cont

Issuing a cont command when execution is stopped causes the program execution to continue normally.

# Printing Variable Values

Whenever the application or applet is stopped, you can display the values of local variables or member variables. Note that if you have an object that has other objects as data members, if you ask jdb to print the data member object before it has been created, jdb complains that it is not a valid variable or object. In fact the object may be valid but is simply null because it has not been created yet. Once it is created, an attempt to print it succeeds.

### locals

Typing locals at the prompt when the application is stopped causes jdb to display all the local variables within the current scope. Remember that in order for jdb to be able to access any local variables, you must have compiled the classes with the -g option. If the program is not stopped, locals displays an error message.

### print <id> [<id>(s)]

Using print, you can print a single value or several values, of any of the local or member variables available within the current scope. The parameter id can be a local variable name, a member variable, a class name followed by . followed by a static class variable, or a Java expression combining these.

For example, part of the class definition of StockTicker is as follows:

```
class StockTicker extends java.awt.Canvas {
        static     int    MAXLENGTH = 1000;
            String  tickerStr = null;
```

When this program is stopped in a StockTicker method which sets the value of tickerStr, the command

```
print tickerStr
```

results in this output:

```
this.tickerStr =      PARQ: 8.5
```

and the command

```
print StockTicker.MAXLENGTH
```

results in this output:

```
"StockTicker" is not a valid field of (StockTicker)0x13a10a8
StockTicker.MAXLENGTH = 1000
```

The print command calls the object's toString() method to format the output.

If a class is not loaded when you type the print command, you must specify the class's full name, and the class is loaded as a side effect.

## *dump* <id> [<id>(s)]

dump prints the values of all the variables for a class or a class instance if you specify a class name or class instance as the id. dump <className> prints the static class variable values, whereas dump this or dump <classInstanceVariableName> prints the member variable values.

If you specify a variable for id, dump prints some other information about the variable as well as its value (such as, for example, the offset and count for a string variable).

---

**Note**

If a class is not loaded when you type the debug command, you must specify the class's full name, and the class is loaded as a side effect.

---

# Examining the Stack

Whenever your program is suspended or stopped at a breakpoint, you can examine the call stack, which is the list of all functions in the current thread which have not yet returned. jdb always has a stack frame context, which means it is focused on a particular line number in a particular function. By default, the context is at level 1, which is the last function that was called. You can move the context up and down the stack and examine variables in any of the functions in the stack.

## *where* [<thread id>] [all]

The where command with no arguments dumps the stack of the current thread (set with the thread command). where all dumps the stack of all threads. where <thread id > dumps the stack of that thread; thread id is the index number of the thread in the current threadgroup. If the thread is suspended or the program is stopped, you can browse the variables with the print and dump commands. If you have moved the stack level context via the up or down command, the where command shows the current level by listing only those frames at the current level and above.

## *up* [n]

The up command with no argument moves the current thread's stack's context up a frame. up n moves the current thread's stack's context up *n* frames. The stack level is indicated in the number in brackets in the jdb prompt. Once you have moved up the stack, you can then examine variables in that frame.

## *down* [n]

The down command with no argument moves the current thread's stack's context down a frame. down n moves the current thread's stack's context down *n* frames. The stack level is indicated in the number in brackets in the jdb prompt. Once you have moved down the stack, you can then examine variables in that frame.

# Exceptions

When an exception occurs for which there isn't a catch statement anywhere in the program's stack, Java normally dumps an exception trace and exits. When run with jdb, however, the exception is treated as a non-recoverable breakpoint, and jdb stops at the statement that caused the exception. You can at that point examine local and instance variables to determine the cause of the exception.

---

**Note**

Note that under jdb a program may throw exceptions that don't occur when run without the debugger. This is because there may be timing differences, especially in the relationships between and among threads. This is not all bad, as these are often caused by not checking for an object's existence or for other initialization. As you add checks for these, your code becomes more robust.

---

You can specify that jdb catch specific exceptions for debugging via the catch command. When the specified exception is thrown, it is treated as if a breakpoint were set on the instruction that caused the exception. You can re-move the exception from the list of exceptions jdb is to catch via the ignore command.

Once jdb stops, either because of an uncaught or a caught exception, in order to list the code at the point the exception occurred, do the following:

Set the jdb thread focus to the thread containing the instruction that caused the exception. To do this type threads, then thread n, where *n* is the index of the thread wanted. Then type where, to see the stack for that thread. Then type up n, where *n* is the number of levels to move up the stack to focus the stack context on your code containing the instruction that caused the excep-tion. Then type list.

### *catch* <class id>

The catch command causes jdb to treat the occurrence of the <class id> ex-ception as a breakpoint. catch with no argument lists the exceptions in the catch list. <class id> can be a Java exception or one you have defined. Examples of catch commands are:

```
catch java.io.IOException
catch StockReader.NoInputException
```

### *ignore* <class id>

The ignore command causes jdb to remove the <class id> exception from the list of exceptions it breaks for. Note that the ignore command only causes jdb to ignore the specified exception; the Java interpreter continues to catch it. ignore with no argument lists the exceptions in the catch list.

# Miscellaneous Commands

These commands are easy to learn and use, but are quite helpful, especially the help command.

## *gc*

gc frees unused objects.

## *help* or *?*

help or ? displays the list of recognized commands with a brief description of each.

## *!!*

!! repeats the previous command.

## *exit* or *quit*

exit or quit exits the jdb debugger.

# A Simple Debugging Example

Here are the steps to get you started debugging.

To compile the program with a symbol table appropriate for debugging:

```
javac -g StockTicker.java
```

To start the debugging session:

```
jdb StockTicker
```

To set breadpoints:

```
stop at StockTicker:181
stop in ShiftPainter.paint
```

To start execution:

```
run
```

Once the program has stopped at the breakpoint, to list the code surrounding the breakpoint:

```
list
```

To list code farther from the breakpoint, surrounding line 150:

```
list 150
```

To display the local variables:

```
locals
```

To print the value of a particular class instance variable:

```
print tickerWin.paintX
```

To dump all member variables of an object:

```
dump tickerWin
```

To execute one line of code:

```
next
```

To find out what the stack looks like, and what the current stack context is:

```
where
```

To move up a level in the stack:

```
up
```

To list the code of the method in the new stack context:

```
list
```

To continue execution:

```
cont
```

To exit jdb:

```
quit
```

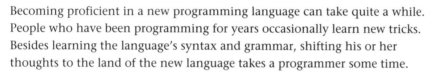

# CHAPTER 18

# Browser Script Language

*by Jerry Ablan*

Becoming proficient in a new programming language can take quite a while. People who have been programming for years occasionally learn new tricks. Besides learning the language's syntax and grammar, shifting his or her thoughts to the land of the new language takes a programmer some time.

At this point in the book, you probably have dozens of ideas for cool applets to implement on your Web site. But writing a complete applet takes time and a decent understanding of the Java language. Wouldn't it be nice to simply add the required functionality to your Web page?

Suppose that you want to create an applet that scrolls information in the help bar of the browser. Coding and testing a complete applet could take several days. Adding a little snippet of code to your Web page to perform that single function would be great. Browser script languages allow you to perform these simple feats without coding entire Java applets.

This chapter will cover the following topics:

- Smart browsers
- JavaScript
- VBScript
- Using scripts in your Web pages

## Power to the Browsers!

Web browsers are fairly unintelligent; they simply request, retrieve, and display the content of documents from various servers. If you want to add something unique to your Web site, you have to create a program on the server that modifies the document before it is sent to the browser. Instead of doing any modifications to the document at the browser, the changes are made before the document is sent. This is referred to as a *server-side* modification because the changes are made at the server's side of the connection. These modifications are performed by scripts and processes called *server-side* programs.

But creating server-side programs can be a headache. And for many people, creating such programs is not even an option; writing these programs involve UNIX programming skills that many people don't have. In addition, if you have a home page with an Internet Service Provider, you may not have the capability to create server-side scripts and programs. Many ISPs offer these services only to their corporate clients.

# A Smarter Browser

Although browsers are large and have many functions, they are essentially unintelligent; they run, retrieve, and browse Web pages, and then they end. Browsers can interact with a variety of servers: HTTP, FTP, and Gopher, to name a few. But the basic browser is a multimedia display tool—nothing more.

To make the browser smarter, you have to add some *client-side* capabilities that allow a retrieved document to modify itself or the retrieving browser. This capability moves the power of server-side programs to the client, in essence empowering the browser and making it smarter.

One client-side capability that is available is a script language. Scripts allow a Web browser to intelligently deal with situations that otherwise would require a program on the Web server. In addition, the user's perception is that the situation is handled much faster, because the browser does not need to send the request to the server and display the response.

# JavaScript

In December 1995, Netscape Communications Corporation and Sun Microsystems announced a new scripting language called JavaScript. JavaScript is an open, cross-platform scripting language that complements the features of Java. JavaScript is easy to learn, even by users who have little or no programming background. JavaScript was first available in the beta versions of Netscape Navigator 2.0.

According to the original press release for JavaScript, 28 companies endorse JavaScript as an open-standard, object scripting language and intend to provide support for it in their future products. These companies include America

Online, Apple Computer, Borland International, Novell, and Oracle. The full press release is available at the following URL:

```
http://java.sun.com/pr951204-03.html
```

## What Is JavaScript?

JavaScript is similar to Java in syntax but is by no means "Java Lite" or a slimmed-down version of Java. JavaScript is a complementary language that provides some of the features of Java without requiring the user to learn object-oriented programming. JavaScript can recognize and respond to various events that are generated by the browser software, including mouse clicks and movements, page loading, and form input.

JavaScript scripts are embedded in Web documents and are executed by the browser at various points of the document's retrieval. This distinction between Java and JavaScript is important. Java applets must be compiled and downloaded by the browser before they are executed; JavaScript scripts are simply downloaded and interpreted.

An excellent use of JavaScript is to perform error checking in online forms. If you have forms that rely on a server-side program to perform error checking, you can perform the check at the client with JavaScript. This allows, for instance, an instantaneous response to a user entering invalid information into a form. An interesting use of form-checking calculations is the 1040-EZ form Web page. Figure 18.1 is what this page looks like. This site is at:

```
http://www.homepages.com/fun/1040EZ.html
```

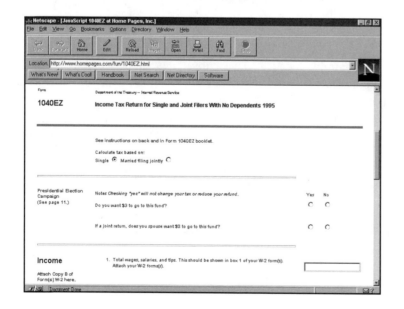

**Fig. 18.1**
The 1040-EZ Web page uses JavaScript to check the form values entered by the user.

III

Writing an Applet

Another use is to perform calculations at the client instead of the server. Perhaps you have a Web site that amortizes home loans. The user inputs his or her data and then submits the form to the server. The server spawns a CGI program to calculate the results, which are sent back to the client for display. With JavaScript, the entire calculation can be performed at the client, by the client, thereby reducing network traffic and the time needed for transmission of data. *Books Galore* is a Web site designed to show off the features of JavaScript. Figure 18.2 shows one of its pages. The site is at:

```
http://weber.u.washington.edu/~davidnf/java/bookstore.html
```

**Fig. 18.2**

This site uses JavaScript to check the total quantities and which books are selected. It automatically calculates the tax and total for a book order as well.

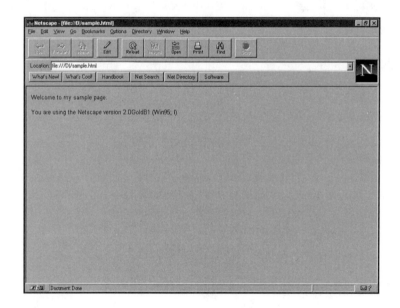

Like a programming language, JavaScript has variables. But conventional programming languages (like C, C++, and Java) require the programmer to declare the type of data that is to be stored in the variable. This is called *static typing* of variables. JavaScript has the opposite of this: *loose typing*. That is to say that variable types are never declared, they are implied. Variables become a certain type depending on the data that is placed inside of them. They may also change type on the fly. If you assign a string value to a variable, you may later change it to a Boolean. Whichever value is currently in the variable defines the type.

For example, if you have a variable called **booFar**, and you initialize it with a string value, the variable then becomes a string.

```
var booFar = "Hi there!";
```

Later in your script, you can place another value type in it like this:

```
var booFar = 3421.34
```

The variable changes to hold the information automatically.

In Java, you must declare the variable as a string before attempting to place any string data into it.

```
String booFar = "Hi there!";
```

Once a type has been chosen in a static typed language, any value other than the original type must be converted before assignment. With JavaScript, this conversion is done for you.

JavaScript is not capable of defining classes. Although you can create instances of internal or Java classes, you cannot create classes with JavaScript. You also cannot inherit new classes from internal or Java classes.

## JavaScript Data Types

JavaScript supports four basic types of variables:

- *Boolean*—This type of variable holds a true or false value.

  ```
  doesThisWork = True;

  isThisBroken = False;
  ```

- *Number*—This type of variable can hold a decimal or floating-point value.

  ```
  aFloat = 123.45;

  anInt = 3492;
  ```

- *String*—This type of variable can hold a sequence of alphanumeric characters.

  ```
  userName = "munster";

  emailAddress = "munster@mcs.net";
  ```

- *Object*—This generic data type can hold a value of any type. This is usually used to store instances of internal or Java classes.

  ```
  today = new Date();

  aDate = new Date( 1971, 4, 12 );
  ```

In addition, JavaScript supports arrays of any data type.

## JavaScript's Object Model

JavaScript is based on the idea that an object is an entity that has defined properties. These properties can be variables or other objects. All properties can be manipulated with JavaScript and are considered to be variables.

An object also can include functions. As in Java, these functions are called *methods*.

Manipulating the property of an object in JavaScript is similar to Java and other programming languages. They use the *dot-notation* to drill-down into the object.

For example, one of the internal objects available to JavaScript is called navigator. This object holds information about the browser the user is running. One of the navigator properties is appName. This string property contains the name of the browser. To get the value of this property, you use dot-notation by placing a period, or dot, in between the object and the property like this:

```
navigator.appName
```

Any property of any object can be interrogated in this fashion. In addition, a property may be another object, so you can drill-down even further to reach the property desired. The next section will introduce you to more of JavaScript's internal objects and have some examples.

---

**Note**

This model is similar to C and C++, as well as to higher-level languages such as Visual Basic, PowerBuilder's PowerScript, and Smalltalk.

---

## JavaScript Objects

JavaScript comes with a rich set of built-in objects. These objects give the programmer access to form controls and to browser, server, and document information. All these objects have their own properties and associated events. The properties of these objects can be manipulated and interrogated. The events generated by these objects can trigger the execution of other scripts as well.

Four very important objects are available with every retrieved document:

- document: contains information about the content of the current document, including type, colors, and forms.
- history: contains information about the URLs that the user has visited.
- location: contains information about the currently loaded document.
- window: contains information about the entire browser window. Each framed window also has its own window object. The window object is the top-level object in the object hierarchy.

Figure 18.3 shows the `window` object hierarchy.

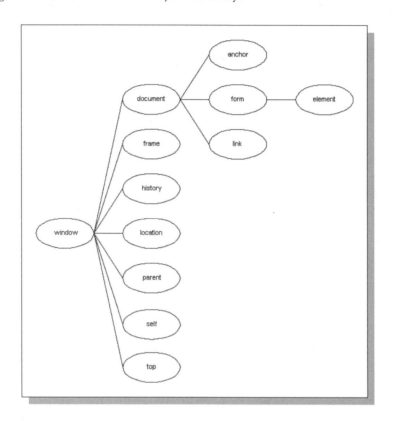

**Fig. 18.3**
The hierarchy of
the `window` object.

To familiarize yourself with these objects, create the sample HTML page
shown in listing 18.1.

**Listing 18.1   Sample HTML Document**

```
<html>
<head>
   <title>Sample HTML Document</title>
</head>
<body text="#000000" bgcolor="#FFFFFF" link="#0000EE" vlink="#551A8B"
alink="#FF0000">
<p>

<script language="JavaScript">
<!-- Non-Aware Browsers will ignore this

//
// Function: handleClick
//
```

(continues)

**Listing 18.1 Continued**

```
// Moves values into the display field.
//

function handleClick( theButton, theForm )
{
    if ( theButton.name == "Button_Me" )
            theForm.total.value = "You pressed me!";
    else
    {
            if ( theButton.name == "Button_Him" )
                    theForm.total.value = "I said to press the other
                    ➥button!!";
            else
                    if ( theButton.name == "Clear" )
                            theForm.total.value = "";
    }
}


// End of script -->
</script>

This is a sample HTML document. </p>

<p>

<form NAME="myForm"><font SIZE=+2>Stuff  </font>
<input name="Total" size=50></input>

<p>
<input  TYPE="button" NAME="Button_Me" VALUE="Press Me"
➥onClick="handleClick( this, this.form )"></input>
<p>
<input  TYPE="button" NAME="Button_Him" VALUE="Press The Other
➥Button" onClick="handleClick( this, this.form )"></input>
<p>
<input  TYPE="button" NAME="Clear" VALUE="Clear Stuff"
➥onClick="handleClick( this, this.form )"></input>
<p>
</form>
<p>
<script language="JavaScript">
<!-- Non-Aware Browsers will ignore this

document.writeln( "Loaded Document: " + location.href + "<br>" );
document.writeln( "Document Title: " + document.title + "<br>" );
document.writeln( "<P>" );
document.writeln( "This document contains " +
➥document.myForm.elements.length + " form elements. <p>" );

for ( var i = 0; i < document.myForm.elements.length; i++ )
{
    document.writeln( "Element #" + ( i + 1 ) + " is named " +
```

```
document.myForm.elements[ i ].name );
    document.writeln( " and has a value of \"" +
    ➥document.myForm.elements[ i ].value + "\"<br>" );
}

// End of script -->
</script>
</body>
</html>
```

Here are some of the object properties used in the above example:

```
location.href = "http://www.netgeeks.com/junk/sample.html"
document.title = "Sample HTML Document"
document.myForm.Button_Me.name = "Button_Me"
```

**Note**

The preceding items are only examples; the values depend on the location and content of the target document.

Figure 18.4 shows the result of the HTML document from listing 18.1.

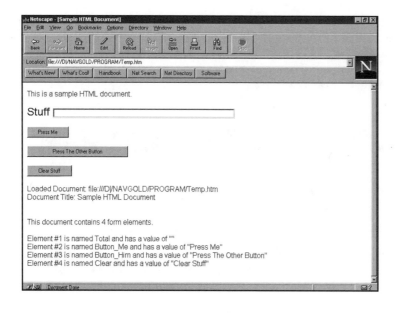

**Fig. 18.4**
The results of loading the sample document.

## JavaScript Resources

Even though JavaScript is relatively new, many Internet resources are already devoted to JavaScript. Following are a few of the better sites:

Netscape's JavaScript Page

```
http://home.netscape.com/comprod/products/navigator/
version_2.0/script/
```

Right from the horse's mouth comes Netscape's very own JavaScript resources page.

**The JavaScript Index**

```
http://www.c2.org/~andreww/javascript
```

This site provides a list of excellent JavaScript resources.

**Gamelan's JavaScript Page**

```
http://www.gamelan.com/frame/Gamelan.javascript.html
```

This site provides another great list of JavaScript resources.

# Visual Basic Script

Another scripting language soon will be available from Microsoft. This language is called Visual Basic Script (VB Script for short). VBScript, which is a slimmed-down version of Visual Basic for Applications (VBA), initially will be available for Microsoft's Internet Explorer.

VB Script is similar to JavaScript in that it lives inside HTML documents. The resemblance, however, ends there. While JavaScript is closer to Java (or C and C++) in syntax, VB Script is actual Visual Basic code. VB Script allows you to embed Visual Basic code into your documents. When a VB Script-enabled Web browser reaches the <SCRIPT> tag, the code is compiled and executed. Listing 18.2 shows a sample VB Script script.

**Listing 18.2  Sample VB Script Script**

```
<SCRIPT>
Sub Button_Me_click
  Total.Text = "He clicked me!"
End Sub
</SCRIPT>
```

VB Script will also be capable of OLE automation. This will allow you to get and set properties of OLE and Java objects that are embedded within an HTML document.

Not much more information was available about VBScript at the time this chapter was written. Developments occur quickly, however, so check out the following Microsoft Web site from time to time:

```
http://www.microsoft.com/intdev
```

# The *<SCRIPT>* Tag

How do script languages find their way into an HTML document? The languages use a new HTML extension: the <SCRIPT> tag.

The <SCRIPT> tag can be placed anywhere in the <BODY> or <HEAD> section of an HTML document. If the script is placed in the <HEAD> portion, however, it is interpreted before the body of the document is fully received. Because of this, you should place functions and initialization code into the <HEAD> portion. That code will be available throughout the life of the document.

You can place <SCRIPT> tags throughout your HTML document. A common practice is to place a <SCRIPT> tag within the <HEAD> portion of a document to hold functions. These functions then are available to the entire document. You can place other <SCRIPT> tags in the <BODY> section of your document to call these functions or to provide information as shown in listing 18.1.

---

**Note**

Remember to follow each <SCRIPT> tag with </SCRIPT>. This tag signifies the end of an HTML script block.

---

**The *LANGUAGE* Parameter**

The <SCRIPT> tag has one optional parameter. This parameter is the LANGUAGE parameter. It is used to specify the language in which the script is written.

This is useful to the browser to ignore scripts in languages that it does not support and allows for other languages to be developed. Currently, the only language that the Netscape Navigator software supports is JavaScript.

III

**Writing an Applet**

# Part IV

# Using Applets in Web Pages

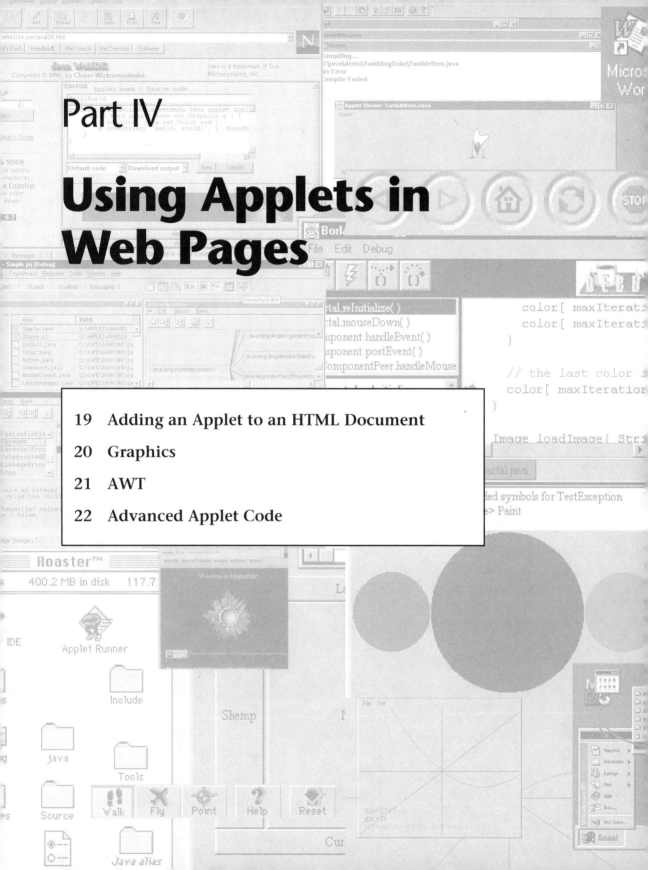

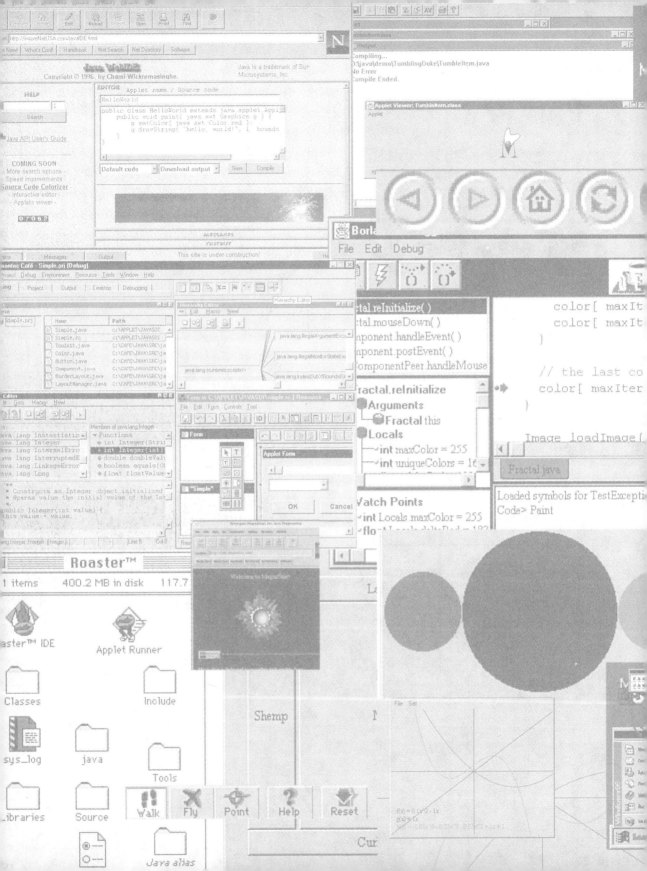

# CHAPTER 19

# Adding an Applet to an HTML Document

*by Kevin M. Krom*

In the last several chapters, you learned how to create a Java applet. But maybe you just want to use a pre-written applet in one of your documents. When the time comes to test your applet, and then later to show it to others, you're going to need to place your applet inside an HTML file so it can be viewed with a Web browser or the appletviewer program.

In this chapter you will learn how

- To use the <APPLET> tag in an HTML document
- To pass parameters to your applet with the <PARAM> tag
- To allow non-Java enabled Web browsers to see alternate HTML
- To use the <APP> tag for the HotJava browser (1.0 alpha 3 release only)
- Java-enabled browsers manage applets

## The <APPLET> Tag

Adding items to an HTML document is done through the use of tags. For example, if you wanted to insert a GIF image file called "somepic.gif," you would put the following in your HTML source document:

```
<IMG src="somepic.gif">
```

**Tip**

Note that the <IMG> tag is case insensitive, i.e., "IMG" and "img" both work. Likewise, both "SRC" and "src" will work for the image source parameter.

However, using the All Caps form of HTML tags may make reading your HTML source easier, because the tags will stand out clearly from parameters and plain text.

## Syntax

A Java applet is done in a similar fashion to images through the use of the <APPLET> tag. The basic syntax of the <APPLET> tag is:

```
<APPLET [codebase=[path¦URL]] code=someclass.class
➡height=applet_height width=applet_width>
</APPLET>
```

As with the <IMG> tag, the <APPLET> tag is case insensitive, except the values of someclass.class, path, and URL.

### Why Does the <APPLET> Tag Need a Closing </APPLET> Tag?

This is not the complete syntax of the <APPLET> tag. In order to specify user parameters for the applet or alternate HTML for browsers which aren't Java-enabled, the applet declaration needs to be bracketed to include potentially any number of other tags inside of it.

The full <APPLET> syntax is specified later in this chapter.

## The Codebase Parameter

The codebase parameter specifies the location of the class file. The value of codebase can either be a pathname relative to the HTML file, or it can be a uniform resource locator (URL) specifying the location of the class.

This parameter is technically optional, but is always needed if the applet's .class file is not in the same directory as the referencing HTML file.

**Using a Relative Path on the Local Host.** For this example, the Foo.class file is located in a subdirectory classes directly underneath the directory Foo.html is located in figure 19.1 (the left side) shows this directory structure. Foo.html then needs to use the codebase parameter to specify the classes subdirectory:

```
<APPLET codebase="classes" code="Foo.class" height=100 width=300>
</APPLET>
```

**Using a URL for Classes on Remote Hosts.** To access a remote class, use the codebase to specify the URL of the directory that contains the class, not the URL of the class itself.

```
<APPLET codebase="http://example.applet.net/html/classes"
➡code="Foo.class" height=100 width=300>
</APPLET>
```

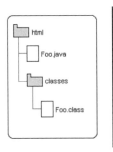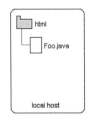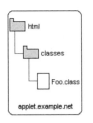

**Fig. 19.1**
Location of the Foo.class file for both local (left) and remote (right) applet calls.

## The Code Parameter

The code parameter specifies the name of the applet class to be executed. For example, if you want to include the applet in the file Foo.class in the same directory as your HTML file, you simply need to specify:

```
<APPLET code="Foo.class" height=100 width=300>
</APPLET>
```

The quotes around the class name are not strictly necessary, but they help maintain good style and consistency.

Test the applet by using appletviewer, included with the Java release, or with Netscape Navigator. To use the appletviewer from the command line, enter the command:

```
appletviewer Foo.html
```

With Netscape Navigator or another Java-enabled browser, simply load the HTML file in the normal manner. For Netscape Navigator, select File, Open File (or use the shortcut Ctrl+O) and then find the correct file to load.

---

**Caution**

Windows 95/NT users need to open a DOS window to get a command line, and should be in the directory with the HTML file, rather than using an absolute or relative pathname.

---

## The Height and Width Parameters

The height and width parameters are both required, and specify how tall or how wide (respectively) the applet will appear in number of pixels. If you want Foo.class to be 300 pixels wide by 100 pixels high, your HTML tag would look like:

```
<APPLET codebase="classes" code="Foo.class" width=300 height=100>
</APPLET>
```

## Summary

To add an applet to an HTML document:

1. Insert an <APPLET> tag at the place in the document where you wish the applet to appear.
2. Specify the name of the applet's class with the code parameter.
3. If the class file is not in the current directory, use the codebase parameter to:
   - Specify the relative path if the class file is on the local filesystem.
   - Specify the URL of the directory containing the class file if it resides on a remote filesystem.
4. Specify the space needed by the applet with the height and width parameters.
5. Close the applet declaration with the </APPLET> tag.

# Including User-Specified Parameters

Applets receive their initialization parameters through the invoking HTML file. In the previous section, you saw the pre-defined parameters code, codebase, height, and width. In this section, you'll learn how to pass additional parameters to applets via the <PARAM> tag.

## Syntax

The syntax for applets with user-specified parameters:

```
<APPLET [codebase=[path¦URL]] code=someclass.class
➥height=applet_height width=applet_width>
{[<PARAM name=parameter_name value=parameter_value>]}
</APPLET>
```

The entire <PARAM> tag, except parameter_value, is case insensitive. Whether parameter_value is case sensitive or not depends on the code that uses it. By default, parameter_value is case sensitive.

The <PARAM> tag needs to be placed between the <APPLET> and </APPLET> tags for the applet it corresponds to. You can use as many different <PARAM> tags as you wish for each applet, each one specifying a different applet parameter.

## Example

When you write an applet, you can search for any number of parameters, of which some, all, or none may be present when the applet is declared in the HTML file. Take Foo.java as the example source. Inside of the init() method, it has code to handle two parameters: color and text.

The getParameter() method allows the programmer to access the parameters specified by the <PARAM> tags. The method always returns a String, and needs to be supplied with the (case-insensitive) name of the parameter to be read. Note the first line of the init() method below—it reads the "COLOR" parameter.

```java
public void init()
{
    String p = getParameter("COLOR");

    if (p == null)
    {
        textcolor = Color.black;
    }
    else if (p.equalsIgnoreCase("red"))
    {
        textcolor = Color.red;
    }

    p = getParameter("TEXT");

    if (p == null)
    {
        textvalue = "Hello world.";
    }
    else
    {
        textvalue = p;
    }}
```

Note that by using the equalsIgnoreCase method (from class String), this applet has made the color parameter case-insensitive.

This is only part of the Foo.java file. With the above initializers, a Foo applet will print the phrase "Hello world." in black if no other parameters are given (see fig. 19.2):

**Fig. 19.2**
Foo applet
without
parameters.

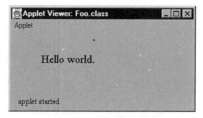

To change the color of the text to red, you can insert a <PARAM> tag, changing the value of the color parameter:

```
<APPLET codebase="classes" code="Foo.class" height=100 width=300>
<PARAM name=color value="red">
</APPLET>
```

And now, to change the text to something else, like "I love creating Java applets!" add another <PARAM> tag (see fig. 19.3):

```
<APPLET codebase="classes" code="Foo.class" height=100 width=300>
<PARAM name=color value="red">
<PARAM name=text value="I love creating Java applets!">
</APPLET>
```

**Fig. 19.3**
Foo applet with
text set to "I love
creating Java
applets!"

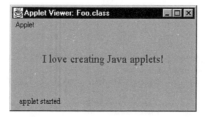

All parameters are passed to the init method of the applet, regardless of whether there is any code written to handle the parameter. As a demonstration, add a third parameter to the applet declaration:

```
<APPLET codebase="classes" code="Foo.class" height=100 width=300>
<PARAM name=color value="red">
<PARAM name=dummy value="bogus">
<PARAM name=text value="I love creating Java applets!">
</APPLET>
```

The result is exactly the same as before. Since there is nothing to handle the dummy parameter, it is simply ignored, without affecting anything else.

## Summary

To add an applet to an HTML document (updated):

1. Insert an <APPLET> tag at the place in the document where you wish the applet to appear.

2. Specify the name of the applet's class with the code parameter.

3. If the class file is not in the current directory, use the codebase parameter to :

   • Specify the relative path if the class file is on the local filesystem.

   • Specify the URL of the directory containing the class file if it resides on a remote filesystem.

4. Specify the space needed by the applet with the height and width parameter.

5. Add any user-defined parameters with <PARAM> tags.

6. Close the applet declaration with the </APPLET> tag.

# Specifying Alternate HTML for Non-Java Browsers

As of this writing, the only browser that supports the finalized 1.0 version of Java is Netscape Navigator 2.0, by Netscape Corporation. While this is one of the more popular Web browsers (perhaps even the most popular), there are people out there using other browsers who will not get to see your Java applets.

The HTML parser in these browsers will simply skip over the <APPLET> and <PARAM> tags, since they don't have the capability to display them. Few, if any, will even recognize these tags as valid HTML. The point is that the rest of the document will be displayed.

You may wish to include something for these browsers, because it's possible that certain things may be out of context once the applet is missing, or perhaps you just want whoever is viewing the page to know that there's more than meets their browser's eyes.

## Syntax

This is the other reason that the </APPLET> closing tag is needed. Anything within the bracketed applet tags will be displayed to the user only if it is a non-Java browser. To display any other HTML test, images, etc., specify the HTML source for these browsers between the <APPLET> and </APPLET> tags of the appropriate applet. This is the final syntax for an HTML applet declaration:

```
<APPLET [codebase=[path¦URL]] code=someclass.class
➥height=applet_height width=applet_width>
{[html¦<PARAM name=parameter_name value=parameter_value>]}
</APPLET>
```

The `html` can occur before, after, around, or even in between your group of
<PARAM> tags. For good style and cleanliness, place the alternative HTML
after all of your <PARAM> tags, if any.

> **Note**
>
> This is not the complete syntax of the <APPLET> tag, but should be all you need to
> use, most if not all the time. For the complete syntax, see the README file distributed
> with the JDK.

Java-enabled browsers will simply ignore the `html`, while non-Java browsers
will ignore everything but the `html`. You can add a "consolation" message to
the Foo applet for non-Java enabled viewers like so:

```
<APPLET codebase="classes" code="Foo.class" height=100 width=300>
<PARAM name=color value="red">
<PARAM name=text value="I love creating Java applets!">
You don't have a <strong>Java</strong>-enabled browser!<p>
</APPLET>
```

Attempting to view this HTML from a non-Java browser (such as the 1.0
alpha 3 HotJava browser) looks something like figure 19.4:

**Fig. 19.4**

Foo applet as
viewed by a non-
Java browser.

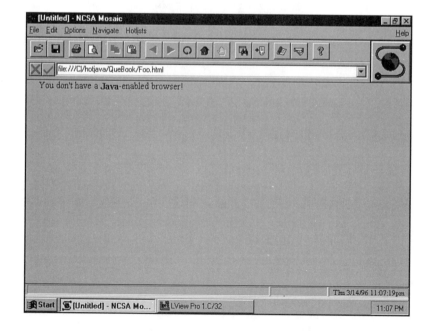

## Summary

To add an applet to an HTML document (updated):

1. Insert an <APPLET> tag at the place in the document where you wish the applet to appear.
2. Specify the name of the applet's class with the code parameter.
3. If the class file is not in the current directory, use the codebase parameter to :
   - Specify the relative path if the class file is on the local file system.
   - Specify the URL of the directory containing the class file if it resides on a remote file system.
4. Specify the space needed by the applet with the height and width parameters.
5. Add any user-defined parameters with <PARAM> tags.
6. Add alternate HTML source for non-Java enabled browsers.
7. Close the applet declaration with the </APPLET> tag.

# Adding Applets to HotJava

At the time of this writing, the latest version of the HotJava browser accepts only applets written in the 1.0 alpha 3 release of the language. If you plan on viewing applets inside of HotJava, make sure you write the source code using that release.

Applets written for any of the beta releases or the finalized 1.0 version of the language will not be viewable inside the HotJava browser.

## The <APP> Tag

The <APPLET> and <PARAM> tags were added in the beta releases. The original HTML tag was the <APP> tag:

```
<APP class=someclass {[param=val]}>
```

Note that since there is no corresponding </APP> tag, alternate HTML cannot be included. Parameters are included inside the <APP> tag, rather than through the use of <PARAM> tags.

The someclass parameter is the name of the applet class (minus the .class extension) to be executed. The parameters param and value are optional.

For a version of Foo written with the alpha 3 release (see fig. 19.5), which is called Foo_a3, the same applet declaration used earlier can be rewritten as:

```
<APP class="Foo_a3" color="red" text="I love creating Java
➥applets!">
```

**Fig. 19.5**
The alpha 3 version of the Foo applet as viewed in HotJava.

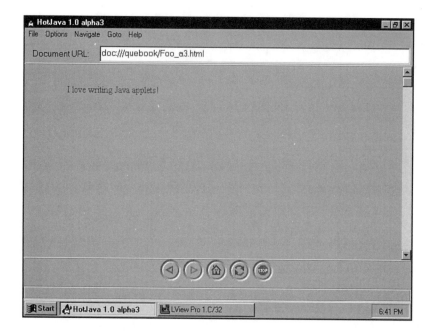

The Foo_a3.class file must be stored in a subdirectory directly underneath the HTML file, and the name of that subdirectory must be `classes`.

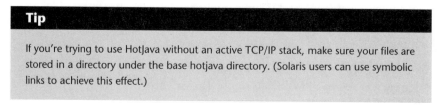

**Tip**

If you're trying to use HotJava without an active TCP/IP stack, make sure your files are stored in a directory under the base hotjava directory. (Solaris users can use symbolic links to achieve this effect.)

Now, you just need to fire up the HotJava browser, and check out your handiwork.

## Putting It All Together

So now you have an alpha 3 applet for HotJava users, and the same applet written with the final 1.0 release for Netscape Navigator users. If you want to present the correct version to the appropriate viewer, with no alternate text for non-Java viewers, you can simply use the <APP> tag as your alternate HTML:

```
<APPLET codebase="classes" code="Foo.class" height=100 width=300>
<PARAM name=color value="red">
<PARAM name=text value="I love creating Java applets!">
<APP class=Foo_a3 color="red" text="I love creating Java applets!">
</APPLET>
```

# Behind the Scenes

So what, exactly, does the browser do when it comes across the <APPLET> tag? First it loads the bytecode for the specified class, then it attempts to run the applet.

## Loading the Byte Code

A Java browser, or more precisely, the Java run-time environment inside the browser, is dynamically extensible, which means that it can add class definitions on the fly. That's what happens when an applet class is loaded—the class actually becomes part of the run-time system.

The Java-enabled browser is then free to create an instance of the applet class, and place it inside of the browser. The initializer will make all of the parameters (specified by the <PARAM> tag) available to the applet.

The browser contains one or more objects to handle bytecode verification and security. If the bytecode doesn't meet the validation checks, the run-time Java environment inside of the browser will reject the byte code, and the class will not be loaded. An appropriate error or warning message will inform you when this occurs.

Likewise, the run-time environment will not allow an applet to violate any security provisions while the applet is running. The response of the browser is somewhat variable, based on the security policy set for the user's system.

If the applet uses additional resources, such as images, audio, or other classes, these are loaded by the browser as needed by the applet, provided that the browser hasn't already had to load the resource previously for another applet.

◄ See "Before We Begin: Java & Security," p. 103, for more information about Java run-time security.

Additional classes, used as resources by an applet, are also subject to byte code verification and security measures.

## Using Packages to Avoid Namespace Conflicts

If a class has already been loaded, the Java run-time will attempt to use that class rather than go through the overhead of loading it in again. This can create problems if multiple classes have the same name.

To avoid namespace conflicts, you might want to use packages.

◄ For information about packages, see "The Parts of the Language," p. 121.

To make sure your Foo applet doesn't create problems if another Foo class comes along, put it in a package called, for example, "SEJava." Figure 19.6 shows the directory layout for using the ficticious SEJava package structure.

(continues)

(continued)

**Fig. 19.6**
Directory structure
for the SEJava
package.

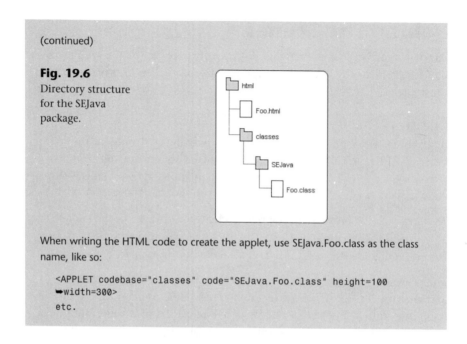

When writing the HTML code to create the applet, use SEJava.Foo.class as the class
name, like so:

```
<APPLET codebase="classes" code="SEJava.Foo.class" height=100
➥width=300>
etc.
```

## Initializing the Applet

Once the byte code is verified, the Java run-time calls the init() method to
give the applet a chance to initialize its resources. Since init() will only be
invoked once, this is the best time to do initialization and preparation for the
applet instance, such as parsing and storing information from the parameters.

After init() is called, the Java run-time calls start(). As seen below, start()
and stop() can be called many times during an applet's lifetime. As such,
start() is the best place to create threads, since the threads should be released by stop().

## Stopping and Restarting

◀ See "The Basics
of Applet
Construction,"
p. 269, for
more details
about the
methods
defined by the
Applet class.

The lifecycle of an applet is fairly straightforward, as shown by figure 19.7
(above). It is based on the inherited methods shown in the diagram. Note
that the paint() method doesn't change the state of the applet at all. It only
makes sense for paint() to be called when the applet is in the "Started" state.

The browser calls the stop() method on the applet when it changes to a new
page, or when it reloads the current page (see note below). However, it is up
to the author of the applet to actually stop the applet's execution within the
stop() method.

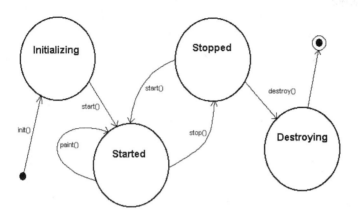

**Fig. 19.7**
An applet's state transition diagram (STD).

When the browser returns to a page with an already loaded applet, it restarts the applet with the start() method again.

> **Note**
>
> What does the browser do with applets when it reloads the page?
>
> This turns out to be browser-specific. Some, such as the appletviewer utility, actually reload the applet, which means that the current applet is cleaned up by stop() and destroy(), and then the applet goes through the entire process from the beginning. Others, like Netscape Navigator, will not reload the applet, but instead will just stop() and then start() the applet again.

Some applets, such as the Foo applet in this chapter, don't really do anything after they've been started, but many applets will have one or more threads running at any given time. If the stop() method doesn't contain code to suspend the current execution, the applet will continue to run, and that could start affecting the user's performance, especially if several applets continue to run unchecked.

To summarize, for applets that "run," the start() method creates the thread or threads which the applet will run in, and the stop() method should stop and then release the thread or threads. (Threads can be released by setting them to null.)

▶ For more information on threads, see "More About Java Applications: Threads," p. 547.

## Cleaning Up

When the time comes for an applet to be deleted, it gets released in two stages. Just like creating an applet calls both the init() and start() methods, deleting an applet will first stop() the applet, then it will destroy() it.

Since stop() should clean up all of the threads, it's unlikely that destroy() actually needs to be over-written by your applet. However, there are some cases, such as in inter-process communication, where it may be desirable to have a more controlled shutdown. In most cases, however, it is probably best to stick with the default destroy() method.

## Summary

A Java-enabled browser loads the applet class and its required resources at run-time, when the HTML source containing the applet declaration is read.

The Java run-time then calls the initialization function init(), at which time the parameters are available to be processed by the applet.

After initialization, the applet is started with the start() method. The browser draws the applet by calling the paint() method.

When the browser is minimized, or the page is exited, it should invoke the stop() method on the applet.

When an applet is deleted, the Java run-time first uses stop() and then destroy() to clean up the applet's resources.

# Complete Source Code for Foo.java

```java
import java.awt.*;

public class Foo extends java.applet.Applet
{
    Color  textcolor;
    String textvalue;

    public void init()
    {
        String p = getParameter("COLOR");
        if (p == null)
        {
            textcolor = Color.black;
        }
        else if (p.equalsIgnoreCase("blue"))
        {
            textcolor = Color.blue;
        }
        else if (p.equalsIgnoreCase("green"))
        {
            textcolor = Color.green;
        }
        else if (p.equalsIgnoreCase("red"))
        {
            textcolor = Color.red;
        }
        else
        {
```

```
            System.out.println("Invalid color... exiting");
            System.exit(0);
    }

     p = getParameter("TEXT");
    if (p == null)
    {
        textvalue = "Hello world.";
    }
    else
    {
       textvalue = p;
    }      }


    public void paint(Graphics g)
    {
     g.setColor(textcolor);
     g.drawString(textvalue, 50, 50);
    }
}
```

# Complete Source Code for Foo_a3.java

```
import browser.Applet;
import awt.Graphics;

class Foo_a3 extends Applet
{
    awt.Color textcolor;
    String    textvalue;

    public void init()
    {
        String att = getAttribute("color");
        if (att == null)
        {
            textcolor = awt.Color.black;
        }
        else if (att.equalsIgnoreCase("blue"))
        {
            textcolor = awt.Color.blue;
        }
        else if (att.equalsIgnoreCase("green"))
        {
            textcolor = awt.Color.green;
        }
        else if (att.equalsIgnoreCase("red"))
        {
            textcolor = awt.Color.red;
        }
        else
        {
```

```
                    System.out.println("Invalid color... exiting");
                    System.exit(0);
            }

      att = getAttribute("text");
      if (att == null)
      {
          textvalue = "Hello world.";
      }
      else
      {
          textvalue = att;
      }    }

      public void paint(Graphics g)
      {
          g.setForeground(textcolor);
          g.drawString(textvalue, 50, 25);
      }
  }
```

# Bibliography

Most of the material in the section covering the lifecycle of an applet was verified by comparison to the tutorial pages written by the Java team at:

**http://java.sun.com/tutorial/**

# CHAPTER 20

# Graphics

*by Mark Wutka*

One of the most important aspects of Java is its ability to display graphical output. You can write Java applets that display lines, shapes, images, and text in different fonts, styles, and colors. You can also create applets that interact with the mouse and keyboard to provide the same kind of programs you find on other windowing systems.

In this chapter, you will learn how to

- Draw various lines and shapes in different colors.
- Select different fonts and font styles for drawing text.
- Create event handlers for interacting with the mouse and keyboard.
- Create flicker-free animation applets.
- Load images and draw them.
- Use the image producer-consumer model to perform powerful image manipulation.

## Paint, Update, and Repaint

As you saw in the simple "Hello World" applet, Java applets can redraw themselves by overriding the `paint` method. You may have wondered how the `paint` method gets called. Your applet actually has three different methods that are used in redrawing the applet, as follows:

- `repaint` can be called anytime the applet needs to be repainted (redrawn).
- `update` is called by `repaint` to signal that it is time to update the applet. The default `update` method clears the applet's drawing area and calls the `paint` method.

- paint actually draws the applet's graphics in the drawing area. The paint method is passed an instance of a Graphics class that it can use for drawing various shapes and images.

# Points, Lines, and Circles

The Graphics class provides methods for drawing a number of graphical figures, including the following:

- Lines
- Circles and Ellipses
- Rectangles and Polygons
- Images
- Text in a variety of fonts

## The Coordinate System

The coordinate system used in Java is a simple Cartesian (x, y) system where *x* is the number of screen pixels from the left-hand side, and *y* is the number of pixels from the top of the screen. The upper-left corner of the screen is represented by (0, 0). Figure 20.1 gives you an example of some coordinates.

**Fig. 20.1**
Unlike math coordinates, where y increases from bottom to top, the y coordinates in Java increase from the top down.

## Drawing Lines

The simplest figure you can draw with the Graphics class is a line. The drawLine method takes two pairs of coordinates—x1,y1 and x2,y2—and draws a line between them. The applet in listing 20.1 uses the drawLine method to draw some lines. The output from this applet is shown in figure 20.2.

**Listing 20.1   Source Code for DrawLines.java**

```
import java.awt.*;
import java.applet.*;

//
// This applet draws a pair of lines using the Graphics class
//
```

```
public class DrawLines extends Applet
{
    public void paint(Graphics g)
    {
// Draw a line from the upper-left corner to the point at (200, 100)
        g.drawLine(0, 0, 200, 100);

    // Draw a horizontal line from (20, 120) to (250, 120)
        g.drawLine(20, 120, 250, 120);
    }
}
```

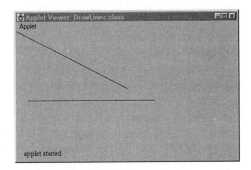

**Fig. 20.2**
Line drawing is one of the most basic graphics operations.

## Drawing Rectangles

Now that you know how to draw a line, you can progress to rectangles and filled rectangles. To draw a rectangle, you use the drawRect method and pass it the *x* and *y* coordinates of the upper-left corner of the rectangle, the width of the rectangle, and its height. To draw a rectangle at (150, 100) that is 200 pixels wide and 120 pixels high, your call would be:

```
g.drawRect(150, 100, 200, 120);
```

The drawRect method draws only the outline of a box. If you want to draw a solid box, you can use the fillRect method, which takes the same parameters as drawRect. You may also clear out an area with the clearRect method, which also takes the same parameters as drawRect. Figure 20.3 shows you the difference between drawRect, fillRect, and clearRect. The rectangle on the left is drawn with drawRect, and the center one is drawn with fillRect. The rectangle on the right is drawn with fillRect, but the clearRect is used to make the empty area in the middle.

## Drawing 3-D Rectangles

The Graphics class also provides a way to draw "3-D" rectangles similar to buttons that you might find on a toolbar. Unfortunately, the Graphics class draws these buttons with very little height or depth, making the 3-D effect difficult to see. The syntax for the `draw3DRect` and `fill3DRect` are similar to `drawRect` and `fillRect`, except that they have an extra parameter at the end—a Boolean indicator as to whether the rectangle is raised or not. The raising/lowering effect is produced by drawing light and dark lines around the borders of the rectangle.

**Fig. 20.3**

Java provides several flexible ways of drawing rectangles.

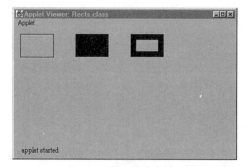

Imagine a light coming from the upper-left corner of the screen. Any 3-D rectangle that is raised would catch light on its top and left sides, while the bottom and right sides would have a shadow. If the rectangle was lowered, the top and left sides would be in shadow, while the bottom and right sides caught the light. Both the `draw3DRect` and `fill3DRect` methods draw the top and left sides in a lighter color for raised rectangles while drawing the bottom and right sides in a darker color. They draw the top and left darker and the bottom and right lighter for lowered rectangles. In addition, the `fill3DRect` method will draw the entire button in a darker shade when it is lowered. The applet in listing 20.2 draws some raised and lowered rectangles, both filled and unfilled.

**Listing 20.2  Source Code for Rect3d.java**

```
import java.awt.*;
import java.applet.*;

//
// This applet draws four varieties of 3-d rectangles.
// It sets the drawing color to the same color as the
// background because this shows up well in HotJava and
// Netscape.

public class Rect3d extends Applet
{
    public void paint(Graphics g)
    {
```

```
// Make the drawing color the same as the background
    g.setColor(getBackground());

// Draw a raised 3-d rectangle in the upper-left
    g.draw3DRect(10, 10, 60, 40, true);
// Draw a lowered 3-d rectangle in the upper-right
    g.draw3DRect(100, 10, 60, 40, false);

// Fill a raised 3-d rectangle in the lower-left
    g.fill3DRect(10, 80, 60, 40, true);
// Fill a lowered 3-d rectangle in the lower-right
    g.fill3DRect(100, 80, 60, 40, false);
    }
}
```

Figure 20.4 shows the output from the Rect3d applet. Notice that the raised rectangles appear the same for the filled and unfilled. This is only because the drawing color is the same color as the background. If the drawing color were different, the filled button would be filled with the drawing color, while the unfilled button would still show the background color.

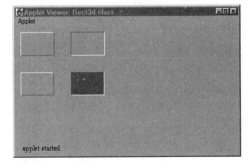

**Fig. 20.4**
The draw3DRect and fill3DRect methods use shading to produce a 3-D effect.

## Drawing Rounded Rectangles

In addition to the regular and 3-D rectangles, you can also draw rectangles with rounded corners. The drawRoundRect and fillRoundRect methods are similar to drawRect and fillRect except that they take two extra parameters: arcWidth and arcHeight. These parameters indicate how much of the corners will be rounded. For instance, an arcWidth of 10 tells the Graphics class to round off the left-most five pixels and the right-most five pixels of the corners of the rectangle. An arcHeight of 8 tells the class to round off the top-most and bottom-most four pixels of the rectangle's corners.

Figure 20.5 shows the corner of a rounded rectangle. The arcWidth for the figure is 30, while the arcHeight is 10. The figure shows an imaginary ellipse with a width of 30 and a height of 20 to help illustrate how the rounding is done.

**Fig. 20.5**

Java uses an imaginary ellipse to determine the amount of rounding.

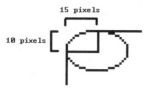

The applet in listing 20.3 draws a rounded rectangle and a filled, rounded rectangle. Figure 20.6 shows the output from this applet.

**Listing 20.3   Source Code for RoundRect.java**

```java
import java.awt.*;
import java.applet.*;

// Example 20.3—RoundRect Applet
//
// This applet draws a rounded rectangle and then a
// filled, rounded rectangle.

public class RoundRect extends Applet
{
   public void paint(Graphics g)
   {
// Draw a rounded rectangle with an arcWidth of 20, and an arcHeight of 20
      g.drawRoundRect(10, 10, 40, 50, 20, 20);

// Fill a rounded rectangle with an arcWidth of 10, and an arcHeight of 8
      g.fillRoundRect(10, 80, 40, 50, 10, 6);
   }
}
```

**Fig. 20.6**

Java's rounded rectangles are a pleasant alternative to sharp cornered rectangles.

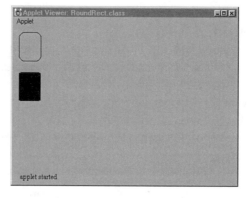

## Drawing Circles and Ellipses

If you are bored with square shapes, you can try your hand at circles. The
Graphics class does not distinguish between a circle and an ellipse, so there is
no drawCircle method. Instead, you use the drawOval and fillOval methods. To draw a circle or an ellipse, first imagine that the figure is surrounded
by a rectangle that just barely touches the edges. You pass drawOval the coordinates of the upper-left corner of this rectangle. You also pass the width and
height of the oval. If the width and height are the same, you are drawing a
circle. Figure 20.7 illustrates the concept of the enclosing rectangle.

**Fig. 20.7**
Circles and Ellipses
are drawn within
the bounds of
an imaginary
enclosing
rectangle.

The applet in listing 20.4 draws a circle and a filled ellipse. Figure 20.8 shows
the output from this applet.

**Listing 20.4   Source Code for Ovals.java**

```java
import java.awt.*;
import java.applet.*;

//
// This applet draws an unfilled circle and a filled ellipse

public class Ovals extends Applet
{
    public void paint(Graphics g)
    {

// Draw a circle with a diameter of 30 (width=30, height=30)
// With the enclosing rectangle's upper-left corner at (0, 0)
    g.drawOval(0, 0, 30, 30);

// Fill an ellipse with a width of 40 and a height of 20
// The upper-left corner of the enclosing rectangle is at (0, 60)
      g.fillOval(0, 60, 40, 20);
    }
}
```

**Fig. 20.8**

Java doesn't know the difference between ellipses and circles, they're all just ovals.

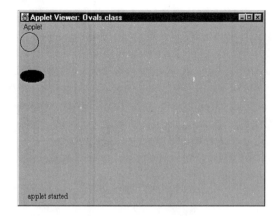

## Drawing Polygons

You can also draw polygons and filled polygons using the Graphics class. You have two options when drawing polygons. You can either pass two arrays containing the *x* and *y* coordinates of the points in the polygon, or you can pass an instance of a Polygon class. The applet in listing 20.5 draws a polygon using an array of points. Figure 20.9 shows the output from this applet.

---

**Listing 20.5   Source Code for DrawPoly.java**

```
import java.applet.*;
import java.awt.*;

//
// This applet draws a polygon using an array of points

public class DrawPoly extends Applet
{
// Define an array of X coordinates for the polygon
   int xCoords[] = { 10, 40, 60, 30, 10 };

// Define an array of Y coordinates for the polygon
   int yCoords[] = { 20, 0, 10, 60, 40 };

   public void paint(Graphics g)
   {
     g.drawPolygon(xCoords, yCoords, 5);   // 5 points in polygon
   }
}
```

---

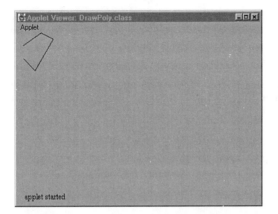

**Fig. 20.9**
Java allows you to draw polygons of almost any shape you can imagine.

---

**Caution**

Notice that in this example, the polygon is not "closed off." In other words, there is no line between the last point in the polygon and the first one. If you want the polygon to be closed, you must repeat the first point at the end of the array.

---

The Polygon class provides a more flexible way to define polygons. You can create a Polygon by either passing it an array of *x* points and an array of *y* points, or you can add points to it one at a time. Once you have created an instance of a Polygon class, you can use the getBoundingBox method to determine the area taken up by this polygon (the minimum and maximum *x* and *y* coordinates):

```
Rectangle boundingBox = myPolygon.getBoundingBox();
```

The Rectangle class returned by getBoundingBox contains variables indicating the *x* and *y* coordinates of the rectangle and its width and height. You can also determine whether or not a point is contained within the polygon or is outside it by calling inside with the x and y coordinates of the point:

```
if (myPolygon.inside(5, 10))
{
// the point (5, 10) is inside this polygon
}
```

You can use this Polygon class in place of the array of points for either the drawPolygon or fillPolygon methods. The applet in listing 20.6 creates an instance of a polygon and draws a filled polygon. Figure 20.10 shows the output from this applet.

**Listing 20.6   Source Code for Polygons.java**

```
import java.applet.*;
import java.awt.*;

//
// This applet creates an instance of a Polygon class and then
// uses fillPoly to draw the Polygon as a filled polygon.

public class Polygons extends Applet
{
// Define an array of X coordinates for the polygon
    int xCoords[] = { 10, 40, 60, 30, 10 };

// Define an array of Y coordinates for the polygon
    int yCoords[] = { 20, 0, 10, 60, 40 };

    public void paint(Graphics g)
    {
// Create a new instance of a polygon with 5 points
        Polygon drawingPoly = new Polygon(xCoords, yCoords, 5);

// Draw a filled polygon
        g.fillPolygon(drawingPoly);
    }
}
```

**Fig. 20.10**
Polygons created
with the Polygon
class look just like
those created from
an array of points.

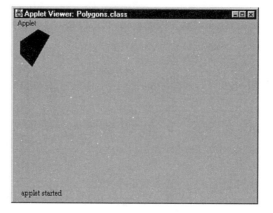

# Color

You may recall learning about the *primary colors* when you were younger.
There are actually two kinds of primary colors. When you are drawing with a
crayon, you are actually dealing with *pigments*. The primary pigments are red,
yellow, and blue. You probably know some of the typical mixtures, such as

red + yellow = orange, yellow + blue = green, and blue + red = purple. Black is formed from mixing all the pigments together, while white indicates the absence of pigment.

Dealing with the primary colors of light is slightly different. The primary colors of light are red, green, and blue. Some common combinations are red + green = brown (or yellow, depending on how bright it is), green + blue = cyan (light blue), and red + blue = magenta (purple). For colors of light, the concept of black and white is the reverse of the pigments. Black is formed by the absence of all light, while white is formed by the combination of all the primary colors. In other words, red + blue + green (in equal amounts) = white. Java uses a color model called the *RGB* color model. This means that colors are described by giving the amount of Red, Green, and Blue light in the color.

You define a color in the RGB color model by indicating how much red light, green light, and blue light are in the color. You can do this either by using numbers between zero and 255 or by using floating-point numbers between 0.0 and 1.0. Table 20.1 indicates the red, green, and blue amounts for some common colors.

**Table 20.1    Common Colors and Their RGB Values**

| Color Name | Red Value | Green Value | Blue Value |
|---|---|---|---|
| White | 255 | 255 | 255 |
| Light Gray | 192 | 192 | 192 |
| Gray | 128 | 128 | 128 |
| Dark Gray | 64 | 64 | 64 |
| Black | 0 | 0 | 0 |
| Red | 255 | 0 | 0 |
| Pink | 255 | 175 | 175 |
| Orange | 255 | 200 | 0 |
| Yellow | 255 | 255 | 0 |
| Green | 0 | 255 | 0 |
| Magenta | 255 | 0 | 255 |
| Cyan | 0 | 255 | 255 |
| Blue | 0 | 0 | 255 |

You can create a custom color three ways:

```
Color(int red, int green, int blue)
```

This creates a color using red, green, and blue values between 0 and 255.

```
Color(int rgb)
```

This creates a color using red, green, and blue values between 0 and 255, but all combined into a single integer. Bits 16–23 hold the red value, 8–15 hold the green value, and 0–7 hold the blue value. These values are usually written in hexadecimal notation, so you can easily see the color values. For instance, 0×123456 would give a red value of 0×12 (18 decimal), a green value of 34 (52 decimal), and a blue value of 56 (96 decimal). Notice how each color takes exactly 2 digits in hexadecimal.

```
Color(float red, float green, float blue)
```

This creates a color using red, green, and blue values between 0.0 and 1.0.

Once you have created a color, you can change the drawing color using the setColor method. For instance, suppose you wanted to draw in pink. A nice value for pink is 255 red, 192 green, and 192 blue. The following paint method sets the color to pink and draws a circle:

```
public void paint(Graphics g)
{
    Color pinkColor = new Color(255, 192, 192);
    g.setColor(pinkColor);
    g.drawOval(5, 5, 50, 50);
}
```

You don't always have to create colors manually. The Color class provides a number of predefined colors:

```
Color.white, Color.lightGray, Color.gray, Color.darkGray,
Color.black, Color.red, Color.pink, Color.orange, Color.yellow,
Color.green, Color.magenta, Color.cyan, Color.blue.
```

Given a color, you can find its red, green, and blue values by using the getRed, getGreen, and getBlue methods:

```
int redAmount, greenAmount, blueAmount;
Color someColor = new Color(0x345678);   // red=0x34, green = 0x56,
                                          ➥blue = 0x78

redAmount = someColor.getRed();    // redAmount now equals 0x34
greenAmount = someColor.getGreen();    // greenAmount now equals 0x56
blueAmount = someColor.getBlue();    // blueAmount now equals 0x78
```

# Drawing Modes

The Graphics class has two different modes for drawing figures: paint mode and XOR mode. Paint mode means that when a figure is drawn, all the points in that figure overwrite the points that were underneath it. In other words, if you draw a straight line in blue, every point along that line will be blue. You probably just assumed that would happen anyway, but it doesn't have to. There is another drawing mode called XOR mode, short for eXclusive-OR.

The XOR drawing mode dates back several decades. You can visualize how the XOR mode works by forgetting for a moment that you are dealing with colors and imagining that you are drawing in white on a black background. Drawing in XOR involves the combination of the pixel you are trying to draw and the pixel that is on the screen where you want to draw. If you try to draw a white pixel where there is currently a black pixel, you will draw a white pixel. If you try to draw a white pixel where there is already a white pixel, you will instead draw a black pixel.

This may sound strange, but it was once very common to do animation using XOR. To understand why, you should first realize that if you draw a shape in XOR mode and then draw the shape again in XOR mode, you erase whatever you did in the first draw. If you were moving a figure in XOR mode, you would draw it once; then to move it, you'd draw it again in its old position, erasing it, then XOR draw it in its new position. Whenever two objects overlapped, the overlapping areas looked like a negative: black was white and white was black. You probably won't have to use this technique for animation, but at least you have some idea where it came from.

> **Note**
>
> When using XOR on a color system, you think of the current drawing color as the white from the above example and identify another color as the XOR color—or the black. Because there are more than two colors, the XOR mode makes interesting combinations with other colors, but you can still erase any shape by drawing it again.

To change the drawing mode to XOR mode, just call the setXORMode and pass it the color you want to use as the XOR color. The applet in listing 20.7 shows a simple animation that uses XOR mode to move a ball past a square.

**Listing 20.7   Source Code for BallAnim.java**

```java
import java.awt.*;
import java.applet.*;
import java.lang.*;

//
// The BallAnim applet uses XOR mode to draw a rectangle
// and a moving ball. It implements the Runnable interface
// because it is performing animation.

public class BallAnim extends Applet implements Runnable
{
   Thread animThread;

   int ballX = 0;      // X coordinate of ball
   int ballDirection = 0;   // 0 if going left-to-right, 1 otherwise

// Start is called when the applet first cranks up. It creates a
   ➥thread for
// doing animation and starts up the thread.

   public void start()
   {
     if (animThread == null)
     {
        animThread = new Thread(this);
        animThread.start();
     }
   }

// Stop is called when the applet is terminated. It halts the animation
// thread and gets rid of it.

   public void stop()
   {
     animThread.stop();
     animThread = null;
   }

// The run method is the main loop of the applet. It moves the ball, then
// sleeps for 1/10th of a second and then moves the ball again.

   public void run()
   {
     Thread.currentThread().setPriority(Thread.NORM_PRIORITY);

     while (true)
     {
        moveBall();
        try {
```

```
            Thread.sleep(100);    // sleep 0.1 seconds
        } catch (Exception sleepProblem) {
// This applet ignores any exceptions if it has a problem sleeping.
// Maybe it should take Sominex
        }
      }
    }

    private void moveBall()
    {
// If moving the ball left-to-right, add 1 to the x coord
      if (ballDirection == 0)
      {
          ballX++;

// Make the ball head back the other way once the x coord hits 100

          if (ballX > 100)
          {
            ballDirection = 1;
            ballX = 100;
          }
      }
      else
      {

// If moving the ball right-to-left, subtract 1 from the x coord
          ballX--;

// Make the ball head back the other way once the x coord hits 0
          if (ballX <= 0)
          {
            ballDirection = 0;
            ballX = 0;
          }
      }

      repaint();
    }

    public void paint(Graphics g)
    {
      g.setXORMode(getBackground());
      g.fillRect(40, 10, 40, 40);
      g.fillOval(ballX, 0, 30, 30);
    }
}
```

Figure 20.11 is a snapshot of the BallAnim applet in action. Notice that the ball changes color as it passes over the square. This is due to the way the XOR mode works.

**Fig. 20.11**
XOR drawing produces an inverse effect when objects collide.

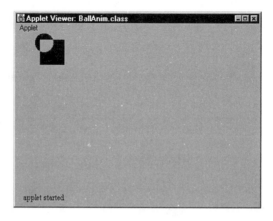

# Drawing Text

The Graphics class also contains methods to draw text characters and strings. As you have seen in the "Hello World" applet, you can use the drawString method to draw a text string on the screen. Before plunging into the various aspects of drawing text, you should be familiar with some common terms for fonts and text, as follows:

**Baseline**—This refers to the imaginary line the text is resting on.

**Descent**—This is how far below the baseline a particular character extends. Some characters, such as *g* and *j*, extend below the baseline.

**Ascent**— This is how far above the baseline a particular character extends. The letter *d* would have a higher ascent than the letter *x*.

**Leading**—This is the amount of space between the descent of one line and the ascent of the next line. If there was no leading, such letters as *g* and *j* would almost touch such letters as *M* and *H* on the next line.

---

**Caution**

The term "ascent" in Java is slightly different from the same term in the publishing world. The publishing term "ascent" refers to the distance from the top of the letter *x* to the top of a character, where the Java term "ascent" refers to the distance from the baseline to the top of a character.

---

Figure 20.12 illustrates the relationship between the descent, ascent, baseline, and leading.

**Fig. 20.12**
Java's font
terminology
originated in the
publishing field,
but some of the
meanings have
been changed.

---

**Note**

You may also hear the terms *proportional* and *fixed* associated with fonts. In a fixed font, every character takes up the same amount of space. Typewriters (if you actually remember those) wrote in a fixed font. Characters in a proportional font only take up as much space as they need. You can use this book as an example.

The text of the book is in a proportional font, which is much easier on the eyes. Look at some of the words and notice how the letters only take up as much space as necessary. (Compare the letters *i* and *m,* for example.) The code examples in this book, however, are written in a fixed font (this preserves the original spacing). Notice how each letter takes up exactly the same amount of space.

---

Now, to draw a string using the `Graphics` class, you simply call `drawString` and give it the string you want to draw and the *x* and *y* coordinates for the beginning of the baseline (that's why you needed the terminology briefing). You may recall the "Hello World" applet used this same method to draw its famous message:

```
public void paint(Graphics g)
{
    g.drawString("Hello World", 10, 30);
}
```

You can also draw characters from an array of characters or an array of bytes. The format for `drawChars` and `drawBytes` is:

```
void drawChars(char charArray[], int offset, int numChars, int x, int y)
void drawBytes(byte byteArray[], int offset, int numChars, int x, int y)
```

The `offset` parameter refers to the position of the first character or byte in the array to draw. This will most often be zero because you will usually want to draw from the beginning of the array. The applet in listing 20.8 draws some characters from a character array and from a byte array.

**Listing 20.8 Source Code for DrawChars.java**

```java
import java.awt.*;
import java.applet.*;

//
// This applet draws a character array and a byte array

public class DrawChars extends Applet
{
    char[] charsToDraw = { 'H', 'i', ' ', 'T', 'h', 'e', 'r', 'e', '!' };

    byte[] bytesToDraw = { 65, 66, 67, 68, 69, 70, 71 }; // "ABCDEFG"

    public void paint(Graphics g)
    {
      g.drawChars(charsToDraw, 0, charsToDraw.length, 10, 20);

      g.drawBytes(bytesToDraw, 0, bytesToDraw.length, 10, 50);
    }
}
```

You may find that the default font for your applet is not very interesting. Fortunately, you can select from a number of different fonts. These fonts have the potential to vary from system to system, which may lead to portability issues in the future; but for the moment, HotJava and Netscape support the same set of fonts.

In addition to selecting between multiple fonts, you may also select a number of font styles: Font.PLAIN, Font.BOLD, and Font.ITALIC. These styles can be added together, so you can use a bold italic font with Font.BOLD + Font.ITALIC.

When choosing a font, you must also give the *point size* of the font. The point size is a printing term that relates to the size of the font. There are 100 points to an inch when printing on a printer, but this does not necessarily apply to screen fonts. A typical point size value for printed text is either 12 or 14. The point size does not indicate the number of pixels high or wide; it is simply a relative term. A point size of 24 is twice as big as a point size of 12.

You create an instance of a font by using the font name, the font style, and the point size. The following declaration creates the Times Roman font that is both bold and italic and has a point size of 12:

```java
Font myFont = new Font("TimesRoman", Font.BOLD + Font.ITALIC, 12);
```

The getFontList method in the Toolkit class returns an array containing the names of the available fonts. The applet in listing 20.9 uses getFontList to display the available fonts in a variety of styles.

**Listing 20.9   Source Code for ShowFonts.java**

```java
import java.awt.*;
import java.applet.*;

//
// This applet uses the Toolkit class to get a list
// of available fonts, then displays each font in
// PLAIN, BOLD, and ITALIC style.

public class ShowFonts extends Applet
{
   public void paint(Graphics g)
   {
     String fontList[];
     int i;
     int startY;

// Get a list of all available fonts
     fontList = getToolkit().getFontList();

     startY = 15;

     for (i=0; i < fontList.length; i++)
     {
// Set the font to the PLAIN version
        g.setFont(new Font(fontList[i], Font.PLAIN, 12));
// Draw an example
        g.drawString("This is the "+
           fontList[i]+" font.", 5, startY);
// Move down a little on the screen
        startY += 15;

// Set the font to the BOLD version
        g.setFont(new Font(fontList[i], Font.BOLD, 12));
// Draw an example
        g.drawString("This is the bold "+
           fontList[i]+" font.", 5, startY);
// Move down a little on the screen
        startY += 15;

// Set the font to the ITALIC version
        g.setFont(new Font(fontList[i], Font.ITALIC, 12));
// Draw an example
        g.drawString("This is the italic "+
           fontList[i]+" font.", 5, startY);

// Move down a little on the screen with some extra spacing
        startY += 20;
     }
   }
}
```

**Fig. 20.13**
Java provides
a number of
different fonts
and font styles.

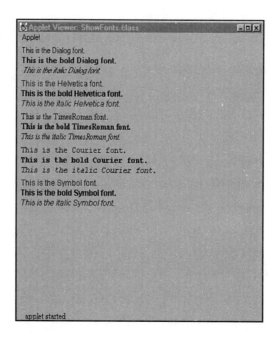

# Drawing Images

The Graphics class provides a way to draw images with the drawImage method:

```
boolean drawImage(Image img, int x, int y, ImageObserver observer)

boolean drawImage(Image img, int x, int y, int width, int height,
    ImageObserver observer)
```

The observer parameter in the drawImage method is an object that is in charge of watching to see when the image is actually ready to draw. If you are calling drawImage from within your applet, you can pass this as the observer because the Applet class implements the ImageObserver interface.

To draw an image, however, you need to get the image first. That is not provided by the Graphics class. Fortunately, the Applet class provides a getImage method that you can use to retrieve images. The applet in listing 20.10 retrieves an image and draws it. Figure 20.14 shows the output from this applet.

**Listing 20.10    Source Code for DrawImage.java**

```
import java.awt.*;
import java.applet.*;

//
// This applet uses getImage to retrieve an image
// and then draws it using drawImage

public class DrawImage extends Applet
{
    private Image samImage;

    public void init()
    {
        samImage = getImage(getDocumentBase(), "samantha.gif");
    }

    public void paint(Graphics g)
    {
        g.drawImage(samImage, 0, 0, this);
    }
}
```

**Fig. 20.14**
You can draw any
.GIF in a Java
applet with the
drawImage method.

One problem you may face in trying to display images is that the images may
be coming over a slow network link (for instance, a 14.4K modem). When
you begin to draw the image, it may not have arrived completely. You can
use a helper class called the MediaTracker to determine whether an image is
ready for display.

To use the MediaTracker, you must first create one for your applet:

```
MediaTracker myTracker = new MediaTracker(this);   // "this" refers to the
                                                    applet
```

Next, try to retrieve the image you want to display:

```
Image myImage = getImage("samantha.gif");
```

Now you tell the MediaTracker to keep an eye on the image. When you add an image to the MediaTracker, you also give it a numeric *id*. This id can be used for multiple images so that when you want to see if an entire group of images is ready for display, you can check it with a single id. As a simple case, you can just give an image an id of zero:

```
myTracker.addImage(myImage, 0);   // Track the image, give an id of 0
```

Once you have started tracking an image, you can load it and wait for it to be ready by using the waitForID method:

```
myTracker.waitForID(0);   // Wait for all images with id of 0 to be
                             ➥ready
```

You can also wait for all images using the waitForAll method:

```
myTracker.waitForAll();
```

You may not want to take the time to load an image before starting your applet. You can use the statusID method to initiate a load, but not wait for it. When you call statusID, you pass the id you want to status and a boolean flag to indicate whether it should start loading the image. If you pass it true, it will start loading the image:

```
myTracker.statusID(0, true);   // Start loading the image
```

A companion to statusID is statusAll, which checks the status of all images in the MediaTracker:

```
myTracker.statusAll(true);   // start loading all the images
```

The statusID and statusAll methods return an integer that is made up of the following flags:

- MediaTracker.ABORTED if any of the images have aborted loading
- MediaTracker.COMPLETE if any of the images have finished loading
- MediaTracker.LOADING if any images are still in the process of loading
- MediaTracker.ERRORED if any images encountered an error during loading

You can also use checkID and checkAll to see if an image has been success-fully loaded. All the variations of checkAll and checkID return a boolean value that is true if all the images checked have been loaded.

```
boolean checkID(int id);
```

This returns `true` if all images with a specific id have been loaded. It does not start loading the images if they are not loading already.

```
boolean checkID(int id, boolean startLoading);
```

This returns `true` if all images with a specific id have been loaded. If `startLoading` is `true`, it will initiate the loading of any images that are not already being loaded.

```
boolean checkAll();
```

This returns `true` if all images being tracked by this `MediaTracker` have been loaded, but does not initiate loading if an image is not being loaded.

```
boolean checkAll(boolean startLoading);
```

This returns `true` if all images being tracked by this `MediaTracker` have been loaded. If `startLoading` is `true`, it will initiate the loading of any images that have not started loading yet.

The applet in listing 20.11 uses the `MediaTracker` to watch for an image to complete loading. It will draw text in place of the image until the image is complete; then it will draw the image.

### Listing 20.11   Source Code for ImageTracker.java

```java
import java.awt.*;
import java.applet.*;
import java.lang.*;
//
// The ImageTracker applet uses the media tracker to see if an
// image is ready to be displayed. In order to simulate a
// situation where the image takes a long time to display, this
// applet waits 10 seconds before starting to load the image.
// While the image is not ready, it displays the message:
// "Image goes here" where the image will be displayed.

public class ImageTracker extends Applet implements Runnable
{
    Thread animThread;    // Thread for doing animation
    int waitCount;        // Count number of seconds we have waited
    MediaTracker myTracker;   // Tracks the loading of an image
    Image myImage;        // The image we are loading

    public void init()
    {
// Get the image we want to show
        myImage = getImage(getDocumentBase(), "samantha.gif");

// Create a media tracker to track the image
        myTracker = new MediaTracker(this);

// Tell the media tracker to track this image
```

(continues)

**Listing 20.11 Continued**

```
      myTracker.addImage(myImage, 0);
   }

   public void run()
   {
      Thread.currentThread().setPriority(Thread.NORM_PRIORITY);

      while (true)
      {
// Count how many times we've been through this loop
         waitCount++;

// If we've been through 10 times, call checkID and tell it to start
// loading the image
         if (waitCount == 10)
         {
            myTracker.checkID(0, true);
         }

         repaint();
         try {
// Sleep 1 second (1000 milliseconds)
            Thread.sleep(1000);   // sleep 1 second
         } catch (Exception sleepProblem) {
         }
      }
   }

   public void paint(Graphics g)
   {
      if (myTracker.checkID(0))
      {
// If the image is ready to display, display it
         g.drawImage(myImage, 0, 0, this);
      }
      else
      {
// Otherwise, draw a message where we will put the image
         g.drawString("Image goes here", 0, 30);
      }
   }

   public void start()
   {
      animThread = new Thread(this);
      animThread.start();
   }

   public void stop()
   {
      animThread.stop();
      animThread = null;
   }

}
```

# Keyboard and Mouse Events

Your applet can receive information about the keyboard and mouse. You can
be notified when a key is pressed and when it is released; when the mouse
enters the applet window and when it leaves the applet window; when the
mouse button is pressed and when it is released; and when the mouse moves
and when the mouse is dragged (moved with the button held down).

## Keyboard Events

The keyDown method is called whenever a key is pressed. Its companion
method, keyUp, is called whenever a key is released. You will normally just be
concerned with a key being pressed, so you can usually ignore the keyUp
method. The format for keyDown and keyUp is the following:

```
public boolean keyDown(Event event, int keyCode)
public boolean keyUp(Event event, int keyCode)
```

Where:

> event is an Event class that contains specific information about the
> keyboard event (the key press or the key release).
>
> keyCode is the key that was pressed.

All of your event handling methods, such as keyDown and keyUp, should
return a value of true.

For regular ASCII characters, the keyCode is the ASCII value of the character
pressed. For instance, if you press the *g* key, the keyCode would be 107. You
could also cast the keyCode to a character value, in which case it would be the
character *g*. If you were to hold down shift and press *g*, the keyCode would be
71, representing the character value *G*. If you hold down control and press *g*,
the keyCode would be 7.

You can also determine if the shift, control, or alt (sometimes called meta)
keys have been pressed by checking the shiftDown, controlDown, and
metaDown methods in the event class. For example:

```
public boolean keyDown(Event event, int keyCode)
{
  if (event.shiftDown())
  {
    // someone pressed shift
  }

  if (event.controlDown())
  {
    // someone pressed control
  }
```

```
    if (event.metaDown())
    {
      // someone pressed meta (or alt)
    }
    return true;
}
```

Because the codes for certain keys vary from system to system, Java defines a number of key codes that can be used on all systems. These key codes are as follows:

| | |
|---|---|
| `Event.F1-Event.F12` | function keys F1 through F12 |
| `Event.LEFT` | left arrow key |
| `Event.RIGHT` | right arrow key |
| `Event.UP` | up arrow key |
| `Event.DOWN` | down arrow key |
| `Event.END` | end key |
| `Event.HOME` | home key |
| `Event.PGDN` | page down key |
| `Event.PGUP` | page up key |

## Mouse Events

You can receive information about the mouse through a number of different methods. The mouseDown event is called whenever the mouse button is pressed:

```
public boolean mouseDown(Event event, int x, int y)
```

Where:

event is the Event class containing information about the event.

x and y are the coordinates where the mouse button was pressed.

You may also want to know when the mouse button is released. You can use the mouseUp method, which takes the same arguments as mouseDown:

```
public boolean mouseUp(Event event, int x, int y)
```

The mouseEnter and mouseExit methods are called whenever the mouse enters the applet area or leaves it. These methods also take the same arguments as mouseDown:

```
public boolean mouseEnter(Event event, int x, int y)
public boolean mouseExit(Event event, int x, int y)
```

You can also track the movement of the mouse with `mouseMove` and `mouseDrag`. `mouseMove` is called whenever the mouse is moved while the button is up; `mouseDrag` is called when the mouse is moved while the button is down. These methods also take the same arguments as `mouseDown`:

```
public boolean mouseMove(Event event, int x, int y)
public boolean mouseDrag(Event event, int x, int y)
```

The applet in listing 20.12 uses keyboard events and mouse events to manipulate shapes. The applet in listing 20.13 makes use of a utility class called `Shape`, which extends the `Polygon` class to enable a polygon to be moved around the screen easily.

### Listing 20.12  Source Code for Shape.java

```
import java.awt.*;
//
// The Shape class is an extension of the Polygon class that adds
// a method for moving the Polygon to a different location. It makes
// a copy of the original coordinates, then when you move it to a new
// location, it just adds the new position to each coordinate. In other words,
// if you moved the shape to (100,100), moveShape would add 100 to each x
// coordinate and each y coordinate. You should give the coordinates relative
// to 0, 0.

public class Shape extends Polygon
{
    private int[] originalXpoints;
    private int[] originalYpoints;

    public int x;
    public int y;

    public Shape(int x[], int y[], int n)
    {
      super(x, y, n);

// Make a copy of the x coordinates
        originalXpoints = new int[n];
        System.arraycopy(x, 0, originalXpoints, 0, n);

// Make a copy of the x coordinates
        originalYpoints = new int[n];
        System.arraycopy(y, 0, originalYpoints, 0, n);

    }
```

(continues)

**Listing 20.12    Continued**

```
    public void moveShape(int newX, int newY)
    {
      int i;

// Add the new X and new Y values to the original coordinates, and
➥make that
// the new position of this shape.

      for (i=0; i < npoints; i++)
      {
          xpoints[i] = originalXpoints[i] + newX;
          ypoints[i] = originalYpoints[i] + newY;
      }
    }
}
```

**Listing 20.13    Source Code for ShapeManipulator.java**

```
import java.awt.*;
import java.applet.*;

//
// The ShapeManipulator applet lets you drag a shape
// around the screen by holding down the left mouse
// button. It uses three different shapes: a triangle,
// a square, and a pentagon. You can switch between these
// by hitting 't', 's', and 'p' respectively.
//
// This applet makes use of the Shape class, which extends
// the functionality of Polygon to enable the polygon to be
// moved to a new location with a single method call.

public class ShapeManipulator extends Applet
{

    private int squareXCoords[] = { 0, 40, 40, 0 };
    private int squareYCoords[] = { 0, 0, 40, 40 };

    private int triangleXCoords[] = { 0, 20, 40 };
    private int triangleYCoords[] = { 40, 0, 40 };

    private int pentXCoords[] = { 0, 20, 40, 30, 10 };
    private int pentYCoords[] = { 15, 0, 15, 40, 40 };

    private int shapeX;    // the X and Y of the current shape
    private int shapeY;

    private Shape currentShape;    // What shape we are dragging

    private Shape triangle;
    private Shape square;
    private Shape pentagon;
```

```
    public void init()
    {
        shapeX = 0;
        shapeY = 0;

        triangle = new Shape(triangleXCoords, triangleYCoords, 3);
        square = new Shape(squareXCoords, squareYCoords, 4);
        pentagon = new Shape(pentXCoords, pentYCoords, 5);

        currentShape = triangle;   // Start with a triangle
    }

    public void paint(Graphics g)
    {
        g.fillPolygon(currentShape);   // Draw the current shape
    }

    public boolean mouseDrag(Event event, int mouseX, int mouseY)
    {
        shapeX = mouseX; // make shape coordinates = mouse coordinates
        shapeY = mouseY;
// Now move the shape to its new coordinates
        currentShape.moveShape(shapeX, shapeY);

// Even though the shape is moved, we still need to call repaint to update
// the display.
        repaint();

        return true;    // always do this in event handlers
    }

    public boolean keyDown(Event event, int keyCode)
    {

// Check the keyCode to see if it is a t, an s, or a p

        if ((char)keyCode == 't')
        {
            currentShape = triangle;
        }
        else if ((char)keyCode == 's')
        {
            currentShape = square;
        }
        else if ((char)keyCode == 'p')
        {
            currentShape = pentagon;
        }

// because we may have changed the shape, make sure the current shape
// is moved to the current shape X and Y
```

(continues)

**Listing 20.13 Continued**

```
      currentShape.moveShape(shapeX, shapeY);

// Make sure the screen shows the current shape
      repaint();

      return true;
    }
}
```

# Clipping

Clipping is a technique in graphics systems to prevent one area from drawing over another. Basically, you draw in a rectangular area, and everything you try to draw outside the area gets "clipped off." Normally, your applet is clipped at the edges. In other words, you cannot draw beyond the bounds of the applet window. You cannot increase the clipping area; that is, you cannot draw outside the applet window, but you can further limit where you can draw inside the applet window. To set the boundaries of your clipping area, use the clipRect method.

The applet in listing 20.14 reduces its drawing area to a rectangle whose upper-left corner is at (10, 10) and is 60 pixels wide and 40 pixels high, and then tries to draw a circle. Figure 20.15 shows the output from this applet.

**Listing 20.14 Source Code for Clipper.java**

```
import java.applet.*;
import java.awt.*;

//
// This applet demonstrates the clipRect method by setting
// up a clipping area and trying to draw a circle that partially
// extends outside the clipping area.
// I want you to go out there and win just one for the Clipper...

public class Clipper extends Applet
{
   public void paint(Graphics g)
   {
// Set up a clipping region
      g.clipRect(10, 10, 60, 40);

// Draw a circle
      g.fillOval(5, 5, 50, 50);
   }
}
```

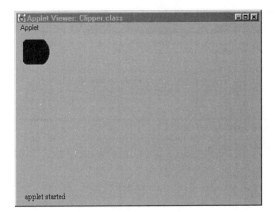

**Fig. 20.15**
The clipRect method reduces the drawing area and cuts off anything that extends outside it.

Within a paint method, once you change your clipping area, you cannot restore the old clipping area. In other words, you can only reduce your drawing area; you can never expand it. Even the clipping area is clipped, so if part of your new clipping area extends outside the old clipping area, only the portion of the new clipping area that falls within the old clipping area will be used. The clipping area lasts for the rest of your paint method; but the next time your paint method is called, the clipping area will be reset.

# Animation Techniques

You may have noticed a lot of screen flicker when you ran the Shape Manipulator applet. It was intentionally written to not eliminate any flicker so you could see just how bad flicker can be. What causes this flicker? One major cause is that the shape is redrawn on the screen right in front of you. The constant redrawing catches your eye and makes things appear to flicker. A common solution to this problem is a technique called *double-buffering*.

The idea behind double-buffering is that you create an off-screen image, and do all your drawing to that off-screen image. Once you are finished drawing, you copy the off-screen image to your drawing area in one quick call so the drawing area updates immediately.

The other major cause of flicker is the update method. The default update method for an applet clears the drawing area, then calls your paint method. You can eliminate the flicker caused by the screen clearing by overriding update to simply call the paint method:

```
public void update(Graphics g)
{
    paint(g);
}
```

---

**Caution**

There is a danger with changing update this way. Your applet must be aware that the screen has not been cleared. If you are using the double-buffering technique, this should not be a problem because you are replacing the entire drawing area with your off-screen image anyway.

---

The ShapeManipulator applet can be modified easily to support double-buffering and eliminate the screen-clear. In the declarations at the top of the class, you add an Image that will be the off-screen drawing area:

```
private Image offScreenImage;
```

Next, you add a line to the init method to initialize the off-screen image:

```
offScreenImage = createImage(size().width, size().height);
```

Finally, you create an update method that does not clear the real drawing area, but makes your paint method draw to the off-screen area and then copies the off-screen area to the screen (see listing 20.15).

---

**Listing 20.15  An Update Method to Support Double-Buffering**

```
public void update(Graphics g)
{
// This update method helps reduce flicker by supporting off-screen
➥drawing
// and by not clearing the drawing area first. It enables you to leave
// the original paint method alone.

// Get the graphics context for the off-screen image
    Graphics offScreenGraphics = offScreenImage.getGraphics();

// Now, go ahead and clear the off-screen image. It is O.K. to clear the
// off-screen image, because it is not being displayed on the screen.
// This way, your paint method can still expect a clear area, but the
// screen won't flicker because of it.

    offScreenGraphics.setColor(getBackground());

// We've set our drawing color to the applet's background color, now
// fill the entire area with that color (i.e. clear it)
    offScreenGraphics.fillRect(0, 0, size().width,
        size().height);

// Now, because the paint method probably doesn't set its drawing color,
// set the drawing color back to what was in the original graphics
    ➥context.
```

```
        offScreenGraphics.setColor(g.getColor());

    // Call the original paint method
        paint(offScreenGraphics);

    // Now, copy the off-screen image to the screen
        g.drawImage(offScreenImage, 0, 0, this);
    }
```

# Manipulating Images

Java's methods for manipulating images are different from some of the more conventional graphics systems. In order to support network-based operations, Java has to support an imaging paradigm that supports the gradual loading of images. You don't want your applet to have to sit and wait for all the images to download. Java's Producer-Consumer model takes the gradual loading of images into account. Java also uses the concept of filters to allow you to change the image as it passes from producer to consumer. It may seem like a strange way to deal with images at first, but it is really very powerful.

## Producers, Consumers, and Observers

Java's model for manipulating images is more complex than on other systems. Java uses the concept of image producers and image consumers. An example of an image producer might be an object responsible for fetching an image over the network, or it might be a simple array of bytes that represent an image. The image producer can be thought of as the source for the image data. Image consumers are objects that make use of the image data.

The image consumers are typically low-level drawing routines that display the image on the screen. The interesting thing about the producer-consumer model is that the producer is "in control." The ImageProducer uses the setPixels method in the ImageConsumer to describe the image to the consumer.

The best way to illustrate this mechanism is to trace the process of loading an image over the network. First of all, the ImageProducer starts reading the image. The first thing it will read from the image is the width and height in the image. It will notify its consumers (notice that a producer can serve multiple consumers) of the dimension of the image using the setDimensions method. Figure 20.16 illustrates the relationship between an ImageProducer and an ImageConsumer.

**Fig. 20.16**
The Image-
Producer reads the
image dimensions
from the image
file and passes the
information to the
ImageConsumer.

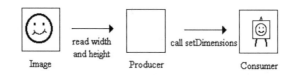

Next, the producer will read the color map for the image. The producer determines from this color map what kind of color model the image uses and calls
the setColorModel method in each consumer. Figure 20.17 illustrates how
the producer passes color information to the consumer.

**Fig. 20.17**
The producer uses
the setColorModel
method to relay
color information
to the consumer.

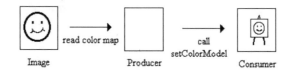

The producer calls the setHints method in each consumer to notify them
how it intends to deliver the image pixels. This enables the consumers to
optimize their pixel handling if possible. Some of the values for the hints
are ImageConsumer.RANDOMPIXELORDER, ImageConsumer.TOPDOWNLEFTRIGHT,
ImageConsumer.COMPLETESCANLINES, ImageConsumer.SINGLEPASS, and
ImageConsumer.SINGLEFRAME. Figure 20.18 illustrates how the producer
passes hints to the consumer.

**Fig. 20.18**
The producer
passes hints to
the consumer to
indicate how it
will send pixels.

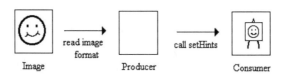

Now, the producer finally starts to "produce" pixels, calling the setPixels
method in the consumers to deliver the image. This may be done in many
calls, especially if it is delivering one scan line at a time for a large image.
Or it may be one single call if it is delivering the image as a single pass
(ImageConsumer.SINGLEPASS). Figure 20.19 shows the producer passing
pixel information to the consumer.

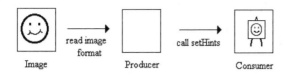

**Fig. 20.19**
The producer uses the setPixels method to pass pixel information to the consumer.

Finally, the producer calls the `imageComplete` method in the consumer to indicate that the image has been delivered. If there was a failure in delivery—
for instance, the network went down as it was being transmitted—
then the `imageComplete` method will be called with a parameter of
`ImageConsumer.IMAGEERROR` or `ImageConsumer.IMAGEABORT`. Another
possible status is that this image is part of a multiframe image (a form of
animation) and there are more frames to come. This would be signaled by
the `ImageConsumer.SINGLEFRAMEDONE` parameter. When everything is truly
complete, `imageComplete` is called with the `ImageConsumer.STATICIMAGEDONE`
parameter. Figure 20.20 shows the producer wrapping up the image transfer
to the consumer.

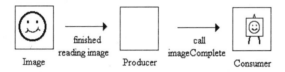

**Fig. 20.20**
The producer uses the imageComplete method to tell the consumer it is through transfer-ring the image.

This method enables Java to load images efficiently while not stopping to
wait for them all to load before it begins. The `ImageObserver` interface is
related to the producer-consumer interface as sort of an "interested third
party." It enables an object to receive updates whenever the producer has
released some new information about the image.

You may recall that when you used the `drawImage` method you passed `this` as
the last parameter. You were actually giving the `drawImage` method a reference to an `ImageObserver`. The `Applet` class implements the `ImageObserver`
interface. The `ImageObserver` interface contains a single method called
`imageUpdate`:

```
boolean imageUpdate(Image img, int flags, int x, int y, int width, int
height)
```

Not all the information passed to the `imageUpdate` method is valid all the time. The `flags` parameter is a summary of flags that tell what information is now available about the image. The possible flags are as follows:

| | |
|---|---|
| `ImageObserver.WIDTH` | Width value is now valid. |
| `ImageObserver.HEIGHT` | Height value is now valid. |
| `ImageObserver.PROPERTIES` | Image properties are now available. |
| `ImageObserver.SOMEBITS` | More pixels are available (x, y, width, height indicate the bounding box of the pixels now available). |
| `ImageObserver.FRAMEBITS` | Another complete frame is now available. |
| `ImageObserver.ALLBITS` | The image has been loaded completely. |
| `ImageObserver.ERROR` | There was an error loading the image. |
| `ImageObserver.ABORT` | The loading of the image was aborted. |

These flags are usually added together, so an `imageUpdate` method might test for the `WIDTH` flag with the following:

```
if ((flags & ImageObserver.WIDTH) != 0) {
  // width is now available
}
```

## Image Filters

The Java image model also enables you to *filter* images easily. The concept of a filter is similar to the idea of a filter in photography. It is something that sits between the image consumer (the film) and the image producer (the outside world). The filter changes the image before it is delivered to the consumer. The `CropImageFilter` is a predefined filter that crops an image to a certain dimension (i.e., it only shows a portion of the whole image). The `FilteredImageSource` class enables you to put a filter on top of an `ImageProducer`. The applet in listing 20.16 takes an image and applies a `CropImageFilter` to it to only display a part of the image. Figure 20.21 contains the output from this applet, showing a full image, and a cropped version of the image.

**Listing 20.16 Source Code for CropImage.java**

```
import java.awt.*;
import java.awt.image.*;
import java.applet.*;

//
```

```
// This applet creates a CropImageFilter to create a
// cropped version of an image. It displays both the original
// and the cropped images.

public class CropImage extends Applet
{
    private Image originalImage;
    private Image croppedImage;
    private ImageFilter cropFilter;

    public void init()
    {
// Get the original image
        originalImage = getImage(getDocumentBase(), "samantha.gif");

// Create a filter to crop the image in a box starting at (25, 30)
// that is 50 pixels wide and 50 pixels high.

        cropFilter = new CropImageFilter(25, 30, 50, 50);

// Create a new image that is a cropped version of the original

        croppedImage = createImage(new FilteredImageSource(
            originalImage.getSource(), cropFilter));
    }

    public void paint(Graphics g)
    {
// Display both images
        g.drawImage(originalImage, 0, 0, this);
        g.drawImage(croppedImage, 0, 150, this);
    }
}
```

**Fig. 20.21**
CropImageFilter
allows you to
display only a
portion of an
image.

## Copying Memory to an Image

One possible type of image producer is an array of integers representing the color values of each pixel. The `MemoryImageSource` class does just that. You create the memory image, then create a `MemoryImageSource` to act as an image producer for that memory image. Next, you create an image from the `MemoryImageSource`. The applet in listing 20.17 creates a memory image, a `MemoryImageSource`, and finally draws the image in the drawing area. Figure 20.22 shows the output from this applet.

**Listing 20.17   Source Code for MemoryImage.java**

```java
import java.applet.*;
import java.awt.*;
import java.awt.image.*;

//
// This applet creates an image using an array of
// pixel values.

public class MemoryImage extends Applet
{
    private final static int b = Color.blue.getRGB();
    private final static int r = Color.red.getRGB();
    private final static int g = Color.green.getRGB();

// Create the array of pixel values. The image will be 10x10
// And resembles a square bull's-eye with blue around the outside,
// green inside the blue, and red in the center.

    int pixels[] = {
        b, b, b, b, b, b, b, b, b, b,
        b, b, b, b, b, b, b, b, b, b,
        b, b, g, g, g, g, g, g, b, b,
        b, b, g, g, g, g, g, g, b, b,
        b, b, g, g, r, r, g, g, b, b,
        b, b, g, g, r, r, g, g, b, b,
        b, b, g, g, g, g, g, g, b, b,
        b, b, g, g, g, g, g, g, b, b,
        b, b, b, b, b, b, b, b, b, b,
        b, b, b, b, b, b, b, b, b, b};

    Image myImage;

    public void init()
    {
// Create the new image from the pixels array. The 0, 10 means start
// reading pixels from array location 0, and there is a new row of
// pixels every 10 locations.
        myImage = createImage(new MemoryImageSource(10, 10,
            pixels, 0, 10));
    }
```

```
    public void paint(Graphics g)
    {
// Draw the image. Notice that the width and height we give for the
// image is 10 times its original size. The drawImage method will
// scale the image automatically.
        g.drawImage(myImage, 0, 0, 100, 100, this);
    }
}
```

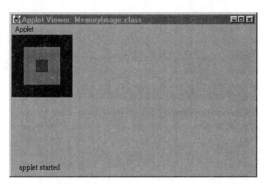

**Fig. 20.22**
MemoryImageSource class allows you to create your own images from pixel values.

## Copying Images to Memory

The PixelGrabber class is sort of an inverse of the MemoryImageSource. Rather than taking an array of integers and turning it into an image, it takes an image and turns it into an array of integers. The PixelGrabber acts as an ImageConsumer. You create a PixelGrabber, give it the dimensions of the image you want and an array in which to store the image pixels, and it gets the pixels from the ImageProducer.

The PixelGrabber is useful if you want to take an existing image and modify it. Listing 20.18 is an applet that uses the PixelGrabber to get the pixels of an image into an array. It then enables you to color sections of the image by picking a crayon and touching the area you want to color. To redisplay the image, it uses the MemoryImageSource to turn the array of pixels back into an image. The applet runs pretty slowly on a 486/100, so you need a lot of patience.

**Listing 20.18   Source Code for Crayon.java**

```
import java.applet.*;
import java.awt.*;
import java.awt.image.*;
//
// The Crayon applet uses the PixelGrabber to create an array of pixel
```

(continues)

**Listing 20.18  Continued**

```
// values from an image. It then enables you to paint the image using
// a set of crayons, and then redisplays the image using the
// MemoryImageSource.
// If you want to use other images with this applet, make sure that
// the lines are done in black, because it specifically looks for black
// as the boundary for an area.
// Also, beware, this applet runs very slowly on a 486/100

public class Crayon extends Applet
{
    private Image coloringBook;   // the original image
    private Image displayImage;   // the image to be displayed

    private int imageWidth, imageHeight;   // the dimensions of the
                                         ➥image

// the following two arrays set up the shape of the crayons

    int crayonShapeX[] = { 0, 2, 10, 15, 23, 25, 25, 0 };
    int crayonShapeY[] = { 15, 15, 0, 0, 15, 15, 45, 45 };

// We use the Shape class defined earlier so we can move the crayons
// to a new location easily.
    private Shape crayons[];

// The color class doesn't provide a default value for brown, so we
    ➥add one.
    private Color brown = new Color(130, 100, 0);

// crayonColors is an array of all the colors the crayons can be.
    ➥You can
// add new crayons just by adding to this array.

    private Color crayonColors[] = {
      Color.blue, Color.cyan, Color.darkGray,
      Color.gray, Color.green, Color.magenta,
      Color.orange, Color.pink, Color.red,
      Color.white, Color.yellow, brown };

    private Color currentDrawingColor;   // the color we are coloring
                                        ➥with

    private int imagePixels[];   // the memory image of the picture

    boolean imageValid = false;   // did we read the image in O.K.?

// blackRGB is just used as a shortcut to get to the black pixel
    ➥value
    private int blackRGB = Color.black.getRGB();

    public void init()
    {
```

```
      int i;
      MediaTracker tracker = new MediaTracker(this);

// Get the image we will color
      coloringBook = getImage(getDocumentBase(), "smileman.gif");

// tell the media tracker about the image
      tracker.addImage(coloringBook, 0);

// Wait for the image, if we get an error, flag the image as invalid
      try {
         tracker.waitForID(0);
         imageValid = true;
      } catch (Exception oops) {
         imageValid = false;
      }

// Get the image dimensions
      imageWidth = coloringBook.getWidth(this);
      imageHeight = coloringBook.getHeight(this);

// Copy the image to the array of pixels
      resetMemoryImage();

// Create a new display image from the array of pixels
      remakeDisplayImage();

// Create a set of crayons. We determine how many crayons to create
// based on the size of the crayonColors array
      crayons = new Shape[crayonColors.length];

      for (i=0; i < crayons.length; i++)
      {
// Create a new crayon shape for each color
         crayons[i] = new Shape(crayonShapeX,
            crayonShapeY, crayonShapeX.length);

// The crayons are lined up in a row below the image
         crayons[i].moveShape(i * 30,
            imageHeight + 10);
      }
// Start coloring with the first crayon
      currentDrawingColor = crayonColors[0];
   }

// resetMemoryImage copies the coloringBook image into the
// imagePixels array.

   private void resetMemoryImage()
   {
      imagePixels = new int[imageWidth * imageHeight];

// Set up a pixel grabber to get the pixels
      PixelGrabber grabber = new PixelGrabber(
         coloringBook.getSource(),
```

(continues)

**Listing 20.18  Continued**

```
                 0, 0, imageWidth, imageHeight, imagePixels,
                 0, imageWidth);

// Ask the image grabber to go get the pixels
      try {
         grabber.grabPixels();
      } catch (Exception e) {
         // Ignore for now
         return;
      }

// Make sure that the image copied correctly, although we don't
// do anything if it doesn't.

      if ((grabber.status() & ImageObserver.ABORT) != 0)
      {
         // uh oh, it aborted
         return;
      }

   }

// getPixel returns the pixel value for a particular x and y
   private int getPixel(int x, int y)
   {
      return imagePixels[y * imageWidth + x];
   }

// setPixel sets the pixel value for a particular x and y
   private void setPixel(int x, int y, int color)
   {
      imagePixels[y*imageWidth + x] = color;
   }

// floodFill starts at a particular x and y coordinate and fills it,
   ➥and all
// the surrounding pixels with a color. The doesn't paint over black
   ➥pixels,
// so they represent the borders of the fill.
// The easiest way to code a flood fill is by doing it recursively:
   ➥you
// call flood fill on a pixel, color that pixel, then it calls flood
   ➥fill
// on each surrounding pixel and so on. Unfortunately, that usually
   ➥causes
// stack overflows because recursion is pretty expensive.
// This routine uses an alternate method. It makes a queue of pixels
   ➥that
// it still has to fill. It takes a pixel off the head of the queue
   ➥and
// colors the pixels around it, then adds those pixels to the queue.
   ➥In other
// words, a pixel is really added to the queue after it has been
   ➥colored.
```

```
// If a pixel has already been colored, it is not added, so eventually, it
// works the queue down until it is empty.

   private void floodFill(int x, int y, int color)
   {
// If the pixel we are starting with is already black, we won't paint
      if (getPixel(x, y) == blackRGB)
      {
         return;
      }

// Create the pixel queue. Assume the worst case where every pixel in the
// image may be in the queue.
      int pixelQueue[] = new int[imageWidth * imageHeight];
      int pixelQueueSize = 0;

// Add the start pixel to the queue (we created a single array of ints,
// even though we are enqueuing two numbers. We put the y value in the
// upper 16 bits of the integer, and the x in the lower 16. This gives
// a limit of 65536x65536 pixels, that should be enough.)

      pixelQueue[0] = (y << 16) + x;
      pixelQueueSize = 1;

// Color the start pixel
      setPixel(x, y, color);

// Keep going while there are pixels in the queue
      while (pixelQueueSize > 0)
      {

// Get the x and y values of the next pixel in the queue
         x = pixelQueue[0] & 0xffff;
         y = (pixelQueue[0] >> 16) & 0xffff;

// Remove the first pixel from the queue. Rather than move all the
// pixels in the queue, which would take forever, just take the one
// off the end and move it to the beginning (order doesn't matter here).

         pixelQueueSize--;
         pixelQueue[0] = pixelQueue[pixelQueueSize];

// If we aren't on the left side of the image, see if the pixel to the
// left has been painted. If not, paint it and add it to the queue
         if (x > 0) {
           if ((getPixel(x-1, y) != blackRGB) &&
             (getPixel(x-1, y) != color))
           {
             setPixel(x-1, y, color);
             pixelQueue[pixelQueueSize] =
               (y << 16) + x-1;
             pixelQueueSize++;
           }
         }
```

(continues)

**Listing 20.18   Continued**

```
// If we aren't on the top of the image, see if the pixel above
// this one has been painted. If not, paint it and add it to the queue
      if (y > 0) {
        if ((getPixel(x, y-1) != blackRGB) &&
            (getPixel(x, y-1) != color))
        {
          setPixel(x, y-1, color);
          pixelQueue[pixelQueueSize] =
            ((y-1) << 16) + x;
          pixelQueueSize++;
        }
      }

// If we aren't on the right side of the image, see if the pixel to the
// right has been painted. If not, paint it and add it to the queue
      if (x < imageWidth-1) {
        if ((getPixel(x+1, y) != blackRGB) &&
            (getPixel(x+1, y) != color))
        {
          setPixel(x+1, y, color);
          pixelQueue[pixelQueueSize] =
            (y << 16) + x+1;
          pixelQueueSize++;
        }
      }

// If we aren't on the bottom of the image, see if the pixel below
// this one has been painted. If not, paint it and add it to the queue
      if (y < imageHeight-1) {
        if ((getPixel(x, y+1) != blackRGB) &&
            (getPixel(x, y+1) != color))
        {
          setPixel(x, y+1, color);
          pixelQueue[pixelQueueSize] =
            ((y+1) << 16) + x;
          pixelQueueSize++;
        }
      }
    }
  }

// remakeDisplayImage takes the array of pixels and turns it into an
// image for us to display
  private void remakeDisplayImage()
  {
    displayImage = createImage(new MemoryImageSource(
      imageWidth, imageHeight, imagePixels, 0, imageWidth));
  }
```

```
// The paint method is written with the assumption that the screen has
// not been cleared ahead of time, that way we can create an update
// method that doesn't clear the screen, but doesn't need an off-screen
// image.

   public void paint(Graphics g)
   {
     int i;

// If we got the image successfully, draw it, otherwise, print a
message
// saying we couldn't get it

      if (imageValid)
      {
         g.drawImage(displayImage, 0, 0, this);
      }
      else
      {
         g.drawString("Unable to load coloring image.", 0, 50);
      }

// Draw the crayons
      for (i=0; i < crayons.length; i++)
      {
// Draw each crayon in the color it represents
         g.setColor(crayonColors[i]);
         g.fillPolygon(crayons[i]);

// Get the box that would enclose the crayon
         Rectangle box = crayons[i].getBoundingBox();

// If the crayon is the current one, draw a black box around it, if not,
// draw a box the color of the background around it (in case the current
// crayon has changed, we want to make sure the old box is erased).

         if (crayonColors[i] == currentDrawingColor)
         {
           g.setColor(Color.black);
         }
         else
         {
           g.setColor(getBackground());
         }

// Draw the box around the crayon
         g.drawRect(box.x, box.y, box.width, box.height);
      }
   }

// Override the update method to call paint without clearing the screen
```

(continues)

**Listing 20.18   Continued**

```
    public void update(Graphics g)
    {
      paint(g);
    }

    public boolean mouseDown(Event event, int x, int y)
    {
      int i;

// Check each crayon to see of the mouse was clicked inside of it.
➥If so,
// change the current color to that crayon's color. We use the
➥"inside"
// method to see if the mouse x,y is within the crayon shape. Pretty
handy!

      for (i=0; i < crayons.length; i++)
      {
        if (crayons[i].inside(x, y))
        {
          currentDrawingColor = crayonColors[i];
          repaint();
          return true;
        }
      }

// If the mouse wasn't clicked on a crayon, see if it was clicked
➥within
// the image. This assumes that the image starts at 0, 0.
      if ((x < imageWidth) && (y < imageHeight))
      {
// If the image was clicked, fill that section of the image with the
// current crayon color
        floodFill(x, y, currentDrawingColor.getRGB());

// Now re-create the display image because we just changed the pixels
        remakeDisplayImage();
        repaint();
        return true;
      }

      return true;
    }
}
```

## Color Models

The image producer-consumer model also makes use of a ColorModel class.
As you have seen, the images passed between producers and consumers are
made up of arrays of integers. Each integer represents the color of a single
pixel. The ColorModel class contains methods to extract the red, green, blue,

and alpha components from a pixel value. You are familiar with the red, green, and blue color components from the earlier discussion on color, but the alpha component may be something new to you.

The alpha component represents the *transparency* of a color. An alpha value of 255 means that the color is completely opaque, while an alpha of zero indicates that the color is completely transparent. The default color model is the RGBdefault model, which encodes the four color components in the form 0xaarrggbb. The left-most eight bits are the alpha value; the next eight bits are the red component followed by eight bits for green and, finally, eight bits for blue. For example, a color of 0x12345678 would have an alpha component of 0x12 (fairly transparent), a red component of 0x34, a green component of 0x56, and a blue component of 0x78. Anytime you need a color model and you are satisfied with using the RGBdefault model, you can use getRGBDefault:

```
ColorModel myColorModel = ColorModel.getRGBDefault();
```

# CHAPTER 21
# AWT

*by Mark Wutka*

## What Is the AWT?

The Abstract Windowing Toolkit (AWT) provides an API for common User Interface components like buttons and menus.

One of the main goals of Java is to provide a platform-independent development environment. The area of Graphical User Interfaces has always been one of the stickiest parts of creating highly portable code. The Windows API is different from the OS/2 Presentation Manager API, which is different from the X-Windows API, which is different from the Mac API. The most common solution to this problem is to take a look at all the platforms you want to use, identify the components that are common to all of them (or would be easy to implement on all of them), and create a single API that you can use. On each different platform, the common API would interface with the platform's native API so that applications using the common API would have the same look and feel as applications using the native API.

The opposite of this approach is to create a single look and feel and then implement that look and feel on each different platform. For Java, Sun chose the common API approach, which allows Java applications to blend in smoothly with their surroundings. Sun called this common API the Abstract Windowing Toolkit, or AWT for short.

In this chapter, you will learn how to:

■ Create and use Components

Components are the building blocks of the user interface. They represent the actual parts of the user interface—the buttons, lists, scrollbars, menus, etc.

- Create and use Containers

  Containers help you organize components into manageable groups. They also provide basic window and dialog services.

- Create and use Layout Managers

  Layout managers arrange components within a container. They allow you to lay out your user interface on the screen without worrying about differences in screen dimensions.

- Use Observables to create a more flexible interface

  Observables allow an object to notify other objects when it changes. Using this concept, you can create more modular classes that can be used over and over again in new applets.

The AWT contains a number of familiar user interface elements. Figure 21.1 shows a Java applet with a sample of some of the components of the AWT.

**Fig. 21.1**
The AWT features a number of familiar compo-nents.

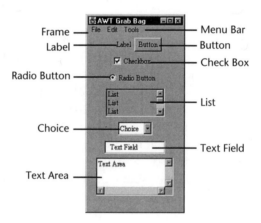

Figure 21.2 shows you a portion of the AWT's inheritance hierarchy.

**Fig. 21.2**
The AWT inherits all its user inter-face components from Component.

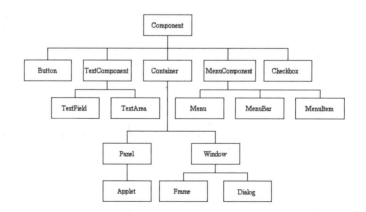

## Components

*Components* are the building blocks of the AWT. The end-user interacts directly with these components. The components provided by the AWT are:

- Buttons
- Labels
- Checkboxes
- Radio Buttons
- Lists
- Choices
- Text Fields
- Text Areas
- Menus
- Canvases
- Scrollbars

## Containers

You need more than just components to create a good user interface. The components need to be organized into manageable groups. That's where containers come in. Containers hold components. You cannot use a component in the AWT unless it is held within a container. A component without a container is like a refrigerator magnet without a refrigerator. The containers defined in the AWT are:

- Windows
- Panels
- Frames
- Dialogs

Even if you don't create a container in your applet, you are still using one. The Applet class is a subclass of the Panel class.

> **Tip**
>
> Containers not only hold components, they are components themselves. This means that a container can hold other containers.

## Layout Managers

Even though you have containers as a place to neatly store your UI components, you still need a way to organize the components within a container. That's where the layout managers come in. Each container is given a *layout manager* that decides where each component should be displayed. The layout managers in the AWT are:

- Flow
- Border
- Grid
- Card
- Grid Bag

# Buttons

Buttons are a simple mechanism, but they are one of the workhorses of any graphical interface. You find buttons on toolbars, dialog boxes, windows, and even in other components such as scrollbars.

## Creating Buttons

The only thing you have to decide when creating a button is whether or not you want the button to be labeled. There are no other options for buttons.

To create an unlabeled button, use this syntax:

```
Button myButton = new Button();
```

Creating a labeled button is an equally simple task:

```
Button myButton = new Button("Press Me");
```

Once you have created a button, you need to add it to a container. Since your applet is already a container, you can add a button directly to your applet:

```
Button myButton = new Button("Press Me");

add(myButton);
```

To change the label of a button, use setLabel:

```
Button.setLabel("Hey!  Press me!");
```

To get the label for a button use getLabel:

```
String buttonLabel = Button.getLabel();
```

> **Note**
>
> You may notice the lack of "image buttons"—that is, buttons that contain an image instead of text. These types of buttons are almost a necessity for creating toolbars. Unfortunately, they are not supported in the AWT. Hopefully, these will show up in a future version of the AWT; but for now, if you want an image button, you'll have to implement it yourself.

## Using Buttons

Now that you are able to create a button and add it to your applet, it's time to learn how to make the button do something.

All the components within the AWT have an `action` method which is called when an action is taken on the component. In the case of the button, `action` is called when the button is pressed. The `action` method is similar to some of the event handling methods you may have come across already like `keyDown` or `mouseDown`.

> **Note**
>
> When an action takes place in a component, the AWT calls the `handleEvent` method in that component with an event type of `ACTION_EVENT`. The default `handleEvent` method calls the *action* method in the component. By default, the component doesn't handle the action, which causes the event to be passed to the `handleEvent` method in the parent container where, by default, the parent's `action` method is called. This continues until the action is either handled or ignored by the top-most container. A component signals that it has handled the event by returning a value of *true* from the event- handling method (`action`, `handleEvent`, or whatever). A return value of `false` from an event-handling method indicates that the component has not handled the event and the event should be passed up to the parent.

The format of the action method in all components is

```
public boolean action(Event event, Object whatAction)
```

where `event` is the Event that has occurred in the component, and `whatAction` indicates what has occurred.

For buttons, `whatAction` is the label of the button that has been pressed. The event parameter contains other information specific to the action, such as the component where the action occurred (`event.target`) and the time the action occurred (`event.when`).

---

**Caution**

You should always check the event.target variable using the `instanceof` operator to make sure that the action is for the object you expect. For instance, if you expect that the action is for a `Button`, then you need to check that (`event.target instanceof Button`) is true.

---

Now that you know how to create a button and check for an action, you can create a button applet. A very simple example is an applet with buttons that change its background color. One way to do this is by putting the name of the color in the button label. Then, in the `action` method, you look at the label of the button that was pressed and set the applet's background color based on that label. For example, the button to turn the background blue could be labeled "Blue." The `action` method would set the background to blue if the button's label was blue. The applet in listing 21.1 demonstrates how to do this:

**Listing 21.1   Filename—Source Code for Button1Applet.java**

```java
import java.applet.*;
import java.awt.*;

// Example 21.1 - Button1Applet
//
// This applet creates two buttons named "Red" and "Blue".  When a
// button is pressed, the background color of the applet is set to
// the color named by that button's label.
//

public class Button1Applet extends Applet
{
    public void init()
    {
        add(new Button("Red"));

        add(new Button("Blue"));

    }

    public boolean action(Event evt, Object whatAction)
    {
// Check to make sure this is a button action, if not,
// return false to indicate that the event has not been handled.
        if (!(evt.target instanceof Button))
        {
            return false;
        }
        String buttonLabel = (String) whatAction;
```

```
        if (buttonLabel == "Red")
        {
            setBackground(Color.red);
        }
        else if (buttonLabel == "Blue")
        {
            setBackground(Color.blue);
        }
        repaint();      // Make the change visible immediately
        return true;
    }
}
```

You will learn a better way to design this applet in the section titled "Object-Oriented Thinking" later in this chapter.

Figure 21.3 shows you the Button1Applet in operation.

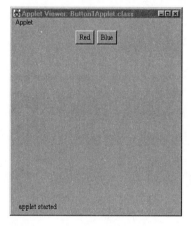

**Fig. 21.3**
The buttons in Button1Applet change the applet's background color.

# Labels

*Labels* are the simplest of the AWT components. They are text strings that are used only for decoration. Since they are "display-only," labels have no `action` method.

> **Note**
>
> For you technical purists, labels do have an `action` method since they inherit from the Component class, and all components have an `action` method. A label's `action` method is never called.

### Creating Labels

There are three different ways to create a label. The simplest is to create an empty label, such as

```
Label emptyLabel = new Label();
```

Of course, an empty label isn't going to do you much good since there is nothing to see. A more useful label is one with some text, as in

```
Label myLabel = new Label("This is a label");
```

Labels can be left-justified, right-justified, or centered. The variables `Label.LEFT`, `Label.RIGHT`, and `Label.CENTER` can be used to set the alignment of a label. Here is an example of how to create a right-justified label:

```
Label myLabel = new Label("This is a right-justified label",
Label.RIGHT);
```

You can change the text of a label with `setText`:

```
myLabel.setText("This is the new label text");
```

You can also get the text of a label with `getText`:

```
String labelText = myLabel.getText();
```

You can change the alignment of a label with `setAlignment`:

```
myLabel.setAlignment(Label.CENTER);
```

You can also get the alignment of a label with `getAlignment`:

```
int labelAlignment = myLabel.getAlignment();
```

Figure 21.4 shows you a sample label.

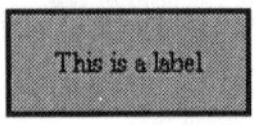

**Fig. 21.4**
Labels are simply
text strings.

This is a label

# Checkboxes and Radio Buttons

*Checkboxes* are similar to buttons except that they are used as "yes-no" or "on-off" switches. Every time you click a checkbox it changes from "off" to "on" or from "on" to "off." A close cousin to the checkbox is the radio button. *Radio buttons* are also "on-off" switches, but they are arranged in special mutually exclusive groups where only one button in the group can be on at a time. Imagine what a radio would sound like if you could have more than one station on at a time!

## Creating Checkboxes

A checkbox has two parts—a label and a state. The label is the text that is displayed next to the checkbox itself, while the state is a Boolean variable that indicates whether or not the box is checked. By default, the state of a checkbox is false, or "off."

To create a checkbox with no label:

```
Checkbox myCheckbox = new Checkbox();
```

To create a checkbox with a label:

```
Checkbox myCheckbox = new Checkbox("Check me if you like Java");
```

You can also create a checkbox while setting its state:

```
Checkbox myCheckbox = new Checkbox("Check me if you like Java",null, true);
```

The null in the preceding code fragment refers to the CheckboxGroup to which the checkbox belongs. You use CheckboxGroup to create a set of radio buttons. For a normal checkbox, the CheckboxGroup will be null.

You may check to see if a checkbox has been checked with getState:

```
if (myCheckbox.getState()) {
    // The box has been checked
} else {
    // The box has not been checked
}
```

## Creating Radio Buttons

Radio buttons are just a special case of a checkbox. There is no RadioButton class. Instead, you create a set of radio buttons by creating checkboxes and putting them in the same checkbox group. The constructor for CheckboxGroup takes no arguments:

```
CheckboxGroup myCheckboxGroup = new CheckboxGroup()
```

Once you have created the group, you create checkboxes that belong to this group by passing the group to the constructor. You can then add them to the applet:

```
add(new Checkbox("Favorite language is Java", myCheckboxGroup, true));
add(new Checkbox("Favorite language is Visual Cobol", myCheckboxGroup, false));
add(new Checkbox("Favorite language is Backtalk", myCheckboxGroup, false));
```

> **Note**
>
> When you add checkboxes to a checkbox group, the last checkbox that was added as *true* is the box that is checked when the group is displayed.

You can find out which radio button is selected by either calling getState on each checkbox, or calling getCurrent on the CheckboxGroup. The getCurrent method returns the checkbox that is currently selected.

## Using Checkboxes and Radio Buttons

The action method for a checkbox or a radio button is called whenever it is clicked. The whichAction parameter of the action method will be an instance of a Boolean class that is true if the checkbox was clicked on, or false if the checkbox was clicked off. If you create an action method for a radio button, you should not rely on the whichAction parameter to contain the correct value. If a radio button is clicked when it is already on, the whichAction contains a false value even though the button is still on. You are safer just using the getState method to check the state of the radio button or the checkbox. You can also use the getLabel method to determine which checkbox has been checked. The following code fragment shows an action method that responds to a box being checked and retrieves the current state of the box:

```
public boolean action(Event evt, Object whichAction)
{
if (evt.target instanceof Checkbox)  // make sure this is a checkbox
    {
        Checkbox currentCheckbox = (Checkbox)evt.target;
        boolean checkboxState = currentCheckbox.getState();

        if (currentCheckbox.getLabel() == "Check me if you like
        ➥Java")
        {
            if (checkboxState)
            {
             // Code to handle "Check me if you like Java"
                ➥being set to on
            }
            else
            {
            // Code to handle "Check me if you like Java"
                ➥being set to off
            }
            return true;  // the event has been handled
```

```
            }
        }
        return false;  // the event has not been handled
    }
```

---

**Note**

Whenever you write an event-handling method like `handleEvent` or `action`, you
should return `true` only in the cases where you actually handle the event. Notice that
the example `action` method for checkboxes only returns `true` in the case where the
event is a checkbox event. It returns `false` in all other cases. You may also have cases
where you handle an event but you still want to allow other classes to handle the
same event. In those cases, you also return `false`.

---

Figure 21.5 shows you some checkboxes and a group of three radio buttons.

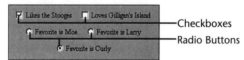
——Checkboxes
——Radio Buttons

**Fig. 21.5**
Checkboxes are
squared boxes with
checks in them.
Radio buttons are
rounded and are
checked with dots.

# Choices

The Choice class provides a pop-up menu of text string choices. The current
choice is displayed as the menu title.

## Creating Choices

To create a choice pop-up menu, you must first create an instance of the
Choice class. Since there are no options for the choice constructor, the creation of a choice should always look something like this:

```
Choice myChoice = new Choice();
```

Once you have created the choice, you can add string items to it using the
*addItem* method:

```
myChoice.addItem("Moe");
myChoice.addItem("Larry");
myChoice.addItem("Curly");
```

You may also change which item is currently selected either by name or by
index. If you wanted Curly to be selected, for instance, you could select him
by name:

```
myChoice.select("Curly");      // Make "Curly" become selected item
```

You could also select Curly by his position in the list. Since he was added third, and the choices are numbered starting at 0, Moe would be 0, Larry would be 1, and Curly would be 2:

```
myChoice.select(2);    // Make the third list entry become selected
```

The getSelectedIndex method will return the position of the selected item. Again, if Curly was selected, getSelectedIndex would return 2. Similarly, the getSelectedItem method returns the string name of the selected item, so if Curly was selected, getSelectedItem would return "Curly."

If you have an index value for an item and you want to find out the name of the item at that index, you can use getItem:

```
String selectedItem = myChoice.getItem(2);
```

Figure 21.6 shows a choice in its usual form, while figure 21.7 shows a choice with its menu of choices pulled down.

**Fig. 21.6**

The choice box displays its current selection.

**Fig. 21.7**

The button on the right of a choice pops up a menu of the possible choices.

## Using Choices

The action method for a choice is called whenever a choice is made, even if it is the same choice. The whatAction parameter contains the name of the selected item. The following code fragment gives an example action method for a choice where the selection is stored in a String variable within the applet:

```
String currentStooge;

public boolean action(Event event, Object whatAction)
{
// Check to make sure this is a choice object, if not
// indicate that the event has not been handled.
    if (!(event.target instanceof Choice))
    {
        return false;
```

```
      }
      Choice whichChoice = (Choice) event.target;
// See if this is an action for myChoice
      if (whichChoice == myChoice)
      {
          currentStooge = (String) whatAction;
          return true; // the event has been handled
      }
      return false;  // it must have been a different Choice
  }
```

# Lists

The List class allows you to create a scrolling list of values that may be selected either individually, or many at a time.

## Creating Lists

You have two options when creating a list. The default constructor for the List class allows you to create a list that does not allow multiple selections:

```
List myList = new List();
```

You may also set the number of list entries that are visible in the list window at any one time, as well as whether or not to allow multiple selections. The following code fragment creates a list with 10 visible entries and multiple selections turned on:

```
List myList = new List(10, true);    // True means allow multiple selections
```

Once you have created the list, you can add new entries to it with the addItem method:

```
myList.addItem("Moe");
myList.addItem("Larry");
myList.addItem("Curly");
```

You may also add an item at a specific position in the list. The list positions are numbered from 0, so if you add an item at position 0, it goes to the front of the list. If you try to add an item at position -1, or try to add an item at a position higher than the number of positions, the item will be added to the end of the list. The following code adds "Shemp" to the beginning of the list, and "Curly Joe" to the end:

```
myList.addItem("Shemp", 0);       // Add Shemp at position 0
myList.addItem("Curly Joe", -1);  // Add Curly Joe to the end of the list
```

## *List* Features

The List class provides a number of different methods for changing the contents of the list. The replaceItem method will replace an item at a given position with a new item:

```
myList.replaceItem("Dr. Howard", 0);
            // Replace the first item in the list with "Dr. Howard"
```

You can delete an item in the list with deleteItem:

```
myList.deleteItem(1);
            // Delete the second item in the list (0 is the first)
```

The deleteItems method deletes a whole range of items from the list. The following code removes items from the list starting at position 2, up to and including position 5:

```
myList.deleteItems(2, 5);
            // Delete from position 2 up to and including position 5
```

You can delete all the items in the list with the clear method:

```
myList.clear();
```

The getSelectedIndex method returns the index number of the currently selected item, or -1 if no item is selected:

```
int currentSelection = myList.getSelectedIndex();
```

You can also get the selected item directly with getSelectedItem:

```
String selectItem = myList.getSelectedItem();
```

For lists with multiple selections turned on, you can get all the selections with getSelectedIndexes:

```
int currentSelections[];
currentSelections = myList.getSelectedIndexes();
```

The getSelectedItems returns all the selected items:

```
String selectedItems[];
selectItems = myList.getSelectItems();
```

---

**Caution**

You should only use getSelectedIndex and getSelectedItem on lists without multiple selections. If you allow multiple selections, you should always use getSelectedIndexes and getSelectedItems.

---

You may make any item become selected by calling the `select` method with the index of the item you want selected. If the list does not allow multiple selections, the previously selected item will be deselected:

```
myList.select(2);        // Select the third item in the list
```

You may deselect any item by calling the `deselect` method with the index of the item you want deselected:

```
myList.deselect(0);      // Deselect the first item in the list
```

The `isSelected` method will tell you whether or not the item at a particular index is selected:

```
if (myList.isSelection(0))
{
        // the first item in the list is selected
}
```

You may turn multiple selections on and off with the `setMultipleSelections` method:

```
myList.setMultipleSelections(true);
            // turn multi-select on, false turns it off
```

The `allowsMultipleSelections` method returns `true` if multiple selections are allowed:

```
if (myList.allowsMultipleSelections())
{
    // multiple selections are allowed
}
```

Sometimes you might make sure a particular item is visible in the list window. You can do just that by passing the index of the item you want to make visible to `makeVisible`. For example, suppose the list was positioned on item 0, but you wanted to make sure item 15 was showing in the window instead, you would call:

```
myList.makeVisible(15);          // Make item 15 in the list visible
```

## Using *Lists*

Unlike the previous User Interface components you have encountered, the `List` class does not make use of the `action` method. Instead, you must use the `handleEvent` method to catch list selection and deselection events. The `handleEvent` method is called whenever you select or deselect an item in a list. The format of `handleEvent` is:

```
public boolean handleEvent(Event event)
```

When an item on a list is selected, event.id will be equal to Event.LIST_SELECT, and event.arg will be an instance of an integer whose value is the index of the selected item. The deselect event is identical to the select event except that event.id is Event.LIST_DESELECT. LIST_SELECT and LIST_DESELECT are declared in the Event class as static variables, as are all the other event types.

The applet in listing 21.2 sets up a List containing several values and uses a label to inform you whenever an item is selected or deselected.

**Listing 21.2  Source Code for ListApplet.java**

```
// Example 21.2 - ListApplet
//
// This applet creates a scrolling list with several choices and
// informs you of selections and deselections using a label.
//

import java.applet.*;
import java.awt.*;

public class ListApplet extends Applet
{
    Label listStatus;
    List scrollingList;

    public void init()
    {

// First, create the List

        scrollingList = new List(3, true);

// Now add a few items to the list

        scrollingList.addItem("Moe");

        scrollingList.addItem("Larry");

        scrollingList.addItem("Curly");

        scrollingList.addItem("Shemp");

        scrollingList.addItem("Curly Joe");

// Set Shemp to be selected

        scrollingList.select(3);

// Finally, add the list to the applet
```

```
        add(scrollingList);
// Now create a label to show us the last event that occurred

        listStatus = new Label("You selected entry Shemp");
        add(listStatus);

    }

    public boolean handleEvent(Event evt)
    {
        String selectionString;
        Integer selection;
// Since we are handling events in the applet itself,
// we need to check to make sure the event is for the scrollingList.

        if (evt.target == scrollingList)
        {
// Check to see if this is a selection event

            if (evt.id == Event.LIST_SELECT)
            {
// selection is the index of the selected item
                selection = (Integer) evt.arg;
// use getItem to get the actual item.
                selectionString = "You selected entry "+
                    scrollingList.getItem(
                        selection.intValue());
// Update the label
                listStatus.setText(selectionString);
            }
            else if (evt.id == Event.LIST_DESELECT)
            {
// If this is a deselection, get the deselected item
// selection is the index of the selected item
                selection = (Integer) evt.arg;
// use getItem to get the actual item.
                selectionString = "You deselected entry "+
                    scrollingList.getItem(
                        selection.intValue());
// Update the label
                listStatus.setText(selectionString);
            }
        }
        return true;
    }
}
```

Figure 21.8 shows the output from ListApplet.

**Fig. 21.8**
The ListApplet
program lets you
select and deselect
list items.

# Text Fields and Text Areas

The AWT provides two different classes for entering text data—TextField
and TextArea. The TextField class handles only a single line of text, while
the TextArea handles multiple lines. Both of these classes share many
similar methods, since they both are derived from a common class called
TextComponent.

## Creating Text Fields

The easiest way to create a text field is

```
TextField myTextField = new TextField();
```

This will create an empty text field with an unspecified number of columns.
If you want to control how many columns are in the text field, you can do so
with:

```
TextField myTextField = new TextField(40);      // Create 40-column
                                                 ➥text field
```

Sometimes you may want to initialize the text field with some text when you
create it:

```
TextField myTextField = new TextField("This is some initial text");
```

Rounding out these combinations is a method for creating a text field initialized with text, having a fixed number of columns:

```
TextField myTextField = new TextField("This is some initial text", 40);
```

## Creating Text Areas

It should come as no surprise to you that the methods to create text areas are
similar to those for text fields. In fact, they are identical, except that when
giving a fixed size for a text area you must give both columns and rows.
You can create an empty text area having an unspecified number of rows
and columns with

```
TextArea myTextArea = new TextArea();
```

If you want to initialize an area with some text:

```
TextArea myTextArea = new TextArea("Here is some initial text");
```

You can give a text area a fixed number of rows and columns with

```
TextArea myTextArea = new TextArea(5, 40 );     // 5 rows, 40 columns
```

Finally, you can create a text area having some initial text and a fixed size with

```
TextArea myTextArea = new TextArea(
        "Here is some initial text", 5, 40); // 5 rows, 40 cols
```

## Common Text Component Features

The TextComponent abstract class implements a number of useful methods that may be used on either TextArea or TextField classes.

You will probably want to put text into the component at some point. You can do that with setText:

```
myTextField.setText("This is the text now in the field");
```

You will certainly want to find out what text is in the component. You can use getText to do that:

```
String textData = myTextArea.getText();
```

You can find out what text has been selected (highlighted with the mouse) by using getSelectedText:

```
String selectedStuff = myTextArea.getSelectedText();
```

You can also find out where the selection starts and where it ends. The getSelectionStart and getSelectionEnd methods return integers that indicate the position within the entire text where the selection starts and ends. For instance, if the selection started at the very beginning of the text, getSelectionStart would return 0:

```
int selectionStart, selectionEnd;
selectionStart = myTextField.getSelectionStart();
selectionEnd = myTextField.getSelectionEnd();
```

You can also cause text to be selected with the select method:

```
myTextField.select(0, 4);
        // Selects the characters from position 0 through 4
```

If you want to select the entire text, you can use selectAll as a shortcut:

```
myTextArea.selectAll();     // Selects all the text in the area
```

You can also use setEditable to control whether the text in the component can be edited (if not, it is read-only):

```
myTextField.setEditable(false);
        // Don't let anyone change this field
```

The isEditable method will return true if the component is editable, or false if it is not.

## Text Field Features

Text fields have some features that text areas do not have. The TextField class allows you to set an echo character that is printed instead of the character that was typed. This is useful when making fields for entering passwords, where you might make '*' the echo character. Setting up an echo character is as easy as calling setEchoCharacter:

```
myTextField.setEchoCharacter('*'); // Print *s in place of what was
                                    ➥typed
```

You can find out the echo character for a field with getEchoChar:

```
char echoChar = myTextField.getEchoChar();
```

The echoCharIsSet method will return true if there is an echo character set for the field, or false if not.

Finally, you can find out how many columns are in the text field (how many visible columns, not how much text is there) by using the getColumns method:

```
int numColumns = myTextField.getColumns();
```

## Text Area Features

Text areas also have special features all their own. Text areas are usually used for editing text, so they contain some methods for inserting, appending, and replacing text. You can add text to the end of the text area with appendText:

```
myTextArea.appendText(
    "This will be added to the end of the text in the area");
```

You can also insert text at any point in the current text with insertText. For instance, if you add text at position 0, you will add it to the front of the area:

```
myTextArea.insertText(
    "This will be added to the front of the text in the area", 0);
```

You can also use replaceText to replace portions of the text. Here is an example that uses the getSelectionStart and getSelectionEnd functions from TextComponent to replace selected text in a TextArea with "[CENSORED]":

```
myTextArea.replaceText("[CENSORED]", myTextArea.getSelectionStart(),
    myTextArea.getSelectionEnd());
```

Finally, you can find out the number of columns and the number of rows in a text area with getColumns and getRows.

## Using Text Fields and Text Areas

Like the List class, the TextArea class does not use the action method. However, in this case, you probably do not need to use the handleEvent method, either. The events you would get for the TextArea would be keyboard and mouse events, and you want the TextArea class to handle those itself. What you should do instead is create a button for the user to press when he or she has finished editing the text. Then you can use getText to retrieve the edited text.

The TextField class does use the action method, but only in the case of the user pressing return. You may find this useful, but again, you could create a button for the user to signal that he or she has finished entering the text (especially if there are a number of text fields he or she must fill out).

Listing 21.3 creates two text fields, a text area with an echo character defined and a text area that displays the value of the text entered in one of the text fields:

---

**Listing 21.3    Source Code for TextApplet.java**

```java
import java.awt.*;
import java.applet.*;

// TextApplet
// This applet creates some text fields and a text area
// to demonstrate the features of each.
//

public class TextApplet extends Applet
{
    protected TextField inputField;
    protected TextField passwordField;

    protected TextArea textArea;

    public void init()
    {
            inputField = new TextField();   // unspecified size
            add(inputField);

            passwordField = new TextField(10); // 10 columns
            passwordField.setEchoCharacter('*'); // print '*' for input
            add(passwordField);

            textArea = new TextArea(5, 40); // 5 rows, 40 cols
            textArea.appendText(
                    "This is some initial text for the text area.");
            textArea.select(5, 12); // select "is some"
```

*(continues)*

---

**Listing 21.3  Continued**

```
                    add(textArea);
        }

// The action method looks specifically for something entered in the
// password field and displays it in the textArea

        public boolean action(Event evt, Object whichAction)
        {
// Check to make sure this is an event for the passwordField
// if not, signal that the event hasn't been handled
                if (evt.target != passwordField)
                {
                        return false;  // Event not handled
                }

// Now, change the text in the textArea to "Your password is: "
// followed by the password entered in the passwordField

                textArea.setText("Your password is: "+
                        passwordField.getText());
                return true;     // Event has been handled
        }
}
```

---

Figure 21.9 shows the text fields and text area set up by the TextApplet example. Notice how small the first text field is because its size was left unspecified.

**Fig. 21.9**
Text fields and
text areas allow
the entry of text.

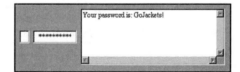

# Scrollbars

The Scrollbar class provides a basic interface for scrolling that can be used in a variety of situations. The controls of the scrollbar manipulate a position value that indicates the scrollbar's current position. You can set the minimum and maximum values for the scrollbar's position as well as its current value. The scrollbar's controls update the position in three ways—"line," "page," and "absolute." The arrow buttons at either end of the scrollbar update the scrollbar position with a "line" update. You can tell the scrollbar how much to add to the position (or subtract from it) for a line update. The default is 1. A "page" update is performed whenever the mouse is clicked on the gap between the slider button and the scrolling arrows. You may also tell the scrollbar how much to add to the position for a page update. The "absolute" update is performed whenever the slider button is dragged in one direction or the other. You have no control over how the position value changes for an absolute update, except that you are able to control the minimum and maximum values.

An important aspect of the `Scrollbar` class is that it is only responsible for updating its own position. It is unable to cause any other component to scroll. If you want the scrollbar to scroll a canvas up and down, you have to add code to detect when the scrollbar changes and update the canvas as needed.

## Creating Scrollbars

You can create a simple vertical scrollbar with

```
Scrollbar myScrollbar = new Scrollbar();
```

You can also specify the orientation of the scrollbar as either `Scrollbar.HORIZONTAL` or `Scrollbar.VERTICAL`:

```
Scrollbar myScrollbar = new Scrollbar(Scrollbar.HORIZONTAL);
```

You can create a scrollbar with a predefined orientation, position, page increment, minimum value, and maximum value. The following code creates a vertical scrollbar with a minimum value of 0, a maximum value of 100, a page size of 10, and a starting position of 50:

```
Scrollbar myScrollbar = new Scrollbar(Scrollbar.VERTICAL, 50, 10, 0, 100);
```

## Scrollbar Features

You can set the scrollbar's line increment with `setLineIncrement`:

```
myScrollbar.setLineIncrement(2);
        // Arrow button increment/decrement by 2 each time
```

You can query the current line increment with `getLineIncrement`:

```
int lineIncrement = myScrollbar.getLineIncrement();
```

You can set the page increment with `setPageIncrement`:

```
myScrollbar.setPageIncrement(20);
        // Page update adds/subtracts 20 each time
```

You can also query the page increment with `getPageIncrement`.

```
int pageIncrement = myScrollbar.getPageIncrement();
```

You can find out the scrollbar's minimum and maximum position values with getMinimum and getMaximum:

```
int minimum = myScrollbar.getMinimum();
int maximum = myScrollbar.getMaximum();
```

The setValue method sets the scrollbar's current position:

```
myScrollbar.setValue(25);      // Make the current position 25
```

You can query the current position with getValue:

```
int currentPosition = myScrollbar.getValue();
```

The getOrientation method will return Scrollbar.VERTICAL if the scrollbar is vertical or Scrollbar.HORIZONTAL if it is horizontal:

```
if (myScrollbar.getOrientation() == Scrollbar.HORIZONTAL)
{
        // Code to handle a horizontal scrollbar
}
else
{
    // Code to handle a vertical scrollbar
}
```

You can also set the position, page increment, minimum value, and maximum value with setValues. The following code sets the position to 75, the page increment to 25, the minimum value to 0, and the maximum to 500:

```
myScrollbar.setValues(75, 25, 0, 500);
```

## Using Scrollbars

Like the List class, the Scrollbar class does not make use of the action method. You must use the handleEvent method to determine when a scrollbar has moved. The possible values of evt.id for events generated by the Scrollbar class are:

- Event.SCROLL_ABSOLUTE when the slider button is dragged.
- Event.SCROLL_LINE_DOWN when the top or left arrow button is pressed.
- Event.SCROLL_LINE_UP when the bottom or right arrow button is pressed.
- Event.SCROLL_PAGE_DOWN when the user clicks in the area between the slider and the bottom or left arrow.
- Event.SCROLL_PAGE_UP when the user clicks in the area between the slider and the top or right arrow.

You may not care which of these events is received. In many cases, you may only need to know that the scrollbar position is changed and you would call the getValue method to find out the new position.

The `IntScrollbar` class introduced later in this chapter in the section titled "Using Observables" demonstrates how to create your own custom scrollbar.

# Canvases

The `Canvas` class is a component with no special functionality. It is mainly used for creating custom graphic components. You create an instance of a `Canvas` with:

```
Canvas myCanvas = new Canvas();
```

However, you will almost always want to create your own special subclass of `Canvas` that does whatever special function you need. You should override the `Canvas` paint method to make your `Canvas` do something interesting. Listing 21.4 creates a `CircleCanvas` class that draws a filled circle in a specific color:

**Listing 21.4   Source Code for CircleCanvas.java**

```
import java.awt.*;

// Example 21.4 CircleCanvas class
//
// This class creates a canvas that draws a circle on itself.
// The circle color is given at creation time, and the size of
// the circle is determined by the size of the canvas.
//

public class CircleCanvas extends Canvas
{
    Color circleColor;

// When you create a CircleCanvas, you tell it what color to use.

    public CircleCanvas(Color drawColor)
    {
        circleColor = drawColor;
    }

    public void paint(Graphics g)
    {
        int circleDiameter, circleX, circleY;

        Dimension currentSize = size();

// Use the smaller of the height and width of the canvas.
// This guarantees that the circle will be drawn completely.


        if (currentSize.width < currentSize.height)
        {
```

(continues)

**Listing 21.4 Continued**

```
            circleDiameter = currentSize.width;
    }
    else
    {
            circleDiameter = currentSize.height;
    }

    g.setColor(circleColor);
// The math here on the circleX and circleY may seem strange.  The
➥x and y
// coordinates for fillOval are the upper-left coordinates of the
➥rectangle
// that surrounds the circle.  If the canvas is wider than the
➥circle, for
// instance, we want to find out how much wider (i.e. width -
➥diameter)
// and then, since we want equal amounts of blank area on both sides,
// we divide the amount of blank area by 2.  In the case where the
➥diameter
// equals the width, the amount of blank area is 0.

    circleX = (currentSize.width - circleDiameter) / 2;
    circleY = (currentSize.height - circleDiameter) / 2;

    g.fillOval(circleX, circleY, circleDiameter,
    ➥circleDiameter);
    }
}
```

The CircleCanvas is only a component, not a runnable applet. Later in this chapter in the section titled "Grid Bag Layouts" you'll use this new class in an example of using the GridBagLayout layout manager.

# Containers

In addition to all of these wonderful components, the AWT provides several useful containers:

- Panel is a "pure" container. It is not a window in itself. Its sole purpose it to help you organize your components in a window.

- Frame is a fully functioning window with its own title and icon. Frames may have pull-down menus and may use a number of different cursor shapes.

- Dialog is a pop-up window, not quite as fully functioning as the frame. Dialogs are used for things like "Are you sure you want to quit?" pop-ups.

# Panels

Since panels are only used for organizing components, there are very few things you can actually do to a panel. You create a new panel with

```
Panel myPanel = new Panel();
```

You can then add the panel to another container. For instance, you might want to add it to your applet:

```
add(myPanel);
```

You can also nest panels—one panel containing one or more other panels:

```
Panel mainPanel, subPanel1, subPanel2;
subPanel1 = new Panel();   // create the first sub-panel
subPanel2 = new Panel();   // create the second sub-panel
mainPanel = new Panel();   // create the main panel

mainPanel.add(subPanel1);  // Make subPanel1 a child (sub-panel) of mainPanel
mainPanel.add(subPanel2);  // Make subPanel2 a child of mainPanel
```

You can nest panels as many levels deep as you like. For instance, in the above example, you could have made subPanel2 a child of subPanel1 (obviously with different results).

Listing 21.5 shows how to create panels and nest subpanels within them:

### Listing 21.5   Source Code for PanelApplet.java

```
import java.awt.*;
import java.applet.*;

// PanelApplet
//
// The PanelApplet applet creates a number of panels and
// adds buttons to them to demonstrate the use of panels
// for grouping components.

public class PanelApplet extends Applet
{
    public void init()
    {
// Create the main panels
            Panel mainPanel1 = new Panel();
            Panel mainPanel2 = new Panel();

// Create the sub-panels
            Panel subPanel1 = new Panel();
            Panel subPanel2 = new Panel();

// Add a button directly to the applet
            add(new Button("Applet Button"));
```

(continues)

**Listing 21.5 Continued**

```
// Add the main panels to the applet
            add(mainPanel1);
            add(mainPanel2);

// Give mainPanel1 a button and a sub-panel
            mainPanel1.add(new Button("Main Panel 1 Button"));
            mainPanel1.add(subPanel1);

// Give mainPanel2 a button and a sub-panel
            mainPanel2.add(new Button("Main Panel 2 Button"));
            mainPanel2.add(subPanel2);

// Give each sub-panel a button
            subPanel1.add(new Button("Sub-panel 1 Button"));

            subPanel2.add(new Button("Sub-panel 2 Button"));
    }
}
```

Figure 21.10 shows the output from PanelApplet.

**Fig. 21.10**
Panels, like other
containers, help
group components
together.

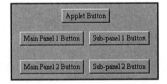

# Frames

Frames are a powerful feature of the AWT. They enable you to create separate
windows for your application. For instance, you might want your application
to run outside the main window of a Web browser. You can also use frames
to build stand-alone graphical applications.

## Creating Frames

You can create a frame that is initially invisible and has no title with:

```
Frame myFrame = new Frame();
```

You can give the frame a title when you create it, but it will still be invisible:

```
Frame myFrame = new Frame("Hi!  This is my frame!");
```

## Frame Features

Once you have created a frame, you will probably want to see it. Before you
can see the frame, you must give it a size. Use the resize method to set the
size:

```
myFrame.resize(300, 100);  // Make the frame 300 pixels wide, 100 high
```

You can use the show method to make it visible:

```
myFrame.show();       // Show yourself, Frame!
```

You can send a frame back into hiding with the hide method. Even though the frame is invisible, it still exists:

```
myFrame.hide();
```

As long as a frame exists, invisible or not, it is consuming some amount of resources in the windowing system it is running on. If you have finished with a frame, you should get rid of it with the dispose method:

```
myFrame.dispose();      // Gets rid of the frame and releases its resources
```

You can change the title displayed at the top of the frame with setTitle:

```
myFrame.setTitle("With Frames like this, who needs enemies?");
```

The getTitle method will return the frame's title:

```
String currentTitle = myFrame.getTitle();
```

The Frame class has a number of different cursors. You can change the frame's cursor with setCursor:

```
myFrame.setCursor(Frame.HAND_CURSOR);         // Change cursor to a hand
```

The available cursors are: Frame.DEFAULT_CURSOR, Frame.CROSSHAIR_CURSOR, Frame.TEXT_CURSOR, Frame.WAIT_CURSOR, Frame.HAND_CURSOR, Frame.MOVE_CURSOR, Frame.N_RESIZE_CURSOR, Frame.NE_RESIZE_CURSOR, Frame.E_RESIZE_CURSOR, Frame.SE_RESIZE_CURSOR, Frame.S_RESIZE_CURSOR, Frame.SW_RESIZE_CURSOR, Frame.W_RESIZE_CURSOR, and Frame.NW_RESIZE_CURSOR.

The getCursorType method will return one of these values indicating the current cursor type.

If you do not want to allow your frame to be resized, you can call setResizable to turn resizing on or off:

```
myFrame.setResizable(false);     // Turn resizing off
```

You can change a frame's icon with setIconImage:

```
myFrame.setIconImage(someIconImage);
            // someIconImage must be an instance of Image
```

## Using Frames to Make Your Applet Run *standalone*

You can create applets that can run either as an applet or as a standalone application. All you need to do is write a main method in the applet that creates a Frame then creates an instance of the applet that belongs to the frame. Listing 21.6 shows an applet that can run either as an applet or as a standalone application:

**Listing 21.6  Source Code for StandaloneApplet.java**

```
import java.awt.*;
import java.applet.*;

// StandaloneApplet is an applet that runs either as
// an applet or a standalone application.  To run
// standalone, it provides a main method that creates
// a frame, then creates an instance of the applet and
// adds it to the frame.

public class StandaloneApplet extends Applet
{
    public void init()
    {
            add(new Button("Standalone Applet Button"));
    }

    public static void main(String args[])
    {
// Create the frame this applet will run in
            Frame appletFrame = new Frame("Some applet");

// Create an instance of the applet
            Applet myApplet = new StandaloneApplet();

// Initialize and start the applet
            myApplet.init();
            myApplet.start();

// The frame needs a layout manager
            appletFrame.setLayout(new FlowLayout());

// Add the applet to the frame
            appletFrame.add(myApplet);

// Have to give the frame a size before it is visible
            appletFrame.resize(300, 100);

// Make the frame appear on the screen
            appletFrame.show();
    }
}
```

## Adding Menus to Frames

You can attach a `MenuBar` class to a frame to provide drop-down menu capabilities. You can create a menu bar with:

```
MenuBar myMenuBar = new MenuBar();
```

Once you have created a menubar, you can add it to a frame using the `setMenuBar` method:

```
myFrame.setMenuBar(myMenuBar);
```

Once you have a menu bar, you can add menus to it. The following code fragment creates a menu called "File" and adds it to the menu bar:

```
Menu fileMenu = new Menu("File");
myMenuBar.add(fileMenu);
```

Some windowing systems allow you to create menus that stay up after you release the mouse button. These are referred to as "tear-off" menus. You can specify that a menu is a "tear-off" menu when you create it:

```
Menu tearOffMenu = new Menu("Tear Me Off", true);
        // true indicates it can be torn off
```

In addition to adding submenus, you will want to add menu items to your menus. Menu items are the parts of a menu the user actually selects. Menus, on the other hand, are used to contain menu items as well as submenus. For instance, the File menu on many systems contains menu items such as New, Open, Save, and Save As. If you created a menu structure with no menu items, the menu structure would be useless. There would be nothing to select. You may add menu items to a menu in two ways. You can simply add an item name with

```
fileMenu.add("Open");     // Add an "Open" option to the file menu
```

You can also add an instance of a `MenuItem` class to a menu:

```
MenuItem saveMenuItem = new MenuItem("Save");
        // Create a "Save" menu item
fileMenu.add(saveMenuItem);        // Add the "Save" option to the file menu
```

You can enable and disable menu items by using `enable` and `disable`. When you disable a menu item, it still appears on the menu, but it usually appears in gray (depending on the windowing system). You cannot select menu items that are disabled. The format for `enable` and `disable` is:

```
saveMenuItem.disable();    // Disables the save option from the file menu
saveMenuItem.enable();     // Enables the save option again
```

In addition to menu items, you can add submenus and menu separators to a menu. A separator is a line that appears on the menu to separate sections of the menu. To add a separator, just call the addSeparator method:

```
fileMenu.addSeparator();
```

To create a submenu, just create a new instance of a menu and add it to the current menu:

```
Menu printSubmenu = new Menu("Print");
fileMenu.add(printSubmenu);
printSubmenu.add("Print Preview");
        // Add print preview as option on Print menu
printSubmenu.add("Print Document");
        // Add print document as option on Print menu
```

You can also create special checkbox menu items. These items function like the checkbox buttons. The first time you select one, it becomes checked or "on." The next time you select it, it becomes unchecked or "off." To create a checkbox menu item:

```
CheckboxMenuItem autoSaveOption = new CheckboxMenuItem("Auto-save");
fileMenu.add(autoSaveOption);
```

You can check to see whether a checkbox menu item is checked or not with getState:

```
if (autoSaveOption.getState())
{
    // autoSaveOption is checked, or "on"
}
else
{
    // autoSaveOption is off
}
```

You can set the current state of a checkbox menu item with setState:

```
autoSaveOption.setState(true);      // Explicitly turn auto-save option on
```

Normally, menus are added to a menu bar in a left to right fashion. Many windowing systems, however, create a special "help" menu that is on the far right of a menu bar. You can add such a menu to your menu bar with the setHelpMenu method:

```
Menu helpMenu = new Menu();
myMenuBar.setHelpMenu(helpMenu);
```

# Using Menus

Whenever a menu item is selected it generates an action. The `whichAction` parameter to the `action` method will be the name of the item selected:

```
public boolean action(Event evt, Object whichAction)
{

// First, make sure this event is a menu selection

    if (evt.target instanceof MenuItem)
    {
        if ((String)whichAction == "Save")
        {
            // Handle save option
        }
    }
    return true;
}
```

Listing 21.7 shows an application that sets up a simple File menu with New, Open, and Save menu items, a checkbox called Auto-Save, and a Print submenu with two menu items on it:

**Listing 21.7  Source Code for MenuApplication.java**

```
import java.awt.*;
import java.applet.*;

public class MenuApplication extends Object
{
    public static void main(String[] args)
    {
// Create the frame and the menubar
        Frame myFrame = new Frame("Menu Example");
        MenuBar myMenuBar = new MenuBar();

// Add the menubar to the frame
        myFrame.setMenuBar(myMenuBar);

// Create the File menu and add it to the menubar
        Menu fileMenu = new Menu("File");
        myMenuBar.add(fileMenu);

// Add the New and Open menuitems
        fileMenu.add(new MenuItem("New"));
        fileMenu.add(new MenuItem("Open"));

// Create a disabled Save menuitem
        MenuItem saveMenuItem = new MenuItem("Save");
        fileMenu.add(saveMenuItem);
        saveMenuItem.disable();
```

(continues)

---

**Listing 21.7   Continued**

```
// Add an Auto-Save checkbox, followed by a separator
        fileMenu.add(new CheckboxMenuItem("Auto-Save"));
        fileMenu.addSeparator();

// Create the Print submenu
        Menu printSubmenu = new Menu("Print");
        fileMenu.add(printSubmenu);
        printSubmenu.add("Print Preview");
        printSubmenu.add("Print Document");

// Must resize the frame before it can be shown
        myFrame.resize(300, 200);

// Make the frame appear on the screen
        myFrame.show();
    }
}
```

---

Figure 21.11 shows the output from the MenuApplication program, with the "Print Document" option in the process of being selected.

**Fig. 21.11**

The AWT provides a number of popular menu features including checked menu items, disabled menu items, and separators.

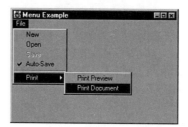

## Dialogs

Dialogs are pop-up windows that are not quite as flexible as frames. You can create a dialog as either "modal" or "non-modal." The term *modal* means the dialog box blocks input to other windows while it is being shown. This is useful for dialogs where you want to stop everything and get a crucial question answered such as "Are you sure you want to quit?" An example of a "non-modal" dialog box might be a control panel that changes settings in an application while the application continues to run.

## Creating Dialogs

You must first have a frame in order to create a dialog. A dialog cannot belong to an applet. However, an applet may create a frame to which the dialog can then belong. You must specify whether a dialog is modal or non-modal at creation time and cannot change its "modality" once it has been created. The following example creates a dialog whose parent is myFrame and is modal:

```
Dialog myDialog = new Dialog(myFrame, true);      // true means model dialog
```

You can also create a dialog with a title:

```
Dialog myDialog = new Dialog(myFrame, "A Non-Modal Dialog", false);
        // false = non-modal
```

> **Note**
>
> Since a dialog cannot belong to an applet, your use of dialogs can be somewhat limited. One solution is to create a dummy frame as the dialog's parent. Unfortunately, you cannot create modal dialogs this way, since only the frame and its children would have their input blocked—the applet would continue on its merry way. A better solution is to use the technique discussed in the "Frames" section of this chapter in which you create a stand-alone application using frames, then have a "bootstrap" applet create a frame and run the real applet in it.

Once you have created a dialog, you can make it visible using the show method:

```
myDialog.show();
```

## Dialog Features

The Dialog class has several methods in common with the Frame class:

```
void setResizable(boolean);
boolean isResizable();
void setTitle(String);
String getTitle();
```

In addition, the isModal method will return true if the dialog is modal.

## A Reusable OK Dialog Box

Listing 21.8 shows the OKDialog class which provides an OK dialog box that displays a message and waits for you to click OK.

**Listing 21.8  Source Code for OKDialog.java**

```java
import java.awt.*;

// Example 21.6 - OK Dialog class
//
// OKDialog - Custom dialog that presents a message and waits for
// you to click on the OK button.
//
// Example use:
//    Dialog ok = new OKDialog(parentFrame, "Click OK to continue");
//    ok.show();      // Other input will be blocked until OK is pressed
// As a shortcut, you can use the static createOKDialog that will
// create its own frame and activate itself:
//    OKDialog.createOKDialog("Click OK to continue");
//

public class OKDialog extends Dialog
{
    protected Button okButton;
    protected static Frame createdFrame;

    public OKDialog(Frame parent, String message)
    {
        super(parent, true);    // Must call the parent's
                                   ➥constructor

// This Dialog box uses the GridBagLayout to provide a pretty good
   ➥layout.

        GridBagLayout gridbag = new GridBagLayout();
        GridBagConstraints constraints = new GridBagConstraints();

// Create the OK button and the message to display
        okButton = new Button("OK");
        Label messageLabel = new Label(message);

        setLayout(gridbag);

// The message should not fill, it should be centered within this
   ➥area, with
// some extra padding.  The gridwidth of REMAINDER means this is the
   ➥only
// thing on its row, and the gridheight of RELATIVE means there
   ➥should only
// be one thing below it.
        constraints.fill = GridBagConstraints.NONE;
        constraints.anchor = GridBagConstraints.CENTER;
        constraints.ipadx = 20;
        constraints.ipady = 20;
        constraints.weightx = 1.0;
        constraints.weighty = 1.0;
        constraints.gridwidth = GridBagConstraints.REMAINDER;
        constraints.gridheight = GridBagConstraints.RELATIVE;
```

```
        gridbag.setConstraints(messageLabel, constraints);
        add(messageLabel);

// The button has no padding, no weight, taked up minimal width, and
// Is the last thing in its column.

        constraints.ipadx = 0;
        constraints.ipady = 0;
        constraints.weightx = 0.0;
        constraints.weighty = 0.0;
        constraints.gridwidth = 1;
        constraints.gridheight = GridBagConstraints.REMAINDER;

        gridbag.setConstraints(okButton, constraints);
        add(okButton);

// Pack is a special window method that makes the window take up the minimum
// space necessary to contain its components.

        pack();

    }

// The action method just waits for the OK button to be clicked and
// when it is it hides the dialog, causing the show() method to return
// back to whoever activated this dialog.

    public boolean action(Event evt, Object whichAction)
    {
        if (evt.target == okButton)
        {
            hide();
            if (createdFrame != null)
            {
                createdFrame.hide();
            }
        }
        return true;
    }

// Shortcut to create a frame automatically, the frame is a static variable
// so all dialogs in an applet or application can use the same frame.

    public static void createOKDialog(String dialogString)
    {
// If the frame hasn't been created yet, create it
        if (createdFrame == null)
        {
            createdFrame = new Frame("Dialog");
        }
// Create the dialog now
```

(continues)

**Listing 21.8   Continued**

```
            OKDialog okDialog = new OKDialog(createdFrame, dialogString);

// Shrink the frame to just fit the dialog
            createdFrame.resize(okDialog.size().width,
                    okDialog.size().height);

// Show the dialog
            okDialog.show();

    }
}
```

The DialogApplet in listing 21.9 pops up an OK dialog whenever a button is pressed:

**Listing 21.9   Source Code for DialogApplet.java**

```
import java.awt.*;
import java.applet.*;

// DialogApplet
//
// Dialog applet creates a button, and when you press
// the button it brings up an OK dialog.  The input
// to the original button should be blocked until
// the OK button in the dialog is pressed.

public class DialogApplet extends Applet
{
    protected Button launchButton;

    public void init()
    {
            launchButton = new Button("Give me an OK");
            add(launchButton);
    }

    public boolean action(Event event, Object whichAction)
    {
// Make sure this action is for the launchButton
            if (event.target != launchButton)
            {
                    return false;
            }

// Create and display the OK dialog
            OKDialog.createOKDialog(
                    "Press OK when you are ready");

// Signal that we've handled the event
            return true;
    }
}
```

Figure 21.12 shows the DialogApplet with the OK dialog popped up.

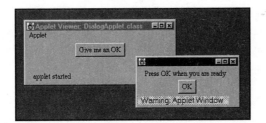

**Fig. 21.12**
The OKDialog class creates a popup dialog box with an OK button.

# Layout Managers

If you haven't noticed already, when you add components to a container you don't have to tell the container where to put a component. By using layout managers, you tell the AWT where you want your components to go relative to the other components. The layout manager figures out exactly where to put them. This helps you make platform-independent software. When you position things by absolute coordinates, it can cause a mess when someone running Windows 95 in 640×480 resolution tries to run an applet designed to fit on a 1280×1024 X-terminal.

The AWT provides five different types of layout managers:

- FlowLayout arranges components from left to right until no more components will fit on a row, then it moves to the next row and continues going left to right.

- GridLayout treats a container as a grid of identically sized spaces. It places components in the spaces in the grid starting from the top left and continuing in left to right fashion just like the FlowLayout. The difference between GridLayout and FlowLayout is that GridLayout gives each component an equal-sized area to work in.

- BorderLayout treats the container like a compass. When you add a component to the container, you ask the BorderLayout to place it in one of five areas: "North," "South," "East," "West," or "Center." It figures out the exact positioning based on the relative sizes of the components.

- CardLayout treats the components added to the container as a stack of cards. It places each component on a separate card, and only one card is visible at a time.

■ GridBagLayout is the most flexible of the Layout Managers. It is also the most confusing. GridBagLayout treats a container as a grid of cells, but unlike GridLayout, a component may occupy more than one cell. When you add a component to a container managed by GridBagLayout, you give it a GridBagConstraint, which has placement and sizing instructions for that component.

## Flow Layouts

A FlowLayout class treats a container as a set of rows. The height of the rows is determined by the height of the items placed in the row. The FlowLayout starts adding new components from left to right. If it cannot fit the next component onto the current row, it drops down to the next row and starts again from the left. It also tries to align the rows using either left-justification, right-justification, or centering. The default alignment for a FlowLayout is centered, which means that when it creates a row of components, it will try to keep it centered with respect to the left and right edges.

### Tip

The FlowLayout layout manager is the default layout manager for all applets.

To create a FlowLayout with centered alignment and attach it to your applet:

```
myFlowLayout = new FlowLayout();
setLayout(myFlowLayout);
```

To create a FlowLayout with a left-justified alignment:

```
myFlowLayout = new FlowLayout(FlowLayout.LEFT);
```

The different types of FlowLayout alignment are FlowLayout.LEFT, FlowLayout.RIGHT, and FlowLayout.CENTER.

You may also give the FlowLayout horizontal and vertical gap values. These values specify the minimum amount of horizontal and vertical space to leave between components. These gaps are given in units of screen pixels. To create a right-justified FlowLayout with a horizontal gap of 10 pixels and a vertical gap of 5 pixels:

```
myFlowLayout = new FlowLayout(FlowLayout.RIGHT, 10, 5);
```

Figure 21.13 shows five buttons arranged in a flow layout.

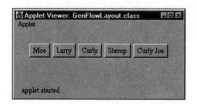

**Fig. 21.13**
The flow layout
places components
from left to right.

## Grid Layouts

A GridLayout class divides a container into a grid of equally sized cells. When
you add components to the container, the GridLayout places them from left
to right starting in the top left cells. When you create a GridLayout class, you
must tell it how many rows you want, or how many columns. If you give it a
number of rows, it will compute the number of columns needed. If instead
you give it a number of columns, it will compute the number of rows needed.
If you add 6 components to a GridLayout with 2 rows, it will create 3 columns. The format of the GridLayout constructor is:

```
GridLayout(int numberOfRows, int numberOfColumns)
```

If you create a GridLayout with a fixed number of rows, you should use 0 for
the number of columns. If you have a fixed number of columns, use 0 for the
number of rows.

> **Note**
>
> If you pass GridLayout non-zero values for both the number of rows and the number
> of columns, it will only use the number of rows. The number of columns will be
> computed based on the number of components and the number of rows.
> GridLayout(3, 4) is exactly the same as GridLayout(3, 0).

You may also specify a horizontal and vertical gap. The following code creates a GridLayout with 4 columns, a horizontal gap of 8, and a vertical gap
of 10:

```
GridLayout myGridLayout = new GridLayout(0, 4, 8, 10);
```

Figure 21.14 shows five buttons arranged in a grid layout.

**Fig. 22.14**
The grid layout allocates equally sized areas for each component.

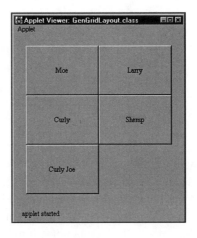

## Border Layouts

A BorderLayout class divides a container up into five areas named "North," "South," "East," "West," and "Center." When you add components to the container, you must use a special form of the add method that includes one of these five area names. These five areas are arranged like the points on a compass. A component added to the "North" area is placed at the top of the container, while a component added to the "West" area is placed on the left side of the container. The BorderLayout class does not allow more than one component in an area. You may optionally specify a horizontal gap and a vertical gap. To create a BorderLayout without specifying a gap:

```
BorderLayout myBorderLayout = new BorderLayout();
```

To create a BorderLayout with a horizontal gap of 10 and a vertical gap of 20:

```
BorderLayout myBorderLayout = new BorderLayout(10, 20);
```

To add myButton to the "West" area of the BorderLayout:

```
myBorderLayout.add("West", myButton);
```

> **Caution**
>
> The BorderLayout class is very picky about how and where you add components. If you try to add a component using the regular add method (without the area name), you will not see your component. If you try to add two components to the same area, you will only see the last component added.

Listing 21.10 shows a BorderLayoutApplet that creates a BorderLayout, attaches it to the current applet, and adds some buttons to the applet:

**Listing 21.10    Source Code for BorderLayoutApplet.java**

```java
import java.applet.*;
import java.awt.*;

// Example 21.8 - BorderLayoutApplet
//
// This applet creates a BorderLayout and attaches it
// to the applet.  Then it creates buttons and places
// in all possible areas of the layout.

public class BorderLayoutApplet extends Applet
{
    public void init()
    {

// First create the layout and attach it to the applet

        setLayout(new BorderLayout());

// Now create some buttons and lay them out

        add("North", new Button("Larry"));
        add("South", new Button("Curly Joe"));
        add("East", new Button("Curly"));
        add("West", new Button("Shemp"));
        add("Center", new Button("Moe"));
    }
}
```

Figure 21.15 shows five buttons arranged in a border layout.

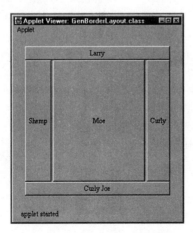

**Fig. 22.15**
The border layout places components at the north, south, east, and west compass points, as well as in the center.

## Grid Bag Layouts

The GridBagLayout class, like the GridLayout, divides a container into a grid of equally sized cells. Unlike the GridLayout, however, the GridBagLayout class decides how many rows and columns it will have, and it allows a component to occupy more than one cell if necessary. The total area that a component occupies is called its "display area." Before you add a component to a container, you must give the GridBagLayout a set of "suggestions" on where to put the component. These suggestions are in the form of a GridBagConstraints class. The GridBagConstraints class has a number of variables to control the placement of a component:

- gridx and gridy are the coordinates of the cell where the next component should be placed (if the component occupies more than one cell, these coordinates are for the upper-left cell of the component). The upper-left corner of the GridBagLayout is at 0, 0. The default value for both gridx and gridy is GridBagConstraints.RELATIVE, which for gridx means the cell just to the right of the last component that was added, while for gridy it means the cell just below the last component added.

- gridwidth and gridheight tell how many cells wide and how many cells tall a component should be. The default for both gridwidth and gridheight is 1. If you want this component to be the last one on a row, use GridBagConstraint.REMAINDER for the gridwidth (use this same value for gridheight if this component should be the last one in a column). Use GridBagConstraint.RELATIVE if the component should be the next to last component in a row or column.

- fill tells the GridBagLayout what to do when a component is smaller than its display area. The default value, GridBagConstraint.NONE, causes the component size to remain unchanged. GridBagConstraint.HORIZONTAL causes the component to be widened to take up its whole display area horizontally, while leaving its height unchanged. GridBagConstraint.VERTICAL causes the component to be stretched vertically while leaving the width unchanged. GridBagConstraint.BOTH causes the component to be stretched in both directions to completely fill its display area.

- ipadx and ipady tell the GridBagLayout how many pixels to add to the size of the component in the x and y direction. The pixels will be added on either side of the component, so an ipadx of 4 would cause the size of a component to be increased by 4 on the left and also 4 on the right.

Remember that the component size will grow by 2 times the amount of padding since the padding is added to both sides. The default for both ipadx and ipady is 0.

■ insets is an instance of an Insets class and it indicates how much space to leave between the borders of a component and edges of its display area. In other words, it creates a "no man's land" of blank space surrounding a component. The Insets class (discussed later in this chapter in the section titled "Insets") has separate values for the top, bottom, left, and right insets.

■ anchor is used when a component is smaller than its display area. It indicates where the component should be placed within the display area. The default value is GridBagConstraint.CENTER, which indicates that the component should be in the center of the display area. The other values are all compass points: GridbagConstraints.NORTH, GridBagConstraints.NORTHEAST, GridBagConstraints.EAST, GridBagConstraints.SOUTHEAST, GridBagConstraints.SOUTH, GridBagConstraints.SOUTHWEST, GridBagConstraints.WEST, and GridBagConstraints.NORTHWEST. As with the BorderLayout class, NORTH indicates the top of the screen, while EAST is to the right.

■ weightx and weighty are used to set relative sizes of components. For instance, a component with a weightx of 2.0 takes up twice the horizontal space of a component with a weightx of 1.0. Since these values are relative, there is no difference between all components in a row having a weight of 1.0 or a weight of 3.0. You should assign a weight to at least one component in each direction. Otherwise, the GridBagLayout will squeeze your components towards the center of the container.

When you want to add a component to a container using a GridBagLayout, you create the component, then create an instance of GridBagConstraints and set the constraints for the component. For instance:

```
GridBagLayout myGridBagLayout = new GridBagLayout();
setLayout(myGridBagLayout);
         // Set the applet's Layout Manager to myGridBagLayout

Button myButton = new Button("My Button");
GridBagConstraints constraints = new GridBagConstraints();
constraints.weightx = 1.0;
constraints.gridwidth = GridBagConstraints.RELATIVE;
constraints.fill = GridBagConstraints.BOTH;
```

Next, you set the component's constraints in the GridBagLayout with:

```
myGridLayout.setConstraints(myButton, constraints);
```

Now you may add the component to the container:

```
add(myButton);
```

The applet in listing 21.11 uses the GridBagLayout class to arrange a few instances of CircleCanvas (created earlier in this chapter):

---

**Listing 21.11   Source Code for CircleApplet.java**

```java
import java.applet.*;
import java.awt.*;

// Example 21.9 CircleApplet
//
// This circle demonstrates the CircleCanvas class we
// created.  It also shows you how to use the GridBagLayout
// to arrange the circles.

public class CircleApplet extends Applet
{
    public void init()
    {
        GridBagLayout gridbag = new GridBagLayout();
        GridBagConstraints constraints = new GridBagConstraints();
        CircleCanvas newCircle;

        setLayout(gridbag);

// We'll use the weighting to determine relative circle sizes. Make the
// first one just have a weight of 1. Also, set fill for both directions
// so it will make the circles as big as possible.

        constraints.weightx = 1.0;
        constraints.weighty = 1.0;
        constraints.fill = GridBagConstraints.BOTH;

// Create a red circle and add it

        newCircle = new CircleCanvas(Color.red);
        gridbag.setConstraints(newCircle, constraints);
        add(newCircle);

// Now, we want to make the next circle twice as big as the previous
// one, so give it twice the weight.

        constraints.weightx = 2.0;
        constraints.weighty = 2.0;

// Create a blue circle and add it

        newCircle = new CircleCanvas(Color.blue);
        gridbag.setConstraints(newCircle, constraints);
        add(newCircle);
```

```
// We'll make the third circle the same size as the first one, so set the
// weight back down to 1.

        constraints.weightx = 1.0;
        constraints.weighty = 1.0;

// Create a green circle and add it.

        newCircle = new CircleCanvas(Color.green);
        gridbag.setConstraints(newCircle, constraints);
        add(newCircle);

    }
}
```

Figure 21.16 shows the three circle canvases from the GridBagApplet.

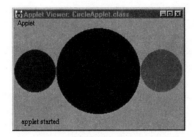

**Fig. 21.16**
The GridBagApplet
creates three circle
canvases.

## *Insets*

Insets are not layout managers, but instructions to the layout manager about
how much space to leave around the edges of the container. The layout manager determines the insets values for a container by calling the container's
insets method. The insets method returns an instance of an Insets class,
which contains the values for the top, bottom, left, and right insets. For example, if you want to leave a 20 pixel gap between the components in your
applet and the applet border, you should create an insets method in your
applet:

```
public Insets insets()
{
    return new Insets(20, 20, 20, 20);
        // Inset by 20 pixels all around
}
```

The constructor for the Insets class takes four inset values in the order top,
left, bottom, and right.

Figure 21.17 shows what the GridBagApplet would look like if it used the previous insets method. The gap between the circles is not from the Insets class, but from the fact that the circles are smaller. The gaps on the top, bottom, left, and right are created by the Insets class.

**Fig. 21.17**

Insets create a gap between components and the edges of their containers.

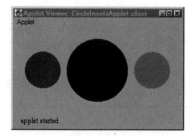

# Object-Oriented Thinking

Now that you have a good understanding of the various parts of the AWT, it's time to delve into a more esoteric area—object-oriented design.

You may have heard all the talk about how wonderful object-oriented languages are, and that's not all hype. However, just because a language is object-oriented does not mean that the programs written in it are. Take a look again at the first applet in this chapter:

```
public class Button1Applet extends Applet
{
    public void init()
    {
        add(new Button("Red"));

        add(new Button("Blue"));

    }

    public boolean action(Event evt, Object whatAction)
    {
        String buttonLabel = (String) whatAction;

        if (buttonLabel == "Red")
        {
            setBackground(Color.red);
        }
        else if (buttonLabel == "Blue")
        {
            setBackground(Color.blue);
        }
        repaint();      // Make the change visible immediately
        return true;
    }
}
```

This applet is not a good example of object-oriented design. The main problem with the applet is that it is very authoritarian. It puts these poor buttons out there and takes all the responsibility on itself to handle the actions when the buttons are pressed. What you should strive for in object-oriented design is just the opposite. You want to create objects that handle as much as possible on their own. You want to get to the point where you create a new application just by using a set of existing objects. Your application becomes nothing more than the "glue holding the objects together." While that isn't so easy to reach, you can try to minimize the amount of work you do every time you sit down to write a program.

Another important feature of object-oriented programs is that they are easy to modify. How easy is this applet to modify? If you want to add 10 more colors what do you do? You have to add 10 more buttons, of course, then you have to go into the action method and add more `else ifs` to check for the other colors. That seems like a lot of work.

Try looking at the original description of the applet through object-oriented eyes. As you will recall, the applet was described as "an applet with buttons that change the background color." The key phrase there is "buttons that change the background color." You want to give that responsibility to the buttons, not heap it onto the applet. What you really want is intelligent buttons. If you had a button that changed the applet background by itself, all the applet would have to do is create buttons—it wouldn't even have an `action` method!

What would it take to create such a button? You'll need be able to give the button a name and a color. It will also need to know what applet it belongs to in order to change the background.

> **Note**
>
> When writing new classes, always ask yourself, "What might I want to do with this in the future?"

Take a second to look at this new button. You were planning to have the button set the background color for an applet. Why restrict it to just an applet? All components have a `setBackground` method. Why not let it set the background on any component? For that matter, why just background? Why can't it set either the foreground or the background? Listing 21.12 shows a ColorButton class that changes the background color of a component:

## A Better Button

**Listing 21.12  Source Code for ColorButton.java**

```java
import java.awt.*;

// Example 21.10 - ColorButton class

public class ColorButton extends Button
{
// Set up some values to indicate whether we want to set
// the foreground or background.

    public static final int FOREGROUND = 1;
    public static final int BACKGROUND = 2;

// Need a placeholder for which component to set the color on
    protected Component whichComponent;

// Need to remember which color to set
    protected Color color;

// Need to remember whether to set foreground or background
    protected int whichColorToChange;

// The constructor for this button will take a label, a color value
// and a whichColor flag telling whether to set foreground or
// background, and the Component it is supposed to modify.

    public ColorButton(String label, Color colorToChoose,
        int whichColor, Component comp)
    {
        super(label);      // Do the regular button creation first

        color = colorToChoose;
        whichColorToChange = whichColor;
        whichComponent = comp;
    }

    public boolean action(Event evt, Object whichAction)
    {

// See whether we are supposed to change the foreground or the
    ➥background

        if (whichColorToChange == FOREGROUND)
        {
            whichComponent.setForeground(color);
        }
        else
        {
            whichComponent.setBackground(color);
```

```
            }
        whichComponent.repaint();      // redraw component

        return true;
    }
}
```

---

> **Note**
>
> For completeness, the `ColorButton` class should also have methods to get and set the color, `whichComponent`, and `whichColorToChange`. You should consider this a standard practice for all the variables in a class that someone else might want to change.

You're probably asking, "This looks like a whole lot more work than I had to do before! Why is this any better? I thought object-oriented meant less work, not more!" Think of object-oriented programming as an investment. You have to put in a little more up front, but you save a lot more later on. The next time you need a button to change the color on a component, you have the `ColorButton` ready to go. Now, how does using this new `ColorButton` affect the applet? Listing 21.13 shows the revised applet:

**Listing 21.13    Source Code for Button2Applet.java**

```
import java.applet.*;
import java.awt.*;

// Example 21.11 - Button2Applet
//
// This applet uses the ColorButton to change its background color.
//

public class Button2Applet extends Applet
{
    public void init()
    {
        add(new ColorButton("Red", Color.red,
            ColorButton.BACKGROUND, this));

        add(new ColorButton("Blue", Color.blue,
            ColorButton.BACKGROUND, this));

    }
}
```

As promised, the applet no longer has an `action` method. Now look what happens if you want to add 10 more colors—you add 10 more buttons. That's it. You don't have to change the `action` method because there isn't one.

# Using *Observables*

One of the most useful classes for creating modular user interfaces isn't part of the AWT at all—the `Observable` class. The concept of `observables` is borrowed from Smalltalk. In Smalltalk, an object may "express interest" in another object, meaning it would like to know when the other object changes. When building user interfaces, you might have multiple ways to change a piece of data, and changing that data might cause several different parts of the display to update. For instance, suppose you want to create a scrollbar that changes an integer value, and in turn, that integer value is displayed on some sort of graphical meter. You want the meter to update as the value is changed, but you don't want the meter to know anything about the scrollbar. If you are wondering why the meter shouldn't know about the scrollbar, what happens if you decide you don't want a scrollbar but want the number entered from a text field instead? You shouldn't have to change the meter every time you change the input source.

You would be better off creating an integer variable that is "observable." It allows other objects to express interest in it. When this integer variable changes, it notifies those interested parties (called observers) that it has changed. In the case of the graphical meter, it would be informed that the value changed and would query the integer variable for the new value and then redraw itself. This allows the meter to display the value correctly no matter what you are using to change the value.

This concept is known as "Model-View-Controller." A "model" is the non-visual part of an application. In the above example, the model is nothing more than a single integer variable. The "view" is anything that visually displays some part of the model. The graphical meter is an example of a view. The scrollbar could also be an example of a view since it updates its position whenever the integer value changes. A "controller" is any input source that modifies the view. The scrollbar in this case is also a controller (it can be both a view and a controller).

In Smalltalk, the mechanism for expressing interest in an object is built right into the `Object` class. Unfortunately, for whatever reason, Sun separated out the observing mechanism into a separate class. This means extra work for you since you cannot just register interest in an Integer class. You must create your own subclass of Observable. The most important methods to you in creating a subclass of Observable are `setChanged` and `notifyObservers`. The `setChanged` method marks the Observable as having been changed, so that when you call `notifyObservers`, the observers will be notified. The `notifyObservers` method checks to see if the `changed` flag has been set, and if not, it will not send any notification. The following code fragment sets the changed flag and notifies the observers of the change:

```
setChanged();           // Flag this observable as changed
notifyObservers();      // Tell observers about the change
```

The `notifyObservers` method can also be called with an argument:

```
public void notifyObservers(Object arg)
```

This argument can be used to pass additional information about the change, for instance, the new value. Calling `notifyObservers` with no argument is equivalent to calling it with an argument of `null`.

Observers may register interest in an Observable by calling the `addObserver` method. Any class that implements the Observer interface can register interest in an Observable with:

```
addObserver(this);      // Whatever "this" object is, it must implement Observer
```

Observers may deregister interest in an Observable by calling `deleteObserver`:

```
deleteObserver(this);
```

Listing 21.14 shows an example implementation of an ObservableInt class:

**Listing 21.14  Source Code for ObservableInt.java**

```
import java.util.*;

// Example 21.11 - ObservableInt class
//
// ObservableInt - an integer Observable
//
// This class implements the Observable mechanism for
// a simple int variable.
// You can set the value with setValue(int)
// and int getValue() returns the current value.

public class ObservableInt extends Observable
{
    int value;      // The value everyone wants to observe

    public ObservableInt()
    {
```

(continues)

**Listing 21.14    Continued**

```
                value = 0;      // By default, let value be 0
        }

        public ObservableInt(int newValue)
        {
                value = newValue;     // Allow value to be set when created
        }

        public synchronized void setValue(int newValue)
        {
//
// Check to see that this call is REALLY changing the value
//
                if (newValue != value)
                {
                    value = newValue;
                    setChanged();       // Mark this class as "changed"
                    notifyObservers();     // Tell the observers about it
                }
        }

        public synchronized int getValue()
        {
                return value;
        }
}
```

The Observable class has a companion interface called Observer. Any class
that wants to receive updates about a change in an observable needs to
implement the Observer interface. The Observer interface consists of a single
method called update that is called when an object changes. The format of
update is:

```
        public void update(Observable obs, Object arg);
```

Where obs is the Observable that has just changed, and arg is a value passed
by the observable when it called notifyObservers. If notifyObservers is
called with no arguments, arg will be null.

Listing 21.15 shows an example of a Label class that implements the Observer interface so it can be informed of changes in an integer variable and
update itself with the new value:

**Listing 21.15    Source Code for IntLabel.java**

```
import java.awt.*;
import java.util.*;
```

```
// Example 21.13 - IntLabel class
//
// IntLabel - a Label that displays the value of
// an ObservableInt.

public class IntLabel extends Label implements Observer
{
    private ObservableInt intValue;      // The value we're observing

    public IntLabel(ObservableInt theInt)
    {
        intValue = theInt;

// Tell intValue we're interested in it

        intValue.addObserver(this);

// Initialize the label to the current value of intValue

        setText(""+intValue.getValue());
    }

// Update will be called whenever intValue is changed, so just update
// the label text.

    public void update(Observable obs, Object arg)
    {
        setText(""+intValue.getValue());
    }
}
```

Now that you have a "model" object defined in the form of the
ObservableInt, and a "view" in the form of the IntLabel, you can create a
"controller"—the IntScrollbar. Listing 21.16 shows the implementation of
IntScrollbar:

**Listing 21.16    File Name—Source Code for IntScrollbar.java**

```
import java.awt.*;
import java.util.*;

// Example 21.14 - IntScrollbar class
//
// IntScrollbar - a Scrollbar that modifies an
// ObservableInt.  This class functions as both a
// "view" of the observable, since the position of
// the scrollbar is changed as the observable's value
// is changed, and it is a "controller" since it also
// sets the value of the observable.
//
// IntScrollbar has the same constructors as Scrollbar,
// except that in each case, there is an additional
```

(continues)

**Listing 21.16  Continued**

```
// parameter that is the ObservableInt.
// Note:  On the constructor where you pass in the initial
// scrollbar position, the position is ignored.

public class IntScrollbar extends Scrollbar implements Observer
{
    private ObservableInt intValue;

// The bulk of this class is implementing the various
// constructors that are available in the Scrollbar class.

    public IntScrollbar(ObservableInt newValue)
    {
        super();      // Call the Scrollbar constructor
        intValue = newValue;
        intValue.addObserver(this);       // Register interest
        setValue(intValue.getValue());    // Change scrollbar
                                         ➥position
    }

    public IntScrollbar(ObservableInt newValue, int orientation)
    {
        super(orientation);          // Call the Scrollbar constructor
        intValue = newValue;
        intValue.addObserver(this);       // Register interest
        setValue(intValue.getValue());    // Change scrollbar
                                         ➥position
    }

    public IntScrollbar(ObservableInt newValue, int orientation,
        int value, int pageSize, int lowValue, int highValue)
    {
        super(orientation, value, pageSize, lowValue, highValue);
        intValue = newValue;
        intValue.addObserver(this);       // Register interest
        setValue(intValue.getValue());    // Change scrollbar
                                         ➥position
    }

// The handleEvent method check with the parent class (Scrollbar) to see
// if it wants the event, if not, just assume the scrollbar value has
// changed and update the observable int with the new position.

    public boolean handleEvent(Event evt)
    {
        if (super.handleEvent(evt))
        {
            return true;      // The Scrollbar class handled it
        }
        intValue.setValue(getValue());       // Update the observable int
        return true;
```

```
        }

// update is called whenever the observable int changes its value

        public void update(Observable obs, Object arg)
        {
            setValue(intValue.getValue());
        }
}
```

This may look like a lot of work, but watch how easy it is to create an applet with an `IntScrollbar` that modifies an `ObservableInt` and an `IntLabel` that displays one. Listing 21.17 shows an implementation of an applet that uses the IntScrollbet, the ObservableInt, and the IntLabel:

**Listing 21.17  Source Code for ObservableApplet1.java**

```
import java.applet.*;
import java.awt.*;

// Example 21.14 - ObservableApplet1 applet

public class ObservableApplet1 extends Applet
{
    ObservableInt myIntValue;

    public void init()
    {

// Create the Observable int to play with

        myIntValue = new ObservableInt(5);

        setLayout(new GridLayout(2, 0));

// Create an IntScrollbar that modifies the observable int

        add(new IntScrollbar(myIntValue,
            Scrollbar.HORIZONTAL,
            0, 10, 0, 100));

// Create an IntLabel that displays the observable int

        add(new IntLabel(myIntValue));
    }
}
```

You will notice when you run this applet that the label value changes whenever you update the scrollbar, yet the label has no knowledge of the scrollbar, and the scrollbar has no knowledge of the label.

Now, suppose you also want to allow the value to be updated from a TextField. All you need to do is create a subclass of TextField that modifies the ObservableInt. Listing 21.18 shows an implementation of an IntTextField.

**Listing 21.18   Source Code for IntTextField.java**

```
import java.awt.*;
import java.util.*;

// Example 21.15 - IntTextField class
//
// IntTextField - a TextField that reads in integer values and
// updates an Observable int with the new value.  This class
// is both a "view" of the Observable int, since it displays
// its current value, and a "controller" since it updates the
// value.

public class IntTextField extends TextField implements Observer
{
    private ObservableInt intValue;

    public IntTextField(ObservableInt theInt)
    {
// Initialize the field to the current value, allow 3 input columns

        super(""+theInt.getValue(), 3);
        intValue = theInt;
        intValue.addObserver(this);       // Express interest in
                                          ➥value
    }

// The action for the text field is called whenever someone presses
    ➥"return"
// We'll try to convert the string in the field to an integer, and if
// successful, update the observable int.

    public boolean action(Event evt, Object whatAction)
    {
        Integer intStr;            // to be converted from a string

        try {    // The conversion can throw an exception
            intStr = new Integer(getText());

// If we get here, there was no exception, update the observable

            intValue.setValue(intStr.intValue());
        } catch (Exception oops) {
// We just ignore the exception
        }
        return true;
    }
```

```
// The update action is called whenever the observable int's value changes.
// We just update the text in the field with the new int value

    public void update(Observable obs, Object arg)
    {
        setText(""+intValue.getValue());
    }
}
```

Once you have created this class, how much code do you think you have
to add to the applet? You add one line (and change GridLayout to have
3 rows). Listing 21.19 shows an implementation of an applet that uses an
ObservableInt, an IntScrollbar, an IntLabel, and an IntTextField.

**Listing 21.19   Source Code for ObservableApplet2.java**

```
import java.applet.*;
import java.awt.*;

// Example 21.16 - ObservableApplet2 applet

public class ObservableApplet2 extends Applet
{
    ObservableInt myIntValue;

    public void init()
    {

// Create the Observable int to play with

        myIntValue = new ObservableInt(5);

        setLayout(new GridLayout(3, 0));

// Create an IntScrollbar that modifies the observable int

        add(new IntScrollbar(myIntValue,
            Scrollbar.HORIZONTAL,
            0, 10, 0, 100));

// Create an IntLabel that displays the observable int

        add(new IntLabel(myIntValue));

// Create an IntTextField that displays and updates the observable
  ➥int

        add(new IntTextField(myIntValue));
    }
}
```

Again, the components that modify and display the integer value have no knowledge of each other, yet whenever the value is changed, they are all updated with the new value. ❖

# CHAPTER 22
# Advanced Applet Code

*by Mark Wutka*

Now that you have learned some of the fundamentals of Java programming, you can concentrate on design issues that will help you create better programs in less time. Writing object-oriented software is not a skill that can be learned overnight. As you begin to realize some of the benefits that object-oriented software brings you, you will start learning to consider these benefits when you first begin to write a program. Pretty soon, it will become second-nature.

One thing you should always keep in mind is that just because a program is written in an object-oriented language, it is not necessarily an object-oriented program. It is just as easy to write bad code in Java as it is in C. You have to put some effort into the design of your code to realize the benefits of object-orientation.

Fortunately, you don't have to get it perfect the first time, just keep refining your code over and over. Pretty soon, you will have a good object-oriented program. This chapter will help you understand some of the issues and techniques involved in improving your code and maximizing its reuse.

In this chapter you will learn

- What code reuse is and how it helps you
- How to refine a design
- How to create flexible classes that can be reused easily
- How to make your applets more configurable
- How to add sound to your applets

# What Is Code Reuse?

One of the highly touted advantages of object-oriented languages is the reusability of code: you don't have to start from scratch every time you write a program. Smalltalk, for instance, comes with a large set of reusable objects that are available to a programmer from the start. These objects are well-designed and provide a large number of commonly used components. This core of objects is one of the reasons that software can be developed in Smalltalk so quickly. There is less new code to write. One thing to remember about creating reusable code is that you sometimes have to take a little extra time up front to realize the benefits of reuse later on.

*Inheritance* and *encapsulation* are two of the features of object-oriented languages that help support code reuse. Java supports both of these features, but you must still be careful in how you use them. Like other features, inheritance and encapsulation can be easily abused.

## Reuse by Inheritance

Inheritance is most often praised as the great instrument of reuse that sets object-oriented languages apart from the rest. Inheritance achieves reuse by taking an existing class as a basis and building on top of it—adding new functionality or changing existing functionality. Inheritance is a very visible form of reuse because it explicitly reuses existing code.

## To Extend, or Not To Extend

One question that comes up frequently is "How do I know when to create a subclass?" The following are a few rules of thumb to help you decide whether you should create a subclass of an existing class or write a new one:

- Create a subclass when you want to change the behavior of a class. In other words, you want to change the way some of the methods work.

- Create a subclass when you want to create a new class that adds new behavior to a class but is still kind of like the old class. For example, a lemon is a kind of fruit, but maybe you want to add a "squeeze" method just for lemons.

- Do not create a subclass when you are trying to reuse the behavior of a class in a new class that is not kind of like the old class. For example, an Orange class may have an orange color and an orange taste, but you should not make OrangeSoda a subclass of Orange just to get the color and taste.

- Do not create a subclass when you are trying to "cheat" the protection scheme by creating a subclass simply to get access to protected variables.

### Reuse by Encapsulation

Encapsulation is an equally useful concept for creating reusable code, but is overlooked by many because it requires more work up front. To reuse by encapsulation means creating a class that has a well-defined interface and performs a specific set of functions and is as self-sufficient as possible. A self-sufficient class contains all the information necessary to perform its job.

Whereas inheritance promotes reuse by actually reusing an existing class, encapsulation creates classes that can be used easily by many other classes. The Graphics class is a well-encapsulated, very reusable class. You use the Graphics class in many applets, yet you never have to create a subclass of it.

The real key to code reuse does not lie in inheritance, but in a large set of flexible classes. Many people have suggested that object-oriented programming will lead to the development of *software ICs,* software that is as easy to put into a new system as integrated circuits. In creating a new system, a hardware designer uses catalogs of existing components. These components have a well-defined interface and perform a specific set of functions. These are, for the most part, self-sufficient. Whether the software industry ever gets to that point is a question that only time will answer.

# Working Through a Design

Rather than trying to grasp all the issues in object-oriented programming all at once, you can start with a basic design problem and see how different ideas affect your design. The design problem is this: *Create an applet that scrolls a text string from right to left in a marquee style.*

To create a marquee text, you need to keep track of the following items:

- You obviously need to know the string you are scrolling.
- You need to remember the string's position, which you continuously change.
- You need to set up a timer to figure out when to move the string.
- You'll want to be able to change the color and font of the text.

Your first try will probably look something like listing 22.1. The output from this applet is shown in figure 22.1.

**Listing 22.1   Source Code for *SimpleMarqueeApplet.java***

```
import java.awt.*;
import java.applet.*;

// SimpleMarqueeApplet
//
// This applet scrolls a text string from right to left like a
// marquee sign.

public class SimpleMarqueeApplet extends Applet implements Runnable
{
    protected String scrollString;      // the string to scroll
    protected int stringX;              // the current string position
    protected Font scrollFont;
    protected Color scrollColor;
    protected int scrollDelay;          // how many milliseconds between
                                        ➥movement
    protected int scrollIncrement;      // how many pixels to scroll

    protected Thread animThread;
    protected Image offscreenImage;         // for flicker prevention
    protected Graphics offscreenGraphics;      // for flicker prevention

// The init method sets up some default values.  The applet provides
➥methods
// to set each of the customizable values.

    public void init()
    {
        scrollFont = new Font("TimesRoman", Font.BOLD, 24);
        scrollString = "Welcome to the very plain, yet fun, Simple
        ➥Marquee Applet.";
        scrollColor = Color.blue;
        scrollDelay = 100;
        scrollIncrement = 2;
        stringX = size().width;

// Create tbe off-screen image for double-buffering
        offscreenImage = createImage(size().width, size().height);
        offscreenGraphics = offscreenImage.getGraphics();
    }

// The run method implements a timer that moves the string and then
// repaints the screen.  It tries to keep the delay time constant by
// figuring out when the next tick should be and only sleeping for
// however much time is left.

    public void run()
    {
        long nextTime, currTime;
        Thread.currentThread().setPriority(Thread.NORM_PRIORITY);
```

```
            while (true)
            {
// Figure out what time the next tick should occur
            nextTime = System.currentTimeMillis() + scrollDelay;

// Scroll the string
            moveString();
// Redraw the string
            repaint();

// See what time it is now
            currTime = System.currentTimeMillis();

// If we haven't gotten to the next tick, sleep for however many
  ➥milliseconds
// are left until the next tick;
            if (currTime < nextTime) {
                try {
                    Thread.sleep((int)(nextTime - currTime));
                } catch (Exception noSleep) {
                }
            }
        }
    }

// moveString updates the string's position
    public void moveString()
    {
        stringX -= scrollIncrement;
    }

// setScrollString changes the string that is being displayed
    public void setScrollString(String newString)
    {
        scrollString = newString;
    }

// setScrollIncrement changes the number of pixels the string is move
// each tick time.
    public void setScrollIncrement(int increment)
    {
        scrollIncrement = increment;
    }

// setScrollDelay changes the number of milliseconds between ticks
    public void setScrollDelay(int delay)
    {
        scrollDelay = delay;
    }

// setScrollFont sets the font for the scroll string
    public void setScrollFont(Font newFont)
    {
        scrollFont = newFont;
    }
```

(continues)

**Listing 22.1   Continued**

```
// setScrollColor sets the color for the scroll string
    public void setScrollColor(Color color)
    {
        scrollColor = color;
    }

// paint redraws the string on the screen
    public void paint(Graphics g)
    {
        FontMetrics currentMetrics;

        g.setFont(scrollFont);
        g.setColor(scrollColor);

        currentMetrics = g.getFontMetrics();

// If the left coordinate of the string is so far to the left that
// the string won't be displayed, move it over to the right again.

        if (stringX < -currentMetrics.stringWidth(scrollString))
        {
            stringX = size().width;
        }
        else
        {
// Compute the baseline as the ascent plus a padding of 5 pixels.
// This means there should be a clearance of 5 pixels between the
// tallest letter and the top of the drawing area.

            int stringBaseline = currentMetrics.getAscent()+5;
            g.drawString(scrollString, stringX, stringBaseline);
        }
    }

// This update method uses an off-screen drawing area to reduce
// applet flicker.  It enables the paint method to assume a cleared
// screen by clearing the off-screen drawing area before calling paint.

    public void update(Graphics g)
    {
        offscreenGraphics.setColor(getBackground());
        offscreenGraphics.fillRect(0, 0, size().width,
            size().height);
        offscreenGraphics.setColor(g.getColor());
        paint(offscreenGraphics);
        g.drawImage(offscreenImage, 0, 0, this);
    }
```

```
    public void start()
    {
        animThread = new Thread(this);
        animThread.start();
    }

    public void stop()
    {
        animThread.stop();
        animThread = null;
    }
}
```

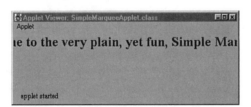

**Fig. 22.1**
SimpleMarqueeApplet
scrolls text from
right to left.

One of the first things you should realize about this applet is that it is not very reusable. One of the problems is that it is one big applet, making it difficult to use this functionality in another applet. For instance, suppose you wanted to make a stock trading applet and you wanted to have stock quotes scrolling across the bottom. To use this marquee code, you have to create a subclass of the SimpleMarqueeApplet. That is a case of subclassing for the wrong reason. The stock trading program is not a kind of marquee, it is something completely different.

> **Note**
>
> Avoid putting all your code into one big applet; concentrate instead on making smaller pieces that can be reused. Your applet should make use of smaller classes while adding as little functionality as possible.

It is useful to think of objects as employees. One of the popular management buzzwords these days is *employee empowerment.* When you empower employees, you give them the authority to perform their jobs, and you trust them to complete their assignments without any interference from supervisors. In the world of objects, you want to "empower" your objects. Give them a specific role and trust them to do it.

Unfortunately, many programmers (and many more managers) do not subscribe to the idea of empowerment. When a manager does not empower the employees, the employees must come through him or her for all decisions. In the programming world, when the objects are not empowered, the applet becomes the big controlling force, only using other objects for simple tasks.

From a reuse standpoint, this is a bad thing. When you put all of your program logic into one big applet, it becomes difficult to reuse portions of it. For instance, suppose car engines were built as one huge part. You could not go down to a junkyard and pick up an old carburetor to replace a bad one.

One of the difficulties with object-oriented programming is figuring out how to split an object into smaller objects. Many times, looking at a description of what an object does can help you break the object into more specialized components.

> **Tip**
>
> If you are having difficulty identifying the subobjects that make up an object, try writing out a description of what the object does and look at the nouns in the description. These are often the subobjects.

The description of the marquee applet earlier was that *it scrolls a text string from right to left in a marquee style.* Wouldn't it be better if the text string knew how to scroll itself? The applet's only job would be to create the marquee text. Any other applet that wanted to have marquee text could also use the marquee text class.

> **Tip**
>
> Remember that object-oriented programming focuses on the interaction of small, "intelligent" objects, not single monolithic programs.

# A *SimpleMarqueeString* Class

Your goal with the SimpleMarqueeString class is to create a text string that can somehow scroll itself from right to left and be used by many applets. In fact, you want to make it as easy to use as the Button or the Label from the AWT library. You can do that by making the SimpleMarqueeString a subclass of a Canvas. Recall that in the SimpleMarqueeApplet, you used a thread to create a timer for moving the string. Because you are moving the responsibility for displaying the string to the `SimpleMarqueeString` class, you move the timer as well.

Remember, you want the applet that uses the `SimpleMarqueeString` to do as little as possible to make it run. As it turns out, it does not take much effort to convert this applet into a `Canvas`. First, you need to change the declaration of the class:

```
public class SimpleMarqueeString extends Canvas implements Runnable
```

Now, you need two additional class variables: `preferredWidth` and `preferredHeight`. In an applet, the width and height are predetermined, but the `Canvas` needs some way of finding out how large you want it to be.

```
protected int preferredWidth;
protected int preferredHeight;
```

Next, you need to create a constructor for the class. It is a good idea to provide a quick constructor for the most common usage and then a full constructor that enables you to set all the options. Listing 22.2 shows a quick constructor:

**Listing 22.2   A Quick Constructor for *SimpleMarqueeString* Class**

```
public SimpleMarqueeString(String string, int width, int height)
{
        scrollString = string;
        scrollFont = new Font("TimesRoman", Font.BOLD, 24);
        scrollColor = Color.blue;
        scrollDelay = 100;
        scrollIncrement = 2;

        preferredWidth = width;
        preferredHeight = height;
        stringX = width;
}
```

Listing 22.3 shows a full constructor that enables you to set all of the parameters:

**Listing 22.3   A Full Constructor for the *SimpleMarqueeString* Class**

```
public SimpleMarqueeString(String string, int width, int height,
        Color color, Font font, int delay, int increment)
{
        scrollString = string;
        scrollFont = font;
        scrollColor = color;
```

(continues)

**Listing 22.3    Continued**

```
        scrollDelay = delay;
        scrollIncrement = increment;
        preferredWidth = width;
        preferredHeight = height;
        stringX = width;
}
```

You need a way to convey the preferred height and width to the layout manager in charge of this Canvas. You can define methods called preferredSize
and minimumSize to do this:

```
public Dimension preferredSize()
{
        return new Dimension(preferredWidth, preferredHeight);
}

public Dimension minimumSize()
{
        return preferredSize();
}
```

Finally, creating an off-screen image is a little trickier with a Canvas because
you cannot create the image reliably from the constructor. However, as
shown in listing 22.4, you can create it in the update method:

**Listing 22.4    A Flicker-Free Update Method for the
*SimpleMarqueeString* Class**

```
public void update(Graphics g)
{
// create off-screen image if it doesn't exist
        if (offscreenImage == null) {
                offscreenImage = createImage(size().width,
                        size().height); // for flicker prevention
                offscreenGraphics = offscreenImage.getGraphics();
        }
        offscreenGraphics.setColor(getBackground());
        offscreenGraphics.fillRect(0, 0, size().width,
                size().height);
        offscreenGraphics.setColor(g.getColor());
        paint(offscreenGraphics);
        g.drawImage(offscreenImage, 0, 0, this);
}
```

# Making Flexible Classes

Another big key to creating reusable code is creating flexible classes. You
wanted the text to scroll from right to left. Maybe someone else wants it to

scroll from left to right—or maybe top to bottom. Maybe there should be options for changing speeds or making the text flash. It may take you a little extra time to add features like these, but remember: this is an investment. Two months later when you need to scroll text a different way, you'll be glad you put all those extra features in there—and so will the other people who use it.

> **Note**
>
> Try to anticipate other uses for a class, and provide methods for them. The more options available, the more likely the class is to be reused.

You will often find that you greatly underestimated the ways someone might want to use a class that you designed. Many times, you will need to add a wider variety of parameters. You can either add new methods to accept these different parameters, or better yet, encapsulate the parameters in an object. Whenever you add features that require more parameters, you can make a subclass of the parameter object.

> **Note**
>
> Try to group configuration parameters for a class into their own class, rather than continually changing and adding constructors. This enables you to expand the class functionality quickly without modifying its interface.

## Choosing Between Public and Protected Variables

There are two schools of thought in how you update member variables in a class. The *Smalltalk* school suggests that you make all the variables private (or at least protected) and that you always access them through methods commonly referred to as *accessor methods*. The most common format is getVariableName and setVariableName. Of course, in Smalltalk, you have to access member variables this way—there is no other choice. The *Direct Access* school suggests just making them public. There are advantages and disadvantages to each approach.

Accessor methods enable you to react to a variable being changed. In other words, if you want an object to perform a series of actions whenever a certain variable is changed, you modify the set method for that variable. Unfortunately, it takes time to write accessor methods for each variable, and in very intensive algorithms, they can add some overhead.

Public variables, on the other hand, are much easier to use and do not add overhead during intense usage. They do make it more difficult to react to changes, however.

> **Note**
>
> Use public variables in data-oriented objects, such as those encapsulating configuration parameters. Use accessor methods for any variable that could possibly trigger some action if changed.

The MarqueeItem class holds the parameters for scrolling a string in four directions: right to left, left to right, top to bottom, and bottom to top (see listing 22.2).

**Listing 22.5  Source Code for *MarqueeItem.java***

```java
import java.awt.*;

public class MarqueeItem extends Object
{
//
// Define some constants for describing the marquee
//
     public static final int RIGHT_TO_LEFT = 1;
     public static final int LEFT_TO_RIGHT = 2;
     public static final int TOP_TO_BOTTOM = 3;
     public static final int BOTTOM_TO_TOP = 4;

// Define the marquee item parameters

     public String marqueeString;    // The string to draw
     public Color marqueeColor;      // The string's color
     public Font marqueeFont;        // The string's font
     public int scrollIncrement;     // how much to move the string
     public int scrollDelay;         // how many milliseconds
                                     // between moves

     public int scrollDirection;     // which way to move the string
                                     // RIGHT_TO_LEFT, LEFT_TO_RIGHT, etc.

// Set up a constructor for creating a MarqueeItem quickly

     public MarqueeItem(String string)
     {
          marqueeString = string;

          marqueeColor = Color.blue;
          marqueeFont = new Font("TimesRoman", Font.BOLD, 24);
          scrollIncrement = 3;
          scrollDelay = 100;
```

```
            scrollDirection = RIGHT_TO_LEFT;
    }

// Set up a full constructor for creating a MarqueeItem

    public MarqueeItem(String string, Color color, Font font,
        int increment, int delay, int direction)
    {
        marqueeString = string;
        marqueeColor = color;
        marqueeFont = font;
        scrollIncrement = increment;
        scrollDelay = delay;
        scrollDirection = direction;
    }
}
```

Now that you have an object to describe the marquee string and its direction,
you can improve the SimpleMarqueeString class to scroll the text in multiple directions. The MarqueeString class is an improved version of
SimpleMarqueeString, using the MarqueeItem class to configure the marquee
string (see listing 22.6).

**Listing 22.6    Source Code for *MarqueeString1.java***

```
import java.awt.*;
import java.applet.*;

// MarqueeString
//
// This canvas scrolls a text string from right to left like a
// marquee sign.

public class MarqueeString extends Canvas implements Runnable
{
    protected MarqueeItem item;

    protected int stringX;              // the current string position
    protected int stringBaseline;       // the current string baseline

    protected Thread animThread;

    protected int preferredWidth;
    protected int preferredHeight;

    protected Image offscreenImage;
    protected Graphics offscreenGraphics;


    public MarqueeString(MarqueeItem newItem, int width, int height)
    {
        item = newItem;
```

(continues)

**Listing 22.6 Continued**

```
            preferredWidth = width;
            preferredHeight = height;

            setScrollPosition();
    }

// Set scroll position sets the initial position for the scrolling string.
    public void setScrollPosition()
    {

        switch (item.scrollDirection)
        {
// For a right to left scroll, place it just off the screen to the right
            case MarqueeItem.RIGHT_TO_LEFT:
                stringX = preferredWidth;
                break;

// For a left to right scroll, place the left end of the string on the
// left side of the screen.  This would be better if you could put the
// whole string just off the left hand side of the screen, but at this
// point we may not be able to get the font metrics.
            case MarqueeItem.LEFT_TO_RIGHT:
                stringX = 0;
                break;

// For a top to bottom scroll, place the string at the just off the top of
// the screen.  Text that extends below the baseline will be immediately
// visible.
            case MarqueeItem.TOP_TO_BOTTOM:
                stringX = 0;
                stringBaseline = 0;
                break;

// For a bottom to top scroll, place the string just below the bottom of
// the screen.
            case MarqueeItem.BOTTOM_TO_TOP:
                stringX = 0;
                stringBaseline = preferredHeight;
                break;

// By default do a right to left scroll

            default:
                item.scrollDirection = MarqueeItem.RIGHT_TO_LEFT;
                stringX = preferredWidth;
        }
    }

// Enable the item parameters to be changed on-the-fly.  Reset the string
// position of the item changes.

    public void setMarqueeItem(MarqueeItem newItem)
    {
```

```
            item = newItem;
            setScrollPosition();
    }

    public Dimension preferredSize()
    {
            return new Dimension(preferredWidth, preferredHeight);
    }

    public Dimension minimumSize()
    {
            return preferredSize();
    }

// The run method implements a timer that moves the string and then
// repaints the screen.  It tries to keep the delay time constant by
// figuring out when the next tick should be and only sleeping for
// however much time is left.

    public void run()
    {
            long nextTime, currTime;
            Thread.currentThread().setPriority(Thread.NORM_PRIORITY);

            while (true)
            {
// Figure out what time the next tick should occur
                nextTime = System.currentTimeMillis() +
                    item.scrollDelay;

// Scroll the string
                moveString();
// Redraw the string
                repaint();

// See what time it is now
                currTime = System.currentTimeMillis();

// If we haven't gotten to the next tick, sleep for however many
// milliseconds are left until the next tick;
                if (currTime < nextTime) {
                    try {
                        Thread.sleep((int)(nextTime - currTime));
                    } catch (Exception noSleep) {
                    }
                }
            }
    }

// moveString updates the string's position
    public void moveString()
    {
            switch (item.scrollDirection)
            {
```

(continues)

**Listing 22.6   Continued**

```
                case MarqueeItem.RIGHT_TO_LEFT:
                    stringX -= item.scrollIncrement;
                    break;

                case MarqueeItem.LEFT_TO_RIGHT:
                    stringX += item.scrollIncrement;
                    break;

                case MarqueeItem.TOP_TO_BOTTOM:
                    stringBaseline += item.scrollIncrement;
                    break;

                case MarqueeItem.BOTTOM_TO_TOP:
                    stringBaseline -= item.scrollIncrement;
                    break;
        }

    }


// checkMarqueeBounds checks to see if the string goes completely off
// the screen, and if so, it moves the string to the other side of the
// screen.  For the horizontal scrolls, it also computes the baseline
// each time.

    public void checkMarqueeBounds(FontMetrics metrics)
    {
        switch (item.scrollDirection)
        {
// For right to left, the string is off the screen when the x is less than
// the negative of the string width (i.e. x + width < 0)

                case MarqueeItem.RIGHT_TO_LEFT:
                    if (stringX < -metrics.stringWidth(
                        item.marqueeString))
                    {
                        stringX = metrics.stringWidth(
                            item.marqueeString);
                    }
                    stringBaseline = metrics.getHeight() + 5;
                    return;

// for left to right, the string is off the screen when X goes past the
// width of the area.
                case MarqueeItem.LEFT_TO_RIGHT:
                    if (stringX > preferredWidth)
                    {
                        stringX = -metrics.stringWidth(
                            item.marqueeString);
                    }
                    stringBaseline = metrics.getHeight() + 5;
                    return;
```

```
// For top to bottom, the string is off the screen when the baseline goes
// beyond the point where baseline + height is still within the screen
            case MarqueeItem.TOP_TO_BOTTOM:
                if (stringBaseline > preferredHeight +
                    metrics.getHeight()) {
                    stringBaseline = -metrics.getHeight();
                }
                return;

// For bottom to top, the string is off the screen when the baseline goes
// below the negative of the string height (baseline + height < 0)

            case MarqueeItem.BOTTOM_TO_TOP:
                if (stringBaseline < -metrics.getHeight()) {
                    stringBaseline = preferredHeight +
                        metrics.getHeight();
                }
                return;
        }
    }

// paint redraws the string on the screen
    public void paint(Graphics g)
    {
        FontMetrics currentMetrics;

        g.setFont(item.marqueeFont);
        g.setColor(item.marqueeColor);

        currentMetrics = g.getFontMetrics();

        checkMarqueeBounds(currentMetrics);

        g.drawString(item.marqueeString, stringX, stringBaseline);
    }

// This update method uses an off-screen drawing area to reduce applet
// flicker.  It enables the paint method to assume a cleared screen
// by clearing the off-screen drawing area before calling paint.

    public void update(Graphics g)
    {
// If the offScreenImage doesn't exist yet, create it
        if (offscreenImage == null) {
            offscreenImage = createImage(size().width,
                size().height);       // for flicker prevention
            offscreenGraphics = offscreenImage.getGraphics();
        }
        offscreenGraphics.setColor(getBackground());
        offscreenGraphics.fillRect(0, 0, size().width,
            size().height);
        offscreenGraphics.setColor(g.getColor());
        paint(offscreenGraphics);
        g.drawImage(offscreenImage, 0, 0, this);
    }
```

(continues)

---

**Listing 22.6  Continued**

```
    public void start()
    {
        animThread = new Thread(this);
        animThread.start();
    }

    public void stop()
    {
        animThread.stop();
        animThread = null;
    }
}
```

---

The `MarqueeApplet` class uses the `MarqueeString` class to display two different marquees. Notice that the applet still just creates the objects that do the work; it doesn't do anything special itself (see listing 22.7).

---

**Listing 22.7  Source Code for *MarqueeApplet1.java***

```
import java.awt.*;
import java.applet.*;

// MarqueeApplet
//
// This applet scrolls two text strings one from right to left,
// the other from top to bottom.

public class MarqueeApplet1 extends Applet
{
    MarqueeString marquee1;
    MarqueeString marquee2;

    public void init()
    {
        marquee1 = new MarqueeString(
            new MarqueeItem("Welcome to the new and improved
marquee!"), 300, 50);
        add(marquee1);
        marquee1.start();

        marquee2 = new MarqueeString(
            new MarqueeItem("This scrolls from top to bottom.",
                Color.red, new Font("TimesRoman",
                    Font.PLAIN, 16), 1, 100,
                MarqueeItem.TOP_TO_BOTTOM), 300, 100);
        add(marquee2);
        marquee2.start();
    }
}
```

---

You probably want to be able to change the text from time to time on the marquee. Because you don't want to change the text in the middle of the scrolling, you want the MarqueeString class to notify you when the text has finished scrolling. What you want here is a callback method. You set up a method in your applet, and the MarqueeString class calls that method when it is finished displaying the text.

> **Note**
>
> Use interfaces to implement callbacks. Interfaces define a set of methods that any object which implements that interface must provide. When you want to create a callback, create an interface that represents that callback, then any object that wants to be called back must implement the interface.

The MarqueeObserver interface defines a callback method that the MarqueeString class calls every time it finishes displaying a string (see listing 22.8).

**Listing 22.8  Source Code for *MarqueeObserver.java***

```
public interface MarqueeObserver
{
// marqueeNotify is called whenever the item scrolls off the screen

    public void marqueeNotify(MarqueeItem item);
}
```

The MarqueeString class needs to be modified to support this new callback. Whenever you change a class, you should be careful not to make it unusable for previous users in the class. In this case, you can add another constructor for the class that sets up the callback. This way, the original applet you wrote can still use the MarqueeString class with no changes.

> **Note**
>
> When adding functionality to a class, try not to remove the existing constructors and methods. You don't want every new addition to break applets that use the class.

To add support for the MarqueeObserver interface to the MarqueeString, you need to add a variable for the observer:

```
    protected MarqueeObserver observer;
```

Next, add a new constructor to create a `MarqueeString` with an observer, but leave the original constructor available for any old applets that may still use it. Listing 22.9 shows the new constructor:

**Listing 22.9   A Constructor for MarqueeString That Supports a MarqueeObserver**

```
public MarqueeString(MarqueeItem newItem, int width, int height,
        MarqueeObserver newObserver)
{
        preferredWidth = width;
        preferredHeight = height;

        setMarqueeItem(newItem);
        observer = newObserver;
}
```

You should also add a method to set the observer manually just in case you want to change the observer after the `MarqueeString` has already been created:

```
public void setObserver(MarqueeObserver newObserver)
{
        observer = newObserver;
}
```

Finally, change the `checkMarqueeBounds` method to call `marqueeNotify` if the string runs off the screen:

```
public void checkMarqueeBounds(FontMetrics metrics)
{
        switch (item.scrollDirection)
        {
// For right to left, the string is off the screen when the x is less
// than the negative of the string width (i.e. x + width < 0)

                case MarqueeItem.RIGHT_TO_LEFT:
                        if (stringX < -metrics.stringWidth(
                                item.marqueeString))
                        {
                                stringX = metrics.stringWidth(
                                        item.marqueeString);
                                if (observer != null) {
                                        observer.marqueeNotify(item);
                                }
                        }
                        stringBaseline = metrics.getHeight() + 5;
                        return;

// for left to right, the string is off the screen when X goes past
// the width of the area.
```

```
                case MarqueeItem.LEFT_TO_RIGHT:
                        if (stringX > preferredWidth)
                        {
                                stringX = -metrics.stringWidth(
                                        item.marqueeString);
                                if (observer != null) {
                                        observer.marqueeNotify(item);
                                }
                        }
                        stringBaseline = metrics.getHeight() + 5;
                        return;
// For top to bottom, the string is off the screen when the baseline goes
// beyond the point where baseline + height is still within the screen
                case MarqueeItem.TOP_TO_BOTTOM:
                        if (stringBaseline > preferredHeight +
                                metrics.getHeight()) {
                                stringBaseline = -metrics.getHeight();
                                if (observer != null) {
                                        observer.marqueeNotify(item);
                                }
                        }
                        return;

// For bottom to top, the string is off the screen when the baseline goes
// below the negative of the string height (baseline + height < 0)

                case MarqueeItem.BOTTOM_TO_TOP:
                        if (stringBaseline < -metrics.getHeight())
    {
                                stringBaseline = preferredHeight +
                                        metrics.getHeight();
                                if (observer != null) {
                                        observer.marqueeNotify(item);
                                }
                        }
                        return;
        }
}
```

## Encapsulating Common Mechanisms

In addition to adding methods to a class, sometimes you can even encapsulate common *mechanisms* for using a class. You frequently perform the same operation on a group of classes. When you do, you should consider creating a class to encapsulate that operation or a group of similar operations. For instance, many applets probably want to change the text once it has finished scrolling. You can create a driver that takes a number of MarqueeItem objects and automatically changes the marquee text whenever it finishes scrolling (see listing 22.10).

> **Note**
>
> Any time you notice you are doing the same thing over and over, try to think of a
> way to capture it in a class. This is the essence of object-oriented programming.

**Listing 22.10  Source Code for *MarqueeDriver.java***

```
// MarqueeDriver
//
// The marquee driver automatically cycles through an
// array of MarqueeItems feeding them to a MarqueeString
// whenever an item has scrolled off the screen.

public class MarqueeDriver extends Object implements MarqueeObserver
{
    MarqueeItem items[];
    MarqueeString marquee;

    int currItem;

    public MarqueeDriver(MarqueeString marqueeString, MarqueeItem
    ↪newItems[])
    {
        items = newItems;
        currItem = 0;

        marquee = marqueeString;

// Ask the marquee string to notify us when an item scrolls off
        marquee.setObserver(this);

    }

    public void marqueeNotify(MarqueeItem item)
    {
        currItem++;      // goto next item

// If we get to the end, start back at the beginning
        if (currItem >= items.length)
        {
            currItem = 0;
        }

// Change the item in the marquee string
        marquee.setMarqueeItem(items[currItem]);
    }
}
```

# Making an Applet Extensible

So far, the applets in this chapter have only created a few objects and set them in action. You can add flexibility to your applets by passing them parameters from HTML using the <PARAM> tag. The applet uses the getParameter method to retrieve parameters passed through <PARAM>.

Parameters are not the only way to make an applet—or any other class—extensible. Inheritance is a useful way of adding functionality to a class, but the class should be designed with inheritance in mind.

> **Note**
>
> Try to break up each action an object performs into separate methods. When you want to change a single action, you should be able to override a single method in the subclass and not affect the rest of the original object.

In a class, such as an applet, pay particular attention to methods that create instances of objects. Try to separate the creation of the instance into a separate method. For example, if you have a method that parses parameters from the getParameters method and then creates an instance of another object, try to separate the creation of the object into a separate method. This is especially useful when creating objects that are likely to be subclassed at some time.

The following applet creates a number of MarqueeItems based on parameters passed via the <PARAM> tag, as well as a MarqueeDriver to cycle through the parameters (see listing 22.11).

### Listing 22.11  Source Code for *MarqueeApplet.java*

```
import java.awt.*;
import java.applet.*;

// MarqueeApplet
//
// This applet scrolls a text string from right to left like a
// marquee sign.  It is configurable via the <PARAM> tag in HTML.
// For each marquee string, the parameters are:
// marqueeName - the string to be displayed
// marqueeFont - the name of the font to use
// marqueeFontHeight - the point height of the font to use
// marqueeFontPlain - if this param is present, make the font plain
// marqueeFontBold - if this param is present, make the font bold
// marqueeFontItalic - if this param is present, make the font bold
// You can specify more than one of the plain/bold/italic parameters
// to get combinations like Bold+Italic
```

(continues)

**Listing 22.11 Continued**

```
// marqueeColor - the color of the text, either a name or an integer RGB
// value scrollIncrement - the number of pixels to scroll each time
// scrollDelay - the number of millisecond to delay between successive
// scrolls
// scrollDirection - either topToBottom, bottomToTop, leftToRight or
// rightToLeft
//
// Each of these parameter names should be followed immediately by a
// number indicating which item it is for.  For instance, to set the
// marqueeName for the first item, the <PARAM> tag would be:
// <PARAM name="marqueeName0" value="This is the first entry">
// the second item would be:
// <PARAM name="marqueeName1" value="This is the second entry">
//

public class MarqueeApplet extends Applet
{
// Set up some arrays to map names to colors

    public static final String colorNames[] = {
        "white", "lightGray", "gray", "darkGray", "black",
        "red", "pink", "orange", "yellow", "green",
        "magenta", "cyan", "blue"
    };
    public static final Color colorValues[] = {
        Color.white, Color.lightGray, Color.gray, Color.darkGray,
        Color.black, Color.red, Color.pink, Color.orange,
        Color.yellow, Color.green, Color.magenta, Color.cyan,
        Color.blue
    };

// Set up some arrays to map direction names to directions

    public static final String directionNames[] = {
        "topToBottom", "bottomToTop", "leftToRight", "rightToLeft"
    };

    public static final int directions[] = {
        MarqueeItem.TOP_TO_BOTTOM, MarqueeItem.BOTTOM_TO_TOP,
        MarqueeItem.LEFT_TO_RIGHT, MarqueeItem.RIGHT_TO_LEFT
    };

    MarqueeString marquee;
    MarqueeItem items[];
    MarqueeDriver driver;

    public void init()
    {
        int i, numParams;

// First, figure out how many parameters there are

        numParams = 0;
```

```
                while (true)
                {
// Stop counting when fetchParameter returns null (which means the
// parameter didn't exist).
                    if (fetchParameter("marqueeString", numParams) == null)
                    {
                        break;
                    }
                    numParams++;
                }


// Now, create an array of items long enough to hold all the strings
            items = new MarqueeItem[numParams];

// Now, loop again and create all the items.
            for (i=0; i < numParams; i++)
            {
                items[i] = fetchMarqueeItem(i);

            }

// If there were no items, be gentle - scroll out a message saying so

            if (items.length == 0)
            {
                items = new MarqueeItem[1];
                items[0] = new MarqueeItem(
                    "No parameters were supplied for this marquee : (");
            }

            marquee = createMarqueeString(items[0], 300, 300);
            add(marquee);

            marquee.start();

            driver = createMarqueeDriver(marquee, items);
        }

// getIntParameter tries to convert a string to an integer.  If the
// conversion isn't successful, return the defaultValue that was
// passed in.

    public int getIntParameter(String str, int defaultValue)
    {
        int radix = 10;
        String convertString = str;

// If the string starts with 0x, it is a hex number

            if ((str.length() > 2) && (str.substring(0, 2).equals("0x") ||
                str.substring(0, 2).equals("0X")))
            {
                radix = 16;
```

(continues)

**Listing 22.11  Continued**

```
            convertString = str.substring(2);  // ignore the 0x now
        }
// otherwise, if it starts with 0, it is an octal number

        else if ((str.length() > 1) && (str.substring(0,
1).equals("0")))
        {
            radix = 8;
            convertString = str.substring(1); // ignore the 0 now
        }

// try to convert the string to an integer
        try {
            return Integer.parseInt(convertString, radix);
        } catch (Exception badConversion) {
// if there was a conversion error, return the default value
            return defaultValue;
        }
    }

// fetchParameter tries to retrieve an applet parameter.  If the
// parameter is unavailable, it returns null.

    public String fetchParameter(String paramPrefix, int index)
    {
        String paramName = paramPrefix+index;
        try {
            return getParameter(paramName);
        } catch (Exception noparameter) {
            return null;
        }
    }

// Create an instance of a MarqueeItem - this enables subclasses
// of this applet to change the creation of MarqueeItems

    public MarqueeItem createMarqueeItem(String name,
        Color color, Font font, int increment, int delay,
        int direction)
    {
        return new MarqueeItem(name, color, font, increment,
            delay, direction);
    }

// Create an instance of a MarqueeString - this enables subclasses
// of this applet to change the creation of MarqueeStrings

    public MarqueeString createMarqueeString(MarqueeItem item,
        int preferredWidth, int preferredHeight)
    {
        return new MarqueeString(item, preferredWidth,
            preferredHeight);
    }
```

```
// Create an instance of a MarqueeDriver - this enables subclasses
// of this applet to change the creation of MarqueeDrivers

    public MarqueeDriver createMarqueeDriver(MarqueeString marquee,
        MarqueeItem items[])
    {
        return new MarqueeDriver(marquee, items);
    }

    public MarqueeItem fetchMarqueeItem(int itemNumber)
    {

        int i;
        String parameter;

        String marqueeName;

        String fontName;
        int fontStyle;

        int fontHeight;

        int colorValue;
        Color color;

        int increment;
        int delay;
        int direction;

        marqueeName = fetchParameter("marqueeString", itemNumber);

// Try getting the font, if not there, default to TimesRoman

        fontName = fetchParameter("marqueeFont", itemNumber);
        if (fontName == null)
        {
            fontName = "TimesRoman";
        }

// Try getting the font height, otherwise, default to 24

        parameter = fetchParameter("marqueeFontHeight", itemNumber);

        if (parameter == null)
        {
            fontHeight = 24;
        }
        else
        {
            fontHeight = getIntParameter(parameter, 24);
        }


// Check for the font style parameters
```

(continues)

**Listing 22.11 Continued**

```
            fontStyle = 0;

            if (fetchParameter("marqueeFontPlain", itemNumber) != null)
            {
                fontStyle += Font.PLAIN;
            }

            if (fetchParameter("marqueeFontBold", itemNumber) != null)
            {
                fontStyle += Font.BOLD;
            }

            if (fetchParameter("marqueeFontItalic", itemNumber) != null)
            {
                fontStyle += Font.ITALIC;
            }


// Try getting the marquee color, default to black if not present

            parameter = fetchParameter("marqueeColor", itemNumber);
            if (parameter == null)
            {
                color = Color.black;
            }
            else
            {
                color = null;

// Try checking to see if it is a color name, first

                for (i=0; i < colorNames.length; i++)
                {
                    if (colorNames[i].equals(parameter))
                    {
                        color = colorValues[i];
                        break;
                    }
                }

// Otherwise, assume it is an RGB value, default to 0 if not a valid
// integer

                if (color == null)
                {
                    color = new Color(
                        getIntParameter(parameter, 0));
                }
            }

// try getting the scroll increment, default to 3 if not present

            parameter = fetchParameter("scrollIncrement", itemNumber);
            if (parameter == null)
```

```
        {
              increment = 3;
        }
        else
        {
              increment = getIntParameter(parameter, 3);
        }
// try getting the scroll delay, default to 100 if not present

        parameter = fetchParameter("scrollDelay", itemNumber);
        if (parameter == null)
        {
              delay = 100;
        }
        else
        {
              delay = getIntParameter(parameter, 100);
        }
// try getting the scroll direction, default to RIGHT_TO_LEFT if not
// present

        parameter = fetchParameter("scrollDirection", itemNumber);
        direction = MarqueeItem.RIGHT_TO_LEFT;
        if (parameter != null)
        {
              for (i=0; i < directionNames.length; i++)
              {
                   if (parameter.equals(directionNames[i]))
                   {
                         direction = directions[i];
                         break;
                   }
              }
        }
// Create a new marquee item

        return createMarqueeItem(marqueeName, color,
              new Font(fontName, fontStyle, fontHeight),
              increment, delay, direction);

    }
}
```

# Adding Sound

One of the nice features of Java is its support for multimedia applications.
You can add sound to an applet through the getAudioClip method. Once
you have an audio clip, you can play it with the play method, stop playing it
with the stop method, or play it in a continuous loop with the loop method.

You can add sound to the marquee very easily. Remember, back in the section titled "Making Flexible Classes," how all the marquee parameters were stored in a class called MarqueeItem? You can add audio parameters by creating an AudioMarqueeItem subclass (see listing 22.12).

**Listing 22.12  Source Code for *AudioMarqueeItem.java***

```java
import java.applet.*;
import java.awt.*;

public class AudioMarqueeItem extends MarqueeItem
{
        public AudioClip audioClip;      // the audio clip to play
        public boolean loopClip;         // should it be played once or looped?

        AudioMarqueeItem(String string, AudioClip clip, boolean loop)
        {
                super(string);
                audioClip = clip;
                loopClip = loop;
        }

// Set up a full constructor for creating a AudioMarqueeItem

        public AudioMarqueeItem(String string, Color color, Font font,
                int increment, int delay, int direction, AudioClip clip,
                boolean loop)
        {
                super(string, color, font, increment, delay, direction);
                audioClip = clip;
                loopClip = loop;
        }
}
```

The AudioMarqueeItem is a good example of adding additional parameters in a non-intrusive way. You can still pass an AudioMarqueeItem to the MarqueeString class; the audio information will just be ignored. To make use of the audio information in the AudioMarqueeItem, you need to make a version of the MarqueeString that supports it (see listing 22.13).

**Listing 22.13  Source Code for *AudioMarqueeString.java***

```java
import java.awt.*;
import java.applet.*;

// AudioMarqueeString
//
// This canvas scrolls a text string from right to left like a
// marquee sign.  It will also play audio clips along with the
// text.
```

```
public class AudioMarqueeString extends MarqueeString
{
    AudioClip currentClip;      // the clip currently playing

// The constructors for AudioMarqueeString are identical to those in
// MarqueeString because the audio-specific items are in the AudioMarqueeItem.

    public AudioMarqueeString(MarqueeItem newItem, int width, int height)
    {
        super(newItem, width, height);
    }

    public AudioMarqueeString(MarqueeItem newItem, int width, int height,
        MarqueeObserver newObserver)
    {
        super(newItem, width, height, newObserver);
    }

// When the item changes, check to see if the new one is an audio
// item and if so, play its audio clip if it has one.

    public synchronized void setMarqueeItem(MarqueeItem newItem)
    {

// Stop playing the old clip if we were playing one
        if (currentClip != null)
        {
            currentClip.stop();
        }

// change the marquee item in the super class

        super.setMarqueeItem(newItem);

// Check to see if this is an audio item
        if (newItem instanceof AudioMarqueeItem)
        {
            AudioMarqueeItem audioItem =
                                    (AudioMarqueeItem)newItem;
// Now see if it has an audio clip
            if (audioItem.audioClip != null)
            {
                currentClip = audioItem.audioClip;
                if (audioItem.loopClip)
                {
                    currentClip.loop();
                }
                else
                {
                    currentClip.play();
                }
            }
        }
    }
}
```

Notice how the AudioMarqueeString class deals almost exclusively with playing audio and is able to leave the rest up to the super class. One of the reasons that it requires so little code to add audio to the MarqueeString is that there is a special method called when the marquee item changes. This is a good example showing why you should try to separate the actions into separate methods. All you need now to play audio clips is an applet that creates an AudioMarqueeString (see listing 22.14).

**Listing 22.14  Source Code for *AudioMarqueeApplet.java***

```
import java.awt.*;
import java.applet.*;

// AudioMarqueeApplet
//
// This applet scrolls a text string from right to left like a
// marquee sign.

public class AudioMarqueeApplet extends MarqueeApplet
{
    public MarqueeItem createMarqueeItem(String marqueeName,
        Color color, Font font, int increment, int delay,
        int direction)
    {
        return new AudioMarqueeItem(marqueeName, color, font,
            increment, delay, direction,
            (AudioClip)null, false);
    }

    public MarqueeString createMarqueeString(MarqueeItem item,
        int preferredWidth, int preferredHeight)
    {
        return new AudioMarqueeString(item, preferredWidth,
            preferredHeight);
    }

    public MarqueeItem fetchMarqueeItem(int itemNumber)
    {

// The fetchMarqueeItem in the super class SHOULD return an
// AudioMarqueeItem
// because it will call createMarqueeItem, which this class overloads
// to create an AudioMarqueeItem.
        MarqueeItem originalItem = super.fetchMarqueeItem(itemNumber);

// Now, just in case something went wrong and originalItem is not an
// instance of an AudioMarqueeItem, just return it and ignore the
// audio parameters
        if (!(originalItem instanceof AudioMarqueeItem))
        {
            return originalItem;
```

```
            }

            AudioMarqueeItem item = (AudioMarqueeItem) originalItem;

// Get the name of the audio clip to play
            String clipName = fetchParameter("audioClip", itemNumber);

            if (clipName != null)
            {
// Try to load the clip
                item.audioClip = getAudioClip(getDocumentBase(),
                    clipName);
            }

// See if the clip should loop or not

            if (fetchParameter("loopAudioClip", itemNumber) != null)
            {
                item.loopClip = true;
            }
            else
            {
                item.loopClip = false;
            }

            return item;
        }
    }
```

Notice how easily the AudioMarqueeApplet adds audio support to the
MarqueeApplet. Because the MarqueeApplet uses separate methods for creating the different objects it uses, it is simple to make it use different objects.
Likewise, because it has a separate method for reading the parameters for an
item, it is easy to add support for additional parameters. ❖

# Part V

# Advanced Java

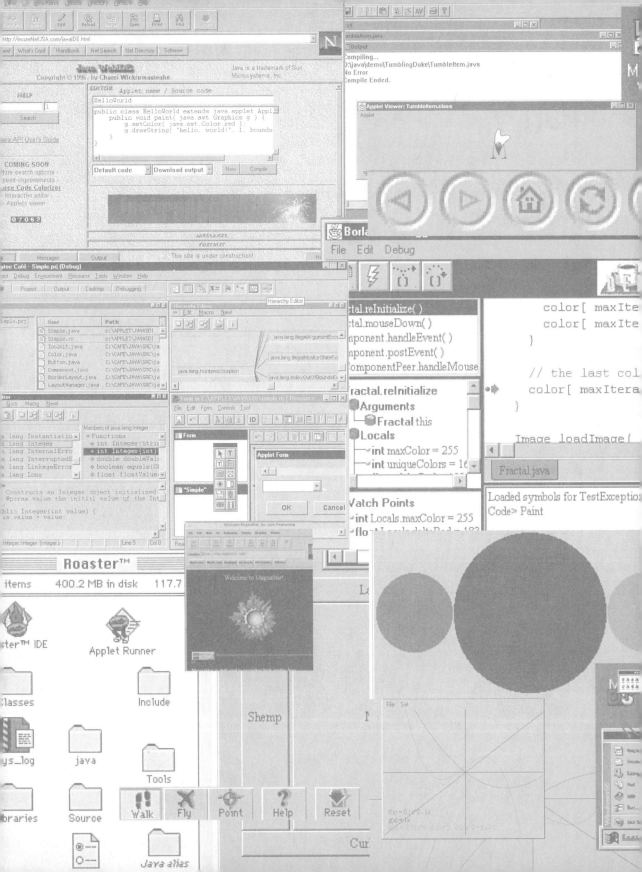

# CHAPTER 23

# Java Applications

Up until now, you have been looking at primarily Java applets. You can also build full-scale stand-alone applications using Java. In fact, the HotJava browser is itself a Java application.

Applications have a wider range of possibilities than applets do because they are not required to inherit from the `Applet` class. Java applications can do just about anything that can be done in a third-generation language (such as C, C++, Smalltalk, Ada, et. al.) limited only by the Java run-time security system.

Topics to be covered in this chapter include:

- Applications vs. Applets

  How Java applications differ from Java applets

- Creating Applications

  How to move from an original concept to a complete Java application

- Running Applications

  How to compile and run a Java application

- Refining Applications

  Applications can be refined and extended to include additional features

## Applications versus Applets

Applets require some third-party support in order to run. Applets always inherit from the AWT class `Applet`, itself a subclass of `Panel`.

Applications, on the other hand, can be run directly from the Java run-time interpreter. "Application" can actually be somewhat of a misleading name, as there isn't a single executable that the user can just go ahead and run.

◀ See "Writing
an Applet Ex-
plored," p. 293,
for more infor-
mation about
writing applets
in general.

What actually happens is that the run-time loads the specified class, as well as other clients of that class, and attempts to call the `main()` function on the class.

Or at least that's the way it works with the current tool set. In the future, look for compilers to be able to generate machine-dependent binaries which can be run as complete applications. These will almost certainly be necessary to acheive the level of performance expected of modern programming languages.

---

**Tip**

There's nothing to stop a class from being both an applet and an application. All you need to do is extend `Applet` and add a `main()` method. Any application that extends the `Panel` class may also be used as an applet—simply extend `Applet` instead of `Panel`.

---

# Building an Application

This section will show how to build a simple application, from a basic concept, through implementation, and finally, running the application. The following sections will build on this basic application by slowly adding complexity through new features.

Please note that all of the examples use the Java Developers Kit. If you are using the alpha3 release, you will need to make several changes to the code, especially where the AWT components are used.

## Coming Up with a Concept

The first step in writing any program is figuring out what the software is sup-posed to do. For personal projects, it's best to set some goals before starting, so you'll know when you're done. In industrial settings, the specification is likely to come in the form of customer requirements.

The example used here is a program that will help the user graph a quadratic equation, in the form of:

$$f(x) = ax^2 + bx + c$$

The concept in the first pass is to compute and print the values of $f(x)$ for $x$ between –10 and 10. This concept will be altered through the set of examples as more features are added to this basic application.

## Coding the Application

Implementation is the step of writing software based on the design. At this level, knowledge of the langauge is the most important element—to be able to come up with a reasonable way to implement the design using Java.

A required element is the `main()` method. `main()` must be a `public` and `static` method on one of the classes in the application, so that the Java runtime has some place to begin. Like `init()` on applets, `main()` is where you can perform your one-time initialization, including reading parameters, which, in the case of applications, come from the command line.

Here's the source code for the first pass of this example, broken down step by step to show exactly what's going on.

```java
public class QuadraticFormula
{
    static final float DEFAULT_MIN_X = -10.0f;
    static final float DEFAULT_MAX_X =  10.0f;
    static final float DEFAULT_INCREMENT = 0.25f;

    /* coefficients for the equation:  ax^2 + bx + c */

    float a;
    float b;
    float c;

    public static void main(String args[])
    {
        if (args.length < 3)
        {
            System.out.println("Usage: QuadraticFormula a b c");
            System.exit(1);
        }
        new QuadraticFormula(Float.valueOf(args[0]).floatValue(),
                        Float.valueOf(args[1]).floatValue(),
                        Float.valueOf(args[2]).floatValue());
    }

    QuadraticFormula(float coeff_a, float coeff_b, float coeff_c)
    {
        a = coeff_a;
        b = coeff_b;
        c = coeff_c;

        float x = DEFAULT_MIN_X;

        while (x <= DEFAULT_MAX_X)
        {
            System.out.println("x = " + x + "    \tf(x) = " +
calculate(x));
            x += DEFAULT_INCREMENT;
        }
    }

    float calculate(float x)
```

```
        {
            return (float) ((a * Math.pow(x, 2.0f)) + (b * x) + c);
        }
    }
```

The first few lines of the QuadraticFormula class declare the constants used by the class. These constants specify the range and the step size for the "x" values of the program. From an overhead standpoint, it's better to make constants static, so each instance of a class won't have to carry around a separate copy; although in this case, only one instance of the class will run at any given time.

Next come the instance variables, or attributes, of the class. Each instance of the class has a separate copy of these variables, which are independent from each other. These attributes are available to any non-static method in QuadraticFormula.

The main() method is the entry point of the application. In QuadraticFormula, it reads the command-line arguments (passed into main() as the parameter args), and creates an instance of the QuadraticFormula class using the command-line parameters. Once the constructor has exited, main() reaches its end, and the application will terminate.

> **Note**
>
> Why not run the whole program from main()?
>
> Because main() is a static method, there is no actual QuadraticFunction object, so main() can't access any of the attributes or the non-static calculate() method.

For the simple example, there's no reason not to just run the entire program from within the constructor of QuadraticFunction, except the part where the equation is evaluated—it makes more sense to break that out into a separate method, which is called calculate(). This will make even more sense in the later examples.

The QuadraticFormula constructor begins by copying the initialization parameters into the attributes of the new object. The remainder of the constructor runs through a loop, which calculates the value of the quadratic equation for a series of values of x, printing the result of each calculation to the user's standard output (usually a terminal).

The calculate() method performs the actual calculation of the quadratic equation. The result is cast to float before the return because the default result of the equation is of type double, and the javac compiler will produce a warning unless there is an explicit cast down to a float.

QuadraticFunction uses three standard library classes: Float, System, and Math, all of which are imported by default from the java.lang package, so no import statements are necessary.

Note that instead of using the power function from the Math class, the $x^2$ term could have been expressed simply as (x*x). However, the power function will be needed by later examples, so it's best to just leave it in.

## Running the Application

Once you have written the code file (for the sake of convenience assume it is called QuadraticFunction.java), you will need to compile it into byte codes, and then call the Java run-time interpreter.

The following instructions assume that you are using the javac compiler from the Java Developer's Kit (JDK):

  **1.** Compile the QuadraticFunction.java source code into bytecodes:

  ```
  javac QuadraticFunction.java
  ```

  **2.** Run the application with the java run-time interpreter:

  ```
  java QuadraticFunction a b c
  ```

Replace "a," "b," and "c" in step 2 with the corresponding coeffecients. Figure 23.1 shows part of the output when run with the parameters –0.1 1 0 (i.e.,–.1$x^2$ + x).

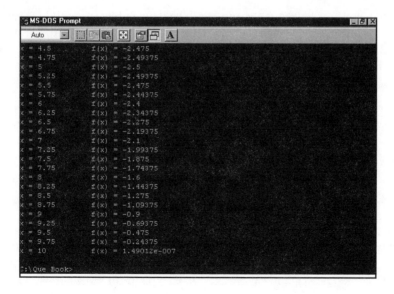

**Fig. 23.1**
Output of: java QuadraticFunction –0.1 1 0 (i.e., –.1$x^2$ + x).

**V**

**Advanced Java**

### Testing the Application Components

Because any class can have `main()` defined, it's possible to design an application where classes are self-testing; for example, each class defines `main()` as a test driver.

So far, there's only a single class, so this doesn't come into play yet.

### Refining the Application

At some point during the development of an application you are likely to come across things that need changing in one way or another.

Concept or requirement changes are common in commercial products, as the end customer may change his or her mind, or may change or add features that only come to mind later. It's best to try and develop the design and implementation with the possibility of requirement changes in mind. The second and third examples in this chapter reflect changes in the concept of the application.

Design changes occur either as a result of requirement changes, errors in the original design, or the designer noticing additional relationships between classes that may not have been evident during the previous design phase. A common case is the modification of inheritance and interface hierarchies to help generalize classes for increased flexibility and reuse potential, as in this chapter's third example.

Implementation changes come from design changes, bug fixes, and rewrites to make code cleaner or more efficient. Once an application is fairly stable, you should try to minimize implementation changes, as each section of code you change will need to be retested; so try to make modifications only when necessary.

Never be afraid to jump back to a previous stage when it's called for. During design or implementation you may uncover missing, conflicting, or unclear requirements. The moral is to never lock yourself into following a set sequence of events—building software is an art, not a science.

# Adding a User Interface

◀ See p. 405, "AWT," for in-depth information about the Advanced Window Toolkit.

A simple text dump of values is all right, but wouldn't a graph of the equation be nicer to look at? The Java language has a built-in graphical user interface (GUI) library, called the Advanced Window Toolkit (AWT), which allows developers to create graphical displays that are platform-independent. Other than adding the graphics, the bulk of the class is built off of the original `QuadraticFormula` above.

```java
import java.awt.*;

public class QuadraticGraph extends Frame
{
    static final float DEFAULT_MIN_X = -10.0f;
    static final float DEFAULT_MAX_X =  10.0f;
    static final float DEFAULT_MIN_Y = -10.0f;
    static final float DEFAULT_MAX_Y =  10.0f;

    /* coefficients for the equation:  ax^2 + bx + c */

    float a;
    float b;
    float c;

    public static void main(String args[])
    {
        if (args.length < 3)
        {
            System.out.println("Usage: QuadraticGraph a b c");
            System.exit(1);
        }

        new QuadraticGraph(Float.valueOf(args[0]).floatValue(),
                           Float.valueOf(args[1]).floatValue(),
                           Float.valueOf(args[2]).floatValue());
    }

    QuadraticGraph(float coeff_a, float coeff_b, float coeff_c)
    {
        super("Quadratic Equation");
        setTitle("Quadratic Equation");

        /* Initialize variables */

        a = coeff_a;
        b = coeff_b;
        c = coeff_c;

        /* Create a generic menu */

        MenuBar menu = new MenuBar();
        Menu m = new Menu("File");
        m.add(new MenuItem("Exit"));
        menu.add(m);
        setMenuBar(menu); // install this menu bar in the frame
        /* draw the graph */

        resize(400, 400);  /* setting a default window size */
        show();
    }

    public void paint(Graphics g)
    {
        int height = size().height - 50;
        int width  = size().width;
```

```
/* clear background */

g.clearRect(0, 0, width, height);

/* draw x-axis and y-axis */

g.setColor(Color.black);

int x_pixel = (int) (-DEFAULT_MIN_X * width /
                    (DEFAULT_MAX_X - DEFAULT_MIN_X));
int y_pixel = (int) (-DEFAULT_MIN_Y * height /
                    (DEFAULT_MAX_Y - DEFAULT_MIN_Y));

if ((x_pixel >= 0) && (x_pixel <= width))
{
    g.drawLine(x_pixel, 0, x_pixel, height);
}

if ((y_pixel >= 0) && (y_pixel <= width))
{
g.drawLine(0, y_pixel, width, y_pixel);
}

/* Draw curve */

g.setColor(Color.red);

x_pixel = 0;
float x = (DEFAULT_MAX_X - DEFAULT_MIN_X) * ((x_pixel /
➥width) - 0.5f);
y_pixel = (int) (height / (DEFAULT_MAX_Y - DEFAULT_MIN_Y) *
                (DEFAULT_MAX_Y - calculate(x)));

if ((y_pixel >= 0) && (y_pixel <= height))
{
    g.drawLine(x_pixel, y_pixel, x_pixel, y_pixel);
}

x_pixel += 1;

while (x_pixel <= width)
{
    int last_y = y_pixel;
    x = (DEFAULT_MAX_X - DEFAULT_MIN_X) *
        (((float) x_pixel / width) - 0.5f);
    y_pixel = (int) (height / (DEFAULT_MAX_Y -
    ➥DEFAULT_MIN_Y) *
                    (DEFAULT_MAX_Y - calculate(x)));

    if ((y_pixel >= 0) && (y_pixel <= height))
    {
        if ((last_y >= 0) && (last_y <= height))
        {
            g.drawLine(x_pixel - 1, last_y, x_pixel,
            ➥y_pixel);
        }

        else
```

```
            {
                g.drawLine(x_pixel, y_pixel, x_pixel, y_pixel);
            }
        }
        x_pixel += 1;
    }

    String equation = "f(x) = ";

    if (a != 0)
    {
        equation = equation + a + "x^2";

        if (b < 0)
        {
            equation = equation + " - " + (-b) + "x";
        }

        else if (b > 0)
        {
            equation = equation + " + " + b + "x";
        }

        if (c < 0)
        {
            equation = equation + " - " + (-c);
        }

        else if (c > 0)
        {
            equation = equation + " + " + c;
        }
    }

    else if (b != 0)
    {
        equation = equation + b + "x";

        if (c < 0)
        {
            equation = equation + " - " + (-c);
        }

        else if (c > 0)
        {
            equation = equation + " + " + c;
        }
    }

    else
    {
        equation = equation + c;
    }

    g.drawString(equation, 10, height-10);
}
```

```
float calculate(float x)
{
    return (float) ((a * Math.pow(x, 2.0f)) + (b * x) + c);
}

public boolean handleEvent(Event e)
{

    if ((e.id == Event.ACTION_EVENT) && (e.target instanceof
MenuItem))
    {
        if (((MenuItem) e.target).getLabel().equals("Exit"))
        {
            System.exit(0);
        }
    }

    return false;
    }
}
```

To use the graphics libraries, the AWT package has to be included. By using the asterisk (*) on the end, the import statement tells the javac compiler to import all classes in the package; otherwise, for this example, there would have to be separate import statements for java.awt.Frame, java.awt.Graphics, java.awt.Color, java.awt.Menu, and java.awt.MenuBar. As applications use more and more components from a single package, it begins to make more sense to include the entire package, rather than individual components.

The QuadraticGraph class inherits from the AWT component Frame, so all instances of QuadraticGraph are also Frames.

Minimum and maximum values of y are included as new constants so that the graph will have a "clipping" area defined, that is, a set region of values to draw. Since the formula will be evaluated on a pixel-by-pixel basis, there is no need for a default step size for x.

The super() method used in the constructor passes arguments to the constructor of the base class, in this case, Frame. super() must be the first command inside of a constructor. The setTitle() method is unnecessary because the Frame constructor should set the title.

A menu bar is added to the window. It has a single menu, "File," with a single option, "Exit." To see how to include multiple menus and multiple options under each menu, skip ahead to the third example in this chapter.

The paint() method is called every time the window is exposed, moved, or resized. That's why size() is called each time—to ensure that paint() will take the current window size into account. The height subtracts 50 pixels for the window's title and menu bars, as size() returns the size of the whole frame, not just the drawing area.

Think of the frame as a canvas. If you don't actually remove what was there before, it won't disappear on it's own. Calling clearRect( ) clears the entire drawing area so old and new lines won't be displayed over each other.

After drawing the x-axis and the y-axis, the first point, if it falls within the range of acceptable y minimum and maximum, is drawn. Because the line will be drawn pixel by pixel, instead of figuring out x_pixel from x, x is figured out from x_pixel. The value of y simply equals calculate(x), so this just skips a step and computes y_pixel directly from x.

The following loop performs the same calculations as above for each x pixel for the entire width of the frame. The current pixel will only be shown if it's within the maximum and minimum values of y. If the last value of y was shown, then a line is drawn from the last pixel to the current pixel; otherwise, only the current pixel is drawn.

The end of the paint() routine uses drawString() to display the text representation of the equation in the lower-left corner of the window.

handleEvent() will be called every time any GUI event occurs. The only event that QuadraticGraph is interested in is when the sole menu item is selected, in which case it exits the application. The return value is false to indicate that the event was not processed—this will only return if the program does not exit.

Figure 23.2 shows the finished product.

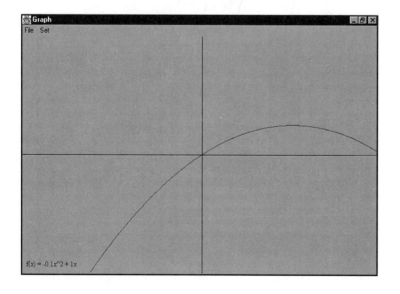

**Fig. 23.2**
A picture is worth a thousand words.

# Refining the Application

The previous example is indeed an improvement on the first pass, but it still seems too dependent on a specific type of problem, namely a quadratic equation.

Wouldn't it be nicer to have a more generic graphing tool that could handle different types of equations? Or more than one equation at a time?

This example is going to implement these ideas, and one or two others, to show a few more useful programming techniques as well as to illustrate how refining an application can make for better software.

Introduced in this example are the following items:

■ Using interfaces and inheritance to produce more generic code

■ More AWT components

Graph.java is the third example file. You will note that it is considerably larger than the others, mostly because it's doing quite a bit more. Because of its size, there won't be a line-by-line description of the file—only the highlights will be pointed out.

## Equation

The first change is that the code for calculating the equation has been moved out of the `Graph` class. An interface (Equation) is the new way to access `calculate()`, and a few other new methods:

```
interface Equation
{
    void setEquation();
    float calculate(float x);
    boolean isValid();
    String toString();
    Color getColor();
}
```

Take a quick look at the other functions:

■ `setEquation()` is the way each `Equation` object can set or update the equation that it represents.

■ `isValid()` returns whether there is a valid equation to be displayed.

■ `toString()` creates a text representation of the equation.

■ `getColor()` returns the color that should be used to draw the curve. (Needed because there can be more than one equation displayed at a time.)

The `EquationDialog` class implements some of these methods, but leaves others to its subclasses, so `EquationDialog` must be declared as `abstract`.

```
abstract class EquationDialog extends Dialog implements Equation
```

EquationDialog also extends the `Dialog` class. This gives the class the ability to pop up a window to accept user input, which the `EquationDialog` sub-classes will use to set their equations.

```
class QuadraticEquation extends EquationDialog
class PolynomialEquation extends EquationDialog
```

There are two subclasses of `EquationDialog`: `QuadraticEquation` and `PolynomialEquation`. The former uses much of the code from the previous example, simply regrouped under the new interface. `PolynomialEquation` is a more generic type of equation, which can accept coefficients for any polynomial equation up to order $x^9$.

In both cases, the interesting parts are the `setEquation()` and `action()` methods. `setEquation()` finishes the layout of the dialog that was started by the `EquationDialog` constructor and then displays the dialog. `action()` responds to the buttons being clicked—simply closing the window on "Cancel;" setting the equation to invalid and closing the window on "Don't Show;" and parsing, validating, and storing the input and closing the window on "OK."

Looking at the `EquationDialog` constructor, you can see the layout of the buttons on the bottom of the pop-up window:

```
Panel p = new Panel();
add("South", p);
p.add(new Button("OK"));
p.add(new Button("Cancel"));
p.add(new Button("Don't Show"));
```

The `setEquation()` methods in the subclasses (the following fragment is from `PolynomialEquation`) add a few more screen elements—text boxes, one editable, the other not:

```
Panel p = new Panel();
add("Center", p);
t = new TextField("Enter coefficients separated by spaces:");
t.setEditable(false);
t.setBackground(Color.lightGray);
p.add(t);
t = new TextField(current, 20);
t.setEditable(true);
t.setBackground(Color.lightGray);
p.add(t);
```

Figure 23.3 shows the layout of the PolynomialEquation dialog.

The other method of note is `action()`, which is called whenever there is a GUI event. In this example, the code is looking for when any of the buttons are pressed:

**Fig. 23.3**

Changing the equation on the fly.

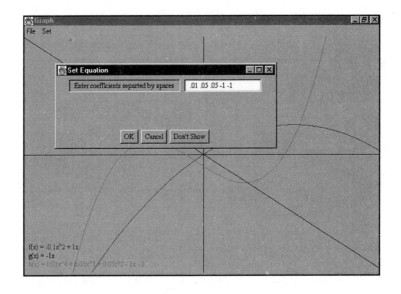

```java
public boolean action(Event e, Object obj)
{
    if ("OK".equals(obj))
    {
        String coefficients = t.getText();
        ...
        valid_equation = true;
        hide();
        return true;
    }

    if ("Cancel".equals(obj))
    {
        hide();
        return true;
    }

    if ("Don't Show".equals(obj))
    {
        valid_equation = false;
        hide();
        return true;
    }

    return true;
}
```

The code for the "OK" portion is actually much more detailed than shown here, as this is where the validation and storage of the new equation is performed. For any of the buttons, `hide()` is called to remove the dialog from the screen.

## Graph

The Graph class contains the drawing information from the QuadraticGraph class and adds support for multiple equations to be displayed at once. It also adds the ability to spawn off other Graph objects, each with its own thread of execution.

```
MenuBar menu = new MenuBar();
Menu m = new Menu("File");
m.add(new MenuItem("Close"));
m.add(new MenuItem("Exit"));
menu.add(m);
m = new Menu("Set");
m.add(new MenuItem("f(x)"));
m.add(new MenuItem("g(x)"));
m.add(new MenuItem("h(x)"));
menu.add(m);
setMenuBar(menu);
```

This shows how to create multiple menus and multiple items under each menu. Each menu, and each menu item under each menu, shows up in the order in which it is added (left to right or top to bottom, as appropriate).

```
Equation function_f;
Equation function_g;
Equation function_h;
```

These are the attributes used to keep track of the multiple equations. Note that each of these could hold any object that implements the Equation interface, and in fact, the Graph constructor uses two different classes to initialize these objects:

```
function_f = new QuadraticEquation(this, Color.red);
function_g = new QuadraticEquation(this, Color.blue);
function_h = new PolynomialEquation(this, Color.green);
```

Figure 23.4 shows the Graph class with all three functions displayed at the same time.

---

### Static vs. Dynamic Association

It's probably not a good idea to hard-code the Equation constructors inside of the Graph class—it makes the Graph class that much less configurable.

How would you fix this?

One approach could be to pass three Equation objects in the constructor of Graph. Another may be to include setFunctionF(), and so on, methods in the Graph class—this will be shown in the fourth and final example. Other possibilites surely exist.

(continues)

(continued)

This is a general class of object-oriented problems, which have to be solved on a case-by-case basis—is it better to define associations between classes at compile time (static associations) or at runtime (dynamic associations)? The answer each time will depend on the specific classes and the specific problem domain.

**Fig. 23.4**
The Graph class allows up to three functions to be displayed at once.

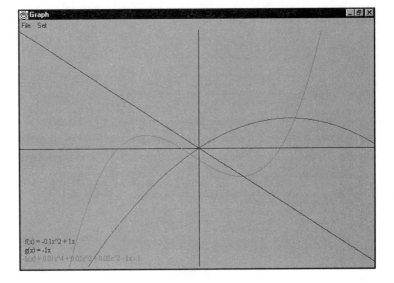

## More Refinement

There are many more improvements that can be made to this example application; some of which, in no particular order, are

- Modifying the Graph constructor to allow Equations to be dynamically attached rather than having a hard-coded set.

- Moving the graphing area and equation displays into separate panels so they don't overwrite each other.

- Using threads to create multiple windows, each with an independent instance of the Graph class.

- Adding comprehensive error-checking and recovery. The current version assumes the user is going to be "good" about entering data.

- More sublasses of `EquationDialog`. How about one that will read in a complete formula (in terms of "x") and generate the appropriate equation (for example, something that could parse: "x^2 + sin(x/2)")?

- Using command-line parameters to specify the scaling of the graph, rather than just using the defaults.
- Writing an event handler for mouse actions so that Graph will show the "y" values of each equation for the current mouse "x."

These are only a few ways in which you can work with this example to create bigger and better applications. Or you may be ready to try an idea or two of your own now that you have the basic feel of writing applications.

The final example is the last pass at the Graph application. The new features are

- Allowing Graph to dynamically add Equation objects
- Creating a GraphApp class as an entry point, so `main()` doesn't have to be rewritten for each configuration of Graph
- Making the Graph class an "appletcation," that is, a class that can be used either as an applet or as an application.

Again, because of the length of the code, there won't be a line-by-line description of the classes.

---

**Note**

Two files are needed because only one class may be decalred "public" in any given Java source file. `GraphApp`, the entry point for the application, must be public so you can call `main()` on it. `Graph` must also be public so it can be used as an applet.

These files are in their own directory because the name Graph.java conflicts with an earlier example.

---

The biggest change is to the Graph class:

```
public class Graph extends Applet
```

Instead of `Frame`, `Graph` now inherits from `Applet`. This will allow the `Graph` class to be used as an applet in an HTML document; however, it also means that `Graph` can no longer control its own menus. Later, you'll see the menus in the `GraphApp` class.

Four methods have been added to Graph:

- `init()`
- `setFunctionF()`
- `setFunctionG()`
- `setFunctionH()`

The first, init(), will be used only when the Graph class is treated as an applet. This will read in the parameters and initialize the equations accordingly. Since Graph doesn't have menus, this version of Graph will not be able to change the equations when used as an applet, so the equations had better be specified through the initialization parameters.

The other three methods are quite simple—they set the appropriate equation equal to the one passed into the function.

One method has been removed from Graph—main(). When Graph is used in an application, it would be better for some Window-based class (as opposed to a Panel-based class such as Applet) to be the entry point, so menus can be added to the user interface. Besides, this allows several different classes to use Graph without having to compile a separate version of Graph for each of its clients.

```
void setEquation(String s);
```

The Equation interface has been modified to include an overloaded version of setEquation(), which takes in a String argument. Rather than popping open a dialog window to prompt the user, this method will create an equation based on the supplied String.

Moving over to the GraphApp.java file, there is only the GraphApp class declared. Note that all of the classes and interfaces used by GraphApp have to be specified with the import statements at the top of the file.

GraphApp keeps a copy of the same Equation objects it passes to Graph. Because all objects are passed by reference, both GraphApp and Graph point to the exact same Equation objects. When any Equation is modified, both the GrapApp and the Graph objects will see the modifications.

GraphApp contains a Graph object and adds it to the visual display using the add() method.

You can compile both files at once, if you wish:

```
javac Graph.java GraphApp.java
```

To run as an application, use GraphApp as the starting class:

```
java GraphApp
```

This should actually run just the same as the previous example, except that not only are the types of the equations preset (in this case, they're all PolynomialEquation objects), but the initial values of the functions are also initialized.

To run Graph as an applet, copy the graph.html file into your working directory, and use either the Applet Viewer, or your Java-enabled web browser (such as Netscape Navigator) to view the HTML file. Figure 23.5 shows Netscape navigator displaying the graph.java file found on the CD-ROM. Naturally, you can produce different graphs by changing the parameters in the applet declaration in the HTML file.

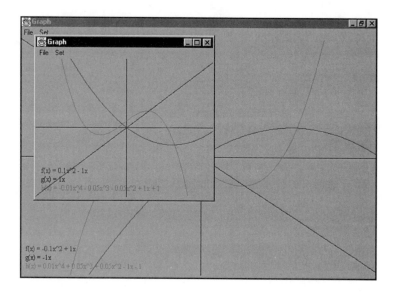

**Fig. 23.5**
Netscape Navigator displaying the graph.html file.

V

**Advanced Java**

# CHAPTER 24

# Managing Applications

*by Joseph L. Weber*

Java applications are a very powerful way to deliver your Java programs. Before you can use Java applications, however, you have to know how to install them. This chapter discusses how to install and maintain applications. The chapter also provides directions for turning your applets into applications.

In this chapter, you learn to do the following things:

- Install applications
- Maintain multiple applications on the same system
- Troubleshoot applications when something goes wrong
- Convert an applet to an application
- Package an application to deliver to your clients

## Installing Applications

Java applications come in many forms, but this chapter discusses the two most common: applications that come packaged as a series of `.class files`, and applications that come as a `single .zip` file.

> **Caution**
>
> When you install someone else's Java applications, you are giving up the security protection that you are guaranteed with an applet. Giving up this security is not necessarily a bad thing; in fact, you may *need* to violate it. Just be aware that installing random Java applications can expose you to all the problems that you may encounter with traditional software schemes, such as viruses and other malicious software.

## Installing Applications from *.class* Files

Installing an application that comes as a set of `.class` files is a bit less entangling than installing applications for `.zip` files. In time, most applications will come with their own installation programs, but for now, you must perform the installation manually.

### Create a Directory for the Application

First, you need to designate a directory in which to place your Clock. This directory need not be associated with the directory where you put your Java JDK. Having a deployment plan for your applications is important, however. This plan can be the same one that you use for installing more traditional programs, such as Netscape, or for installing something unique to your Java applications.

> **Caution**
>
> Keeping backup copies of applications that you value is important. Don't expect applications to become corrupted, but don't ignore that possibility, either.

### Copy the Files

After you create the directory in which you want to place the application, copy all the `.class` files to it. You should make sure you maintain any directory structure that has already been set up for the application. If you have subdirectories for packages, make sure that you keep the classes in them.

> **Note**
>
> To copy an entire subdirectory on a DOS machine, use the following command:
>
> ```
> xcopy c:\original\directory\*.class
> c:\destination\directory /s
> ```
>
> On UNIX machines, the command is
>
> ```
> cp -r /original/directory /destination/directory
> ```

> **Caution**
>
> If you are deploying an application that you have written, and you are still updating the program, don't make your working copy the same one that you have users accessing. If you happen to be compiling your application at the same time that a user tries to start it, unexpected and undesirable effects may occur.

### Make Sure That Everything Works

Now make sure that everything is running the way that it should. Go to the directory in which you placed the Clock application, and type **Java Clock**. If everything is going as planned, a clock window should appear on-screen as shown in figure 24.1. If not, something has gone wrong; make sure that you followed all the procedures correctly. You should also make sure that you have the Java executable in your path. If you have been following through the rest of the book, and you have installed the Java Developer Kit, the Java executable should already be in your path.

**Fig. 24.1**
The Clock application as it appears under Solaris.

V

Advanced Java

## Finishing the Installation

After you copy all the .class files to the correct directory, the next task is to create a script or batch file that you will use to run the application.

You can automate this process so that your users don't always have to type **Java Clock**. Your users will be much happier if they can just type **Clock** to invoke the Clock program, without having to also type **Java**. Making this possible, however, takes you in a different direction, depending on your platform. Ideally, you will be able to follow the same path that you would use for UNIX and Windows 95/NT.

## Finishing Installing Applications for UNIX

In explaining how to install an application under UNIX, this section specifically covers how to do this under Solaris 2.4 using Korn shell. Your implementation may differ slightly, based on your particular operating system and shell.

### Create a Wrapper Script

Automating the usage of a Java application under UNIX is done by creating a Wrapper Script. The Wrapper Script is essentially a standard script file that "wraps" all the commands for a Java Application together. The first task is creating the script. You can create the script with vi, nedit, or your favorite text editor. Listing 24.1 shows an example script for Clock. Note that there are several variables you may need to change for your particular installation.

---

**Listing 24.1    Clock**

```
#Add the applications directory to the CLASSPATH
#set to the directory you have placed the application
#Note, I insert the application directory first to avoid
#having classes from other applications getting called first

CLASSPATH=/ns-home/docs/que/Clock/:$CLASSPATH

#Set the location in which you hold java.
#This directory is probably the same as below
#If you have java in your global path, this line is
#not really necessary

Java_Home=/optl/java/bin/java

#Specify the name of the application.
#Important: Remember this is the name of the class, not the
#file

App=Clock

#Now run the actual program.
#If you have any additional parameters which you need to
#pass to the application, you can add them here.

$Java_Home $App
```

---

### Test the Script

Copy the text from listing 24.1 to a file called Clock, and make sure that the script is functioning correctly. To test it, simply type the name of the wrapper script, as follows:

```
Clock &
```

Your application should start and look something like figure 24.2; if it doesn't, make sure that you made the script executable. You can make the script executable by typing the following:

```
chmod a+x Clock
```

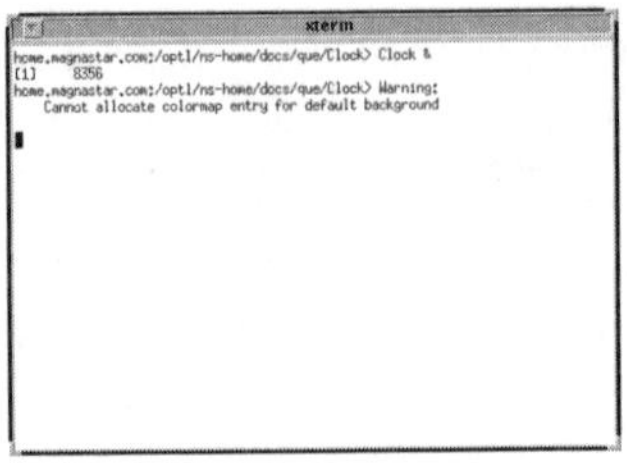

**Fig. 24.2**

Type the name of the wrapper script to test the Clock application.

Don't do this if you don't want everyone to execute your script. If that is the case, check with your system administrator to determine the proper setting to use for chmod.

### Copy the Script to a Common Location

It is probably a good idea to place your new wrapper script in the /usr/bin directory so that anyone who has access to the system can run the new script.

## Finishing Installing an Application for Windows

This section discusses how to install applications under Windows 95. Aside from a few particulars, the procedures are the same under Windows NT.

You can install an application under Windows in two ways: by creating a batch file, or by using the .pif file.

### Create a Wrapper Batch File

To install the application with a batch file, use your favorite editor. You can use the Edit command supplied with DOS, Notepad under Windows, or any other text editor. Create a batch file called Clock.bat that contains the lines shown in listing 24.2.

**Tip**

If your application does not use the Windows environment, or if you need to be able to see the output on System.out, use java instead of javaw.

**Listing 24.2   Clock.bat**

```
rem add the location where java.exe is located. If it
rem is already in your path don't add this line.
rem change c:\java\bin to the directory you have
rem installed for the JDK - see chapter 3

set PATH=%PATH%;c:\java\bin

rem Set this line to be the directory where your new
rem application is located.

set CLASSPATH = c:\appdir\;%CLASSPATH%

rem Run the actual application, change the applClass to be
rem the correct class for the application you are installing

javaw applClass
```

### Troubleshooting

If your application does not run, and you see an error message similar to `Can't find class classname`, first make sure that the .zip file is included in your `CLASSPATH` variable. Next, make sure that the length of the `CLASSPATH` variable does not exceed the maximum limit, which on Windows machines is 128 characters.

### Caution

Despite the documentation provided with java.exe at Sun's **www.javasoft.com** site and that given when you type **java**, *CLASSPATH* on Windows machines is not separated by a colon (:). The separation between the elements in the CLASSPATH is accomplished with a semicolon (;). In short, the syntax of *CLASSPATH* is the same syntax that you use to set your *PATH* variable.

Wrong syntax:

```
set CLASSPATH=c:\java\lib\classes.zip:c:\application\
```

Correct syntax:

```
CLASSPATH=c:\java\lib\classes.zip;c:\application\
```

### Test the Batch File

To run the application, type **Clock** at a DOS prompt. The application should start as shown in figure 24.3. Pay special attention to any extra parameters that you have to send to the application. Note that since Clock is a DOS batch file, it is actually case-insensitive, so you can run the file as Clock, clock or cLOCK if you would like.

**Fig. 24.3**
The Clock application running under windows.

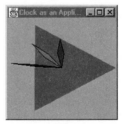

### Add the Application to Windows

To add this batch file to your Windows environment, switch back to the Windows environment (if necessary), and select the folder in which you want to place the application. Make sure you can actually see the folder's contents, not just the folder icon.

Now create a new shortcut (<u>F</u>ile, <u>N</u>ew, <u>S</u>hortcut). Fill in the information for your new batch file (in this case **c:\que\Clock.bat**), and specify the name under which you want the application to appear on your desktop. The short-cut window should appear as shown in figure 24.4.

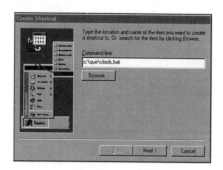

**Fig. 24.4**
The shortcut window appears after you add the Clock batch file.

When you finish creating the shortcut, double-click it. An MS-DOS window appears, and your Clock should start. Now, if you're like most people, having a DOS window pop up in order to start an application is downright annoy-ing. Normally you don't care what is going to System.out, and having a big black obstruction on the screen causes most people to just close the window. Here are a few pointers to make this a bit less obtrusive to you and your users.

To make the MS-DOS window less obtrusive, first, stop the DOS window from appearing on the screen and second, have the DOS window exit on its own as soon as the Java application has started. To make these changes, open the properties for your new application. Right-click on the Clock icon. A pop-up menu should appear. Choose P<u>r</u>operties from this menu.

The properties window shown in figure 24.5 should appear. Now switch to the Program tab. Change the <u>R</u>un option to Minimized; this will make it so that the DOS Window does not appear. Next, select Close on E<u>x</u>it, which will force the DOS session to exit automatically after the Java application has started. Finally, click OK.

Now, if you double-click the Clock icon, the application starts without the obtrusive DOS window.

### Add Applications to Windows Another Way
The other method of adding an application to Windows requires you to know the following:

1. Where `java.exe` is located.  Alternatively, `java.exe` must be in the path.

2. Where the `classes.zip` file is located

3. Where your new application is located

**Fig. 24.5**
In the Properties
Window, change
the Run option
and select Close
on Exit.

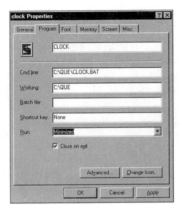

First, select the folder in which you want your new application to appear.
Then create a new shortcut, as described in the preceding section. When you
are prompted to enter the command line option, however, enter the following line as seen in figure 24.6:

```
c:\java\bin\javaw.exe -classpath c:\java\lib\classes.zip;c:\appDir\
➥applicationClass
```

**Fig. 24.6**
Enter the complete
command line
in the Create
Shortcut window.

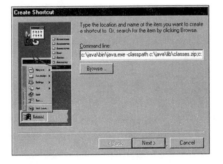

You want to replace all the directories and the class name with the ones that
apply to your application. If your application does not seem to load, try using
java.exe instead of javaw.exe. javaw.exe is an alternative version of Java that
returns right away and ignores all the error messages that ordinarily are generated when an application starts. javaw.exe is great for abstracting your users
from what is going on, but it makes it difficult to see what is really happening
when things don't work correctly.

**Caution**

When you use the `-classpath` variable, you must be careful to include the classes.zip file in java\lib. Not including this file makes it impossible for any application to start.

## Installing Applications from a *classes.zip* File

With the advent of JDK 2, support was added to deliver Java applications with a `single.zip` file. This addition makes it easier to deliver an application, because only the zip file and the wrapper are required. In fact, as more and more applications are delivered to market, they undoubtedly will use this method for distribution.

When you install an application from a zip file, be aware of the following things:

- When you run an application from a zip file, you must include the file in the CLASSPATH environment variable. You must actually specify the zip file, not just the path in which the file is located.

- When you include multiple applets in your CLASSPATH variable, make sure that the applications that you are installing do not use classes that have the same name but refer to different classes.

The second point here is important. Suppose that you have the applet SkyTune installed in CLASSPATH. SkyToon, which calculates the likelihood that the sky will fall today, has a class called Tune, which deals with the color of the sky. You also have an applet called CDTunes installed; you use this applet to play music CDs in your CD-ROM drive. CDTunes has a class called Tune that handles all the audio input and output from the CD. What happens in this situation where two applications have a class called Tune? When you run CDTunes, the Java interpreter looks down your class path, finds the first instance of the class Tune, finds the class in SkyToons...and chokes.

You can prevent this problem by carefully naming all your classes and/or putting them in packages. If you are running someone else's program, however, there is no guarantee that this problem won't occur. You need to be aware of the possibility in case your applications stop working one day. (You may have this problem when you run applications that come in .class form, too, but the problem is a bit more obvious when it occurs.)

Now you are ready to install an application sent in zip format. Although zip-distributed classes are somewhat trickier to deal with in a management sense than .class distributions, you have to make only one change in your wrapper script or batch file.

If you are using UNIX, refer to the script in listing 24.1, and make the following change:

```
CLASSPATH="/ns-home/docs/appDir/:$CLASSPATH"
```

to

```
CLASSPATH="/ns-home/docs/appDir/application.zip:$CLASSPATH"
```

If you are using Windows, refer to the batch file in listing 24.2, and make the following change:

```
set CLASSPATH = c:\appdir\;%CLASSPATH%
```

to

```
set CLASSPATH = c:\appdir\application.zip;%CLASSPATH%
```

These examples assume that the zip file that you received with the application is called `application.zip`. In reality, the file probably is called `classes.zip`. The examples simply demonstrate the fact that the file may have any name.

# Maintaining Multiple Applications on the Same System

Maintaining multiple Java applications on a single system is not as simple as maintaining several normal programs compiled in binary code, for the following reasons:

- Java byte code depends on the Virtual Machine. As a result, changes in the VM can cause bugs to appear and disappear in all your Java programs.
- Java programs are not compiled to a single file. Each class for the program is contained in its own file. Code is installed based on its class name.
- Java applications that reuse parts of other programs are affected if those other programs are changed.

You can solve the last two problems yourself. The first problem, however, will have to be resolved by the Virtual Machine vendors.

Consider an example situation. You have been using a Java-based word processor for months. One night, you or your system administrator installs a new version of Java. This new version of Java is 300 times faster (which is the minimum that you can expect from the next generation of VMs), but it has an interesting side effect: it switches the characters *a* and *z*. This switch probably is the result of a bug, but what happens to your word processor? Worse, what happens if you don't notice the change for a few days, and you have saved several old documents in the new format? Only one thing can completely prevent such an event: don't upgrade without making absolutely certain that your new Java machine is 100 percent compatible with previous versions. Developers working before the final Java release went through some growing pains with each new release of the JDK (from JDK pre-beta to JDK 1, and so on. Lest you be scared off from upgrading your VM, most of the problems were very minor, but they almost always required a small code change, and if you don't have the source code, you may not have this luxury.

The second problem deals with the fact that Java is compiled to files that bear the name `Something.class`. Each class for an applet is contained in its own `.class` file, and each application can contain dozens of class files.

With each of your Java applications having dozens of classes, it's difficult to avoid using applications that have one or more classes bearing the same name as classes from another application. One solution is to place the classes in packages and give each of the packages a unique name. What happens, though, when package names overlap? This situation is not likely to occur if you follow good programming practice, but you may not be able to avoid the problem entirely.

To prevent this class name problem from crashing your applications, you should always place the current application directory or zip file at the beginning of the classpath list. In situations where there is code sharing, make sure that the items you include in the *CLASSPATH* are correct for the application you are actually running. If you think you are pulling the wrong class, strip your *CLASSPATH* down to nothing and rebuild it with only the required directories. Ultimately, though, you have to put your faith in the programmers. As with upgrading your Virtual Machine, time will tell if good methods will be developed to prevent these situations.

Finally, what do you do about applications that share code with other applications or that load part of their code from the Internet? When you make changes in one application, you must ensure that the changes are backward-compatible. Normally, code that is being deployed is not subject to frequent change, but when you install a new version of an application, you need to make sure that no other programs depend on the code in the old version.

If some programs do depend on code from the old version, maintain the legacy code just in case you need to reinstall the code for other applications. You will look at one minor change of this sort which breaks all applications using the class in the section titled "Paying Attention to Your Constructor" later in this chapter.

In all, the procedure is not quite as simple as installing a new version of Microsoft Word, but it isn't like reinstalling your operating system, either. The key when installing applications is being aware of the downwind effects that every change will cause.

# Converting an Applet to an Application

Now that you know how to install and convert an application, you're ready to learn more about Java code. In this section, you convert the applet Clock to the application that you just finished installing.

First though, you need to realize something. Prepare yourself—everything the press has told you over the last year is about to be shattered.

Not everyone in the world has realized that the Internet exists. Some people and companies do, but do not yet have access to the Internet, and many companies have access to the Internet but do not allow their users to surf the World Wide Web.

As a result, before long, you probably will want to present your applets to people and companies that are not yet familiar with the Net, or you may want to present your applets to people without forcing them to be connected to the Internet. A perfect example of this is when you want to deliver your applets on a CD-ROM. With Java, there is no reason why the application you deliver on a CD should be any different from what you display on the Net. Imagine being able to develop a single application that will run on every platform and that can work over the World Wide Web, Enterprise Network, and CD-ROM.

The key to Java applications (as opposed to applets) is that they do not require a browser to live in. The applications do require a Java VM, but that's less costly to include when sending your applications out, than Netscape.

Why should you have your applets function as applications if you can just bundle appletviewer? Applications have four advantages over appletviewer:

- Windows generated from an application do not display the yellow "warning applet window." This can be a source of confusion to inexperienced users.

- Applications do not require an HTML file to tell them what to load.

■ Applications are much cleaner because they are executed just like normal executable programs.

■ Your clients undoubtedly will consider applications to be full-fledged programs, and based on the name alone, they will consider applets to be miniature programs. Clients probably will be willing to pay more for something that they perceive to be a complete program than for a partial one.

In the following sections, you learn how to upgrade an applet to an application. In this example you will convert the applet Clock into the application we installed earlier in this chapter.

## Changing the Applet Code to an Application

The first task is adding a main() method to the application. To do so, open Clock.java in your favorite text editor. Page all the way down until you reach the closing brace (}). Directly before that brace, add the code shown in listing 24.3.

**Listing 24.3   New Main Method for Clock.java**

```
static boolean inApplet =true;
public static void main(String args[]){
 /*set a boolean flag to show if we are in an applet or not */
 inApplet=false;

/*Create a Frame to place our application in. */
 /*You can change the string value to show your desired label*/
 /*for the frame */
 Frame myFrame = new Frame ("Clock as an Application");

 /*Create a clock instance. */
 Clock myApp = new Clock();


 /*Add the current application to the Frame */
 myFrame.add ("Center",myApp);

 /*Resize the Frame to the desired size, and make it visible */
 myFrame.resize(200,200);
 myFrame.show();

 /*Run the methods the browser normally would */
 myApp.init();
 myApp.start();
 }
```

The following paragraphs explain the changes that you made.

```
    inApplet=false;
```

First, as you will learn later, you often must do a few things differently when you have an applet that is not actually running in a browser, such as appletviewer or Netscape. As a result, a Boolean variable (inApplet) has been added to the class. The declaration for this variable should be placed at the top with the rest of your variables, but it's easier to see it here. Notice that the variable is declared to be static. If you miss this keyword, the compiler growls at you about referencing a nonstatic variable in a static method. main() must be static and public for you to run the method as an application.

```
Frame myFrame = new Frame ("Clock as an Application");
```

Next, you create a frame in which to put your new clock. The parameter "Clock as an Application" is placed in the title bar of the Frame. Indicating that the program is being run as an application is good practice; this indication helps eliminate confusion on the part of the user. If you don't want to set the title in the Constructor for some reason, you can create an untitled frame and change the title later, using setTitle(String), if you prefer.

```
Clock myApp = new Clock();
```

The next line indicates that you want to create a new instance of the class Clock. A perfectly legitimate question at this point is, why not use this? After all, this is an instantiation of the class Clock already. The primary reason to create a new instance of Clock is to avoid rewriting any of the applet methods to make them static. Just as it is not legitimate to change the variable inApplet if it is nonstatic, it is not legitimate to try to access a nonstatic method. It is, however, legitimate to access the nonstatic methods of a variable. Bearing that in mind, create a new instance variable of the class Clock called myApp, and add it to the frame.

```
myFrame.add ("Center",myApp);
```

◀ See "Layout Managers," p. 408

The next line adds the new Clock variable to the Frame. This is important, because the Clock can't be displayed until you attach it to something.

```
myFrame.resize(200,200);
 myFrame.show();
```

Next, you add the lines myFrame.resize(200,200) and myFrame.show() to the Clock.java file. myFrame.resize(200,200) tells the application to make the frame's size 200 by 200. Normally, when you convert an applet to an application, you know the ideal size for your applet. When in doubt, go ahead and copy the WIDTH and HEIGHT values from your most commonly used HTML file. On those rare occasions when you want the size to be adjustable, use the techniques covered in defaulting, where you learn how to account for parameter data, to read in the size from the command line.

**V**

Advanced Java

> **Caution**
>
> When the applet has been added to the frame, technically, you could go through the normal applet methods `init()` and `start()` right there. Contrary to popular belief, however, this procedure is not a good idea. If your applet uses double buffering or requires any other image that is built with the `createImage(x,y)` method, the procedure will not work until the frame has been `shown()`. The drawback is that you will see a flicker as the frame comes up with nothing in it. Keep this fact in the back of your mind even if you're not using `createImage(x,y)` now, because this minor fact is not documented anywhere and has caused this author hours of headaches.

```
myApp.init();
myApp.start();
```

Finally, you add the lines `myApp.init()` and `myApp.start()` to your function. Because your application is not running in the browser, the `init()` and `start()` methods are not called automatically, as they would be if the program were running as an applet. As a result, you must simulate the effect by calling the methods explicitly. It should be pointed out that if your application does not appear, you may want to add the line `myApp.repaint()` to the end of the `main()` method.

```
import java.awt.Frame
```

Before you save your new copy of Clock.java, you need to make one more change. Go to the top of the file in which you are performing your imports, and make sure that you are importing java.awt.Frame. Then go ahead and save the file.

## Compiling the Application

The next step is recompiling the application. Recompiling an application is no different from compiling an applet. In this case, type the following:

```
javac Clock.java
```

## Testing the Application

Now you can test your application. To do so, you need to invoke the Java Virtual Machine, followed by the class name, as follows:

```
java Clock
```

The application should now appear as shown in figure 24.7.

> **Tip**
>
> Be sure to maintain proper capitalization at all times.

**Fig. 24.7**

The Clock running as an Application.

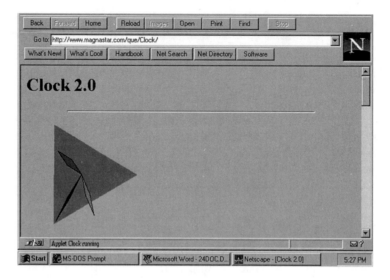

## Accounting for Other Applet Peculiarities

The most difficult problem to deal with when you convert applets to applications has to do with duplicating the effect of a parameter tag and other applet-specific tasks. You can handle this situation in many ways; the following sections discuss two of the most common solutions.

### Defaulting

The first solution is defaulting. In defaulting, the idea is to provide the application with all the information that it would be getting anyway from the HTML file. In a sense, this solution is exactly what you did when you told the frame what size you wanted to use with resize(x,y). To do this for the <param> items requires rewriting the getParameter method.

Clock has several parameters that it receives in <param> tags. If you have run the Clock up to this point, you no doubt have noticed that the current Clock displays a bit differently from the one that you originally saw in Netscape. This is because the parameters that normally come from the Clock.html file are not present. Take a look at the number of <param> tags in listing 24.4.

---

**Listing 24.4   Clock.html**

```
<TITLE>Clock 2.0</TITLE>
<H1>Clock 2.0</H1>
<HR ALIGN=CENTER WIDTH=75%>
<applet code="Clock.class" width=200 height=200>
<param name=num_lines value=3>
<param name=hour_len value=60>
<param name=minute_len value=75>
```

```
<param name=second_len value=95>
<param name=hour_col value=ff0000 >
<param name=minute_col value=00ff00>
<param name=second_col value=0000ff>
<param name=border_col value=00ffff>
<param name=background_col value=cccc22>
<param name=timezone value=1>
</applet>
```

To mimic these effects in your new application, add the method shown in listing 24.5 to your current `Clock.java` file.

**Listing 24.5   getParameter() Method for Clock.java**

```
public String getParameter (String name){
  String ST;
  if (inApplet)
  return super.getParameter(name);
  //If we are not in an applet we default all of the values.
  if (name == "num_lines")
  return "3";
  if (name == "hour_len")
  return "60";
  if (name == "minute_len")
  return "75";
  if (name == "second_len")
  return "95";
  if (name == "hour_col")
  return "ff0000" ;
  if (name == "minute_col")
  return "00ff00";
  if (name == "second_col")
  return "0000ff";
  if (name == "border_col")
  return "00ffff";
  if (name == "background_col")
  return "cccc22";
  if (name == "timezone")
  return "1";
  return null;
}
```

### Caution

If you are going to have several parameters, you should use a switch statement. A switch, however, requires an integer, which you can get by using the `hashCode()` of the String. Since multiple Strings can have the same `hashCode()` you must then make sure you really have the correct String. This makes the solution much more involved. Nonetheless, if you are working with several <param> tags, consider using this alternative method.

V

Advanced Java

This method replaces the duties that are normally performed by the java.applet.Applet class with your own default values. Notice that the first thing you do is check to see whether you are in an applet (if (inApplet)). If so, you use the getParameter(String) method from your super class (java.applet.Applet). Doing this maintains your normal pattern of operation when you go back and use Clock as an applet again. The idea is to have one program that can run as both an application and an applet, as shown in figure 24.8.

---

**Note**

A better way to handle the getParameter is to implement appletStub, but without a complete explanation of interfaces, such an explanation would be purely academic. If you plan to implement several aspects of java.applet.Applet, refer to chapter 12 for more information.

---

**Fig. 24.8**
Running the Clock applet.

### Second Way to Add <param> Information

Defaulting is a quick and easy way to get into an application the extraneous information that you normally leave in an HTML file. Odds are, however, that if you took the time to include a parameter tag in the first place, you don't want the values to be fixed. After all, you could have hard-coded the values to start with, and then you wouldn't have this problem in the first place. How do you get information into your application from the outside world? The easiest answer is to get it from the command line.

As you recall, the main method takes an array of Strings as an argument. You can use this array to deliver information to an application at run-time. This section addresses one of the simplest cases: sending the WIDTH and HEIGHT information to the application from the command line. While the section doesn't explain how to insert the information for a <param>, you should be able to deduce from this example how to do it for <param> tags on your own.

To use the information from the command line, you need to make a few modifications in the main() method. Listing 24.6 shows the new version.

**Listing 24.6  New main Method**

```
public static void main(String args[]){
/*set a boolean flag to show if we are in an applet or not */
inApplet=false;

/*Create a clock instance. */
Clock myApp = new Clock();

/*Create a Frame to place our application in. */
/*You can change the string value to show your desired label*/
/*for the frame */
Frame myFrame = new Frame ("Clock as an Applet");

/*Add the current application to the Frame */
myFrame.add ("Center",myApp);

/*Resize the Frame to the desired size, and make it visible */
if (argv.length>=2)
/*resize the Frame based on command line inputs */
myFrame.resize(Integer.parseInt(args[0]),Integer.parseInt(args[1]));
else
myFrame.resize(200,200);
myFrame.show();

/*Run the methods the browser normally would */
myApp.init();
myApp.start();
}
```

Make the necessary changes, and recompile the program. Now you can run the Clock at any size you want. Try the following:

```
java Clock 100 100
```

At first glance, your new main method is almost identical to the one in listing 24.3. The main difference is a group of six lines:

```
/*Resize the Frame to the desired size, and make it visible */
if (argv.length>=2)
/*resize the Frame based on command line inputs */
myFrame.resize(Integer.parseInt(args[0]),Integer.parseInt(args[1]));
else
myFrame.resize(200,200);
```

The first line of actual code checks to see whether the user put enough information in the command line. This check prevents null pointer exceptions caused by accessing information that isn't really there. Besides, you probably want the user to be able to run Clock at its normal size without specifying the actual size.

The next line is the one that does most of the work. It should be fairly obvious to you what is happening in this code, but you should know why you need to use Integer.parseInt on the array values. At run-time, the Java machine isn't aware of what is coming in from the command line; it simply sees a string. To convert a String to an int, you need to use the class Integer's `parseInt(String)` method.

---

**Caution**

To be complete, the `parseInt` method should be surrounded by a `try{}` `catch{}` block, in case something other than an integer is typed in the command line.

---

## Making the Window Close Work

By now, you probably have noticed that to close your new Clock application, you have to press Ctrl+C or in some other way cause the operating system to close your application. This section reveals to you the secret method by which all MagnaStar, Inc., applications and applets close their frames by a normal method.

The answer is to not use the frame from java.awt.Frame. This frame ignores the `Event.WINDOW_DESTROY` event and doesn't bother to pass it along to its container objects. To get around this situation, use the goodFrame class shown in listing 24.7.

**Listing 24.7   goodFrame.java**

```
/* ---------------------------------------------------------------
 * goodFrame , Copyright  1995 MagnaStar Inc, All Rights Reserved.
 * Permission to use, copy, modify, and distribute this software and its
 * documentation for NON-COMMERCIAL purposes and without fee is hereby
 * granted, provided that this copyright notice and appropriate
   ➥documentation
 * appears in all software that contains this code, or is derived
   ➥from it.
 *
 * MagnaStar Inc. MAKES NO REPRESENTATIONS OR WARRANTIES ABOUT THE
 * SUITABILITY OF THE SOFTWARE, EITHER EXPRESS OR IMPLIED, INCLUDING
   ➥BUT NOT
 * LIMITED TO THE IMPLIED WARRANTIES OF MERCHANTABILITY, FITNESS FOR A
 * PARTICULAR PURPOSE, OR NON-INFRINGEMENT. MagnaStar Inc. SHALL NOT
   ➥BE LIABLE
 * FOR ANY DAMAGES SUFFERED BY LICENSEE AS A RESULT OF USING, MODIFYING OR
 * DISTRIBUTING THIS SOFTWARE OR ITS DERIVATIVES.
 *
 * You may reach MagnaStar Inc. at info@magnastar.com
 * P.O. Box 70, Waupun, WI 53963
 *
 * For more information see:
 * http://www.magnastar.com */

import java.awt.Event;
```

```
import java.awt.Component;
/** GoodFrame extends java.awt.Frame and acknowledges standard window
 * Close and minimize commands */

public class goodFrame extends java.awt.Frame{

//Constructors duplicate those from java.awt.Frame
public goodFrame (){
 super();
}

public goodFrame(String title){
 super(title);
}

public boolean handleEvent(Event evt){
 //Acknowledge minimize requests
 if (evt.id== Event.WINDOW_ICONIFY){
 hide();
 return false;
 }
 //Acknowledge window close requests
 if (evt.id == Event.WINDOW_DESTROY){
 //Pass the destroy event along to the components.
 //This should be used to stop all Threads
 Component c[] = getComponents();
 for (int x=0;x<c.length;x++)
 c[x].handleEvent(evt);
 //Destroy the current Frame
 dispose();
 return false;
 }
 //Default to the normal handleEvent
 return super.handleEvent(evt);
}

 }
```

To implement this class, copy goodFrame.java to the directory in which the Clock.java class is located. Next, edit Clock.java. Replace all the instances of Frame with goodFrame, and make one more change: rather than import java.awt.Frame at the top of the program, import goodFrame. Now recompile the program. Everything should work exactly as it did before, with one change: if you click the close icon, the application disappears.

Now you need to make one more change to Clock to get it to quit completely. Add the following method to your Clock applet:

```
public boolean handleEvent(Event evt){
  if (evt.id == Event.WINDOW_DESTROY){
  if(inApplet){
  stop();
  destroy();
```

```
return true;
}
else {
System.exit(0);
}
}
return super.handleEvent(evt);
}
```

This method causes Clock to run through the standard exit procedures under an applet (if (inApplet)). The real key, however, is that when you run it as an application, Clock calls System.exit(0). Before you do one more recompilation of Clock.java, add one more line to the top of Clock.java to import the Event class:

```
import java.awt.Event;
```

Now, recompile and run Clock one last time. If you click the window close icon, Clock now exits like a normal program.

## Checking All the Applet Methods

When you convert your own applets to applications, you need to perform one last step. You need to search for all methods in java.applet.Applet that are valid only with respect to a browser. Most commonly, you need to search for the methods described in the following sections.

### getAppletContext()

Fortunately, most of the things that you will do with getAppletContext(), you can ignore with applications. showDocument(), for example, has no meaning without a browser. Attempting to execute getAppletContext().showDocument() produces an error on System.out, but the application shouldn't crash because of it.

Similarly, showStatus() usually is not relevant with applications. In applets that use the applet context to display information, the easiest thing to do usually is to surround the specific code with an if (inApplet){} block, and ignore it if you're not in an applet.

What do you do if you really have to see that information? You can select the top and bottom 20 lines of the frame and write into the paint method a section that displays the applet-context information there. Why do you select the top *and* the bottom? Due to a strange quirk between the UNIX version of Frame peer and the Windows 95 version of Frame peer, each system chops out a 20-line area in which it can display its "warning applet" message. On Windows machines, this area is the top 20 lines; on UNIX machines, it is the bottom 20 lines.

If you're not convinced, go to the following URL:

```
http://www.magnastar.com/ultra_nav
```

If you are on a Windows machine, you should see an information bar at the top of the frame. If you're on a UNIX machine, that bar is at the bottom. The bar is being drawn at both the top and the bottom; you are just seeing one.

### getCodeBase() and getDocumentBase()

getCodeBase() and getDocumentBase() are a bit trickier to deal with. Both of these methods return an URL, and you don't want to limit yourself to having the user connected to the Internet. After all, if the user can access your Web site, you probably have him or her downloading the applet directly from you, so you would have no need to turn the applet into an application.

You usually deal with getCodeBase() and getDocumentBase() on a case-by-case basis. If you can get away without the information, ignore it. If you really need the information from getCodeBase() or getDocumentBase(), you may have to give it a hard-coded URL or one that you read from the command line.

### Paying Attention to Your Constructor

Frequently, when converting applets you will find yourself creating a constructor for your class other than the null constructor. Creating a custom constructor is a perfectly desirable thing to do to pass information from the command line or other information. If you do this, however, make sure that you add the null constructor back in manually (the null constructor is the constructor which does not take any paramenters on input). If you create another constructor, Java doesn't automatically generate a null one for you. You won't even notice that you need one until you are working on a project and another class needs to create an instance of your applet, for a thread or something. When this situation occurs, the class attempts to access the null constructor. Now, even though you didn't actually delete the null constructor from the class, it is no longer there. The error message that you get will look something like this:

```
java.lang.NoSuchMethodError
 at sun.applet.AppletPanel.run(AppletPanel.java:200)
 at java.lang.Thread(Thread.java)
```

Notice that nothing in the error message tells you anything about your classes. The error doesn't even look like one that involves your class; it looks like a bug in AppletPanel. If you encounter this situation, the first thing to do is delete *.class and recompile the whole program. Then the compiler will be able to catch the missing Constructor call.

*createImage*

If you are using `createImage`, and the `Image` variable is being returned as null when you convert your applet to an application, make sure that you have made the frame visible first. See the caution under "Converting the Applet Code to an Application" in the section titled "Changing the Applet Code to an Application" for more information.

# Packaging Your Applications in ZIP format

Now that you have converted your applets to applications, you can send them to your clients. The best way to deliver the applications is in a single zip file.

When you package your own applications in zip format, make sure that you don't use compression. Due to the way that the Java interpreter uses the zip files, the files can only be stored in the zip file—not compressed.

| Caution |
| --- |
| Be aware that you cannot deliver applets in the `.zip` format. Sun and Netscape may see the wisdom of this in the future, but at least in JDK version 1.0, you cannot package applets in zip format. |

## Under Windows

Currently, PKZIP, the most popular zip program, does not have support for long file names, so you have to use an alternative zip compression program. When PKZIP does support long file names, however, the command should be:

```
pkzip -e0 classes.zip *.class
```

## Under UNIX

On UNIX machines, you can use Zip. Zip 2.0.1, from Info-ZIP, is available at a variety of FTP sites. The URL for the Web site is **http://quest.jpl. nasa.gov/Info-Zip/Info-Zip.html**. The command for Info-Zip to zip `.class` files is:

```
zip -0 classes.zip *.class
```

> **Note**
>
> When you deliver applications, be sure to include directions for your users on how to get the JDK (if you are not including it with your application). In general, it is also a good idea to include both a batch file and a script file to allow both UNIX and Windows users to access your applications.

# CHAPTER 25

# More About Java Applications: Threads

*by Joseph L. Weber*

A unique property of Java is its built-in support for threads. This chapter covers how threads are used in Java applications.

In this chapter, you will learn

- What threads are
- How and why threads are used
- About a threaded program
- How to synchronize data between threads
- How to change thread properties
- How to change thread priority

## What Are Threads?

Think about a typical corporation. In almost every company there are at least three interdependent departments: management, accounting, and manufacturing/sales. For an efficient company to run, all three of these operations need to be done at the same time. If accounting fails to do its job the company will go bankrupt. If management fails, the company will simply fall apart, and if manufacturing doesn't do its job, the company will have nothing with which to make money.

Many software programs operate under the same conditions as your company. In a company, you get all the tasks done at the same time by assigning them to different people. Each person goes off and does his or her appointed task. With software you (usually) have only a single processor, and that single processor has to take on the tasks of all these groups. To manage this, a concept called *multitasking* was invented. In reality, the processor is still doing only one thing at any one time, but it switches between them so fast that it seems like it is doing them all simultaneously. Fortunately, modern computers work much faster than human beings, so you hardly even notice that this is happening.

Now, let's go one step deeper. Have you ever noticed that the accounting person is really doing more than one thing? For instance, that person spends time photocopying spreadsheets, calculating how many widgets the company needs to sell in order to corner the widget market, and adding up all the books and making sure the bills get paid.

In operating system terms, this is what is known as *multithreading*. Think about it this way: each program is assigned a particular person to carry out a group of tasks, called a process. That person then breaks up his or her time even further into *threads*.

# Why Use Threads?

So, you're saying to yourself, "Why should I care how the computer works, so long as it runs my programs?" Multithreading is important to understand because one of the great advances Java makes over its fellow programming languages is that at the very heart of the language is support for threading. By using threading, you can avoid long pauses between what your users do and when they see things happen. Better yet, you can send tasks such as printing off into the background where the user doesn't have to worry about them—the user can continue typing his or her dissertation or perform some other task.

In Java, currently the most common utilization of a thread is to allow your applet to go off and do something while the browser continues to do its job. Any application you're working on that requires two things to be done at the same time is probably a great candidate for threading.

# How To Make Your Classes Threadable

You canmake your applications and classes run in separate threads in two ways, by extending the Thread class or by implementing the Runnable interface. It should be noted that making your class *able* to run as a thread does not automatically make it run as such. A section later in this chapter explains this.

### Extend Thread

You can make your class runnable as a thread by extending the class java.lang.Thread. This gives you direct access to all the thread methods directly.

```
public class GreatRace extends Thread
```

### Implement *Runnable*

Usually, when you want to make a class able to run in its own thread, you will also want to extend the features of some other class. Because Java doesn't support multiple inheritance, the solution to this is to implement Runnable. In fact Thread actually implements Runnable itself. The Runnable interface has only one method: run(). Anytime you make a class implement Runnable, you will need to have a run() method in your class. It is in the run() method that you actually do all of the work you want to have done by that particular thread.

```
public class GreatRace extends java.applet.Applet implements
Runnable
```

# Synchronization

When dealing with multiple threads, consider this: What happens when two or more threads want to access the same variable at the same time, and at least one of them wants to change it? If they were allowed to do this at will, chaos would reign. For example, while one thread reads Joe Smith's record, another thread tries to change his salary (Joe has earned a $0.50 raise). The problem is that this little change causes the thread reading the file in the middle of the update to see something somewhat random, and it thinks Joe has gotten a $500 raise. That's a great thing for Joe, but not such a great thing for the company, and probably a worse thing for the programmer who will lose his job because of it. How do you resolve this?

Well, the first thing to do is to declare the method that will change the data and the method that will read to be synchronized. Java's key word, synchronized, tells the system to put a lock around a particular method. At most, one thread may be in *any* synchronized method at a time. Listing 25.1 shows an example of two synchronized methods.

**Listing 25.1   Two Synchronized Methods**

```
public synchronized void setVar(int){
  myVar=x;
}

public synchronized int getVar (){
   return myVar;
}
```

Don't just make all your methods synchronized or you won't be able to do any multithreading at all. But even with only a couple of methods declared as synchronized, what happens when one thread starts a synchronized method, and then stops until some condition that needs to be set by another thread? The solution lies in the dining philosopher's problem.

## Speaking with a Forked Tongue

What is the dining philosopher's problem? Well, I won't go into all the details, but let me lay out the scenario for you.

Five philosophers are sitting around a table with a plate of food in front of them. One chopstick (or fork) lies on the table between each philosopher, for a total of 5 chopsticks. What happens when they all want to eat? They need two chopsticks to eat the food, but there are not enough chopsticks to go around. At most, two of them can eat at any one time—the other three will have to wait. How do you make sure that each philosopher doesn't pick up one chopstick, and none of them can get two? This will lead to starvation because no one will be able to eat. (The philosophers are too busy thinking to realize that one of them can go into the kitchen for more chopsticks; that isn't the solution.)

There are a number of ways to solve this ancient problem (at least in terms of the life of a computer). I won't even try to solve this problem for you. But it's important to realize the consequences. If you make a method synchronized, and it is going to stop because of some condition that can only be set by another thread, make sure you exit the method, and return the chopstick to the table. If you don't, it is famine waiting to happen. The philosopher won't return his chopstick(s) to the table, and he will be waiting for something to happen that can't happen because his fellow thinker doesn't have utensils to be able to start eating.

# The Great Thread Race

Now that you have looked at the fundamental philosophies, such as synchronization and making your class runnable, let's take a look at a thread example. The source code for two classes follows GreatRace, a class that adds several items of the class Threader. Threader operates in its own thread and races along a track to the finish line.

## Sample Class Using a Thread: *GreatRace.java*

**Listing 25.2     *GreatRace.java***

```
import goodFrame;
import java.awt.Graphics;
import java.awt.GridLayout;
import Threader;


public class GreatRace extends java.applet.Applet implements Runnable{
Threader theRacers[];
static int racerCount = 3;
Thread     theThreads[];
Thread     thisThread;
static boolean inApplet=true;
int     numberofThreadsAtStart;


public void init(){
  //we will use this later to see if all our Threads have died
  numberofThreadsAtStart = Thread.activeCount();

  //Specify the layout.  We will be adding all of the racers one on top
  //of the other.

  setLayout(new GridLayout(racerCount,1));

  //Specify the number of racers in this race, and make the arrays for the
  //Theaders and the actual threads the proper size.
  theRacers = new Threader [racerCount];
  theThreads = new Thread[racerCount];

  //Create a new Thread for each racer, and add it to the panel
  for (int x=0;x<racerCount;x++){
    theRacers[x]=new Threader ("Racer #"+x);
    theRacers[x].resize(size().width,size().height/racerCount);
    add (theRacers[x]);
    theThreads[x]=new Thread(theRacers[x]);

  }
}
```

(continues)

V

Advanced Java

**Listing 25.2 Continued**

```java
public void start(){
  //Start all of the racing threads
  for (int x=0;x<racerCount;x++)
    theThreads[x].start();

  //Create a thread of our own.  We will use this to monitor the
  ➥state of
  //the racers and determine when we should quit all together
  thisThread= new Thread (this);
  thisThread.start();
}


public void stop(){
  thisThread.stop();
}

public void run(){
  //Loop around until all of the racers have finished the race.
  while(Thread.activeCount()>numberofThreadsAtStart+2){
    try{
      thisThread.sleep(100);
      } catch (InterruptedException e){
        System.out.println("thisThread was interrupted");
        }
    }

  //Once the race is done, end the program
  if (inApplet){
    stop();
    destroy();
    }
  else
    System.exit(0);
}


public static void main (String argv[]){
  inApplet=false;

  //Check to see if the number of racers has been specified on the
  ➥command line
  if (argv.length>0)
    racerCount = Integer.parseInt(argv[0]);

  //Create a new frame and place the race in it.
  goodFrame theFrame = new goodFrame("The Great Thread Race");
  GreatRace theRace = new GreatRace();
  theFrame.resize(400,200);
  theFrame.add ("Center",theRace);
  theFrame.show();
  theRace.init();
  theFrame.pack();
```

```
      theRace.start();
   }

}//end class GreatRace
```

## Sample Class Implementing Runnable: *Threader.java*

```java
import java.awt.Graphics;
import java.awt.Color;

public class Threader extends java.awt.Canvas implements Runnable {
int myPosition =0;
String myName;
int numberofSteps=600;

//Constructor for a threader.  We need to know our name when we
//create the threader
public Threader (String inName){
  myName=new String (inName);
}

public synchronized void paint(Graphics g){
  //Draw a line for the 'racing line'
  g.setColor (Color.black);
  g.drawLine (0,size().height/2,size().width,size().height/2);

  //Draw the round racer;
  g.setColor (Color.yellow);
  g.fillOval((myPosition*size().width/numberofSteps),0,15,size().height);
}


public void run(){
  //loop until we have finished the race
  while (myPosition <numberofSteps){
    //move ahead one position
    myPosition++;
    repaint();

    //Put ourselves to sleep so the paint thread can get around to painting.
    try{
      Thread.currentThread().sleep(10);
      }catch (Exception e){System.out.println("Exception on sleep");}
    }
  System.out.println("Threader:"+myName+" has finished the race");
}


}//end class Threader
```

# Understanding the GreatRace

Most of the code in `Threader.java` and `GreatRace.java` should be fairly easy for you to understand by now. Let's take a look at the key sections of the code that deal with the actual threads. The first one to look at is the `for` loop in the `init()` method of `GreatRace`.

---

**Listing 25.4**   *for* **Loop from** *init( )* **in GreatRace**

```
for (int x=0;x<racerCount;x++){
    theRacers[x]=new Threader ("Racer #"+x);
    theRacers[x].resize(size().width,size().height/racerCount);
    add (theRacers[x]);
    theThreads[x]=new Thread(theRacers[x]);

    }
}
```

---

In the `for` loop, the first thing to do is to create an instance of the class `Threader`. As you can see from the previous page, `Threader` is an ordinary class that happens to also implement the `Runnable` interface. After an instance of `Threader` is created, it is added to the panel and new thread is created with using our `Threader`. Don't confuse the `Threader` class with the Thread Class. `Threader` is the name of the class we created in listing 25.3.

---

**Caution**

The new `Thread` can be created only from an object extending `thread` or an object that implements `Runnable`. In either case, the object must have a `run()` method. However, when you first create the thread, the `run()` method is not called. That will happen later.

---

The next important set of code is in the `start()` method, again of `GreatRace.java`.

---

**Listing 25.5**   *start()* **Method of** *GreatRace*

```
public void start(){
  //Start all of the racing threads
  for (int x=0;x<racerCount;x++)
    theThreads[x].start();

  //Create a thread of our own.  We will use this to monitor the
  ➥state of
  //the racers and determine when we should quit all together
  thisThread= new Thread (this);
```

```
    thisThread.start();
  }
```

The first task is to start up all the threads created in the `init()` method.
When the thread is started, it calls the `run()` method right away. In this case,
it will be the `run()` method of the `Threadable` that was passed to the constructor back in the `init()` method.

Notice that once the racers are all started, a thread is created for the actual
applet. This thread will be used to monitor what is going on with all the
threads. If the race finishes, you might as well end the program.

Finally, take a look at the last set of important code—the `run()` method of
`Threader`.

**Listing 25.6**  *run()* **Method of** *Threadable* **(Racer)**

```
public void run(){
  //loop until we have finished the race
  while (myPosition <numberofSteps){
    //move ahead one position
    myPosition++;
    repaint();

    //Put ourselves to sleep so the paint thread can get around to
painting.
    try{
      Thread.currentThread().sleep(10);
      }catch (Exception e){System.out.println("Exception on sleep");}
    }
  System.out.println("Threader:"+myName+" has finished the race");
  }
```

Notice that you start a fairly long loop in the `run()` method. `run()` is called
only once when the thread is started . If you plan to do a lot of repetitive
work, which is usually the case in a thread, you need to stay within the confines of the `run()`. In fact, it isn't a bad idea to think of the `run()` method as
being a lot like typical `main()` methods in other structured languages.

Look down a few lines and you will notice that you put the thread to sleep a
bit, in the middle of each loop (`Thread.currentThread().sleep(10)`). This is
a very important task. You should always put your threads to sleep once in a
while. This prevents other threads from going into starvation. It is true that
under Windows you can get away without doing this in some cases. This
works under Windows because Windows doesn't really behave like it should
with respect to the priority of a Thread, as we will discuss later.  However, this

**V**

**Advanced Java**

is a bad idea, and it probably will not be portable. UNIX machines in particular will look like the applet has hung, and the Macintosh will do the same thing. This has to do with the priority assigned to the paint thread, but there are a lot of other reasons to give the system a breather from your thread.

# Try the Great Thread Race Out

Go ahead and compile the GreatRace, and run it by typing

> **java GreatRace**

**Fig. 25.1**

GreatRace run as an application.

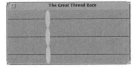

You can also access it using your browser, by opening the index.html file (see fig. 25.2).

**Fig. 25.2**

Greate Race as an applet.

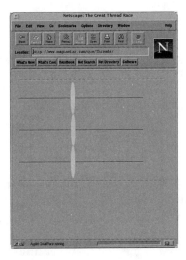

You just saw three rather boring ovals run across the screen. Did you notice that they all ran at almost the same speed, yet they were really all processing separately? You can run the GreatRace with as many racers as you want by typing

> **java GreatRace 5**

The racers should all make it across the screen in about the same time.

If you run the race a number of times, you will see that the race is actually quite fair, and each of the racers wins just about an equal number of times. If you show the Java Console under Netscape (Options Show Java Console) or look at the window you ran Java GreatRace from, you can actually see the order in which the Racers finish the race (see fig. 25.3).

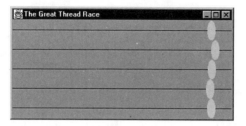

**Fig. 25.3**
GreatRace and the DOS window it was run from.

# Changing the Priority

There are two methods in `java.lang.Thread` that deal with the priority of a thread. These are:

- `setPriority(int)`
- `getPriority()`

`getPriority` is used to obtain the current priority of a thread, and `setPriority` is used to set a new priority for a thread.

Now, let's see what happens when you tell the computer you want it to treat each of the Racers a bit differently by changing the priority.

Change the `init()` method in `GreatRace.java` by adding the following line into the `for` loop:

```
theThreads[x].setPriority(Thread.MIN_PRIORITY+x);
```

The `for` loop now looks like this:

**Listing 25.7  New *for* Loop for *init()* Method**

```
for (int x=0;x<racerCount;x++){
    theRacers[x]=new Threader ("Racer #"+x);
    theRacers[x].resize(size().width,size().height/racerCount);
    add (theRacers[x]);
    theThreads[x]=new Thread(theRacers[x]);

    theThreads[x].setPriority(Thread.MIN_PRIORITY+x);
    }
```

V

Advanced Java

Recompile the GreatRace now, and run it again (see fig. 25.4).

**Fig. 25.4**

New Great Race
run—mid race.

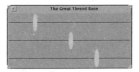

By changing the priority on the Racers, now all of a sudden the bottom Racer
always wins. The reason for this is that the highest priority thread always gets
to use the processor when it is not sleeping. This means that every 10ms the
bottom racer always gets to advance towards the finish line, stopping the
work of the other racers. The other racers get a chance to try to catch up only
when that racer decides to go to sleep. Unlike the hare in the story about the
tortoise and the hare though, the highest priority thread always wakes back
up in 10ms, and rather quickly out paces the other racers all the way to the
finish. As soon as that racer finishes though, the next racer becomes the
highest priority and gets to move every 10ms, leaving the next racer further
behind.

To change the priority of the thread, the method `setPriority(int)` from
`Thread` was used. Note that you did not just give it a number. The priority
was set relative to the `MIN_PRIORITY` variable in `Thread`. This is a very important step. The `MIN_PRIORITY` and `MAX_PRIORITY` are variables that could be set
differently for a particular machine. Currently, the `MIN_PRIORITY` on all machines is 1 and the `MAX_PRIORITY` is 10. It is important not to exceed these
values. Doing so will cause an `IllegalArgumentException` to be thrown.

# A Word About Thread Priority,
# Netscape and Windows

If youran the updated version of the GreatRace under Windows, no doubt
you're wondering why your race did not turn out the same as it showed before. The trailing two racers stayed very close together until the first one won.

If you ran it with Netscape under Windows, you may even be wondering why
your last racer didn't even win!

The reason for this discrepancy is that threads under Windows don't have
nearly the amount of control in terms of priority as do threads under UNIX
or Macintosh machines. In fact, threads that have nearly the same priority
are treated almost as if they had the same priority under Netscape. That is the
reason that under Netscape the last two racers seem to have a nearly equal
chance at winning the race. To make the last racer always win, you must

increase the priority difference (see fig. 25.5). Try changing the line in the GreatRace `init()` method to read like this (see fig. 25.6):

```
theThreads[x].setPriority(Thread.MIN_PRIORITY+x*3);
```

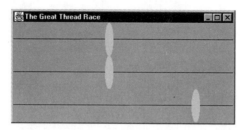

**Fig. 25.5**
New Great Race under Windows 95.

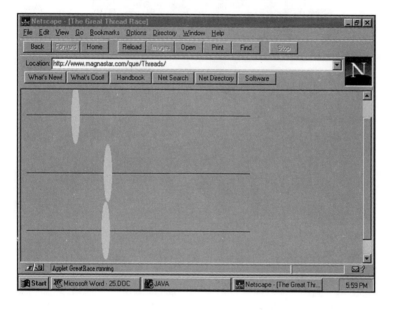

**Fig. 25.6**
New Great Race run as an applet under Windows 95.

**V**

**Advanced Java**

Now if you try the race under Windows 95, the last racer should always win by a good margin (see fig. 25.7).

If you run the same thing under Netscape, the last racer will also still win, but just barely.

This difference is very important to realize. If you're going to depend on the priority of your threads, make sure that you test the application on both a Windows and on a Macintosh or UNIX machine. If you don't have the luxury of a UNIX machine or a Macintosh, it seems that running the program as a Java application (see fig. 25.8) instead of a Java applet is a closer approximation to how the thread priorities should be handled, as you saw in the last two figures.

**Fig. 25.7**

Great Race with increased priorities under Windows 95.

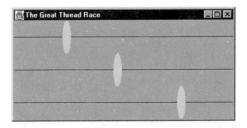

**Fig. 25.8**

Great Race with increased priorities as an applet under Window 95.

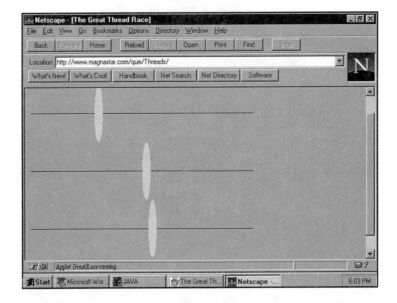

---

## Caution

These thread priority differences make it very dangerous to not put your threads to sleep occasionally if you're using only a Windows 95 machine. The paint thread, which is a low priority thread, will get a chance at the processor under Windows, but only because it will be able to keep up just as the racers did. However, this will not work under a Macintosh or UNIX machine.

---

# Changing the Running State of the Threads

Threads have a number of possible states. Let's take a look at how to change the state and what the effects are. The methods covered here are

- `start()`
- `stop()`
- `sleep(long)`, `sleep(long,int)`
- `suspend()`
- `resume()`
- `yield()`
- `destroy()`

`start()` and `stop()` are relatively simple operations for a thread. `start()` tells a thread to start the `run()` method of its associated `Runnable` object. `stop()` tells the thread to stop. Now really there is more that goes into `stop()`. `stop()` actually throws a `ThreadDeath` object at the thread. Under almost every situation, you should not try to catch this object. The only time you will need to consider doing so will be if you have a number of extraordinary things you need to clean up before you can stop.

> ### Caution
>
> If you catch the `ThreadDeath` object, be sure to throw it again. If you don't do this the thread will not actually stop and, because the error handler won't notice this, nothing will ever complain.

You have already briefly looked at the `sleep` method, when putting the `Threadable`'s to sleep in the GreatRace was talked about. Putting a thread to sleep essentially tells the Virtual Machine that "I'm done with what I am doing right now, wake me back up in a little while." By putting a thread to sleep you are allowing lower priority threads a chance to get a shot at the processor. This is especially important when there are very low priority threads that are doing tasks that, while not as important, still need to be done periodically. Without stepping out of the way occasionally, your thread can put these threads into starvation.

The `sleep` method comes in two varieties, the first is `sleep(long)`, which tells the interpreter that you want to go to sleep for a certain number of milliseconds.

```
thisThread.sleep(100);
```

A millisecond, while only an instant for humans, is an awfully long time for a computer. Even on a 486/33 computer, this is enough time for the processor to do 25,000 instructions. On high-end workstations, hundreds of thousands of instructions can be done in 1 millisecond. As a result, there is a second incantation, `sleep(long,int)`. With this version of the sleep command, you can put a thread to sleep for a number of milliseconds, plus a few nanoseconds.

```
thisThread.sleep(99,250);
```

`suspend()` and `resume()` are two pairs of threads that you can use to put the thread to sleep until some other event has occurred. One such example would be if you were about to start a huge mathematical computation, such as finding the millionth prime number, and you don't want the other threads to be taking up any of the processor. Incidentally, if you're really trying to find the millionth prime number, I would suggest you write the program in a language other than Java, and get yourself a very very large computer.

`yield()` works a bit differently than `suspend()`. `yield()` is much closer to `sleep()`, in that with `yield` you're telling the interperter that you would like to get out of the way of the other threads, but when they are done, you would like to pick back up. `yield()` does not require a `resume()` to start back up when the other threads have stopped, gone to sleep, or died.

The last method to change a threads running state is `destroy()`. In general, don't use `destroy()`. `destroy()` does not do any clean up on the thread. It just destroys it. Because it is essentially the same as shutting down a program in progress, you should use `destroy()` only as a last resort.

# Obtaining the Number of Threads That Are Running

`Java.lang.Thread` has one method that deals with determining the number of threads that are running. This is `activeCount()`.

`Thread.activeCount()` returns an integer number of the number of threads that are running in the current *ThreadGroup*. This is used in the GreatRace to find out when all of the threads have finished executing. Notice that in the `init()` method you check the number of threads that are running when you start your program. In the `run()` method, you then compare this number +2 to the number of threads that are currently running to see if your racers have finished the race.

```
while(Thread.activeCount()>numberofThreadsAtStart+2){
```

Why +2? You need to account for two additional threads that do not exist before the race is started. The first one is the thread which is made out of GreatRace(thisThread) which actually runs through the main loop of GreatRace. The other thread that has not started up at the point the `init()`

method is hit is the Screen_Updater thread. This thread does not start until it is required to do something.

> **Note**
>
> As with most programming solutions, there are many ways to determine if all the racers have finished. You can use thread messaging with PipedInputStream and PipedOutputStream, or check to see if the threads are alive.

# Finding All the Threads That Are Running

Sometimes it's necessary to be able to see all the threads that are running. For instance, what if you did not know that there were two threads you needed to account for in the main() loop of the GreatRace? There are three methods in java.lang.Thread that help us show just this information:

- enumerate(Thread [])
- getName()
- setName(String)

enumerate(Thread []) is used to get a list of all the threads that are running in the current ThreadGroup.

getName() is used to get the name assigned to the thread, while its counter-part setName(String) is used to set this name. By default, if you do not pass in a name in the constructor of a thread, it is assigned the default name Thread-x where x is a unique number for that thread.

Let's modify the GreatRace a bit to show all the threads that are running. Change the run() method to look like this:

> **Listing 25.8  New *run()* Method for GreatRace**

```
public void run(){
  Thread allThreads[];
  //Loop around until all of the racers have finished the race.
  while(Thread.activeCount()>1){
    try{
      //create a Thread array for allThreads
      allThreads = new Thread[Thread.activeCount()];
      //obtain a link to all of the current Threads.
      Thread.enumerate (allThreads);
      //Display the name of all the Threads.
```

(continues)

V

Advanced Java

**Listing 25.8  Continued**

```
        System.out.println("****** New List ***** ");
        for (int x=0;x<allThreads.length;x++)
          System.out.println("Thread:"+allThreads[x].getName()
          ➥+":"+allThreads[x].getPriority()+":"+allThreads[x].is
          ➥Daemon());
        thisThread.sleep(1000);
        }  catch (InterruptedException e){
          System.out.println("thisThread was interrupted");        }
      }

  //Once the race is done, end the program
  if (inApplet){
    stop();
    destroy();
    }
  else
    System.exit(0);
  }
```

The new set of lines is at the very beginning of the while() loop. These lines create an array of threads, utilize the enumerate method which was just talked about, and write out the name of each of the threads to System.out.

Go ahead and recompile the program and run it. Under Netscape, make sure you show the Java Console (Properties, Show Java Console) (see fig. 25.9).

**Fig. 25.9**
Great Race under Netscape with the Java Console showing.

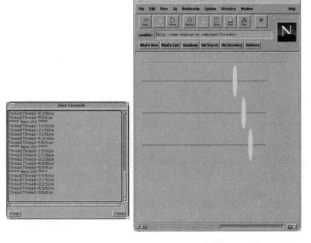

As the race progresses and each of the racers completes the race, you will be able to see that the number of active threads does really decrease. In fact, run the application and give it a number higher than three (see fig. 25.10). In other words, try

**java GreatRace 2**

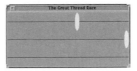

**Fig. 25.10**
Great Race run with 2 racers.

# The Daemon Property

Threads can be one of two types: a user thread or a Daemon thread.

What is a Daemon any way? Well, *Webster's Dictionary* says it is "a supernatural being or force, not specifically evil." In a sense, Webster's is right. While the thread is not actually supernatural and it is definitely not evil, a Daemon thread is not a natural thread either. You can set off Daemon threads on a path without ever worrying whether they come back. Once you start a Daemon thread, you don't need to worry about stopping it. When the thread reaches the end of the tasks it was assigned, it will stop and change its state to being inactive.

A very important difference between Daemon threads and user threads though is that Deamon threads can run all the time. If the Java interpretor determines that only Daemon threads are running, it will exit, without worrying if the Daemon threads have finished. This is very useful because it allows you to start threads that do things such as monitoring; they will die on their own when there is nothing else running. The usefulness of this technique is limited for graphical Java applications because, by default, several base threads are not set to be Daemon. These include AWT-Input, AWT-Motif, Main, and Screen_Updater. Unfortunately, this means that any application using the AWT class will have non-daemon threads that will prevent the application from exiting.

Two methods in `java.lang.Thread` deal with the daemonic state assigned to a thread. They are:

- `isDaemon()`
- `setDaemon(boolean)`

The first method, `isDaemon()`, is used to test the state of a particular thread. Occasionally this is useful to an object running as a thread so it can determine if it is running as a Daemon or as a regular thread. `isDaemon()` will return `true` if the thread is a Daemon and `false` otherwise.

The second method, `setDaemon(boolean)`, is used to change the daemonic state of the thread. To make a thread a Daemon, you indicate this by setting the input value to `true`. To change it back to a user thread, you set the Boolean value to `false`.

If you had wanted to make each of the racers in the GreatRace Daemon threads, you could have done so. In the `init()` for loop this would have looked like listing 25.9:

**Listing 25.9  New *for* Loop for *init()* Method in GreatRace.java**

```
for (int x=0;x<racerCount;x++){
    theRacers[x]=new Threader ("Racer #"+x);
    theRacers[x].resize(size().width,size().height/racerCount);
    add (theRacers[x]);
    theThreads[x]=new Thread(theRacers[x]);
    theThreads[x].setDaemon(true);
}
```

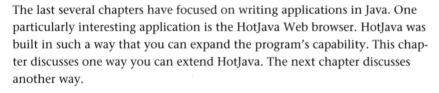

# CHAPTER 26
# Protocol Handlers

*by Eric Blossom*

The last several chapters have focused on writing applications in Java. One particularly interesting application is the HotJava Web browser. HotJava was built in such a way that you can expand the program's capability. This chapter discusses one way you can extend HotJava. The next chapter discusses another way.

Each document on the web is served up to your browser by a server program. The browser is then a client of the server program. Each server program understands a particular protocol. The protocol is designed so that the server can serve it's clients. The protocol is a rigid structure for the conversation between the client and server programs. HotJava can be extended by writing code to handle a new protocol. This lets HotJava talk to any server that understands the new protocol.

For more information on HotJava you can start with Sun's White Paper on the subject. It is available on the Web at

**http://www.javasoft.com/HotJava/overview/**

In this chapter, you will

- Create a new package to handle the finger protocol for HotJava
- Define a new `Handler` class in the package
- Define a new `fingerConnection` class
- Write a trivial Web browser in lieu of HotJava so you can test your new protocol handler

**Netscape Plug-ins**

Netscape uses a different scheme to extend its Navigator browser. You create something it calls a *plug-in*. Essentially, you write a plug-in in C or some other language. Presumably it could be in Java. Navigator then has an API that the plug-in uses to communicate to Navigator. There is also an API that the plug-in must implement. The first API lets the plug-in use the browser. The second API lets the browser use the plug-in. For more information, see Netscape's Web site:

> **http://home.netscape.com/comprod/products/navigator/
> version_2.0/plugins/**

This chapter discusses how to enable HotJava to talk to new types of servers. When any client program such as HotJava uses a server program, it uses a protocol to give structure to its conversation. Each server has its own protocol and HotJava (and all other browsers) knows several protocols. However, HotJava doesn't know some protocols, and therefore, it can't talk to some servers. By defining a "protocol handler," you can instruct HotJava in the new protocol.

# Anatomy of an URL

Documents on the Web are specified by *Universal Resource Locators* (URLs). They always start with a single word followed by a colon. The most common one is *http:,* which stands for *HyperText Transport Protocol.* This first word in the URL is where a browser gets the needed tip about what protocol to use to get the document specified. What follows the protocol in the URL may vary from one protocol to another. This is because different protocols have different needs. Generally, the format is *protocol://host:port/document.* For more information on URLs, you can consult a primer on the Web or the standard documents defining URLs.

> **http://www.ncsa.uiuc.edu/demoweb/url-primer.html ftp://
> ftp.internic.net/rfc/rfc1738.txt ftp://ftp.internic.net/rfc/
> rfc1808.txt**

Let's teach HotJava how to use the *finger protocol* by writing a finger protocol handler. This simple protocol gives information about a user on a particular system.

Open a connection to the other machine on port 79. This will connect you to the finger server. Then send a user name to the finger server. It will then send

back some information in plain text about the user you named. If you send
the server an empty line, it will send back a list of users currently logged onto
the server's system.

For all the details about the finger protocol, consult the current standard
document on the Web at

**ftp://ftp.internic.net/rfc/rfc1288.txt**

The finger URL is of the form:

```
finger://host/user
```

where *host* is the domain name of the server machine and user is the name
of the user. *user* can be blank—if it's blank and the server allows such a
query, a list of all users will be returned.

# Creating the New Finger Package

When HotJava encounters a URL such as finger://somehost.somwhere.com/
someone, it looks for a package named sun.net.www.protocol.finger.
The last word in the package must match the protocol at the beginning of the URL. HotJava wants to create an object of the class
sun.net.www.protocol.finger.Handler. Your job is to write that
class and put it in the right place so that HotJava can find it.

This new package must contain at least two public classes. One must be
named Handler. It must be an extension of the sun.net.ContentHandler
class. The other can be any name you choose. The one in this chapter follows
(loose) convention and is named fingerConnection. It must be an extension
of the sun.net.URLConnection class.

# Defining the New *Handler* Class

Listing 26.1 shows the Java code for the new Handler class. It must go in a file
named Handler.java. The compiler will insist on it.

**Listing 26.1   The Finger Protocol Handler**

```
1    package sun.net.www.protocol.finger;
2
3    // Finger Protocol Handler
4
5    import java.net.URL;
6    import java.net.URLConnection;
7    import java.net.URLStreamHandler;
```

(continues)

**Listing 26.1    Continued**

```
 8
 9    import sun.net.www.protocol.finger.fingerConnection;
10
11    public class Handler extends URLStreamHandler {
12
13        public URLConnection openConnection( URL u ) {
14
15            return new fingerConnection( u );
16
17        }
18
19    }
```

Now try to compile Handler.java with javac. You will get an error. Javac
wants to know what a fingerConnection is. So your job will get a little
harder. But, let's look at what you have so far.

1. First, import three standard objects that you need (see lines 5–7 of
   listing 26.1). They are all part of the java.net package that comes with
   the JDK.

   - An URL is a Universal Resource Locator object. Anyone who has
     worked with the Web knows that it refers to a document some-
     where out on the Web. The java.net.URL class knows how to go
     get the document and make it available to a Java program. This
     hides a lot of work for you. One need only create a URL and use
     its getContent() method to get a document from the Internet.

   - An URLConnection is a Java object that represents the connection
     between our machine and the one serving up the document.
     It's an abstract class. You can only use subclasses of it.

   - An URLStreamHandler handles the conversation—protocol—
     between the Web browser and the server. It's what you are
     building. This is another abstract class. The class you build will
     be a subclass.

2. Next, import the mysterious fingerConnection (line 9). Later, you will
   create the fingerConnection class.

3. Declare the Handler to be a subclass of URLStreamHandler (line 11).
   Now you know that you can do anything a generic URLStreamHandler
   can do. HotJava will be using your Handler class and will expect it
   to be a URLStreamHandler. This is why your class must extend
   URLStreamHandler.

**4.** Provide a method for other objects to open this connection. All you do
here is return a new `fingerConnection` object. So now you had better
look at creating a `fingerConnection`.

# Defining a New Type of URLConnection: The *fingerConnection*

Listing 26.2 shows the Java code for the new `fingerConnection` class. It must
go in a file named `fingerConnection.java`. Now there are two files, one for
each class. Recall that a Java source file can have only one public class. Because both the `Handler` and `fingerConnection` classes must be public, they
must each have a source file.

---

**Listing 26.2  The *fingerConnection* Subclass of *URLConnection***

```
1    package sun.net.www.protocol.finger;
2
3    import java.net.URL;
4    import java.net.URLConnection;
5    import java.net.Socket;
6    import java.io.InputStream;
7    import java.io.PipedInputStream;
8    import java.io.SequenceInputStream;
9    import java.io.DataOutputStream;
10   import java.io.PipedOutputStream;
11   import java.io.IOException;
12
13   public class fingerConnection extends URLConnection {
14       Socket socket;
15
16       public fingerConnection( URL u ) {
17
18           super( u );
19
20       }
21
22       public String getHeaderField( String label ) {
23
24           if ( label.equalsIgnoreCase( "content-type" ) )
25               return "text/plain";
26           return null;
27
28       }
29
30       public void connect() throws IOException {
31
32           if ( -1 < this.url.getPort() ) {
```

(continues)

Advanced Java

**Listing 26.2 Continued**

```
33              this.socket = new Socket( this.url.getHost(),
           ➡this.url.getPort() );
34          } else {
35              this.socket = new Socket( this.url.getHost(), 79 );
36          }
37
38          DataOutputStream out = new
           ➡DataOutputStream(this.socket.getOutputStream());
39          out.writeBytes( this.url.getFile().substring( 1 ) +
           ➡"\r\n" );
40          out.flush();
41
42      }
43
44
45      public InputStream getInputStream() throws IOException {
46
47          this.connect();
48          return this.socket.getInputStream();
49
50      }
51
52  }
```

## Declaring the *fingerConnection* Class

Lines 3-11 of listing 26.2 import the necessary Java objects and line 13 declares the new fingerConnection class. It's a kind of URLConnection. It handles a connection to something else that will serve up the document. You saw one of these in the Handler. Remember how the Handler returned a fingerConnection? If you look at the declaration, you see that it's supposed to return a URLConnection. Well, now this makes sense because a fingerConnection *is* a kind of URLConnection.

There is one more thing that a fingerConnection has that a generic URLConnection doesn't—a Socket. Line 14 declares the Socket attribute. We will use the Socket to send the user name to the server and to get the server's response.

## Defining a *fingerConnection* Constructor

Now you need to define a constructor for your new class. Lines 16-20 define a constructor for the fingerConnection. Construct a generic URLConnection and then set the socket to null. You'll get a new socket later.

## Setting the Content Type

Different documents can contain different types of data. The MIME standard has defined seven content types. Each type is extended by several subtypes. The type of a document's content is specified in a Content-type field at the head of the document.

The MIME standard describes the content-type field in detail. The standard is available on the Net from:

**ftp://ftp.internic.net/rfc/rfc1521**

The standard says that the default content type is text/plain. So if a document does not have a Content-type field, it should be considered to be of type text/plain. However, the current version 1.0 Final of the JDK sets it to content/unknown. Hopefully, this will be changed in a future version of the JDK and of HotJava. What this means for us is that you will need to override the method that sets the content type. This is because there is no Content-type field in the reply from the finger server. Hence, you will want to set your content type to text/plain.

Do this by overriding the getHeaderFields() method of a URLConnection class. Lines 22 to 28 of listing 26.2 do this. The method in the JDK just returns null. Return text/plain when asked for the value of the Content-type field.

## Defining a *connect* Method

One cannot declare an instance of a plain old URLConnection because it is an abstract class. The only way it can be made concrete is to extend it as you did with fingerConnection. What makes it an abstract class is that it contains an abstract method. The connect method of a URLConnection is abstract. It has a declaration but it does not have any implementation. So to make the fingerConnection concrete, you must provide a connect() method that matches the abstract connect() method defined in java.net.URLConnection.

Now you need to show how to connect to the server and send the user name. Lines 30-42 show the connect() method. This is where this.socket is used, along with a local DataOutputStream.

What's a DataOutputStream? Once upon a time, the developers of UNIX thought files were too complicated, partly because of things like record structures and access methods. They decided that it would be simpler to have files just be a sequence of bytes. That way they would look a lot like a sequence of bytes coming in over a communications line or a sequence of bytes going to a terminal screen. This decision simplified a lot of software. Programs no longer needed to be concerned with where the bytes were coming from or where they were going to. If you don't know what "record structure" and "access method" means, don't worry. You don't need to.

A Web browser can make good use of this concept. Sometimes a document is coming from a server far away. Sometimes it's coming from a local file. The protocol handlers deal with this and make an InputStream available to whatever object needs to read the document.

Java Streams fit in with this idea. InputStreams are streams of bytes that come into the program. OutputStreams are bytes going away. You can write() to an OutputStream and read() from an InputStream. A process can produce data by writing to an OutputStream. Another can consume data by reading from an InputStream. An intermediate process can filter data by reading data from an InputStream, modifying it, and writing it to an OutputStream.

You'll be using one to send the user name to the server. Okay. But what's a DataOutputStream? Streams deal in arrays of bytes. A DataOutputStream has additional methods for writing other types of data and converting them automatically. You don't want to write the user name one byte at a time. It is much more convenient to write the whole string at once.

## Getting a Socket to the Server

Next up is plugging into the server (see lines 32 to 36 of listing 26.2). Sockets connect to a host at a port number. A host has many ports just as Japan has many ports. A different service is available at each port. The finger service is usually available at port 79 if at all. Many folks think it's not a good idea to let others know who is on their systems. So, often the finger service is not available.

---

**Note**

There is a java.net.ServerSocket class. Don't be confused. The ServerSocket class is for server programs. HotJava is a client program. Hence, our protocol handler is part of a client program. It should use the Socket class, not the ServerSocket class.

## Sockets

Sockets are an abstraction developed at the University of California at Berkeley to make network programming easier. UCB had added networking code to UNIX and needed a way for programmers to use it. Theoretically, it can be independent of the underlying network protocols. Practically, it has been tied to TCP/IP. It has been very successful as an API. One can find implementations of the UCB sockets API in just about any operating system that supports TCP/IP. In the early 90s a version of the sockets API was created for Microsoft's Windows operating environment. It is called WinSock. This has helped in porting UNIX networking programs to the PC. Currently, work is underway to define a second version of WinSock, which will try to fulfill the promise of lower-layer independence. Java's Socket class is an even more convenient way to do network programming.

The URL may have a port specified, in which case we use that port. Otherwise we use the standard port 79. If the URL was something like "finger:// somehost.somewhere.com:2088/someone," we would use port 2088.

A Java URL has methods to reveal the host and port. In this chapter's example `self.url.getHost()` returns *somehost.somewhere.com* and `self.url.getPort()` returns *2088*. If the port number was not assigned `self.url.getPort()` returns *-1*.

## Getting an *OutputStream* to the Server

To send bytes to the server, you want an `OutputStream`. A `Socket` object provides just such a thing. This is what line 38 of listing 26.2 shows.

Actually, you need to get a `DataOutputStream` to the `Socket`. A Java `Socket` will kindly provide any kind of `OutputStream` with its `getOutputStream()` method. You then "wrap" it in a `DataOutputStream` so that you can write a `String` all in one go. Otherwise you'd have to send the bytes out one-by-one.

## Sending the User Name to the Server

Line 39 of listing 26.2 sends the user name to the server. The `writeChars()` method of a `DataOutputStream` object will write a `String`. The `DataOutputStream` will, in turn, send the bytes to the `Socket`'s `OutputStream`. The `Socket` will then pass them on to the server.

Remember the format of a finger URL: `finger://somehost.somewhere.com/`*someone*. The user name *someone* is where the file name would be in an HTTP or FTP URL. Use the getFile() method to find out the user's name. That method, however, returns the slash before the name as well. That's why you need to use the substring() method to get just the bytes after the first. Don't forget the carriage return and line feed characters after the user name.

Now you just writeBytes() on the DataOutputStream and off they go to the server. The flush() method makes sure they go right away rather than waiting around for other things in the system to settle.

## Making the Document Available to the Browser

Lines 45–50 of listing 26.2 define the getInputStream() method. This makes the document available to the browser. HotJava will be calling the getInputStream() method of the fingerConnection. The browser will then be able to read bytes on the InputStream returned by this method. Of course, you just get it from your socket. Use your connect() method to get the socket connected to the server and then return the socket's InputStream.

This makes a lot of sense. Our protocol handler should handle the protocol entirely. No other object should need to know anything about it. This handler can talk to the server and just deliver the document. Luckily, the finger protocol is a very simple one.

# Putting It All Together

In this section, you will put the package together so that HotJava can use it. There are several steps you need to take to accomplish this.

1. Create a directory for the finger package.
2. Compile the classes that make up the package.
3. Put the classes in the directory you created in step 1.
4. Modify your CLASSPATH environment variable to let Java know where you put the package.

## Creating a Directory for the New Package

The classes that came with the JDK are kept in a file named classes.zip. This file is in the subdirectory "lib" of the directory where you installed the JDK. So if you installed the JDK in /usr/local/java, for example, the classes would be in /usr/local/java/lib/classes.zip. This is one place you can put your new package. It has the advantage that Java already knows about this directory and will look for your package there.

An alternative is to create another directory for your own packages. This has the advantage of making it clearer which packages came with Java and which you added. On a multi-user system, you may have do take this alternative because you might not have access to the directory where the JDK was installed. You might create a subdirectory called myclasses in your home directory.

In either case, you will need to create a chain of subdirectories of the directory you have chosen for your packages. Because HotJava is looking for the package `sun.net.www.protocol.finger`, you need to have a new directory sun/net/www/protocol/finger/. This is the directory where you will put the `.class` files.

For example, suppose you have chosen the second option above on your UNIX system. The command mkdir -p myclasses/sun/net/www/protocol/finger issued from your home directory should do the trick.

## Compiling the Classes

You need to compile both of your classes but you must compile the `fingerConnection` class before the `Handler` class. This is because the `Handler` class uses a `fingerConnection` object. If the `Handler` class has not been compiled, the compiler will not be able to find it when you try to compile the `fingerConnection` class.

## Putting the *.class* Files in the Package Directory

The 1.0 release of the JDK has all the classes zipped up in an archive named `classes.zip`. On UNIX systems this will often be in /usr/local/java/lib. Don't zip your new classes into this archive. Use the directory you created in step 1. Copy the files `Handler.class` and `fingerConnection.class` to this directory.

## Modifying Your *CLASSPATH*

Your operating system needs to know where to look for programs to run. You let the operating system know where to look by specifying the PATH environment variable. Similarly, Java needs to know where to look for classes. You let Java know where to look by specifying the CLASSPATH environmental variable.

Set it to include the classes that came with the JDK and your classes. Another convenience, especially when developing and testing, is to specify that the current directory is also a place to look for classes.

Suppose you've chosen /usr/local/java/classes to put your packages in. This means that the classes will go in /usr/local/java/classes/sun/net/www/protocol/finger. You need to set your CLASSPATH this way:

```
export CLASSPATH=.:/usr/local/java/classes:/usr/local/java/lib/
.classes.zip
```

Notice that there are three components to the CLASSPATH, separated by colons.

**1.** A period (.)—this means look in the current directory.

**2.** Where you expect to find your package (and, perhaps, other classes and/or packages you may have defined for other purposes). Do not specify the sun/net/www/protocol/finger portion of the path. This is because that is your package name. Java knows to tack on the rest of the full path name to each path it finds in the CLASSPATH environment variable.

**3.** The compressed classes that you got with the JDK.

The order of these components is significant. You can keep newer versions of packages and classes under your current directory. They will be found before the other class libraries are searched. This lets you work on experimental versions without disturbing more stable versions in your classes directory.

# Testing the New Handler

Sun has not yet released the new version of HotJava. The current version of HotJava uses the 1.0 Alpha3 API. This leaves you with a problem—how to test it. You can't just tap your foot until HotJava 1.0 Final is released. A solution is to build a trivial browser to stand in for HotJava.

## Building a Trivial Browser

You need a trivial browser that will work with your new classes. It uses the same URL object that HotJava will use. Hopefully, if your protocol handler works with this, it will work with HotJava.

Toward that end, create a file named GoGet.java. Its contents are listed in listing 26.3.

### Listing 26.3 The Trivial Browser—*GoGet*

```
1    import java.net.URL;
2    import java.net.MalformedURLException;
3
4    public class GoGet {
5
6        public static void main( String args[] ) {
7
8            URL url = null;
```

```
 9          Object o = null;
10
11          try {
12             url = new URL( args[0] );
13             o = url.getContent();
14             System.out.println( o.toString() );
15
16          } catch (ArrayIndexOutOfBoundsException e) {
17             System.err.println( "usage: java tester URL " );
18
19          } catch (MalformedURLException e) {
20             System.err.println( "Malformed URL: " + args[0] );
21             System.err.println( e.toString() );
22
23          } catch (Exception e) {
24             System.err.println( e.toString() );
25
26          }
27
28      }
29
30  }
```

The trivial browser is an application run through the Java interpreter. Its usage is:

```
java GoGet URL
```

Notice that this listing never called anything in the finger package. It doesn't import anything from it, either. Behind the scenes, the URL takes apart the String passed to it. It finds the protocol and looks for a package that implements it. Guess where it looks? That's right, in sun/net/www/protocol/finger, just where you put it. When you think about it, that had to be the case. Sun isn't going to change HotJava for every oddball protocol someone wants to write. So they found a general way for you to plug something in.

Line 12 of listing 26.3 creates an URL; line 13 gets the content in; line 14 converts it to a String (with the toString() method) and puts it out on stdout. The rest of it catches exceptions.

If no URL is specified on the command line, the args[] array will be empty. This will throw an ArrayIndexOutOfBoundsException. So line 16 catches that exception; line 17 gives a hint about usage.

If the URL specified on the command line is illegal, the URL constructor will throw a MalformedURLException. Lines 19 to 21 report that.

Lines 23 and 24 catch and report any other Exception that might get thrown.

**V**

**Advanced Java**

## Trying It Out

Now try it out. Listing 26.4 shows what happened when the author tried it out on his system. First he tried it with a URL of just **finger:**. The host portion should default to the local host. An empty `finger` command should return all the users logged in at the current time.

---

**Listing 26.4   Just the Protocol Part of the URL**

```
bash$ java GoGet finger:
Login    Name               Tty  Idle  Login Time   Office
➥Office Phone
eric     Eric Blossom        1   4:48  Feb 25 08:40 West
➥510 841-3338
eric     Eric Blossom        p0         Feb 25 08:40 [ :0.0 ]
```

---

Listing 26.5 shows an attempt using the author's user name. Again the default host should be taken.

---

**Listing 26.5   The Protocol and User Name**

```
bash$ java GoGet finger:eric
Login: eric                        Name: Eric Blossom
Directory: /home/eric              Shell: /bin/bash
Office: West, 510 841-3338
On since Sun Feb 25 08:40 (PST) on tty1,  idle 4:49
On since Sun Feb 25 08:40 (PST) on ttyp0 from :0.0
No Mail.
Plan:
to (dare I say it?) rule the world!
```

---

Listing 26.6 shows an attempt with a different host. The author's user name on that host is "elb."

---

**Listing 26.6   The Full URL, Protocol, Host, and User**

```
bash$ java GoGet finger://shell/elb
Login: elb                         Name: Eric Blossom
Directory: /home/elb               Shell: /bin/tcsh
Never logged.in.
No Mail.
No Plan.
```

---

Listing 26.7 shows what happened when the author tried to see who else was using another host.

**Listing 26.7  Just the Protocol and Host Portions of the URL**

```
bash$ java GoGet finger://shell
must provide username
```

Remember that the administrators of some machines think it's not such a good idea to run a finger server. Others will run finger, but only reply if a user name is asked for. The machine named "shell" in the author's domain is such a machine. The response "must provide username" is from the finger server on shell.

# Comparing Protocol Handlers and Applets

Another way to connect to a server using another protocol is to write an applet. This has some advantages over writing a protocol handler and some disadvantages.

With a protocol handler, your Web page would have a link that looks like any other link. Only the URL it points to is different. You could write an applet that functions like a link and even looks like a link (or like a button). This applet would have to be downloaded and run before the user can click on it to retrieve the document to which it points.

An applet can be used in any browser that supports Java, not just the HotJava browser. It can also have a better, more lively appearance, perhaps downloading the document referred to without requiring (or allowing) user action.

A protocol handler is not restricted by the security constraints of an applet. It can connect to servers other than the one from which it got the containing page. This gives you far more flexibility in pointing to other resources.

A protocol handler must be installed on the client machine where an applet can be downloaded over the net. The HotJava White Paper talks about protocol handlers being downloaded on demand. However, the version 1.0 Alpha3 of HotJava does not support this. It doesn't seem likely that the next version of HotJava will, either.

# Security Considerations

Using a custom protocol handler should be about as risky as installing a browser. If you trust the producer or can examine the source code, you will likely be able to trust the software.

V

Advanced Java

Having the protocol handler downloaded automatically is another concern. This makes it roughly as risky as an applet. If the protocol handler is still free of an applet's security restrictions, it would be riskier than an applet. However, as mentioned previously, this may not be a worry if HotJava doesn't support downloadable protocol handlers.

# Some Unanswered Questions

Protocol handlers have not yet been a widely used feature of HotJava. There are still questions about their use and value that need to be answered. Here are some of them.

- What is Sun's commitment to HotJava?

  Do they intend to continue developing it or defer to their licensees, like Netscape and Microsoft? There may be some pressure for Sun not to compete with their licensees.

- Will protocol handlers be downloadable?

  The HotJava White Paper talks of protocol handlers being loaded on request from the server that has the content. This doesn't seem to be the case, yet. It is not clear how this would work, anyway. Presumably one would need another protocol of some sort to download the handler. Of course, this would have to be a second protocol. Otherwise, it would be catch-22.

- Will other browsers support protocol handlers?

  From here it looks like Netscape has already gone to plug-ins instead. What will Microsoft do? Sun moved the protocol handlers out from the java.net packages and into the sun.net packages. This may be a sign that protocol handlers will not be supported by other vendors. That would make them considerably less valuable. Any protocol handler you wrote would only work with HotJava. This would limit your market quite severely.

# CHAPTER 27

# Content Handlers

*by Eric Blossom*

Documents found on the Web are of many different types. A document may contain text, an image, sound, etc. HotJava and other Web browsers are able to display a variety of different documents.

However, new types of content come online all the time. HotJava and other browsers have software built-in to handle the types they know about. But what about new types? Many browsers support the notion of helper applications. You can associate a particular content type with an application. For example, Microsoft defined a format for document interchange called Rich Text Format (RTF). You can associate the RTF content type with Microsoft Word. Now when you download a document containing text in RTF, your browser will launch Microsoft Word with your document loaded. This is pretty convenient. But, it pops open a whole new application in a different window. There is another way.

With HotJava, you can define new classes to handle new types of content. These new classes are called content handlers. HotJava was designed to accept new content handlers allowing it to handle new types of content directly, without any helper application. The content handlers effectively become a part of HotJava.

With a content handler instead of a helper application, the document will be displayed in the browser's window. No helper application needs to be launched.

In this chapter you will:

- Explore the notion of a MIME content type.
- Briefly describe the text/enriched content type.
- Build an enriched text content handler.

- Expand the trivial browser of chapter 26 to be able to use content handlers in general.
- Test our text/enriched content handler with the modified browser.

# Understanding MIME Content Types

When a Web browser gets a document, it tries to figure out what the document contains. Part of the HyperText Transport Protocol (HTTP) tells the browser what the coming document contains. For other protocols, the browser will try to deduce the content type from the file name extension.

A standard way of specifying content types comes from MIME (Multipurpose Internet Mail Extensions). The Web and the Hypertext Transport Protocol specify content type in exactly the same way. This is why content types are often referred to as MIME types.

**ftp://ftp.internic.net/rfc/rfc1521.txt**

In mail messages the content type is specified in a header field labeled "Content-type:". Its value is of the form <type>/<subtype>. The content type of most Web pages is "text/html." HotJava knows how to handle this kind of content and many others. Still, you can define others and teach HotJava how to handle them. You will write a handler for the standard content-type of text/enriched.

**ftp://ftp.internic.net/rfc/rfc1526.txt**

## Enriched Text

The people who invented the MIME standard also came up with a simple format for encoding text a little richer than plain ASCII. It uses tags similar to HTML. The tags come in pairs of <TAG> and </TAG>

<bold> bold text </bold>
<italic> italic text </italic>
<fixed> text in a monospaced font </fixed>
<smaller> text in a smaller font </smaller>
<bigger> text in a larger font </bigger>
<underline> underlined text </underline>
 centered text 
<flushleft> text aligned on the left margin </flushleft>
<flushright> text aligned on the right margin </flushright>
<flushboth> text spread out to align on both margins </flushboth>
<nofill> verbatim text with new lines honored </nofill>

&lt;indent&gt; indented text &lt;/indent&gt;
&lt;indentright&gt; text with a wider right margin &lt;/indentright&gt;
&lt;excerpt&gt; text excerpted from another source &lt;/excerpt&gt;
&lt;param&gt; specialized commands &lt;/param&gt;

A literal "&lt;" is represented by doubling it "&lt;&lt;". Sequences of consecutive newline characters in the input are decreased by one. Isolated newline characters are converted to a single space. This effectively makes newline characters into paragraph separators.

## Separating Lines of Text

Plain ASCII text is not so plain when it comes to separating lines of text. Some systems (like DOS) use two characters, a carriage return (CR) and a line feed (LF), to signal a new line. Some (like UNIX) use a single LF character. Some (like Macintosh) use a single CR character. Standard C language functions for reading and writing text use the notion of a newline character. The newline character is encoded with '\n'. The standard C functions handle conversion to and from whatever the local convention is.

In Java, newline is also coded as \n. However, content handlers use a data stream that bypasses the standard C language IO functions. Text from the internet generally arrives with lines separated by pairs of CR and LF characters. Your content handler will see the CR as \r and the LF as \n.

Generally you will want to convert whatever comes over the net as a newline to a single \n character.

The author noticed when using the text/plain content handler with Alpha3 HotJava on Windows, that the CR characters showed up in the viewing panel as little rectangles. Modifying the text/plain content handler to strip out the \r characters fixed this.

V

Advanced Java

# Creating a Content Handler Step-by-Step

Your content handler will be a minimal one. It will strip the tags from the enriched text and honor only the &lt;nofill&gt; and &lt;/nofill&gt; tags. It will also strip out anything between &lt;param&gt; and &lt;/param&gt; tags.

Chapter 27—Content Handlers

## Declaring the Package

Content handlers must be part of a package named for the type. The package will contain a class for each subtype. So for the type text we will need a text package. In that package there should be classes for plain, html, etc. URL objects look for these packages with the prefix sun.net.www.content. So **sun.net.www.content.text** is the text package. This package already exists in the JDK. The text/plain handler is there. The first line in our source code declares this to be part of that package.

```
package sun.net.www.content.text;
```

## Importing Standard Classes

The next thing you need to do is import the standard classes that you will use or extend in your handler.

```
import java.net.ContentHandler;
import java.net.URLConnection;
import java.io.InputStream;
import java.io.IOException
```

Your handler will be a subtype of the `java.lang.ContentHandler` class. It provides a `getContent()` method useful to browsers. You will be overriding that method.

An URLConnection gives you control of a connection to a server on the Internet. You will use its `getInputStream()` method to provide an InputStream from the server that you can read.

An InputStream is a stream of characters that can be read.

It is actually an abstract class. Any objects returned of type InputStream will actually be of some subtype of InputStream. This will not matter to you. All that matters is that you can use the `read()` method to get characters. Since the abstract class InputStream has such a method, all its subclasses must also have that method.

An IOException is what can get thrown back to from some of the methods you will be using.

You, in turn, will throw the IOException back to whatever is using your method. This exception will get thrown if there is trouble getting characters from the server.

## Declaring the class

You declare the class as extending the java.net.ContentHandler class. It is the only public class you will need. Its name must match the name of the MIME subtype. In your case that is "enriched." Here is an empty version showing out to declare the class. You will fill it in later.

```
public class enriched extends ContentHandler {
}
```

## Defining the *getContent()* Method

You override the getContent() method of the ContentHandler class. It must be declared to be the same as the one in the ContentHandler class. Its single parameter is the URLConnection from where the data are coming. It can throw an IOException back to the caller.

Notice that the method returns an Object. Any kind of object can be returned. You will be returning a string. However, you could return a graphic widget containing the text rendered in varying fonts complete with a scrolling mechanism to view it with. A graphic browser would be able to take such a widget and display it in one of its panels. It might also be able to accept a String and put it in a text box of some sort for display.

Your trivial browser will just write a string to the standard output. So a String will be just fine for your purposes. Here is the enriched class again. This time with an empty getContent() method. This shows how to define the method. You will fill it in later.

```
public class enriched extends ContentHandler {
    public Object getContent( URLConnection urlc ) throws IOException {
    }
}
```

## Reading the InputStream

Now you put in a loop to read data from the URLConnection and build a StringBuffer with them. The StringBuffer is then returned to the caller as a String. This is pretty much just what the text/plain content handler does. It gets an InputStream from the URLConnection passed to it. Then it reads characters one at a time from the InputStream and appends them to a StringBuffer. The last line returns the characters converted to a String object.

Here is your `getContent()` method filled in enough to do this.

```
        public Object getContent( URLConnection urlc ) throws
    IOException {
            StringBuffer out = new StringBuffer();
            int c;

        InputStream in = urlc.getInputStream();
        c = in.read();
        while( 0 <= c ) {
            out.append( (char) c );
            c = in.read();
        }
        in.close();
        return out.toString();
    }
```

## Transforming the Content

At last you get to parsing the enriched text. The full content handler is given in listing 27.1 below. The basic loop is the same. However, within that loop you check for tags and convert newline sequences appropriately. This code may look a lot like C. This is because it is a fairly direct translation from the C code given in RFC 1526.

The main loop is just as it was except for a large if statement inside it. That statement is checking for a < that may be starting a tag.

You also have three context variables. One keeps track of how long the current sequence of newline characters is. Another, paramct, shows how deeply nested you are in <param>, </param> tags. The third, nofill, shows how deeply nested you are between <nofill> and </nofill> tags.

If there are no tags or < characters in the text, only the code in lines 50 to 58 will get exercised within the if, else statement starting at line 26.

Line 50 checks to see if you are between any <param>, </param> pairs. If you are, just ignore the current character.

In line 52, you check to see if your character is a newline. If it is and you are not in a nofill section, the newline is counted. If the sequence is now more than one newline long (i.e. the previous character was also a newline) then the newline is emitted. Otherwise it is just counted.

At line 54, you know that the character is not a newline. If the newline sequence was exactly one character long, then a space is emitted in line 55. In line 56 you set your newline count to zero, because you know that the current character is not a newline. Line 57 emits the current character.

If 0 < nofill then the newline count will not be incremented. In this case, line 57 will just emit them as they come.

Now let's look at what happens when you encounter a <. Line 27 will emit a space if the previous character was a single newline and line 29 gets the next character. If the next character is also a <, then line 31 emits it. Otherwise you probably have a tag.

You read in the rest of the tag in lines 33 to 36 and convert it to a String in line 37. Lines 39 to 47 adjust the appropriate context variable based on the tag just encountered.

**Listing 27.1   Enriched Text Content Handler**

```
1    // Enriched Text Content Handler.
2
3    package sun.net.www.content.text;
4
5    import java.net.ContentHandler;
6    import java.net.URLConnection;
7    import java.io.InputStream;
8    import java.io.IOException;
9
10   public class enriched extends ContentHandler {
11
12      public Object getContent( URLConnection urlc ) throws IOException {
13         StringBuffer out = new StringBuffer();
14         StringBuffer ts = new StringBuffer();
15         String token = new String();
16         InputStream in;
17         int c;
18         int newlinect = 0;
19         int paramct = 0;
20         int nofill = 0;
21
22         in = urlc.getInputStream();
23         try {
24            c = in.read();
25            while( -1 < c ) {
26               if ( '<' == c ) { // We may have a command.
27                  if ( 1 == newlinect ) { out.append( ' ' ); }
28                  newlinect = 0;
29                  c = in.read();
30                  if ( '<' == c ) { // We have a quoted <
31                     if ( paramct < 1 ) out.append( (char)c );
32                  } else { // We have a command.
33                     while ( -1 < c && '>' != c ) {
34                        ts.append( (char)c );
35                        c = in.read();
36                     }
37                     token = ts.toString();
```

(continues)

---

**Listing 27.1   Continued**

```
38                        ts.setLength( 0 );
39                        if ( token.equalsIgnoreCase( "param" ) ) {
40                            paramct++;
41                        } else if ( token.equalsIgnoreCase( "nofill") ) {
42                            nofill++;
43                        } else if ( token.equalsIgnoreCase( "/param") ) {
44                            paramct--;
45                        } else if ( token.equalsIgnoreCase( "/nofill") ) {
46                            nofill--;
47                        }
48                    }
49                } else { // It's text.
50                    if ( 0 < paramct )
51                        ; // ignore params
52                    else if ( c == '\n' && nofill < 1 ) {
53                        if ( 1 < ++newlinect ) out.append( (char)c );
54                    } else {
55                        if ( 1 == newlinect ) out.append( ' ' );
56                        newlinect = 0;
57                        out.append( (char)c );
58                    }
59                }
60                c = in.read();
61            }
62        } finally {
63            in.close();
64        }
65        out.append( '\n' );
66        return out.toString();
67    }
68 }
```

---

# Testing Our Content Handler

The trivial browser you used for testing in chapter 26 needs to be extended to test your content handler. Listing 27.2 shows the new version of GoGet.

The big change here is the addition of a ContentHandlerFactory. The URLConnection will use the ContentHandlerFactory's createContentHandler() method to create the correct content handler for a MIME type. A ContentHandlerFactory is not a class, but an interface. This means that you need to define every method in the interface. The only method in the interface is the createContentHandler method.

Having defined your ContentHandlerFactory, you need to let the URLConnection know we have done so. That is the purpose of line 40. Of course, to set the URLConnection's content handler factory, we need the URLConnection. That is the purpose of line 39. Line 39 actually establishes communication with the server. In the previous version that happened behind the scene when getObject() was used. In this case, getObject() realizes that the connection is already established.

Your factory in lines 13 to 22 gives back your enriched handler for enriched text and the plain handler for other subtypes of type text and for objects of unknown content. You do not have handlers for any other content types, so you should return a null pointer in those cases.

**Listing 27.2    A Trivial Browser—GoGet Revisited**

```
1     import java.net.URL;
2     import java.net.URLConnection;
3     import java.net.MalformedURLException;
4
5     import java.net.ContentHandler;
6     import java.net.ContentHandlerFactory;
7
8
9     class ourContentHandlerFactory implements ContentHandlerFactory {
10
11        public ContentHandler createContentHandler( String mimetype ) {
12
13            if ( mimetype.equalsIgnoreCase( "text/enriched" ) ) {
14                return new sun.net.www.content.text.enriched();
15
16            } else if ( mimetype.startsWith( "text/" ) ) {
17                return new sun.net.www.content.text.plain();
18
19            } else if ( mimetype.equalsIgnoreCase( "content/unknown") ) {
20                return new sun.net.www.content.text.plain();
21
22            }
23
24            return null;
25        }
26
27    }
28
39
30    public class GoGet {
31
32        public static void main( String args[] ) {
33
34            URL url = null;
35            Object o = null;
```

(continues)

**Listing 27.2   Continued**

```
36
37          try {
38              url = new URL( args[0] );
39              URLConnection c = url.openConnection();
40              c.setContentHandlerFactory( new ourContentHandlerFactory() );
41              o = c.getContent();
42              System.out.println( o.toString() );
43
44          } catch (ArrayIndexOutOfBoundsException e) {
45              System.err.println( "usage: java tester URL " );
46
47          } catch (MalformedURLException e) {
48              System.err.println( "Malformed URL: " + args[0] );
49              System.err.println( e.toString() );
50
51          } catch (Exception e) {
52              System.err.println( e.toString() );
53
54          }
55
56      }
57
58
59  }
```

## Creating Test Data

You need to create a file containing some enriched text to see if you can
GoGet it.

```
Here's a bit of <bold>enriched</bold> text.
This should be the second sentence in the first paragraph.
It should all be one long line.

Did this start a second line
with no blank line before it?


Did this start a second paragraph
with a single blank line before it?
<nofill>
This sentence should
be on two lines.
</nofill>
```

## Associating MIME Types with File Fame Suffixes

Mosaic and Netscape use a file named mime.types to associate MIME types
with file name suffixes. Each line of the file consists of a MIME type and one
or more suffixes separated by spaces.

Unfortunately, the final version of the JDK appears to consult an internal table to make these associations. This will make it a bit harder to test our code. The problem is letting the URLConnection object know what the content type is.

## One More Adjustment

One way to get around the problem mentioned above is to change line 17 in listing 27.2 to read the same as line 14. This will treat all text files as enriched text. Then rename the test file test.txt so that it will be associated with the content type text/plain.

For the more adventurous, another way is to modify the URLConnection.java file and recompile it. To do this, you need find a series of lines of the form:

```
setSuffix(".text", "text/plain");
```

Then you need to add one that reads:

```
setSuffix(".enriched", "text/enriched");
```

Then you can recompile and replace the URLConnection.class in the classes.zip file. Don't forget to make a backup of classes.zip first!

## Running the Test

At last we can try it. This shows what happened when the author ran the test:

```
bash$ java GoGet file:test.txt
Here's a bit of enriched text. This should be the second sentence
paragraph. It should all be one long line.                in the first
Did this start a second line with no blank line before it?

Did this start a second paragraph with a single blank line before
This sentence should                                      it?
be on two lines.
```

# Open Questions

Installing content handlers is about as risky as installing protocol handlers. See chapter 26 for a discussion of those risks.

Sun's HotJava White Paper describes content handlers being downloaded on the fly if HotJava encounters a content type it doesn't have a handler for. However, Neither the alpha nor beta APIs seem to support this. Will future versions of the API support it?

This would be very convenient. It would also be a security risk. Sun (and other browser makers who wanted to use content handlers) would need to decide if the risk is worth it. They may decide to allow it, but with security restrictions similar to those imposed on applets.

One of the great benefits of content handlers is that one can create a new type of content and a handler to go with it. The MIME standard says that when you do such a thing you should give it a subtype starting with X-. HotJava needs for you to then define a class whose name starts with X-. However the Java compiler will reject such a name. Class names cannot contain a hyphen. Javac will report a syntax error. How will Sun deal with this problem?

Perhaps Sun could modify HotJava. When confronted with such a type or subtype name, HotJava could seek a class named the same except for an underline character in place of the hyphen. e.g. for a content type of text/x-mystuff, HotJava would look for a class named x_mystuff in the text package. If you don't want to wait for Sun to make this change, you could use a prefix of X_ rather than the standard X-. You would not be quite standard, but your new name would probably not collide with any new standard names either. ❖

# CHAPTER 28

# Communications and Networking

*by Ira Krakow*

Connectivity to the Internet is probably one of the reasons you are interested in Java. The future of computing may be that Java applets from all over the Internet be capable of running instantly—the same way that HTML pages are publishable today. In this chapter, I discuss the special network-aware classes in Java (in the java.net package) that make writing programs for communication over the Internet easier than in most other languages.

In this chapter we will:

- Introduce the Java socket classes
- Explain how the Internet uses sockets
- Write a prototype Internet telnet server for remote login
- Write a prototype telnet client that talks to our server
- Write a prototype program that sends a datagram packet
- Write a prototype program that receives a datagram packet
- Explore security issues that may shape the future of Java network programming

## The Java Socket Classes

Java has the same UNIX roots as the Internet. It's designed from the ground up as a networking language. I will first discuss the URL class, which provides a number of ways of specifying an Internet resource. Then I will discuss how Java makes network programming easier by encapsulating connection functionality in *socket classes*. I will discuss the following socket classes:

- Socket is the basic object in Internet communication, which supports the TCP protocol. TCP is a reliable stream network connection. The

Socket class provides methods for stream I/O, which make reading from and writing to `Socket` easy. If you want to write programs that communicate on the Internet, you almost cannot avoid using this class. You will see the steps in writing a simple Telnet server (for login to a remote computer) using `Socket`, as well as a prototype client program that talks to our Telnet server.

■ `ServerSocket` is an object used for Internet server programs for listening to client requests. `ServerSocket` does not actually perform the service; instead, it creates a `Socket` object on behalf of the client. The communication is performed through that object.

■ `DatagramSocket` is an object that uses the *Unreliable Datagram Protocol* (UDP). Datagram sockets are not as reliable as TCP-based sockets. (For one thing, the packets aren't guaranteed to arrive at their destination.) However, communication using datagram sockets is faster because there is no connection made between the sender and receiver. On UNIX servers, functions such as getting the time of day are usually implemented using UDP because of speed considerations.

■ `SocketImpl` is an abstract class that enables you to implement your own flavor of data communication. As with all abstract classes, you subclass `SocketImpl` and implement its methods, as opposed to instantiating `SocketImpl` itself. If your application has specialized communication requirements, such as implementing a firewall (TCP is an unsecured protocol) or communicating with specialized equipment such as a bar code reader or a differential analyzer, you may need to "roll your own" socket class. (You could also subclass `Socket` or `DatagramSocket` if their methods are a useful starting point.)

A commercial example of customized transmission protocol is Netscape's *Secure Sockets Layer* (SSL) for ensuring that such transactions as credit card purchases can be transmitted securely over the Internet (see **http://www.netscape.com/info/security-doc.html**).

I will also touch on security considerations inherent in this new vision of distributed worldwide applets. The goal is to lay the foundation for whatever Java network programming your application might require.

# How the Internet Uses Sockets

In chapter 26, "Protocol Handlers," the author used the Socket class to develop a Finger protocol. You can think of an Internet server as a set of Socket classes that provide additional capabilities—generally called *services*.

Examples of services are electronic mail, *Telnet* for remote login, and *File Transfer Protocol* (FTP) for transferring files around the network. If the server to which you are attached provides Web access, then there is a Web service available as well.

## Ports and Services

Each service is associated with a *port*. A port is a numeric address through which service requests (such as asking for a Web page) are processed. On a UNIX system, the particular services provided are in the /etc/services file. Here are a few lines from a typical /etc/services file:

```
daytime      13/udp
ftp          21/tcp
telnet       23/tcp        telnet
smtp         25/tcp        mail
www          80/tcp
```

The first column displays system name of the service (daytime). The second column displays the port number and the protocol, separated by a slash (13/udp). The third column displays an alias to the service, if any. For example, smtp (the standard Simple Mail Transfer Protocol), also known as *mail,* is the implementation of e-mail service.

Communication of Web related information takes place at Port 80 using the TCP protocol. To emulate this in Java, you use the Socket class. `Daytime`, the service to get the system date and time, occurs at Port 13 using the UDP protocol. A `daytime` server to emulate this in Java would use the `DatagramSocket` object.

## The URL Class Revisited

The URL class contains constructors and methods for managing a URL: an object or service on the Internet. The TCP protocol requires two pieces of information: the IP address and the port number. So how is it possible that when you type

**http://www.yahoo.com**

you get Yahoo's home page?

First, Yahoo has registered its name, allowing yahoo.com to be assigned an IP address (say 205.216.146.71).

> **Note**
>
> Actually it's a bit more complicated than that. There's a service called DNS, for Domain Naming Service, that translates www.yahoo.com into 205.216.146.71. This enables you to type **www.yahoo.com** instead of having to remember the IP address.
>
> An interesting sidelight is that *one* network name can map to *many* IP addresses. This may be necessary for a site, like Yahoo, that accommodates large volumes of traffic and needs more than one IP address to service the traffic. The actual internal name for 205.216.146.71, for example, is **www7.yahoo.com**. DNS can translate a list of IP addresses assigned to yahoo into www.yahoo.com. This is a useful feature, but also opens up a security hole, which is discussed in "Will Security Considerations Disable Java Applets?" later in this chapter.

So the IP address is known.

Now what about the port number? If not specified, the server's port in /etc/services is used.

> **Note**
>
> The /etc/services is the filename on UNIX servers. On other platforms, the filename will probably be different. On a Windows NT server, for example, the file may be called simply **services**. Ask your server administrator.

The usual Web service port is 80, so if it is not specified, the Yahoo server uses that port. The actual URL specification is `filename:port`. Test this. If you type

> **http://www.yahoo.com:80**

you also get Yahoo's home page.

> **Note**
>
> There's no hard and fast rule that the Web server reside on port 80. This is, however, becoming the Internet custom. In the early days of the Web, you'd find URLs with strange port addresses. Using port 80 saves keystrokes. URLs are hard enough to remember without having to remember the port number as well.

An interesting sidelight: If you request another protocol, such as in **ftp://ftp.microsoft.com,** the port number is derived from the protocol. So if Microsoft's FTP port was 21 (in their /etc/services file), the server would

map the `ftp:` protocol name to Port 21 using the IP address
**ftp.microsoft.com.**

The first part of the URL (http) means that we're using the *HyperText Trans-mission Protocol,* the protocol for handling Web documents. And if no file is specified, most Web servers are configured to fetch the file called index.html. So the IP address and the port are determined either by explicit specification of all the parts of the URL or by using defaults.

The URL class allows for these variations in specification. There are four con-structors, as follows:

```
public URL(String spec) throws MalformedURLException;
public URL(String protocol, String host, int port, String file)
➥throws MalformedURLException;
public URL(String protocol, String host, String file) throws
MalformedURLException;
public URL(URL context, String spec) throws MalformedURLException;
```

You can thus specify each piece of the URL, as in
`URL("http","www.yahoo.com",80,"index.html")`, or enable the defaults to take over, as in `URL("http://www.yahoo.com")`, letting Yahoo figure out all the pieces.

## Mapping Java Sockets to Internet Sockets

Sockets are based on a client/server model. One program (the server) provides the service at a particular IP address and port. The server listens for service re-quests, such as requests for Web pages, and fills the order. Any program that wants to be serviced (a client, such as a Web browser) needs to know the IP address and port to communicate with the server.

An advantage of the socket model over other forms of data communication is that the server doesn't care where the client requests come from. As long as the client is sending requests according to the TCP/IP protocol, the requests will reach the server—provided the server is up and the Internet isn't too busy. (What the particular server program does with the request is another matter. The Finger server of chapter 26, "Protocol Handlers," could be pro-grammed to reject requests from external clients, as many Finger servers are.)

This also means that the client can be any type of computer. No longer are we restricted to UNIX, Macintosh, DOS, or Windows platforms. Any com-puter that supports TCP/IP can talk to any other computer that supports it through this socket model. This is a potentially revolutionary development in computing. Instead of maintaining armies of programmers to *port* a system from one platform to another, you write it once—in Java. Any computer with a Java virtual machine can run it.

Java socket classes fit nicely into this picture. You implement a server by creating subclasses of Thread, overriding the run() method. The Java virtual machine can then perform the thread management without the program having to worry. So with a few lines of code, you can write a server that can handle as many data communications sessions as you want. And data transmission is simply a matter of calling the Socket methods.

# Creating a Telnet Server

The procedure for creating a server is to create a ServerSocket object, which listens on a particular port for client requests. When it recognizes a valid request, it creates a Socket object through which the data conversation can take place. This socket is like a pipe through which data can pass back and forth. In fact, it's very similar to a UNIX pipe. The stream classes are used to route data back and forth efficiently.

The following program is a prototype for a line-oriented Telnet server, enabling remote logins to a network on the Internet. The server prompts the client for ID and password and, if the user is authorized, prints a welcome message. For our network, the Telnet service is on port 23.

**Listing 28.1   TelnetServer.java—A Prototype Telnet Server**

```
1. import java.net.ServerSocket;
2. import java.net.Socket;
3. import java.io.IOException;
4. import java.io.DataInputStream;
5. import java.io.PrintStream;


6. public class TelnetServer extends Thread {
7.   protected ServerSocket server_listening_socket;

8.   public static void fail(Exception exception, String msg) {
9.     System.err.println(msg + "." + exception);
10.    System.exit(1);
11.  }

12.  public TelnetServer() {
13.    try {server_listening_socket = new ServerSocket(23, 5); }
14.    catch (IOException ioexception) fail(ioexception,
15.          "Could not start Telnet Server");
16.    System.out.println("Telnet Server Started");
17.    this.start();
18.  }

19.  public void run() {
20.    try {
21.      while (true) {
22.        Socket client_socket = server_listening_socket.accept();
23.        TelnetConnection connection = new
            ➡TelnetConnection(client_socket);
```

```
24.      }
25.    }
26.    catch (IOException e) fail(e, "Listening loop failed.");
27.  }

28. public static void main (String[] args) {
29.   new TelnetServer();
30. }
}

31. class TelnetConnection extends Thread {
32.   protected Socket telnet_client;
33.   protected DataInputStream from_client;
34.   protected PrintStream to_client;

35.   // initialize the stream, start the thread.
36.   public TelnetConnection (Socket client_socket) {
37.     telnet_client = client_socket;
38.     try {
39.       from_client = new DataInputStream(telnet_client .getInput Stream());
40.       to_client  = new PrintStream(telnet_client.getOutputStream());
41.     }
42.     catch (IOException ioexception) {
43.       try telnet_client.close(); catch (IOException anIOException);
44.       System.err.println("Unable to set up socket streams." +
45.               ioexception);
46.       return;
47 .    }
48.     this.start();
49. }

50.   public void run() {
51.     String login_id;
52.     String password;
53.     int len;
54.     try {
55.       for(;;) {
56.         //prompt, then read login_id
57.         to_client.println("Login: ");
58.         login_id = from_client.readLine();
59.         if (login_id == null) break;

60.         // prompt, then read password
61.         to_client.println("Password: ");
62.         password = from_client.readLine();
63.         if (password == null) break;

64.         // check for valid login ID and password. If the user is
65.         // authorized, tell the client …
66.         to_client.println("Welcome! You're online! Enter command.");
67.         // then continue conversation between client and server
68.         // to close conversation, set a boolean to false, and code
69.         if (boolean_var == false) break;
70.       }
71.     }
72.     catch (IOException e);
```

```
73.     finally try telnet_client.close() ; catch (IOException
        ↪anIOexception);
74.  }
75. }
```

OK, now let's break it down. (The following line numbers refer to listing 28.1.)

## Classes Used by the Server Program

From java.net, you use the ServerSocket class (to create a socket where the server listens for remote login requests) and the Socket class (to create the socket through which the Telnet conversation occurs).

From java.io, you use the IOException class (to handle errors). The DataInputStream class handles traffic from the client to the server (i.e., input to the server). The PrintStream class handles traffic from the server to the client ("printing" to the client).

## Creating the Telnet Server Class

Note that your Telnet server is a subclass of Thread. A ServerSocket object (server_listening_object), declared on line 7 of listing 28.1, will later do the work of listening for client Telnet requests.

An error handling routine called fail(), defined from lines 8 to 11, takes two arguments (an Exception object and a String object), prints an error message if there is any problem starting the server, and exits.

The constructor (lines 12–18) creates and starts a ServerSocket thread. An error message is produced if there's a problem. Note the statement on line 13 that actually constructs the server socket:

```
server_listening_socket = new ServerSocket(23, 5);
```

This form of the ServerSocket constructor takes two integer arguments. The first argument, the port number, is 23 because we've defined the Telnet service to be on Port 23. The second argument is a count of the number of concurrent Telnet services that we want to allow. We will allow five Telnet sessions in this example. The actual setting is a server configuration issue. If we allow more sessions, we also allocate more server memory. The potential for overloading the server exists because each session requires additional memory.

## The *Run()* Method: Listening for Client Requests

The server's run() method (lines 19–27 of listing 28.1), as with all threads that implement the Runnable interface, is where the work is done. In this case, the server goes into an infinite loop and "listens" for client requests. When the server "hears" the client, the server calls the ServerSocket's accept() method, which accepts the connection. Then the server creates a TelnetConnection thread, passing it a Socket object where the Telnet conversation actually occurs.

## The *Main()* Method: Starting the Server

The main() method (lines 28–31) is very simple. Just create an instance of TelnetServer, print a message to the console that the server has started, and it can figure everything else out.

## The Telnet Thread: The Work Gets Done

The TelnetConnection thread (lines 32–75) is where the conversation actually takes place. TelnetConnection creates a DataInputStream object (from_client), which retrieves input from the client using the GetInputStream() method, and a PrintStream object (to_client), which enables the server to write output to the client using the GetOutputStream() method. Thus, a two-way conversation can occur. If this happens successfully, the Telnet session starts.

After the server connects, it issues the Login: prompt by printing it to the client using the println() method of the to_client object (line 57). On line 58, the server uses the readLine() method to store the login ID in the string variable, login_id. The server now needs the password, so it uses the println() method of the to_client object to issue the Password: prompt. Then the server issues another readLine(), storing the user's entry in another string variable, password.

From this point, it's up to the program to verify the login ID and password. Perhaps there's a login ID table, which contains the password. If the password is stored in encrypted format, this would be the place to decrypt it. If the user is authorized, the session can begin using the stream objects that have been set up. Typically, the server prompts for a command and uses a case statement to either perform the command or deny access.

When it's time to log off, the server issues a break to exit the loop. This causes the finally statement to execute, closing the client socket. Closing the socket is critical because, otherwise, you'll exhaust server memory before long. The finally clause ensures that. You can't count on Java's garbage collection to close the socket.

V

Advanced Java

Note that the server is multithreaded, as each client that connects gets its own thread in the server. This is quite an impressive result in so few lines of code!

# Writing a Client Program To Communicate with the Server

Below is a prototype for a client program that talks to our Telnet server.

**Listing 28.2  TelnetClient.java—A Prototype Telnet Client**

```
1. import java.net.Socket;
2. import java.io.IOException;
3. import java.io.DataInputStream;
4. import java.io.PrintStream;

5. public class TelnetClient {

6.  public static void main(String[] args) {
7.    Socket s = null;

8.    try {
9.      s = new Socket("krakow.com",23);

10.       DataInputStream server_in = new
          ➥DataInputStream(s.getInputStream());
11.       PrintStream server_out = new PrintStream(s.getOutputStream());

12.       DataInputStream input = new DataInputStream(System.in);

13.       String line;

14.       while (true) {
15.         line = server_in.readLine();
16.         if (line == null) break;
17.         System.out.println(line);

18.         line = input.readLine();
19.         if (line == null) break;
20.         server_out.println(line);
21.       }
22.   }

23.   catch (IOException e) System.out.println(e);
24.   finally {
25.     try if (s != null) s.close() ; catch (IOException e2);
26.   }
27.   }
28. }
```

The client program is simpler. Create a Socket object, specifying the host address and port. The client must know both of these before connecting to the server. We'll assume that the host is "krakow.com". The Telnet port we already know is Port 23.

After connecting successfully with the server, we create two DataInputStream objects: one to get data from the server and the other to get data from the user (System.in). We also create a PrintStream object so we can "print" to the server. The client goes into a read/write loop until it receives no more input from the server, at which time it closes the socket.

The line numbers in the following sections refer to listing 28.2.

## Classes Used by the Client Program

The client needs only the Socket class from the java.net package. The client uses the getInputStream() method to receive data from the server and the getOutputStream() methods to send data to the server. These methods support TCP, ensuring reliable data communication across the network.

From the java.io package, the program imports IOException (for I/O error handling), DataInputStream (for reading input from a stream), and DataOutputStream (for writing to a stream).

## The *Main()* Method

TelnetClient has only one method—main() —which makes it a stand-alone program. On line 9, a Socket object (s) is created. Socket takes two arguments: the Internet address ("krakow.com") and the Telnet port (23). After the Socket object is created, the following three streams are created:

- server_in is a DataInputStream object used to read data from the server using the socket.
- server_out is a PrintStream object used to write data to the server using the socket.
- input is a DataInputStream object for reading input from the terminal.

The program then goes into an infinite loop (lines 14–21). The code from lines 15–17 reads input from the server (line 15), exits if no input is received (line 16), and prints the input on the terminal (line 17). After the socket was established, the server printed out Login: using the println() method on its PrintStream object. On line 15, the client reads it. On line 17, the client prints it to the terminal.

Lines 18–20 are the response from the terminal. On line 18, the client uses the readLine() method, getting the login ID from the user. The readLine() method waits for a carriage return before continuing. On line 20, the client uses the println() method on its PrintStream object (attached to the same socket as the server) to print back to the server.

The exchange continues to get the password, announcing that the connection succeeded (or failed). We have established a line-oriented conversation between client and server. What happens after that depends on the particular application's requirements and is beyond the scope of this discussion.

# Communicating with Datagram Sockets

Communicating using datagram sockets is simpler than using the TCP based sockets (Socket and ServerSocket) that we used for our Telnet server. Communications is also faster because there is no connection overhead. There's also no attempt to send packets again if an error occurs or sequencing of multiple packets, as occurs in TCP transmissions.

A datagram packet is sent simply as an array of bytes to a receiving program, presumably listening at a particular IP address and port. If the receiving program gets the datagram and wants to send a reply, it becomes the sender addressing a datagram back to a known IP address and port. The conversation style is a bit like those old movies in which the pilot sends a message, says "over," and waits for ground control to respond.

You might use datagram socket communication if you're writing an interactive game or, as in many UNIX systems, for returning a small piece of information, such as the time, when you don't want the overhead of establishing a connection and/or (in the case of the time server) when the communication takes place locally.

## Sending a Datagram Packet

Here's a prototype program for sending a datagram packet (see listing 28.3). I am going to send a 12-byte message ("Ira says Hi!") to the IP address mapped to "krakow.com" at port number 1000. When you try this, use an IP address and port that you know is available. I purposely left out error handling to make the prototype more readable. You should insert the appropriate try blocks and catch statements to handle errors gracefully.

**Listing 28.3    DatagramSend.java—A Prototype Program To Send a Datagram Packet**

```
1. import java.net.DatagramPacket;
2. import java.net.DatagramSocket;
3. import java.net.InetAddress;

4. public class DatagramSend {
5.  public static void main (String args[]) throws Exception {

6.     byte[] byte_greeting = new byte[12];
7.     String string_greeting = "Ira says hi!";
8.     int message_length = 12;
9.     int port = 1000;

10.    InetAddress internet_address =
11.      InetAddress.getByName("krakow.com");
12.    string_greeting.getBytes(0 , 12 , byte_greeting , 0 );

13.    DatagramPacket packet = new DatagramPacket( byte_greeting,
14.            message_length, internet_address , port);
15.    DatagramSocket socket = new DatagramSocket();
16.    socket.send(packet);
17.    socket.close();
18.  }
19. }
```

We need to use only one socket: the DatagramSocket. There is no concept of the server listening for client requests. The idea is just to establish a DatagramSocket object and then send and receive messages. The messages are sent in a DatagramPacket object. An additional object—InetAddress— is needed to construct the IP address to send the packet.

The DatagramSend class has only one method—main()—so it's a stand-alone Java program. This demonstration program only sends one message. You can, of course, modify main() to pass any message to any IP address and port. Because main() throws Exception, I have declared that I'm not handling errors in this class.

The DatagramPacket constructor that I use has the following four arguments:

- byte_greeting is a byte array containing the message I'm sending.
- message_length is an integer specifying the length of the message.
- internet_address is an iNetAddress object containing the IP address to send the message.
- port is an integer specifying the port number.

V

Advanced Java

Another form of the constructor requires only the first two arguments. It's designed for local communication when the IP address and port are already known. You'll see it in action later in the next section, "Receiving a Datagram Packet."

The following line numbers refer to listing 28.3.

The statement on line 6 creates the byte array form of our greeting message. On line 7 is the declaration and initialization of the greeting. On line 10, the getBytes() instance method of the java.lang.String class converts string into byte array form, storing the converted string in byte_greeting.

The getByName() method of InetAddress (on line 8) converts a string into an Internet address in the form that the DatagramPacket constructor accepts.

On lines 11 and 12, an instance of DatagramPacket is created with the above arguments. Finally, on line 13, the packet is sent using the send() instance method of the DatagramPacket.

## Receiving a Datagram Packet

The packet is on its way, so it's time to receive it. Here's the receiving program (see listing 28.4).

**Listing 28.4   DatagramReceive.java—A Prototype Program To Receive a Datagram Packet**

```
1. import java.net.DatagramSocket;
2. import java.net.DatagramPacket;

3. public class DatagramReceive {
4. public static void main (String args[]) throws Exception {

5.     String greeting;
6.     byte[] buffer = new byte[2048];
7.     DatagramPacket rcv_packet = new DatagramPacket(buffer,
       ➥buffer.length);
8.     DatagramSocket rcv_socket = new DatagramSocket(1000);

9.     rcv_socket.receive( rcv_packet );
10.    greeting = new String(buffer ,0 ,0 , rcv_packet.getLength());
11.    System.out.println(greeting);
12.    rcv_socket.close();
13. }
14. }
```

The DatagramReceive class, like the DatagramSend class, uses the DatagramSocket and DatagramPacket classes from java.net. First, create a buffer large enough to hold the message. Our buffer (buffer) is a 2K byte array. Your buffer size may vary. Just make sure it will hold the largest packet you'll receive.

Then we create a datagram packet. Note that the receive program already knows its IP address and port, so it can use the two-argument form of the constructor. On line 8 of listing 28.4, the `DatagramSocket` is set up to receive data at Port 1000.

The `receive()` method of Datagram receives the packet as a byte array. The `String` (greeting) is constructed out of the byte array and the greeting is printed on the terminal. Finally, the socket is closed, freeing memory instead of waiting for Java's garbage collection.

> ## Tip
>
> To get the IP address of the network you're running on, call the `getLocalHost()` and `getAddress()` methods of the class `java.net.InetAddress`. First, `getLocalHost()` returns an `iNetAddress` object. Then, you use the `getAddress()` method, which returns a byte array consisting of the four bytes of the IP address, as in the following example:
>
> ```
> InetAddress internet_address = InetAddress.getLocalHost();
> byte[] ipaddress = internet_address.getAddress();
> ```
>
> If the IP address of the network you're running on is 221.111.112.23, then
>
> ipaddress[0] = 221
>
> ipaddress[1] = 111
>
> ipaddress[2] = 112
>
> ipaddress[3] = 23

# Why Create a Custom Socket Type?

The Internet does not provide built-in security. The socket-oriented communications methods I've discussed do not verify whether any particular request for reading or writing data is coming from a source that should have such access.

A number of solutions have been proposed. As mentioned at the beginning of this chapter, Netscape has proposed the Secure Sockets Layer (SSL) protocol. SSL is a protocol that resides between the services, such as Telnet, FTP, and http, and the TCP/IP connection sessions that I've illustrated here. SSL would check that the client and server networks are valid, provide data encryption, and ensure that the message does not contain any embedded commands or programs. SSL would thus provide for secure transactions to occur across the Internet.

Another proposal is to write a server that provides security from the start. This is the idea behind *Secure HyperText Transfer Protocol* (S-HTTP) developed by Enterprise Information Technologies (EIT), RSA Labs, and the National Center for Supercomputer Applications (NCSA).

> **Note**
>
> NCSA is the group that developed Mosaic, the the original Web browser for Microsoft Windows. The Mosaic design team went on to fame and fortune by completely rewriting Mosaic to create a new and original Web browser. The result was Netscape.

You can find the S-HTTP specifications at **http://www.commerce. net:80/ software/Shttpd**

In your organization, you might want to provide a firewall between the public and private areas of your networks, so there are a number of reasons you might need more protection for your network than TCP-IP provides.

Java provides a set of methods for implementing this strategy called `SocketImpl`, which is an abstract class. To use it, you create a subclass and implement its methods, such as connecting to the server, accepting client requests, getting file information, writing to local files, and so on. Even if you never write your own server or create a custom socket class, it's nice to know that it's possible to do it in Java.

# Will Security Considerations Disable Java Applets?

Imagine a world in which Java applets on any network can set up client/ server communications of the type I've discussed in this chapter. Perhaps an applet on my network can call a method in an applet on your network or run a program on your network remotely. For example, an applet connects to a quote server, determines that the price of a certain stock has reached the target price, and then connects to a user's machine on a network, displaying a message and requesting permission to buy. Or perhaps the applet can run an Excel spreadsheet macro to update the portfolio every 10 minutes. Many powerful applets could be written.

With this power comes potential danger. How can we prevent the applet from deleting files, downloading unauthorized data, or even being aware of the existence of such files? In this world of distributed objects, there's a profound tension between enabling more capabilities for an applet and fear of unwanted use.

This is why the debate on object access is fierce. The main stage is a standard called *Common Object Request Broker Architecture*:

### http://www.acl.lanl.gov/CORBA

This is a consortium of many computer companies that allows requests and responses to be made securely from distributed objects. Microsoft is, of course, one of the participants. They have a protocol for requesting objects called *Object Linking and Embedding* (OLE). OLE's main purpose is for one Windows application to access information in another Windows application. OLE is more platform-specific than CORBA. It's worth watching the progress of the debate. Will Java applets be allowed to run Windows DLLs so they can communicate with Windows objects? How *open* will OLE become?

Currently, applets loaded from a network not only cannot run Windows DLLs on the local machine, but are forbidden to run local commands, such as the DOS dir command, that would find out the names of files on the client. In addition, applets cannot make network connections except to the network they're on.

> **Note**
>
> These limitations apply only to applets loaded from a network. Locally loaded applets are not restricted like this.

The debate between power and security seems to be veering towards the security side. An example is a recent "bug" that Drew Dean, Ed Felten, and Dan Wallach of Princeton University, found in Netscape 2.0 running a Java applet. They were able to trick the Domain Name Service (DNS) (the program that translates addresses, such as **www.yahoo.com**, into those funny IP addresses) by disguising their origin. They were able to make DNS believe they were actually from another computer, and then they were able to breach security on it. Netscape acknowledged the situation and has provided an update (Version 2.01) that provides more close control over how an IP address is resolved.

This situation caused a real stir. Concerns about Internet security are rampant. Also, concerns about restricting applet access to the point where the usefulness of the applications are diminished greatly are also rampant. It will be interesting to see which side prevails.

Sun has suggested a naming convention for running applets across networks. The convention would be based on the IP address of the network where the applet resides. Perhaps in the future, digital signatures will be attached to applets before they run. Take a look at

**http://www.sun.com/sfaq**

(Frequently Asked Questions about Java and applet security) for developments. ❖

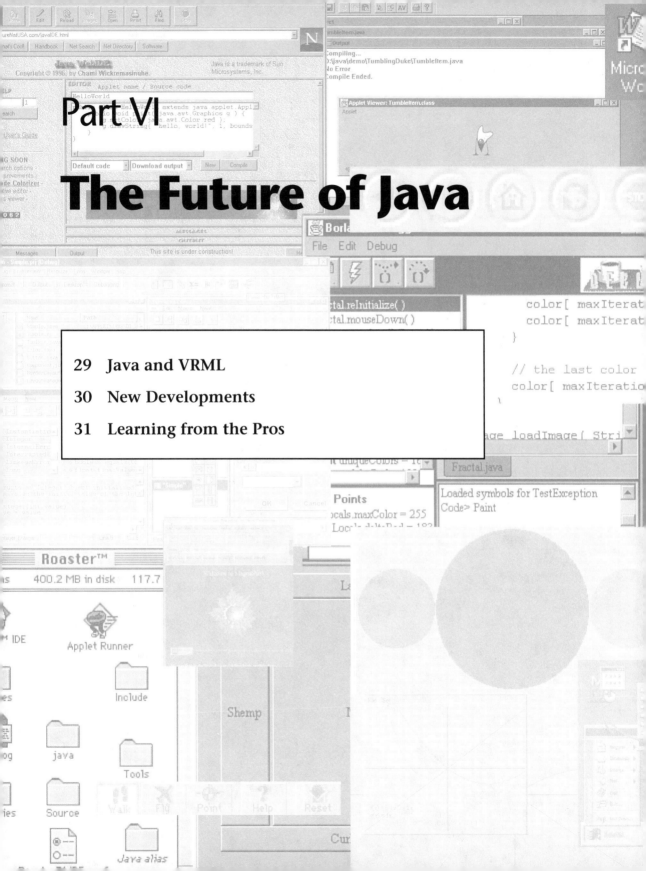

# Part VI

# The Future of Java

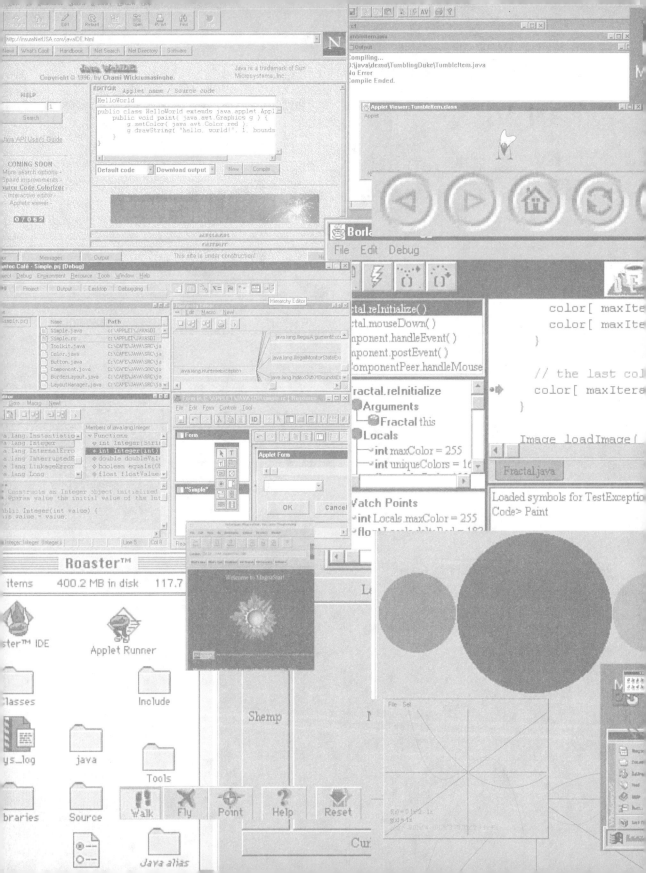

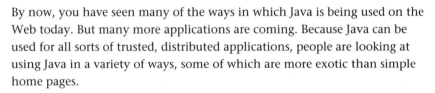

# CHAPTER 29

# Java and VRML

*by Mark Waks*

By now, you have seen many of the ways in which Java is being used on the Web today. But many more applications are coming. Because Java can be used for all sorts of trusted, distributed applications, people are looking at using Java in a variety of ways, some of which are more exotic than simple home pages.

This chapter explores the interaction of Java and another new technology: Virtual Reality. Java and Virtual Reality appear to be separate but actually are vital parts of a whole. For even while Java is changing the Net by allowing users to interact with programs on the Web, Virtual Reality, in the form of VRML, is allowing users to start building spaces in which that interaction can take place.

## Virtual Reality

Virtual Reality (VR) is one of the hottest topics in the computing world today—so much so that the term is overused, sometimes when it isn't even appropriate. Virtual Reality is the art of simulating reality within the computer and presenting that "reality" to the user as best the computer can.

The exact details of this presentation can vary quite widely. In the simplest cases, the system displays a 3-D image on a conventional monitor, and the user navigates around in this world by moving the mouse. In some of the most sophisticated systems, the user is outfitted with a helmet that provides a fully responsive stereoscopic image, and with gloves (or even a full bodysuit) that capture and respond to the user's movements. But although the details differ, the basic concept is the same: allowing the user to explore an artificial version of reality and trying to make that reality reasonably convincing.

VR is starting to develop into a mature set of technologies. A reasonably well-equipped personal computer or workstation now can display (or render) a three-dimensional display fast enough to present a convincing imitation of reality as the user moves through it. Specialized enhancement boards that speed this display are beginning to appear on the market, and the newest operating systems often include built-in 3-D libraries, so that proprietary libraries are less necessary. VR-based games are almost commonplace by now.

# Cyberspace and the History of VRML

Over the past decade, science-fiction authors have frequently used the term *cyberspace*—a term that William Gibson coined in his book *Neuromancer*. Although no two authors agree on precisely what cyberspace would look like, most concur on the basic model: a shared virtual place (or places), where people interact both with objects in that place, and with other people in the same place. The idea is a powerful, almost mythic one, with people interacting on a level higher than the physical one, where almost anything is possible.

People began to realize years ago that a cyberspace of sorts already exists, in the form of the Internet. The Net is a common place for communication and activity, bearing little resemblance to the physical world. Granted, the communication is text-based, but the idea is similar to that of the fictional cyberspace.

Finally, people around the world started arriving at a common idea. We have relatively mature and cheap Virtual Reality technology, and we have a network that covers the entire world, in the form of the World Wide Web. If we combine the two ideas, we could get something very much like Gibson's idea of cyberspace: a world-spanning VR system, which anyone can enter at will and to which anyone can add their own personal areas.

The idea gelled at the first WWW conference, which was held in Geneva, Switzerland, in May 1994. People who were interested in the idea met at the conference and began to talk seriously. Dave Raggett coined the name Virtual Reality Markup Language, or VRML (later changed to Virtual Reality Modeling Language), for the new language that would provide the underpinnings of cyberspace, in homage to HTML. Afterward, the group set up a mailing list. The list attracted enormous attention in a remarkably short time, and the process of creating cyberspace was started.

To avoid reinventing the wheel, the members of the VRML mailing list decided to use an existing VR language as its basis. After considerable discussion and debate, the group adopted the Open Inventor ASCII format as a starting point. This format is the human-readable input language for Silicon Graphics' Inventor system, one of the better-established 3-D modeling packages. The group (led in particular by several developers, including Mark Pesce, Tony Parisi, and Gavin Bell) stripped the language down to its bare bones, and added a few new Web-specific features, resulting in the first attempt at putting virtual reality on the Web: VRML 1.0.

# The VRML 1.0 Language

A full description of the VRML language is beyond the scope of this book. You can find the complete language specification at the following URL:

**http://www.vrml.org/**

---

**Note**

For a comprehensive treatment of VRML, see *Using VRML, Special Edition* (Que). This book covers the language itself, as well as VRML browsers, utilities, and advanced programming topics.

---

This chapter concentrates on the major ideas behind the language, so that you can understand how Java relates to it.

VRML is all about creating a *scene*: the collection of objects that users look at. The scene is held together in a *scene graph*, a hierarchical description of the scene, and how the objects relate to each other. Figure 29.1 shows the scene graph for a very simple scene, containing a red cube, a green sphere, and a blue cone. The corresponding VRML code looks like this:

```
#VRML V1.0 ascii
Group {
  Separator {
    Material {
      ambientColor 1 0 0  # Red
    }
    Translation {
      translation -3 0 0  # Left
    }
    Cube { }
  }
  Separator {
    Material {
```

VI

The Future of Java

```
        ambientColor 0 1 0  # Green
      }
      Sphere { }
    }
    Separator {
      Material {
        ambientColor 0 0 1  # Blue
      }
      Translation {
        translation 3 0 0   # Right
      }
      Cone { }
    }
  }
```

**Fig. 29.1**

A very simple
VRML scene.

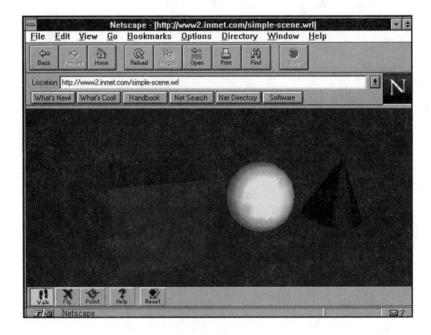

The graph consists of a collection of *nodes*—specific objects or groupings of
objects, which are laid out hierarchically. The VRML language is mainly just a
listing of the different kinds of nodes that you can use in a scene graph and
the simple syntax that holds them together.

## Fields

Before you learn the syntax, understanding the kinds of fields that may be present in a VRML file is useful. You can think of a *field* as being a parameter to a node. A Cube node, for example, has the fields `width`, `height`, and `depth`, and a `DirectionalLight` node has the fields `on`, `intensity`, `color`, and `direction`.

VRML has several classes of fields, and each named field falls into one of these classes. These classes in turn fall into two broad categories: single-valued and multi-valued fields. A *single-valued* field describes exactly one thing. (However, a single-valued field may involve several numbers. A three-dimensional vector, for example, requires three numbers, but it is only one vector.) *Multi-valued* fields list a number of values of the same kind—for example, a list of colors or vectors. By convention, the names of classes for single-valued fields start with SF, and those for multi-valued fields start with MF.

Table 29.1 shows the fields that are available in VRML 1.0.

| Table 29.1 Node Classes in VRML 1.0 | |
| --- | --- |
| **Class Name** | **Description** |
| SFBitMask | A bit mask |
| SFBool | A true/false value |
| SFColor | A single color, written as an RGB triplet |
| SFEnum | A collection of named options |
| SFFloat | A single floating-point number |
| SFImage | A bitmap image, which can be grayscale or RGB |
| SFLong | A single long integer |
| SFMatrix | A 4x4 transformation matrix |
| SFRotation | A rotation around a specified axis |
| SFString | An ASCII string |
| SFVec2f | A two-dimensional vector, with floating-point values |
| SFVec3f | A three-dimensional vector |
| MFColor | A list of colors |
| MFLong | A list of long integers |
| MFVec2f | A list of two-dimensional vectors |
| MFVec3f | A list of three-dimensional vectors |

Single-valued fields are simply given as values after the field name. The direction field of a DirectionalLight node, for example, looks like this:

```
direction 1 .5 .35
```

direction is a SFVec3f field—a three-dimensional vector—and the three numbers after the name of the field specify the value of that field.

Multi-valued fields are placed in brackets after the field name, and the values are separated by commas. The ambientColor field of the Material node, for example, describes a list of colors, which the various faces of later objects may take. A typical ambientColor field might look like this:

```
ambientColor [.2 .5 .8, 1 0 .5, .9 .4 .65]
```

ambientColor is a MFColor field. The field in the preceding example lists three colors, separated by commas, each listing the RGB triplet that describes the color.

## Nodes

As mentioned earlier, the language is mainly about describing nodes. Several kinds of nodes exist. Most nodes describe a physical object, such as a cube or a cylinder. Other nodes provide other information, such as the colors or transformations to be applied to subsequent objects.

## Node Syntax

Nodes have an extremely simple syntax, as follows:

```
node-name {
  field
  field
  ... }
```

You start with the name of the node and follow with the names of the fields, surrounded by braces. Every node expects specific named fields, but default values often exist, so sometimes you can omit fields.

A simple cube can be described as follows:

```
Cube {
  width 1    # Note that all three fields are of
  height 1   # class SFFloat
  depth 1 }
```

By default, a cube is size 2 in every direction, so Cube {} is equivalent to the following:

```
Cube {
  width 2
  height 2
  depth 2 }
```

## Node Types

Table 29.2 lists the types of nodes that are available in VRML 1.0.

### Table 29.2   Types of Nodes in VRML 1.0

| Node Name | Description |
| --- | --- |
| AsciiText | Strings to display in 3-D |
| Cone | A simple cone |
| Coordinate3 | A list of coordinates for later nodes to use |
| Cube | A simple cube |
| Cylinder | A simple cylinder |
| DirectionalLight | A light source that shines in a specific direction |
| FontStyle | Describes the font for later AsciiText nodes |
| Group, Separator, Switch, and TransformSeparator | See below |
| IndexedFaceSet | An object described by a list of polygons |
| IndexedLineSet | A different way of drawing an arbitrary shape |
| Info | Essentially a comment in the graph |
| LOD | Formerly LevelOfDetail; see below |
| Material | Describes colors for later shapes |
| MaterialBinding | Describes how those colors are mapped to shapes |
| MatrixTransform | Transforms a shape via a matrix |
| Normal | Describes the normals (vectors related to the faces) to a shape, for efficiency in rendering that shape |
| NormalBinding | Describes how those normals are mapped to shapes |
| OrthographicCamera | See below |
| PerspectiveCamera | See below |
| PointLight | An omnidirectional light at a location |
| PointSet | A collection of points for use in later nodes |
| Rotation | Describes how to rotate subsequent objects |
| Scale | Describes how to scale subsequent objects |
| ShapeHints | Provides hints for optimizing the rendering process |
| Sphere | A simple sphere |
| SpotLight | A fixed, conical light source |
| Texture2, Texture2Transform, and TextureCoordinate2 | Describes and applies two-dimensional textures to objects |

**VI**

**The Future of Java**

*(continues)*

| Table 29.2 Continued | |
|---|---|
| **Node Name** | **Description** |
| Transform | Allows arbitrary transformation of later objects |
| Translation | Describes how to move subsequent objects |
| WWWAnchor | A link, very much like the `<a href="">` construct in HTML |
| WWWInline | Includes an object from any URL |

The purpose of this section is simply to familiarize you with the concepts in VRML, so the section will not go into much further detail about the nodes; see the language specification for full details. A few nodes, however, warrant more discussion.

## Properties

Several of the node types, such as Transform and Material, are used in later nodes; these nodes are known as *properties*. Properties are related to the concept of *scene traversal*, which is how the browser understands the scene graph. After loading the graph, the VRML browser performs a depth-first traversal of the graph, putting everything together as it goes. So when the browser reaches (for example) a Translation node, it knows to move all the subsequent objects appropriately.

The various kinds of transformations are particularly special, because they are cumulative. If, for example, you have a node that scales up by 2 and another node that scales up by 3, all subsequent objects are scaled up by a factor of 6.

## Groups

*Groups* are nodes that collect objects together. For example, no primitive object called Chair exists, but you can make a chair out of suitable pieces— perhaps Cylinders for the legs and back, and a Cube (or a rectangular prism, anyway) for the seat. You collect these pieces in some type of Group node. Figure 29.2 shows a chair made this way.

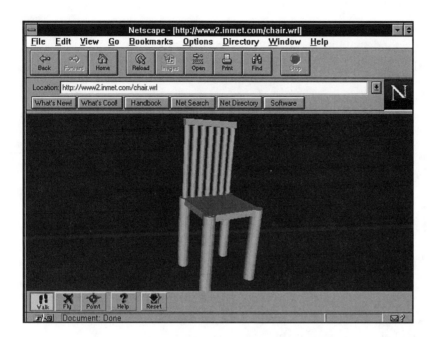

**Fig. 29.2**
A basic chair, as
displayed in
Netscape Live 3D.

Several kinds of Group nodes exist. The basic Group simply allows you to collect objects in a single higher-level object; there collected objects are called
*child nodes*. The syntax for children is simple: children are contained within
the parent. To group a cube and a sphere, the syntax would be something like
the following:

```
Group {
  Cube {
    width 3
    height 2
    depth 1
  }

  Sphere {
    radius 3
  } }
```

Basic groups are used relatively rarely, for one reason: properties. You usually
want to define objects by using some properties internally—for example, using a Translation node to move a chair leg 6 inches to the right. But as mentioned earlier, transformations simply accumulate. You don't want the chair
to cause everything in the scene graph to shift 6 inches.

**VI**

**The Future of Java**

The solution is a `Separator` node, which is the most commonly used node type for describing objects. A `Separator` is just like a group, except that when the browser is traversing the scene graph, it preserves the properties (such as transformations) before entering the `Separator` and restores them after leaving the `Separator`. Thus, any properties that are specified as children of the `Separator` do not affect any objects outside that `Separator`. Most objects use `Separator` as their top-level node.

> **Note**
>
> `TransformSeparator` is just like the normal `Separator`, except that it saves only the transformations, not any other properties. `Switch` allows you to choose one of several children to activate.

## Cameras

You view the VRML scene through a *camera*. If a camera is established in the scene, it usually is used as the initial viewing location (although most browsers allow you to move within the scene).

Two kinds of cameras exist. The `PerspectiveCamera` shows everything in perspective, and the `OrthographicCamera` displays everything with no shrinkage in the distance.

## LOD

`LOD` is a special node whose main purpose is efficiency. The `LOD` node lists a collection of distances and objects. As you draw closer to the `LOD` node, the displayed object changes.

This effect can be used for object animation (actually, changing the object as you come closer), but it is used mainly to control the level of detail. (`LOD` is a modification of the `LevelOfDetail` node from Open Inventor, the language VRML evolved from.) `LOD` allows the browser to show only a very simple object, with little detail, when the user is far away and the object appears small (the screen resolution does not permit great detail anyway) and to show more and more detail as the user draw near. This way, the browser needs to load only the more-detailed objects (which presumably have larger files) as needed.

## WWWAnchor

The WWWAnchor node is what makes VRML a Web-based language. This node is a Group like the Groups described earlier in the chapter; it behaves like a Separator. But when the user selects one of the children of WWWAnchor (usually, by clicking it), this action tells the browser to go to some other URL. This can be a simple hypertext-like link to a URL, or the browser can include the 3-D position of the click within the WWWAnchor as part of the URL, similar to how imagemaps work in HTML.

## General Syntax

Every VRML file must begin with a standard header that identifies it as such, as follows:

```
#VRML V1.0 ascii
```

After that, everything is nodes and fields. Notice that the entire file is a single high-level node—generally, a Group or Separator that contains various children.

Anything else that appears on a line after a pound sign (#) is considered to be a comment; the browser ignores comments.

## Instancing

One last concept is useful for reading and understanding VRML: *instancing*, which is how you can share a node (and its children, if any) in multiple places in the file. The DEF command, placed before a node, assigns a name to that node. If that name is used in a USE command anywhere else in that file, the same node is used in place of the USE command. The following Group contains two spheres of different sizes:

```
Group {
 DEF sphere1 Sphere {
  radius 3
 }

 Scale {
  scalefactor .5 .5 .5
 }

 USE sphere1 }
```

Instancing usually is used with groups, so as not to waste file space in describing the same object in multiple places.

# VRML 1.0 and Java

So how does Java fit in with VRML? Java and VRML make an excellent pair, because the strengths of Java fit so well with the weaknesses of VRML.

VRML 1.0 has a few major flaws. One flaw is that VRML is oriented toward a single user. You upload a VRML scene in your browser and then prowl around in it, much as you examine a normal HTML Web page. This is all well and good, but it doesn't match one of the main requirements of cyberspace: that it be a place for people to interact. VRML 1.0 is a good way to distribute 3-D models on the Net, but it isn't a particularly effective communications medium otherwise.

Also, VRML 1.0 is static. Nothing in VRML 1.0 alone really allows objects to move and change. In the real world, things are changing all the time, and many objects react to all sorts of stimuli. Again, VRML 1.0 falls a bit short of being full cyberspace.

All of these problems are understandable; VRML 1.0 was an attempt to get something put together quickly and to serve as a base standard that people could begin to use. But more is needed, to address these failings. In particular, VRML worlds need multiple-user communications and *behaviors*—objects that react to the world around them.

Given the fact that VRML and Java came onto the Internet scene at about the same time, people naturally thought about melding the two, and several companies are trying to do just that in a variety of ways. The following section talks about one of those approaches: Liquid Reality.

## Liquid Reality

Liquid Reality is a particularly relevant implementation of VRML, in that it is itself written in Java. Liquid Reality is based on Ice, a 3-D library for Java, and comes from Dimension X, a high-end Web-site company in California. You can find Liquid Reality at the following URL:

**http://www.dimensionx.com/lr/**

Liquid Reality implements VRML as a collection of Java classes. Due to the flexibility of Java, the product has remarkable extensibility. When the Liquid Reality browser encounters a node type that it doesn't understand, it goes back to the server and asks for a class that implements that node type. Thus, Liquid Reality provides extensibility to VRML much as the HotJava browser provides extensibility to HTML.

Liquid Reality provides Java with a large class library, which essentially covers all the capabilities of VRML. A class exists for each kind of field (such as SFColor or MFLong). Each class implements setValue() and getValue() methods; multi-valued fields also implement methods to return the number of values in the field and set a particular value.

Similarly, a class exists for each kind of node—for example, class CubeNode or SeparatorNode. The node's fields are public members of the class; when a field is changed, it notifies the node that contains it, so that the node can (if necessary) be redrawn. Each node has methods that do the following things:

- Set or get the name of the node
- Get the fields of the node
- Determine whether the node has been modified
- Read or print the node
- Handle events such as mouse clicks

Several methods deal with scene traversal, including the following:

- Save and restore the state (as Separator nodes do)
- Set up geometry and transformations
- Control lighting and cameras

By using Liquid Reality in a Java-based environment, you extend the capabilities of VRML as needed. You can have Java routines modify the scene graph on the fly, and you can add new node classes to make up for the gaps in VRML 1.0. Overall, Liquid Reality makes the basic VRML language considerably more interactive and interesting.

These capabilities soon may be available to everyone who uses VRML, due to a new proposal for revising the language: Moving Worlds.

# The Future: VRML 2.0 and Moving Worlds

Perhaps the greatest potential lies in the next revision of VRML. The VRML community has generally accepted the facts that VRML 1.0 is just a first step and that the time has come to advance the standard to incorporate behavior and multiple-user capability, which means integrating VRML with some sort of programming language.

At the time when this chapter was written, the shape of VRML 2.0 had not yet been determined; various vendors of major tools had proposed several possibilities. Probably the most interesting of the proposals is Moving Worlds, submitted by Silicon Graphics and backed by several major VRML vendors, including Sony, Worldmaker, Netscape, Intervista, Paper Software, and Chaco. This section discusses Moving Worlds and how it relates to Java.

The Moving Worlds proposal is still being discussed, and the details are still up in the air, so this section does not provide the complete details; instead, the section discusses the broad scope of how this proposal changes VRML. For more details, see the Moving Worlds page at the following URL:

**http://webspace.sgi.com/moving-worlds/**

At the time when this chapter was written, Netscape had produced a beta implementation of Moving Worlds named Live3D, running with Netscape 2.0; the illustrations in this chapter were displayed with Live3D (which also works with VRML 1.0). For more information, see the Netscape site at the following URL:

**http://home.netscape.com/**

Bear in mind that the spec still is in a state of flux. The examples in this section should give you a good idea of how things work, but the details may have changed by the time you read this chapter.

Moving Worlds is a ground-up rewrite of VRML. The syntax and many nodes are mostly the same as in version 1.0, but the proposal attempts to address all the major failings of the first version. Moving Worlds includes the following features:

- New static capabilities, including sound, fog, and scene backdrops
- Prototyping: mechanisms to create well-defined, reusable objects
- Sensors, which detect actions by the user or the passage of time
- Scripting, which allows you to connect applets to your VRML worlds

# Static Capabilities

Most of the new static capabilities aren't world-shaking, but they are useful. Elements such as sound can make a virtual world considerably more real to the user. Numerous small tweaks have been made in the various nodes, so don't assume that any given node is exactly the same in version 2.0 as it is in version 1.0.

A few nodes have been added to make creating and using objects easier. The `Separator` node from VRML 1.0 has been replaced by an enhanced `Transform` node, which has many of the characteristics of the old `Separator` but combines those capabilities with the transformations (such as size and orientation) that apply to the node. Also, a new node—`Shape`—has been added, which can be used to collect the geometry for an object. `Shape` has the fields `appearance` (which defines things such as the `Materials` for the object) and `geometry` (which defines the actual form of the object).

To understand how Moving Worlds differs from VRML 1.0, consider an example (courtesy of Silicon Graphics). The files in listings 29.1 and 29.2 show a simple scene that includes a red cone, a blue sphere, and a green cylinder. The first file shows how you might represent these objects in VRML 1.0; the second file shows how you might represent them in Moving Worlds.

### Listing 29.1   A Simple Scene in VRML 1.0

```
#VRML V1.0 ascii
Separator {
 Transform {
   translation 0 2 0
 }
 Material {
   diffuseColor 1 0 0
 }
 Cone { }

 Separator {
   Transform {
     scaleFactor 2 2 2
   }
   Material {
     diffuseColor 0 0 1
   }
   Sphere { }

   Transform {
     translation 2 0 0
   }
   Material {
     diffuseColor 0 1 0
   }
   Cylinder { }
 } }
```

**Listing 29.2   The Same Scene in VRML 2.0**

```
#VRML V2.0 ascii
Transform {
  translation 0 2 0
  children [
    Shape {
      appearance Appearance {
        material Material {
          diffuseColor 1 0 0
        }
      }
      geometry Cone { }
    },

    Transform {
      scaleFactor 2 2 2
      children [
        Shape {
          appearance Appearance {
            material Material {
              diffuseColor 0 0 1
            }
          }
          geometry Sphere { }
        },

        Transform {
          translation 2 0 0
          children [
            Shape {
              appearance Appearance {
                material Material {
                  diffuseColor 0 1 0
                }
              }
              geometry Cylinder { }
            }
          ]
        }
      ]
    }
  }
] }
```

The file in listing 29.2 is a bit wordier than the one in listing 29.1, but also a bit more elegant. The Shape nodes allow you to collect the appearance of an object and its geometry, making it a little clearer how things relate to one another. Combining the Separator and Transform nodes makes sense, because they usually are used together.

# Prototyping

Prototyping is a welcome addition to VRML that any object-oriented programmer will understand. Recall that in VRML 1.0 the only way to reuse a node is with the DEF and USE commands. These commands do not take any parameters, and don't really provide any good way to create a new node class.

Prototyping addresses these concerns. With the new PROTO keyword, you can define a prototype object, which is conceptually close to a class. This prototype exposes certain fields (which are used internally to set the fields of the objects that comprise the prototype) and certain events. (Events are described later in this section.) Effectively, PROTO allows you to define new VRML node types, which you then can use just like the built-in ones.

Listing 29.3 shows part of the code for a simple bookshelf, whose back and bottom can be painted in colors specified as a field.

### Listing 29.3 VRML 2.0 Prototype for a Bookshelf

```
PROTO Bookshelf [ field MFColor backColor .5 .5 .5
    field MFColor baseColor .2 .2 .2 ] {
Transform {
 children [

  Shape { # back of the bookcase
  appearance Appearance {
   material Material { diffuseColor IS backColor }
  }
  geometry Cube { ... }
  },

  Shape { # bottom of the bookcase
  appearance Appearance {
   material Material { diffuseColor IS baseColor }
  }
  geometry Cube { ... }
  }
 ] # End of the children
} # End of the Transform } # End of the prototype
```

Bookshelf is a top-level Transform node (which acts as a kind of Group) that contains two children: the back and the base. The IS command in each Material node (such as diffuseColor IS backColor) tells the browser to take the value specified in the backColor field, and use it for the diffuseColor field of Material. Therefore, the fields of the prototype are propagated into the bookshelf's subsidiary objects and used appropriately.

Prototypes enable you to create libraries of reusable VRML objects.

# Sensors and Routes

Sensors are objects that generate *events*, which are messages that can be passed between nodes. You can use sensors and events to make your worlds truly interactive. Kinds of sensors include the following:

- BoxProximitySensor
- ClickSensor
- CylinderSensor
- DiskSensor
- PlaneSensor
- SphereSensor
- TimeSensor

BoxProximitySensor generates an event when the user gets close to it. ClickSensor detects mouse movement and clicks. CylinderSensor, DiskSensor, PlaneSensor, and SphereSensor detect mouse drags and map them to various kinds of rotations and movements, so that you can allow users to manipulate objects. Finally, TimeSensor generates clock ticks, which other nodes can use to change over time.

You can use the events generated by sensors by specifying them in ROUTE commands. ROUTEs are not nodes and are not part of the scene graph; they are browser commands to the browser that connect nodes.

A ROUTE connects an output event from one node to an input to another node. In general, most fields of most nodes have a corresponding set event. A Transform node, for example, can take set_rotation events, set_scale events, and so on. You can think of these events as being input events. By using a ROUTE, you can connect the outputs from a Sensor (or some other node that generates events) to these inputs and cause things to change. The following code causes object myCylinder to rotate:

```
DEF myCylinder Transform {
  children [
   DEF Rotator CylinderSensor { }
   Cylinder { ... }
  ] }
...
ROUTE Rotator.rotation TO myCylinder.set_rotation
```

Rotator interprets mouse drags as meaning cylindrical rotation and generates events of type SFRotation. The ROUTE command sends these SFRotation events from Rotator to myCylinder, where they are used to set the rotation for myCylinder, turning it appropriately.

Some more code is necessary to completely flesh out the example, but you get the idea: ROUTEs send events from the output of one object to the input of another.

# Scripting

The most critical new node in the Moving Worlds roster is the Script node. Although the analogy is inexact, you can think of Scripts as being the VRML equivalents of applets.

A Script node has the following fields:

```
MFString   behavior
SFString   scriptType
FBool      mustEvaluate
SFBool     directOutputs
```

A Script node also has any number of eventIns, eventOuts, and fields. In general, the syntax is similar to that of the PROTO construct. The behavior field provides the class of the applet. scriptType indicates the language of the applet. (Moving Worlds is not restricted to Java, although that language is used the most.) mustEvaluate tells the browser whether it can buffer events or must send them to the applet immediately. directOutputs tells the browser whether this applet can send events directly to other nodes and receive events from other nodes.

The Script node receives events just as any other node does. The node passes those events to the related applet, which processes them and (usually) generates other events to change the state of the virtual world.

# The API

The applet uses an API, which is defined as part of the standard, and which defines how Java accesses the outside world. Many routines are defined in this API, but the routines fall into a small number of categories.

First is a `Field` class, which extends Java's `Object` class by default and therefore inherits all the capabilities of `Object`. For each type of VRML field, a class defines a read-only (constant) Java version of that field. For the `SFColor` field type (which defines a single color value), the corresponding read-only class is:

```
class ConstSFColor extends Field {
public float[] getValue(); }
```

These constant classes typically are used for input values from VRML to Java applets, so they have only the single routine `getValue()`. Notice that `ConstSFColor` uses an array of floats. A color is an RGB value, so it needs three floating-point numbers to represent it.

For each field, the API also defines a class which can be written as well as read:

```
class SFColor extends Field {
public float[] getValue();
public void setValue(float[] value)
 throws ArrayIndexOutOfBoundsException; }
```

Single-valued `Fields` have only `getValue()` and `setValue()` methods. For multiple-value `Fields`, the options are slightly more complex, as the following code shows:

```
class MFColor extends Field {
public float[][] getValue();
public void setValue(float[][] value)
 throws ArrayIndexOutOfBoundsException;
public void setValue(ConstMFColor value);
public void set1Value(int index, float[] value); }
```

In this case, you can set the value of the entire collection of colors from an array of arrays of floats (that is, an array of colors), set all of the colors from a `ConstMFColor` object (essentially copying the constant to a variable object), or set a single color within the list.

Notice that `setValue()` throws an exception. In general, all `Fields` define a `setValue()` method, and many of them can throw exceptions. Be prepared to write exception handlers when necessary.

The API currently defines two interfaces, one describing how Java interprets events, and one describing the basic capabilities of a node:

```
interface EventIn {
public String getname();
public SFTime getTimeStamp();
public ConstField getValue(); }
interface Node {
public ConstField getValue(String fieldName)
 throws InvalidFieldException;
```

```
public void postEventIn(String eventName, Field eventValue)
 throws InvalideventInException; }
```

These interfaces are useful in fleshing out the rest of the interface, particularly the `Script` class, which is the superclass for most Java programs that will interact with VRML:

```
class Script implements Node {
public void processEvents(Events [] events)
 throws Exception;
public void eventsProcessed()
 throws Exception;
protected Field getEventOut(String eventName)
 throws InvalidEventOutException;
protected Field getField(String fieldName)
 throws InvalidFieldException; }
```

All `Scripts` should be subclasses of `Script`. Notice that the `Exceptions` are left generalized, so that `Scripts` can tailor their exceptions to their needs. The methods of `Script` are shown and described below, in the examples.

The API also defines a `Browser` class, which has several methods. These methods examine the state of the virtual world, find out where the camera is pointing, set the major characteristics of the virtual world (how foggy it is, for example), and load new geometry from specified URLs.

## Example TextureAnchor

To better understand how `Scripts` and applets work, as well as how you build objects in Moving Worlds, consider the examples  (courtesy of Silicon Graphics) shown in listings 29.4 and 29.5.

**Listing 29.4   The TextureAnchor Node and Related Java Class**

```
PROTO TextureAnchor [
 field SFString name ""
 field SFString target ""
 field MFNode children [ ] {
 Group {
   children [
     DEF CS ClickSensor { },
     Group {
       children IS children
     }
   ]
 }

DEF S Script {
   field SFString name IS name
   field SFString target IS target
   eventIn SFVec2f hitTexCoord
```

VI

The Future of Java

(continues)

**Listing 29.4 Continued**

```
      behavior "TextureAnchor.java"
  }

  ROUTE CS.hitTexCoord TO S.hitTexCoord }

TextureAnchor.java _____
import "vrml.*"
class TextureAnchor extends Script {
  SFString name = (SFString) getField("name");
  SFString target = (SFString) getField("target");

  public void hitTexCoord(ConstSFVec2f value, SFTime ts) {
    // construct the string
    String str;
    sprintf(str, "%s?%g,%g target=%s",
        name.getValue(),
        value.getValue()[0],
        value.getValue()[1],
        target.getValue());

    Browser.loadURL(str);
  } }
```

This example defines a somewhat improved version of the WWWAnchor node. The original anchor node was trying, more or less, to duplicate the concept of the HTML image map; the node had some problems with that procedure, however, because the application domain is a little different from HTML. In particular, you aren't clicking a single image, generally, but a texture that has been applied to a surface and that might repeat. What you really want is to know where in the texture you are, which is provided by this node.

TextureAnchor takes three parameters:

- The URL to which this anchor goes
- The window in which to display that URL (called the *target*)
- Children that define the geometry of the anchor

The ClickSensor node can do a variety of things. The node generates a hitTexCoord event, for example, whenever the user clicks the mouse button. This event is a 2-D value, giving the location of the click on the texture below the mouse. (In other words, if you have a surface with a texture tiled on it, and you click that surface, the ClickSensor tells you the coordinates *within the texture* that you clicked.)

The work is done by the `hitTexCoord()` method in the Java class `TextureAnchor`. Notice that the way that this method is called isn't particularly evident. The related event occurs in VRML, and the method seems to just get called. In fact, the method is being called indirectly.

Remember that the basic `Script` class (shown above) defines a `processEvents()` method. By default, this method takes a list of events that the browser has queued up and calls the appropriate method for each event, passing to that method the data from the event and the time when the event occurred. Thus, when a `hitTexCoord` event occurs in the browser, that event is queued up and sent to `processEvents()`, which takes the vector value (because the event is an `SFVec2f`), which now is a `Java ConstSFVec2f`, and passes that value and the time to the `hitTextCoord()` method. `processEvents()` always passes the time to methods, because the time is useful so often.

Although you can override `processEvents()` to gain more control of your event processing, this model usually works well. You do not need to get involved with creating or reacting to events directly; you can simply assume that the connection between VRML and Java is established.

> **Note**
>
> You also can define an `eventsProcessed()` method, which will be called after `processEvents()` has dealt with all of the pending events. This technique sometimes is useful to build up your data and then deal with all of it at the same time.

So the `hitTexCoord()` method is invoked. This method builds a URL, using the usual image-map syntax (anything after a question mark is interpreted as coordinates). The name and target values were given in the instance of the node; you get those values by using the `getField()` method. The `TextureAnchor` class gets the value of the `name` field from the node, extracts the X and Y coordinates of the mouse click from the value that was passed in (an `SFVec2f`, remember), and combines the name and coordinates to make up the URL. Finally, `hitTextCoord()` calls `Browser.LoadURL` to actually load in the new URL.

## Example Chopper

The next example is a little more sophisticated; it sends events as well as receives them, providing semi-intelligent control of a simple animation. The example shown in listing 29.5 describes a helicopter with spinning rotors.

Notice that Chopper simply pulls the Rotor node over the network and uses it; this section is examining the control logic, which turns the rotors on and off when the user clicks the mouse, and assumes that Rotor works correctly.

**Listing 29.5  The Chopper Node and Corresponding Java**

```
EXTERNPROTO Rotor [
  eventIn MFFloat Spin
  field MFNode children ]
 "http://somewhere/Rotor.wrl" # Where to look for implementation
PROTO Chopper [
  field SFFloat maxAltitude 30
    field SFFloat rotorSpeed 1 ]
{
  Group {
    children [
      DEF CLICK ClickSensor { }, # Get click events
      Shape { ... body... },
      DEF Top Rotor { ... geometry ... },
      DEF Back Rotor { ... geometry ... }
    ]
  }

  DEF SCRIPT Script {
    eventIn SFBool startOrStopEngines
    field maxAltitude IS maxAltitude
    field rotorSpeed IS rotorSpeed
    field SFNode topRotor USE Top
    field SFNode backRotor USE Back

    scriptType "java"
    behavior "chopper.java"
  }

  ROUTE CLICK.isActive TO SCRIPT.startOrStopEngines }


DEF MyScene Group {
  DEF MikesChopper Chopper { maxAltitude 40 } }


chopper.java: _____- import "vrml.*"
public class Chopper extends Script {
  SFNode TopRotor = (SFNode) getField("topRotor");
  SFNode BackRotor = (SFNode) getField("backRotor");

  float fRotorSpeed = ((SFFloat) getField("rotorSpeed")).getValue();

  boolean bEngineStarted = FALSE;

  public void startOrStopEngines(ConstSFBool value, SFTime ts) {
    boolean val = value.getValue();

    // Don't do anything on mouse-down:
    if (val == FALSE) return;
```

```
      // Otherwise, start or stop engines:
      if (bEngineStarted == FALSE) {
        StartEngine();
      }
      else {
        StopEngine();
      }
    }

    public void SpinRotors(fInRotorSpeed, fSeconds) {
        MFFloat rotorParams;
        float[] rp = rotorParams.getValue();

        rp[0] = 0;
        rp[1] = fInRotorSpeed;
        rp[2] = 0;
        rp[3] = fSeconds;
      TopRotor.postEventIn("Spin", rotorParams);

        rp[0] = fInRotorSpeed;
        rp[1] = 0;
        rp[2] = 0;
        rp[3] = fSeconds;
      BackRotor.postEventIn("Spin", rotorParams);
    }

    public void StartEngine() {
      // Sound could be done either by controlling a PointSound node
      // (put into another SFNode field) OR by adding/removing a
      // PointSound from the Separator (in which case the Separator
      // would need to be passed in an SFNode field).

        SpinRotors(fRotorSpeed, 3);
        bEngineStarted = TRUE;
    }

    public void StopEngine() {
        SpinRotors(0, 6);
        bEngineStarted = FALSE;
    } }
```

EXTERNPROTO, at the top of the listing, loads the Rotor node over the network, and provides a brief spec for the visible events and fields of the Rotor. Spin describes the orientation and speed at which the rotor turns; the children describe the geometry of the rotor.

PROTO describes a Chopper prototype—essentially, a class. Chopper takes two parameters: maxAltitude (don't worry about it for this example) and rotorSpeed (how fast the rotors should turn).

Group at the top of Chopper contains the geometry of the helicopter and the rotors, and ClickSensor detects when the user clicks the helicopter. Then come the definitions of the Script node and its fields, as well as a ROUTE command from ClickSensor to that Script, so that the Script receives events when the user clicks the mouse.

The corresponding Java class Chopper starts out by getting the Fields with which it is concerned: pointers to the Rotor nodes and the overall rotor speed.

When the user clicks the mouse, the ClickSensor detects that action and generates an isActive event (two events, actually—a FALSE event when the mouse button goes down and a TRUE event when it goes up again). That event is routed to the Script's startOrStopEngines event. As described in the preceding example, the event gets queued up for processEvents(), which then dispatches the data to the startOrStopEngines() method.

The method checks the value that has been passed in. If the value is FALSE, the user just clicked the mouse button down; the method doesn't do anything in that case, but waits for the user to release the button. If the value is TRUE, the button has been released, so the method continues. The method checks the bEngineStarted variable, which keeps track of whether the rotors are running, and calls either StartEngine() or StopEngine(). These methods, in turn, call SpinRotors(), which has a speed of 0 (meaning that the rotors should stop) or the speed that the object specified (to turn the rotors on).

SpinRotors builds up a rotorParams variable—an MFFloat that corresponds to the elements of the Spin eventIn on the Rotor object. SpinRotors uses this variable to send Spin events to both TopRotor and BackRotor, turning them on or off as appropriate.

# And On to Cyberspace

A full example of multiple-user cyberspace would be too involved to present in this chapter, but how this example would be presented is clear. As demonstrated in the examples above, you can use Java applets to modify the virtual world in arbitrary ways. The examples only looked at user clicks and uploading files or starting animations, but the sky is essentially the limit; you can use events to set virtually any characteristic of the scene graph.

The next step is obvious: hook people together. Using Java, you can create communication links among multiple users who are viewing the same world. You could use those links to pass information back and forth. Each user could be embodied by an *avatar*—a visible geometric representation of where the user is and what he or she is doing. Although avatars in virtual-reality systems can be quite fancy, looking like lifelike humans, they also can be quite simple—basic geometric objects, chosen by the user, that are only complex enough to show which way the user is facing.

You could track each user's movement by attaching events to the user's viewpoint and send those movements to the other users in the same room, moving avatars just as the camera moves. If you combine these avatars with a simple chat or voice interaction, you begin to get a useful area in which people can meet.

With a little imagination, even more capabilities are possible. The objects in rooms can have dynamic characteristics, for example, and the communications links can keep track of these characteristics. Thus, when one user flicks on a light switch in a room, this actions sends a message to the browsers of all the other users who are present, telling their lights to turn on as well. The synchronization issues aren't simple, but they are solvable, now that you have the necessary tools. ❖

# CHAPTER 30

# New Developments

*by Alexander Newman*

Where do we go from here? In 30 or so chapters, dozens of diagrams, and hundreds of lines of code, we've covered cutting edge changes in computing. Like it or not, Java has revolutionized what people expect from the World Wide Web. The question is "Is Java here to stay?" The answer, as with all prognostication, is a little murky.

Among those people who care about Java and the World Wide Web, there are basically three camps: converts, realists, and reactionaries. But to keep things in perspective, there are hundreds of millions of people to whom Java means nothing. Not because they have other things to do or worry about, but because they don't interact with the Web or even the Internet. At last report, about one in every ten Americans had never used the Internet at all—and of those 25 million people, only one in ten used the Internet regularly. Out of those two and a half million people, only (you guessed it) about one in ten used the World Wide Web on a regular basis. That means that only about a quarter of a million people use the Web on a regular basis. Now, no study has been done yet, but looking at everything else, if you had to guess how many of those people were using Java or a Java-compatible browser, you might guess close to...one in ten.

To be honest, we don't know. Sun Microsystems claims that "millions" of copies of Java have been downloaded. Of course, many of those downloads were probably performed by the same people as each new iteration of Java appeared. Nonetheless, Java seems to be a phenomenon that is bucking the bell curve.

In this chapter we'll look at:

- An overview of JDBC
- Kona, Sun's minimalist operating system

- Low-cost internet hardware (Hollow Boxes)
- Who's shaping the future of Java?

# What Is JDBC?

As the popularity of Java swells, many information specialists are using Java to provide a unique role in client-server databases: use of Java as a platform-independent client for network-accessible databases. Java allows the database programmers to focus on the functionality of the database without worrying about platform-specific issues, and for outside access to databases, an easy way to download the client to the user's specific machine.

The Java DataBase Connectivity (JDBC) Specification takes this one step further: database application designers write database-independent Java clients, which will in turn be able to connect to a wide variety of databases. Just as Java itself helped application designers write programs without worrying about the final user platform, programs written to conform to the JDBC specification are developed without worrying about the final database platform the user will choose.

Before the JDBC specification, database designers needed to take care of the interaction between the Java application and the standard database tools themselves. They usually accomplished this by running a helper application or server on a network-accessible machine, which would translate data between a Java applet on a user's machine and the database on the local system. The helper applications needed to be hand coded for each type of environment: one wrapper for ODBC databases, another for I/Net systems, another for Oracle databases, and so on. In addition, there were some performance issues related to funneling all processing through a particular helper interface, in order to satisfy the strict Java security requirements.

The JDBC specification removes the hassle of writing that helper application. Java applications and applets are able to speak through the JDBC layer to the required databases, and the JDBC drivers are able to handle all of the database connectivity. If the database designer uses fairly standard SQL syntax when implementing his or her Java application, then any database product with a JDBC-compliant driver may be used, transparently to the database programmer.

The JDBC is not a product; it is a specification of an interface between a client application and an SQL database. It is up to the various database vendors and third-party software vendors to actually implement JDBC-compliant drivers to connect to Java applications to their commercial and free database engines. One of the first such drivers is expected to be the JDBC driver for ODBC-compliant databases, which will give Java programmers easy access to any ODBC-compliant database. The JDBC/ODBC driver (now, that's a mouthful) is expected to be available by June, 1996.

All of the major database vendors have committed to developing JDBC drivers for their on-line databases. As they become available, Java programmers using JDBC will have the flexibility to choose database engines which meet their needs and budget—without rewriting any part of their Java code. At the time of this writing, there are almost 20 different companies who have endorsed the JDBC API.

## Simple Examples of JDBC Usage

The most common example of database functionality embedded in a Java application is to perform a database search for a given set of criteria. Using JDBC, the code fragment to perform the search might look like

```
ResultSet rs = stmnt.executeQuery("SELECT compid, comp_name,
comp_city FROM companies");
```

The select statement is passed through to the database engine by the JDBC driver, which in turn performs the search itself (hopefully, very rapidly), and returns the results back up through the JDBC layer to the client program. The client program may then step through the results of the search and use the information in its interaction with the user. The results for the current row are obtained by fairly simple methods, such as

```
rs.next();
// Moves to next row in result
Numeric compid = rs.getNumeric(1);
String comp_name = rs.getString(2);
```

The interface may be used also to update or insert rows within the database, using a similar type of statement:

```
Statement cmd = con.createStatement();
int num_rows = cmd.execute(
   "update companies set comp_name = \"Leepfrog\"
   where compid = 8337");
```

The JDBC specification also supports dynamic statements, where "placeholders" are given in the SQL string or when which columns are returned from a query are not known in advance and must be discovered at run-time. The above could have been written:

```
Statement cmd = con.prepareStatement(
   "update companies set comp_name= ? where compid = ?");
cmd.setVarChar(1, "Leepfrog");
cmd.setInteger(2, 9337);
cmd.execute();
```

VI

The Future of Java

Of course, the values could easily have been variables reflecting user input or program calculations.

When using data types whose representation varies from database engine to database engine, you must use a special syntax so that the database driver may change the representation into one that the engine can understand. Such data types include date, time, and timestamp (date/time fields). Similar handling is done for scalar functions, which in some databases are done by keyword (such as using "TODAY" to mean "today's date").

Advanced features of modern RDBMSs are accessible also through the JDBC interface. For example, if a database engine supports stored features, that procedure may be called by a Java applet through the JDBC driver, and outer joins between tables may be specified in an engine-independent manner, and the JDBC driver will translate the statement into an appropriate syntax for the database engine. The "update company name" may be a stored procedure in the database, with associated side effects. This could be called as:

```
cmd.execute("{ call update_compname[8337, \"Leepfrog\"] }");
```

The JDBC drivers allow client Java programs to query for the functionality available from a database engine. For example, if the database engine does not support outer joins, the client program may choose to use two SQL statements with a "UNION" to get the same results. The meta-information includes lists of callable scalar functions, permissions information regarding the current user, sorting order for NULL values, how the engine handles many of the different idiosyncrasies of the different SQL dialects, transaction handling, schema information, and so on.

## Relationship Between ODBC and JDBC

The JDBC specification is very similar to Microsoft's ODBC specification, largely because both specifications are based on the X/Open SQL CLI (Call Level Interface). Database programmers who are familiar with either of those specifications will find that using the JDBC is a direct application of the concepts learned in their previous projects. In many ways, the JDBC is easier to use than ODBC, because the interface is naturally strongly typed to work with Java. Many of ODBC's shortcomings—such as string overflow, handling of very large binary objects, and miscast pointers—either are easier to handle with Java, or don't even exist because of the way that Java handles data types of unknown size. The JDBC specification states that ease of implementation using common SQL APIs (ODBC, in particular) is a strong goal of JDBC; therefore, much of JDBC "tastes like" ODBC.

The main differences between JDBC and ODBC concern how the data is passed back and forth between the caller and the driver. Since ODBC is a C-based API, it makes use of "(void *)" casting to pass column results back to the calling procedure. Since Java is strongly typed, it uses methods that return the expected types to the caller directly, which removes a frequent source of ODBC errors. Since Java is not limited to static array sizes, concern with string overflow and the host of different character sizes needed by the database can be easily handled within Java. Retrieving large amounts of data from a database BLOB is much easier using a Java iostream than it is to use the corresponding ODBC methods.

JDBC also provides more flexibility in specifying a database's namespace, which allows users to "find" databases on large networks more easily. Because Java applets frequently have no knowledge of the user's file system configuration and naming conventions, the JDBC specification gives applet programmers the ability to choose the JDBC driver that will be able to correctly provide data access, and from there give the driver enough information to find the database on the local network or out on the Internet.

JDBC provides levels of security that are not present in ODBC, which faithfully reflects Java's overall approach to trusted/untrusted applets. Because Java's strict rules on security cannot be propagated through the ODBC layer, the Java security model may lead to an overly-strict enforcement by the JDBC manager in charge of the ODBC driver. In general, handling a trusted/untrusted mix of applets and device drivers seems to be a fairly sticky proposition, and users may be tempted to disable JDBC security entirely rather than deal with conflicting driver/applet permissions.

JDBC does not support scrollable cursors, or ODBC-style bookmarks, although this may change in the future.

## Structure of the JDBC and JDBC Manager

As a Java program executes, it may have several JDBC drivers accessible for its use. One driver connects to ODBC-compliant databases, another connects to Informix databases accessible by I/Net, and a third provides access to any database following a well-published protocol. Each driver "registers" itself to the JDBC manager during initialization so that the manager has an overview of the drivers available. The manager also tracks the "trusted" state of each driver so that an untrusted applet may download an appropriate driver itself if one does not already exist on the system.

During a database connection attempt, the Java program passes a database URL to the JDBC manager. The JDBC manager then calls each loaded JDBC driver until one is able to open the requested URLs. Each driver ignores URLs that request databases that it cannot connect to. Java client programs may also bypass the "driver hunt" and specify explicitly which driver is to be used, if the Java client knows ahead of time which driver is appropriate.

JDBC URLs are in the form `jdbc:subprotocol:subname`. The subprotocol is the name of the connection protocol, and the subname is the name of the specific database within the domain of the protocol. If the subname contains information about the host and port numbers, then it is strongly suggested that the subname be encoded in the URL-standard `//hostname:port/subname` manner.

For example, the ODBC database customers may be specified by the URL `jdbc:odbc:customers`. The textbooks database accessible on the machine walker using the connection protocol ixnet would have a URL of `jdbc:ixnet://walker/textbooks`. To avoid collision between different subprotocols with the same name (which would confuse the JDBC drivers), JavaSoft provides information registration for URLs. Drivers will also likely be available which will allow URLs to use a formal named lookup mechanism (such as DCE), which would provide even greater flexibility in changing between different JDBC databases.

Each client may have multiple database connections open, each of which is an instance of a class derived from jva.sql.connection. The multiple connection may come from the same JDBC driver, or may be spread across a variety of different drivers. In many cases, the Java program will not care which connection goes where, but when the application needs to track which database features are available to the client, care must be taken not to confuse which connection has which features.

## Security Issues

In keeping with its overall security module, Java keeps track of the trusted status of each database driver. Untrusted drivers have the same restrictions that untrusted applets have: they cannot access the local file system or network hosts other than their home. The JDBC manager will go even one step further: untrusted drivers will be used only on applets downloaded from the same host. During the connection attempt and "hunt" for an appropriate JDBC driver, the manager skips over untrusted drivers from different hosts. This may result in many copies of a particular kind of driver on a user's machine, but it prevents a malicious driver writer from hijacking a harmless applet that calls it.

Trusted JDBC database drivers must be careful not to extend their credentials upwards to untrusted applets who call it, particularly when it comes to other hosts on the network or the local file system. In particular, it is important that JDBC drivers that access real data do not allow untrusted applets to corrupt that data.

## What's on the Horizon for JDBC?

As the various database vendors release drivers for their databases, the database programmer will be able to swap their clients around with different databases. Simple demos or beginning users may use small database systems and then graduate up to larger, more expensive, more reliable database systems as their data needs grow. As they move, none of their investment in the Java/JDBC clients is lost; in fact, the client may be able to access the new databases without modification. The design, programming, and training investment with the old system is not lost—it is directly usable by the new database engine.

In addition to the flexibility of code reuse, there will be an exciting market of published data forms accessible over the Internet. Companies or organizations that maintain collections of information may allow remote querying of their information over the Internet. The schema and protocols (and possibly even custom JDBC drivers) for such data will be published, and Java applet writers may then spread out across the Internet to gather various information. As an example, a company that expends considerable effort compiling an accurate database of people in the United States may sell query subscriptions to its service. A data-entry applet can query on-the-fly the people database for records that match what has been entered so far, and the record populated. The company can publish the information as up-to-date as possible, and the subscribers see updates and changes as soon as they are entered into the database, rather than waiting for the next CD-ROM release. There are already a variety of data servers on the Internet, but in general they do not offer a common means of accessing them. JDBC will change that.

Even more interesting are the application design tools that can be built on top of Java and the JDBC specification. Coming up just around the next bend, programmers will be able to develop easily, in Java, an entire database application using high-level visual design tools. The final result will be a cohesive graphical interface to a particular database *design*, which will run on any machine supporting Java, and can utilize any database engine that support the JDBC specification. Once written, the same application can be used both by Macintosh users who access a FoxPro database on their local machines, all the way up to a user on a high-end SGI workstation who accesses a large distributed Informix On-Line database over a fiber optic network.

**VI**

**The Future of Java**

Database vendors are working also on ways of extending the functionality of the database engine itself, by providing programming hooks that will allow a wide variety of data types to be stored in the database. No longer will database columns be constrained to the mundane char, int, date, time, interval data types, but any user-definable data type may be stored within the database proper and searched by the database engine using normal SQL statements. Geographical positions (what is located near here?), graphic pictures (find me other things which look like that), HTML files (what documents have links pointing to here?) and so on will be accessible directly from SQL—and through JDBC, from any Java client running on any platform. The future of database client development is poised to change drastically, and Java/JDBC will be on the edge of the new technology.

The JDBC specification is very well written and easy to follow, and provides the header files for the JDBC database drivers, along with a couple of examples of JDBC usage. The specification can be found on the web, at URL **http://splash.javasoft.com/jdbc**.

The major database vendors also are the best source of information about how their databases can be accessed using the JDBC specification. They are also the best source on the availability and schedule for their database drivers. Many vendors also are announcing additional Java classes for use with their engines, which enhance the Java environment even further. For up-to-date information, check out their home page on the Web.

# Back to the Future

There are three ways to make software popular: make it easy to get, make it easy to use, make it easy to run. Sun, by following Netscape's Internet play model of marketing, has made Java easy to get. It's free. More than free, they've established multiple websites where you can download Java at the touch of a button. You can get Java.

Sun hasn't done a particularly good job of making Java easy to use. The online documentation is limited, both in scope and volume. Supporting a product which you're not going to make any money off of just doesn't make that much business sense. Most of the support for Java comes from outside Sun in the rapidly developing Java community. Local user groups are springing up all over, and a national Java user group (Java-SIG) appeared last December. Sun does host a few electronic mailing lists, but they aren't moderated and there's no guarantee that you'll get an answer to your question.

One of the models floating around the net that seems to be picking up support is OpenDoc. OpenDoc is a multi-platform component software architecture that is designed to work across Mac OS, Windows, OS/2 and UNIX. Component software allows users to select the features they need to get the job done without forcing them to run burdensome monolithic applications. This means that when a user goes to create a presentation she doesn't have to build tables in her spreadsheet, graphics in a draw program and text in a word processor before lumping it all into a presentation application. Instead, she starts with a blank page and adds information using components that consist of specialized text, graphics or spreadsheet tools. OpenDoc supporters assert that OpenDoc would bring a whole new level of capabilities to Java programmers and applet users, allowing applets to be integrated seamlessly and complex applications to be constructed of interchangeable components.

Developers worldwide have been attracted to OpenDoc since its introduction. By creating an architecture where smaller, more specialized software components can interoperate, OpenDoc provides an ideal environment for both independent software vendors and entrepreneurial developers. Since Apple made OpenDoc 1.0 available on the World Wide Web in November 1995, the site has averaged more than 1000 OpenDoc downloads each day. For more information about OpenDoc, visit Apple's OpenDoc Web site at:

**http://opendoc.apple.com/**.

OpenDoc components are based on industry standards set by Component Integration Laboratories, an association of industry leading companies including Apple, Adobe Systems, IBM, Lotus, Novell, and Oracle. OpenDoc 1.0 for Mac OS shipped in November 1995, and OpenDoc for Windows is expected later this year. More than 300 developers have committed to delivering OpenDoc component software products, and Apple plans to introduce this year an OpenDoc-based Internet application suite (code-named CyberDog) as well as a series of parts and viewers that will allow easy integration of Apple technology, such as QuickDraw 3D, into OpenDoc-aware applications.

Many people believe Java is OpenDoc's best potential platform: a highly productive cross-platform environment with broad industry support and a rapidly growing audience.

More information about the OpenDoc for Java movement is available at:

**http://summary.net/~breck/java-opendoc.html**.

We've already seen a variety of self-styled Java "experts" appear. Hot on their heels we've already started to see Java consulting firms and Java VARs. You may well ask "how does one become a VAR for a free product?" The key is the "VA" part of "VAR." VARs are Value Added Resellers. Obviosuly a

**VI**

**The Future of Java**

company can't resell Java. Even if you could legally, the fact that Sun is giving it away would certainly cut into your market. However, the Java craze has created a niche for people to market packages on top of Java or related to Java: bundles of applets, Java "gunslingers" for hire, and more. You can already get Java training from a number of places besides Sun. Once the fervor dies down, you'll start to see some of these consultants and instructors get shaken out of the marketplace, or merged together for survival.

As for making Java easy to use, Sun and a variety of other companies have come up with a novel solution to that problem.

Java is, after all, a computing language. You still need a computer to do anything with it. But Sun, as well as Oracle and a few other companies, have announced their intentions to develop low-end machines designed exclusively to run Web applications well.

These machines, called variously "hollow boxes," "virtual boxes," and "network access devices," depend on Java's "virtual machine" specification. As we've discussed, the virtual machine defines a high-level instruction set for which the Java compiler generates bytecode, takes care of garbage collection, and also provides a minimalist interface to the underlying machine and operating system. Sun and other computer companies got people talking with the notion of a network computer.

The network, or "hollow" computer paradigm has a lot of support, particularly from longtime computer users who feel that Microsoft and Intel have an unbreakable lock on the home computing market. Hollow computing supporters say their approach breaks this grip, which is based on Microsoft's Windows operating system and Intel Corp. processors. Currently, about 80 percent of desktop computers are Intel machines.

In theory, these machines could draw applications and even their operating system from large servers, or even over the Internet, as needed—but that's not going to happen. In February, Sun conceded that, despite the hype, "hollow computers" will still require some operating software. Their solution? Codename: Kona.

# Kona

Even though Sun chief executive Scott McNealy has gone on record as saying "the whole idea is not to give you an operating system," Sun's own version of the hollow computer is going to include a "minimal operating system layer." Sun's hollow box was demonstrated at the Uniforum tradeshow in early

1996. Uniforum is a conference focused on the UNIX operating system widely used by businesses for network purposes.

Sun's "Java client" (their name for the hollow box) is supposed to be ready by the end of 1996. To support the Java Client, Sun is developing its own operating system, code-named Kona. The Kona operating system is going to go head-to-head with other low-level operating systems, such as Oracle's Network Computer Operating System (NCOS). If both Sun and Oracle bring operating systems to market, you're going to have to choose one, with no guarantee that they'll run the same programs.

Kona "tricks" Sun's network device. Kona essentially makes the network server believe that the hollow box is a fully functioning machine. At a minimum, the operating system for a hollow computer would have to provide support for network connections and multithreading. However, it wouldn't have to support many of the operations that today's desktop operating systems support: features like files systems, memory protection, or virtual memory.

Hollow boxes also are more secure than many of today's typical servers or other machines that are attached to the Internet twenty-four hours a day. With the hollow box model, you only attach to the Internet when you need to retrieve a piece of data, much like dialing up to an service provider with your home computer. Like your home computer, a hollow box is connected to the Internet for short periods of time only. By keeping your connect times short, you greatly narrow the window of opportunity for intrusion from the Net.

Kona supports Sun's Hot Java browser, although it's currently unclear which other browser the hollow box will support. Netscape? Maybe. We hope so. The only thing we know for sure is that Sun doesn't plan to develop any browsers other than HotJava.

Sun has always been a leading advocate of network computing. And that makes sense. In order for there to be network computing, you need servers, and Sun controls the majority share of the network server market.

Sun has been providing only sketchy details of its network device. The price for different versions would vary widely depending on which of Sun's many microprocessors end up in the machine, and on what sort of battery the machine uses in wireless implementations. Also, the Java client is being designed to connect to a variety of devices. Add a joystick, and you've got yourself a game machine; add a touch screen if you want a kiosk; or add the simple keyboard and mouse and you've got an all-purpose office tool. Essentially, Sun is covering all the bases. They're hoping to be able to stay on top by moving where opportunities come up, and they're going to try to move there fast.

# Who's Shaping the Future?

Naturally, when we say "the future," we mean the future of Java. Well, there are a lot of players, each with his own agenda. Like anything else, they're not all going to succeed. Some are directly opposed to one another (like Sun and Oracle on the matter of hollow boxes), and some just won't catch the wave at the right time. After all, the only reason VHS is the standard for video cassette recorders is because Beta isn't.

## Sun and Java Chips

Not a lot is currently known about Sun's "Java Chips," except how they are going to be executed. At this time, we don't know if they are going to be for "Java accelerators" or full-blown Java systems. More importantly, we don't know whether they're an entirely new design, or just a lightweight RISC state machine with a Java software front-end. The evidence seems to support the former (use of the Java Virtual Machine's machine code natively) partially eliminating the interpretation, but nothing is definite yet.

In February, 1996, in a move "to better reflect the division's breadth and depth," Sun Microsystem's SPARC Technology Business division announced a new corporate name and divisional restructuring. The newly entity named "Sun Microelectronics" was tasked with delivering merchant-market processing solutions, including the industry's highest performance networked computing microprocessor cores, chips, chipsets, boards, and services. In support of its business in networked embedded applications as well as the low-end of the newly-announced Java processor family, the division announced its Embedded Product Group.

Besides the fact that Sun Microelectronics sells Sun's UltraSPARC, SuperSPARC, and microSPARC technologies, it's not a division which has been in the spotlight a lot. They recently kicked off their Embedded Products group, which is developing, marketing, and selling SPARC and Java processors into the emerging networked embedded marketplace. With their new family of Java processors, Sun hopes to open up a vast new spectrum of solutions for Internet and multimedia applications.

More information on Sun Microelectronics is available via the World Wide Web at

**http://www.sun.com/stb**.

## Java and IBM

In the latter half of 1995, a team led by IBM Fellow Mike Cowlishaw at IBM's Hursley laboratory spent several months evaluating the Java environment. The team initially ported one of the versions to both OS/2 and AIX. In January, 1996, they released the JDK 1 for OS/2 and JDK 1 for AIX.

IBM is continuing work on ports to MVS and OS/400, as well as to Win16. The Win16 port is the one that is closest to completion. The chief technical problems that needed to be addressed were threads and long file names. They seem to be progressing towards the stage of a complete implementation of the JDK by use of existing code and raw intelligence, but no dates yet.

## America Online and Other Online Services

You wouldn't ordinarily think of an online service, no matter how large, as having an impact on software development. That's not true in the case of Java and America Online. When they introduced their own built-in browser, AOL, with something on the order of three million subscribers, brought the Web to the masses. Now America Online has announced that they've "endorsed" Java. What does that mean to AOL subscribers? Probably that we'll see a Java-only compatible browser built into AOL by the end of 1996.

The real question is, "What does this mean for Java?" If AOL's web browser is Java-capable, than Java has just been introduced to millions of users who might not otherwise have access to it. In the first place, it's going to be a brutal field-testing. Every bug, every flaw, and every possible configuration of Java hardware (at both the server and client ends) will be stress-tested in a matter of months—if not weeks. If Java passes this battery of assaults, it could truly establish itself as the language for network programming. If it fails in something, those failures are going to be well-publicized.

There's the additional element that your average America Online user's craving for Java may be satisfied with just the browser. After all, AOL doesn't currently offer individual homepages, so there's little need for their users to want to start writing their own applets. There may be some "trickle down," as AOL users expect to see more animation and interactivity on the pages they visit, but that's not the same thing as encouraging people to develop their own applets.

One online service provider that does allow people limited access to Java for their own Webpages is Boston-based Software Tool & Die. Their online service, called The World, offers its customers a chance to use Java on their own web pages. By placing a variety of parameter-intensive applets in a publicly accessible directory, along with some on-line examples, users with almost no

Java experience and only limited HTML experience can pull together sophisticated webpages using only simple tools. Users currently can't compile their own Java source into bytecode, but that's not too far off.

# What's Wrong with Java?

Throughout this book, we've been discussing what's right with Java, and how to get the most out of the Java language. That's because we truly believe that Java is a valuable resource that will continue to change the World Wide Web. However, we'd be remiss in our responsibilities if we didn't at least touch on some of the negative aspects of Java.

As we've discussed throughout this book, the Java language is a series of trade-offs. Each feature begets a limitation, and while the value of those features strongly out-weighs the detriments of the limitations, that doesn't mean there are no limitations.

Java is free. That's great; you don't have to pay anything for it. It also means that there's no single company supporting the language. Despite Sun's ownership of Java, the documentation, as we've said, is sketchy at best, which means that support for Java is going to have to come from elsewhere.

Java is secure, but that security places some unfortunate limitations on what files and devices a Java applet has access to, which limits Java's usefulness. Also, questions remain about how secure Java really is. Lack of security isn't a major shortcoming in an increasingly open environment, and we feel that if the Java development team hadn't made such an issue out of Java's security, people wouldn't be as focused on Java security as they are.

Nonetheless, even within the fairly stringent parameters that come with the programming language, the potential for abuse exists. For example, it's a fairly trivial matter to use JavaScript to grab the e-mail address of everyone who visits your webpage. It's equally trivial to automatically send e-mail to those people about your product, services, hobbies, etc. If you want to see how it works, visit

**http://www.popco.com/grabtest.html**.

Before you rush right out and implement this code, think about this: Not only is this intrusive to the casual Web browser (think of it as the moral equivalent of junk mail), it's probably illegal. Certainly, if you're a commercial site, utilizing a script like this one (and configuring it to gather even more information) violates the US laws regarding consumer privacy. What impact will that have on overseas sites? That will vary from place to place, but that's one of the wonders of the World Wide Web.

# In Closing

We expect to see Java spawn a small industry within an industry. Look for a whole range of software tools to help you write better, faster, and smaller applets. Imagine a helper application where you could combine several applets from a large library of pre-existing applets to come up with a new applet—all with but a few clicks of the mouse. You won't have to wait too long; several companies are working on these helper programs even as we speak. Be patient as these start to appear; the first one to market isn't always the best.

Also, look for applet swaps to start up. Applets are small, portable (you can fit them on a floppy), and run the range from utilitarian to amusing to creative. They could become high-tech baseball cards. People will bring their applets on a disk to a single site, with a Java compatible machine. Programmers can show off their creations and pick up a few new ones while they're at it, in a casual atmosphere.

There are several conferences and magazines focusing on Java in the works. Like most things, some will stick, the conferences will become annual events, and some will fail. One such magazine is JavaWorld Online, from the publishers of SunWorld Online. You can find them at:

   **http://www.javaworld.com.**

You can also check the newsgroup comp.lang.java on a regular basis for updates from the world of Java.

We hope this book has done what you hoped it would, whether that was to provide you with a general overview of this hot new programming language, or to provide you with the knowledge you needed to design and implement your own applets and applications. This is just the beginning for Java, and all of us who work with Java are looking forward to seeing where the future takes us! ❖

**VI**

**The Future of Java**

# CHAPTER 31

# Learning from the Pros

*by Mark Wutka*

Even though you have now learned how to use Java, you may still be wondering what to do with it. This chapter will introduce you to some companies that are doing Java development in the real world, show you some of the ways they are using Java, and give you some idea of how to take advantage of Java's unique features.

In this chapter you will see:

- How the University of Michigan uses Java to distribute weather information across the Internet

- How the Creative Media Cauldron is creating a framework of reusable objects that help them develop new applets faster

- How MagnaStar has committed to developing 100% of their code in Java, and how they are successful with it

- How Pioneer Technologies is using Java to create a flexible client-server architecture

## Graphical Data Over the Internet

The University of Michigan Weather Underground has been providing weather information to Internet users since 1991. At that time, the only way this data was available was through the text-based telnet interface. In 1993, the Weather Underground decided it was time to go graphical, so they hired Alan Steremberg. Alan created "Blue Skies," a graphical front end to the weather system that ran on the Macintosh computer. Unfortunately, this left other users such as PC and UNIX workstation out in the cold. Now, thanks to the wonders of Java, Alan, along with Christopher Schwerzler, has made graphical weather data available to a much wider audience.

This new Java version of "Blue Skies" can display textual weather information on top of a graphical map. As the mouse passes over a city on the map, the status bar at the top is updated with that city's current conditions. Users can get the National Weather Service forecast for a city just by clicking that city. "Blue Skies" also allows users to zoom in on a particular area. The following figure shows a sample weather map from the "Blue Skies" applet.

**Fig. 31.1**
The "Blue Skies" applet displays a map of precipitation.

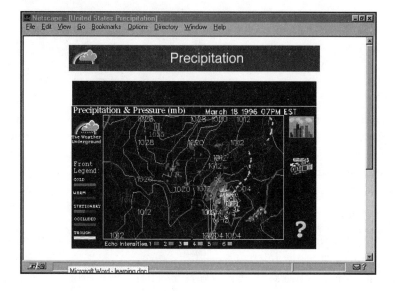

You can find "Blue Skies" on the World Wide Web at the address:

**http://cirrus.sprl.umich.edu**

This is just one of the many ways that Java can be used to access data that was once only available in text form.

# Creative Media Cauldron

Creative Media Cauldron is an up-and-coming Web development shop located in New York City's "Silicon Alley." The company develops cutting-edge Internet content and tools that are both high-impact and cost-effective. They blend a rare mixture of artistic design sense and technology expertise.

## Developing a Framework for Reuse

Creative Media Cauldron has made great use of Java's Object-Oriented features by creating a framework of reusable objects. They sell a number of useful components that they call "Plug-In Playlets." These playlets are applets that you can use to add neat features to your Web pages. Among the playlets currently available are Streaming Animation, Temporal ImageMap, HotButton Panel, and Invisible Download.

The Streaming Animation playlet is used for displaying simple animation sequences while larger sequences are still downloading. This allows your page to be "active" faster, while still allowing you to display complex animation sequences. For instance, you might display a simple 2-frame animation that the user can interact with while you are downloading a much nicer 20-frame animation.

The Temporal ImageMap playlet is a neat variation on the old clickable image that you find on many Web pages. Rather than provide one image with different sections you can click, the Temporal ImageMap shows you different images at different times, allowing you to click any one you like. This allows you to create a large number of clickable images, yet display them in an area the size of a single image. The following two figures show snapshots of the Temporal ImageMap at two separate times. Notice that the icons on the left and right have changed.

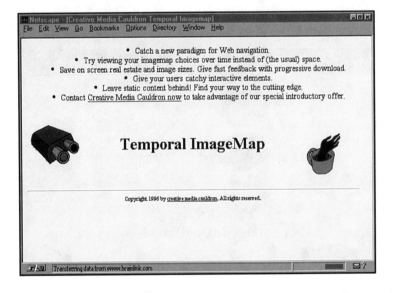

**Fig. 31.2**
Each icon in a Temporal ImageMap leads to a different Web page.

The HotButton Panel playlet creates a button that is "alive." When you pass the mouse over the button, it changes. For instance, you could create a button that displayed an image, but when the mouse passed over it, you could also display a text description of the button. This is similar to the concept of the "Hot Zone" in windows, where you see the name of a button if you leave the mouse pointer on the button for a few seconds. The following two figures show a hot button before the mouse passes over it, and while the mouse is sitting on top of the button. Notice the text that appears while the mouse is on top of the button.

**Fig. 31.3**
Temporal ImageMaps conserve space by cycling images through the same area.

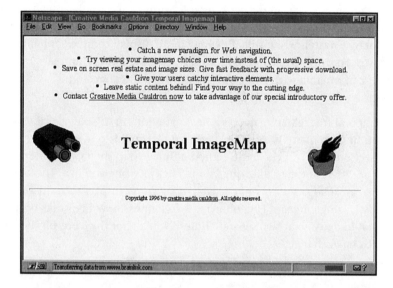

**Fig. 31.4**
The HotButton looks just like a normal image.

The Invisible Download playlet allows you to download images and other items and have them cached for later use. For instance, you might have a main Web page with a link to an image page containing 20 different images. You can use the Invisible Download playlet from the main page to start downloading the images for the image page ahead of time. That way, when a user clicked the link for the image page, some or all of the images would already be loaded.

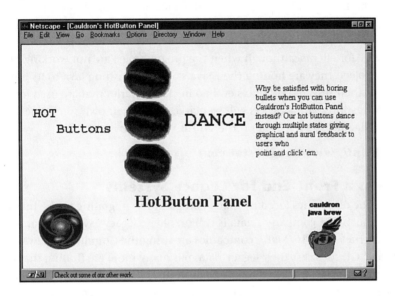

**Fig. 31.5**
The HotButton changes its appearance when the mouse passes over it.

Since Creative Media Cauldron has developed these playlets on top of a core set of objects, much of the code for these playlets is shared. One of the advantages of having a large amount of shared code is that once the code for one playlet is downloaded, the other playlets using that same code will not have to wait for it to be downloaded. From a development standpoint, Creative Media Cauldron can develop new playlets very quickly because they have built a framework that handles many common tasks for them.

Creative Media Cauldron is very excited about the opportunities presented by Java. According to Andruid Kerne of Creative Media Cauldron, "Java inside of Netscape is the most powerful cross-platform development environment ever created. We are excited to create truly interactive distributed environments across the Internet."

Creative Media Cauldron can be found on the World Wide Web at the address:

**http://www.brainlink.com/~cauldron**

# MagnaStar—A Java Development Company

MagnaStar Inc. was the first company to be formed for the express purpose of doing 100% Java coding. They provide consulting, training and lecturing in Java, in addition to programming. MagnaStar's primary focus is in doing custom work for clients, although when the programmers are not working on a client project, they are honing their Java skills and pushing Java to its limits. Many of their research products end up in class libraries that are used for client applications, while others will be marketed on their own sometime in the future. MagnaStar's location on the World Wide Web is:

> **http://www.magnastar.com**

## Java as a Front-End for Legacy Systems

One of the difficulties faced by many companies in migrating to the Internet is that much of a company's data is still on older "legacy" systems that aren't very Internet friendly. Many companies are using the Common Gateway Interface (CGI) to access their legacy data, but many more are finding that CGI just isn't interactive enough to suit their needs. MagnaStar uses Java to create network front-ends for their clients' legacy systems. Java's graphical user interface and networking capabilities make it an ideal tool for accessing legacy data. Using Java, a salesperson out on the road can access the company's ordering system over the Internet through a Java applet.

## Creating Customizable Applications

Java promises to provide greater flexibility in common applications and reduce the size of these applications. One of the reasons that packages such as word processors are so large these days is because of the number of features they provide. The problem is that everyone uses a different set of features, and only in very rare circumstances does one person use every single feature provided. A word processor written in Java could allow you to add a thesaurus only when you needed it. Someone who never used a thesaurus would never have the thesaurus code in their application. Java supports the concept of "dynamic loading" of classes—it can add new classes "on-the-fly." For example, you could suddenly decide that you need a thesaurus, and Java could download the thesaurus from the Internet while you were still running your word processor. MagnaStar's "Universal Applications" program, still under development, is aimed towards achieving this kind of dynamic application.

## Java Adds Smarts to Web Pages

Java provides a number of features that can help make a Web page more effective. One of the most useful features is the ability to jump to other URLs. Rather than using the old static text link, or even an image map, you can create unique, lively ways of displaying links to other Web pages.

MagnaStar has written several applets that help enhance Web pages. The UltraNav navigation tool helps users navigate through a hierarchy of information the same way that a file manager navigates through files and directories. For instance, you might want to organize your information into categories such as "Business," "Education," and "Games." You might want to further break "Business" down into "Sales" and "Finance." If you were doing this with static Web pages, you would have a link to the Business page, which would then have links to the Sales and Finance pages. UltraNav lets you create a shortcut. Rather than having to pull up three different pages to get to Sales, UltraNav shows you the choices and lets you navigate down to Sales from within UltraNav, then when you select Sales, you jump directly to the Sales page. In other words, UltraNav uses Java to help you create Web shortcuts, saving users time, and also presenting a sort of "overhead view" of the page hierarchy. Figure 31.6 shows UltraNav in action.

UltraNav is available over the World Wide Web for demonstration:

> **http://www.magnastar.com/ultra_nav**

MagnaStar's Carousel provides yet another way to create interesting links. It presents a number of images in the form of a 3-D kiosk. You can use the mouse to spin the carousel around to see the different images, then when you see one you are interested in, you can click the image and visit the page to which it refers. The following figure shows Carousel in action:

You can try out Carousel on the World Wide Web:

> **http://www.magnastar.com/Carousel**

**Fig. 31.6**
MagnaStar's
Carousel presents
a rotating kiosk of
images.

## Keeping People on Your Web Page Longer

MagnaStar also creates games in Java to help make a page more interesting.
Someone surfing the Web might stop at a page for ten seconds, but if there's
a game on the page, they might stay a little longer. That is significant if you
are trying to put advertising on your pages.

## Full-Blown Applications in Java

Java isn't just for sprucing up your Web pages. It is a powerful language,
well-suited for application development. In fact, MagnaStar is so confident
in Java's suitability for development that they develop 100% of their code in
Java. Some of the advantages that Java provides over some of the more traditional languages like C++ are:

- Platform Independence—Java programs can be run on any hardware
  platform that supports Java. You can develop a Java program on your
  486 running Windows 95, and turn around and run it on a SparcCenter
  2000 with no changes. That is a huge boon to shops trying to develop
  products that run on multiple platforms.

- Shorter Development Time—MagnaStar reports that the time it takes
  them to develop an application in Java is about half the amount of time
  to develop the same application in C++. Java has the potential to approach the quick development times of Smalltalk, once a larger core set
  of classes is developed.

- On-the-fly Loading—Java's ability to load and unload classes on-the-fly
  gives it a unique advantage over languages like C++. While it is true
  that Dynamic Linking Libraries (DLLs) allow languages like C++ to load
  in new classes at runtime, Java's "network awareness" gives it the added
  ability to load new classes across the network.

MagnaStar has created a database system called "Products Unlimited" that allows users to browse through a large catalog of company products and locate them quickly. According to Joe Weber of MagnaStar, "The unique user interface makes it trivial for Web viewers to find the products they are looking for, and because the entire system is coded in Java, without any modifications, users of Products Unlimited can present their information on the World Wide Web and CD-ROM for every platform, all with the same friendly interface."

# Pioneer Technologies and Client-Server Computing

Pioneer Technologies Inc. (PTI) has already seen some success creating Web pages, now it is looking to branch into online client-server computing using Java. PTI hopes to offer a variety of online services, available through a server on the Internet.

## A Dynamic Client-Server Architecture

Pioneer Technologies's architecture consists of a single server program, which can dynamically load any number of service objects, and a client applet, that can dynamically load objects to provide custom graphical interfaces for various services.

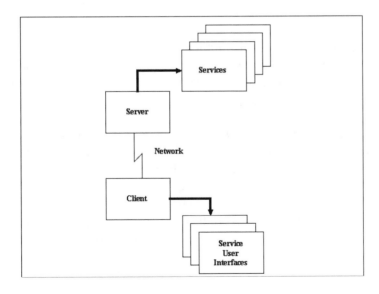

**Fig. 31.7**
The PTI Architecture Features a Server with Multiple Services and a Client with multiple user interfaces.

Java's ability to load classes dynamically is a key to PTI's online technology. PTI uses a single server program—no matter what services are running, it always uses the same code for the server. The server program can be configured to provide a certain set of services, and can also add services on-the-fly.

On the client side, the story is very similar. PTI uses a single client applet to communicate with the server program. Whenever a user requests a service, the client checks to see if it already has the user interface class for that service loaded. If not, it downloads the user interface class from the server and proceeds on.

## Taking Advantage of Interfaces

Another key to PTI's architecture is the concept of interfaces. In order to support multiple services, Pioneer Technologies has designed a common interface between server and service. The server may query the service for information such as its version and the version of the client software required to use it. The server also uses the interface to pass client messages on to the service. Because each service supports the same interface, the server program never needs to be changed in order to support new services.

Interfaces are just as important on the client side in PTI's architecture. The user interface classes all provide the same interface for the client applet. The client applet can query a user interface class for its version, and also pass on messages from the server. For instance, suppose the server provides a banking service where you can check your account balance. When a user requests the banking service, the client applet asks the server what version of the banking service user interface is required. It then sees if it has the banking service user interface loaded already, and if so, what version it is. If the versions do not match, it automatically loads the newer version. This allows services to be upgraded on the server on-the-fly.

## Using Panels to Hide Implementation Details

In designing the client applet, Pioneer Technologies took advantage of the AWT's Panel class. The client applet divides its interface into two portions— the server interface and the service interface. The server interface allows clients to log onto the server, see what services are available, and select a service. The service interface contains the user interface to a particular service. For instance, a user running the server interface would see something like

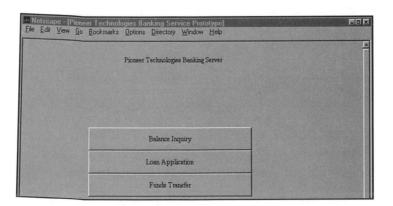

**Fig. 31.8**
The PTI client applet allows users to choose among a variety of services.

Once a service like the funds transfer service is selected, the client applet would look like:

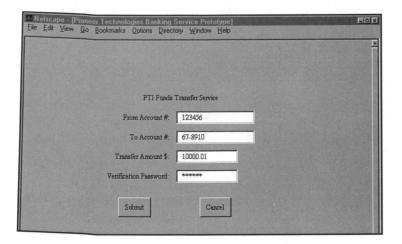

**Fig. 31.9**
Each service in the PTI client has its own panel, and is presented on a card layout.

Each service user interface is a separate instance of a Panel class. The client applet simply displays the user interface Panel for a service when the user selects that service. By using the CardLayout layout manager, the Client applet is able to switch between server interfaces at any time.

Pioneer Technologies hopes to be able to provide their own online services, as well as license this technology to other companies. They are located on the World Wide Web at **http://www.pioneertech.com/pti**. ❖

**VI**

**The Future of Java**

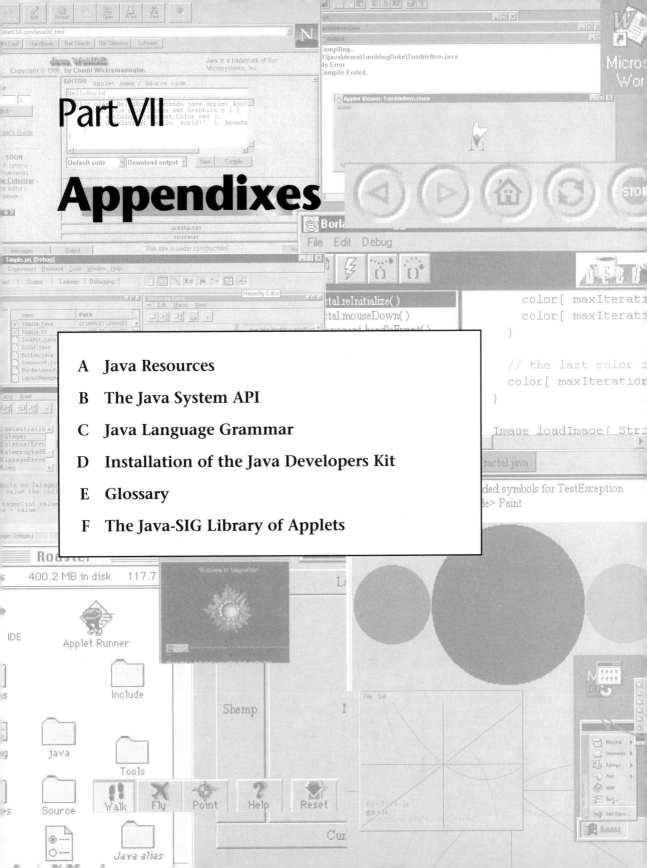

# Part VII

# Appendixes

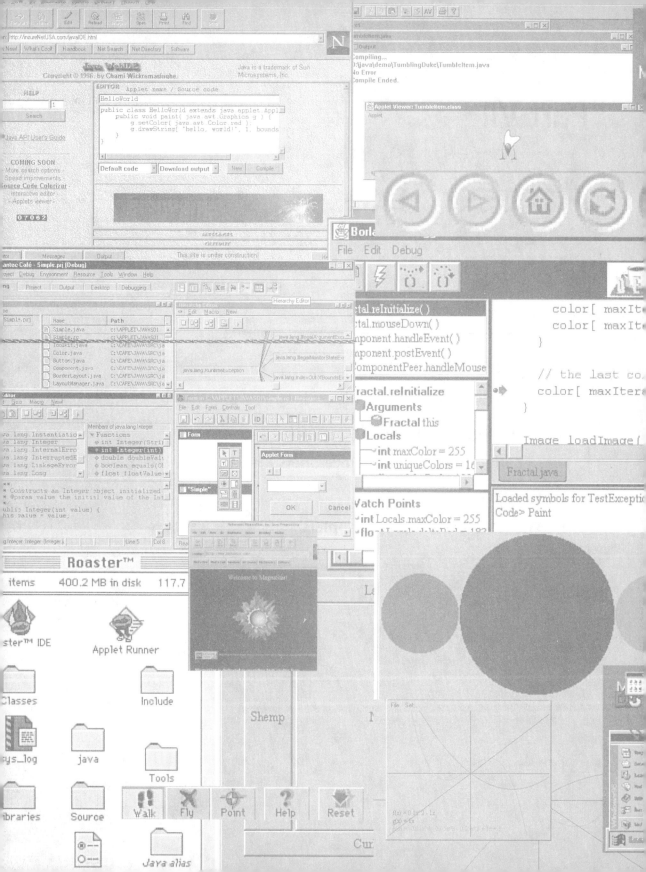

# Java Resources

## Java-SIG: The National Java Users' Group

In early December, 1995, the Sun User Group (SUG) announced the creation of Java-SIG, a national special interest group for users and developers of Sun Microsystem's Java and HotJava technology. Java-SIG offered (and still offers) a unique opportunity for the global electronic community to get a head start on the technology that was already changing the Web forever. According to the Executive Director of the Sun User Group, "Java-SIG allows the computer users of today to help shape the technology of tomorrow."

Java-SIG acts as the national user group for anyone interested in developing, publishing, or even just playing with Java, HotJava, and related technologies and applications. Many smaller local Java users' groups have already appeared, and Java-SIG unites these groups into a global information network.

Java-SIG is a source of hot news and information about the latest developments from Sun Microsystems and other licensed Java developers. Those currently working with Java who want to share their developments and discoveries will find a grateful audience in the members of Java-SIG. Or, for people who don't know the difference between an applet and a piglet, but want to know what all the buzz is about, Java-SIG is a great place to get started!

### Java-SIG Benefits and Services

Java-SIG is a membership organization, and one of the best ways to attract members is to provide them with services and benefits. Java-SIG does its best to add new and different services all the time. As someone once said, "membership has its privileges." Following are some of the privileges of membership in the national Java user group, Java-SIG.

### Electronic Mailing List

As one of the benefits of membership, Java-SIG runs a moderated mailing list that provides a forum for discussion by Java and HotJava users. This noncommercial network allows Java-SIG members to post questions or items of interest and get quick responses from hundreds of Java users worldwide.

### *Java-Cites*

*Java-Cites* is one of the many services available at Java-SIG's Web site. *Java-Cites* is an online bibliography of articles about Java, Java technology, and Java's impact on the industry. This site provides readers with a comprehensive listing of the articles, books, and other documents that have helped shape and describe Java during its first year.

It's an exciting service. Many sites offer links to online documentation, but this is the first directory of offline writing about Java. While there is a great deal of information available about Java online, *Java-Cites* is the first listing of the in-depth material and commentary that is available universally.

The index is maintained by Marisa A. Urgo. Ms. Urgo, who has a Master's degree in Library Sciences from Catholic University, is a frequent contributor to trade journals such as *InfoManage* and *The One-Person Library*.

*Java-Cites* can be accessed through the World Wide Web at **http://www.sug.org/Java-Cites.html** and is available to anyone, whether a member of Java-SIG or not. Individuals who want to add citations to the list can send them to Ms. Urgo at **cc001304@interramp.com**, or contact the Sun User Group at (617)232-0514.

### The Java-SIG Library of Applets

The Java-SIG Library of Applets (JLA) CD-ROM is a collection of hundreds of ready-to-use applets for Sun's platform-independent Java programming language.

The JLA spotlights the impressive versatility of Java. Applets included in the JLA range from simple text manipulation and 3-D animated graphics to systems or network management tasks. Best of all, the JLA allows users to add these applets to their Web pages instantaneously by simply copying the appropriate files from the CD-ROM.

VII

Appendixes

Literally hundreds of applets from developers all over the world are included on this CD, which features some of the most innovative, useful, and amusing work being done in Java. One of the CD's developers feels ". . . that the diversity of the contributors to this project is a testament to Java's universal appeal. . . that theme of diversity runs throughout the entire project. It's amazing how differently two people can address the same problem with the same set of tools. This disk includes utilities, animations, games, simulations, and tools. It's a very practical demonstration of Java's limitless flexibility."

In addition to being the first library of its kind, Java-SIG's Library of Applets is an excellent learning and development tool for those interested in Java and the changes it is introducing to the Web. It includes:

■ Source and byte-code for each applet

■ Examples of each applet in use

■ An easy-to-use HTML format

■ All available documentation

The JLA was released in April, 1996, with future volumes to follow. Because Java-SIG is dedicated to furthering the use and development of Java applets, applications, and development tools, they tried to keep the price down. The JLA sells for $50.00, with discounts available to Java-SIG members.

Some applets from future volumes of the JLA can be seen in advance of the final release on Java-SIG's "Cool Applet of the Week" page at this URL:

**http://www.sug.org/java-cool.html**

## The Future of Java-SIG

Future plans for Java-SIG include FILTER, a Java and HotJava newsletter to compliment the regular Java column in *Readme*, the newsletter of the Sun User Group; "Instant Coffee," a guidebook to using Java technology; and an online archive of Java programs or "applets."

For information about joining Java-SIG, contact **java-sig@sug.org** or call (617)232-0514. You can also access Java-SIG via the World Wide Web at **http://www.sug.org/java-sig.html**.

Its address is:

Java-SIG/Sun User Group
1330 Beacon Street, Suite 344
Brookline, MA   02146-3202

Phone: (617)232-0514
FAX: (617)232-1347
E-mail: **office@sug.org**

# Local User Groups—Within the United States (By State)

Local user groups are popping up all over as Java's popularity—and the desire to learn about it—spreads. Some local Java user groups (commonly called "JUGs") are formal affairs with dues and regular meetings; others are more casual. The term "local" is used loosely; JUGs have appeared around the world as well as around the country.

The following pages provide details on most of the JUGs. If you'd like more information about a particular group, use the provided contact information. Java-SIG maintains a list of JUGs that is updated on a regular basis. The URL is:

**http://www.sug.org/java-groups.html**

## CALIFORNIA: SacJUG (Sacramento Java Users' Group)
**Geographic area(s) serviced (city and state):**

Sacramento, CA

**Number of members:**

25 or so were at the first meeting in January, 1996.

**Charge dues?**

Not yet implemented, but soon.

**How often are meetings held?**

Once a month. So far, every fourth Thursday.

**Web address:**

**http://www.calweb.com/~statenet/sacjug**

We hope to have our own domain soon. It should be **http://www.sacjug.org**.

**Name and address of person to contact about this group:**

Michael F. Smith, Jr.
4429 F. Street
Sacramento, CA  95819

**E-mail address of contact person:**

> **michaels@statenet**
> or **sacjug@ns.net**

**Phone number for contact person:**

(916)444-0840

**Other information:**

We are a small but quickly growing group of Webmasters, programmers, and basic Internet and computer users who want to learn more about Java. Our philosophy is to share all the information we have with everyone and create an environment that is conducive to learning and growing. We hope to become a resource for Java programming and consulting in our region.

**Sponsors:**

> KDS Engineering  **http://www.kdeng.com**
>
> Calweb  **http://www.calweb.com**
>
> Ns Net  **http://www.ns.net**

## CALIFORNIA: Silicon Valley Java Users' Group

**Geographic area(s) serviced (city and state):**

At this time, we will be meeting in Palo Alto, CA. Geographically speaking, Silicon Valley Computer Society (SVCS) serves Silicon Valley, which encompasses many cities.

**Number of members:**

SVCS has about 250 members.

**Charge dues?**

SVCS costs $38 annually.

**How often are meetings held?**

Once a month, on the fourth Tuesday.

**Web address:**

> **http://www.best.com/~rickloek/javasig.html**

**Name and address of person to contact about this group:**

Rick Loek
6433 Cottle Rd.
San Jose, CA 95123

**E-mail address of contact person:**

**rickloek@best.com**

**Phone number for contact person:**

(415)843-6179

**Other information:**

The Silicon Valley Java Users' Group is still forming; we had our first meeting in February of 1996. The primary purpose of SVCS is to educate the community through public forums for discussion of personal computing. We are holding the meetings at OmniCell Technologies. (OmniCell makes point-of-use inventory control systems for use in hospitals.)

## COLORADO: BJUG (Boulder Java Users Group)
**Geographic area(s) serviced (city and state):**

Boulder, CO

**Number of members:**

Around 75 and growing.

**Charge dues?**

No.

**How often are meetings held?**

Once a month, third Wednesday of every month.

**Web address:**

N/A

**Electronic mailing list, if any:**

Unmoderated Discussion: **bjug-discuss@xor.com**

Moderated Announcements: **bjug-announce@xor.com**

**Name and address of person to contact about this group:**

Tim Miller
3445 Penrose Place, Suite 225
Boulder, CO    80301

**E-mail address of contact person:**

**timothy@rmii.com**

**Phone number for contact person:**

(303)415-9525

**Other information:**

First meeting was held in February 1996 and 45 attended. Very technical crowd who want to share technical issues and observations with one another.

## COLORADO: DAMJUG (Denver Area Metro Java Users' Group)

**Geographic area(s) serviced (city and state):**

Denver, CO

**Number of members:**

Approximately 40.

**Charge dues?**

No.

**How often are meetings held?**

Once a month.

**Web address:**

**http://www.webset.com/webset/java/JUG/DAMJUG.html**

**Electronic mailing list, if any:**

We do not have a listserver or reflecter yet, but will be implementing one in the near future.

**Name and address of person to contact about this group:**

Corey Klaasmeyer
910 16th Street, Suite 231
Denver, CO  80202

**E-mail address of contact person:**

corey@webset.com

**Phone number for contact person:**

(303)575-9258

**Other information:**

DAMJUG focuses primarily, but not exclusively, on topics related to programming and design in Java. As of January, DAMJUG had a membership of approximately 40 people who are excited about Java on professional, academic, and intellectual levels.

## ILLINOIS: I-JUG (Illinois Java Users' Group)
**Geographic area(s) serviced (city and state):**

Illinois and neighboring communities

**Number of members:**

10.

**Charge dues?**

No.

**How often are meetings held?**

Once a month—twice, if possible.

**Web address:**

http://www.xnet.com/~rudman/java/ijug.html

**Electronic mailing list, if any:**

ijug@petrified.cic.net
("subscribe" in body to **ijug-request@petrified.cic.net**)

**Name and address of person to contact about this group:**

Dan Rudman
725 Constitution Drive #5
Palatine, IL  60074-1945

**E-mail address of contact person:**

rudman@xnet.com

VII

Appendixes

**Phone number for contact person:**

(847)776-8964 (9AM–9PM CST)

**Other information:**

The Illinois Java Users' Group is dedicated to the education of its members and the development of business-oriented applets that demonstrate Java's powerful future. Ours is a unique philosophy in which we accelerate learning by dividing our members into small "Dream Teams" that attack a local Java topic and then present back to the group. This method has been shown to provide enthusiasm and quick results from its participants.

## MARYLAND: MAJUG (Mid-Atlantic Java Users' Group)
**Geographic area(s) serviced (city and state):**

Baltimore–Washington Metropolitan Area (MD, DC, VA)

**Number of members:**

Approximately 250.

**Charge dues?**

No.

**How often are meetings held?**

About once a month, so far. We are looking into creating SIGs to meet more frequently in subgroups.

**Web address:**

> **http://www.rssi.com/info/majug.html**

**Electronic mailing list:**

General membership: **majug@rssi.com**

Organizers only: **jug@rssi.com**

**Name and address of person to contact about this group:**

John Zukowski
Rapid Systems Solutions
8850 Stanford Blvd, Suite 4000
Columbia, MD  21045

**E-mail address of contact person:**

**john.zukowski@rssi.com**

**Phone number for contact person:**

voice (410)312-0777

FAX (410)312-1666

**Other information:**

The group started in December, 1995, in the ice and snow. The philosophy is fairly open. We try to meet people doing Java and learn/network. Meetings tend to have one user-focused presentation and one vendor-focused one. Special Interest Group meetings are in the planning stages, so meetings will be more frequent and more focused. Make-up includes both commercial and government people, along with several of the independent variety. The group is sponsored by Rapid Systems Solutions, one of Washington Technology's Fast 50 Corporations for 1996.

## NORTH CAROLINA: RTP Java Users' Group (Research Triangle Park)

**Geographic area(s) serviced (city and state):**

Central North Carolina

**Number of members:**

80 attendees at the last meeting; 155 people on mailing list.
We are just starting membership.

**Charge dues?**

Yes. $50/year, or $5/event.

**How often are meetings held?**

1-2 events/month.

**Web address:**

**http://jughead.trinet.com**

**Name of person to contact about this group:**

Rayme Jernigan

**E-mail address of contact person:**

   **rayme@vnet.net**

**Other information:**

The Research Triangle Park Java Users' Group has been established to provide Java-related information to its members, to facilitate contacts between its members, and to promote the use of Java technology in the Mid-North Carolina area. The RTP JUG is being organized as a vendor-independent organization.

The RTP JUG plans to move toward using digital telecommunications as a primary vehicle for group and inter-member communication. Initial tests providing audio or audiovisual content to the members' desktops are under discussion.

At the present, we have two categories of supporters: sustaining partners and contributing partners. Our sustaining partner is Trinet Services, and our contributing partners are Daniels and Daniels Attorneys at Law, Institute for Academic Technology, Strategic Technologies, Sun Microsystems, Inc., and RTP Information.

We welcome vendor information! If you have Java-related marketing collateral you would like distributed at our meetings, or products you would like to demo or have demonstrated, please contact Rayme Jernigan at **rayme@vnet.net**, or Sam Matheny at **matheny@interpath.net**.

## OHIO: CinJUG

**Geographic area(s) serviced (city and state):**

Cincinnati, OH

**Number of members:**

Approximately 20.

**Charge dues?**

Not established yet.

**How often are meetings held?**

Once a month, on the fourth Wednesday of every month.

**Web address:**

N/A

**Name and address of person to contact about this group:**

Attn: Dennis M. Hartsock
CIS–Cars Information Systems
4000 Executive Park Dr.
Cincinnati, OH  45230

**E-mail address of contact person:**

hartsock@carsinfo.com

**Phone number for contact person:**

(513)563-4543

**Other information:**

Currently, our new group is small and is primarily comprised of people from the Cincinnati/Dayton areas interested in being developers—they use the meetings to absorb as much technical information as possible. On the average, we receive one to two request(s) for membership everyday. A few of our area members are Sun Microsystems CEs, who provide much of the up-to-date information and technical expertise needed to maintain the interests. Additionally, we promote sharing through trading code (applets), ideas, and technical support.

## OREGON: OJIG (Oregon Java Interest Group)
**Geographic area(s) serviced (city and state):**

Eugene, OR

**Number of members:**

At last count, 26. About half show up at any one time.

**Charge dues?**

No.

**How often are meetings held?**

Once every two weeks.

**Web address:**

http://www.cs.uoregon.edu/ojig

**Name and address of person to contact about this group:**

Sean Russell
Department of Physics
University of Oregon
Eugene, OR   97403

**E-mail address of contact person:**

ser@jersey.uoregon.edu

**Other information:**

We have no sponsor. At this point, meetings resemble tutorials more than anything else, but we're working hard to get past that point. Our philosophy is to grok Java and similar technologies.

## PENNSYLVANIA:  P-JUG

**Geographic area(s) serviced (city and state):**

Philadelphia, PA and the Delaware Valley

**Number of members:**

About 15.

**Charge dues?**

No.

**How often are meetings held?**

Once per month.

**Web address:**

http://www.iliad.com/PhillyJUG

**Electronic mailing list, if any:**

PhillyJUG@iliad.com

**Name of person to contact about this group:**

Luke Cassady-Dorion

**E-mail address of contact person:**

luke@iliad.com

**Other information:**

We are a small group of programmers who are really excited about what Java means not only for the WWW, but also as it applies to any client/server system. We are dedicated to learning all that we can about the language as it progresses through its development.

## TENNESSEE: VandyJUG (Vanderbilt University)
**Geographic area(s) serviced (city and state):**

Nashville, TN (Vanderbilt University)

**Number of members:**

Approximately 25.

**Charge dues?**

No.

**How often are meetings held?**

It's decided in the newsgroup.

**Web Address:**

N/A

**Name and address of person to contact about this group:**

Andrew Warner
Vanderbilt University
Box 1005 Station B
Nashville, TN    37235

**E-mail address of contact person:**

   **andy@andy.net**

**Phone number for contact person:**

(615)421-8070

## TEXAS: JavaMUG (Java Metroplex Users' Group)
**Geographic area(s) serviced (city and state):**

Dallas/Fort Worth, TX

**Number of members:**

Approximately 40—but we don't have "members." The meetings are free and open.

**Charge dues?**

No.

**How often are meetings held?**

Once a month.

**Web address:**

> **http://www.utdallas.edu/orgs/javamug/**

**Electronic mailing list:**

> **javamug@utdallas.edu**

**Name of person to contact about this group:**

Billy Barron

**Other information:**

We're small—open to everyone of any knowledge level. We are sponsored by the University of Texas at Dallas (**http://www.utdallas.edu/**), which hosts our Web page and provides meeting space.

## TEXAS: Austin Java Klatch

**Geographic area(s) serviced (city and state):**

Austin, TX

**Number of members:**

Approximately 45.

**Charge dues?**

No.

**How often are meetings held?**

Monthly, on the fourth Tuesday of the month.

**Web address:**

> **http://www.webwords.com/austin_java_klatch.html**

**Electronic mailing list:**

> **javagroup@lists.webedge.com**

**Name and address of person to contact about this group:**

Bill Tschumy
2505 Greenlee Dr.
Austin, TX    78703

**E-mail address of contact person:**

> **bill@otherwise.com**

**Phone number for contact person:**

(512)474-5533

**Other information:**

The Austin Java Klatch was founded in November of 1995. There is no formal membership procedure—just come to the meetings if you are interested. We currently have around 45 people attending. Meetings are informal and are designed to bring together people with an interest in Java. Much of the meeting is taken up with a general gab session where people can discuss whatever Java-related thing is on their minds. We also generally try to have some sort of presentation for each meeting.

## VIRGINIA:  Southern Virginia Java Users' Group
**Geographic area(s) serviced (city and state):**

Richmond, Roanoke, and Tidewater, VA

**Number of members:**

Around 30 people attended the first meeting; expect overall membership to reach (in about one year) around 100 people.  The first meeting was held March, 1996.

**Charge dues?**

No.

**How often are meetings held?**

Once a month.

**Web address:**

N/A

**Name and address of person to contact about this group:**

George H. Pickering
CTO
Apexx Software, Inc.
101 St. Johns' Street
Warsaw, VA   22572

**E-mail address of contact person:**

  **gpickering@msn.com**

**Phone number for contact person:**

(703)222-3286

**Other information:**

The Southern Virginia Java Users Group is in the startup phase. We expect to be a medium-sized group with the goal of providing a forum for technical discussion about Java, Javascript, and VRML. We expect to hold a meeting every month. The meeting will consist of a brief business meeting, one or two Java-based demos from our members, and a technical discussion period to end the meeting. We will try to keep the first part of every meeting at a level where managers, users, and students can come and learn about Java's capabilities without being bogged down with technical details. The group expects to provide online access to demos and briefing materials through the SVJUG Web page following each meeting.

## WASHINGTON STATE: SeaJUG
### Geographic area(s) serviced (city and state):

Seattle, WA—including Redmond, Bellevue

**Number of members:**

60.

**Charge dues?**

No.

**How often are meetings held?**

Monthly, the third Wednesday of the month.

**Web address:**

> **http://www.seajug.org**

**Electronic mailing list:**

> **seajug@sealevelsoftware.com**
> (see **www.seajug.org** for details on joining)

**Name and address of person to contact about this group:**

Daniel Lipkie
Hewlett-Packard ELSE
101 Stewart St #700
Seattle, WA   98101

**E-mail address of contact person:**

> **daniel@elseware.com**

**Phone number for contact person:**

(206)269-4006

**Other information:**

This is a newly formed group—the first meeting was held in January, 1996. It's open to people with all levels of interest in Java/JavaScript—for example, users of Java, Web page designers, beginning Java coders, and experienced Java coders.

# Local User Groups—Outside the United States (By Country)

## BRAZIL: UFPE Java Group
**Geographic area(s) serviced:**

Recife–PE–Brazil

**Number of members:**

10.

**Charge dues?**

No.

**How often are meetings held?**

Twice a month.

**Web address:**

> **http://www.di.ufpe.br/java/**

**Electronic mailing list:**

> **java-l@di.ufpe.br**

**Name and address of person to contact about this group:**

Jorge Henrique Cabral Fernandes
Departamento de Informatica
Universidade Federal de Pernambuco
Av. Professor Luiz Freire, s/n
Cidade Universitaria–Recife–PE
BRAZIL  50.740-540

**E-mail address of contact person:**

> **jhcf@di.ufpe.br**

**Phone number for contact person:**

55-81-271-8430

**Other information:**

We are a small academic group, created in October, 1995, led by Professor Silvio Meira, and mostly composed of graduate and undergraduate students at the Department of Informatics of the Federal University of Pernambuco. Our main objective is to explore the research and application possibilities of Java and the Web model in society. We are a nonprofit group and have created and taught two different introductory courses in Java to our undergraduate and graduate peers. Our meetings occur on a demand basis, depending on the Department of Informatics (our sponsor).

## CANADA: TorJUG (Toronto Java Users' Group)
**Geographic area(s) serviced:**

Toronto, Ontario, Canada (although people from all over southern Ontario attend our meetings and people from all over the world have subscribed to our mailing list)

**Number of members:**

Approximately 150.

**Charge dues?**

No.

**How often are meetings held?**

Monthly.

**Web address:**

> **http://www.jug.org**

**Electronic mailing list:**

> **jug@jug.org**
> (to subscribe, send an e-mail message with "subscribe jug" in the body to **majordomo@jug.org**)

**Name and address of person to contact about this group:**

Greg Nenych / Geoff Wells / Rick Yazwinski
c/o Solect Technology Group
33 Yonge Street, 6th Floor
Toronto, Ontario, Canada
M5E 1G4

**E-mail address of contact person:**

> **greg.nenych@solect.com**
> or **jug-info@jug.org**

**Other information:**

We are not that old, but old for a Java user group, and are still an evolving entity. Our sponsors are Sun Microsystems of Canada, Solect Technology Group, Imagine That!, and Rogers.

## CANADA: JaVan Group

**Geographic area(s) serviced:**

Vancouver (Metro area), British Columbia, Canada

**Number of members:**

We're just starting, so only 1 at the present time.

**Charge dues?**

Free at the present time (changes will be decided by the group).

**How often are meetings held?**

Monthly.

**Web address:**

N/A

**Name and address of person to contact about this group:**

Dr. Mehrzad Tabatabaian
P.O. Box 31076
Port Moody, BC V3H 4T4

**E-mail address of contact person:**

**mehrzadt@dowco.com**

**Other information:**

Group is new. Philosophy: Provide up-to-date info, tutorial sessions, and discussion sessions for Java users.

## INDIA: IIJUG (India Internet Java Users' Group)

**Geographic area(s) serviced:**

Based in Mumbai, India (formerly known as Bombay). However, with the Internet, the world is our stage. The charter sports the idea of proliferating Java on a global platform.

**Number of members:**

We do not maintain a quantitative list of members. Just about anybody who is genuinely interested in Java or anything pertaining to Java is a member of the group.

**Charge dues?**

Not yet.

**How often are meetings held?**

Because there is no collective body as such, this question cannot be answered.

**Web address:**

**http://www.neca.com/~vmis**

This is a Java tutorial with a comprehensive list of articles related to Java, applets they like, and so on. Recently, a Spanish version of the tutorial was also put up by an Internet friend who happened to be enamored by the site. That can be found at:

**http://www.upc.edu.pe/java/**

**Name and address of person to contact about this group:**

Vijay Mukhi
B-13, Everest Building, tardeo,
Mumbai, India 400 034

**E-mail address of contact person:**

**vijaymukhi@eworld.com**

**Phone number for contact person:**

91-022-496 4335

**Other information:**

Basically, we set out to be a sort of body like the rest of the users' groups, members and all, but with the burgeoning cyber-culture, that seemed to be a rather narrow idea. We are interested in dealing with people who have even a remote real interest in Java. The achievements of the group (as yet) include:

- Organizing a one-day workshop on Java at NASSCOM 96, which is the largest software-driven exhibition in the IT history of India. The three-day international cyber-conference with exhibition is sponsored by the likes of Silicon Graphics, Apple Industries, and Sun Microsystems themselves.

- Putting up a tutorial on the Net that caters to the need of newbies as well as the developers, dispensing with the teasing techno-babble.

- An interactive live demo with a workshop for college students (the future programmers, that is), which was sponsored and organized by Metropolis, a newspaper from The (famous) Times group.

- A one-day conference for the Java-crazed press. The journalists were shown how Java is all set to change lives.

- A whole ongoing series of college demonstrations about Java. It is organized by IIJUG to acquaint the youth with the Internet as well as the elements that are conditioning its future (with Java being a protagonist).

- The National Association Of Computer Trainers (NACT) is organizing an International Conference on how to teach Java so that it does not turn out to be a "Revenge of the Nerds."

The group regularly interacts with the other Java developers and JUGs around the world to keep abreast of the latest happenings.

## MEXICO: Java Users' Group—ITESM Mexico City Campus

**Geographic area(s) serviced:**

Mexico City (Federal District) and Metro Area

**Number of members:**

Approximately 20.

**Charge dues?**

The equivalent of US$10.00/year.

**How often are meetings held?**

Monthly.

**Web address:**

> **http://www.ccm.itesm.mx/~enrique/EECDOCS/ myNewWebPage/JavaSUG/paginasWebJava.html**

**Electronic mailing list:**

> **eespinos@campus.ccm.itesm.mx**

**Name and address of person to contact about this group:**

Enrique David Espinosa Carrillo
Calle del Puente 222 Ejidos de Huipulco
Mexico D.F. 14380  MEXICO

**E-mail address of contact person:**

> **eespinos@campus.ccm.itesm.mx**

Alternatively, contact:

> **abueno@campus.ccm.itesm.mx**
> or **ejimenez@campus.ccm.itesm.mx**

**Phone number for contact person:**

(525)673-1000 x4231

**Other information:**

We're just getting started—in a *big* way! Our first meeting was March 7, 1996. We are working closely together with Sun Microsystems, Mexico, in three areas of technological innovation:

- Long-distance education using Java

- Applied artificial intelligence (intelligent agents) for education

- Education technology (i.e., intelligent tutoring systems)

We will bring together developers and researchers from all over the Metro Area, in a joint effort to make a difference in the growth of Mexico's Information Systems.

## UNITED KINGDOM:  iJUGGL (Independent Java Users' Group - Greater London)

**Geographic area(s) serviced:**

We focus on the area inside the M25, Greater London, but as long as you don't mind not being able to get to the meetings, we welcome Internet members from anywhere.

**Number of members:**

The Membership side is still forming up. Currently, if you turn up or participate electronically, you are a member.

**Charge dues?**

Money? Tsk! Never!

**How often are meetings held?**

We're aiming for once a month...

**Web address:**

> **http://www.compulink.co.uk/~java/**

**Name of person to contact about this group:**

Gordon Hundley or D.J. Walker-Morgan

**E-mail address of contact person:**

> **gh@compulink.co.uk**
> or **dj@popera.compulink.co.uk**

**Other information:**

We're an informal friendly lot who talk Java. We aren't sponsored but there are people we thank for use of their resources. Most of all, we are independent.

# Newsgroups

Two newsgroups are currently available:

- **comp.lang.java**—about the Java language and programming
- **alt.www.hotjava**—about the HotJava World Wide Web browser

> **Note**
>
> Please be aware that not all news servers make the **alt.** hierarchy of newsgroups available to their subscribers. If you're having trouble locating it, contact your news administrator.

The Northeast Parallel Architecture Server at Syracuse University tracks **comp.lang.java**, among other newsgroups. This is a handy way to get all of the **comp.lang.java** postings regarding "garbage collection," for example.

# Mailing Lists

In addition to the mailing list administered by Java-SIG, and the lists run by various smaller groups, there are a few lists run out of Sun.

> **Caution**
>
> This is an extremely high-traffic group, with over 20,000 subscribers and dozens of posts everyday. The list isn't moderated, so this isn't a place for you if you're easily overwhelmed.

The address for the list is:

**java-interest@java.sun.com**

You can subscribe to the list by sending the words "subscribe java-interest" in the body of your message to **majordomo@java.sun.com**

All the traffic on the Sun lists is gated to **comp.lang.java**, so there's no need to both read the mailing list and the newsgroup. For more information about Sun's mailing lists, take a look at:

**http://java.sun.com/mail.html**

# Training

Sun makes Java training available to its customers and the general public. The courses vary in length, cost, and quality. More information can be found at:

**http://www.sun.com/sunservice/wh/10-17-95-press-1.html**

Java-SIG holds classes on Java and other topics at its "SUG Lab" facilities in Boston, Massachusetts. The classes are small—limited to 12 students per session—and hands-on. Each student is provided with his or her own work-station. One of the courses is even taught by Jay Cross (one of the authors of this book!). For more information about SUGLabs, contact the Sun User Group at **office@sug.org** or call (617)232-0514.

# Support for Porting Issues

Java is a popular language and there are a lot of people doing their level best to see that it becomes a truly universal one by porting it to as many platforms as possible. Following is a listing of where to connect with some of the porters.

# Amiga Porting Issues

Mattias Johansson (**matj@o.lst.se**) in Sweden, runs P'Jami—which stands for **P**orting **J**ava to **Ami**ga.

**E-mail:**

There are three lists:

- **amiga-hotjava-dev@mail.iMNet.de** is a closed list. Participants must be approved by the list administrator.

- **amiga-hotjava@mail.iMNet.de** is an open mailing list for the exchange of information. To subscribe, send the words "subscribe amiga-hotjava" in the body of your message to **majordomo@mail.iMNet.de**

- The last list is: **amiga-hotjava-announce@mail.iMNet.de**, which broadcasts announcements of Amiga ports. To subscribe, send the words "subscribe amiga-hotjava-announce" in the body of a message to **majordomo@mail.iMNet.de**

# DEC Alpha OSF/1 Port

Patches and information about a DEC Alpha port. Page maintained by Greg Stiehl.

**Web site:**

> **http://www.NetJunkies.Com/Java/osf1-port.html**

**E-mail:**

> **stiehl@NetJunkies.com**

# Linux Porting Issues

Linux is the free, IBM-compatible version of UNIX. Karl Asha (**karl@blackdown.org**) maintains several resources for people interested in porting and using Java and HotJava with Linux.

**Web site:**

> **http://www.blackdown.org/java-linux.html**

**E-mail:**

There are two mailing lists for Linux issues. They are **java-linux** and **java-linux-announce**. The first is a discussion list, the second is a broadcast list.

The address for the mailing list is **java-linux@java.blackdown.org**

To subscribe to this list, send the word "subscribe" in the subject line of a message to **java-linux-request@java.blackdown.org** or **java-linux-announce-request@java.blackdown.org**

**FTP:**

An anonymous distribution of the Linux Java port is available from **ftp://substance.blackdown.org:/pub/Java**

## NEXTSTEP Porting Issues
**E-mail:**

Bill Bumgarner (**bbum@friday.com**) maintains an open mailing list for discussion of porting and integration esoteria that are unique to the NeXT platform.

To subscribe, send the word "subscribe" in the BODY of a message to **next-java-request@friday.com** The address to mail to the list is **next-java@friday.com**. ❖

# APPENDIX B
# The Java System API

This appendix is designed to provide you with a detailed summary of the Java Application Programming Interface (API). The Java API is a set of classes developed by the authors of the Java language designed to assist you in developing your own classes, applets, and applications.

The classes in the Java API are grouped into packages each of which may have several classes and interfaces. Furthermore, each of these items may also have several properties such as fields and/or methods.

While it is possible to program in Java without knowing too much about the API, every class that you develop will be dependent on at least one class within the API. Consequently, when you begin to develop more complex programs that deal with strings, sockets, and graphical interfaces, it is extremely helpful for you to know the objects provided to you by Sun as well as the properties of these objects.

The following appendix lists all objects defined in the Java API along with their superclass, interfaces, methods, and fields when applicable. There are however, a few details to note:

- Only public or *protected* classes, methods, and fields are listed in this appendix. This is because all other classes, methods, and fields are not accessible outside of the API packages. As a result, they are not readily available to the Java programmer in developing his own classes and packages.

- If an access modifier is not specified, the method or field is assumed to be public.

- The constructor methods of every class are the first methods listed under the "Method" heading. They can easily be identified by the fact that they have the same name as the class itself.

- All classes, interfaces, exceptions, and errors derive from the java.lang.Object class. Consequently, for those classes that do not list a superclass, the superclass is assumed to be java.lang.Object. (Except in the case of java.lang.Object which has no superclass.)

- Due to the encapsulation with which these packages were designed, almost all parent objects employed by the following objects are drawn from the same package. Consequently, unless otherwise noted, the parent object of the object listed can be found in the same package.

- All exceptions and errors are listed by themselves at the end of the appendix.

- All exceptions and errors are derived from java.lang.Exception and java.lang.Error respectively which in turn are derived from java.lang.Throwable. While powerful objects, most exception and error classes consist merely of two constructors for the given class—leaving the rest of their implementation to their superclasses. Consequently, while these two constructor methods are present in most exception and error classes, they are only listed in java.lang.Exception and java.lang.Error.

Finally note that this information (as well as explanations of each field and method) is also available in summarized form at **http://www.javasoft .com/JDK-1.0/api/packages.html**, or you can download and peruse the Java source code itself from **http://www.javasoft.com/**.

# java.applet

Although the smallest, this package is the most notable as a result of the Applet class. Full of useful methods, the Applet class lays the foundation for all applets and is able to provide you with information regarding the applet's surroundings via the AppletContext interface.

## Classes

**Applet extends java.awt.Panel**
**Methods**

void **destroy**( )

AppletContext **getAppletContext**( )

String **getAppletInfo**( )

AudioClip **getAudioClip**(*URL* url, *String* name)

AudioClip **getAudioClip**(*URL* url)

URL **getCodeBase**( )

URL **getDocumentBase**( )

Image **getImage**(*URL* url, *String* name)

Image **getImage**(URL url)

String **getParameter**(String name)

String[ ][ ] **getParameterInfo**( )

void **init**( )

Boolean **isActive**( )

void **play**(URL url, String name)

void **play**(URL url)

void **resize**(Dimension d)

void **resize**(int width, int height)

void **setStub**(AppletStub stub)

void **showStatus**(String msg)

void **start**( )

void **stop**( )

## Interfaces

### AppletContext
### Methods

Applet **getApplet**(String name)

Enumeration **getApplets**( )

AudioClip **getAudioClip**(URL url)

Image **getImage**(URL url)

void **showDocument**(URL url, String target)

void **showDocument**(URL url)

void **showStatus**(String status)

### AppletStub
### Methods

void **appletResize**(int width, int height)

AppletContext **getAppletContext**( )

URL **getCodeBase**( )

URL **getDocumentBase**( )

String **getParameter**(String name)

Boolean **isActive**( )

**AudioClip**
**Methods**

    void **loop**( )

    void **play**( )

    void **stop**( )

# java.awt

The Java Abstract Window Toolkit (AWT) consists of resources to enable you to create rich, attractive, and useful interfaces in your applets. The AWT not only contains managerial classes such as GridBagLayout, but also has several concrete interactive tools such as Button and TextField. More important, however, is the Graphics class which provides you with a wealth of graphical abilities, including the ability to draw shapes and display images.

## Classes

**BorderLayout implements LayoutManager**
**Methods**

    **BorderLayout**( )

    **BorderLayout**(int hgap, int vgap)

    void **addLayoutComponent**(String name, Component comp)

    void **layoutContainer**(Container target)

    Dimension **minimumLayoutSize**(Container target)

    Dimension **preferredLayoutSize**(Container target)

    void **removeLayoutComponent**(Component comp)

    String **toString**( )

**Button extends Component**
**Methods**

    **Button**( )

    **Button**(String label)

    *synchronized* void **addNotify**( )

    String **getLabel**( )

    *protected* String **paramString**( )

    void **setLabel**(String label)

VII

Appendixes

**Canvas extends Component**
**Methods**

    **Canvas**( )

    *synchronized* void **addNotify**( )

    void **paint**(Graphics g)

**CardLayout implements LayoutManager**
**Methods**

    **CardLayout**( )

    **CardLayout**(int hgap, int vgap)

    void **addLayoutComponent**(String name, Component comp)

    void **first**(Container parent)

    void **last**(Container parent)

    void **layoutContainer**(Container parent)

    Dimension **minimumLayoutSize**(Container parent)

    void **next**(Container parent)

    Dimension **preferredLayoutSize**(Container parent)

    void **previous**(Container parent)

    void **removeLayoutComponent**(Component comp)

    void **show**(Container parent, String name)

    String **toString**( )

**Checkbox extends Component**
**Methods**

    **Checkbox**( )

    **Checkbox**(String label)

    **Checkbox**(String label, CheckboxGroup group, Boolean state)

    *synchronized* void **addNotify**( )

    CheckboxGroup **getCheckboxGroup**( )

    String **getLabel**( )

    Boolean **getState**( )

    *protected* String **paramString**( )

    void **setCheckboxGroup**(CheckboxGroup g)

    void **setLabel**(String label)

    void **setState**(Boolean state)

**CheckboxGroup**
**Methods**

> **CheckboxGroup**( )
>
> Checkbox **getCurrent**( )
>
> *synchronized* void **setCurrent**(Checkbox box)
>
> String **toString**( )

**CheckboxMenuItem extends MenuItem**
**Methods**

> **CheckboxMenuItem**(String label)
>
> *synchronized* void **addNotify**( )
>
> Boolean **getState**( )
>
> String **paramString**( )
>
> void **setState**(Boolean state)

**Choice extends Component**
**Methods**

> **Choice**( )
>
> *synchronized* void **addItem**(String item)
>
> *synchronized* void **addNotify**( )
>
> int **countItems**( )
>
> String **getItem**(int index)
>
> int **getSelectedIndex**( )
>
> String **getSelectedItem**( )
>
> *protected* String **paramString**( )
>
> void **select**(String str)
>
> *synchronized* void **select**(int pos)

**final Color**
**Fields**

> final **black**
>
> final **blue**
>
> final **cyan**
>
> final **darkGray**
>
> final **gray**
>
> final **green**
>
> final **lightGray**
>
> final **magenta**

final **orange**

final **pink**

final **red**

final **white**

final **yellow**

## Methods

**Color**(int rgb)

**Color**(float red_value, float green_value,

    float blue_value)

**Color**(int red_value, int green_value, int blue_value)

**Color** brighter( )

**Color** darker( )

Boolean **equals**(Object obj)

int **getBlue**( )

static Color **getColor**(String nm, int v)

static Color **getColor**(String nm, Color v)

static Color **getColor**(String nm)

int **getGreen**( )

static Color **getHSBColor**(float hue, float saturation,

    float brightness)

int **getRed**( )

int **getRGB**( )

int **hashCode**( )

static int **HSBtoRGB**(float hue, float saturation,

    float brightness)

static float[ ] **RGBtoHSB**(int red, int green, int blue,

    float hsbvals[ ])

String **toString**( )

*abstract* **Component implements ImageObserver**
## Methods

Boolean **action**(Event evt, Object what)

void **addNotify**( )

Rectangle **bounds**( )

int **checkImage**(Image image, int width, int height, ImageObserver observer)

int **checkImage**(Image image, ImageObserver observer)

Image **createImage**(int width, int height)

Image **createImage**(ImageProducer producer)

void **deliverEvent**(Event e)

*synchronized* void **disable**( )

void **enable**(Boolean cond)

*synchronized* void **enable**( )

Boolean **gotFocus**(Event evt, Object what)

Boolean **handleEvent**(Event evt)

*synchronized* boolean **inside**(int x, int y)

Boolean **keyDown**(Event evt, int key)

Boolean **keyUp**(Event evt, int key)

void **list**(PrintStream out, int indent)

void **list**(PrintStream out)

void **list**( )

Component **locate**(int x, int y)

Boolean **lostFocus**(Event evt, Object what)

Boolean **mouseDown**(Event evt, int x, int y)

Boolean **mouseDrag**(Event evt, int x, int y)

Boolean **mouseEnter**(Event evt, int x, int y)

Boolean **mouseExit**(Event evt, int x, int y)

Boolean **mouseMove**(Event evt, int x, int y)

Boolean **mouseUp**(Event evt, int x, int y)

Color **getBackground**( )

*synchronized* ColorModel **getColorModel**( )

Font **getFont**( )

FontMetrics **getFontMetrics**(Font f)

Color **getForeground**( )

Graphics **getGraphics**( )

Container **getParent**( )

ComponentPeer **getPeer**( )

VII

Appendixes

Toolkit **getToolkit**( )

*synchronized* void **hide**( )

Boolean **imageUpdate**(Image img, int flags, int x, int y, int width, int height)

void **invalidate**( )

Boolean **isEnabled**( )

Boolean **isShowing**( )

Boolean **isValid**( )

Boolean **isVisible**( )

void **layout**( )

Point **location**( )

Dimension **minimumSize**( )

void **move**(int x, int y)

void **nextFocus**( )

void **paint**(Graphics g)

void **paintAll**(Graphics g)

*protected* String **paramString**( )

Boolean **postEvent**(Event e)

Boolean **prepareImage**(Image image, int width, int height, ImageObserver observer)

Dimension **preferredSize**( )

Boolean **prepareImage**(Image image, ImageObserver observer)

void **print**(Graphics g)

void **printAll**(Graphics g)

void **repaint**(int x, int y, int width, int height)

void **repaint**(long tm, int x, int y, int width,

void **repaint**(long tm)

void **repaint**( )

*synchronized* void **removeNotify**( )

void **requestFocus**( )

*synchronized* void **reshape**(int x, int y, int width, int height)

void **resize**(Dimension d)

void **resize**(int width, int height)

*synchronized* void **setBackground**(Color c)

*synchronized* void **setFont**(Font f)

*synchronized* void **setForeground**(Color c)

void **show**(boolean cond)

*synchronized* void **show**( )

Dimension **size**( )

String **toString**( )

void **update**(Graphics g)

void **validate**( )

## Container extends Component
## Methods

**Container**( )

*synchronized* Component **add**(String name, Component comp)

*synchronized* Component **add**(Component comp, int pos)

Component **add**(Component comp)

*synchronized* void **addNotify**( )

int **countComponents**( )

void **deliverEvent**(Event e)

*synchronized* Component **getComponent**(int num) throws ArrayIndexOutOfBoundsException

*synchronized* Component[ ] **getComponents**( )

LayoutManager **getLayout**( )

*synchronized* void **layout**( )

void **list**(PrintStream out, int indent)

Component **locate**(int x, int y)

*synchronized* Dimension **minimumSize**( )

void **paintComponents**(Graphics g)

*protected* String **paramString**( )

*synchronized* Dimension **preferredSize**( )

void **printComponents**(Graphics g)

*synchronized* void **remove**(Component comp)

*synchronized* void **removeNotify**( )

void **setLayout**(LayoutManager mgr)

*synchronized* void **validate**( )

**Dialog extends Window**
**Methods**

> **Dialog**(Frame parent, String title, Boolean modal)
>
> **Dialog**(Frame parent, boolean modal)
>
> *synchronized* void **addNotify**( )
>
> Boolean **isModal**( )
>
> Boolean **isResizable**( )
>
> *protected* String **paramString**( )
>
> void **setTitle(**String title)

**Dimension**
**Fields**

> int **height**
>
> int **width**

**Methods**

> **Dimension**( )
>
> **Dimension**(Dimension d)
>
> **Dimension**(int width, int height)
>
> String **toString**( )

**Event**
**Fields**

> final static int **ACTION_EVENT**
>
> final static int **ALT_MASK**
>
> Object **arg**
>
> int **clickCount**
>
> final static int **CTRL_MASK**
>
> final static int **DOWN**
>
> Event **evt**
>
> final static int **F1**
>
> final static int **F2**
>
> final static int **F3**
>
> final static int **F4**
>
> final static int **F5**

final static int **F6**

final static int **F7**

final static int **F8**

final static int **F9**

final static int **F10**

final static int **F11**

final static int **F12**

final static int **GOT_FOCUS**

final static int **HOME**

int **id**

int **key**

final static int **KEY_ACTION**

final static int **KEY_ACTION_RELEASE**

final static int **KEY_PRESS**

final static int **KEY_RELEASE**

final static int **LEFT**

final static int **LIST_DESELECT**

final static int **LIST_SELECT**

final static int **LOAD_FILE**

final static int **LOST_FOCUS**

final static int **META_MASK**

int **modifiers**

final static int **MOUSE_DOWN**

final static int **MOUSE_DRAG**

final static int **MOUSE_ENTER**

final static int **MOUSE_EXIT**

final static int **MOUSE_MOVE**

final static int **MOUSE_UP**

final static int **PGDN**

final static int **PGUP**

final static int **RIGHT**

final static int **SAVE_FILE**

final static int **SCROLL_ABSOLUTE**

final static int **SCROLL_LINE_DOWN**

final static int **SCROLL_LINE_UP**

final static int **SCROLL_PAGE_DOWN**

final static int **SCROLL_PAGE_UP**

final static int **SHIFT_MASK**

Object **target**

final static int **UP**

long **when**

final static int **WINDOW_DEICONIFY**

final static int **WINDOW_DESTROY**

final static int **WINDOW_EXPOSE**

final static int **WINDOW_ICONIFY**

final static int **WINDOW_MOVED**

int **x**

int **y**

**Methods**

**Event**(Object target, int id, Object arg)

**Event**(Object target, long when, int id, int x, int y, int key, int modifiers)

**Event**(Object target, long when, int id, int x, int y, int key, int modifiers, Object arg)

Boolean **controlDown**( )

Boolean **metaDown**( )

*protected* String **paramString**( )

Boolean **shiftDown**( )

String **toString**( )

void **translate**(int x, int y)

**FileDialog extends Dialog**
**Fields**

final static **LOAD**

final static **SAVE**

**Methods**

**FileDialog**(Frame parent, String title, int mode)

**FileDialog**(Frame parent, String title)

*synchronized* void **addNotify**( )

String **getDirectory**( )

String **getFile**( )

FilenameFilter **getFilenameFilter**( )

int **getMode**( )

*protected* String **paramString**( )

void **setDirectory**(String dir)

void **setFile**(String file)

## FlowLayout implements LayoutManager
**Fields:**

final static int **CENTER**

final static int **LEFT**

final static int **RIGHT**

## Methods

**FlowLayout**( )

**FlowLayout**(int align)

**FlowLayout**(int align, int hgap, int vgap)

void **addLayoutComponent**(String name, Component comp)

void **layoutContainer**(Container target)

Dimension **minimumLayoutSize**(Container target)

Dimension **preferredLayoutSize**(Container target)

void **removeLayoutComponent**(Component comp)

String **toString**( )

## Font
**Fields**

final static int **BOLD**

final static int **ITALIC**

*protected* String **name**

final static int **PLAIN**

*protected* int **size**

*protected* int **style**

## Methods

**Font**(String name, int style, int size)

Boolean **equals**(Object obj)

String **getFamily**( )

static Font **getFont**(String nm)

static Font **getFont**(String nm, Font font)

String **getName**( )

int **getSize**( )

int **getStyle**( )

int **hashCode**( )

Boolean **isBold**( )

Boolean **isItalic**( )

Boolean **isPlain**( )

String **toString**( )

## FontMetrics
### Fields

*protected* Font font

### Methods

*protected* **FontMetrics**(Font f)

int **bytesWidth**(byte data[ ], int offset, int len)

int **charsWidth**(char data[ ], int offset, int len)

int **charWidth**(char ch)

int **charWidth**(int ch)

int **getAscent**( )

int **getDescent**( )

Font **getFont**( )

int **getHeight**( )

int **getMaxAdvance**( )

int **getMaxAscent**( )

int **getMaxDecent**( )

int **getMaxDescent**( )

int[ ] **getWidths**( )

int **stringWidth**(String str)

String **toString**( )

## Frame extends Window implements MenuContainer
### Fields

final static int **CROSSHAIR_CURSOR**

final static int **DEFAULT_CURSOR**

final static int **E_RESIZE_CURSOR**

final static int **HAND_CURSOR**

final static int **MOVE_CURSOR**

final static int **NE_RESIZE_CURSOR**

final static int **NW_RESIZE_CURSOR**

final static int **N_RESIZE_CURSOR**

final static int **SE_RESIZE_CURSOR**

final static int **SW_RESIZE_CURSOR**

final static int **S_RESIZE_CURSOR**

final static int **TEXT_CURSOR**

final static int **WAIT_CURSOR**

final static int **W_RESIZE_CURSOR**

**Methods**

**Frame**( )

**Frame**(String title)

*synchronized* void **addNotify**( )

*synchronized* void **dispose**( )

int **getCursorType**( )

Image **getIconImage**( )

MenuBar **getMenuBar**( )

String **getTitle**( )

Boolean **isResizable**( )

*protected* String **paramString**( )

*synchronized* void **remove**(MenuComponent m)

void **setCursor**(int cursorType)

void **setIconImage**(Image image)

*synchronized* void **setMenuBar**(MenuBar mb)

void **setResizable**(Boolean resizable)

void **setTitle**(String title)

***abstract* Graphics**
**Methods**

*protected* **Graphics**( )

*abstract* void **clearRect**(int x, int y, int width, int height) *abstract* void **clipRect**(int x, int y, int width, int height)

*abstract* void **copyArea**(int x, int y, int width,

Graphics **create**(int x, int y, int width, int height)

*abstract* Graphics **create**( )

void **draw3DRect**(int x, int y, int width, int height, Boolean raised)

*abstract* void **drawArc**(int x, int y, int width, int height, int startAngle, int arcAngle)

*abstract* void **drawLine**(int x1, int y1, int x2, int y2)

*abstract* void **drawOval**(int x, int y, int width, int height)

void **drawRect**(int x, int y, int width, int height)

*abstract* void **drawRoundRect**(int x, int y, int width, int height, int arcWidth, int arcHeight)

void **fill3DRect**(int x, int y, int width, int height, Boolean raised)

*abstract* void **fillOval**(int x, int y, int width, int height)

*abstract* void **fillRect**(int x, int y, int width, int height)

*abstract* void **fillRoundRect**(int x, int y, int width, int height, int arcWidth, int arcHeight)

*abstract* void **dispose**( )

void **drawBytes**(byte data[ ], int offset, int length, int x, int y)

void **drawChars**(char data[ ], int offset, int length, int x,  int y)

*abstract* Boolean **drawImage**(Image img, int x, int y, int width, int height, Color bgcolor, ImageObserver observer)

*abstract* Boolean **drawImage**(Image img, int x, int y, Color bgcolor, ImageObserver observer)

*abstract* Boolean **drawImage**(Image img, int x, int y, int width, int height, ImageObserver observer)

*abstract* Boolean **drawImage**(Image img, int x, int y, ImageObserver observer)

void **drawPolygon**(Polygon p)

*abstract* void **drawPolygon**(int xPoints[ ], int yPoints[ ], int nPoints)

*abstract* void **drawString**(String str, int x, int y)

*abstract* void **fillArc**(int x, int y,  int width, int height, int startAngle,int arcAngle)

void **fillPolygon**(Polygon p)

*abstract* void **fillPolygon**(int xPoints[ ], int yPoints[ ], int nPoints)

void **finalize**( )

*abstract* Rectangle **getClipRect**( )

*abstract* Color **getColor**( )

*abstract* Font **getFont**( )

*abstract* FontMetrics **getFontMetrics**(Font f)

FontMetrics **getFontMetrics**( )

*abstract* void **setColor**(Color c)

*abstract* void **setFont**(Font f)

*abstract* void **setPaintMode**( )

*abstract* void **setXORMode**(Color c1)

*abstract* void **translate**(int x, int y)

String **toString**( )

## GridBagConstraints implements Cloneable
### Fields

**int** anchor

final static int **BOTH**

final static int **CENTER**

final static int **EAST**

int **fill**

int **gridheight**

int **gridwidth**

int **gridx**

int **gridy**

final static int **HORIZONTAL**

Insets **insets**

int **ipadx**

int **ipady**

final static int **NONE**

final static int **NORTH**

final static int **NORTHEAST**

final static int **NORTHWEST**

final static int **RELATIVE**

final static int **REMAINDER**

final static int **SOUTH**

final static int **SOUTHEAST**

final static int **SOUTHWEST**

final static int **VERTICAL**

double **weightx**

double **weighty**

final static int **WEST**

## Methods

**GridBagConstraints**( )

Object **clone**( )

## GridBagLayout implements LayoutManager
## Fields

double **columnWeights[ ]**

int **columnWidths[ ]**

*protected* Hashtable **comptable**

*protected* GridBagConstraints **defaultConstraints**

*protected* GridBagLayoutInfo **layoutInfo**

*protected* final static int **MAXGRIDSIZE**

*protected* final static int **MINSIZE**

*protected* final static int **PREFERREDSIZE**

int **rowHeights[ ]**

double rowWeights[ ]

## Methods

**GridBagLayout**( )

void **addLayoutComponent**(String name, Component comp)

*protected* void **AdjustForGravity**(GridBagConstraints constraints, Rectangle r)

*protected* void **ArrangeGrid**(Container parent)

*protected* void **DumpConstraints**(GridBagConstraints constraints)

*protected* void **DumpLayoutInfo**(GridBagLayoutInfo s)

GridBagConstraints **getConstraints**(Component comp)

int[ ][ ] **getLayoutDimensions**( )

*protected* GridBagLayoutInfo **GetLayoutInfo**(Container parent, int sizeflag)

Point **getLayoutOrigin**( )

double[ ][ ] **getLayoutWeights**( )

*protected* Dimension **GetMinSize**(Container parent, GridBagLayoutInfo info)

void **layoutContainer**(Container parent)

Point **location**(int x, int y)

*protected* GridBagConstraints **lookupConstraints**(Component comp)

Dimension **minimumLayoutSize**(Container parent)

Dimension **preferredLayoutSize**(Container parent)

void **removeLayoutComponent**(Component comp)

void **setConstraints**(Component comp, GridBagConstraints constraints)

String **toString**( )

**GridLayout implements LayoutManager**
**Methods**

**GridLayout**(int rows, int cols)

**GridLayout**(int rows, int cols, int hgap, int vgap)

void **addLayoutComponent**(String name, Component comp)

void **layoutContainer**(Container parent)

Dimension **minimumLayoutSize**(Container parent)

Dimension **preferredLayoutSize**(Container parent)

void **removeLayoutComponent**(Component comp)

String **toString**( )

***abstract* Image**
**Fields**

final static Object **UndefinedProperty**

**Methods**

**Image**( )

*abstract* Graphics **getGraphics**( )

*abstract* int **getHeight**(ImageObserver observer)

*abstract* Object **getProperty**(String name)

*abstract* void **flush**( )

*abstract* ImageProducer **getSource**( )

*abstract* int **getWidth**(ImageObserver observer)

## Insets implements Cloneable
## Fields

int **bottom**

int **left**

int **right**

int **top**

## Methods

**Insets**(int top, int left, int bottom, int right)

Object **clone**( )

String **toString**( )

## Label extends Component
## Fields

final static int **CENTER**

final static int **RIGHT**

## Methods

**Label**( )

**Label**(String label)

**Label**(String label, int alignment)

*synchronized* void **addNotify**( )

int **getAlignment**( )

String **getText**( )

*protected* String **paramString**( )

void **setAlignment**(int alignment)

void **setText**(String label)

## List extends Component
## Methods

**List**( )

**List**(int rows, Boolean multipleSelections)

*synchronized* void **addItem**(String item, int index)

*synchronized* void **addItem**(String item)

*synchronized* void **addNotify**( )

int **countItems**( )

String **getItem**(int index)

*synchronized* void **removeNotify**( )

*synchronized* void **replaceItem**(String newValue, int index)

Boolean **allowsMultipleSelections**( )

*synchronized* void **clear**( )

*synchronized* void **delItem**(int position)

*synchronized* void **delItems**(int start, int end)

*synchronized* void **deselect**(int index)

int **getRows**( )

*synchronized* int **getSelectedIndex**( )

*synchronized* int[ ] **getSelectedIndexes**( )

*synchronized* String **getSelectedItem**( )

*synchronized* String[ ] **getSelectedItems**( )

int **getVisibleIndex**( )

*synchronized* Boolean **isSelected**(int index)

void **makeVisible**(int index)

Dimension **minimumSize**( )

Dimension **minimumSize**(int rows)

*protected* String **paramString**( )

Dimension **preferredSize**( )

Dimension **preferredSize**(int rows)

*synchronized* void **select**(int index)

void setMultipleSelections(Boolean v)

## MediaTracker
## Fields

final static int **ABORTED**

final static int **COMPLETE**

final static int **ERRORED**

## Methods

**MediaTracker**(Component comp)

*synchronized* void **addImage**(Image image, int id, int width, int height)

void **addImage**(Image image, int id)

*synchronized* Boolean **checkAll**(Boolean load)

Boolean **checkAll**( )

*synchronized* Boolean **checkID**(int id, Boolean load)

Boolean **checkID**(int id)

*synchronized* Object[ ] **getErrorsAny**( )

*synchronized* Object[ ] **getErrorsID**(int id)

*synchronized* Boolean **isErrorAny**( )

*synchronized* Boolean **isErrorID**(int id)

int **statusAll**(Boolean load)

int **statusID**(int id, Boolean load)

*synchronized* Boolean **waitForAll**(long ms) throws InterruptedException

void **waitForAll**( ) throws InterruptedException

*synchronized* Boolean **waitForID**(int id, long ms) throws InterruptedException

void **waitForID**(int id) throws InterruptedException

## Menu extends MenuItem implements MenuContainer
## Methods

**Menu**(String label)

**Menu**(String label, Boolean tearOff)

void **add**(String label)

*synchronized* MenuItem **add**(MenuItem mi)

*synchronized* void **addNotify**( )

void **addSeparator**( )

int **countItems**( )

MenuItem **getItem**(int index)

Boolean **isTearOff**( )

*synchronized* void **remove**(MenuComponent item)

*synchronized* void **remove**(int index)

*synchronized* void **removeNotify**( )

## MenuBar extends MenuComponent implements MenuContainer
## Methods

**MenuBar**( )

*synchronized* Menu **add**(Menu m)

*synchronized* void **addNotify**( )

    int **countMenus**( )

    Menu **getHelpMenu**( )

    Menu **getMenu**(int i)

    *synchronized* void **remove**(MenuComponent m)

    *synchronized* void **remove**(int index)

    void **removeNotify**( )

    *synchronized* void setHelpMenu(Menu m)

## MenuComponent
## Methods

    **MenuComponent**( )

    MenuContainer **getParent**( )

    MenuComponentPeer getPeer( )

    Font **getFont**( )

    *protected* String **paramString**( )

    Boolean **postEvent**(Event evt)

    void **removeNotify**( )

    void **setFont**(Font f)

    String **toString**( )

## MenuItem extends MenuComponent
## Methods

    **MenuItem**(String label)

    *synchronized* void **addNotify**( )

    void **disable**( )

    void **enable**(Boolean cond)

    void **enable**( )

    String **getLabel**( )

    Boolean **isEnabled**( )

    String **paramString**( )

    void **setLabel**(String label)

## Panel extends Container
## Methods

    **Panel**( )

    *synchronized* void **addNotify**( )

**VII**

**Appendixes**

**Point**
**Fields**

    int **x**

    int **y**

**Methods**

    **Point** (int x, int y)

    Boolean **equals**(Object obj)

    int **hashCode**( )

    void **move**(int x, int y)

    String **toString**( )

    void **translate**(int x, int y)

**Polygon**
**Fields**

    int **npoints**

    int **xpoints**[ ]

    int **ypoints**[ ]

**Methods**

    **Polygon**( )

    **Polygon**(int xpoints[ ], int ypoints[ ], int npoints)

    void **addPoint**(int x,  int y)

    Rectangle **getBoundingBox**( )

    Boolean **inside**(int x, int y)

**Rectangle**
**Fields**

    int **height**

    int **width**

    int **x**

    int **y**

**Methods**

    **Rectangle**( )

    **Rectangle**(Dimension d)

    **Rectangle**(int x, int y, int width, int height)

    **Rectangle**(int width, int height)

    **Rectangle**(Point p)

**Rectangle**(Point p, Dimension d)

void **add**(Rectangle r)

void **add**(Point pt)

void **add**(int newx, int newy)

Boolean **equals**(Object obj)

void **grow**(int h, int v)

int hashCode( )

Boolean **inside**(int x, int y)

Rectangle **intersection**(Rectangle r)

Boolean **intersects**(Rectangle r)

Boolean **isEmpty**( )

void **move**(int x, int y)

void **reshape**(int x, int y, int width, int height)

void **resize**(int width, int height)

String **toString**( )

void **translate**(int x, int y)

Rectangle **union**(Rectangle r)

## Scrollbar extends Component
### Fields

final static int **HORIZONTAL**

final static int **VERTICAL**

### Methods

**Scrollbar**( )

**Scrollbar**(int orientation)

**Scrollbar**(int orientation, int value, int visible, int minimum, int maximum)

*synchronized* void **addNotify**( )

int **getLineIncrement**( )

int **getMaximum**( )

int **getMinimum**( )

int **getOrientation**( )

int **getPageIncrement**( )

int **getValue**( )

int **getVisible**( )

*protected* String **paramString**( )

void **setLineIncrement**(int l)

void **setPageIncrement**(int l)

void **setValue**(int value)

void **setValues**(int value, int visible, int minimum, int maximum)

## TextArea extends TextComponent
## Methods

**TextArea**( )

**TextArea**(int rows, int cols)

**TextArea**(String text)

**TextArea**(String text, int rows, int cols)

*synchronized* void **addNotify**( )

void **appendText**(String str)

int **getColumns**( )

int **getRows**( )

void **insertText**(String str, int pos)

Dimension **minimumSize**( )

Dimension **minimumSize**(int rows, int cols)

*protected* String **paramString**( )

Dimension **preferredSize**( )

Dimension **preferredSize**(int rows, int cols)

void **replaceText**(String str, int start, int end)

## TextComponent extends Component
## Methods

String **getSelectedText**( )

int **getSelectionEnd**( )

int **getSelectionStart**( )

Boolean **isEditable**( )

*protected* String **paramString**( )

void **select**(int selStart, int selEnd)

void **selectAll**( )

void **setEditable**(Boolean t)

**TextField extends TextComponent**
**Methods**

    **TextField**( )

    **TextField**(int cols)

    **TextField**(String text)

    **TextField**(String text, int cols)

    *synchronized* void **addNotify**( )

    Boolean **echoCharIsSet**( )

    int **getColumns**( )

    char **getEchoChar**( )

    Dimension **minimumSize**( )

    Dimension **minimumSize**(int cols)

    *protected* String **paramString**( )

    Dimension **preferredSize**( )

    Dimension **preferredSize**(int cols)

    void setEchoCharacter(char c)

**Toolkit**
**Methods**

    **Toolkit**( )

    *protected abstract* ButtonPeer **createButton**(Button target)

    *protected abstract* CanvasPeer **createCanvas**(Canvas target)

    *abstract* int **checkImage**(Image image, int width, int height, ImageObserver observer)

    *abstract* CheckboxPeer **createCheckbox**(Checkbox target)

    *abstract* Image **createImage**(ImageProducer producer)

    *protected abstract* CheckboxMenuItemPeer **createCheckboxMenuItem**(CheckboxMenuItem target)

    *protected abstract* ChoicePeer **createChoice**(Choice target)

    *protected abstract* LabelPeer **createLabel**(Label target)

    *protected abstract* ListPeer **createList**(List target)

    *protected abstract* MenuPeer **createMenu**(Menu target)

    *protected abstract* MenuBarPeer **createMenuBar**(MenuBar target)

    *protected abstract* MenuItemPeer **createMenuItem**(MenuItem target)

    *protected abstract* PanelPeer **createPanel**(Panel target) *abstract* Boolean **prepareImage**(Image image, int width, int height,ImageObserver observer)

*protected abstract* ScrollbarPeer **createScrollbar**(Scrollbar target)

*protected abstract* TextAreaPeer **createTextArea**(TextArea target)

*protected abstract* TextFieldPeer **createTextField**(TextField target)

*protected abstract* WindowPeer **createWindow**(Window target)

*protected abstract* DialogPeer **createDialog**(Dialog target)

*protected abstract* FileDialogPeer **createFileDialog**(FileDialog target)

*protected abstract* FramePeer **createFrame**(Frame target)

*abstract* ColorModel **getColorModel**( )

static *synchronized* Toolkit **getDefaultToolkit**( )

*abstract* String[] **getFontList**( )

*abstract* FontMetrics **getFontMetrics**(Font f)

*abstract* Image **getImage**(URL url)

*abstract* Image **getImage**(String filename)

*abstract* int **getScreenResolution**( )

*abstract* Dimension **getScreenSize**( )

*abstract* void **sync**( )

**Window extends Container**
**Methods**

**Window**(Frame parent)

*synchronized* void **addNotify**( )

*synchronized* void **dispose**( )

Toolkit **getToolkit**( )

final String **getWarningString**( )

*synchronized* void **pack**( )

*synchronized* void **show**( )

void **toBack**( )

void **toFront**( )

## Interfaces

**LayoutManager**

void **addLayoutComponent**(String name, Component comp)

void **layoutContainer**(Container parent)

Dimension **minimumLayoutSize**(Container parent)

Dimension **preferredLayoutSize**(Container parent)

void **removeLayoutComponent**(Component comp)

**MenuContainer**
**Methods**

Font **getFont**( )

Boolean **postEvent**(Event evt)

void **remove**(MenuComponent comp)

# java.awt.image

Closely related to the java.awt package, this package consists of tools designed to handle and manipulate images coming across a network. Because all classes and interfaces in this package are closely related, you will see that many of the methods appear multiple times.

## Classes

### *abstract* ColorModel
**Fields**

*protected* int **pixel_bits**

**Methods**

**ColorModel**(int bits)

*abstract* int **getAlpha**(int pixel)

*abstract* int **getBlue**(int pixel)

*abstract* int **getGreen**(int pixel)

int **getPixelSize**( )

*abstract* int **getRed**(int pixel)

int **getRGB**(int pixel)

static ColorModel **getRGBdefault**( )

### CropImageFilter extends ImageFilter
**Methods**

**CropImageFilter**(int x, int y, int w, int h)

void **setDimensions**(int width, int height)

void **setPixels**(int x, int y, int w, int h, ColorModel model, int pixels[ ], int offset, int scansize) void **setPixels**(int x, int y, int w, int h, ColorModel model, byte pixels[ ], int offset, int scansize)

void **setProperties**(Hashtable props)

## DirectColorModel extends ColorModel
### Methods

**DirectColorModel**(int bits, int rmask, int gmask, int bmask)

**DirectColorModel**(int bits, int rmask, int gmask, int bmask, int amask)

final int **getAlpha**(int pixel)

final int **getAlphaMask**( )

final int **getBlue**(int pixel)

final int **getBlueMask**( )

final int **getGreen**(int pixel)

final int **getGreenMask**( )

final int **getRed**(int pixel)

final int **getRedMask**( )

final int **getRGB**(int pixel)

## FilteredImageSource extends Object implements ImageProducer
### Methods

**FilteredImageSource**(ImageProducer orig, ImageFilter imgf)

*synchronized* void **addConsumer**(ImageConsumer ic)

*synchronized* Boolean **isConsumer**(ImageConsumer ic)

void **startProduction**(ImageConsumer ic)

*synchronized* void **removeConsumer**(ImageConsumer ic)

void requestTopDownLeftRightResend(ImageConsumer ic)

## ImageFilter implements ImageConsumer, Cloneable
### Fields

*protected* ImageConsumer **consumer**

### Methods

**ImageFilter**( )

Object **clone**( )

ImageFilter **getFilterInstance**(ImageConsumer ic)

void **imageComplete**(int status)

void **resendTopDownLeftRight**(ImageProducer ip)

void **setColorModel**(ColorModel model)

void **setDimensions**(int width, int height)

void **setHints**(int hints)

void **setPixels**(int x, int y, int width, int height, ColorModel model, int pixels[ ], int offset, int scansize)

void **setPixels**(int x, int y, int w, int h, ColorModel model, byte pixels[ ], int offset, int scansize)

void **setProperties**(Hashtable props)

## IndexColorModel extends ColorModel
## Methods

**IndexColorModel**(int bits, int size, byte r[ ], byte g[ ], byte b[ ])

**IndexColorModel**(int bits, int size, byte r[ ], byte g[ ], byte b[ ], int trans)

**IndexColorModel**(int bits, int size, byte r[ ], byte g[ ], byte b[ ], byte a[ ])

final int **getAlpha**(int pixel)

final void **getAlphas**(byte a[ ])

final int **getBlue**(int pixel)

final void **getBlues**(byte b[ ])

final int **getGreen**(int pixel)

final void **getGreens**(byte g[ ])

final int **getMapSize**( )

final int **getRed**(int pixel)

final void **getReds**(byte r[ ])

final int **getRGB**(int pixel)

final int getTransparentPixel( )

## MemoryImageSource implements ImageProducer
## Methods

**MemoryImageSource**(int w, int h, ColorModel cm, byte pix[ ], int offset, int scan)

**MemoryImageSource**(int w, int h, ColorModel cm, byte pix[ ], int offset, int scan, Hashtable props)

**MemoryImageSource**(int w, int h, ColorModel cm, int pix[ ], int offset, int scan)

**MemoryImageSource**(int w, int h, ColorModel cm, int pix[ ], int offset, int scan, Hashtable props)

**MemoryImageSource**(int w, int h, int pix[ ], int offset, int scan)

**MemoryImageSource**(int w, int h, int pix[ ], int offset, int scan, Hashtable props)

*synchronized* void **addConsumer**(ImageConsumer ic)

*synchronized* Boolean **isConsumer**(ImageConsumer ic)

void **startProduction**(ImageConsumer ic)

*synchronized* void **removeConsumer**(ImageConsumer ic)

void **requestTopDownLeftRightResend**(ImageConsumer ic)

## PixelGrabber implements ImageConsumer
## Methods

**PixelGrabber**(Image img, int x, int y, int w, int h, int pix[ ], int offset, int scansize)

**PixelGrabber**(ImageProducer ip, int x, int y, int w, int h, int pix[ ], int offset, int scansize)

*synchronized* Boolean **grabPixels**(long ms) throws InterruptedException

Boolean **grabPixels**( ) throws InterruptedException

void **setColorModel**(ColorModel model)

void **setDimensions**(int width, int height)

void **setHints**(int hints)

void **setPixels**(int srcX, int srcY, int srcW, int srcH, ColorModel model, byte pixels[ ], int srcOff, int srcScan)

void **setProperties**(Hashtable props)

*synchronized* int **status**( )

void **setPixels**(int srcX, int srcY, int srcW, int srcH, ColorModel model, int pixels[ ], int srcOff, int srcScan)

*synchronized* void **imageComplete**(int status)

## RGBImageFilter extends ImageFilter
## Fields

*protected* Boolean **canFilterIndexColorModel**

*protected* ColorModel **newmodel**

*protected* ColorModel **origmodel**

**Methods**
>**RGBImageFilter( )**
>
>IndexColorModel **filterIndexColorModel**(IndexColorModel icm)
>
>void **filterRGBPixels**(int x, int y, int w, int h, int pixels[ ], int offset, int scansize)
>
>void **setColorModel**(ColorModel model)
>
>void **substituteColorModel**(ColorModel oldcm, ColorModel newcm)
>
>void **setPixels**(int x, int y, int width, int height, ColorModel model, int pixels[ ], int offset, int scansize)
>
>void **setPixels**(int x, int y, int width, int height, ColorModel model, byte pixels[ ], int offset, int scansize)
>
>*abstract* int **filterRGB**(int x, int y, int rgb)

# java.awt.peer

The interfaces outlined in this package serve as intermediaries between your code and the computer on which your code is running. While it is beneficial to understand what the peers do, you probably will have no need to work directly with this package.

## Interfaces

**ButtonPeer extends ComponentPeer**
**Methods**
>*abstract* void **setLabel**(String label)

**CanvasPeer extends ComponentPeer**

**CheckboxMenuItemPeer extends MenuItemPeer**
**Methods**
>*abstract* void **setState**(Boolean t)

**CheckboxPeer extends ComponentPeer**
>*abstract* void **setCheckboxGroup**(CheckboxGroup g)
>
>*abstract* void **setLabel**(String label)
>
>*abstract* void **setState**(Boolean state)

**ChoicePeer extends ComponentPeer**
>*abstract* void **addItem**(String item, int index)
>
>*abstract* void **select**(int index)

VII

**ComponentPeer**
**Methods**

*abstract* int **checkImage**(Image img, int w, int h, ImageObserver o)

*abstract* Image **createImage**(int width, mint height)

*abstract* Image **createImage**(ImageProducer producer)

*abstract* void **disable**( )

*abstract* void **dispose**( )

*abstract* void **enable**( )

*abstract* ColorModel **getColorModel**( )

*abstract* FontMetrics **getFontMetrics**(Font font)

*abstract* Graphics **getGraphics**( )

*abstract* Toolkit **getToolkit**( )

*abstract* Boolean **handleEvent**(Event e)

*abstract* void **hide**( )

*abstract* Dimension **minimumSize**( )

*abstract* void **nextFocus**( )

*abstract* void **paint**(Graphics g)

*abstract* Dimension **preferredSize**( )

*abstract* Boolean **prepareImage**(Image img, int w, int h, ImageObserver o)

*abstract* void **print**(Graphics g)

*abstract* void **repaint**(long tm, int x, int y, int width, int height)

*abstract* void **requestFocus**( )

*abstract* void **reshape**(int x, int y, int width, int height)

*abstract* void **setBackground**(Color c)

*abstract* void **setFont**(Font f)

*abstract* void **setForeground**(Color c)

*abstract* void **show**( )

**ContainerPeer extends ComponentPeer**
**Methods**

*abstract* Insets **insets**( )

**DialogPeer extends WindowPeer**
**Methods**

*abstract* void **setResizable**(Boolean resizeable)

*abstract* void **setTitle**(String title)

**FileDialogPeer extends DialogPeer**

> *abstract* void **setDirectory**(String dir)
>
> *abstract* void **setFile**(String file)
>
> *abstract* void **setFilenameFilter**(FilenameFilter filter)

**FramePeer extends WindowPeer**

> *abstract* void **setCursor**(int cursorType)
>
> *abstract* void **setIconImage**(Image im)
>
> *abstract* void **setMenuBar**(MenuBar mb)
>
> *abstract* void **setResizable**(Boolean resizeable)
>
> *abstract* void **setTitle**(String title)

**LabelPeer extends ComponentPeer**
**Methods**

> *abstract* void **setAlignment**(int alignment)
>
> *abstract* void **setText**(String label)

**ListPeer extends ComponentPeer**
**Methods**

> *abstract* void **addItem**(String item, int index)
>
> *abstract* void **clear**( )
>
> *abstract* void **delItems**(int start, int end)
>
> *abstract* void **deselect**(int index)
>
> *abstract* int[ ] **getSelectedIndexes**( )
>
> *abstract* void **makeVisible**(int index)
>
> *abstract* Dimension **minimumSize**(int v)
>
> *abstract* Dimension **preferredSize**(int v)
>
> *abstract* void **select**(int index)
>
> *abstract* void **setMultipleSelections**(Boolean v)

**MenuBarPeer extends MenuComponentPeer**
**Methods**

> *abstract* void **addHelpMenu**(Menu m)
>
> *abstract* void **addMenu**(Menu m)
>
> *abstract* void **delMenu**(int index)

**MenuComponentPeer**
**Methods**

    *abstract* void **dispose**( )

**MenuItemPeer extends MenuComponentPeer**

    *abstract* void **disable**( )

    *abstract* void **enable**( )

    *abstract* void **setLabel**(String label)

**MenuPeer extends MenuItemPeer**

    *abstract* void **addItem**(MenuItem item)

    *abstract* void **addSeparator**( )

    *abstract* void **delItem**(int index)

**PanelPeer extends ContainerPeer**

**ScrollbarPeer extends ComponentPeer**
**Methods**

    *abstract* void **setLineIncrement**(int l)

    *abstract* void **setPageIncrement**(int l)

    *abstract* void **setValue**(int value)

    *abstract* void **setValues**(int value, int visible, int minimum, int maximum)

**TextAreaPeer extends TextComponentPeer**

    *abstract* void **insertText**(String txt, int pos)

    *abstract* Dimension **minimumSize**(int rows, int cols)

    *abstract* Dimension **preferredSize**(int rows, int cols)

    *abstract* void **replaceText**(String txt, int start, int end)

**TextComponentPeer extends ComponentPeer**
**Methods**

    *abstract* int **getSelectionEnd**( )

    *abstract* int **getSelectionStart**( )

    *abstract* String **getText**( )

    *abstract* void **select**(int selStart, int selEnd)

    *abstract* void **setEditable**(Boolean editable)

    *abstract* void **setText**(String l)

**TextFieldPeer extends TextComponentPeer**
**Methods**

>*abstract* Dimension **minimumSize**(int cols)
>
>*abstract* Dimension **preferredSize**(int cols)
>
>*abstract* void **setEchoCharacter**(char c)

**WindowPeer extends ContainerPeer**
**Methods**

>*abstract* void **toBack**( )
>
>*abstract* void **toFront**( )

## Interfaces

**ImageConsumer**
**Fields**

>final static int **COMPLETESCANLINES**
>
>final static int **IMAGEABORTED**
>
>final static int **IMAGEERROR**
>
>final static int **RANDOMPIXELORDER**
>
>final static int **SINGLEFRAME**
>
>final static int **SINGLEFRAMEDONE**
>
>final static int **SINGLEPASS**
>
>final static int **STATICIMAGEDONE**
>
>final static int **TOPDOWNLEFTRIGHT**

**Methods**

>*abstract* void **setColorModel**(ColorModel model)
>
>*abstract* void **setDimensions**(int width, int height)
>
>*abstract* void **setHints**(int hintflags)
>
>*abstract* void **setPixels**(int x, int y, int w, int h, ColorModel model, byte pixels[ ], int offset, int scansize)
>
>*abstract* void **setPixels**(int x, int y, int w, int h, ColorModel model, int pixels[ ], int offset, int scansize)
>
>*abstract* void **imageComplete**(int status)

**ImageObserver**
**Fields**

>final static int **ABORT**
>
>final static int **ALLBITS**

final static int **ERROR**

final static int **FRAMEBITS**

final static int **HEIGHT**

final static int **SOMEBITS**

final static int **WIDTH**

**Methods**

*abstract* Boolean **imageUpdate**(Image img, int infoflags, int x, int y, int widfinal static int PROPERTIES)

**ImageProducer**
**Methods**

*abstract* void **addConsumer**(ImageConsumer ic)

*abstract* Boolean **isConsumer**(ImageConsumer ic)

*abstract* void **removeConsumer**(ImageConsumer ic)

*abstract* void **requestTopDownLeftRightResend**(ImageConsumer ic)
*abstract* void **startProduction**(ImageConsumer ic)

# java.io

The java.io package serves as the standard input/output library for the Java language. This package provides you with the ability to create and handle streams of data in several manners. To this end, it provides you with types as simple as a String and as complex as a StreamTokenizer. Furthermore, because this package is heavily dependent on the basic InputStream and OutputStream classes as well as the interfaces, it would be a wise idea to examine their code details.

## Classes

### BufferedInputStream extends FilterInputStream
**Fields**

*protected* byte **buf**[ ]

*protected* int **count**

*protected* int **marklimit**

*protected* int **markpos**

*protected* int **pos**

**Methods**

**BufferedInputStream**(InputStream in)

**BufferedInputStream**(InputStream in, int size)

*synchronized* int **available**( ) throws IOException

*synchronized* void **mark**(int readlimit)

Boolean **markSupported**( )

*synchronized* int **read**(byte b[ ], int offset, int len) throws IOException

*synchronized* int **read**( ) throws IOException

*synchronized* void **reset**( ) throws IOException

*synchronized* long **skip**(long num) throws IOException

## BufferedOutputStream extends FilterOutputStream
## Fields

*protected* byte **buf**[ ]

*protected* int **count**

## Methods

**BufferedOutputStream**(OutputStream out)

**BufferedOutputStream**(OutputStream out, int size)

*synchronized* void **flush**( ) throws IOException

*synchronized* void **write**(byte b[ ], int offset, int len) throws IOException

*synchronized* void **write**(int b) throws IOException

## ByteArrayInputStream extends InputStream
## Fields

*protected* byte **buf**[ ]

*protected* int **count**

*protected* int **pos**

## Methods

**ByteArrayInputStream**(byte buf[ ])

**ByteArrayInputStream**(byte buf[ ], int offset, int length)

*synchronized* int **available**( )

*synchronized* int **read**(byte b[ ], int offset, int len)

*synchronized* int **read**( )

*synchronized* void **reset**( )

*synchronized* long **skip**(long num)

## ByteArrayOutputStream extends OutputStream
## Fields

*protected* byte **buf**[ ]

*protected* int **count**

**Methods**

    **ByteArrayOutputStream**( )

    **ByteArrayOutputStream**(int size)

    *synchronized* void **reset**( )

    int **size**( )

    *synchronized* byte[ ] **toByteArray**( )

    String **toString**(int hibyte)

    String **toString**( )

    *synchronized* void **write**(int b)

    *synchronized* void **write**(byte b[ ], int offset, int len)

    *synchronized* void **writeTo**(OutputStream out) throws IOException

**DataInputStream extends FilterInputStream implements DataInput**
**Methods**

    **DataInputStream**(InputStream in)

    final int **read**(byte b[ ], int offset, int len) throws IOException

    final int **read**(byte b[]) throws IOException

    final Boolean **readBoolean**( ) throws IOException

    final byte **readByte**( ) throws IOException

    final char **readChar**( ) throws IOException

    final double **readDouble**( ) throws IOException

    final float **readFloat**( ) throws IOException

    final void **readFully**(byte b[ ], int offset, int len) throws IOException

    final void **readFully**(byte b[ ]) throws IOException

    final int **readInt**( ) throws IOException

    final String **readLine**( ) throws IOException

    final long **readLong**( ) throws IOException

    final short **readShort**( ) throws IOException

    final int **readUnsignedByte**( ) throws IOException

    final int **readUnsignedShort**( ) throws IOException

    final static String **readUTF**(DataInput in) throws IOException

    final String **readUTF**( ) throws IOException

    final int **skipBytes**(int num) throws IOException

**DataOutputStream extends FilterOutputStream implements DataOutput**

**Fields**

*protected* int **written**

**Methods**

**DataOutputStream**(OutputStream out)

void **flush**( ) throws IOException

final int **size**( )

*synchronized* void **write**(byte b[ ], int offset,int len) throws IOException

*synchronized* void **write**(int b) throws IOException

final void **writeBoolean**(Boolean v) throws IOException

final void **writeByte**(int v) throws IOException

final void **writeBytes**(String s) throws IOException

final void **writeChar**(int v) throws IOException

final void **writeChars**(String s) throws IOException

final void **writeDoubl**e(double v) throws IOException

final void **writeFloat**(float v) throws IOException

final void **writeInt**(int v) throws IOException

final void **writeLong**(long v) throws IOException

final void **writeShort**(int v) throws IOException

final void **writeUTF**(String str) throws IOException

**File**

**Fields**

final static String **pathSeparator**

final static char **pathSeparatorChar**

final static String **separator**

final static char **separatorChar**

**Methods**

**File**(String path)

**File**(File dir, String name)

**File**(String path, String name)

Boolean **canRead**( )

Boolean **canWrit**e( )

Boolean **delete**( )

    Boolean **equals**(Object obj)

    Boolean **exists**( )

    String **getAbsolutePath**( )

    String **getName**( )

    String **getParent**( )

    String **getPath**( )

    int **hashCode**( )

    Boolean **isAbsolute**( )

    Boolean **isDirectory**( )

    Boolean **isFile**( )

    long **lastModified**( )

    long **length**( )

    String[ ] **list**(FilenameFilter filter)

    String[ ] **list**( )

    Boolean **mkdir**( )

    Boolean mkdirs( )

    Boolean **renameTo**(File dest)

    String **toString**( )

**FileDescriptor**
**Fields**

    final static FileDescriptor **err**

    final static FileDescriptor **in**

    final static FileDescriptor **out**

**Methods**

    **FileDescriptor**( )

    Boolean **valid**( )

**FileInputStream extends InputStream**
**Methods**

    **FileInputStream**(FileDescriptor descriptorObject)

    **FileInputStream**(File file) throws FileNotFoundException

    **FileInputStream**(String name) throws FileNotFoundException

    int **available**( ) throws IOException

    void **close**( ) throws IOException

*protected* void **finalize**( ) throws IOException

final FileDescriptor **getFD**( ) throws IOException

int **read**(byte b[ ], int offset, int len) throws IOException

int **read**(byte b[ ]) throws IOException

int **read**( ) throws IOException

long **skip**(long num) throws IOException

## FileOutputStream extends OutputStream
## Methods

**FileOutputStream**(FileDescriptor fdObj)

**FileOutputStream**(File file) throws IOException

**FileOutputStream**(String name) throws IOException

void **close**( ) throws IOException

*protected* void **finalize**( ) throws IOException

final FileDescriptor **getFD**( ) throws IOException

void **write**(byte b[ ], int offset, int len) throws IOException

void **write**(byte b[ ]) throws IOException

void **write**(int b) throws IOException

## FilterInputStream extends InputStream
## Fields

*protected* InputStream **in**

## Methods

**FilterInputStream**(InputStream in)

int **available**( ) throws IOException

void **close**( ) throws IOException

*synchronized* void **mark**(int readlimit)

Boolean **markSupported**( )

int **read**(byte b[ ], int offset, int len) throws IOException

int **read**(byte b[ ]) throws IOException

int **read**( ) throws IOException

*synchronized* void **reset**( ) throws IOException

long **skip**(long num) throws IOException

## FilterOutputStream extends OutputStream
## Fields

*protected* OutputStream **out**

## Methods

**FilterOutputStream**(OutputStream out)

void **close**( ) throws IOException

void **flush**( ) throws IOException

void **write**(byte b[ ], int offset, int len) throws IOException

void **write**(byte b[ ]) throws IOException

void **write**(int b) throws IOException

## abstract InputStream
## Methods

**InputStream**( )

int **available**( ) throws IOException

void **close**( ) throws IOException

*synchronized* void **mark**(int readlimit)

Boolean markSupported( )

*abstract* int **read**( ) throws IOException

int **read**(byte b[ ], int offset, int len) throws IOException

int **read**(byte b[ ]) throws IOException

*synchronized* void **reset**( ) throws IOException

long **skip**(long num) throws IOException

## LineNumberInputStream extends FilterInputStream
## Methods

**LineNumberInputStream**(InputStream in)

int available( ) throws IOException

int **getLineNumber**( )

void **mark**(int readlimit)

int **read**(byte b[ ], int offset, int len) throws IOException

int **read**( ) throws IOException

void **reset**( ) throws IOException

void **setLineNumber**(int lineNumber)

long **skip**(long num) throws IOException

*abstract* **OutputStream**

**Methods**

> **OutputStream**( )
>
> void **close**( ) throws IOException
>
> void **flush**( ) throws IOException
>
> void **write**(byte b[ ], int offset, int len) throws IOException
>
> void **write**(byte b[ ]) throws IOException
>
> *abstract* void **write**(int b) throws IOException

**PipedInputStream extends InputStream**

**Methods**

> **PipedInputStream**( )
>
> **PipedInputStream**(PipedOutputStream src) throws IOException
>
> void **close**( ) throws IOException
>
> void **connect**(PipedOutputStream src) throws IOException
>
> *synchronized* int **read**(byte b[ ], int offset, int len) throws IOException
>
> *synchronized* int **read**( ) throws IOException

**PipedOutputStream extends OutputStream**

**Methods**

> **PipedOutputStream**( )
>
> **PipedOutputStream**(PipedInputStream snk) throws IOException
>
> void **close**( ) throws IOException
>
> void **connect**(PipedInputStream snk) throws IOException
>
> void **write**(byte b[ ], int offset, int len) throws IOException
>
> void **write**(int b) throws IOException

**PrintStream extends FilterOutputStream**

**Methods**

> **PrintStream**(OutputStream out)
>
> **PrintStream**(OutputStream out, Boolean autoflush)
>
> Boolean **checkError**( )
>
> void **close**( )
>
> void **flush**( )
>
> void **print**(Boolean b)
>
> void **print**(double d)

VII

void **print**(float f)

void **print**(long l)

void **print**(int i)

void **print**(char c)

*synchronized* void **print**(char s[ ])

*synchronized* void **print**(String s)

void **print**(Object obj)

*synchronized* void **println**(Boolean b)

*synchronized* void **println**(double d)

*synchronized* void **println**(float f)

*synchronized* void **println**(long l)

*synchronized* void **println**(int i)

*synchronized* void **println**(char c)

*synchronized* void **println**(char s[ ])

*synchronized* void **println**(String s)

*synchronized* void **println**(Object obj)

void **println**( )

void **write**(byte b[ ], int offset, int len)

void **write**(int b)

## PushbackInputStream extends FilterInputStream
## Fields

*protected* int **pushBack**

## Methods

**PushbackInputStream**(InputStream in)

int **available**( ) throws IOException

Boolean **markSupported**( )

int **read**(byte bytes[ ], int offset, int length) throws IOException

int **read**( ) throws IOException

void **unread**(int ch) throws IOException

## RandomAccessFile implements DataOutput, DataInput
## Methods

**RandomAccessFile**(File file, String mode) throws IOException

**RandomAccessFile**(String name, String mode) throws IOException void **close**( ) throws IOException

final FileDescriptor **getFD**( ) throws IOException

long **getFilePointer**( ) throws IOException

long **length**( ) throws IOException

int **read**(byte b[ ]) throws IOException

int **read**(byte b[ ], int offset, int len) throws IOException

int **read**( ) throws IOException

final Boolean **readBoolean**( ) throws IOException

final byte **readByte**( ) throws IOException

final char **readChar**( ) throws IOException

final double **readDouble**( ) throws IOException

final float **readFloat**( ) throws IOException

final void **readFully**(byte b[ ], int offset, int len) throws IOException

final void **readFully**(byte b[ ]) throws IOException

final int **readInt**( ) throws IOException

final String **readLine**( ) throws IOException

final long **readLong**( ) throws IOException

final short **readShort**( ) throws IOException

final int **readUnsignedByte**( ) throws IOException

final int **readUnsignedShort**( ) throws IOException

final String **readUTF**( ) throws IOException

void **seek**(long pos) throws IOException

int **skipBytes**(int num) throws IOException

void **write**(byte b[ ], int offset, int len) throws IOException

void **write**(byte b[ ]) throws IOException

final void **writeBoolean**(Boolean v) throws IOException

final void **writeByte**(int v) throws IOException

final void **writeBytes**(String s) throws IOException

final void **writeChar**(int v) throws IOException

final void **writeChars**(String s) throws IOException

final void **writeDouble**(double v) throws IOException

final void **writeFloat**(float v) throws IOException

final void **writeInt**(int v) throws IOException

final void **writeLong**(long v) throws IOException

final void **writeShort**(int v) throws IOException

final void **writeUTF**(String str) throws IOException

## SequenceInputStream extends InputStream
### Methods

**SequenceInputStream**(InputStream s1, InputStream s2)

**SequenceInputStream**(Enumeration e)

void **close**( ) throws IOException

int **read**(byte buf[ ], int pos, int len) throws IOException

int **read**( ) throws IOException

## StreamTokenizer
### Fields

double **nval**

String **sval**

final static int **TT_EOF**

final static int **TT_EOL**

final static int **TT_NUMBER**

final static int **TT_WORD**

### Methods

**StreamTokenizer**(InputStream I)

void **commentChar**(int ch)

void **eolIsSignificant**(Boolean flag)

int **lineno**( )

void **lowerCaseMode**(Boolean fl)

int **nextToken**( ) throws IOException

void **ordinaryChar**(int ch)

void **ordinaryChars**(int low, int hi)

void **parseNumbers**( )

void **pushBack**( )

void **quoteChar**(int ch)

void **resetSyntax**( )

void **slashSlashComments**(Boolean flag)

void **slashStarComments**(Boolean flag)

String **toString**( )

void **whitespaceChars**(int low, int hi)

void **wordChars**(int low, int hi)

### StringBufferInputStream extends InputStream
### Fields

*protected* String **buffer**

*protected* int **count**

*protected* int **pos**

### Methods

**StringBufferInputStream**(String s)

*synchronized* int **available**( )

*synchronized* int **read**(byte b[], int offset, int len)

*synchronized* int **read**( )

*synchronized* void **reset**( )

*synchronized* long **skip**(long num)

## Interfaces

### DataInput
### Methods

*abstract* Boolean **readBoolean**( ) throws IOException

*abstract* byte **readByte**( ) throws IOException

*abstract* char **readChar**( ) throws IOException

*abstract* double **readDouble**( ) throws IOException

*abstract* float **readFloat**( ) throws IOException

*abstract* void **readFully**(byte b[ ], int offset, int len) throws IOException

*abstract* void **readFully**(byte b[]) throws IOException

*abstract* int **readInt**( ) throws IOException

*abstract* long **readLong**( ) throws IOException

*abstract* short **readShort**( ) throws IOException

*abstract* int **readUnsignedByte**( ) throws IOException

*abstract* int **readUnsignedShort**( ) throws IOException

*abstract* String **readUTF**( ) throws IOException

*abstract* int **skipBytes**(int num) throws IOException

**DataOutput**
**Methods**

> *abstract* void **write**(byte b[ ], int offset, int len) throws IOException

> *abstract* void **write**(byte b[ ]) throws IOException

> *abstract* void **write**(int b) throws IOException

> *abstract* void **writeBoolean**(Boolean v) throws IOException

> *abstract* void **writeByte**(int v) throws IOException

> *abstract* void **writeBytes**(String s) throws IOException

> *abstract* void **writeChar**(int v) throws IOException

> *abstract* void **writeChars**(String s) throws IOException

> *abstract* void **writeDouble**(double v) throws IOException

> *abstract* void **writeFloat**(float v) throws IOException

> *abstract* void **writeInt**(int v) throws IOException

> *abstract* void **writeLong**(long v) throws IOException

> *abstract* void **writeShort**(int v) throws IOException

> *abstract* void **writeUTF**(String str) throws IOException

**FilenameFilter**
**Methods**

> *abstract* Boolean **accept**(File dir, String name)

# java.lang

These classes are essentially the "heart" of the java language. It provides you not only with the basic data types, such as `Integer` and `String`, but also means of handling errors through the `Throwable` and `Error` classes. Furthermore, the `SecurityManager` and `System` classes supply you with some degree of control over the Java Run-Time System.

## Classes

**Boolean**
**Fields**

> final static Boolean **FALSE**

> final static char **MAX_VALUE**

> final static char **MIN_VALUE**

> final static Boolean **TRUE**

**Methods**

> **Boolean**(String s)
>
> **Boolean**(Boolean value)
>
> Boolean **BooleanValue**( )
>
> Boolean **equals**(Object obj)
>
> static Boolean **getBoolean**(String name)
>
> int **hashCode**( )
>
> String **toString**( )
>
> static Boolean **valueOf**(String s)

**Character**
**Fields**

> **Character**(char value)
>
> char **charValue**( )
>
> static int **digit**(char ch, int radix)
>
> Boolean **equals**(Object obj)
>
> static char **forDigit**(int digit, int radix)
>
> int **hashCode**( )
>
> static Boolean **isDigit**(char ch)
>
> static Boolean **isLowerCase**(char ch)
>
> static Boolean **isSpace**(char ch)
>
> static Boolean **isUpperCase**(char ch)
>
> final static int **MAX_RADIX**
>
> final static int **MIN_RADIX**
>
> static char **toLowerCase**(char ch)
>
> String **toString**( )
>
> static char **toUpperCase**(char ch)

**Class**
**Methods**

> static Class **forName**(String className) throws
> ClassNotFoundException
>
> ClassLoader **getClassLoader**( )
>
> Class[ ] **getInterfaces**( )
>
> String **getName**( )

Class **getSuperclass**( )

Boolean **isInterface**( )

Object **newInstance**( ) throws InstantiationException, IllegalAccessException

String **toString**( )

## ClassLoader

*protected* **ClassLoader**( )

*abstract* Class **loadClass**(String name, Boolean resolve) throws ClassNotFoundException

final Class **defineClass**(byte data[ ], int offset, int length)

final Class **findSystemClass**(String name) throws ClassNotFoundExcept

final void **resolveClass**(Class c)

## Compiler
## Methods

static Object **command**(Object any)

static Boolean **compileClass**(Class clazz)

static Boolean **compileClasses**(String string)

static void **disable**( )

static void **enable**( )

## Double extends Number
## Fields

final static double **MAX_VALUE**

final static double **MIN_VALUE**

final static double **NaN**

final static double **NEGATIVE_INFINITY**

final static double **POSITIVE_INFINITY**

## Methods

**Double**(double value)

**Double**(String s) throws NumberFormatException

static long **doubleToLongBits**(double value)

double **doubleValue**( )

Boolean **equals**(Object obj)

float **floatValue**( )

int **hashCode**( )

int **intValue**( )

Boolean **isInfinite**( )

static Boolean **isInfinite**(double v)

Boolean **isNaN**( )

static Boolean **isNaN**(double v)

static double **longBitsToDouble**(long bits)

long **longValue**( )

String **toString**( )

static String **toString**(double d)

static Double **valueOf**(String s) throws NumberFormatException

## Float extends Number
**Fields**

final static float **MAX_VALUE**

final static float **MIN_VALUE**

final static float **NaN**

final static float **NEGATIVE_INFINITY**

final static float **POSITIVE_INFINITY**

**Fields**

**Float**(String s) throws NumberFormatException

**Float**(double value)

**Float**(float value)

double **doubleValue**( )

Boolean **equals**(Object obj)

static int **floatToIntBits**(float value)

float **floatValue**( )

int **hashCode**( )

static float **intBitsToFloat**(int bits)

int **intValue**( )

Boolean **isInfinite**( )

static Boolean **isInfinite**(float v)

Boolean **isNaN**( )

static Boolean **isNaN**(float v)

long **longValue**( )

String **toString**( )

static String **toString**(float f)

static Float **valueOf**(String s) throws NumberFormatException

## Integer extends Number
### Fields

final static int **MAX_VALUE**

final static int **MIN_VALUE**

### Methods

**Integer**(int value)

**Integer**(String s) throws NumberFormatException

double **doubleValue**( )

Boolean **equals**(Object obj)

float **floatValue**( )

static Integer **getInteger**(String nm, Integer val)

static Integer **getInteger**(String nm, int val)

static Integer **getInteger**(String nm)

int **hashCode**( )

int **intValue**( )

long **longValue**( )

static int **parseInt**(String s) throws NumberFormatException

static int **parseInt**(String s, int radix) throws NumberFormatException

String **toString**( )

static String **toString**(int i)

static String **toString**(int i, int radix)

static Integer **valueOf**(String s) throws NumberFormatException

static Integer **valueOf**(String s, int radix) throws
NumberFormatException

## Long extends Number
### Fields

final static long **MAX_VALUE**

final static long **MIN_VALUE**

**Methods**

**Long**(String s) throws NumberFormatException

**Long**(long value)

double **doubleValue**( )

Boolean **equals**(Object obj)

float **floatValue**( )

static Long **getLong**(String nm, Long val)

static Long **getLong**(String nm, long val)

static Long **getLong**(String nm)

int **hashCode**( )

int **intValue**( )

long **longValue**( )

static long **parseLong**(String s) throws NumberFormatException

static long **parseLong**(String s, int radix) throws
NumberFormatException

String **toString**( )

static String **toString**(long i)

static String **toString**(long i, int radix)

static Long **valueOf**(String s) throws NumberFormatException

static Long **valueOf**(String s, int radix) throws
NumberFormatException

## Math
**Fields**

final static double **E**

final static double **PI**

**Methods**

static double **abs**(double a)

static float **abs**(float a)

static long **abs**(long a)

static int **abs**(int a)

static double **acos**(double a)

static double **asin**(double a)

static double **atan**(double a)

static double **atan2**(double a, double b)

static double **ceil**(double a)

static double **cos**(double a)

static double **exp**(double a)

static double **floor**(double a)

static double **IEEEremainder**(double f1, double f2)

static double **log**(double a) throws ArithmeticException

static double **max**(double a, double b)

static float **max**(float a, float b)

static long **max**(long a, long b)

static int **max**(int a, int b)

static double **min**(double a, double b)

static float **min**(float a, float b)

static long **min**(long a, long b)

static int **min**(int a, int b)

static double **pow**(double a, double b) throws ArithmeticException

static *synchronized* double **random**( )

static double **rint**(double a)

static long **round**(double a)

static int **round**(float a)

static double **sin**(double a)

static double **sqrt**(double a) throws ArithmeticException

static double **tan**(double a)

## *abstract* **Number**
## **Methods**

**Number**( )

*abstract* double **doubleValue**( )

*abstract* float **floatValue**( )

*abstract* int **intValue**( )

*abstract* long **longValue**( )

## **Object**
## **Methods**

**Object**( )

*protected* Object **clone**( ) throws CloneNotSupportedException

Boolean **equals**(Object obj)

*protected* void **finalize**( ) throws Throwable

final Class **getClass**( )

int **hashCode**( )

final void **notify**( )

final void **notifyAll**( )

String **toString**( )

final void **wait**( ) throws InterruptedException

final void **wait**(long timeout, int nanos) throws InterruptedException

final void **wait**(long timeout) throws InterruptedException

**Process**
**Methods**

**Process**( )

*abstract* void **destroy**( )

*abstract* int **exitValue**( )

*abstract* InputStream **getErrorStream**( )

*abstract* InputStream **getInputStream**( )

*abstract* OutputStream **getOutputStream**( )

*abstract* int **waitFor**( ) throws InterruptedException

**Runtime**
**Methods**

Process **exec**(String cmdarray[ ], String envp[ ]) throws IOException

Process **exec**(String cmdarray[ ]) throws IOException

Process **exec**(String command, String envp[ ]) throws IOException

Process **exec**(String command) throws IOException

void **exit**(int status)

long **freeMemory**( )

void **gc**( )

InputStream **getLocalizedInputStream**(InputStream in)

OutputStream **getLocalizedOutputStream**(OutputStream out)

static Runtime **getRuntime**( )

*synchronized* void **load**(String filename)

*synchronized* void **loadLibrary**(String libname)

void **runFinalization**( )

long **totalMemory**( )

void **traceInstructions**(Boolean on)

void **traceMethodCalls**(Boolean on)

## *abstract* **SecurityManager**

**Fields**

*protected* Boolean **inCheck**

**Methods**

*protected* **SecurityManager**( )

void **checkAccept**(String host, int port)

void **checkAccess**(ThreadGroup g)

void **checkAccess**(Thread g)

void **checkConnect**(String host, int port, Object context)

void **checkConnect**(String host, int port)

void **checkCreateClassLoader**( )

void **checkDelete**(String file)

void **checkExec**(String cmd)

void **checkExit**(int status)

void **checkLink**(String lib)

void **checkListen**(int port)

void **checkPackageAccess**(String pkg)

void **checkPackageDefinition**(String pkg)

void **checkPropertiesAccess**( )

void **checkPropertyAccess**(String key, String def)

void **checkPropertyAccess**(String key)

void **checkRead**(String file, Object context)

void **checkRead**(String file)

void **checkRead**(FileDescriptor fd)

void **checkSetFactory**( )

Boolean **checkTopLevelWindow**(Object window)

void **checkWrite**(String file)

void **checkWrite**(FileDescriptor fd)

*protected* int **classDepth**(String name)

*protected* int **classLoaderDepth**( )

*protected* ClassLoader **currentClassLoader**( )

*protected* Class[ ] **getClassContext**( )

Boolean **getInCheck**( )

Object **getSecurityContext**( )

*protected* Boolean **inClass**(String name)

*protected* Boolean **inClassLoader**( )

## String
## Methods

**String**( )

**String**(StringBuffer buffer)

**String**(byte ascii[ ], int hibyte)

**String**(byte ascii[ ], int hibyte, int offset, int count)

**String**(char value[ ], int offset, int count)

**String**(char value[ ])

**String**(String value)

char **charAt**(int index)

int **compareTo**(String anotherString)

Boolean **equals**(Object anObject)

Boolean **equalsIgnoreCase**(String anotherString)

void **getBytes**(int srcBegin, int srcEnd, byte dst[ ], int dstBegin)

void **getChars**(int srcBegin, int srcEnd, char dst[ ], int dstBegin)

int **length**( )

Boolean **regionMatches**(Boolean ignoreCase, int toffset, String other, int offset, int len)

Boolean **regionMatches**(int toffset, String other, int offset, int len)

String **concat**(String str)

static String **copyValueOf**(char data[ ])

static String **copyValueOf**(char data[ ], int offset, int count)

Boolean **endsWith**(String suffix)

int **hashCode**( )

int **indexOf**(String str, int fromIndex)

int **indexOf**(String str)

int **indexOf**(int ch, int fromIndex)

int **indexOf**(int ch)

String **intern**( )

int **lastIndexOf**(String str, int fromIndex)

int **lastIndexOf**(String str)

int **lastIndexOf**(int ch, int fromIndex)

int **lastIndexOf**(int ch)

String **replace**(char oldChar, char newChar)

Boolean **startsWith**(String prefix)

Boolean **startsWith**(String prefix, int toffset)

String **substring**(int beginIndex, int endIndex)

String **substring**(int beginIndex)

char[ ] **toCharArray**( )

String **toLowerCase**( )

String **toString**( )

String **toUpperCase**( )

String **trim**( )

static String **valueOf**(double d)

static String **valueOf**(float f)

static String **valueOf**(long l)

static String **valueOf**(int i)

static String **valueOf**(char c)

static String **valueOf**(Boolean b)

static String **valueOf**(char data[ ], int offset, int count)

static String **valueOf**(char data[ ])

static String **valueOf**(Object obj)

## StringBuffer
## Methods

**StringBuffer**(String str)

**StringBuffer**(int length)

**StringBuffer**( )

int **capacity**( )

*synchronized* char **charAt**(int index)

*synchronized* void **ensureCapacity**(int minimumCapacity)

*synchronized* void **getChars**(int srcBegin, int srcEnd, char dst[ ], int dstBegiint length( )

*synchronized* void **setLength**(int newLength)

StringBuffer **append**(double d)

StringBuffer **append**(float f)

StringBuffer **append**(long l)

StringBuffer **append**(int i)

*synchronized* StringBuffer **append**(char c)

StringBuffer **append**(Boolean b)

*synchronized* StringBuffer **append**(char str[ ], int offset, int len)

*synchronized* StringBuffer **append**(char str[ ])

*synchronized* StringBuffer **append**(String str)

*synchronized* StringBuffer **append**(Object obj)

StringBuffer **insert**(int offset, double d)

StringBuffer **insert**(int offset, float f)

StringBuffer **insert**(int offset, long l)

StringBuffer **insert**(int offset, int i)

*synchronized* StringBuffer **insert**(int offset, char c)

StringBuffer **insert**(int offset, Boolean b)

*synchronized* StringBuffer **insert**(int offset, char str[ ])

*synchronized* StringBuffer **insert**(int offset, Object obj)

*synchronized* StringBuffer **insert**(int offset, String str)

*synchronized* void **setCharAt**(int index, char ch)

String **toString**( )

## System
## Fields

static PrintStream **err**

static InputStream **in**

static PrintStream **out**

## Methods

static void **arraycopy**(Object src, int src_position, Object dst, int dst_posistion, int length) static SecurityManager **getSecurityManager**( )

static void **setSecurityManager**(SecurityManager s)

static void **exit**(int status)

static void **gc**( )

static String **getenv**(String name)

static Properties **getProperties**( )

static String **getProperty**(String key, String def)

static String **getProperty**(String key)

static void **load**(String filename)

static void **loadLibrary**(String libname)

static void **runFinalization**( )

static void **setProperties**(Properties props)

## Thread implements Runnable
## Fields

final static int **MAX_PRIORITY**

final static int **MIN_PRIORITY**

final static int **NORM_PRIORITY**

## Methods

**Thread**( )

**Thread**(Runnable target)

**Thread**(Runnable target, String name)

**Thread**(ThreadGroup group, Runnable target)

**Thread**(ThreadGroup group, Runnable target, String name)

**Thread**(ThreadGroup group, String name)

**Thread**(String name)

static int **activeCount**( )

int **countStackFrames**( )

static Thread **currentThread**( )

void **destroy**( )

static int **enumerate**(Thread tarray[ ])

final String **getName**( )

final int **getPriority**( )

final ThreadGroup **getThreadGroup**( )

void **interrupt**( )

static Boolean **interrupted**( )

Boolean **isInterrupted**( )

final *synchronized* void **join**(long millis, int nanos) throws InterruptedException

final *synchronized* void **join**(long millis) throws InterruptedException

final void **resume**( )

void **run**( )

final void **setName**(String name)

final void **setPriority**(int newPriority)

static void **sleep**(long millis, int nanos) throws InterruptedException

static void **sleep**(long millis) throws InterruptedException

*synchronized* void **start**( )

final *synchronized* void **stop**(Throwable o)

final void **stop**( )

final void **suspend**( )

static void **yield**( )

void **checkAccess**( )

static void **dumpStack**( )

final Boolean **isDaemon**( )

final void **join**( ) throws InterruptedException

final void **setDaemon**(Boolean on)

String **toString**( )

**ThreadGroup**

**ThreadGroup**(String name)

**ThreadGroup**(ThreadGroup parent, String name)

*synchronized* int **activeCount**( )

*synchronized* int **activeGroupCount**( )

final void **checkAccess**( )

final *synchronized* void **destroy**( )

int **enumerate**(ThreadGroup list[ ], Boolean recurse)

int **enumerate**(ThreadGroup list[ ])

int **enumerate**(Thread list[], Boolean recurse)

int **enumerate**(Thread list[ ])

final int **getMaxPriority**( )

final String **getName**( )

final ThreadGroup **getParent**( )

final Boolean **isDaemon**( )

*synchronized* void **list**( )

final Boolean **parentOf**(ThreadGroup g)

final *synchronized* void **resume**( )

final void **setDaemon**(Boolean daemon)

final *synchronized* void **setMaxPriority**(int pri)

final *synchronized* void **stop**( )

final *synchronized* void **suspend**( )

String **toString**( )

void **uncaughtException**(Thread t, Throwable e)

**Throwable**
**Methods**

**Throwable**( )

**Throwable**(String message)

**Throwable** fillInStackTrace( )

String **getMessage**( )

void **printStackTrace**(PrintStream s)

void **printStackTrace**( )

String **toString**( )

## Interfaces

**Cloneable**

**Runnable**

## Methods

*abstract* void **run**( )

# java.net

Inasmuch as Java is a networked-based language, this comparatively small package is very useful. Most importantly, it provides you with the ability to communicate with other sources of information—by creating or connecting to sockets or making use of URLs.

# Classes

*abstract* **ContentHandler**
**Methods**

> **ContentHandler**( )
>
> *abstract* Object **getContent**(URLConnection urlc) throws IOException

**DatagramPacket**
**Methods**

> **DatagramPacket**(byte ibuf[ ], int ilength)
>
> **DatagramPacket**(byte ibuf[ ],int ilength, InetAddress iaddr, int iport)
>
> InetAddress **getAddress**( )
>
> byte[ ] **getData**( )
>
> int **getLength**( )
>
> int **getPort**( )

**DatagramSocket**
**Methods**

> **DatagramSocket**(int port) throws SocketException
>
> **DatagramSocket**( ) throws SocketException
>
> *protected synchronized* void **finalize**( )
>
> int **getLocalPort**( )
>
> *synchronized* void **receive**(DatagramPacket p) throws IOException
>
> void **send**(DatagramPacket p) throws IOException

**final InetAddress**
**Methods**

> static *synchronized* InetAddress[ ] **getAllByName**(String host) throws
> UnknownHostException
>
> static InetAddress **getLocalHost**( ) throws UnknownHostException
>
> Boolean **equals**(Object obj)
>
> byte[ ] **getAddress**( )
>
> static *synchronized* InetAddress **getByName**(String host) throws
> UnknownHostExction
>
> String **getHostName**( )
>
> int **hashCode**( )
>
> String **toString**( )

**ServerSocket**
**Methods**

> **ServerSocket**(int port) throws IOException
>
> **ServerSocket**(int port, int count) throws IOException
>
> Socket **accept**( ) throws IOException
>
> void **close**( ) throws IOException
>
> InetAddress **getInetAddress**( )
>
> int **getLocalPort**( )
>
> String **toString**( )
>
> static *synchronized* void **setSocketFactory**(SocketImplFactory fac) throws IOException

**Socket**
**Methods**

> **Socket**(InetAddress address, int port, Boolean stream) throws IOException
>
> **Socket**(InetAddress address, int port) throws IOException
>
> **Socket**(String host, int port, Boolean stream) throws IOException
>
> **Socket**(String host, int port) throws UnknownHostException, IOException
>
> *synchronized* void **close**( ) throws IOException
>
> InetAddress **getInetAddress**( )
>
> InputStream **getInputStream**( ) throws IOException
>
> int **getLocalPort**( )
>
> OutputStream **getOutputStream**( ) throws IOException
>
> int **getPort**( )
>
> static *synchronized* void **setSocketImplFactory**(SocketImplFactory fac) throws IOException
>
> String **toString**( )

*abstract* **SocketImpl**
**Fields**

> *protected* InetAddress **address**
>
> *protected* FileDescriptor **fd**
>
> *protected* int **localport**
>
> *protected* int **port**

## Methods

**SocketImpl**( )

*protected abstract* void **accept**(SocketImpl s) throws IOException

*protected abstract* int **available**( ) throws IOException

*protected abstract* void **bind**(InetAddress host, int port) throws IOException

*protected abstract* void **close**( ) throws IOException

*protected abstract* void **connect**(InetAddress address, int port) throws IOException

*protected abstract* void **connect**(String host, int port) throws IOException

*protected abstract* void **create**(Boolean stream) throws IOException

FileDescriptor **getFileDescriptor**( )

*protected* InetAddress **getInetAddress**( )

*protected abstract* InputStream **getInputStream**( ) throws IOException

*protected* int **getLocalPort**( )

*protected abstract* OutputStream **getOutputStream**( ) throws IOException

*protected* int **getPort**( )

*protected abstract* void **listen**(int count) throws IOException

String **toString**( )

### URL

**URL**(String protocol, String host, int port, String file) throws MalformedURLException

**URL**(URL context, String spec) throws MalformedURLException

**URL**(String spec) throws MalformedURLException

**URL**(String protocol, String host, String file) throws MalformedURLException

int **getPort**( )

String **getProtocol**( )

Boolean **equals**(Object obj)

final Object **getContent**( ) throws IOException

String **getFile**( )

String **getHost**( )

String **getRef**( )

int **hashCode**( )

URLConnection **openConnection**( ) throws IOException

final InputStream **openStream**( ) throws IOException

Boolean sameFile(URL other)

*protected* void **set**(String protocol, String host, int port, String file, String ref)

static *synchronized* void
**setURLStreamHandlerFactory**(URLStreamHandlerFactory fac)

String **toExternalForm**( )

String **toString**( )

## *abstract* **URLConnection**
### **Fields**

*protected* Boolean **allowUserInteraction**

*protected* Boolean **connected**

*protected* Boolean **doInput**

*protected* Boolean **doOutput**

*protected* long **ifModifiedSince**

*protected* URL **url**

*protected* Boolean **useCaches**

### **Methods**

*abstract* void **connect**( ) throws IOException

Boolean **getAllowUserInteraction**( )

Object **getContent**( ) throws IOException

String **getContentEncoding**( )

int **getContentLength**( )

String **getContentType**( )

long **getDate**( )

Boolean **getDoInput**( )

Boolean **getDoOutput**( )

long **getExpiration**( )

String **getHeaderField**(int num)

String **getHeaderField**(String name)

long **getHeaderFieldDate**(String name, long Default)

int **getHeaderFieldInt**(String name, int Default)

String **getHeaderFieldKey**(int num)

InputStream **getInputStream**( ) throws IOException

long **getLastModified**( )

OutputStream **getOutputStream**( ) throws IOException

URL **getURL**( )

void **setAllowUserInteraction**(Boolean allowuserinteraction)

static void **setDefaultAllowUserInteraction**(Boolean default)

void **setDoInput**(Boolean doinput)

void **setDoOutput**(Boolean dooutput)

String toString( )

**URLConnection**(URL url)

static Boolean **getDefaultAllowUserInteraction**( )

static String **getDefaultRequestProperty**(String key)

Boolean **getDefaultUseCaches**( )

long **getIfModifiedSince**( )

String **getRequestProperty**(String key)

Boolean **getUseCaches**( )

static *synchronized* void
**setContentHandlerFactory**(ContentHandlerFactory fac)

static void **setDefaultRequestProperty**(String key, String value)

void **setDefaultUseCaches**(Boolean defaultusecaches)

void **setIfModifiedSince**(long ifmodifiedsince)

void **setRequestProperty**(String key, String value)

void **setUseCaches**(Boolean usecaches)

static String **guessContentTypeFromName**(String fname)

static String **guessContentTypeFromStream**(InputStream is) throws
IOException

**URLEncoder**
**Methods**

static String **encode**(String s)

*abstract* **URLStreamHandler**
**Methods**

**URLStreamHandler**( )

*abstract* URLConnection **openConnection**(URL url) throws IOException

void **parseURL**(URL url, String spec, int start, int limit)

void **setURL**(URL url, String protocol, String host, int port, String file, String ref)

String **toExternalForm**(URL url)

## Interfaces

### ContentHandlerFactory
**Methods**

*abstract* ContentHandler **createContentHandler**(String mimetype)

### SocketImplFactory

*abstract* SocketImpl **createSocketImpl**( )

### URLStreamHandlerFactory
**Methods**

*abstract* URLStreamHandler **CreateURLStreamHandler**(String protocol)

# java.util

This package is esentially a smorgasbord of useful classes that did not truly fit in any of the other packages. Among these handy classes are the Date class, designed to manage and handle operations with dates; the Hashtable class; and classes to develop ADTs such as Stack and Vector.

## Classes

### BitSet implements java.lang.Cloneable
**Methods**

**BitSet**( )

**BitSet**(int nbits)

void **and**(BitSet set)

void **clear**(int bit)

Object **clone**( )

Boolean **equals**(Object obj)

Boolean **get**(int bit)

int **hashCode**( )

void **or**(BitSet set)

void **set**(int bit)

int size( )

String **toString**( )

void **xor**(BitSet set)

**Date**
**Methods**

**Date**( )

**Date**(int year, int month, int date)

**Date**(int year, int month, int date, int hrs, int min)

**Date**(String s)

**Date**(int year, int month, int date, int hrs, int min, int sec)

Boolean **after**(Date when)

Boolean **before**(Date when)

Boolean **equals**(Object obj)

int **getDate**( )

int **getDay**( )

int **getHours**( )

int **getMinutes**( )

int **getMonth**( )

int **getSeconds**( )

long **getTime**( )

int **getTimezoneOffset**( )

int **getYear**( )

int **hashCode**( )

static long **parse**(String s)

void **setDate**(int date)

void **setHours**(int hours)

void **setMinutes**(int minutes)

void **setMonth**(int month)

void **setSeconds**(int seconds)

void **setTime**(long time)

void **setYear**(int year)

String **toGMTString**( )

String **toLocaleString**( )

String **toString**( )

static long **UTC**(int year, int month, int date, int hrs, int min, int sec)

### *abstract* **Dictionary**

**Dictionary**( )

*abstract* Enumeration **elements**( )

*abstract* Object **get**(Object key)

*abstract* Boolean **isEmpty**( )

*abstract* Enumeration **keys**( )

*abstract* Object **put**(Object key, Object value)

*abstract* Object **remove**(Object key)

*abstract* int **size**( )

### **Hashtable  extends Dictionary implements java.lang.Cloneable**

**Hashtable**( )

**Hashtable**(int initialCapacity)

**Hashtable**(int initialCapacity, float loadFactor)

*synchronized* void **clear**( )

*synchronized* Object **clone**( )

*synchronized* Boolean **contains**(Object value)

*synchronized* Boolean **containsKey**(Object key)

*synchronized* Enumeration **elements**( )

*synchronized* Object **get**(Object key)

Boolean isEmpty( )

*synchronized* Enumeration **keys**( )

*synchronized* Object **put**(Object key, Object value)

*protected* void **rehash**( )

*synchronized* Object **remove**(Object key)

int **size**( )

*synchronized* String **toString**( )

### **Observable**

**Observable**( )

*synchronized* void **addObserver**(Observer o)

*protected synchronized* void **clearChanged**( )

*synchronized* int **countObservers**( )

*synchronized* void **deleteObserver**(Observer o)

*synchronized* void **deleteObservers**( )

*synchronized* Boolean **hasChanged**( )

*synchronized* void **notifyObservers**(Object arg)

void **notifyObservers**( )

protected synchronized void **setChanged**( )

## Properties extends Hashtable
## Fields

*protected* Properties **defaults**

## Methods

**Properties**( )

**Properties**(Properties defaults)

String **getProperty**(String key, String defaultValue)

String **getProperty**(String key)

void **list**(PrintStream out)

*synchronized* void **load**(InputStream in) throws IOException

Enumeration **propertyNames**( )

*synchronized* void **save**(OutputStream out, String header)

## Random

**Random**( )

**Random**(long seed)

double **nextDouble**( )

float **nextFloat**( )

*synchronized* double **nextGaussian**( )

int **nextInt**( )

long **nextLong**( )

*synchronized* void **setSeed**(long seed)

## Stack  extends Vector

**Stack**( )

Boolean **empty**( )

Object **peek**( )

Object **pop**( )

Object **push**(Object item)

int **search**(Object o)

## StringTokenizer implements Enumeration

**StringTokenizer**(String str)

**StringTokenizer**(String str, String delim)

**StringTokenizer**(String str, String delim, Boolean returnTokens)

int **countTokens**( )

Boolean **hasMoreElements**( )

Boolean **hasMoreTokens**( )

Object **nextElement**( )

String **nextToken**(String delim)

String **nextToken**( )

## Vector implements java.lang.Cloneable
## Fields

*protected* int **elementCount**

*protected* Object **elementData**[ ]

## Methods

**Vector**( )

**Vector**(int initialCapacity)

**Vector**(int initialCapacity, int capacityIncrement)

final *synchronized* void **addElement**(Object obj)

final int **capacity**( )

*protected* int **capacityIncrement**

*synchronized* Object **clone**( )

final Boolean **contains**(Object elem)

final *synchronized* void **copyInto**(Object anArray[ ])

final *synchronized* Object **elementAt**(int index)

final *synchronized* Enumeration **elements**( )

final *synchronized* void **ensureCapacity**(int minCapacity)

final *synchronized* Object **firstElement**( )

final *synchronized* int **indexOf**(Object elem, int index) final int **indexOf**(Object elem)

final *synchronized* void **insertElementAt**(Object obj, int index)

final Boolean **isEmpty**( )

final *synchronized* Object **lastElement**( )

final *synchronized* int **lastIndexOf**(Object elem, int index)

final int **lastIndexOf**(Object elem)

final *synchronized* void **removeAllElements**( )

final *synchronized* Boolean **removeElement**(Object obj)

final *synchronized* void **removeElementAt**(int index)

final *synchronized* void **setElementAt**(Object obj, int index)

final *synchronized* void **setSize**(int newSize)

final int **size**( )

final *synchronized* String **toString**( )

final *synchronized* void **trimToSize**( )

## Interfaces

### Enumeration
### Methods

*abstract* Boolean **hasMoreElements**( )

*abstract* Object **nextElement**( )

### Observer

*abstract* void **update**(Observable o, Object arg)

# sun.tools.debug

The sun.tools.debug package is designed to provide for remote debugging with the Java Debugger (JDB). Examining these classes will provide you with some understanding of this process. While normal code will have no need to make use of this package, this package provides you with the ground-work on which you may build a more useful and user-friendly debugger—something the Sun openly encourages.

## Classes

### RemoteArray  extends RemoteObject

VII

Appendixes

**Methods**

String arrayTypeName(int type)

final RemoteValue getElement(int index) throws Exception

final RemoteValue[ ] getElements(int beginIndex, int endIndex) throws Exception

final RemoteValue[ ] getElements( ) throws Exception

final int getElementType( ) throws Exception

final int getSize( )

String typeName( )

String description( )

String toString( )

**RemoteBoolean extends RemoteValue**
**Methods**

Boolean get( )

String toString( )

String typeName( )

**RemoteByte extends RemoteValue**
**Methods**

byte get( )

String toString( )

String typeName( )

**RemoteChar extends RemoteValue**
**Methods**

char get( )

String toString( )

String typeName( )

**RemoteClass extends RemoteObject**
**Methods**

void catchExceptions( ) throws Exception

String clearBreakpoint(int pc) throws Exception

String clearBreakpointLine(int lineno) throws Exception

String clearBreakpointMethod(RemoteField method) throws Exception

String description( )

RemoteObject getClassLoader( ) throws Exception

RemoteField getField(String name) throws Exception

RemoteField getField(int num) throws Exception

RemoteField[ ] getFields( ) throws Exception

RemoteValue getFieldValue(String name) throws Exception

RemoteValue getFieldValue(int num) throws Exception

RemoteField getInstanceField(int num) throws Exception

RemoteField[ ] getInstanceFields( ) throws Exception

RemoteClass[ ] getInterfaces( ) throws Exception

RemoteField getMethod(String name) throws Exception

String[ ] getMethodNames( ) throws Exception

RemoteField[ ] getMethods( ) throws Exception

String getName( ) throws Exception

InputStream getSourceFile( ) throws Exception

String getSourceFileName( )

RemoteField[ ] getStaticFields( ) throws Exception

RemoteClass getSuperclass( ) throws Exception

void ignoreExceptions( ) throws Exception

Boolean isInterface( ) throws Exception

String setBreakpointLine(int lineno) throws Exception

String setBreakpointMethod(RemoteField method) throws Exception

String toString( )

String typeName( ) throws Exception

**RemoteDebugger**
**Methods**

RemoteDebugger(String host, String password, DebuggerCallback client, Boolean verbose) throws Exception

RemoteDebugger(String javaArgs, DebuggerCallback client, Boolean verbose) throws Exception

void close( )

RemoteClass findClass(String name) throws Exception

int freeMemory( ) throws Exception

void gc(RemoteObject save_list[ ]) throws Exception

VII

Appendixes

RemoteObject get(Integer id)

String[ ] getExceptionCatchList( ) throws Exception

String getSourcePath( ) throws Exception

void itrace(Boolean traceOn) throws Exception

String[ ] listBreakpoints( ) throws Exception

RemoteClass[ ] listClasses( ) throws Exception

RemoteThreadGroup[ ] listThreadGroups(RemoteThreadGroup tg)
throws Exception

RemoteThreadGroup run(int argc, String argv[ ]) throws Exception

void setSourcePath(String pathList) throws Exception

int totalMemory( ) throws Exception

void trace(Boolean traceOn) throws Exception

### RemoteDouble extends RemoteValue
**Methods**

double get( )

String toString( )

String typeName( )

### RemoteField extends Field
**Methods**

String getModifiers( )

String getName( )

String getType( )

Boolean isStatic( )

String toString( )

### RemoteFloat extends RemoteValue
**Methods**

float get( )

String toString( )

String typeName( )

### RemoteInt extends RemoteValue
**Methods**

int get( )

RemoteInt(int i)

String toString( )

String typeName( )

**RemoteLong extends RemoteValue**
**Methods**

long get( )

String toString( )

String typeName( )

**RemoteObject extends RemoteValue**
**Methods**

String description( )

final RemoteClass getClazz( )

RemoteField getField(String name) throws Exception

RemoteField getField(int num) throws Exception

RemoteField[] getFields( ) throws Exception

RemoteValue getFieldValue(String name) throws Exception

RemoteValue getFieldValue(int num) throws Exception

final int getId( )

String toString( )

String typeName( ) throws Exception

**RemoteShort extends RemoteValue**
**Methods**

short get( )

String toString( )

String typeName( )

**RemoteStackFrame extends StackFrame**
**Methods**

int getLineNumber( )

RemoteStackVariable getLocalVariable(String name) throws Exception

RemoteStackVariable[] getLocalVariables( ) throws Exception

String getMethodName( )

int getPC( )

RemoteClass getRemoteClass( )

VII

**RemoteStackVariable extends LocalVariable**
**Methods**

String getName( )

RemoteValue getValue( )

Boolean inScope( )

**RemoteString extends RemoteObject**
**Methods**

String description( )

String toString( )

String typeName( )

String typeName( )

**RemoteThread extends RemoteObject**
**Methods**

void cont( ) throws Exception

void down(int nFrames) throws Exception

RemoteStackFrame[ ] dumpStack( ) throws Exception

RemoteStackFrame getCurrentFrame( ) throws Exception

int getCurrentFrameIndex( )

String getName( ) throws Exception

RemoteStackVariable getStackVariable(String name) throws Exception

RemoteStackVariable[ ] getStackVariables( ) throws Exception

String getStatus( ) throws Exception

Boolean isSuspended( )

void next( ) throws Exception

void resetCurrentFrameIndex( )

void resume( ) throws Exception

void setCurrentFrameIndex(int iFrame)

void step(Boolean skipLine) throws Exception

void stop( ) throws Exception

void suspend( ) throws Exception

void up(int nFrames) throws Exception

**RemoteThreadGroup extends RemoteObject**
**Methods**

String getName( ) throws Exception

RemoteThread[ ] listThreads(Boolean recurse) throws Exception

void stop( ) throws Exception

### RemoteValue
### Methods

String description( )

static int fromHex(String hexStr)

final int getType( )

final Boolean isObject( )

static String toHex(int num)

*abstract* String typeName( ) throws Exception

### StackFrame
### Methods

StackFrame( )

String toString( )

### LocalVariable

*The sun.tools.debug.LocalVariable class is not a public class, but rather one restricted for use only within the sun.tools.debug package. This is due to the fact that the class itself and all its fields are defined with the "friendly" (no access modifiers specified). Although it is not meant for use by the Java developer, it is nevertheless listed here due to the dependence on this class by other classes in the package.*

### Fields

Boolean methodArgument;

String name;

String signature;

int slot;

## Interface

### DebuggerCallback

*abstract* void breakpointEvent(RemoteThread t)

*abstract* void exceptionEvent(RemoteThread t, String errorText) throws Exception

*abstract* void printToConsole(String text) throws Exception

*abstract* void quitEvent( ) throws Exception

*abstract* void threadDeathEvent(RemoteThread t) throws Exception

# Exceptions

Exceptions provide you with a means of managing the ordinary run-time problems that may be encountered during execution of your program. Exceptions are thrown by methods and are handled with try-catch blocks.

All exceptions are derived from the `java.lang.Exception` class and most consist only of two constructor methods. Consequently, only the constructor methods for the `java.lang.Exception` class are listed here. Unless otherwise noted, all exceptions may be created with no paramters or with a descriptive string as a paramter.

## java.awt

**AWTException**

> **AWTException**(String message)

## java.io

**EOFException extends IOException**

**FileNotFoundException extends IOException**

**IOException extends java.lang.Exception**

**InterruptedIOException extends IOException**

**UTFDataFormatException extends IOException**

## java.lang

**ArithmeticException extends RuntimeException**

**ArrayIndexOutOfBoundsException extends IndexOutOfBoundsException**
**Constructors**

> ArrayIndexOutOfBoundsException( )
>
> ArrayIndexOutOfBoundsException(int invalid_index)
>
> ArrayIndexOutOfBoundsException(String message)

**ArrayStoreException extends RuntimeException**

**ClassCastException extends RuntimeException**

**ClassNotFoundException extends Exception**

**CloneNotSupportedException extends Exception**

**Exception extends Throwable**

**Methods**
    Exception(String mesage)
    Exception( )

**IllegalAccessException extends Exception**

**IllegalArgumentException extends RuntimeException**

**IllegalMonitorStateException extends RuntimeException**

**IllegalThreadStateException extends RuntimeException**

**IndexOutOfBoundsException extends RuntimeException**

**InstantiationException extends Exception**

**InterruptedException extends Exception**

**NegativeArraySizeException extends RuntimeException**

**NoSuchMethodException extends Exception**

**NullPointerException extends RuntimeException**

**NumberFormatException extends IllegalArgumentException**

**RuntimeException extends Exception**

**SecurityException extends RuntimeException**

**StringIndexOutOfBoundsException extends
IndexOutOfBoundsException**
**Constructors**
    StringIndexOutOfBoundsException( )
    StringIndexOutOfBoundsException(int invalid_index)
    StringIndexOutOfBoundsException(String)

# java.net
**MalformedURLException extends java.lang.IOException**

**ProtocolException extends java.lang.IOException**

**SocketException extends java.lang.IOException**

**UnknownHostException extends java.lang.IOException**

**UnknownServiceException extends java.lang.IOException**

# java.util
**EmptyStackException extends java.lang.RuntimeException**
**Constructors**
    **EmptyStackException( )**

**NoSuchElementException extends java.lang.RuntimeException**

# Errors

While errors and exceptions are both based on the `java.lang.Throwable` class, errors are designed to manage more critical run-time errors. Errors may be handled in a similar manner to exceptions, but unless you clearly understand the problem and have devised a suitable way of resolving it, error-handling is not something that should be used in your code.

Similar to exceptions, all errors are derived from `java.lang.Error`. Most errors contain only constructor methods and most contain only two ErrorName( ) and ErrorName(String message). While all errors are listed here, only those errors whose constructors do not conform to the principle are listed here.

## java.awt

**AWTError extends java.lang.Error**
**Constructors**
    **AWTError( )**

## java.lang

***Abstract*MethodError extends IncompatibleClassChangeError**

**ClassCircularityError extends LinkageError**

**ClassFormatError extends LinkageError**

**Error extends Throwable**
**Methods**
    Error(String mesage)

    Error( )

**IllegalAccessError extends IncompatibleClassChangeError**

**IncompatibleClassChangeError extends LinkageError**

**InstantiationError extends IncompatibleClassChangeError**

**InternalError extends VirtualMachineError**

**LinkageError extends Error**

**NoClassDefFoundError extends LinkageError**

**NoSuchFieldError extends IncompatibleClassChangeError**

**NoSuchMethodError extends IncompatibleClassChangeError**

**OutOfMemoryError extends VirtualMachineError**

**StackOverflowError extends VirtualMachineError**

**ThreadDeath extends Error**
**Constructors**
    ThreadDeath( )

**UnknownError extends VirtualMachineError**

**UnsatisfiedLinkError extends LinkageError**

**VerifyError extends LinkageError**

**VirtualMachineError extends Error**

# Java Language Grammar

A language grammar (sometimes called a *statement of syntax*) like the one contained in this appendix is intended as an aid to understanding. You shouldn't try to use it in isolation because it doesn't contain an exact statement of the language. In particular, you could write Java code that conforms to the "letter of the law" as stated in the grammar, but that doesn't follow the rules laid out elsewhere in the book, and you would end up with code that doesn't compile and won't run.

For example, the grammar for statements and expressions is carefully laid out in this appendix. But from chapters 9 and 13, you know that Java doesn't allow arbitrary combinations of data types. A statement or expression that conforms only to this grammar but that doesn't follow the type rules won't compile successfully.

As another example, this grammar describes legal forms for the declaration and use of variables. But Java imposes additional rules on variables that aren't covered in a grammar. The compiler goes to some lengths, for example, to make sure that variables are initialized before they are used; if the compiler thinks you are trying to use an uninitialized variable, it will give you an error. Those sorts of rules are not covered in the grammar of the language.

The formal specification for the Java language, including the grammar, is available online from JavaSoft. The main documentation page is located at **http://java.sun.com/doc.html** . Documentation specific to the JDK is available at **http://java.sun.com/JDK-1.0/index.html**.

The following grammatical elements refer to the corresponding character from the ASCII character set:

|  |  |
|---|---|
| *ASCII-CR* | Carriage return |
| *ASCII-LF* | Line feed |
| *ASCII-SP* | Space |
| *ASCII-HT* | Horizontal tab |
| *ASCII-FF* | Form feed |

The following elements are as defined in the Unicode standard:

|  |  |
|---|---|
| *UnicodeLetter* | A letter in the Unicode character set |
| *UnicodeDigit* | A digit in the Unicode character set |

> **Note**
>
> The subscript *opt* indicates that the element is optional; the element being defined will be legal (according to the grammar) with or without the optional element present.

# Lexical Structure

## Unicode Escapes and Character Input

*EscapedInputCharacter:*

> *UnicodeEscape*
>
> *RawInputCharacter*

*UnicodeEscape:*

> \ *UnicodeMarker HexDigit HexDigit HexDigit HexDigit*

*UnicodeMarker:*

> u
>
> *UnicodeMarker*u

*RawInputCharacter:*

> *any Unicode character*

*HexDigit: one of*

> 0 1 2 3 4 5 6 7 8 9 a b c d e f A B C D E F

# Input Lines

*LineTerminator:*

    *ASCII-CR  ASCII-LF*

    *ASCII-CR*

    *ASCII-LF*

*InputCharacter:*

    *EscapedInputCharacter, but not ASCII-CR or ASCII-LF*

# Tokens

*Input:*

    *InputElements$_{opt}$*

*InputElements:*

    *InputElement*

    *InputElements InputElement*

*InputElement:*

    *Comment*

    *WhiteSpace*

    *Token*

*WhiteSpace:*

    *ASCII-SP*

    *ASCII-HT*

    *ASCII-FF*

    *LineTerminator*

*Token:*

    *Keyword*

    *Identifier*

    *Literal*

    *Separator*

    *Operator*

## Comments

*Comment:*

> */ * NotStar TraditionalComment*
>
> */ * * DocComment*
>
> */ / InputCharacters$_{opt}$ LineTerminator*

*TraditionalComment:*

> *\* /*
>
> *InputCharacter TraditionalComment*
>
> *LineTerminator TraditionalComment*

*DocComment:*

> */*
>
> *InputCharacter TraditionalComment*
>
> *LineTerminator TraditionalCommentTraditionalComment*

*InputCharacters:*

> *InputCharacter*
>
> *InputCharacters InputCharacter*

## Keywords

*Keyword: one of*

| | | |
|---|---|---|
| abstract | boolean | break |
| byte | byvalue | case |
| cast | catch | char |
| class | const | continue |
| default | do | double |
| else | extends | final |
| finally | float | for |
| future | generic | goto |
| if | implements | import |
| inner | instanceof | int |
| interface | long | native |
| new | null | operator |
| outer | package | private |

| | | |
|---|---|---|
| protected | public | rest |
| return | short | static |
| super | switch | synchronized |
| this | throw | throws |
| transient | try | var |
| void | volatile | while |

## Identifiers

*Identifier:*

    *UnicodeLetter*

    *Identifier UnicodeLetter*

    *Identifier UnicodeDigit*

## Literals

*Literal:*

    *IntegerLiteral*

    *FloatingPointLiteral*

    *BooleanLiteral*

    *CharacterLiteral*

    *StringLiteral*

*IntegerLiteral:*

    *DecimalLiteral IntegerTypeSuffix$_{opt}$*

    *HexLiteral IntegerTypeSuffix$_{opt}$*

    *OctalLiteral IntegerTypeSuffix$_{opt}$*

*IntegerTypeSuffix: one of*

    l L

*DecimalLiteral:*

    *NonZeroDigit Digits$_{opt}$*

*Digits:*

    *Digit*

    *Digits Digit*

*Digit: one of*

    0 1 2 3 4 5 6 7 8 9

*NonZeroDigit: one of*

    1 2 3 4 5 6 7 8 9

*HexLiteral:*

    *0x  HexDigit*

    *0X  HexDigit*

    *HexLiteral  HexDigit*

*OctalLiteral:*

    *0*

    *OctalLiteral  OctalDigit*

*OctalDigit: one of*

    0 1 2 3 4 5 6 7

*FloatingPointLiteral:*

    *Digits . Digits$_{opt}$ ExponentPart$_{opt}$ FloatTypeSuffix$_{opt}$*

    *. Digits ExponentPart$_{opt}$ FloatTypeSuffix$_{opt}$*

    *Digits ExponentPart$_{opt}$ FloatTypeSuffix$_{opt}$*

*ExponentPart:*

    *ExponentIndicator  SignedInteger*

*ExponentIndicator: one of*

    e  E

*SignedInteger:*

    *Sign$_{opt}$  Digits*

*Sign: one of*

    +  −

*FloatTypeSuffix: one of*

    f  F  d  D

*BooleanLiteral: one of*

    true  false

*CharacterLiteral:*

    ' *SingleCharacter* '

    ' *Escape* '

*SingleCharacter:*

    *InputCharacter, but not ' or \*

*Escape: one of*

    \b  \t  \n  \f  \r

    \"  \'  \\

    *OctalEscape*

*OctalEscape:*

    \ *OctalDigit*

    \ *OctalDigit  OctalDigit*

    \ *ZeroToThree  OctalDigit  OctalDigit*

*ZeroToThree: one of*

    0 1 2 3

*StringLiteral:*

    " *StringCharacters* "

*StringCharacters:*

    *StringCharacter*

    *StringCharacters  StringCharacter*

*StringCharacter:*

    *InputCharacter, but not " or \*

    *Escape*

## Separators

*Separator: one of*

    (  )     {     }     ;

    [  ]     ,     .

## Operators

*Operator: one of*

| | | | | |
|---|---|---|---|---|
| = | > | < | ! | ~ |
| == | <= | >= | != | && |
| \|\| | ++ | −− | + | − |
| * | / | & | \| | ^ |
| % | << | >> | >>> | += |
| −= | *= | /= | &= | \|= |
| ^= | %= | <<= | >>= | >>>= |
| ? | = | | | |

# Types and Variables

*Type:*

> *PrimitiveType*
>
> *ClassType*
>
> *InterfaceType*
>
> *ArrayType*

*PrimitiveType: one of*

| | | | | |
|---|---|---|---|---|
| boolean | char | byte | short | int |
| long | float | double | | |

*ClassType:*

> *Name*

*InterfaceType:*

> *Name*

*ArrayType:*

> *Type* [ ]

# Program Structure

*CompilationUnit:*

> *PackageStatement$_{opt}$  ImportStatements$_{opt}$  TypeDeclarations$_{opt}$*

*PackageStatement:*

> package  *PackageName* ;

*PackageName:*

> *PackageNameComponent*
>
> *PackageName . PackageNameComponent*

*PackageNameComponent:*

> *Identifier*

*ImportStatement:*

> *PackageImportStatement*
>
> *TypeImportStatement*
>
> *TypeImportOnDemandStatement*

*PackageImportStatement:*

> import  *PackageName* ;

*TypeImportStatement:*

> import  *PackageName . Identifier* ;

*TypeImportOnDemandStatement:*

> import  *PackageName . * ;

*TypeDeclarations:*

> *TypeDeclaration*
>
> *TypeDeclarations TypeDeclaration*

*TypeDeclaration:*

> *ClassDeclaration*
>
> *InterfaceDeclaration*

# Classes and Interfaces

*ClassDeclaration:*

> *ClassModifiers$_{opt}$* class *Identifier Super$_{opt}$ Interfaces$_{opt}$ ClassBody*

*ClassModifiers:*

    *ClassModifier*

    *ClassModifiers  ClassModifier*

*ClassModifier: one of*

    abstract                final                public

*Super:*

    extends  *TypeName*

*Interfaces:*

    implements  *TypeNameList*

*ClassBody:*

    { *FieldDeclarations$_{opt}$* }

## Field Declarations

*FieldDeclarations:*

    *FieldDeclaration*

    *FieldDeclarations  FieldDeclaration*

*FieldDeclaration:*

    *FieldVariableDeclaration*

    *MethodDeclaration*

    *ConstructorDeclaration*

    *StaticInitializer*

## Variable Declarations

*FieldVariableDeclaration:*

    *VariableModifiers$_{opt}$  Type  VariableDeclarators* ;

*VariableModifiers:*

    *VariableModifier*

    *VariableModifiers  VariableModifier*

*VariableModifier: one of*

    public    protected    private

    static     final        transient

    volatile

*VariableDeclarators:*

    *VariableDeclarator*

    *VariableDeclarators , VariableDeclarator*

*VariableDeclarator:*

    *DeclaratorName*

    *DeclaratorName = VariableInitializer*

*DeclaratorName:*

    *Identifier*

    *DeclaratorName* [ ]

*VariableInitializer:*

    *Expression*

    { *ArrayInitializers*$_{opt}$ ,$_{opt}$ }

*ArrayInitializers:*

    *VariableInitializer*

    *ArrayInitializers ,*

## Method Declarations

*MethodDeclaration:*

    *MethodModifiers*$_{opt}$ *ResultType MethodDeclarator Throws*$_{opt}$ *MethodBody*

*MethodModifiers:*

    *MethodModifier*

    *MethodModifiers MethodModifier*

*MethodModifier: one of*

    public    private    protected

    static    abstract    final

    native    synchronized

*ResultType:*

    *Type*

    void

*MethodDeclarator:*

    *DeclaratorName* ( *ParameterList$_{opt}$* )

    *MethodDeclarator* [ ]

*ParameterList:*

    *Parameter*

    *ParameterList , Parameter*

*Parameter:*

    *TypeDeclaratorName*

*Throws:*

    throws *TypeNameList*

*TypeNameList:*

    *TypeName*

    *TypeNameList , TypeName*

*MethodBody:*

    *Block*

    ;

## Constructor Method Declarations

*ConstructorDeclaration:*

    *ConstructorModifier$_{opt}$ ConstructorDeclarator Throws$_{opt}$ ConstructorBody*

*ConstructorDeclarator:*

    *TypeName* ( *ParameterList$_{opt}$* )

*ConstructorModifier: one of*

    public    protected    private

*ConstructorBody:*

    { *ExplicitConstructorCallStatement$_{opt}$ BlockBody* }

*ExplicitConstructorCallStatement:*

    this ( *ArgumentList$_{opt}$* ) ;

    super ( *ArgumentList$_{opt}$* ) ;

### Static Initialization

*StaticInitializer:*

>   static *Block*

### Interface Declarations

*InterfaceDeclaration:*

>   *InterfaceModifiers$_{opt}$ interface Identifier ExtendsInterfaces$_{opt}$ InterfaceBody*

*InterfaceModifiers:*

>   *InterfaceModifier*
>   *InterfaceModifiers  InterfaceModifier*

*InterfaceModifier: one of*

>   public       abstract

*ExtendsInterfaces:*

>   extends  *TypeNameList*

*InterfaceBody:*

>   {  *FieldDeclarations*  }

# Arrays

*ArrayInitializer:*

>   {  *ElementInitializers$_{opt}$  ,$_{opt}$*  }

*ElementInitializers:*

>   *Element*
>   *ElementInitializers  ,  Element*

*Element:*

>   *Expression*
>   *ArrayInitializer*

# Blocks and Statements

*Block:*

   { *LocalVarDeclarationsAndStatements* }

*LocalVarDeclarationsAndStatements:*

   *LocalVarDeclarationOrStatement*

   *LocalVarDeclarationsAndStatements  LocalVarDeclarationOrStatement*

*LocalVarDeclarationOrStatement:*

   *LocalVariableDeclarationStatement*

   *Statement*

*LocalVariableDeclarationStatement:*

   *TypeSpecifier  VariableDeclarators* ;

*Statement:*

   *EmptyStatement*

   *LabeledStatement*

   *ExpressionStatement*  ;

   *SelectionStatement*

   *IterationStatement*

   *JumpStatement*

   *GuardingStatement*

*EmptyStatement:*

   ;

*LabeledStatement:*

   *Identifier  :  Statement*

   case *ConstantExpression  :  Statement*

   default *:  Statement*

*ExpressionStatement:*

   *Assignment*

   *PreIncrement*

   *PreDecrement*

> *PostIncrement*
>
> *PostDecrement*
>
> *MethodCall*
>
> *AllocationExpression*

*SelectionStatement:*

> if  *( Expression )  Statement*
>
> if  *( Expression )  Statement* else  *Statement*
>
> switch  *( Expression )  Block*

*IterationStatement:*

> while  *( Expression )  Statement*
>
> do  *Statement* while  *( Expression )  ;*
>
> for  *( ForInit Expression$_{opt}$ ; ForIncr$_{opt}$ )*

*ForInit:*

> *ExpressionStatements ;*
>
> *LocalVariableDeclarationStatement*

*ForIncr:*

> *ExpressionStatements*

*ExpressionStatements:*

> *ExpressionStatement*
>
> *ExpressionStatements , ExpressionStatement*

*JumpStatement:*

> break  *Identifier$_{opt}$ ;*
>
> continue  *Identifier$_{opt}$ ;*
>
> return  *Expression$_{opt}$ ;*
>
> throw  *Expression ;*

*GuardingStatement:*

> synchronized  *( Expression )  Statement*
>
> try  *Block  Finally*
>
> try  *Block  Catches*
>
> try  *Block  Catches  Finally*

*Catches:*

> *Catch*
>
> *Catches  Catch*

*Catch:*

> *catch  (  Argument  )  Block*

*Finally:*

> *finally  Block*

# Expressions

## Primary Expressions

*PrimaryExpression:*

> *Name*
>
> *NotJustName*

*NotJustName:*

> *AllocationExpression*
>
> *ComplexPrimary*

*ComplexPrimary:*

> *Literal*
>
> *(  Expression  )*
>
> *ArrayAccess*
>
> *FieldAccess*
>
> *MethodCall*

*Name:*

> *QualifiedName*
>
> this
>
> super
>
> null

*QualifiedName:*

> *Identifier*
>
> *QualifiedName  .  Identifier*

## Array and Field Access

*ArrayAccess:*

>   *Name [ Expression ]*
>
>   *ComplexPrimary [ Expression ]*

*FieldAccess:*

>   *PrimaryExpression . Identifier*

## Method Calls

*MethodCall:*

>   *MethodAccess ( ArgumentList$_{opt}$ )*

*MethodAccess:*

>   *Name*
>
>   *PrimaryExpression . Identifier*

*ArgumentList:*

>   *Expression*
>
>   *ArgumentList , Expression*

## Allocation Expressions

*AllocationExpression:*

>   new *TypeName ( ArgumentList$_{opt}$ )*
>
>   new *TypeName DimExprs Dims$_{opt}$*

*TypeName:*

>   *TypeKeyword*
>
>   *QualifiedName*

*TypeKeyword: one of*

| | | |
|---|---|---|
| boolean | char | byte |
| short | int | float |
| long | double | |

*ArgumentList:*

>   *Expression*
>
>   *ArgumentList , Expression*

*DimExprs:*

> *DimExpr*
>
> *DimExprs DimExpr*

*DimExpr:*

> *[ Expression ]*

*Dims:*

> *[ ]*
>
> *Dims [ ]*

## Unary Operators

*PostfixExpression:*

> *PrimaryExpression*
>
> *PostIncrement*
>
> *PostDecrement*

*PostIncrement:*

> *PrimaryExpression ++*

*PostDecrement:*

> *PrimaryExpression --*

*UnaryExpression:*

> *PreIncrement*
>
> *PreDecrement*
>
> *+ UnaryExpression*
>
> *- UnaryExpression*
>
> *UnaryExpressionNotPlusMinus*

*PreIncrement:*

> *++ PrimaryExpression*

*PreDecrement:*

> *-- PrimaryExpression*

*UnaryExpressionNotPlusMinus:*

> *PostfixExpression*

~  *UnaryExpression*

!  *UnaryExpression*

*CastExpression*

*CastExpression:*

( *TypeKeyword* )  *UnaryExpression*

( *TypeExpression* )  *UnaryExpressionNotPlusMinus*

# Arithmetic Operators

*MultiplicativeExpression:*

*UnaryExpression*

*MultiplicativeExpression* * *UnaryExpression*

*MultiplicativeExpression* / *UnaryExpression*

*MultiplicativeExpression* % *UnaryExpression*

*AdditiveExpression:*

*MultiplicativeExpression*

*AdditiveExpression* + *MultiplicativeExpression*

*AdditiveExpression* – *MultiplicativeExpression*

# Shift Operators

*ShiftExpression:*

*AdditiveExpression*

*ShiftExpression* << *AdditiveExpression*

*ShiftExpression* >> *AdditiveExpression*

*ShiftExpression* >>> *AdditiveExpression*

# Relational and Equality Operators

*RelationalExpression:*

*ShiftExpression*

*RelationalExpression* < *ShiftExpression*

*RelationalExpression* > *ShiftExpression*

*RelationalExpression* <= *ShiftExpression*

*RelationalExpression* >= *ShiftExpression*

*RelationalExpression* instanceof *TypeSpecifier* $Dims_{opt}$

*EqualityExpression:*

> *RelationalExpression*
>
> *EqualityExpression* == *RelationalExpression*
>
> *EqualityExpression* != *RelationalExpression*

## Bitwise and Logical Operators

*AndExpression:*

> *EqualityExpression*
>
> *AndExpression* & *EqualityExpression*

*ExclusiveOrExpression:*

> *AndExpression*
>
> *ExclusiveOrExpression* ^ *AndExpression*

*InclusiveOrExpression:*

> *ExclusiveOr*
>
> *InclusiveOrExpression* | *ExclusiveOrExpression*

## Conditional Operators

*ConditionalAndExpression:*

> *InclusiveOrExpression*
>
> *ConditionalAndExpression* && *InclusiveOrExpression*

*ConditionalOrExpression:*

> *ConditionalAndExpression*
>
> *ConditionalOrExpression* || *ConditionalAndExpression*

*ConditionalExpression:*

> *ConditionalOrExpression*
>
> *ConditionalOrExpression* ? *Expression* : *ConditionalExpression*

## Assignments

*AssignmentExpression:*

> *ConditionalExpression*
>
> *Assignment*

*Assignment:*

> *UnaryExpression  AssignmentOperator  AssignmentExpression*

*AssignmentOperator: one of*

| | | | | |
|---|---|---|---|---|
| = | *= | /= | %= | += |
| -= | <<= | >>= | >>>= | &= |
| ^= | \|= | | | |

*Expression:*

> *AssignmentExpression*

# Installation of the Java Developers Kit

Since Java is being billed as "Programming for the Internet," it makes the most sense that one would download the Java Developers Kit (JDK) off of the Internet. There are a number of ways of going about this, the easiest of which is to use your favorite World Wide Web browser to grab it from either the JavaSoft Web site, or one of the several mirrors. In this appendix, we'll cover the basics of downloading the JDK from the JavaSoft site and how to install it on the various supported platforms. We will be assuming that you already have some familiarity with the Internet and the World Wide Web and know the basics of using a Web browser.

## Downloading the JDK

The first thing you will need to download the JDK is a computer with a connection to the Internet that can use a Web browser. The particular Web browser doesn't really matter all that much, but for our examples we will be using the Netscape Navigator browser.

The second thing you will need is some (well, actually, quite a bit) of free hard disk space on the machine to which you are planning on downloading the JDK. Just to download the JDK to a Solaris machine, you will need about 5.4 megabytes worth of free disk space. To uncompress and unpack it, you will need another 10 meg of space. On a Windows 95/NT machine, you will need 4.4 meg for the JDK and about 6.5 meg to uncompress it. On a Macintosh, you will need 2.5 meg of free disk space and another 6 meg to install it.

> **Note**
>
> The Sun Java Developers Kit is also located on the *Special Edition Using Java* CD-ROM.

If you have some free disk space and a browser handy, you're ready to download. Let's get started!

1. Launch your Net connection and your Web browser. If you are unsure of how to do this, consult your system administrator, your friends who know how to use computers, the manuals, or a book on using the World Wide Web.

2. Point your browser at the JavaSoft JDK download site, at

   **http://www.javasoft.com/JDK-1.0/installation.html**

   You will be presented with a list of the currently supported platforms. The platforms currently supported by Sun are

   - Sun Solaris 2.3, 2.4, and 2.5 for SPARC-based machines
   - Microsoft Windows NT and Windows 95 for Intel x86-based machines
   - Macintosh System 7.5 for 68030, 68040, and PowerPC-based Macs

3. Click on the link appropriate for your machine. Follow the directions on the page. After reading the copyright and readme files, you can then go ahead and click on one of the links to download the JDK for your machine. If you don't get any response, the server may be overloaded, and you will either have to try again or try one of the mirror sites.

   Here is a list of the URLs for the various JDK releases. These are taken directly from the JavaSoft site. These are provided in case the JavaSoft site is unavailable, or if you want to use normal FTP to get the files.

   - For Sun Solaris 2.3, 2.4, 2.5 on SPARC machines:

     **ftp://ftp.javasoft.com/pub/JDK-1_0_1-solaris2-sparc.tar.Z** (ftp.javasoft.com server at Sun)

     **ftp://www.blackdown.org/pub/Java/pub/JDK-1_0_1-solaris2-sparc.tar.Z** (Mirror site at the Blackdown Organization, USA)

   - For Windows 95 and Windows NT/x86 machines:

     **ftp://ftp.javasoft.com/pub/JDK-1_0_1-win32-x86.exe** (ftp.javasoft.com server at Sun)

     **ftp://www.blackdown.org/pub/Java/pub/JDK-1_0_1-win32-x86.exe** (Mirror site at the Blackdown Organization, USA)

   - For Macintoshes running System 7.5 or later, and with a 68030 or higher processor, and PowerMacs:

     MacBinary (*.bin) format: **ftp://ftp.javasoft.com/pub/JDK-beta1-mac.sea.bin** (ftp.javasoft.com server at Sun)

Macintosh HQX format: **ftp://ftp.javasoft.com/pub/JDK-beta1-mac.sea.hqx** (ftp.javasoft.com server at Sun)

MacBinary (*.bin) format: **ftp://ftp.blackdown.org/pub/Java/pub/mac/JDK-beta1-mac.sea.bin** (Mirror site at the Blackdown Organization, USA)

MacBinary (*.bin) format: **ftp://ftp.dimensionx.com/pub/JDK-beta1-mac.sea.bin** (Mirror site at Dimension X)

Macintosh HQX format: **ftp://ftp.blackdown.org/pub/Java/pub/mac/JDK-beta1-mac.sea.hqx** (Mirror site at the Blackdown Organization, USA)

Macintosh HQX format: **ftp://ftp.dimensionx.com/pub/JDK-beta1-mac.sea.hqx** (Mirror site at Dimension X)

> **Note**
>
> If you have a platform that is not listed above, there may or may not be a port for your particular machine, and it will not be supported by Sun. For information on obtaining or helping develop third party ports of the Java Developers Kit for your particular platform, try the Java External Related Mailing Lists and Resources page at
>
> **http://www.javasoft.com/Mail/external_lists.html**
>
> This page has lists for resources and ports outside of Sun, such as the DEC Alpha, Amiga, and Linux ports.

**4.** Wait while it downloads. The JDK is a pretty big file, and downloading is going to take a while. How long it takes depends on how fast your connection is, the user load on the ftp server at that particular moment, the network load on the Internet at the time of day you are downloading the file, the beating of a butterfly's wings somewhere on the planet, sunspots, blind luck, and a large number of other factors that are even more difficult to predict. If the file transfer is going too slow for your taste, try connecting at another time. Depending on where you are on the planet, good times to connect will vary, again depending on many of the same factors as control the transfer rate.

Hopefully, you've now got the JDK for your machine on your hard disk. Now you are ready to install it, so take a deep breath, get up, walk around the room, sit back down, and dive into the next section—"Installing Java."

# Installing Java

Now that you know a little about Java, and you know where to get it, you'll probably want to install it on your computer so you can start using it.

This section focuses on Java installation, including instructions for

- Installing the Java Developers Kit (JDK) on Solaris
- Installing the JDK on Windows
- Installing the JDK on Macintosh

## The Solaris Installation

These instructions are for the JDK only. If you have a Java package from a third-party provider, please refer to the instructions provided with your package.

The JDK is normally distributed as a compressed tape archive (a file with a .tar.Z extension); the name of the file indicates its version.

> **Caution**
>
> It is probably well worth your while to archive your current installation, either through the use of tar or your standard system backup process, prior to beginning the installation of a new version.

1. Choose a directory for the installation. These instructions assume an installation location of /usr1/java. If you choose a different base directory, simply replace usr1 with the name of your installation directory. For example, if you choose to install under your home directory, everywhere you see usr1, replace it with ~ or $HOME.

   > **Caution**
   >
   > Do not install the JDK over a previous release! Especially if the previous release is one of the pre-beta or beta 1 versions.
   >
   > Rename the java directory with a command similar to:
   >
   >     mv java java.old
   >
   > If the installation fails for any reason, you can restore the previous version directly from java.old. Otherwise, after the installation is complete, you can move any additional files, such as documentation, from your old installation into your new installation before removing it from your system.

2. Verify that you have write permissions for the installation directory. Use this command to check the current permissions:

```
ls -ld /usr1
```

The options to the `ls` command specify long listing, which includes information about ownership and permission, and also specifies to `ls` not to list the contents of the directory, which is the default. For more information about the `ls` command, see your system manuals.

The output of the command should be similar to the following:

```
drwxr-xr-x  root  other  512     Feb 18  21:34    /usr
```

In this case, the directory is owned by `root` (the system administrator), and neither the group `other` nor the general user community have permission to write to this directory. If you run into this situation, and you are not `root`, you will need the assistance of your system administrator if you want to install in that directory.

3. Move or copy the JDK distribution file to `/usr1`.

4. Extract the JDK with this command:

```
zcat JDK-1.0-solaris.tar.Z ¦ tar xvfB -
```

The `zcat` command prints an uncompressed version of the compressed file to standard output. The pipe command passes the output of `zcat` into the input of `tar`. The options on `tar` tell it to extract files, be verbose (print messages saying what is being extracted), read from the specified file (- specifies standard input), and expect the input to come from a pipe.

5. Verify that the following subdirectories were created under `/usr1`:

6. Set your PATH environment variable:

for the C shell and its derivatives use

```
setenv PATH $PATH:/usr1/java/bin
```

for the Korn shell and its derivatives use

```
PATH= $PATH;/usr1/java/bin
export PATH
```

7. Set your CLASSPATH environment variable:

for the C shell and its derivatives use

```
setenv CLASSPATH /usr1/java/lib/classes.zip
```

for the Korn shell and its derivitives use

```
CLASSPATH= CLASSPATH /usr1/java/lib/classes.zip
export CLASSPATH
```

**Tip**

Rather than set these variables from the command line each time, you probably should add the commands to set the PATH and CLASSPATH variables in your shell resource file—.shrc, .cshrc, .profile, and so on. If you are a system administrator installing the JDK as a network development tool, you may want to add these parameters to the default configuration files.

## Windows Installation

These instructions are for the JDK only. If you have a Java package from a third-party provider, please refer to the instructions provided with your package.

You need Windows 95 or Windows NT to run Java; it will not run under Windows versions 3.0, 3.1, or 3.11—including Windows for Workgroups.

**Troubleshooting**

*Why can't they make Java work under Windows 3.x?*

At the time of this writing, no one has had the time, much less the patience, to produce a production-quality version of Java for earlier versions of Windows. There are several reasons for this, but the biggest ones seem to be these:

- Difficulty in creating a multithreaded environment under an operating environment that does not support preemptive multitasking
- TCP/IP support
- The 8.3 file format requires a rewrite of the Java interpreter, which expects certain file extensions

The JDK is normally distributed as a self-extracting compressed file; the name of the file indicates its version.

**Caution**

It is probably well worth your while to archive your current installation, either through the use of PKZIP or your standard system backup program, prior to beginning the installation of a new version.

1. Choose a directory for the installation. These instructions assume an installation location of `c:\java`. If you choose a different base directory, simply append the appropriate path (and change the drive letter, if appropriate). For example, if you want to install to `e:\tools\java`, replace `c:` with `e:\tools` whenever it shows up in the instructions.

> **Caution**
>
> Do not install the JDK over a previous release! Especially if the previous release is one of the pre-beta or beta 1 versions.
>
> Rename the `java` directory (for example, to `oldjava`) using the Explorer in Windows 95 or File Manager on Windows NT. If the installation fails for any reason, you can restore the previous version directly from `oldjava`. Otherwise, after the installation is complete, you can move any additional files, such as documentation, from your old installation into your new installation before removing it from your system.

2. If you plan on installing to a networked drive, make sure you have permission to write to the desired directory.

3. Move or copy the JDK distribution file to `c:\`.

4. Extract the JDK by running the self-extracting program (double-clicking the icon in Explorer or File Manager works just fine).

5. Verify that the following subdirectories were created on drive `c`:

6. Add `c:\java\bin` to your PATH statement in your autoexec.bat file:

   ```
   set PATH=c:\windows;c:\dos;...;c:\java\bin
   ```

7. Set your CLASSPATH environment variable in your autoexec.bat file:

   ```
   set CLASSPATH=c:\java\lib\classes.zip
   ```

> **Tip**
>
> If you want to squeeze a little more performance out of Java (at the cost of a little more disk space), move the classes.zip file to `c:\java\classes` (you need to create this directory), and use PKUNZIP to extract the files. You can then remove the classes.zip file.
>
> If you choose this option, you will need to change your CLASSPATH environment variable to `c:\java\classes`.

8. Reboot your computer for the environment variables to take effect.

## Macintosh Installation

These instructions are for installing the JDK only. If you have a package from a third-party developer, please refer to the instructions provided with your package.

The JDK is normally distributed as a stuffed, bin-hexed archive (a file with a .hqx.sit extension). The file version is indicated in its name. This version runs on '040 generation Macs as well as PowerPCs.

> **Caution**
>
> Currently, there is only one version of the JDK available for the Mac (1.0b1). This version runs on both '040 and PPC class machines. As newer versions are released, you will want to install them; make sure to archive your current version before installing a newer version.

1. After following the above instructions for downloading the MacJDK, you should have an installer titled MacintoshJDK1.0b1.sea. Double-click on this installer, and it will launch into a fairly standard Macintosh installer dialog.

> **Caution**
>
> The Macintosh allows users to name directories and files in a manner that chokes UNIX. This includes the naming of folders with slashes (/). This causes problems with the JDK because when the JDK attempts to locate your files, it uses a mixed UNIX/Mac method of tracking paths. Thus, a slash in the name of a folder is interpreted as a change of directory.
>
> UNIX also has a few problems with names that include spaces. As of this release, you should follow the UNIX file and directory naming conventions used by the developers. That means you shouldn't use spaces, slashes, asterisks, and most other punctuation characters in your file and directory names. You can, however, use as many periods as you want, and the filename can be as long as you want it to be (as long as it's less than 32 characters long).

2. In the lower left-hand corner of the installer dialog, there is a box labeled "Install Location." From that dialog, you can specify where you want to install the JDK. After selecting the appropriate drive and directory, you can then click on the "Install" button to run the installer. It will put all of the Mac JDK in a folder called MacJDK1.0b1 at whatever

location you specified in the installer. The default installation location is the root level of your startup disk.

You now have a working copy of the JDK on your hard drive folder. This includes two essential programs: the Java Compiler and the Applet Viewer. You are now ready to move onto the next (and much more fun) parts of Java development. ❖

# APPENDIX E
# Glossary

**abstract class**   A class that is not instantiated directly. Abstract classes exist so that subclasses can inherit variables and methods from them.

**access control**   A way to restrict access to a class's variables and methods. The modifiers `public`, `private`, `protected`, and `private protected` placed before a variable name or function declaration specify the kind of access granted.

**action**   An applet method that can be defined to identify the kind of event that has occurred and act on that event.

**API**   *Application Programming Interface*. The Java API contains classes a developer can use to build applications and applets. Currently, the Java API provides classes to support the language itself, I/O capability, network capability, user interfaces, applets, image management, interaction with a platform-specific toolkit, and general utilities.

**applet**   A Java program that runs in the context of a Java-capable browser or the appletviewer. Java applets extend the content of Web pages beyond just graphics and text.

**appletviewer**   A tool created by SUN to run applets without a browser.

**array**   An indexed set of data, where each data item is of the same type. An element of an array is referenced by its index.

**attribute**   A specifier for an HTML tag (for example, `code` is an attribute of the `<APPLET>` tag).

**attributes**   An object's variables, or state information.

**AWT**   The *Abstract Windowing Toolkit*, or group of classes for writing programs with graphical user interfaces. The AWT contains classes for `Components` (for example, `Button`, `TextField`, `Canvas`, `Choice`, `List`, `TextArea`,

Checkbox, List, MenuItem, Scrollbar, Label), classes for Containers (for example, Window, Frame, Panel, Dialog, FileDialog), and classes to help with layout, graphics, and images.

**behavior**   Describes the way a class reacts to events in the environment, messages, and changes to variables. Behavior depends on the state of an object. A class maintains state information in its variables and reacts to its environment through its methods.

**browser**   A program used for reading, displaying, and interacting with objects on the World Wide Web.

**bytecode**   The machine-independent output of the Java compiler and input to the Java interpreter.

**cast**   To coerce an object of one data type to another type.

**class**   A collection of variables and methods that an object can have, or a template for building objects.

**.class file**   A file containing machine-independent Java bytecodes. The Java compiler generates .class files for the Java interpreter to read.

**CLASSPATH**   An environment variable used to define all the directories where .class files can be found.

**class variable**   A variable allocated once per class. Class variables have global class scope and belong to the entire class instead of an instance.

**code**   An attribute of the HTML <APPLET> tag that specifies the class to load. The term "code" also refers to source code, which is the syntactical representation of a program.

**codebase**   An attribute of the HTML <APPLET> tag that specifies the location of the classes to load.

**compiler**   A language translator. A program that transforms source code into another format without executing the program.

**conditionals**   Programming constructs that support branching or execution of different statements when different conditions are true. Java conditionals are case statements, if statements, and the ? (conditional) operator.

**constructor**   A method that is used to create an instantiation of a class.

**content handler**   A Java routine used to process a particular MIME type (for example, text/html).

`destroy()`   An applet method used to do final cleanup before an applet unloads. Applets override this method when resources need to be released that are not released by the `stop()` method.

**double buffering**   A technique used to reduce flicker in animations. The image or drawing is painted into a temporary space. Then the finished object is drawn to the screen all at once.

**DTD**   Abbreviation for *Document Type Definition*. A DTD file formally describes a particular markup language, such as HTML.

**encapsulation**   A way to contain data and methods in a class so that its methods and variables may be added, changed, or deleted without requiring the code that uses the class to change. This object-oriented programming technique makes a class look like a black box to the outside world.

**event handling**   Identifying events (for example, mouse clicks and button presses) and reacting to them. Events can be handled with the `action` method, a method corresponding to the event (for example, `MouseDown`), or the `handleEvent` method.

**exception**   A signal that something has happened to stop normal execution of a program, usually an error.

**exception handler**   Code that responds to and attempts to recover from an exception.

**expression**   Mathematical, comparative, and other kinds of operations that can be evaluated to a single value. For example, `1+3+9*7+Math.pow(45,3.3)` is an expression.

`extends`   A keyword used to make one class a subclass of another, for example, `class subclass extends superclass`.

**final**   A modifier that prevents subclass definition, makes variables constant, and prevents a subclass from overriding a method.

`finalize`   A method that is called when there are no further references to an object and it is no longer needed. This method releases resources and does any other necessary cleanup that Java does not handle during garbage collection.

**Gamelan**   A registration site on the Web for Java applets and applications. Items registered here often contain the Java source.

**garbage collection thread**   A Java thread that automatically frees memory that is no longer needed by objects.

**GUI**    *Graphical User Interface*. In Java, the AWT provides classes to support user interface construction.

**HotJava**    A Java-capable browser from Javasoft.

**hspace**    An attribute of the HTML <APPLET> tag that specifies the amount of horizontal space (to the left and right) between the applet and the text on the page.

**HTML**    *Hypertext Markup Language*, the language used to create Web pages.

**inheritance**    A property of object-oriented languages where a class assumes the methods and variables of more general classes. A subclass automatically contains all of the methods and variables that its superclasses contain. Note that access modifiers such as private can place restrictions on the use of inherited items in Java.

**init()**    An applet method used to do one-time initialization before an applet begins executing.

**instance**    A concrete representation of a class or object. A class can have many instances.

**instance variable**    A variable allocated once per instance of a class.

**instantiate**    To create a concrete object from a class "template." New objects are instantiated with new.

**interface**    A collection of methods and variables that other classes may implement. A class that implements an interface provides implementations for all of the methods in the interface.

**interpreter**    A program that performs both language translation and program execution. java is the Java interpreter.

**java**    The program used to invoke the Java interpreter, which executes Java programs.

**Java**    An object-oriented language that can be used to create machine-independent applications and applets.

**.java file**    A file containing Java source code.

**java.applet**    Java package that supports applet development. This package provides the ability for an applet to get information about its context, communicate with other applets, load images, and play sounds.

**java.awt**    Java package that supports the development of user interfaces.

**java.awt.image**   Java package that supports image processing.

**java.awt.peer**   Java package that links Java user interface code with a platform-dependent toolkit like Motif or Windows.

**java.io**   Java package that supports reading and writing of files, strings, sockets, and so on.

**java.lang**   Java package that supports the basic features of the language. This class does not have to be explicitly imported into Java programs; it is imported automatically.

**java.net**   Java package that supports network connections.

**java.util**   Java package that provides useful utility classes like random number generation and growable arrays.

**javac**   A command for running the Java compiler.

**javac_g**   A command for running a non-optimized version of the Java compiler. The `javac_g` command can be used with debuggers, such as `jdb`.

**Java-capable browser**   A Web browser that can run Java applets. Also called a Java-enabled or Java-enhanced browser.

**javadoc**   A command that is used to generate API-style HTML documentation automatically.

**javah**   A command that can create C include files and stubs from a Java `.class` file. The resulting C files allow C code to access parameters passed from Java, return values to Java, and access Java class variables.

**javah_g**   A command that can create C `include` files and stubs with debug information from a Java `.class` file.

**javap**   A command that disassembles Java `.class` files.

**JavaScript**   A Java-based scripting language.

**Java-SIG**   The Sun User Group's Special Interest Group for Java.

**jdb**   The Java debugger.

**JDBC**   A database access API from JavaSoft that allows developers to access databases with Java programs.

**JDK**   The *Java Developers Kit.*

**literals**   Numbers or character values. `'x'`, `'2'`, and `'1.22'` are all literals.

**loops**   Programming constructs that support repetitive execution of one or more statements. Java has `while`, `do-while`, and `for` loops.

`main()`   The entry point into a Java application.

**method**   A routine that belongs to a class.

**method prototype**   The format of a method that specifies the name of the method, the return type, and the parameter list. A method prototype is also called a signature.

**MIME**   Abbreviation for *Multipurpose Internet Mail Extensions*. The MIME specification supports electronic mailing of many kinds of messages (for example, audio files, images, and HTML).

**modifier**   A Java keyword that is applied to a method or variable declaration to control access, control execution, or provide additional information. The keywords `private`, `public`, `protected`, `final`, `native`, `synchronized`, and `volatile` are Java modifiers.

**multiple inheritance**   The ability for a class to inherit from multiple classes. Java does not support multiple inheritance.

**multithreaded**   Having multiple threads of execution so that parts of a program can execute concurrently.

`native` **methods**   Methods that are declared in Java with the keyword `native` but are implemented in another language. Usually, `native` methods are written to do something that the Java API does not already do, to interact with a particular computer's hardware or operating system or to improve performance. Since `native` methods are not portable across platforms, applets cannot contain native methods.

`new`   The Java operator that is used to create a new instance of a class, for example, `MyClass c = new MyClass()`.

**object**   An instantiation of a class.

**OOP**   *Object-Oriented Programming* is the ultimate extension of the concept of modular programming.

**override**   To replace a method inherited from a superclass. For example, applets frequently override the `init()`, `start()`, `stop()`, `destroy()`, and `paint()` methods inherited from the applet class.

**package**   A Java keyword used to assign the contents of a file to a package. Packages are Java's mechanism for grouping classes. Packages simplify reuse, and they are very useful for large projects.

**pointers**   Variables that contain machine addresses of data instead of the data itself. The Java language does not support pointers.

`private`   An access control modifier that limits access to within the class itself.

**private protected**   An access control modifier that limits access to a class and its superclasses.

`protected`   An access control modifier that limits access to a class, the package, and its subclasses. A subclass, however, cannot access a superclass's protected variables.

**protocol handler**   A Java routine that interprets a protocol, generally for a browser.

`public`   An access control modifier that allows access to a variable or method from anywhere.

**Runnable interface**   An interface that allows a class the ability to run in a distinct thread without being a subclass of `Thread`.

**scope**   Defines where a method or variable is visible. A variable defined in a method is visible only within the method; it has local scope. A variable or method defined within a class is visible inside the class; it has class scope.

**ServerSocket**   A Java class that supports network connections for server objects.

**SGML**   *Standard Generalized Markup Language*, the grandfather of HTML.

**signature**   The format of a method. A signature specifies the name of the method, the return type, and the parameter list. Also called a method prototype.

**Socket**   A Java class that supports the creation of network connections.

`start()`   An applet method used to begin execution and resume execution after an applet has been temporarily stopped. Applets override this method when they need to do processing after a one-time initialization and anticipate stopping temporarily (for example, when the user leaves the applet's page) and restarting.

**statement**   A Java construct that controls program flow, controls execution of critical sections of code, makes an assignment, imports a package, or declares membership in a package.

`static`   A Java keyword used to indicate that a variable is a class variable, allocated once per class (for example, `static int myinteger`). When class variables change, they change for every instance of a class.

**stop()**    An Applet method that is overridden to stop execution (for example, stop sounds when the user leaves the applet's page). Usually, `stop()` and `start()` are implemented together, so `stop()` should be implemented in a way that permits the `start()` method to resume execution.

**streams**    Controlled flows of data from one source to another. Java supplies several classes to create and manage streams. Classes that handle input data are derived from class `InputStream`, and classes that handle output data are derived from class `OutputStream`.

**string**    A sequence of characters enclosed in double quotes in the generic sense. In Java, strings are instances of the `String` class. Even the statement `String mystring = "This is my string.";` creates a `String` object.

**stub**    Part of the interface between Java code and a `native` method. A stub allows a `native` method to access Java parameters, access Java class variables, and return data to Java.

**subclass**    A class that inherits methods and variables from another class. The statement `class SubClass extends SuperClass` means that `SubClass` is a subclass of `Superclass`.

**super**    A reserved word that refers to a class's immediate superclass.

**super()**    Shorthand for the superclass's constructor method.

**superclass**    A generalization of another class. X is a superclass of Y if Y inherits variables and methods from X.

**synchronized**    A Java keyword that prevents more than one thread from executing inside a method at once.

**this**    A reserved word that refers to the current class.

**token**    The smallest unit in a language that a compiler can recognize.

**type**    A specific kind of data in a program or programming language. In the Java statement `int my_integer = 1;`, the `int` keyword indicates that `my_integer` is an integer instead of some other data type.

**virtual machine**    An abstract, logical model of a computer used to execute Java bytecodes. A Java virtual machine has an instruction set, registers, a stack, a heap, and a method area.

**VRML**    *Virtual Reality Modeling Language.*

**vspace**    An attribute of the HTML <APPLET> tag that specifies the amount of vertical space above and below the applet and the text on the page.

# The Java-SIG Library of Applets

You have in your hands a CD stuffed full of applets, source code, and HTML pages for 200 of the best Java programs available. There are handy utilities, educational tours de force, games, graphics experiments, thought experiments, and programming experiments.

In addition to this massive compilation of Java, the Java-SIG Library of Applets includes Sun's Java Development Kit (JDK) to save you the time of downloading these large files. And, as an added bonus, Que has provided the Java-SIG with over 1,100 pages of reference material on C++, HTML, CGI, and JavaScript that is included on the CD-ROM.

This CD-ROM, which was developed by the Sun User Group's Java Special Interest Group (Java-SIG), sells through the user group for $50 but is included with this book for no extra charge. (If you are interested in membership in the Sun User Group, Java-SIG, or any of its products, you can contact the groups at (617) 232-0514 or by e-mail at **cdrom@sug.org** or check out its Web page at **http://www.sug.org** for more information.)

This appendix will take a brief look at the contents of the CD and where on it you will find topics of interest. The appendix does not provide a "laundry list" of all of the contents of the CD, so you'll want to explore the CD itself to discover all of the treasures.

## The Java Programs

These programs have been selected by the experts of Java-SIG and pulled together in one place on this CD-ROM. The CD contains not only the applets themselves but also source code, HTML pages showing how to use them, and byte code for most of the programs.

All told, there are some 200 Java programs on the CD. These have been organized into categories such as

- Utilities
- Education
- Games

and placed into corresponding directories (or folders, depending on your operating system) on the CD-ROM.

When you look at the type of programs on the CD, don't expect to find spreadsheet programs, the next version of *Doom*, a Smalltalk environment, or a process control system for a robot assembly line in an automated factory. The applets here are written by people groping to figure out how Java works, and who are sharing their findings with the world.

Some of it will be the start of something insanely great. That's why all the source code is included. You should run the applets, study the code, figure out what you like, discover how they did it, and finally, take a stab at improving it.

The following few sections describe a sample of the sorts of things you'll find on the disk.

## Boltzmann Machine

This is a neat demonstration of something called "constraint satisfaction networks." The problem is how to simulate decision-making when the criteria of selection is dependent on initial conditions, but not completely so. One answer is essentially to roll dice, and have those dice rolls influenced by relational conditions you've slowly built up over time. That's what this applet demonstrates, though it isn't completely obvious what's going on.

The demo is a perception test. You get the eight points that form the vertices of a cube, and the question is to decide which of the two sensible patterns for connecting the dots to choose. Your eye does it by picking a focus point, and filling everything else in. The program forms a random start state, builds a model of relationships to get to the next prediction, and runs a probability test to get to the next test state. Over time, the model tends toward one of the two sensible configurations. You can run through the test in either single steps, or groups of 20 iterations, and you can also get a mapping of the current relationships in the model.

## Dining Philosophers

Slow to run (it took two minutes to load into Netscape on a PowerMac 9500) and difficult to follow, this is an applet well worth the effort put into it. In brief, it is a simulation designed to demo synchronization theory. Five philosophers talk, think, and eat, hopefully without coming into conflict.

You don't get to do much besides watch as the philosophers go through their programmed behavior, but a nice thing about this applet is that each philosopher gets his own thread to do calculations in. The implementation of this scheme is well worth the study. You do get to play with the sound (which doesn't seem to work quite right) and tinker with the speed of the simulation and the parameters the philosophers work under, but this is mostly a show-and-tell applet.

The applet is visually stunning, so not getting to interact much isn't such a let-down. Still, I hope you've got a macho machine for this one.

## Hex Calculator

The problem with most calculator programs is that using a handheld calculator works better. Things which appear on the computer screen need something extra to compete with the handier handheld models.

The something extra in this case is optional hexadecimal notation—useful for programmers debugging without other adequate tools. This is a 64–bit calculator with simple functions: +, –, /, *, ^, &, |, ~, <<, and >>. It's got one storage location, and will display results in binary, decimal, or hexadecimal form.

## Lisp Interpreter

In the foreword to Abelson and Sussman's *Structure and Interpretation of Computer Programs*, Alan Perlis wrote, "Lisp has such a simple syntax and semantics that parsing can be treated as an elementary task." Apparently, one can write an evaluator in Java in about a dozen screens of code, and end up with about forty of the most common primitives and atoms.

This interpreter is set up primarily to enter expressions on the fly. It has a code entry area, three save buttons to save on retyping, a button to evaluate the entered expression, and a button to wipe out everything and start over.

## Ringtris

Ringtris is a fun little Tetris variant on a spiderweb board; the garish pieces start along the outer edge and spiral inwards. You can move them around on the Web, and fold or unfold them as you change their orientation. Whenever a ring becomes completely filled by playing pieces, it collapses, and everything outward of it moves inward. The game ends when a starting piece can't get on the board because the piece is already fully occupied.

This game is simple and addicting. The board is eerily pretty, the colors are mesmerizing, and the play gets intense.

# The Sun JDK

To save you the trouble of downloading this large file, the Sun JDK is included on the CD-ROM. It is in the same compressed format on the CD-ROM that it is on the Java Web site. The JDK is included for all three platforms that Sun currently supports: Windows (NT and 95), SPARC/Solaris, and the Macintosh OS. You'll find these in the JDK directory (folder) on the CD-ROM with subdirectories for Solaris, Windows, and Mac.

Detailed installation directions for the JDK are provided in appendix D, "Installation of the Java Development Kit."

# C++, HTML, CGI, and JavaScript Reference Material

This portion of the Java-SIG Library of Applets consists of chapters from several books published by Que. We hope that this additional reference material will be of value to anyone interested in Java. In total, there are over 1,100 pages of reference material from four best-selling books, covering the topics of C++, HTML, JavaScript, and CGI.

All of this material is included on the CD-ROM in HTML format for use with any web browser. (The exception is C++ *by Example*, which is included in Adobe PDF format.) To access any of these, open the contents.htm file in the Quebooks directory (folder) in your Web browser.

The material is taken from the following books:

### C++ *By Example*

The first book included is C++ *by Example*. Since Java has so much in common with C and C++, it is natural that Java programmers may have some questions along the way about C++. This book is included in its entirety, with over 700 pages of reference and examples.

> **Note**
>
> This book is included in Adobe Acrobat PDF format. Adobe Acrobat readers (and Acrobat plug-ins for Netscape) are included on this CD in the /quebooks/cbyexamp/ acrobat directory (or folder, depending on your OS). Versions for Windows, Mac, SPARC/Solaris, and several other platforms are included. If you need more information about Acrobat installation, use, support for other OSs not included, or newer versions, please see the Adobe web pages at **http://www.adobe.com**.

## *Special Edition Using HTML,* **Second Edition**

The next book appearing on the CD-ROM is *Special Edition Using HTML,* Second Edition. While it's likely that most everyone using Java will already have some knowledge of HTML, it's impossible to know everything about all of the nuances of the languages and available tools. So we have included five intermediate and advanced chapters from this book, representing over 100 pages of advanced reference on topics such as Netscape-specific extensions, image map handling, and verification.

## *Special Edition Using JavaScript*

Also included are chapters from *Special Edition Using JavaScript.* While this book had not yet been published at the time this CD-ROM was compiled, we wanted to include this material since there is so little quality reference information available on JavaScript. We have included five chapters representing over 180 pages of reference material on the topics of JavaScript objects, events, browser objects, and much more.

## *Special Edition Using CGI*

Finally, while Java has garnered much attention these days, CGI is still a valuable tool for any Webmaster or Internet programmer. With that in mind, we have included five chapters from *Special Edition Using CGI.* These chapters represent over 140 pages of material covering CGI database query scripts, server-side includes, using Java as a CGI language, security, and more. ❖

# Index

**literals, 137-141, 823**
Boolean, 137
character, 137-139
decimal-integer, 140
hexadecimal-integer, 140
integer, 140
octal escape, 138-139
octal-integer, 140
string, 140-142
**LOD node, 624**
**logical comparison operators, 147**
**logical expressions, 235-238**
**logical operations of bitwise operators, 236**
**logical operators**
binary, 237
unary, 238
**loops, 823**

# M

**Macintosh, installing Java, 816-817**
**macros, 87, 88**
**MagnaStar, Inc**
closing applications and applets, 540-542
Java programming, 664-667
**mailing lists, Java-SIG, 697-698**
**main( ) method, 503-506, 603-606, 824**
**MAJUG (Mid-Atlantic Java Users' Group), 681-682**
**manager structure, JDBC, 647-648**
**MarqueeApplet.java source code (listing 22.11), 487-493**
**MarqueeDriver.java source code (listing 22.10), 486**
**MarqueeItem.java source code (listing 22.5), 476-477**
**Marqueestring.java source code (listing 22.6), 477-482**
**MediaTracker, 377**
**memory, automatic management, 114**

# X

XOR (eXclusive OR)
 graphic mode,
 369-371

# Y

yield( ) method,
 561-562

# Z

Zip Find utility, 84
ZIP format,
 packaging of
 applications, 544
  UNIX, 544-545
  Windows, 544

# NOTES

# NOTES

# NOTES

# NOTES

# NOTES

# NOTES

# NOTES

# NOTES

# NOTES

# NOTES

# NOTES

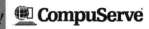

A VIACOM SERVICE

# The Information SuperLibrary™

| Bookstore | Search | What's New | Reference | Software | Newsletter | Company Overviews |

| Yellow Pages | Internet Starter Kit | HTML Workshop | Win a Free T-Shirt! | Macmillan Computer Publishing | Site Map | Talk to Us |

## CHECK OUT THE BOOKS IN THIS LIBRARY.

You'll find thousands of shareware files and over 1600 computer books designed for both technowizards and technophobes. You can browse through 700 sample chapters, get the latest news on the Net, and find just about anything using our massive search directories.

*All Macmillan Computer Publishing books are available at your local bookstore.*

We're open 24-hours a day, 365 days a year.

You don't need a card.

We don't charge fines.

And you can be as **LOUD** as you want.

The Information SuperLibrary

http://www.mcp.com/mcp/   ftp.mcp.com

# Complete and Return this Card for a *FREE* Computer Book Catalog

Thank you for purchasing this book! You have purchased a superior computer book written expressly for your needs. To continue to provide the kind of up-to-date, pertinent coverage you've come to expect from us, we need to hear from you. Please take a minute to complete and return this self-addressed, postage-paid form. In return, we'll send you a free catalog of all our computer books on topics ranging from word processing to programming and the internet.

Mr. ☐     Mrs. ☐     Ms. ☐     Dr. ☐

Name (first) [              ]     (M.I.) ☐     (last) [                          ]

Address [                                    ]
        [                                    ]

City [                    ]     State [  ]     Zip [    ] [   ]

Phone [  ] [   ] [   ] [   ]     Fax [   ] [   ] [   ]

Company Name [                                ]

E-mail address [                                ]

## 1. Please check at least (3) influencing factors for purchasing this book.

Front or back cover information on book ........................ ☐
Special approach to the content ..................................... ☐
Completeness of content................................................ ☐
Author's reputation ...................................................... ☐
Publisher's reputation .................................................. ☐
Book cover design or layout ......................................... ☐
Index or table of contents of book ............................... ☐
Price of book................................................................. ☐
Special effects, graphics, illustrations ......................... ☐
Other (Please specify): _____ ☐

## 2. How did you first learn about this book?

Saw in Macmillan Computer Publishing catalog ........... ☐
Recommended by store personnel .................................. ☐
Saw the book on bookshelf at store ............................... ☐
Recommended by a friend .............................................. ☐
Received advertisement in the mail ............................... ☐
Saw an advertisement in: _____ ☐
Read book review in: _____ ☐
Other (Please specify): _____ ☐

## 3. How many computer books have you purchased in the last six months?

This book only ....... ☐     3 to 5 books...................... ☐
2 books ................... ☐     More than 5 ...................... ☐

## 4. Where did you purchase this book?

Bookstore ................................................................... ☐
Computer Store ........................................................... ☐
Consumer Electronics Store ....................................... ☐
Department Store ........................................................ ☐
Office Club ................................................................. ☐
Warehouse Club .......................................................... ☐
Mail Order .................................................................. ☐
Direct from Publisher ................................................. ☐
Internet site ................................................................ ☐
Other (Please specify): _____ ☐

## 5. How long have you been using a computer?

☐ Less than 6 months     ☐ 6 months to a year
☐ 1 to 3 years              ☐ More than 3 years

## 6. What is your level of experience with personal computers and with the subject of this book?

|  | With PCs | With subject of book |
|---|---|---|
| New | ☐ | ☐ |
| Casual | ☐ | ☐ |
| Accomplished | ☐ | ☐ |
| Expert | ☐ | ☐ |

Source Code ISBN: 0-7897-0604-0

## 7. Which of the following best describes your job title?

- Administrative Assistant ☐
- Coordinator ☐
- Manager/Supervisor ☐
- Director ☐
- Vice President ☐
- President/CEO/COO ☐
- Lawyer/Doctor/Medical Professional ☐
- Teacher/Educator/Trainer ☐
- Engineer/Technician ☐
- Consultant ☐
- Not employed/Student/Retired ☐
- Other (Please specify): _____ ☐

## 8. Which of the following best describes the area of the company your job title falls under?

- Accounting ☐
- Engineering ☐
- Manufacturing ☐
- Operations ☐
- Marketing ☐
- Sales ☐
- Other (Please specify): _____ ☐

## 9. What is your age?

- Under 20 ☐
- 21-29 ☐
- 30-39 ☐
- 40-49 ☐
- 50-59 ☐
- 60-over ☐

## 10. Are you:

- Male ☐
- Female ☐

## 11. Which computer publications do you read regularly? (Please list)

_____
_____
_____
_____
_____
_____
_____
_____
_____
_____

*Comments*: _____
_____
_____

Fold here and scotch-tape to mail.

# The People Who Know Sun™...

## ...Are The People Who Know Java™

**Java-SIG** is the international organization for people who work with Java. Whether you're just beginning to use Java, or you're an experienced developer, **Java-SIG** has something to offer you. **Java-SIG** is part of the Sun User Group – and Sun Microsystems is the company that brought the world Java. The Sun User Group's long-standing ties with Sun allow us to bring our members the most up-to-date Java news, the coolest applets, and the best training anywhere!

As a **Java-SIG** member, you'll get great benefits like:
- Discounts on hardware and software!
- Access to two electronic mailing lists!
- Great rates on great books from all the leading technical publishers!
- A newsletter, with tips, tricks, product reviews, and more!

**Java-SIG** membership is only $50 per year ($65 outside the United States)! To join, just fill out the form below. Or you can join over the telephone at (617) 232-0514, via the Worldwide Web at **http://www.sug.org/java-sig.html**, or by sending e-mail to *office@sug.org*.

---

**Mail to:** Sun User Group • 1330 Beacon St., #344 • Brookline, MA • 02146-3202

Name: _____

Adress: _____

_____

City: _____

State: __ Zip: _____ Country: _____

Phone: _____

Email: _____

☐ *Please add me to the Java-SIG e-mail list*

**Payment Information
$50/year ($65 outside the U.S.A.)**

☐ I have enclosed a check made out to "Sun User Group"

Please charge my ☐ Visa ☐ Mastercard

☐ American Express

Card No.: _____

Exp. Date: _____

Signature: _____